The Editor

GORDON TESKEY is Professor of English and American Literature and Language at Harvard University, where he teaches Renaissance poetry. He is the author of *Allegory and Violence* (1996) and of *Delirious Milton*, forthcoming from Harvard University Press.

A NORTON CRITICAL EDITION

John Milton
PARADISE LOST

AUTHORITATIVE TEXT
SOURCES AND BACKGROUNDS
CRITICISM

Edited by

GORDON TESKEY
HARVARD UNIVERSITY

W • W • NORTON & COMPANY • *New York* • *London*

W. W. Norton & Company has been independent since its founding in 1923, when William Warder Norton and Mary D. Herter Norton first published lectures delivered at the People's Institute, the adult education division of New York City's Cooper Union. The Nortons soon expanded their program beyond the Institute, publishing books by celebrated academics from America and abroad. By mid-century, the two major pillars of Norton's publishing program—trade books and college texts—were firmly established. In the 1950s, the Norton family transferred control of the company to its employees, and today—with a staff of four hundred and a comparable number of trade, college, and professional titles published each year—W. W. Norton & Company stands as the largest and oldest publishing house owned wholly by its employees.

This title is printed on permanent paper containing
30 percent post-consumer waste recycled fiber.

Printed in the United States of America
First Edition.
Composition by Binghamton Valley Composition, LLC.

Manufacturing by the Courier Companies—Westford Division.
Book design by Antonina Krass.
Production manager: Ben Reynolds.

Library of Congress Cataloging-in-Publication Data

Milton, John, 1608–1674.
Paradise lost : an authoritative text, sources and backgrounds, criticism /
John Milton;
edited by Gordon Teskey.
p. cm.—(A Norton critical edition)
Includes bibliographical references (p.).

ISBN 0-393-92428-9 (pbk.)

1. Bible. O.T. Genesis—History of Biblical events—Poetry. 2. Milton, John, 1608–1674. Paradise lost. 3. Adam (Biblical figure)—Poetry. 4. Eve (Biblical figure)—Poetry. 5. Fall of man in literature. 6. Fall of man—Poetry. I. Teskey, Gordon, 1953- II. Title. III. Series.

PR3560.A2T47 2004
821'.4—dc22
2004054779

W. W. Norton & Company, Inc., 500 Fifth Avenue, New York, N.Y. 10110
www.wwnorton.com

W. W. Norton & Company Ltd., Castle House,
75/76 Wells Street, London W1T 3QT

8 9 0

This edition of Milton's *Paradise Lost* is dedicated to my mother,
Ann Camilla Teskey

Contents

Preface and Acknowledgments

This edition of Milton's *Paradise Lost* is intended for the general reader and for students encountering the poem for the first time. Spelling and punctuation have been modernized, the latter, however, as I shall explain in a moment, within limits imposed by Milton's syntax. The few words whose spelling probably reflects how Milton pronounced them, for example, *contemned, sovran,* and *hunderd,* are not, in my view, different enough to warrant retaining. But I have retained *heighth* (which is spelled *highth* in the early editions), *stupendious* and *amarantine*. Speeches are introduced with a colon but are not enclosed in quotation marks, which are used only at a second remove—that is, when a speaker in the poem is quoting someone else. In a few places I have indented to make extra verse paragraphs.

I have capitalized outright personifications such as *Death* and, when appropriate, rhetorical personifications such as *Shame* (9.1058). What I would term *vestigial personifications* are frequent in *Paradise Lost,* especially before the Fall, when created beings such as the Sun and the Ocean seem to oscillate between the states of being an object and being a person: "The Sun that light imparts to all receives / From all his alimental recompense / In humid exhalations and at ev'n / Sups with the Ocean" (5.423–26). The most celebrated moment in which vestigial personifications appear is when Eve eats the forbidden fruit: "she plucked, she eat: / Earth felt the wound, and Nature from her seat / Sighing through all her works gave signs of woe / That all was lost" (9.781–84). See 3. 710–13 and note.

Place names such as *Heaven, Hell,* and *Earth* are capitalized; but the *heavens* within the created universe are not; nor is the *earth* when it is named as a thing and not as a person or place. Especially important terms, such as *Man* (but not *mankind*) and *Adversary* (a more literal rendering of the Hebrew meaning of Satan's name), have been capitalized. The somewhat old-fashioned practice of capitalizing terms referring to God—*the Father, the Son, the Spirit, th' Almighty, Anointed King, Messiah*—as well as pronouns referring to God (*Thou, Thee, Him*) is useful in a poem in which God is on a different level of being from other characters. But for the sake of clarity I have often put in lowercase pronouns referring to the Son. And when the capitalization of pronouns of God becomes obtrusive, for example, when He is speaking of Himself, I have reverted to lower case.

The syntax of *Paradise Lost* is looser and more complex, and the clauses more subtly blended with one another, than fully modern punctuation allows. The stricter logic of modern punctuation can have a flattening effect on Milton's verse at some moments, forcing the sense in one direction alone when two possibilities should be held in suspense for a time.

The punctuation of the two editions of *Paradise Lost* to appear in Milton's lifetime has, in my judgment, no authority. The supposition that the original punctuation reflects the poet's intentions has caused a fashion for centaur-like editions of *Paradise Lost* in which the spelling is modernized and the heavy, often misleading seventeenth-century punctuation retained. In Milton's day punctuation was more the concern of copyists and printers than of poets, still less of blind poets. In a letter to a European correspondent (Peter Heimbach, 15 August 1666) Milton mentions as exceptional that the person taking dictation does not know how to spell or to punctuate, forcing him to do so himself. Clearly, specifying punctuation was not something Milton usually did. In the only sample we have of unrhymed narrative verse in Milton's hand—the Trinity manuscript *Comus*—the punctuation is extremely light: commas are infrequent and in many places even periods are omitted. Milton was formed as a poet by the discipline of composing Latin verse. He would have believed that all significant relationships between the words in a poem should inhere in those words and their syntactical arrangement. I have therefore punctuated as lightly as possible, that is, only where for lack of a comma the reader would take a wrong turn and be forced to go back.

Light punctuation is also crucial for hearing the rhythm. Milton's poems are not so much works on the page, meant to be interpreted as texts, as they are structures of sound meant to be heard, to be listened to, even when one is silently reading. *Paradise Lost* is modeled on the epic poems of Homer and Virgil, which were intended for memorization and oral recitation, and Milton's verse is strongly influenced by Greek and Latin oratory, which was written to be publicly declaimed. (There is as much Cicero as Virgil in the fabric of *Paradise Lost*.) It is this declamatory character of *Paradise Lost* that prompted Samuel Johnson to call it "that wonderful performance," and that is what *Paradise Lost* is: a wonderful performance, which the reader recaptures by listening to the poem as physical effort and physical sound. The one piece of advice I would offer the first-time reader of *Paradise Lost* is to take the poem in as a performance, not as a riddle.

The poetic line in *Paradise Lost* is generally (though not without exception; see 2.27 n.) ten syllables long. But a considerable amount of elision and contraction is needed, especially for North American speakers of English, to recapture the rhythm intended. I have given in the notes some help with pronunciation, but the reader will soon become accustomed to such things as *the* being contracted when it appears before nouns beginning with a vowel (*th' Almighty*), *Heaven* being pronounced in one syllable (*Heav'n*), the letters *ie*, as in *disobedience*, being pronounced like a *j* (dis-o-bee-jence), and so on. All such indications and helps are approximate. Sometimes (although not as often as might be supposed) there is more than one way to say a line. In such cases I have indicated the way that to my ear sounds best. There are no hard and fast rules for the scansion of Milton's verse, but the general pattern, to the reader who cares about such things, soon becomes clear.

Growing to understand *Paradise Lost* is a lifelong adventure. The same may be said of the rhythms of *Paradise Lost:* appreciating them fully is an ongoing project, not a question of getting everything right the first time. Nor is the rhythm of *Paradise Lost* confined to the single verse line, as it most often is, for example, in the poetry of Pope and even of Chaucer. Like Shakespeare's later verse, Milton's lines are heavily enjambed (running on without a pause at the end of the line), opening them to the longer and more complex rhythms of the glorious sentences of *Paradise Lost*. (The verse paragraph has no prosodic significance.) Developing longer rhythms, like ocean swells, than are possible in the single verse line is Milton's most important technical contribution to later verse in English, notably that of the English Romantics, especially Wordsworth and Keats, but also that of American poets from Walt Whitman to A. R. Ammons.

The notes in this edition are intended to elucidate difficulty, not to interpret the poem. As a rule, I have given biblical and classical sources only when they are important enough to be quoted. For these quotations I have used the Authorized (King James) Version of the Bible and have translated the classical sources myself. Latin and Greek verbs referred to in the notes are given in the first person singular. The texture of Milton's verse is thickened by an extraordinary number of exotic place names (Milton is the first truly global poet of the modern world), not all of which need to be looked up immediately. A glossary has been added to make it possible to keep the notes within compass and to separate, so far as is possible, the semantic and syntactic axes of difficulty. Semantic difficulties are dealt with mostly in the glossary, and problems of syntax, the heart of Milton's verse, are explained in the notes. I have also used the glossary to give fuller accounts of such things as Eden, Angels, Chaos, Typhon, Sin, Death, and the Son. References to Milton's prose are from *The Complete Prose Works of John Milton*, 7 vols., ed. Don M. Wolfe et al. (New Haven, Conn.: Yale University Press, 1953–1980), abbreviated as *YP*.

It is a pleasure to acknowledge the support of the Department of English at Cornell University, the Harvard Department of English and American Literature and Language, and the Harvard College Faculty of Arts and Sciences. It is also a pleasure to acknowledge the enthusiasm and patience (hard virtues to reconcile) of the staff of W. W. Norton & Company, especially Carol Bemis. I am indebted, as all editors of Milton are, to a tradition of scholarship and editorial work on the poet that goes back three hundred years. The spirit of that tradition is very much alive today in the community of Miltonists. For valuable discussion on textual matters relating to seventeenth-century poetry I thank Roy Flannagan, John Leonard, Jennifer Lewin, Charles Mahoney, Arthur Marotti, and John T. Shawcross. I have benefited from the editions of Flannagan, Leonard, and Shawcross as well as those of Douglas Bush, Gordon Campbell, Alastair Fowler, and Christopher Ricks. I should like particularly to acknowledge my Milton teacher in graduate school, H. R. MacCallum, and two distinguished Miltonists at Cornell whom it was my privilege to have as colleagues, Mary Ann Radzinowicz, who has taught us so much about the scope and power of Milton's mind, and the late Scott Elledge, the editor of the first Norton Critical Edition of *Paradise Lost*. As always in matters concerning English poetry, my greatest debt is to William Blissett.

Four former students and one present student have assisted me with this edition: my former doctoral student at Cornell, Professor Joseph Campana; Elise Cavaney, who studied Milton with me at Cornell and has worked with me ever since on this edition; Michael Zacchilli, who studied seventeenth-century poetry with me at Harvard; and my present student at Harvard, Yulia Ryzhik, without whose dedication and accuracy this project would still be far from complete. Work on this project began in discussions of the text of *Paradise Lost* in a reading course I did at Cornell with Ellen Devine. I wish to thank also the many students who have read Milton with me over the past twenty years. Although I am responsible for any errors and misjudgments, it may be said of this edition that students, to use the words of the publisher of Shakespeare's sonnets, are its "only begetters."

GORDON TESKEY
Cambridge, Massachusetts

Introduction

The Life of John Milton

John Milton was born on December 9, 1608, in London, into an upper-middle-class, deeply religious Puritan family. The family home, and the father's place of business, was in Bread Street, Cheapside, where the well-to-do lived, in the westerly part of the old city, on Ludgate Hill. Just steps away, dominating the neighborhood and indeed the entire city, stood the huge cathedral of Saint Paul's, one of the largest in Europe. To the east, downstream on the Thames, was London Bridge, which backed up the river to form a broad expanse of water. Below the bridge, farther downstream, lay the massive fortress of the Tower. To the west were the Inns of Court, Charring Cross, and, around the bend in the Thames, the City of Westminster, with Westminster Abbey, the Court, and the Houses of Parliament. In Milton's day London was still a walled, medieval city of narrow lanes, muddy streets, and mostly wooden buildings. But it was already becoming one of the most important trading centers in the world, and what was once open country between it and Westminster was rapidly filling up. One could still walk out of the city into the countryside to the north. At a dramatic moment in *Paradise Lost*, when Satan first catches sight of Eve alone, Milton briefly diverts our attention from the action at hand, comparing Satan's taking pleasure in Paradise, and especially in the sight of Eve, to the pleasure of walking out of the city on a summer morning:

> As one who long in populous city pent
> Where houses thick and sewers annoy the air,
> Forth issuing on a summer's morn to breathe
> Among the pleasant villages and farms
> Adjoined, from each thing met conceives delight—
> The smell of grain or tedded grass, or kine
> Or dairy, each rural sight, each rural sound—
> If chance with nymph-like step fair virgin pass
> What pleasing seemed for her now pleases more,
> She most, and in her look sums all delight.
>
> (9.445–54)

Queen Elizabeth I had died in 1603 and James I was on the throne. The tensions between the king and parliament, and between the Anglican Church and the puritans, which would lead to civil war and the execution of James's son, Charles I, were already great. As always in times of trouble, literature flourished. The Authorized (King James) Version of the Bible would appear in 1611, Shakespeare was writing his last plays, John Donne's poems were circulating in manuscript, and Ben Jonson and his literary entourage were still gathering at the Mermaid Tavern on Bread Street to drink its superior (and more expensive) wine.

Milton was educated at home and at Saint Paul's school, beside the cathedral, and later at Christ's College, Cambridge. Saint Paul's was perhaps the best school in England at the time and excelled in humanistic studies, especially the teaching of Latin and Greek. By the time he went to Cambridge, at age seventeen, Milton had read an impressive range of ancient authors and was accomplished at Latin composition in prose and verse. Milton's father, John, a successful scrivener (a profession that combined money lending, investing, and drawing up contracts), was a musician and a composer of some repute. In most middle-class homes before the age of radio and television music was a regular part of family life, but it was exceptionally so in Milton's home. The poet played the organ and the viola da gamba, and even in old age he sang.[1] The many descriptions of music in *Paradise Lost* betray deep passion for it as well as exceptional knowledge.

In addition to sending his son to an expensive and challenging school Milton's father hired tutors to instruct the boy in subjects not taught at Saint Paul's, among which were modern languages, especially French and Italian. Hebrew was taught to the senior boys at Saint Paul's, but Milton might have been tutored in it earlier, at home. By the time he went to Cambridge he was proficient in at least three languages other than English and expert in two, Latin and Greek. So avid was the boy for his studies that from the age of twelve his father arranged for a servant to sit up with him (no doubt keeping the candles trimmed) while he studied until midnight.

While at Cambridge Milton wrote much Latin poetry and, at age twenty-one, his first undoubted masterpiece in English, "Ode on the Morning of Christ's Nativity." In this poem we see already formed, though in brief outline, the human and cosmic concerns of Milton's mature poems, including a complete Christian vision of history. The Nativity Ode also shows Milton's lifelong preoccupation with using classical poetic forms to express Christian events and ideas. This artistic success confirmed Milton in his ambition to rival the Greek and Latin poets of antiquity by applying what he had learned from

1. The biographer John Aubrey said, "He would be cheerful even in his gout fits, and sing."

them to the Christian vision of history. He could not have known then that this ambition would not be fulfilled until he was in his mid-fifties. He did know that it would take him some time. In a sonnet written for his twenty-fourth birthday (that is, upon completing his "three-and-twentieth year"), Milton expresses his concern that at that advanced age he had as yet achieved very little: "my late spring no bud or blossom show'th." But he concludes with a remarkably mature statement of confidence in himself and in God's will:

> Yet be it less or more, or soon or slow,
> It shall be still in strictest measure even
> To that same lot, however mean or high,
> Toward which Time leads me, and the will of Heav'n.
> All is, if I have grace to use it so,
> As ever in my great Task-Master's eye.

After taking his B.A. in March 1630, Milton remained at Cambridge two more years, took his M.A. in July 1632, and then embarked on another six years of arduous private study in the country, to which his parents had retired, first at Hammersmith, upstream from London on the Thames, and then at Horton, in Buckinghamshire. Both places were near London, which the poet visited often to buy books and to see friends. The beautiful poems "L'Allegro" (the cheerful man) and "Il Penseroso" (the thoughtful, melancholy man) were likely written at this time.

Milton's parents intended him (and he had shared the intention) to enter the priesthood in the Anglican Church. But disillusionment with the conservatism, worldliness, and increasing authoritarianism of the Church caused him to abandon that course and to devote himself exclusively to poetry and learning—not without causing his father some anxiety. In addition to acquiring immense erudition and making the by no means easy transition from brilliant student to serious scholar, Milton composed two major poetical works: the court drama, or masque, subsequently called *Comus*, and the funeral elegy "Lycidas," the most intellectually intense and emotionally powerful short poem (or shorter poem: 193 lines) in the English language. He was not yet thirty years old.

To round out his education (still at his father's expense) Milton departed, with a manservant, for what would prove to be a fifteen-month tour of the European continent, passing almost all of that time in Italy, the faded home of the Renaissance. (It was in Paris, however, a city with a brilliant future rather than a brilliant past, that Milton met the great jurist and theorist of international law, Hugo Grotius, who was also a poet.) Milton made intellectual and literary friends in Florence, Rome, and Naples; and while in Florence he visited (in nearby Fiesole) the most important man in Europe at the time, Galileo, whom Milton recalls in *Areopagitica* and mentions on more than one occasion in *Paradise Lost*. (Indeed, it can be said that Galileo is implicitly mentioned in *Paradise Lost* every time the order of the cosmos is seen or discussed, as so often it is.)

When he arrived in Naples Milton was befriended by a person who, although they knew each other for only several weeks, had a decisive influence on him. This was the seventy-eight-year-old Giovanni Manso, the marquis of Villa, who recognized the quality of Milton's genius and cultivated the poet's friendship with many marks of respect. Manso was venerable in Milton's eyes because he had been the patron and biographer of the famous Italian epic poet Torquato Tasso, whom Manso cared for at the end of that poet's life. In his *Jerusalem Liberated* (*Gerusalemme liberata*, 1581), Tasso demonstrated two things that would prove crucially important to Milton: that an epic poem in the tradition of Homer and Virgil could be written in the modern age and that the specific conventions of the epic poem—set battles and single combats, noble speeches and debates, elaborate descriptions and similes, supernatural interventions and omens, and, not the least of these, invocations of the muse—could be adapted to a Christian subject.

In a Latin poem addressed to Manso, Milton discloses his ambition to write an epic poem. Although uncertain as to subject, Milton was considering a patriotic work on King Arthur, following the example of Spenser's *Faerie Queene*. As Manso conducted Milton to places of interest in the area around Naples, it is inconceivable they would not have visited the spectacular site of ancient Cumae, with its temple of Apollo and its mysterious underground passages of pre-Roman Samnite construction—the haunt, in antiquity, of the Cumaean Sibyl. It is there that Virgil has his hero Aeneas descend to the underworld to receive a prophetic vision of the future of Rome. That episode would be transformed into the mountaintop vision of history that the angel Michael accords Adam in the final two books of *Paradise Lost*. Of perhaps still greater significance to the future author of *Paradise Lost* is the visible presence, southeast of Naples, of Mount Vesuvius, which with Mount Etna, in Sicily, is one of two active volcanoes in Europe. In this region of intense geologic activity there had been two major earthquakes, and an eruption of Vesuvius, in the previous decade. Milton knew the ancient legend that Zeus pinned the monster Typhon beneath Etna (and, Pindar adds, the "sea-enclosed cliffs above Cuma"), where he now heaves in his torment, vomiting lava and fire. (See Glossary, TYPHON.) Milton would situate his Hell away from the earth, far off in chaos, but his explosive, sublime description of it (and chaos) would be inspired by the ancient authors' accounts of this region between Naples and Sicily.

Milton's plans to visit Sicily, rich in Greek antiquities, and to sail to Greece itself were cut short by the news of dangerously escalating religious and political tensions at home. The political left (as we would now call it), the English Puritans and Scottish Presbyterians, was, with growing effectiveness, challenging the legitimacy of the Anglican Church, which became, with the support of King Charles I, more uncompromisingly hierarchical and dogmatic in response to that challenge. When Parliament was recalled after an absence of a decade, it shook the authority of King Charles I, who had been attempting throughout that period to rule, and to collect taxes, without it. This "Short Parliament," as it was called, was soon dismissed. But political circumstances and desperation for money made it impossible for the king's personal rule to continue any longer. The momentous "Long Parliament," which would soon be in arms against the king, was summoned.

Milton's love of liberty, his English patriotism, his hatred of tyranny and especially of political control over spiritual matters, made him the ally of the Presbyterians, who dominated the Long Parliament. But he would eventually find them, as successful revolutionaries often are, more rigidly authoritarian than what they overthrew. Their hypocrisy would inspire the sonnet "On the New Forcers of Conscience Under the Long Parliament" with its hard-hitting final line: "New Presbyter is but old Priest writ large."

Some years later Milton would say, when explaining his early return from Italy, that he thought it wrong for him to be traveling for his personal improvement while his countrymen were fighting for liberty at home. Still, he was in Italy, and his return was unhurried. Traveling north, he passed several months in Rome and Florence to consult works in the Vatican and Laurentian libraries and to confer with learned men.

After crossing the Apennine Mountains, which run down the spine of the Italian peninsula, and traveling northeast through Bologna and Ferrara, Milton passed a month in Venice, where he added musical scores (Venetian music was the most advanced in Europe at that time) to the many books he had already collected. He then traveled west on the rich Lombardy plain to Verona (with its huge Roman amphitheater) and the great city of Milan before heading north on the arduous journey across the Alps to Switzerland and along Lake Leman to Geneva. The journey across the Alps, which was no easy undertaking in those days, and along the beautiful Lake Leman must have been thrilling to Milton, who had a passion for geography, for the complex, physical reality of the earth, which is everywhere apparent in *Paradise Lost* and is equaled by no other great poet. The mountains and plateaus of central Asia, the torrid sands of the Sahara, the icebergs and violent winds of the arctic, and the dangerous sea route around Africa into the Indian Ocean are all vividly imagined.

Geneva was then the center of the Protestant Reformation in

Europe. It was there Milton met and spent much time with the Protestant theologian Giovanni Diodati, the uncle of his boyhood friend Charles Diodati. Milton had probably already learned by letter of the death of his friend, for whom he would write a moving Latin elegy. In that elegy he again reflects on his ambition to write an epic poem on an English theme. Although he enjoyed Italy immensely, Milton must have felt relieved to be again among people whose religious views were close to his own. In the autograph book of the humanist scholar Camillo Cerdogni (it was fashionable in those days to collect samples of the handwriting of eminent and potentially eminent persons), Milton modified a verse from Horace, wittily altering its original meaning. Criticizing travel, Horace said that those who travel across the seas change their skies but not their minds, which remain as dull as when they left. Milton says that when he travels overseas he changes his skies—the skies of England for those of Italy—but never his mind. The trip north through France and home to England soon followed. Milton had fallen in love with Italy, with its language, its learning, its brilliant culture (perhaps especially its music), its affable scholars, and its astonishing sights and sounds. But his exposure in Italy to the oppressive spirit of the Counter-Reformation confirmed Milton in his hostility to Roman Catholicism and in his determination to oppose the Romanizing tendencies of the Anglican Church at home.

The next twenty years were tumultuous for Milton, as they were for England, which was first convulsed by a civil war that was atrociously destructive of human life and then governed by a regime that never achieved the one thing indispensable to a government if it is to last: legitimacy. The king was executed in 1649. The Long Parliament was reduced to a more compliant "Rump Parliament" (as it was derisively called) and then to a still smaller "Barebones Parliament" of religious fanatics, which would give way in turn to the "Protectorate" of Oliver Cromwell. Milton took up a means of livelihood as a schoolmaster, married seventeen-year-old Mary Powell (he was thirty-three at the time); became engaged in the bitter controversies over church government, which were, in effect, the opening salvos of the English civil war; was abandoned by his wife; wrote some remarkable works in prose (including *Reason of Church Government; Areopagitica,* the great work on intellectual freedom; and the forward-looking, but at the time notorious, pamphlets on divorce); and was reconciled with his wife. With her he had three daughters—Anne, Mary, and Deborah—and a son, John, who died when he was just over a year old. He also published *Poems of Mr. John Milton* (1646, dated 1645 because the year then changed in March), containing most of his Latin and English poems up to that date. The collection also contains a Greek epigram and a translation into Greek of Psalm 114, an early experiment (Milton did it as a teenager) in grafting the style of the heroic epic onto the subject matter of the Hebrew scriptures. The subject of Psalm 114 was a favorite of Milton's: the exodus of the Hebrew nation from bondage in Egypt and its joyous entry into the Promised Land. It would be Milton's metaphor for the English revolution.

Early in 1652, after some years of weakening eyesight, Milton became totally blind. Only months later his wife, Mary, died after the birth of their daughter Deborah. Thus it was that by the middle of 1652, little more than a decade after returning to England young, brilliant, ardently idealistic and hopeful, and with the best education possible at that time (and equal to the best at any time), Milton found himself widowed and blind with three daughters to raise, the oldest of whom was six. For a devoted teacher and an accurate scholar, one who had worked all his life with his eyes, Milton might well have thought that his education and talents were now useless and his ambition to serve God with his pen an unrealizable dream from his past. Sonnet 19, "When I Consider How My Light Is Spent," is a response to precisely these thoughts. Milton speaks first, with moving force, of the poetic talent that lies now useless within him, and he asks, "Doth God exact day labor, light denied?" But to this the voice of Patience answers from a place deeper within him:

God doth not need
Either man's work or His own gifts. Who best
Bear His mild yoke, they serve Him best. His state
Is kingly: thousands at His bidding speed
And post o'er land and ocean without rest.
They also serve who only stand and wait.

From 1649, after the execution of King Charles I, which he defended in *The Tenure of Kings and Magistrates*, Milton had worked for the new, revolutionary government as secretary for foreign tongues to the Council of State. It was in this capacity that his energies were absorbed, and his weak eyesight destroyed, defending the new English Commonwealth against covert royalist attacks from within and open attacks from abroad. He became famous for his responses to the latter, fulminating across Europe in brilliant Latin prose. Inevitably, his duties were relaxed after he went blind (that they continued at all shows how indispensable he was), and he was accorded an assistant in his work, the poet Andrew Marvell.

In 1656 Milton married Katherine Woodcock. Both she and the child she bore to him died in 1658. She is remembered (if the sonnet is addressed to her and not, as some scholars think, to Milton's first wife, Mary) in the moving sonnet 23, "Methought I Saw My Late-Espousèd Saint." If the sonnet is addressed to Katherine, it is particularly interesting to read when one recalls that Milton never saw her. He says that in sleep he thought he *saw* his wife come back to him from the grave. Her face, he thought, was veiled, and yet (as can happen in sleep) her entire person shone with more sweetness and love than could ever be expressed in a face:

> Her face was veiled, yet to my fancied sight
> Love, sweetness, goodness in her person shined
> So clear as in no face with more delight.
> But O! as to embrace me she inclined
> I waked, she fled, and day brought back my night.

With the death of his second wife the catastrophes of Milton's middle years were far from over. Later in 1658 the death of Oliver Cromwell, the brilliant general of the later phase of the civil war, the leader of the Council of State after the war, the perpetrator of brutal atrocities in Ireland, and, at his death, the reluctant, baffled dictator of the English Commonwealth, set in motion events that would lead, by 1660, to the Restoration: the triumphal return from the continent of Charles II, the son of the executed Charles I. The mood of most of the English at Cromwell's death is reflected in the diary of John Evelyn, who says of the funeral (at which Milton, Marvell, and Dryden were official mourners) that it was "the joyfullest funeral that ever I saw for there was none that cried but dogs, which the soldiers hooted away." Whatever his shortcomings (old Puritans, including Milton, were shocked by the gay life at court), Charles II's return was immensely popular.

The Restoration was not so much the triumph of royal authority, however, which would henceforth be much more restricted, especially after the "Glorious Revolution" (*glorious* because it was bloodless) of 1688, as it was a triumph of representative, parliamentary rule. The Rump Parliament, itself only recently reinstated after its dismissal by Cromwell, was diluted when the members excluded in Pride's Purge (1648) were recalled, fatally weakening republican resistance to the return of the king. In his diary, Samuel Pepys describes the bonfires and roasting of pork rumps on the London street corners, celebrating the end of the Rump and also the end of the petty, interfering despotism of Cromwell's major generals. The revolution in which Milton had placed his hopes, comparing the English struggle for liberty to the Israelites' escape from Egypt and their journey through the wilderness to the Promised Land, had come to its inevitable, ignominious end. Yet the principles by which Milton was guided in defending the English Revolution, even in its last, indefensible stages, were important for the future of English liberalism and would also inspire the fathers of the American Revolution.

We do not know for certain when Milton began composing *Par-*

adise Lost, but sometime in 1658 may be supposed. In that year (as we saw) Milton's second wife (and their child) died and the political stability Cromwell had imposed on the realm, under the Protectorate, began to fail with the Protector himself. The moral questions of *Paradise Lost* cannot be reduced to narrowly political ones, but the political adventure of the interregnum—the period between the reigns of Charles I and Charles II—was the cause to which Milton devoted himself and for which he sacrificed his eyesight. It gave him the experience of the world—of practical affairs, of sharp conflict, of the conduct of people under intense responsibility and pressure—that is necessary for a poet to be great.

Why the revolution failed, why the English chose "a captain back for Egypt," in the stern phrase of *The Ready and Easy Way* (the courageous appeal Milton published—twice—in the months before the Restoration), is the question that inspired him and drove him on in the composition of *Paradise Lost*. The question is framed in the widest terms possible. The failure of the English people at their supreme moment of opportunity opened a radical reflection—*radical* in the sense of going to the root of the matter—on the meaning of history itself and the place of human liberty in it. History begins at the Fall, when Adam and Eve lose the perfect liberty they had in the garden of Eden. If God's plan for history is the increase of human liberty, partly by human means, partly by divine aid, what causes a nation to surrender its liberty? Is it cowardice or the desire for physical comfort, or both? To pose such questions is only to raise a deeper question: "What is evil?" That is the mysterious question of *Paradise Lost*. Milton's dogmatic answer—*disobedience of God*—never silences the question or dispels the aura of mystery it raises. That is so largely because the question is embodied in one of the grandest characters in English literature: Milton's rebel angel, his seductive antagonist, Satan.

In Milton's Satan we do not see the horrible figure of the medieval imagination, chewing and excreting the damned in Hell. We see the darkened splendor and the reserved, explosive power of an archangel: "He above the rest / In shape and gesture proudly eminent / Stood like a tower" (1.589–91). We may or may not agree with Baudelaire that this power, hardened by Satan's resolute vengefulness yet softened by his deep unhappiness, makes him "the most perfect type of virile beauty" (cited in Armand Himy, *Milton*, pp. 480–81). But we cannot help being drawn to and fascinated by the commander who is so moved at the sight of his defeated companions in revolt: "Thrice he assayed [to speak] and thrice, in spite of scorn, / Tears such as angels weep burst forth" (1.619–20). Nor can we fail to be impressed when he exclaims, "Better to reign in Hell than serve in Heav'n" (1.263). Only gradually does Satan become what he is when we last see him, in the annual punishment to which he and the other devils are subjected, chewing the fruit that turns to dust and ashes in his mouth: "A monstrous serpent on his belly prone" (10.514).

Years before beginning *Paradise Lost*, indeed not long after he returned from Italy, Milton produced four drafts of a tragedy he called *Paradise Lost* and, alternatively, *Adam Unparadized*. At some later time Milton composed verses for the opening of this tragedy that survive in Book Four of *Paradise Lost* (32–41) as Satan's address to the sun, which Satan delivers when he has just landed on the earth, on the top of Mount Niphates:

> O thou that with surpassing glory crowned
> Look'st from thy sole dominion like the god
> Of this new world, at whose sight all the stars
> Hide their diminished heads, to thee I call
> But with no friendly voice and add thy name,
> O Sun, to tell thee how I hate thy beams
> That bring to my remembrance from what state
> I fell, how glorious once above thy sphere
> Till pride and worse ambition threw me down,
> Warring in Heav'n against Heav'n's matchless King.

As much as anything Satan says in the epic, these verses convey the glamour, even the majesty of evil, without diminishing, so to speak, the evil of evil.

Somehow in this period Milton managed to complete, among other projects, a very interesting theological treatise, in Latin, on the foundations of Christian faith, with every argument and point tagged to a passage in the Bible. The authorship of *On Christian Doctrine* (*De Doctrina Christiana*) has recently been questioned, and persuasively defended, but in either case it provides a useful commentary on the ideas underlying *Paradise Lost:* on the death of the soul and the body together, on the materiality of all being, including the source of all being, God the Father, on the subordination of the Son to the Father, and, most important, on Christian liberty and reason.

Although a general amnesty was proclaimed at the Restoration, Milton's name was proposed in Parliament for the list of those excluded from amnesty and therefore liable to prosecution. His friends concealed him through the summer months, when a warrant was out for his arrest. Nine of the men who had signed Charles I's death warrant were executed (against Charles II's wishes, but on the insistence of Parliament) by the terrible punishment of disemboweling, drawing, and quartering. Another Commonwealth leader, Sir Henry Vane the Younger, to whom Milton had addressed a sonnet in 1652, would also be dispatched. In 1661 the corpses of Cromwell and two of Charles I's judges were exhumed, dragged to the place of execution on Tyburn hill, beheaded, and the heads exhibited on pikes. (These events are alluded to in *Samson Agonistes*, lines 680–96.) Through the influence of friends such as Marvell, who had gone into Parliament as the member for Hull, Milton's name was not among those formally excluded from the Act of Pardon at the end of August 1660. He could come out of hiding. But through a misunderstanding (if that is what it was), Milton was arrested anyway, in November, and imprisoned into December. His feelings in this period, which reveal his resolution as an artist and a prophet, are recorded in verses from the invocation to Book Seven (lines 24–28) of *Paradise Lost:*

> I sing with mortal voice unchanged
> To hoarse or mute though fall'n on evil days,
> On evil days though fall'n and evil tongues,
> In darkness and with dangers compassed round
> And solitude.

Were he more inclined to self-pity, Milton might have added "and poverty," since, with the collapse of the Excise Bank and other severe financial misfortunes, he was left after the Restoration in difficult circumstances, which were not eased by his being charged vindictively ruinous fees upon his release from prison.

Living now in relative obscurity, Milton gave his nights and his mornings to the composition of *Paradise Lost*, his afternoons to an increasing flow of visitors from the Continent, where his Latin defenses of the Commonwealth had made him famous. He also received a younger generation of English admirers and poets, such as John Dryden. In 1663 he married Elizabeth Minshull, who would outlive him, and by 1665, before retiring to the country during the Great Plague (1665–66), he completed *Paradise Lost*. Milton's young Quaker friend Thomas Ellwood, to whom he taught Latin in exchange for assistance with reading, recalls being asked, almost casually, to look over a certain manuscript, which the poet then called to have brought to him. It was the manuscript of *Paradise Lost*. Ellwood reports that when he next saw Milton they discussed the poem for some time before Ellwood asked, half in jest, what Milton could now say about "paradise found." Milton made no reply at that time, but he would answer with *Paradise Regained*. Unfortunately, Ellwood says nothing of the substance of their discussion of *Paradise Lost*.

Milton was back in London in 1666, in time to witness (for he could feel it and hear it) the apocalyptic destruction caused by the Great Fire, or Fire of London, in which his boyhood home on Bread Street, the only property left to him, was lost. The fire destroyed the whole city except for its eastern and northeastern edges, including eighty-nine of its ninety-seven parish churches. The great cathedral of Saint Paul's burned with the rest. Pepys's description of the event—of the noise and explosions, of the terrifying smoke and heat, of an entire city in panic, and of pigeons, as they flew, catching fire—is unforgettable.

The fire also destroyed the shops and equipment of many printers and booksellers, which were concentrated around Saint Paul's. When *Paradise Lost* was at last published, in 1667, after further delays obtaining a license (for Milton was still regarded with suspicion by the authorities), it was an immediate success, being mentioned in Parliament, accorded the highest praise by John Dryden, and, not incidentally, selling well. Even readers who were implacably hostile to Milton on political grounds acknowledged the poem's greatness.

In 1670 or 1671 (it was licensed in 1670) Milton published in a single volume the two other long poems of his mature years, *Paradise Regained*, the brilliant and still under-appreciated sequel to *Paradise Lost* recounting Christ's mental fight with Satan in the desert, and *Samson Agonistes*, a tragedy intended for reading rather than for the stage. (The date of *Samson* has been contested in the past, but the evidence is strongly in favor of its being a post-Restoration work. It is generally accepted as the last poem Milton wrote.) The two poems complement each other and make a fascinating study in contrasts. Whereas *Paradise Regained* is subdued in tone and intensely cerebral, *Samson Agonistes* is an explosively passionate work, the poet's *cri de coeur* over the political disappointments and personal afflictions of his life. Yet *Samson* ends—and these are probably the last words of Milton's poetic career—with "calm of mind, all passion spent."

In 1673 Milton published an enlarged edition of the shorter poems of 1645–46, including, among other things, the superb political sonnets written in the intervening years, poems that would make Wordsworth wish Milton were "living at this hour." In the summer of 1674 the second and final edition (in the poet's lifetime) of *Paradise Lost* was published. Milton died the following November, perhaps on the ninth, a month before his sixty-sixth birthday. He was buried beside his father in the London church of Saint Giles, Cripplegate. For a revolutionary, an antimonarchist, and an enemy of the Anglican Church, the poets' corner in Westminster Abbey, where Edmund Spenser rests, was out of the question. But the funeral was attended, as a contemporary reported, by all classes of persons. There was an awareness that there had passed from the scene a great national poet who took, as he said, "these British islands as my world" (*YP* 1.812).

Before the publication of *Paradise Lost*, when he was almost sixty years old, Milton was hardly known as a poet, except to a small circle.

He was known as a political controversialist, as a disestablishmentarian (someone who opposes an "established," state-run church), as an enemy of bishops and of "hireling priests" (ministers paid for their work), as a proponent of divorce, as a defender of regicide, and as the chief propagandist of the English Commonwealth under the dictatorship of Oliver Cromwell—in short, as a vigorous proponent of everything that, after 1660, was regarded by many in England as criminal and seditious. This view of Milton did not fade away after 1667, with the appearance of *Paradise Lost*. But it was entirely subordinated to the conviction, which would only grow more intense in the following century (during which about one hundred editions of *Paradise Lost* would be published), that Milton is one of the very greatest poets of the modern world. Yet he is a poet around whom argument and controversy on the most central issues—on religion, history, politics, and gender relations, in short, on freedom, authority, and power—have never ceased to rage.

The standard scholarly biography is Barbara K. Lewalski's *The Life of John Milton* (London, 2000). Valuable sources are Gordon Campbell, *A Milton Chronology* (London, 1997); John S. Diekhoff, ed., *Milton on Himself*, 2nd ed. (London, 1965); and Helen Darbishire, ed., *The Early Lives of Milton* (New York, 1965). Until Lewalski's *Life* appeared, the standard biography was William Riley Parker, *Milton: A Biography*, 2 vols. (Oxford, 1968; revised ed. Gordon Campbell, 1996). It is still worth consulting. All modern students of Milton are indebted to David Masson's monumental nineteenth-century work *The Life of John Milton, Narrated in Connexion with the Political, Ecclesiastical and Literary History of his Time*, 7 vols. (London, 1881–94). Excellent shorter biographies are A. N. Wilson, *The Life of John Milton* (Oxford and New York, 1983), and Douglas Bush, *John Milton: A Sketch of his Life and Writings* (London, 1965). For readers of French there is an excellent biography by Armand Himy, *John Milton* (Paris, 2003), and a parallel-text translation, also by Himy, with a valuable critical introduction: *Le Paradis perdu* (Paris, 2001).

On the Text of *Paradise Lost*

In 1667, *Paradise Lost: A Poem Written in Ten Books by John Milton* appeared in quarto without either the "arguments" (the prose summaries at the head of each book) or the poet's note on the verse. Although the poem was divided into only ten books, it was substantially complete, only a handful of verses shorter than the later, twelve-book version. Of this first edition there were six issues (essentially reprintings, with minor alterations) between 1667 and 1669, after which the run of some thirteen hundred copies was sold out.

To the fourth issue of this first edition, in 1668, the arguments and the note on the verse were added to the front of the volume, in response to complaints (as the publisher informs us) that the narrative is hard to follow and that the poem "rhymes not." The new arguments could not be placed before their respective books until a new edition was published, which occurred in 1674, only months before the poet's death.

The title page of this second edition, in the smaller octavo format, reads *Paradise Lost: A Poem in Twelve Books. The Author John Milton . . . revised and augmented by the same author. Redistributed* would be a better term than *augmented:* Book Seven was divided to become Books Seven and Eight (accordingly, Book Eight became Nine and Nine became Ten), and the former Book Ten was divided to produce Books Eleven and Twelve. Brief transitional passages of three and a half and five lines, respectively, were added to the new Books Eight and Twelve, and three lines (485–87) were added to Book Eleven. Other changes were very minor.

The text on which this edition is based is 1674, with a few emendations and some adoptions, which are noted below, from the first edition and from the scribal manuscript of book one, in the Pierpont Morgan library, New York.

Emendations and Adoptions

1.230	The manuscript is punctuated to attach the clause *and such appeared in hue* to *fire* (229). Editions 1667 and 1674 imply that the clause is attached to what follows. The manuscript reading is more logical.
1.530	*fainting* 1674; *fainted* 1667 and manuscript
1.703	*founded* manuscript and 1667; *found out* 1674
1.754	*trumpets'*; *Trumpets* 1667, 1674; and *trumpets* manuscript
2.282	*where* 1667; *were* 1674
2.375	*originals* 1667; *original* 1674
2.483	*their* 1667; *her* 1674
2.527	*his* 1667; *this* 1674
2.1001	*your*, an early emendation; *our* 1667 and 1674
4	Argument, line 18; *find him out* 1668; *find him* 1674
4.451	*on* 1667; *of* 1674
4.567	*descried*; *described* 1667, 1674.
4.472	*shalt*; *shall* 1667 and 1674. Robert Martin Adams's argument (p. 90) that *shall* should be retained, ungram-

matically, because it allows the text to read both "he shall enjoy thy soft embraces" and "thou shalt enjoy him" is ingenious but unpersuasive.

4.592	*whether*, emendation of *whither* 1667, 1674, which means both "whether" (as *or* in line 594 requires) and "whither."
4.705	*shadier* 1667; *shady* 1674
4.928	*The* 1667; *Thy* 1674
5.627	*now* added in 1674
5.637–38	printing 1667 reads: "they eat, they drink, and with refection sweet / Are fill'd before th' all–bounteous King, who showrd"
6.115	*fealty*; *realtie* 1667, 1674. (See Shawcross, 2002, p. 392.) Cf. 3.204, 8.344, 9.262.
6.326	*sheared*, emendation of *shared* 1667, 1674.
6.352	*limn*; *Limb* 1667, 1674. (See note to this line and Shawcross, 2002, p. 392.)
7.139	*least* 1667, 1674. Some have emended to *last*, unnecessarily.
7.321	*swelling*, emendation of *smelling* 1667, 1674, probably caught from 319.
7.322	*and* 1674; *add* 1667. Some editors have adopted the 1667 reading.
7.366	*her* 1674; *his* 1667. Some editors adopt the 1667 reading, *his*, taking the "morning planet" to be Lucifer, not Venus. But the gender of the wearer of these *horns* appears to have been carefully corrected in 1674 to *her*.
7.451	*soul* emendation of *Fowle* 1667 and *Foul* 1674. See line 388.
7.563	*stations* 1667; *station* 1674.
8.1–3	Added in 1674, when Book Seven became Books Seven and Eight.
8.4	1667 reads: "To whom thus Adam gratefully, repl'd."
8.269	*as* 1667; *and* 1674
8.553	*Loses*; Looses 1667, 1674
9.213	*hear* 1667; *bear* 1674
9.394	*Likest* 1667; *Likeliest* 1674
9.922	*hast* 1667; *hath* 1674
9.944	*lose*; *loose* 1667, 1674
9.854	*too*; to 1667, 1674.
9.1019	*we* 1667; *me* 1674
9.1092	*for* 1667; *from* 1674
9.1093	*from* 1667; *for* 1674
9.1183	*women* 1667, 1674. Sometimes emended to *woman*.
10.58	*may* 1667; *might* 1674

10.241	*avengers* 1667; *avenger* 1674
10.408	*prevail* 1667; *prevails* 1674
10.550	*fair fruit* 1667; *Fruit* 1674
10.989	*so Death*. Editions of 1667, 1674: *So Death* begins line 990, rendering both lines metrically deficient.
11.427	*that sin* 1667; *that* 1674
11.485–87	Added in 1674.
11.651	*tacks* 1667; *makes* 1674
12.1–5	Added in 1674.
12.238	*what they besought* 1674; *them their desire* 1667

PARADISE LOST

The Verse

The measure is English heroic verse without rhyme, as that of Homer in Greek, and of Virgil in Latin, rhyme being no necessary adjunct or true ornament of poem or good verse, in longer works especially, but the invention of a barbarous age, to set off wretched matter and lame meter; graced indeed since by the use of some famous modern poets, carried away by custom, but much to their own vexation, hindrance and constraint to express many things otherwise, and for the most part worse than else they would have expressed them. Not without cause therefore some both Italian and Spanish poets of prime note have rejected rhyme both in longer and shorter works, as have also long since our best English tragedies, as a thing of it self, to all judicious ears, trivial and of no true musical delight, which consists only in apt numbers, fit quantity of syllables, and the sense variously drawn out from one verse into another, not in the jingling sound of like endings, a fault avoided by the learned ancients both in poetry and all good oratory. This neglect then of rhyme so little is to be taken for a defect, though it may seem so perhaps to vulgar readers, that it rather is to be esteemed an example set, the first in English, of ancient liberty recovered to heroic poem from the troublesome and modern bondage of rhyming.

The Verse.
This somewhat aggressive note on the verse was added to a later issue (the fourth) of the first edition, in 1668, apparently in response to complaints that the poem, as the publisher said, "rhymes not."

1. *English heroic verse* is ten-syllable, iambic pentameter verse.

2. *a barbarous age*: The Middle Ages, after the fall of the Roman Empire and the disappearance of classical culture.

5–6. *famous modern poets*, such as Ariosto, Tasso, and Spenser, all of whom employed rhyme; *modern* means after the Middle Ages, in what we call the Renaissance.

11. *our best English tragedies* refers to Shakespeare principally, but also to Marlowe, Webster, and others.

13–14. *apt numbers* refers, probably, to the number of syllables in the line (ten, eleven for "feminine" lines, in which the line ends with an extra, unaccented syllable). *fit quantity of syllables* refers, perhaps, to the length of time a syllable is sounded or to whether the vowel is long or short. (The term *quantity* alludes to Greek and Latin *quantitative* meter, which is entirely different from Milton's verse. He may have used the term here chiefly to intimidate.) *the sense variously drawn out from one verse into another*, the most important part of this statement, refers to the use of enjambment to run one line into another without a pause, allowing the rhythms of the syntax to assert themselves on a longer scale than that of the individual line.

15. The *learned ancients* avoided alliteration and rhyme.

Book One

The Argument

This first book proposes first, in brief, the whole subject: Man's disobedience and the loss thereupon of Paradise wherein he was placed; then touches the prime cause of his fall, the serpent, or rather Satan in the serpent, who revolting from God and drawing to his side many legions of angels was by the command of God driven out of Heaven with all his crew into the great deep. Which action passed over, the poem hastes into the midst of things, presenting Satan with his angels now fallen into Hell—described here, not in the center (for Heaven and Earth may be supposed as yet not made, certainly not yet accursed) but in a place of utter darkness fitliest called chaos. Here, Satan with his angels lying on the burning lake, thunder-struck and astonished, after a certain space recovers, as from confusion, calls up him who next in order and dignity lay by him. They confer of their miserable fall. Satan awakens all his legions, who lay till then in the same manner confounded. They rise: their numbers, array of battle, their chief leaders named, according to the idols known afterwards in Canaan and the countries adjoining. To these Satan directs his speech, comforts them with hope yet of regaining Heaven, but tells them lastly of a new world and new kind of creature to be created, according to an ancient prophecy or report in Heaven. (For that angels were long before this visible Creation was the opinion of many ancient fathers.) To find out the truth of this prophecy, and what to determine thereon, he refers to a full council. What his associates thence attempt: Pandemonium, the palace of Satan, rises, suddenly built out of the deep. The infernal peers there sit in council.

Of Man's first disobedience and the fruit
Of that forbidden tree whose mortal taste
Brought death into the world and all our woe
With loss of Eden till one greater Man
Restore us and regain the blissful seat
Sing Heav'nly Muse, that on the secret top
Of Oreb or of Sinai didst inspire
That shepherd who first taught the chosen seed,

Book One

The Argument. From the Latin *argumentum*, a summary of the underlying subject matter of a poetical work, often placed before a play.

1. *Man's*: mankind's. *disobedience* has four syllables: 'dis-o-bee-jence.'
4. *Man*: Jesus.
5. *seat*: home, throne.
6. *Muse*: recalling the epic muse of Homer and Virgil, but here the Holy Ghost, God's creative power.
8. *shepherd.* Moses, who was first called by God (on Mount Oreb) while pasturing sheep. The account of Creation, in Genesis, was attributed to Moses.

In the beginning, how the heav'ns and earth
Rose out of chaos. Or if Sion hill
Delight thee more and Siloa's brook that flowed
Fast by the oracle of God, I thence
Invoke thy aid to my advent'rous song
That with no middle flight intends to soar
Above th' Aonian mount while it pursues
Things unattempted yet in prose or rhyme.
And chiefly thou, O Spirit, that dost prefer
Before all temples th' upright heart and pure
Instruct me, for thou know'st, thou from the first
Wast present and with mighty wings outspread
Dove-like sat'st brooding on the vast abyss
And mad'st it pregnant. What in me is dark
Illumine, what is low raise and support,
That to the heighth of this great argument
I may assert Eternal Providence
And justify the ways of God to men.
  Say first, for Heav'n hides nothing from thy view,
Nor the deep tract of Hell, say first what cause
Moved our grand parents in that happy state,
Favored of Heav'n so highly, to fall off
From their Creator and transgress His will
For one restraint, lords of the world besides.
Who first seduced them to that foul revolt?
Th' infernal Serpent. He it was whose guile
Stirred up with envy and revenge deceived
The mother of mankind, what time his pride
Had cast him out from Heav'n with all his host
Of rebel angels, by whose aid aspiring
To set himself in glory 'bove his peers
He trusted to have equaled the Most High
If he opposed, and with ambitious aim

10. *Sion*: After mentioning the mountain associated with Moses' creation narrative in Genesis, the poet mentions Mount Zion, which is associated with the Psalms, attributed to King David, some of which are concerned with Creation (e.g., Psalm 104).

12. *oracle*: On Mount Zion, in Jerusalem, where God inspired the kings David and Solomon. Recalls the oracle of Apollo at Delphi, also on a mountain, and the stream where Apollo prophesied through his priestess.

17. *Spirit*: the Holy Ghost, the *Muse* of line 6, the inner experience of faith. *Spirit* is usually pronounced as one syllable: 'speart.'

18. *upright heart*: the temple of the Spirit. See Genesis 1:2.

24. *argument*: subject.

25. *Providence*: God's foresight and plan for history.

29. *grand parents*: Adam and Eve.

32. *one restraint*: the command not to eat the fruit of the Tree of Knowledge of Good and Evil.

34. *Serpent*: In the Genesis account, the serpent tempts Eve to eat the fruit. In Christian tradition this serpent was identified with Satan. See Revelation 12:9 and 20:1–3.

Against the throne and monarchy of God
Raised impious war in Heav'n and battle proud
With vain attempt. Him the Almighty Pow'r
Hurled headlong flaming from th' ethereal sky
With hideous ruin and combustion down
To bottomless perdition, there to dwell
In adamantine chains and penal fire
Who durst defy th' Omnipotent to arms.
Nine times the space that measures day and night
To mortal men he with his horrid crew
Lay vanquished rolling in the fiery gulf
Confounded though immortal. But his doom
Reserved him to more wrath, for now the thought
Both of lost happiness and lasting pain
Torments him. Round he throws his baleful eyes
That witnessed huge affliction and dismay
Mixed with obdúrate pride and steadfast hate.
At once as far as angels' ken he views
The dismal situation waste and wild:
A dungeon horrible on all sides round
As one great furnace flamed yet from those flames
No light but rather darkness visible
Served only to discover sights of woe,
Regions of sorrow, doleful shades, where peace
And rest can never dwell, hope never comes
That comes to all but torture without end
Still urges and a fiery deluge fed
With ever-burning sulfur unconsumed.
Such place Eternal Justice had prepared
For those rebellious, here their pris'n ordained
In utter darkness and their portion set
As far removed from God and light of Heav'n
As from the center thrice to th' utmost pole.
O how unlike the place from whence they fell!

44. *Pow'r*: power, pronounced with one syllable: 'paar.'
45. *ethereal*: has three syllables: 'eth-ear-yal.'
46. *hideous* has two syllables: 'hid-jus.'
48. *adamantine*: made of the legendary hardest substance, *adamant*. The word is from a Homeric epithet of the king of the underworld, Hades (*Iliad* 9.158): *adamastos*, "untamable, incapable of being overpowered" (*a* "un" + *damnaô* "to overpower, subjugate, master").
50. *Nine times*: recalls the titans in Greek myth (Hesiod, *Theogony* 720 f.), who fell nine days to earth and nine more into the pit of Tartarus. Milton's rebel angels are not the devils of medieval myth but huge cosmic powers. See lines 197–200.
59. *ken*: sight. Possibly a verb ("can see"), probably a noun.
74. *center*: of the earth. *pole*: of the created universe, not of the earth. Milton's Hell is situated not in the interior of the earth but outside the created universe altogether, far off in Chaos. The distance referred to here would be many times the distance from the center of the earth to the upper pole of the cosmos.

There the companions of his fall o'erwhelmed
With floods and whirlwinds of tempestuous fire
He soon discerns. And welt'ring by his side
One next himself in pow'r and next in crime,
Long after known in Palestine and named
Beëlzebub. To whom th' Arch-Enemy,
And thence in Heav'n called *Satan*, with bold words
Breaking the horrid silence thus began:
If thou beest he (but O how fall'n! how changed
From him who in the happy realms of light
Clothed with transcendent brightness didst outshine
Myriads, though bright!), if he whom mutual league,
United thoughts and counsels, equal hope
And hazard in the glorious enterprise
Joined with me once (now misery hath joined
In equal ruin), into what pit thou seest
From what heighth fall'n, so much the stronger proved
He with His thunder (and till then who knew
The force of those dire arms?), yet not for those
Nor what the potent Victor in His rage
Can else inflict do I repent or change,
Though changed in outward luster, that fixed mind
And high disdain from sense of injured merit
That with the Mightiest raised me to contend
And to the fierce contention brought along
Innumerable force of spirits armed
That durst dislike His reign and, me preferring,
His utmost pow'r with adverse pow'r opposed
In dubious battle on the plains of Heav'n
And shook His throne. What though the field be lost?
All is not lost: th' unconquerable will
And study of revenge, immortal hate
And courage never to submit or yield—
And what is else not to be overcome?
That glory never shall His wrath or might
Extort from me: to bow and sue for grace
With suppliant knee and deify His pow'r
Who from the terror of this arm so late
Doubted His empire! That were low indeed,
That were an ignominy and shame beneath
This downfall, since by fate the strength of gods

81–82. *Arch Enemy . . . Satan*. Satan's name is from the Hebrew word for "adversary."
84–94. *If . . . if . . . into . . . yet . . .* Milton makes Satan's syntax deliberately obscure to show passion dominating over reason. Satan will later use such syntax to confuse Eve.
114. *Doubted*: feared the loss of. *Who* [God] is the subject of *Doubted*.
115. *ignominy* and *and* are elided to four syllables: 'ignomin'yand.'

And this empyreal substance cannot fail,
Since through experience of this great event,
In arms not worse, in foresight much advanced,
We may with more successful hope resolve
To wage by force or guile eternal war
Irreconcilable to our grand Foe
Who now triúmphs and in th' excess of joy
Sole reigning holds the tyranny of Heav'n.
So spake th' Apostate Angel though in pain,
Vaunting aloud but racked with deep despair.
And him thus answered soon his bold compeer:
O prince, O chief of many thronèd pow'rs
That led th' embattled seraphim to war
Under thy conduct and in dreadful deeds
Fearless endangered Heav'n's perpetual King
And put to proof His high supremacy
(Whether upheld by strength, or chance, or fate)
Too well I see and rue the dire event
That with sad overthrow and foul defeat
Hath lost us Heav'n and all this mighty host
In horrible destruction laid thus low
As far as gods and Heav'nly essences
Can perish. For the mind and spirit remains
Invincible and vigor soon returns
Though all our glory extinct and happy state
Here swallowed up in endless misery.
But what if He our conqueror (whom I now
Of force believe almighty since no less
Than such could have o'erpow'red such force as ours)
Have left us this our spirit and strength entire
Strongly to suffer and support our pains
That we may so suffice His vengeful ire
Or do Him mightier service as His thralls
By right of war, whate'er His business be:
Here in the heart of Hell to work in fire
Or do His errands in the gloomy deep?
What can it then avail, though yet we feel
Strength undiminished or eternal being,
To undergo eternal punishment?
Whereto with speedy words th' Arch-Fiend replied:
Fall'n cherub, to be weak is mis'rable,

117. *empyreal substance*. The fiery, flexible material of which angels are made. (The Greek root *pyr* means "fire.") *fail*: perish.
131. *perpetual* has three syllables: 'per-pet-chal.'
141. *glory* and *extinct* are elided: 'glor-yextinct.'
146. *spirit* has one syllable.

Doing or suffering, but of this be sure:
To do aught good will never be our task
But ever to do ill our sole delight
As being the cóntrary to His high will
Whom we resist. If then His providence
Out of our evil seek to bring forth good
Our labor must be to pervert that end
And out of good still to find means of evil,
Which ofttimes may succeed so as perhaps
Shall grieve Him, if I fail not, and disturb
His inmost counsels from their destined aim.
But see! The angry victor hath recalled
His ministers of vengeance and pursuit
Back to the gates of Heav'n. The sulph'rous hail
Shot after us in storm o'erblown hath laid
The fiery surge that from the precipice
Of Heav'n received us falling. And the thunder,
Winged with red lightning and impetuous rage,
Perhaps hath spent his shafts and ceases now
To bellow through the vast and boundless deep.
Let us not slip th' occasion, whether scorn
Or satiate fury yield it from our Foe.
Seest thou yon dreary plain forlorn and wild,
The seat of desolation, void of light
Save what the glimmering of these livid flames
Casts pale and dreadful? Thither let us tend
From off the tossing of these fiery waves,
There rest (if any rest can harbor there)
And reassembling our afflicted pow'rs
Consult how we may henceforth most offend
Our enemy, our own loss how repair,
How overcome this dire calamity,
What reinforcement we may gain from hope,
If not what resolution from despair.
   Thus Satan talking to his nearest mate
With head uplift above the wave and eyes
That sparkling blazed. His other parts besides,
Prone on the flood, extended long and large,
Lay floating many a rood in bulk as huge
As whom the fables name of monstrous size:

161. *being* has one syllable.
167. *fail*: mistake. Imitating a similar expression in Latin.
171–74. The storm of thunder that pursues the rebel angels through Chaos shoots over them to form the lake into which they fall.
179. *satiate*: satisfied. Two syllables: 'say-shut.'
196. *rood*: a measure of distance, six to eight yards.

Titanian or Earth-born that warred on Jove,
Briareos or Typhon whom the den
By ancient Tarsus held or that sea-beast
Leviathan which God of all His works
Created hugest that swim th' ocean stream.
Him haply slumb'ring on the Norway foam
The pilot of some small night-foundered skiff
Deeming some island, oft, as seamen tell,
With fixèd anchor in his scaly rind
Moors by his side, under the lee, while Night
Invests the sea and wishèd morn delays.
So stretched out huge in length the Arch-Fiend lay
Chained on the burning lake. Nor ever thence
Had ris'n or heaved his head but that the will
And high permission of all-ruling Heav'n
Left him at large to his own dark designs
That with reiterated crimes he might
Heap on himself damnation while he sought
Evil to others and enraged might see
How all his malice served but to bring forth
Infinite goodness, grace, and mercy shown
On Man by him seduced, but on himself
Treble confusion, wrath and vengeance poured.
Forthwith upright he rears from off the pool
His mighty stature. On each hand the flames
Driv'n backward slope their pointing spires and, rolled
In billows, leave i' th' midst a horrid vale.
Then with expanded wings he steers his flight
Aloft incumbent on the dusky air
That felt unusual weight till on dry land
He lights—if it were land that ever burned
With solid as the lake with liquid fire,
And such appeared in hue. As when the force
Of subterranean wind transports a hill

198–202. Satan's monstrous size is compared to that of the titans and giants of classical mythology who warred against Jove and the Olympians, and to the biblical sea-monster Leviathan, which is "king over all the children of pride" (Job 41:34).

202. *hugest* should perhaps be pronounced as one syllable, *huge*, in which case the *the* before *ocean* should not be contracted.

203. The mention of Norway suggests Milton knew how plentiful whales were in northern latitudes.

204–8. *skiff*: a small sea-going rowboat carried on ships; used in whaling. *night-foundered*: separated from its ship, which has perhaps sunk (foundered). The sailors in the skiff are overcome by darkness. They fasten anchor to what they suppose to be an island but is in fact a whale. The whale dives, dragging them down with it—a symbol of the devil.

208. *invests*: covers, as with a robe.

230–37. Milton's appropriation of a ranting passage in Virgil: "Aetna thunders with horrifying ruin while hurling forth black clouds and balls of flame that lick the stars, vomiting from its depths, with a roar, its entrails of boulders and liquefied stone" (*Aeneid* 3.570–77).

Torn from Pelorus or the shattered side
Of thund'ring Etna whose combustible
And fueled entrails thence conceiving fire
Sublimed with mineral fury aid the winds
And leave a singèd bottom all involved
With stench and smoke: such resting found the sole
Of unblest feet. Him followed his next mate,
Both glorying to have 'scaped the Stygian flood
As gods and by their own recovered strength,
Not by the suff'rance of Supernal Pow'r.
  Is this the region, this the soil, the clime,
Said then the lost archangel, this the seat
That we must change for Heav'n, this mournful gloom
For that celestial light? Be it so, since He
Who now is Sov'reign can dispose and bid
What shall be right. Farthest from Him is best
Whom reason hath equaled, force hath made supreme
Above His equals. Farewell happy fields
Where joy forever dwells! Hail horrors, hail
Infernal world! And thou, profoundest Hell,
Receive thy new possessor, one who brings
A mind not to be changed by place or time!
The mind is its own place and in itself
Can make a Heaven of Hell, a Hell of Heaven.
What matter where, if I be still the same
And what I should be: all but less than He
Whom thunder hath made greater? Here at least
We shall be free. Th' Almighty hath not built
Here for His envy, will not drive us hence.
Here we may reign secure, and in my choice
To reign is worth ambition, though in Hell:
Better to reign in Hell than serve in Heaven!
But wherefore let we then our faithful friends,
Th' associates and copartners of our loss,
Lie thus astonished on th' oblivious pool
And call them not to share with us their part
In this unhappy mansion or once more

235. *sublimed*: vaporized.

240. *gods*: The devils will set themselves up as gods in the world after the Fall. Milton follows the Christian tradition that the gods of the Greeks and Romans were devils in disguise. See lines 1.364–75.

241. *suff'rance*: permission.

248–49. I.e., God, whom we have equaled with our reason, but whom mere force has raised above us.

262–63. "In heav'n they scorn'd to serve, so now in hell they reigne" (Phineas Fletcher, *The Purple Island* 7.10).

266. *oblivious pool* suggests one of the rivers of Hell: Lethe, "forgetfulness."

With rallied arms to try what may be yet
Regained in Heaven or what more lost in Hell?
  So Satan spake and him Beëlzebub
Thus answered: Leader of those armies bright
Which but th' Omnipotent none could have foiled,
If once they hear that voice (their liveliest pledge
Of hope in fears and dangers, heard so oft
In worst extremes and on the perilous edge
Of battle when it raged, in all assaults
Their surest signal) they will soon resume
New courage and revive though now they lie
Grov'ling and prostrate on yon lake of fire
As we erewhile, astounded and amazed—
No wonder, fall'n such a pernicious heighth!
  He scarce had ceased when the superior fiend
Was moving toward the shore. His ponderous shield,
Ethereal temper, massy, large and round,
Behind him cast. The broad circumference
Hung on his shoulders like the moon whose orb
Through optic glass the Tuscan artist views
At evening from the top of Fesolè
Or in Valdarno to descry new lands,
Rivers or mountains in her spotty globe.
His spear (to equal which the tallest pine
Hewn on Norwegian hills to be the mast
Of some great admiral were but a wand)
He walked with to support uneasy steps
Over the burning marl (not like those steps
On Heaven's azure) and the torrid clime
Smote on him sore besides, vaulted with fire.
Nathless he so endured till on the beach
Of that inflamèd sea he stood and called
His legions, angel forms who lay entranced
Thick as autumnal leaves that strew the brooks

285. *Ethereal temper*: The shield is made of empyreal (fiery) substance of Heaven and tempered in the cool *aether* just beneath the region of fire.

286. *Behind*: Greek soldiers slung their shields behind them when in retreat.

288. *Tuscan artist*: Galileo, who is called *Tuscan* because he lived in Tuscany, where the young Milton visited him, in *Fiesole,* which overlooks the valley of the Arno river, *Valdarno*. Galileo is called *artist* in the sense of an *artifex*, one who invents mechanical devices. To observe the heavens, Galileo and Lippershey greatly improved the telescope, formerly a naval instrument.

294. *admiral*: The principal ship of a fleet, having the tallest mast (for signaling). Such a mast would be a mere wand in comparison with Satan's spear.

302–11. Two similes in succession, a natural followed by a biblical: (1) The devils cover the surface of the fiery lake as thickly as fallen leaves cover brooks in the shadowy vale (hence the name *Vallombrosa*) of Tuscany, the region of Italy anciently known as *Etruria*, the home of the pre-Roman Etruscans. (2) The devils are strewn on the fiery lake as reedy plants, uprooted by violent winds brought by the constellation Orion, strew the coast of

In Vallombrosa where th' Etrurian shades
High overarched embow'r, or scattered sedge
Afloat when with fierce winds Orion armed
Hath vexed the Red Sea coast whose waves o'erthrew
Busiris and his Memphian chivalry
While with perfidious hatred they pursued
The sojourners of Goshen, who beheld
From the safe shore their floating carcasses
And broken chariot wheels. So thick bestrewn,
Abject and lost lay these, covering the flood,
Under amazement of their hideous change.
He called so loud that all the hollow deep
Of Hell resounded: Princes! Potentates!
Warriors! the flow'r of Heav'n once yours, now lost,
If such astonishment as this can seize
Eternal Spirits! Or have ye chos'n this place
After the toil of battle to repose
Your wearied virtue for the ease you find
To slumber here as in the vales of Heav'n?
Or in this abject posture have ye sworn
T' adore the Conqueror, who now beholds
Cherub and seraph rolling in the flood
With scattered arms and ensigns till anon
His swift pursuers from Heaven gates discern
Th' advantage and descending tread us down,
Thus drooping, or with linkèd thunderbolts
Transfix us to the bottom of this gulf?
Awake! Arise, or be for ever fall'n!
  They heard and were abashed and up they sprung
Upon the wing, as when men wont to watch
On duty, sleeping found by whom they dread,
Rouse and bestir themselves ere well awake.
Nor did they not perceive the evil plight
In which they were or the fierce pains not feel,
Yet to their gen'ral's voice they soon obeyed
Innumerable. As when the potent rod
Of Amram's son in Egypt's evil day

---

the Red Sea. The Red Sea closed over the army of Pharoah (*Busiris*) and his Egyptian cavalry (*Memphian chivalry*) when they were pursuing the Israelites, who were formerly encamped at *Goshen* and who now behold the destruction of their pursuers (Exodus 14: 21–31).

338. *Innumerable* has four syllables: 'in-núm-rable.' *potent rod*: Moses' staff, which has magical powers given by God. "And Moses stretched forth his rod over the land of Egypt . . . And the locusts went up over all the land of Egypt . . . they covered the face of the whole earth, so that the land was darkened" (Exodus 10:13–15).

339. *Amram's son*: Moses (Exodus 6:20).

Waved round the coast upcalled a pitchy cloud
Of locusts warping on the eastern wind
That o'er the realm of impious Pharaoh hung
Like night and darkened all the land of Nile,
So numberless were those bad angels seen
Hovering on wing under the cope of Hell
'Twixt upper, nether, and surrounding fires
Till as a signal giv'n th' uplifted spear
Of their great sultan waving to direct
Their course in even balance down they light
On the firm brimstone and fill all the plain:
A multitude like which the populous north
Poured never from her frozen loins to pass
Rhene or the Danaw when her barbarous sons
Came like a deluge on the south and spread
Beneath Gibraltar to the Libyan sands.
Forthwith from every squadron and each band
The heads and leaders thither haste where stood
Their great commander: godlike shapes and forms
Excelling human, princely dignities
And pow'rs that erst in Heaven sat on thrones,
Though of their names in Heav'nly records now
Be no memorial, blotted out and razed
By their rebellion from the books of life.
Nor had they yet among the sons of Eve
Got them new names, till wand'ring o'er the earth
Through God's high suff'rance, for the trial of Man,
By falsities and lies the greatest part
Of mankind they corrupted to forsake
God their Creator and th' invisible
Glory of Him that made them, to transform
Oft to the image of a brute adorned
With gay religions full of pomp and gold,
And devils to adore for deities!
Then were they known to men by various names
And various idols through the heathen world.
Say, Muse, their names then known, who first, who last,

342. *impious* has two syllables: 'imp-yus.'

351–55. The devils' landing on the solid ground of Hell is compared to the barbarian hordes that poured out of the north to destroy the Roman empire, crossing the Rhine and Danube rivers and not only invading Italy but descending through Spain into North Africa.

363. *books of life*: "Let them be blotted out of the book of the living, and not be written with the righteous" (Psalms 69:28).

376. It is a convention of epic poetry to re-invoke the muse before any long, encyclopedic list. Homer does so before the catalog of Achaean (Greek) leaders, who lay siege to Troy: "Tell me now you muses who have your homes on Olympus, for you are goddesses, and

Roused from the slumber on that fiery couch
At their great emperor's call, as next in worth,
Came singly where he stood on the bare strand
While the promiscuous crowd stood yet aloof.
The chief were those who from the pit of Hell
Roaming to seek their prey on Earth durst fix
Their seats long after next the seat of God,
Their altars by His altar, gods adored
Among the nations round, and durst abide
Jehovah thund'ring out of Zion throned
Between the cherubim, yea, often placed
Within His sanctuary itself their shrines,
Abominations, and with cursèd things
His holy rites and solemn feasts profaned
And with their darkness durst affront His light.
First Moloch, horrid king, besmeared with blood
Of human sacrifice and parents' tears
Though for the noise of drums and timbrels loud
Their children's cries unheard that passed through fire
To his grim idol. Him the Ammonite
Worshipped in Rabba and her wat'ry plain,
In Argon and in Basan to the stream
Of utmost Arnon. Nor content with such
Audacious neighborhood the wisest heart
Of Solomon he led by fraud to build
His temple right against the templ' of God
On that opprobrious hill and made his grove
The pleasant valley of Hinnom, Tophet thence

---

are present to aid me, and you know all things" (*Iliad* 2.484–85). Virgil does so before the catalog of ancient, Italic leaders: "Spread open Helicon, O goddesses, and move your song . . . for you, being goddesses, can remember and can tell" (*Aeneid* 7.641–45).

379. *singly*: one by one.

380. *promiscuous*: mixed, not distinguished from one another, as the leading devils will be.

383–91. Pagan deities worshipped near and even on the Temple Mount in Jerusalem, brought thither by the foreign wives of kings such as Solomon: "Then did Solomon build an high place for Chemosh, the abomination of Moab, in the hill that is before Jerusalem, and for Molech, the abomination of the children of Ammon. And likewise did he for all his strange wives, which burnt incense and sacrificed unto their gods" (1 Kings 11:1–9).

385. *nations*: i.e., non-Hebrew peoples, gentiles.

387. *cherubim*: gold statues in the Hebrew sanctuary (later in the temple) of angelic beings whose wings overshadow the mercy seat and the ark of the covenant. "Give ear, O Shepherd of Israel, thou that dwellest between the cherubims, shine forth" (Psalms 80:1). See Exodus 37:7–8 and 1 Kings 8:6.

388. *sanctuary* has three syllables: 'sank-cherry.' "[Manasseh] built altars in the house of the Lord . . . for all the host of heaven" (2 Kings 21:4–5). "Host of heaven" here means false gods, not loyal angels.

402. *Temple* and *of* are elided: 'Temp-lov-God.'

403. *opprobrious hill*: the Mount of Olives, which faces the Temple Mount, Zion, to the west.

404. "And they have built the high places of Tophet, which is in the valley of the son of Hinnom, to burn their sons and their daughters in the fire" (Jeremiah 7:21). *valley* and *of* are elided: 'val-yov.'

And black Gehenna called, the type of Hell.
  Next Chemos, th' óbscene dread of Moab's sons,
From Aroer to Nebo and the wild
Of southmost Abarim, in Hesebon
And Horonaim, Seon's realm, beyond
The flow'ry dale of Sibma clad with vines
And Elealè to th' Asphaltic Pool.
Peor his other name when he enticed
Israel in Sittim on their march from Nile
To do him wanton rites which cost them woe.
Yet thence his lustful orgies he enlarged
Ev'n to that hill of scandal by the grove
Of Moloch homicide (lust hard by hate)
Till good Josiah drove them thence to Hell.
  With these came they who from the bord'ring flood
Of old Euphrates to the brook that parts
Egypt from Syrian ground had general names
Of Baälim and Ashtaroth, those male,
These feminine, for spirits when they please
Can either sex assume or both, so soft
And uncompounded is their essence pure,
Not tied or manacled with joint or limb
Nor founded on the brittle strength of bones
Like cumbrous flesh but in what shape they choose,
Dilated or condensed, bright or obscure,
Can execute their airy purposes
And works of love or enmity fulfill.
For those the race of Israel oft forsook
Their Living Strength and unfrequented left
His righteous altar, bowing lowly down
To bestial gods, for which their heads as low
Bowed down in battle, sunk before the spear
Of despicáble foes. With these in troop

406. *obscene*: ominous (Latin), but also repulsive, as might be said of a god whose priests were reputed to defecate ritually before his shrine. Chemos is associated with Peor, whose name means to open or to stretch out. Many of the horrific details of Milton's devils' future careers as the false gods of the Old Testament are from John Selden's *De Diis Syris* ("On the Gods of Syria and Palestine," 1617). Selden denies this detail about Chemos/Peor, however.

413. *march from Nile*: The Exodus from Egypt, during which the temptation to couple with foreign women and to worship foreign gods caused much trouble. "And Israel abode in Shittim, and the people began to commit whoredom with the daughters of Moab. And [the Moabites] called the people unto the sacrifices of their gods; and the people did eat, and bowed down to their gods" (Numbers 25:1–2).

418. "And the groves, and the carved images, and the molten images [Josiah] brake in pieces, and made dust of them. . . . And he burnt the bones of the priests upon their altars, and cleansed Judah and Jerusalem" (2 Chronicles 34:4–5).

419–21. Throughout Palestine (Syria, as Milton called it), from the upper Euphrates in the north to the brook in the south that forms the boundary with Egypt.

Came Astoreth whom the Phoenicians called
Astartè, Queen of Heav'n, with crescent horns,
To whose bright image nightly by the moon
Sidonian virgins paid their vows and songs,
In Sion also not unsung where stood
Her temple on th' offensive mountain, built
By that uxorious king whose heart, though large,
Beguiled by fair idolatresses, fell
To idols foul. Thammuz came next behind
Whose annual wound in Lebanon allured
The Syrian damsels to lament his fate
In amorous ditties all a summer's day
While smooth Adonis from his native rock
Ran purple to the sea, supposed with blood
Of Thammuz yearly wounded. The love-tale
Infected Sion's daughters with like heat
Whose wanton passions in the sacred porch
Ezekiel saw when by the vision led
His eye surveyed the dark idolatries
Of alienated Judah. Next came one
Who mourned in earnest when the captive ark
Maimed his brute image, head and hands lopped off
In his own temple on the grunsel edge
Where he fell flat and shamed his worshippers:
Dagon his name, sea monster, upward man
And downward fish, yet had his temple high
Reared in Azotus, dreaded through the coast
Of Palestine, in Gath and Ascalon
And Accaron and Gaza's frontier bounds.

444. *uxorious king*: i.e., Solomon. (Latin *uxor*, "wife.") "And he had seven hundred wives, princesses, and three hundred concubines" (1 Kings 11:3). See 383–91 n.

450–52. The river Adonis was discolored annually, supposedly by the blood of the dying god Adonis, actually by ferrous mud stirred up by rains or, more poetically, by the petals of the anemone, or windflower, the Adonis (James G. Frazer, *Adonis, Attis, Osiris: Studies in Oriental Religion*, 3rd ed., vol. 1, p. 30). Since Milton says the river is *purple*, he is most likely thinking of the petals as the cause. The *love tale* is the story, told, e.g. in Shakespeare's *Venus and Adonis*, of Venus's (Aphrodite's) love for the boy Adonis, who is killed by a boar. Venus changes Adonis into a flower, which dies and revives annually.

452–57. In Ezekiel 8 the prophet is carried in spirit to Jerusalem and shown various sacrileges being committed there, among which were women sitting by the gate of temple precinct weeping for Thammuz (identified by Saint Jerome with Adonis) and men inside the temple committing the *dark idolatry* of turning their backs to the altar and facing east to worship the sun. In facing the physical light of the sun, they are in mental and moral darkness. The kingdom of *Judah* is *alienated* because its religious and political leaders, including Ezekiel, are in captivity in Babylon.

457–61. When the Philistines captured the ark of the covenant they placed it in their temple to Dagon: "And when they arose early on the morrow morning, behold, Dagon was fallen upon his face to the ground before the ark of the Lord; and the head of Dagon and both the palms of his hands were cut off upon the threshold; only the stump of Dagon was left to him" (1 Samuel 5:4).

460. *grunsel*: threshold.

Him followed Rimmon whose delightful seat
Was fair Damascus on the fertile banks
Of Abbana and Pharphar, lucid streams.
He also 'gainst the house of God was bold.
A leper once, he lost and gained a king,
Ahaz, his sottish conqueror, whom he drew
God's altar to disparage and displace
For one of Syrian mode whereon to burn
His odious offerings and adore the gods
Whom he had vanquished. After these appeared
A crew who under names of old renown,
Osiris, Isis, Orus and their train,
With monstrous shapes and sorceries abused
Fanatic Egypt and her priests to seek
Their wand'ring gods disguised in brutish forms
Rather than human. Nor did Israel 'scape
Th' infection when their borrowed gold composed
The calf in Oreb and the rebel king
Doubled that sin in Bethel and in Dan,
Lik'ning his Maker to the grazèd ox,
Jehovah, who in one night when he passed
From Egypt marching equaled with one stroke
Both her first-born and all her bleating gods.
Belial came last, than whom a spirit more lewd
Fell not from Heaven or more gross to love
Vice for itself. To him no temple stood
Or altar smoked. Yet who more oft than he
In temples and at altars when the priest
Turns atheist, as did Eli's sons, who filled
With lust and violence the house of God?
In courts and palaces he also reigns
And in luxurious cities where the noise

476–89. The gods of Egypt, especially debased in Milton's eyes because they have animal heads. See Glossary, *Typhon*. The Egyptian aberration was imitated by the Hebrews when they worshipped the Golden Calf during the march out of Egypt (Exodus 32:1–6) and again when the *rebel king*, Jeroboam *doubled* the sin by making two calves. These were placed for worship in the northern and southernmost points of the northern kingdom: "Whereupon the king took counsel, and made two calves of gold and said unto them, It is too much for you to go up to Jerusalem: behold thy gods, O Israel, which brought thee up out of the land of Egypt. And he set the one in Bethel, and the other put he in Dan" (1 Kings 12:28–29).

488. *equaled*: killed. "For I will pass through the land of Egypt this night, and will smite all the firstborn in the land of Egypt, both man and beast; and against all the gods of Egypt I will execute judgment: I am the Lord" (Exodus 12:12).

492–98. Belial has no temple because he represents shamelessness and sexual violence, which can occur anywhere, e.g. in the *courts*, *palaces*, and *luxurious cities*.

495–96. The sons of the high priest Eli were themselves priests: "Now the sons of Eli were sons of Belial; they knew not the Lord" (1 Samuel 2:12).

498. *luxurious* has three syllables: 'lug-shur-yus.' *riot* has one syllable ('raat'); *loftiest* has two ('lof-tyest').

Of riot ascends above their loftiest tow'rs,
And injury and outrage. And when night
Darkens the streets then wander forth the sons
Of Belial flown with insolence and wine.
Witness the streets of Sodom and that night
In Gibeah when the hospitable door
Exposed a matron to avoid worse rape.
  These were the prime in order and in might.
The rest were long to tell though far renowned:
Th' Ionian gods of Javan's issue, held
Gods, yet cónfessed later than Heav'n and Earth,
Their boasted parents: Titan, Heav'n's first-born,
With his enormous brood and birthright seized
By younger Saturn. He from mightier Jove
(His own and Rhea's son) like measure found:
So Jove usurping reigned. These first in Crete
And Ida known, thence on the snowy top
Of cold Olympus ruled the middle air,
Their highest heav'n, or on the Delphian cliff
Or in Dodona and through all the bounds
Of Doric land, or who with Saturn old
Fled o'er Adria to th' Hesperian fields
And o'er the Celtic roamed the utmost isles.
All these and more came flocking but with looks
Downcast and damp, yet such wherein appeared
Obscure some glimpse of joy t' have found their chief
Not in despair, t' have found themselves not lost
In loss itself which on his count'nance cast
Like doubtful hue. But he his wonted pride
Soon recollecting with high words that bore
Semblance of worth, not substance, gently raised
Their fainting courage and dispelled their fears.
Then straight commands that at the warlike sound
Of trumpets loud and clarions be upreared
His mighty standard. That proud honor claimed
Azazel as his right, a cherub tall
Who forthwith from the glittering staff unfurled

500–5. The "sons of Belial" attempted to rape the angels who visited Lot in Sodom (Genesis 19:1–11). They later attempted to rape the Levite guest of a pious Jew in Gibeah. The Levite sent his concubine out to them and they raped her to death (Judges 19).

502. *flown*: flushed.

508–21. The gods of Greek myth as described in Hesiod's *Theogony* (literally, "sexual generation of the gods"), maiming, mating with, and overthrowing one another. The Greeks were thought to descend from one of the three sons of Noah, Japhet. The Greek gods are to Milton obviously false gods because in Hesiod's account they are *later* than heaven (*Ouranos*) and earth (*Gaia*), from whom they are generated.

520. Over the Adriatic Sea, on Italy's east coast, to the Atlantic. The *i* in *Adria* is long.

Th' imperial ensign which full high advanced
Shone like a meteor streaming to the wind
With gems and golden luster rich emblazed,
Seraphic arms and trophies, all the while
Sonorous metal blowing martial sounds
At which the universal host upsent
A shout that tore Hell's concave and beyond
Frighted the reign of Chaos and old Night.
All in a moment through the gloom were seen
Ten thousand banners rise into the air
With orient colors waving. With them rose
A forest huge of spears; and thronging helms
Appeared and serried shields in thick array
Of depth immeasurable. Anon they move
In perfect phalanx to the Dorian mood
Of flutes and soft recorders, such as raised
To heighth of noblest temper heroes old
Arming to battle, and instead of rage
Deliberate valor breathed, firm and unmoved
With dread of death to flight or foul retreat,
Nor wanting pow'r to mitigate and swage
With solemn touches, troubled thoughts, and chase
Anguish and doubt and fear and sorrow and pain
From mortal or immortal minds. Thus they
Breathing united force with fixèd thought
Moved on in silence to soft pipes that charmed
Their painful steps o'er the burnt soil. And now
Advanced in view they stand a horrid front
Of dreadful length and dazzling arms in guise
Of warriors old with ordered spear and shield
Awaiting what command their mighty chief
Had to impose. He through the armèd files
Darts his experienced eye and soon traverse
The whole battalion views, their order due,

536. *ensign*: military banner.

546. *orient*: adjective describing the color of the sun rising in the east; lustrous, like a pearl.

548. *serried*: in close order.

549–55. *phalanx*: A tightly packed, heavily armed rank of foot soldiers in ancient Greek warfare. *Dorian mood*: a musical mode suited to military discipline, favored for this reason by Plato in the *Republic* (399A). The ancient Spartans, who were distinguished for valor, went calmly into battle to the sound of flutes, impervious to fear or to rage (Plutarch *Lycurgus* 22.3). In Homer, the clamorous Trojans are contrasted with the Achaeans (Greeks), who "move in silence, breathing strength" (*Iliad* 3.7).

554–55: *unmoved . . . retreat*: fear of death cannot move them to fly or to retreat.

563. *horrid front*. Latin *horror*, "bristling, trembling and inspiring cold terror." Seen from the front, their ranks bristle with arms and cause a chill of horror.

567–68. *files . . . traverse*: Satan walks along the side of his army, darting his eye down the lanes between each rank to inspect it.

569. *battalion*: the main body of an army.

Their visages and stature as of gods,
Their number last he sums. And now his heart
Distends with pride and, hard'ning in his strength,
Glories. For never since created Man
Met such embodied force as named with these
Could merit more than that small infantry
Warred on by cranes, though all the giant brood
Of Phlegra with th' heroic race were joined
That fought at Thebes and Ilium, on each side
Mixed with auxiliar gods, and what resounds
In fable or romance of Uther's son
Begirt with British and Armoric knights
And all who since, baptized or infidel,
Jousted in Aspramont or Montalban,
Damasco, or Morocc' or Trebisond,
Or whom Biserta sent from Afric shore
When Charlemagne with all his peerage fell
By Fontarrábia. Thus far these beyond
Compare of mortal prowess yet observed
Their dread commander. He above the rest
In shape and gesture proudly eminent
Stood like a tower. His form had yet not lost
All her original brightness nor appeared
Less than archangel ruined and th' excess
Of glory obscured, as when the sun, new ris'n,
Looks through the horizontal misty air
Shorn of his beams or from behind the moon
In dim eclipse disastrous twilight sheds
On half the nations and with fear of change
Perplexes monarchs. Darkened so, yet shone
Above them all th' archangel, but his face
Deep scars of thunder had entrenched and care
Sat on his faded cheek, but under brows
Of dauntless courage and consid'rate pride
Waiting revenge. Cruel his eye, but cast
Signs of remorse and passion to behold
The fellows of his crime, the followers rather
(Far other once beheld in bliss) condemned

573. *since created Man*: since Man was created.

573–87. 'To the largest army of men ever amassed add the following: the giants who fought the Olympians, all the heroes in two separate Greek wars (at Troy and at Thebes), the Olympian gods who became involved in those Greek wars, and all the knights of medieval romance. Such an army would still be as puny, compared with this army of rebel angels, as the army of pygmies (mentioned in *Iliad* 3.3–6), which fought against cranes.'

594. *glory* and *obscured* are elided: 'glor-yobscured.'

603. *consid'rate*: calculating.

For ever now to have their lot in pain,
Millions of spirits for his fault amerced
Of Heav'n and from eternal splendors flung
For his revolt. Yet faithful how they stood,
Their glory withered. As when heaven's fire
Hath scathed the forest oaks or mountain pines,
With singèd top their stately growth though bare
Stands on the blasted heath. He now prepared
To speak, whereat their doubled ranks they bend
From wing to wing and half enclose him round
With all his peers. Attention held them mute.
Thrice he assayed and thrice, in spite of scorn,
Tears such as angels weep burst forth. At last
Words interwove with sighs found out their way:
  O myriads of immortal spirits, O Pow'rs
Matchless but with th' Almighty (and that strife
Was not inglorious though th' event was dire
As this place testifies and this dire change,
Hateful to utter). But what pow'r of mind
Foreseeing or presaging from the depth
Of knowledge past or present could have feared
How such united force of gods, how such
As stood like these, could ever know repulse?
For who can yet believe, though after loss,
That all these puissant legions whose exíle
Hath emptied Heav'n shall fail to re-ascend,
Self-raised, and repossess their native seat?
For me be witness all the host of Heav'n
If counsels different or danger shunned
By me have lost our hopes! But He who reigns
Monarch in Heav'n till then as one secure
Sat on His throne upheld by old repute,
Consent or custom, and His regal state
Put forth at full but still His strength concealed,
Which tempted our attempt and wrought our fall.
Henceforth His might we know, and know our own,
So as not either to provoke or dread
New war provoked. Our better part remains
To work in close design by fraud or guile
What force effected not, that He no less
At length from us may find who overcomes

609. *amerced*: deprived.
622. *myriad* is two syllables: 'myr-yad.' *Spirits* is one syllable: 'spearts.'
632. *puissant*: powerful. Two syllables: 'pwée-sant.'
642. *tempted our attempt*: i.e., God's not revealing his strength is to blame for our fall, for that concealment tempted us to try to overthrow him.

By force hath overcome but half His foe!
Space may produce new worlds whereof so rife
There went a fame in Heav'n that He ere long
Intended to create and therein plant
A generation whom His choice regard
Should favor equal to the sons of Heav'n.
Thither, if but to pry, shall be perhaps
Our first eruption, thither or elsewhere.
For this infernal pit shall never hold
Celestial spirits in bondage, nor th' abyss
Long under darkness cover! But these thoughts
Full counsel must mature. Peace is despaired,
For who can think submission? War then, war
Open or understood, must be resolved!
He spake, and to confirm his words out flew
Millions of flaming swords drawn from the thighs
Of mighty cherubim. The sudden blaze
Far round illumined Hell. Highly they raged
Against the High'st and fierce with graspèd arms
Clashed on their sounding shields the din of war,
Hurling defiance toward the vault of Heav'n.
There stood a hill not far whose grisly top
Belched fire and rolling smoke. The rest entire
Shone with a glossy scurf, undoubted sign
That in his womb was hid metallic ore,
The work of sulphur. Thither winged with speed
A num'rous brígade hastened, as when bands
Of pioneers with spade and pickaxe armed
Forerun the royal camp to trench a field
Or cast a rampart. Mammon led them on,
Mammon the least erected spirit that fell
From Heav'n, for ev'n in Heav'n his looks and thoughts
Were always downward bent, admiring more
The riches of Heav'n's pavement, trodden gold,
Than aught divine or holy else enjoyed
In vision beatific. By him first
Men also, and by his suggestion taught,
Ransacked the center and with impious hands
Rifled the bowels of their mother Earth
For treasures better hid. Soon had his crew

651. *fame*: rumor.
653. *a generation*: human beings.
672. *scurf*: scaly crust.
674. *work of sulphur*: Metals were supposed to be formed by the combination of sulfur and mercury.
676. *pioneers*: military engineers, sappers, responsible for fortifications, bridges, etc.

Opened into the hill a spacious wound
And digged out ribs of gold. Let none admire
That riches grow in Hell: that soil may best
Deserve the precious bane! And here let those
Who boast in mortal things and wond'ring tell
Of Babel and the works of Memphian kings
Learn how their greatest monuments of fame
And strength and art are easily outdone
By spirits reprobate, and in an hour
What in an age they with incessant toil
And hands innumerable scarce perform.
Nigh on the plain in many cells prepared
That underneath had veins of liquid fire
Sluiced from the lake, a second multitude
With wondrous art founded the massy ore,
Severing each kind, and scummed the bullion dross.
A third as soon had formed within the ground
A various mold and from the boiling cells
By strange conveyance filled each hollow nook,
As in an organ from one blast of wind
To many a row of pipes the soundboard breathes.
Anon out of the earth a fabric huge
Rose like an exhalation with the sound
Of dulcet symphonies and voices sweet,
Built like a temple where pilasters round
Were set and Doric pillars overlaid
With golden architrave, nor did there want
Cornice or frieze with bossy sculptures grav'n.
The roof was fretted gold. Not Babylon
Nor great Alcairo such magnificence
Equaled in all their glories to enshrine
Belus or Sérapis their gods, or seat
Their kings, when Egypt with Assyria strove
In wealth and luxury. Th' ascending pile

694. References to the two great wicked construction works of the Bible, the Tower of Babel and Pharaoh's building project in Exodus.
698. *they*: the wicked builders.
700. *cells*: separated pools.
702. *sluiced*: channeled.
703. *founded*: in the 1667 printing; *found out* in 1674. The change to *found out* was perhaps motivated by a desire to be more technically correct, since the ore is being separated from the rock. *Founded* is better. *To found* metal means to melt it and pour it into a mold, a meaning that is adequate to the process Milton describes.
705–17. Milton thinks of the rising of this palace of Hell as a kind of visual music. Hence the comparison with the organ (which Milton played), where one blast of air is sent over the *sound board* into pipes of different length. From these pipes all kinds of musical structures develop, just as pillars, cornices, and friezes (architectural features) evolve as Satan's palace rises in the air.

Stood fixed her stately heighth, and straight the doors,
Op'ning their brazen folds, discover wide
Within her ample spaces o'er the smooth
And level pavement. From the archèd roof
Pendent by subtle magic many a row
Of starry lamps and blazing cressets fed
With naphtha and asphaltus yielded light
As from a sky. The hasty multitude
Admiring entered and the work some praise
And some the architect. His hand was known
In Heav'n by many a towered structure high
Where sceptred angels held their residence
And sat as princes, whom the Súpreme King
Exalted to such power and gave to rule
Each in his hierarchy the orders bright.
Nor was his name unheard or unadored
In ancient Greece and in Ausonian land.
Men called him Mulciber, and how he fell
From Heav'n they fabled, thrown by angry Jove
Sheer o'er the crystal battlements. From morn
To noon he fell, from noon to dewy eve,
A summer's day, and with the setting sun
Dropped from the zenith like a falling star
On Lemnos th' Aegean isle. Thus they relate,
Erring. For he with his rebellious rout
Fell long before, nor aught availed him now
T' have built in Heav'n high tow'rs, nor did he 'scape
By all his engines but was headlong sent
With his industrious crew to build in Hell.
Meanwhile the wingèd heralds by command
Of sovereign pow'r with awful ceremony

727. *many* and *a* are elided: 'man-ya.'

728. *cressets*: metal cups suspended from above, containing such flammable materials as *naphtha* and *asphaltus* (tar) in the next line.

732. *the architect*: Mammon, symbolizing worldly wealth and the overvaluing of wealth, is here aligned with the Greek and Roman gods of the forge, Hephaistos and Mulciber, or Vulcan.

740–46. The fall of Hephaistos, when Zeus threw him from heaven, is described by Hephaistos himself in *Iliad* 1.591–93: "Seizing me by the foot, he threw me from the enchanted threshold of Olympos and I fell for an entire day, falling together with the sun, until I plunged down onto the isle of Lemnos."

746. The difficult meter of this line can be read in two ways: (1) "On Lemnós th' Aegéan isle" or (2) "On Lémnos th' Aégean isle."

746–48. Milton regards classical myths as deformations (often beautiful deformations) of biblical truth. Homer's account of Hephaistos being thrown from Olympos, which Hephaistos recounts amid divine laughter in the very place from which he was thrown, is a beautiful deformation of the stern truth that Mammon was driven into Hell by God's fiery thunder, never to return.

And trumpets' sound throughout the host proclaim
A solemn council forthwith to be held
At Pandemonium the high capital
Of Satan and his peers. Their summons called
From every band and squarèd regiment
By place or choice the worthiest, they anon
With hundreds and with thousands trooping came
Attended. All accéss was thronged. The gates
And porches wide, but chief the spacious hall
(Though like a covered field where champions bold
Wont ride in armed and at the soldan's chair
Defied the best of paynim chivalry
To mortal combat or career with lance)
Thick swarmed both on the ground and in the air,
Brushed with the hiss of rustling wings. As bees
In spring time when the sun with Taurus rides
Pour forth their populous youth about the hive
In clusters, they among fresh dews and flow'rs
Fly to and fro or on the smoothèd plank,
The suburb of their straw-built citadel,
New rubbed with balm, expatiate and confer
Their state affairs, so thick the airy crowd
Swarmed and were straitened, till the signal giv'n,
Behold, a wonder! They but now who seemed
In bigness to surpass Earth's giant sons
Now less than smallest dwarfs in narrow room
Throng numberless like that Pygméan race
Beyond the Indian mount or fairy elves
Whose midnight revels by a forest side
Or fountain some belated peasant sees,
Or dreams he sees, while overhead the moon
Sits arbitress and nearer to the earth
Wheels her pale course. They on their mirth and dance
Intent with jocund music charm his ear.

756. *Pandemonium* has four syllables: 'pan-de-moan-yum.' The word is Milton's coinage, formed from Greek *pan*, "all"; *daimon*, "demon, supernatural being"; and the suffix *-ion*, indicating a place of worship, a building.

761. *all accés*: all entrances.

763. *covered field*: a field covered with a huge, decorated, sideless tent.

764–68. *soldan*: sultan. Christian knights boldly ride beneath the tent roof up to the sultan's throne, where they issue a challenge to fight the strongest pagan knights. Although the hall of Pandemonium is as large as such a covered field, still it is thick with swarming devils, whose wings brush the building and also one another.

765. *paynim*: pagan.

768–75. The comparison of the rebel angels to swarming bees leads to their actual diminution, making it possible for them all to enter Pandemonium.

786. *They*: the fairies.

At once with joy and fear his heart rebounds!
Thus incorporeal spirits to smallest forms
Reduced their shapes immense and were at large,
Though without number still amidst the hall
Of that infernal court. But far within
And in their own dimensions like themselves
The great seraphic lords and cherubim
In close recess and secret conclave sat,
A thousand demi-gods on golden seats
Frequent and full. After short silence then
And summons read the great consúlt began.

Book Two

The Argument

The consultation begun, Satan debates whether another battle be to be hazarded for the recovery of Heaven: some advise it, others dissuade. A third proposal is preferred, mentioned before by Satan, to search the truth of that prophecy or tradition in Heaven concerning another world and another kind of creature equal or not much inferior to themselves, about this time to be created. Their doubt who shall be sent on this difficult search. Satan, their chief, undertakes alone the voyage, is honored and applauded. The council thus ended, the rest betake them several ways and to several employments as their inclinations lead them to entertain the time till Satan return. He passes on his journey to Hell gates, finds them shut and who sat there to guard them, by whom at length they are opened, and discover to him the great gulf between Hell and Heaven. With what difficulty he passes through, directed by Chaos, the power of that place, to the sight of this new world which he sought.

High on a throne of royal state which far
Outshone the wealth of Ormus and of Ind
Or where the gorgeous East with richest hand
Show'rs on her kings barbaric pearl and gold
Satan exalted sat, by merit raised

789. *incorporeal* has four syllables: 'incorpor-yal.' *spirits* has one syllable.
793. *their own dimensions*: retaining their own size, unlike the less important rebel angels.
795. *conclave*: an assembly of Roman Catholic cardinals.
797. *Frequent*: crowded (Latin *frequens*, "full, crowded, thronging").

Book Two

The Argument, final sentence. Satan is given directions by Chaos, who is the reigning power of the realm of chaos (*that place*). These directions lead Satan to the distant sight of the created universe (*this new world*), which Satan had been seeking. Once inside that universe Satan will seek out the earth.

To that bad eminence and from despair
Thus high uplifted beyond hope aspires
Beyond thus high, insatiate to pursue
Vain war with Heav'n, and by success untaught
His proud imaginations thus displayed:
  Pow'rs and Dominions, deities of Heav'n,
For since no deep within her gulf can hold
Immortal vigor, though oppressed and fall'n,
I give not Heav'n for lost. From this descent
Celestial Virtues rising will appear
More glorious and more dread than from no fall
And trust themselves to fear no second fate.
Me though just right and the fixed laws of Heav'n
Did first create your leader, next free choice
With what besides in counsel or in fight
Hath been achieved of merit, yet this loss,
Thus far at least recovered, hath much more
Established in a safe unenvied throne
Yielded with full consent. The happier state
In Heav'n which follows dignity might draw
Envy from each inferior. But who here
Will envy whom the highest place exposes
Foremost to stand against the Thund'rer's aim,
Your bulwark, and condemns to greatest share
Of endless pain? Where there is then no good
For which to strive no strife can grow up there
From faction. For none sure will claim in Hell
Precedence, none whose portion is so small
Of present pain that with ambitious mind
Will covet more! With this advantage then
To union and firm faith and firm accord,
More than can be in Heav'n, we now return
To claim our just inheritance of old,
Surer to prosper than prosperity
Could have assured us, and by what best way—
Whether of open war or covert guile—
We now debate. Who can advise may speak.
  He ceased, and next him Moloch, sceptered king

15. *Celestial Virtues*: powers of heaven, referring to the rebel angels.

18–26. I.e., By the law of Heaven, by your own free choice, and by the merit of my own achievements, I am your leader. But our fall (though already we begin to undo it, as you see) has made me even more secure on my throne, which you readily consent to my having and do not envy, as you might envy me if I were on a happier throne (*happier state*) in Heaven.

27. A "feminine" line, which means an eleven-syllable line in which the final syllable of the last word is unaccented.

Stood up, the strongest and the fiercest spirit
That fought in Heav'n, now fiercer by despair.
His trust was with th' Eternal to be deemed
Equal in strength and rather than be less
Cared not to be at all. With that care lost
Went all his fear. Of God or Hell or worse
He recked not and these words thereafter spake:
  My sentence is for open war: of wiles,
More unexpért, I boast not: them let those
Contrive who need or when they need, not now.
For while they sit contriving shall the rest—
Millions that stand in arms and longing wait
The signal to ascend—sit lingering here
Heav'n's fugitives and for their dwelling place
Accept this dark opprobrious den of shame,
The prison of His tyranny who reigns
By our delay? No! Let us rather choose
Armed with hell flames and fury all at once
O'er Heav'n's high tow'rs to force resistless way,
Turning our tortures into horrid arms
Against the Torturer when to meet the noise
Of His almighty engine He shall hear
Infernal thunder and for lightning see
Black fire and horror shot with equal rage
Among His angels and His throne itself
Mixed with Tartarean sulphur and strange fire,
His own invented torments. But perhaps
The way seems difficult and steep to scale
With upright wing against a higher foe.
Let such bethink them (if the sleepy drench
Of that forgetful lake benumb not still)
That in our proper motion we ascend
Up to our native seat. Descent and fall
To us is adverse. Who but felt of late
When the fierce Foe hung on our broken rear
Insulting and pursued us through the deep
With what compulsion and laborious flight
We sunk thus low? Th' ascent is easy then.
Th' event is feared? Should we again provoke

52. *unexpert*: unexperienced (in wiles).
65. *engine*: contrivance (the thunder with which the rebel angels were vanquished).
74. *forgetful lake*: the lake of fire on which the rebel angels lay unconscious, suggesting Lethe, the river of oblivion. Cf. 1.266, *oblivious pool*.
78. *rear*: rear guard of the army.
79. *Insulting*: springing upon and trampling.
82. *event*: consequence.

Our Stronger some worse way His wrath may find
To our destruction—if there be in Hell
Fear to be worse destroyed! What can be worse
Than to dwell here driv'n out from bliss, condemned
In this abhorrèd deep to utter woe
Where pain of unextinguishable fire
Must exercise us without hope of end,
The vassals of His anger, when the scourge
Inexorably and the torturing hour
Calls us to penance? More destroyed than thus
We should be quite abolished and expire.
What fear we then? What doubt we to incense
His utmost ire which to the heighth enraged
Will either quite consume us and reduce
To nothing this essential, happier far
Than, miserable, to have eternal being?
Or if our substance be indeed divine
And cannot cease to be we are at worst
On this side nothing and by proof we feel
Our power sufficient to disturb His Heav'n
And with perpetual inroads to alarm,
Though inaccessible, His fatal throne,
Which if not victory is yet revenge.
He ended frowning and his look denounced
Desperate revenge and battle dangerous
To less than gods. On th' other side up rose
Belial in act more graceful and humane:
A fairer person lost not Heav'n! He seemed
For dignity composed and high explóit,
But all was false and hollow though his tongue
Dropped manna and could make the worse appear
The better reason to perplex and dash
Maturest counsels. For his thoughts were low,
To vice industrious but to nobler deeds
Timorous and slothful. Yet he pleased the ear
And with persuasive accent thus began:
I should be much for open war, O peers,
As not behind in hate, if what was urged

91. *torturing* has two syllables: 'torch-ring.'
94. *doubt*: fear.
97. *essential*: fundamental substance. The immortal substance of angels' bodies. *Happier* has two syllables: 'hap-yer.'
98. *miserable* has three syllables: 'mis-rable.' *being* has one syllable: 'beeng.'
100–101. I.e., We are already in the worst state possible, short of annihilation.
106. *denounced*: proclaimed.
120–23. I.e., if the reason given (by Moloch) for immediate counterattack were not the best argument against it.

Main reason to persuade immediate war
Did not dissuade me most and seem to cast
Ominous conjecture on the whole success.
When he who most excels in fact of arms—
In what he counsels and in what excels
Mistrustful—grounds his courage on despair
And utter dissolution as the scope
Of all his aim after some dire revenge.
First, what revenge? The tow'rs of Heav'n are filled
With armèd watch that render all accéss
Impregnable. Oft on the bord'ring deep
Encamp their legions or with óbscure wing
Scout far and wide into the realm of Night,
Scorning surprise. Or could we break our way
By force and at our heels all Hell should rise
With blackest insurrection to confound
Heav'n's purest light, yet our great Enemy
All incorruptible would on His throne
Sit unpolluted and th' ethereal mould,
Incapable of stain, would soon expel
Her mischief and purge off the baser fire,
Victorious. Thus repulsed our final hope
Is flat despair: we must exasperate
Th' almighty victor to spend all His rage.
And that must end us, that must be our cure:
To be no more. Sad cure! For who would lose,
Though full of pain, this intellectual being,
Those thoughts that wander through eternity,
To perish rather, swallowed up and lost
In the wide womb of uncreated night
Devoid of sense and motion? And who knows,
Let this be good, whether our angry Foe
Can give it or will ever? How He can
Is doubtful. That He never will is sure.
Will He, so wise, let loose at once His ire,
Belike through impotence, or unaware,
To give His enemies their wish and end
Them in His anger whom His anger saves
To punish endless? "Wherefore cease we then?"
Say they who counsel war, "We are decreed,
Reserved and destined to eternal woe

124. *fact of arms*: acts of valor (Latin *facio*, "to make, to do").
139. *ethereal mould*: heavenly structure, which would of itself expel the foreign substance of infernal fire.
152. *Let this be good*: Even if we allow annihilation to be desirable.

Whatever doing. What can we suffer more?
What can we suffer worse?" Is this then worst,
Thus sitting, thus consulting, thus in arms?
What, when we fled amain pursued and strook
With Heav'n's afflicting thunder and besought
The deep to shelter us? This Hell then seemed
A refuge from those wounds. Or when we lay
Chained on the burning lake? That sure was worse!
What if the breath that kindled those grim fires
Awaked should blow them into sev'nfold rage
And plunge us in the flames? Or from above
Should intermitted vengeance arm again
His red right hand to plague us? What if all
Her stores were opened and this firmament
Of Hell should spout her cataracts of fire,
Impendent horrors threat'ning hideous fall,
One day upon our heads while we, perhaps
Designing or exhorting glorious war,
Caught in a fiery tempest shall be hurled
Each on his rock transfixed, the sport and prey
Of racking whirlwinds, or for ever sunk
Under yon boiling ocean, wrapped in chains,
There to converse with everlasting groans,
Unréspited, unpitied, unreprieved,
Ages of hopeless end? This would be worse!
War, therefore, open or concealed alike
My voice dissuades. For what can force or guile
With Him? Or who deceive His mind, whose eye
Views all things at one view? He from Heav'n's heighth
All these our motions vain sees and derides,
Not more almighty to resist our might
Than wise to frustrate all our plots and wiles.
Shall we then live thus vile, the race of Heav'n
Thus trampled, thus expelled to suffer here
Chains and these torments? Better these than worse
By my advice since fate inevitable

174. See Horace, *Odes* 1.2.2–3, where Jove strikes the sacred hills of Rome "with his red right hand."
175. *Her*: Hell's.
177. *Impendent*: overhanging.
188–89. The implied main verb is *accomplish*; i.e., what can force or guile accomplish against God?
191. "He that sitteth in the heavens shall laugh: the Lord shall have them in derision" (Psalms 2:4).
192–93. I.e., God is no less wise in anticipating our subterfuges than he is powerful to repel our attacks.
197. A feminine line. See line 27 n.

Subdues us and omnipotent decree,
The victor's will. To suffer, as to do,
Our strength is equal nor the law unjust
That so ordains. This was at first resolved,
If we were wise, against so great a Foe
Contending and so doubtful what might fall.
I laugh when those who at the spear are bold
And vent'rous, if that fail them shrink and fear
What yet they know must follow: to endure
Exile or ignominy or bonds or pain,
The sentence of their conqueror. This is now
Our doom which if we can sustain and bear
Our súpreme Foe in time may much remit
His anger and perhaps thus far removed
Not mind us not offending, satisfied
With what is punished, whence these raging fires
Will slacken if His breath stir not their flames.
Our purer essence then will overcome
Their noxious vapor or inured not feel,
Or changed at length and to the place conformed
In temper and in nature will receive
Familiar the fierce heat. And void of pain
This horror will grow mild, this darkness light,
Besides what hope the never-ending flight
Of future days may bring, what chance, what change
Worth waiting since our present lot appears
For happy though but ill, for ill not worst,
If we procure not to ourselves more woe.
  Thus Belial with words clothed in reason's garb
Counseled ignoble ease and peaceful sloth,
Not peace, and after him thus Mammon spake:
  Either to disenthrone the King of Heav'n
We war, if war be best, or to regain
Our own right lost. Him to unthrone we then
May hope when everlasting Fate shall yield
To fickle Chance and Chaos judge the strife.

203. *fall*: occur.
207. *ignominy* and *or* are elided: 'ignomin-yor.'
224–25. I.e., Although our condition now isn't a happy one, it is also not the worst. It will remain not the worst so long as we do not provoke God to further ire.
229–35. Mammon attributes both futile alternatives to the former two speakers: the first, war, is attributed to Moloch, the second, to wait for better times to overthrow God, to Belial. The latter is an inexact summary of Belial's position, since Belial does not propose overthrowing God at some time in the future. Yet this aim might still be attributed to Belial, as an inevitable implication of his position. That is exactly what Mammon does in the sentence following. But his argument comes to much the same as Belial's: let us make the best of it in Hell.

The former vain to hope argues as vain
The latter. For what place can be for us
Within Heav'n's bound unless Heav'n's Lord supreme
We overpower? Suppose He should relent
And publish grace to all on promise made
Of new subjection. With what eyes could we
Stand in His presence humble and receive
Strict laws imposed to celebrate His throne
With warbled hymns and to His Godhead sing
Forced hallelujahs while He lordly sits
Our envied sov'reign and His altar breathes
Ambrosial odors and ambrosial flowers,
Our servile offerings? This must be our task
In Heav'n, this our delight. How wearisome
Eternity so spent in worship paid
To whom we hate! Let us not then pursue—
By force impossible, by leave obtained
Unacceptable, though in Heav'n—our state
Of splendid vassalage but rather seek
Our own good from ourselves and from our own
Live to ourselves, though in this vast recess,
Free and to none accountable, preferring
Hard liberty before the easy yoke
Of servile pomp. Our greatness will appear
Then most conspicuous when great things of small—
Useful of hurtful, prosperous of adverse—
We can create and in what place soe'er
Thrive under evil and work ease out of pain
Through labor and endurance. This deep world
Of darkness do we dread? How oft amidst
Thick clouds and dark doth Heav'n's all-ruling Sire
Choose to reside, His glory unobscured,
And with the majesty of darkness round
Covers His throne from whence deep thunders roar,
Must'ring their rage, and Heav'n resembles Hell?
As He our darkness, cannot we His light
Imitate when we please? This desert soil
Wants not her hidden luster: gems and gold!
Nor want we skill or art from whence to raise
Magnificence. And what can Heav'n show more?
Our torments also may in length of time

252. *vassalage*: servility, as with medieval vassals.
258. *conspicuous* has three syllables: 'conspic-yus.'
259. *prosperous* has two syllables: 'pros-prus.'
261. A hypermetrical line. Although it can be regularized by giving *evil* one syllable, "eel," it sounds well as is.

Become our elements, these piercing fires
As soft as now severe, our temper changed
Into their temper, which must needs remove
The sensible of pain. All things invite
To peaceful counsels and the settled state
Of order, how in safety best we may
Compose our present evils with regard
Of what we are and where, dismissing quite
All thoughts of war. Ye have what I advise.
He scarce had finished when such murmur filled
Th' assembly as when hollow rocks retain
The sound of blust'ring winds which all night long
Had roused the sea, now with hoarse cadence lull
Seafaring men o'erwatched whose bark by chance
Or pinnace anchors in a craggy bay
After the tempest. Such applause was heard
As Mammon ended, and his sentence pleased,
Advising peace, for such another field
They dreaded worse than Hell, so much the fear
Of thunder and the sword of Michaël
Wrought still within them and, no less, desire
To found this nether empire which might rise
By policy and long procéss of time
In emulation opposite to Heav'n.
Which when Beëlzebub perceived (than whom,
Satan except, none higher sat) with grave
Aspéct he rose and in his rising seemed
A pillar of state. Deep on his front engrav'n
Deliberation sat and public care
And princely counsel in his face yet shone,
Majestic though in ruin. Sage he stood
With Atlantéan shoulders fit to bear
The weight of mightiest monarchies. His look
Drew audience and attention still as night
Or summer's noontide air while thus he spake:
Thrones and Imperial Pow'rs, offspring of Heav'n,
Ethereal Virtues, or these titles now

284–88. Comparison of a murmuring crowd to a rising (or, here, a falling) storm at sea is traditional in epic poetry. See *Iliad* 2.142–46; *Aeneid* 10.96–99.
287. The subject of *lull* is *winds*.
297. *policy*: political manipulation. *process*: an advance or forward march; Milton preserves the Latin military sense of the word.
302. *pillar* and *of* are elided: 'pill-rov.'
306. *Atlantéan*: like Atlas, who bears the weight of the sky on his shoulders. The name *Atlas* means, paradoxically, "one who does not bear, or suffer."
310. *Imperial* has three syllables: 'im-peer-yal.' *Powers* has one syllable: 'paars.'
311. *Ethereal* has three syllables: 'ee-thee-ryal.'

Must we renounce and changing style be called
Princes of Hell? For so the popular vote
Inclines, here to continue and build up here
A growing empire. Doubtless! while we dream
And know not that the King of Heav'n hath doomed
This place our dungeon not our safe retreat
Beyond His potent arm to live exempt
From Heav'n's high jurisdiction in new league
Banded against His throne, but to remain
In strictest bondage, though thus far removed,
Under th' inevitable curb reserved,
His captive multitude. For He, be sure,
In heighth or depth still first and last will reign
Sole king and of His kingdom lose no part
By our revolt but over Hell extend
His empire and with iron scepter rule
Us here as with His golden those in Heav'n.
What sit we then projecting peace and war?
War hath determined us and foiled with loss
Irreparable, terms of peace yet none
Vouchsafed or sought. For what peace will be giv'n
To us enslaved but custody severe
And stripes and arbitrary punishment
Inflicted? And what peace can we return
But to our pow'r hostility and hate,
Untamed reluctance and revenge, though slow,
Yet ever plotting how the Conqueror least
May reap His conquest and may least rejoice
In doing what we most in suffering feel?
Nor will occasion want nor shall we need
With dangerous expedition to invade
Heav'n whose high walls fear no assault or siege
Or ambush from the deep. What if we find
Some easier enterprise? There is a place,
If ancient and prophetic fame in Heav'n

312. *style*: manner of writing (or of being designated in writing); from Latin *stilus*, "pen."
314. *continue* and *and* are elided, with a total of three syllables.
327. *scepter*: a rod, symbol of royal authority, but also a weapon. "Thou shalt break them with a rod of iron; thou shalt dash them in pieces like a potter's vessel" (Psalm 2:9).
336. *to our power*: with all our might.
337. *reluctance*: struggling back, against. See 6.58 n.
338. *Conqueror* has two syllables.
345–53. It was debated whether humanity was created before or after the fall of the rebel angels. Milton has humanity created after the fall of the rebel angels. See Argument, Book One. The divine plan is for humans to rise eventually to heaven and there replace, to the exact number, the fallen angels. Milton invents a rumor in heaven by which Satan and Beëlzebub obtain this information. See 1.650–54. That rumor here becomes a formal pronouncement and oath by God.

Err not, another world, the happy seat
Of some new race called Man about this time
To be created like to us though less
In pow'r and excellence but favored more
Of Him who rules above. So was His will
Pronounced among the gods and by an oath
That shook Heav'n's whole circumference confirmed.
Thither let us bend all our thoughts to learn
What creatures there inhabit, of what mould
Or substance, how endued and what their power
And where their weakness, how attempted best
By force or subtlety. Though Heav'n be shut
And Heav'n's high Arbitrator sit secure
In His own strength, this place may lie exposed,
The utmost border of His kingdom left
To their defense who hold it. Here perhaps
Some advantageous act may be achieved
By sudden onset, either with Hell fire
To waste His whole creation or possess
All as our own and drive, as we were driven,
The puny habitants, or if not drive
Seduce them to our party that their God
May prove their foe and with repenting hand
Abolish His own works. This would surpass
Common revenge and interrupt His joy
In our confusion and our joy upraise
In His disturbance when His darling sons
Hurled headlong to partake with us shall curse
Their frail originals and faded bliss—
Faded so soon! Advise if this be worth
Attempting or to sit in darkness here
Hatching vain empires. Thus Beëlzebub
Pleaded his devilish counsel first devised
By Satan and in part proposed. For whence
But from the author of all ill could spring
So deep a malice to confound the race
Of mankind in one root and Earth with Hell
To mingle and involve, done all to spite

353. The heavens shake when the king of the gods in classical verse—Zeus in Homer and Jove in Virgil—takes an oath. See *Iliad* 1.530 and *Aeneid* 9.106. Jehovah shakes heaven and earth too—not, however, when he takes an oath but when he exercises his wrath, a premonition of the apocalypse: "Therefore I will shake the heavens, and the earth shall remove out of her place, in the wrath of the Lord of Hosts, and in the day of his fierce anger" (Isaiah 13:13).

375. *frail originals*: Adam and Eve.

379. *devilish* has two syllables: 'dev-lish.'

The great Creator? But their spite still serves
His glory to augment. The bold design
Pleased highly those infernal states and joy
Sparkled in all their eyes. With full assent
They vote, whereat his speech he thus renews:
  Well have ye judged, well ended long debate,
Synod of gods, and like to what ye are
Great things resolved which from the lowest deep
Will once more lift us up, in spite of fate,
Nearer our ancient seat, perhaps in view
Of those bright confines whence with neighboring arms
And opportune excursion we may chance
Re-enter Heav'n. Or else in some mild zone
Dwell not unvisited of Heav'n's fair light
Secure and at the bright'ning orient beam
Purge off this gloom. The soft delicious air
To heal the scar of these corrosive fires
Shall breathe her balm. But first whom shall we send
In search of this new world, whom shall we find
Sufficient? Who shall tempt with wand'ring feet
The dark unbottomed infinite abyss
And through the palpable obscure find out
His uncouth way or spread his airy flight
Upborne with indefátigable wings
Over the vast abrupt ere he arrive
The happy isle? What strength, what art can then
Suffice or what evasion bear him safe
Through the strict senteries and stations thick
Of angels watching round? Here he had need
All circumspection and we now no less
Choice in our suffrage, for on whom we send
The weight of all and our last hope relies.
  This said, he sat and expectation held
His look suspense, awaiting who appeared
To second or oppose or undertake
The perilous attempt. But all sat mute,

391–92. I.e., being great yourselves, you have resolved upon great actions.

395. *neighboring* has two syllables: 'neighb-ring.'

397–402. As we see in *Paradise Regained*, after the Fall of Man the rebel angels will escape Hell and take up residence in the *soft delicious air*, the sky. That will be the base from which they will go to earth to set themselves up as pagan gods and draw human worship away from the true God.

406. *obscure* (noun): darkness so thick it can be felt (*palpable*).

407. *uncouth*: unknown (from Old English *cunnan*, "to know").

409. *abrupt*. Latin *abruptus*, "broken off"; used of places that are steep (like a cliff), inaccessible (like the abyss), or all but impossible to cross (like the sea). *palpable obscure* (line 406) and *vast abrupt* are typically Miltonic, sublime locutions.

412. *senteries*: sentries.

Pondering the danger with deep thoughts and each
In other's count'nance read his own dismay,
Astonished. None among the choice and prime
Of those Heav'n-warring champions could be found
So hardy as to proffer or accept
Alone the dreadful voyage till at last
Satan, whom now transcendent glory raised
Above his fellows with monarchal pride
Conscious of highest worth, unmoved thus spake:
  O progeny of Heav'n, Empyreal Thrones,
With reason hath deep silence and demur
Seized us, though undismayed. Long is the way
And hard that out of Hell leads up to light.
Our prison strong, this huge convéx of fire
Outrageous to devour immures us round
Ninefold and gates of burning adamant
Barred over us prohibit all egress.
These passed (if any pass) the void profound
Of unessential Night receives him next
Wide gaping and with utter loss of being
Threatens him plunged in that abortive gulf.
If thence he 'scape into whatever world
Or unknown region what remains him less
Than unknown dangers and as hard escape?
But I should ill become this throne, O peers,
And this imperial sov'reignty adorned
With splendor, armed with pow'r, if aught proposed
And judged of public moment in the shape
Of difficulty or danger could deter
Me from attempting. Wherefore do I assume
These royalties and not refuse to reign,
Refusing to accept as great a share
Of hazard as of honor, due alike
To him who reigns? And so much to him due

430. *Empyreal* has three syllables: 'em-peer-yal.'

432–33. Paraphrasing the famous lines of the sibyl in *Aeneid* 6.126–29: "Easy is the descent to Avernus, where night and day the door of the dark lord stands open, but to make one's way back up again and escape to the upper air, that is the task, that is the labor." See 3.19–21.

435. *immures*: encloses with walls. *outrageous*: cruelly eager.

439. *unessential*: having no foundation in one substance.

440. *being* has one syllable: 'beeng.'

441. *abortive*. Latin *abortivus*, "prematurely born." The meaning is that the gulf of chaos, which has not been created, is an actual thing or place only in an anticipatory and premature sense, for chaos is not really a thing or place at all.

449. *difficulty* and *or* are elided: 'difficul-chor.'

452–56. *hazard* as well as *honor* is the ruler's due. The higher the ruler sits above those he rules, the more danger he should be willing to be exposed to.

Of hazard more as he above the rest
High honored sits. Go therefore, mighty Pow'rs,
Terror of Heav'n though fall'n: intend at home
(While here shall be our home) what best may ease
The present misery and render Hell
More tolerable if there be cure or charm
To respite or deceive or slack the pain
Of this ill mansion. Intermit no watch
Against a wakeful foe while I abroad
Through all the coasts of dark destruction seek
Deliverance for us all! This enterprise
None shall partake with me. Thus saying rose
The monarch and prevented all reply:
Prudent, lest from his resolution raised
Others among the chief might offer now
(Certain to be refused) what erst they feared
And so refused might in opinion stand
His rivals, winning cheap the high repute
Which he through hazard huge must earn. But they
Dreaded not more th' adventure than his voice
Forbidding, and at once with him they rose.
Their rising all at once was as the sound
Of thunder heard remote. Towards him they bend
With awful reverence prone and as a god
Extol him equal to the High'st in Heav'n.
Nor failed they to express how much they praised
That for the gen'ral safety he despised
His own: for neither do the spirits damned
Lose all their virtue, lest bad men should boast
Their specious deeds on earth which glory excites,
Or close ambition varnished o'er with zeal.
Thus they their doubtful consultations dark
Ended rejoicing in their matchless chief.
As when from mountain tops the dusky clouds
Ascending while the north wind sleeps o'erspread
Heav'n's cheerful face, the louring element
Scowls o'er the darkened landscape snow or show'r,
If chance the radiant sun with farewell sweet
Extend his evening beam, the fields revive,

457. *intend*: stretch your minds.
460. *tolerable* has three syllables: 'tol-rable.'
484. *glory* and *excites* are elided: 'glor-yexcites.'
482–85. I.e., Fallen angels do not lose all their "virtue" (power). Otherwise, bad men who accomplish great deeds (though motivated thereto by concealed ambition and desire of glory) would be able to boast that their deeds alone make them good, not the inner intentions by which those deeds were accomplished.

s their notes renew and bleating herds
eir joy, that hill and valley rings.
O shame to men! Devil with devil damned
Firm concord holds. Men only disagree
Of creatures rational, though under hope
Of Heav'nly grace and, God proclaiming peace,
Yet live in hatred, enmity and strife
Among themselves and levy cruel wars,
Wasting the earth each other to destroy—
As if (which might induce us to accord)
Man had not hellish foes enow besides
That day and night for his destruction wait!
  The Stygian council thus dissolved and forth
In order came the grand infernal peers.
Midst came their mighty paramount and seemed
Alone th' Antagonist of Heav'n, nor less
Than Hell's dread Emperor with pomp supreme
And God-like imitated state. Him round
A globe of fiery seraphim enclosed
With bright emblazonry and horrent arms.
Then of their session ended they bid cry
With trumpets' regal sound the great result.
Towards the four winds four speedy cherubim
Put to their mouths the sounding alchemy
By herald's voice explained. The hollow abyss
Heard far and wide and all the host of Hell
With deaf'ning shout returned them loud acclaim.
Thence more at ease their minds and somewhat raised
By false presumptuous hope the rangèd pow'rs
Disband and wand'ring each his several way
Pursues as inclination or sad choice
Leads him perplexed where he may likeliest find
Truce to his restless thoughts and entertain
The irksome hours till his great chief return.
Part on the plain or in the air sublime
Upon the wing or in swift race contend

499–500. I.e., Although God proclaims peace, men live in hatred and at war.

513. *horrent*: bristling, standing upright (Latin *horresco*, "to stand on end, bristle, be rough"). Various forms of the word are often used of armies before battle or as an epithet of Mars, god of war.

517. *sounding alchemy*: trumpets fashioned of gold or of a metal resembling gold, obtained by alchemy.

518. *Hollow* and *abyss* are elided: 'holl-wabis.'

523–24. *each . . . pursues*. Note the change of focus from the rebel angels as a crowd, showing the psychology of crowds, to the solitude of each rebel angel's experience of Hell: *wand'ring, sad, perplexed, restless thoughts, irksome hours*.

As at th' Olympian games or Pythian fields.
Part curb their fiery steeds or shun the goal
With rapid wheels or fronted brígades form,
As when to warn proud cities war appears
Waged in the troubled sky and armies rush
To battle in the clouds. Before each van
Prick forth the airy knights and couch their spears
Till thickest legions close. With feats of arms
From either end of heav'n the welkin burns.
Others with vast Typhoean rage more fell
Rend up both rocks and hills and ride the air
In whirlwind: Hell scarce holds the wild uproar.
As when Alcides from Oechalia crowned
With conquest felt th' envenomed robe and tore
Through pain up by the roots Thessalian pines,
And Lichas from the top of Oeta threw
Into th' Euboic Sea. Others more mild,
Retreated in a silent valley, sing
With notes angelical to many a harp
Their own heroic deeds and hapless fall
By doom of battle and complain that fate
Free virtue should enthrall to force or chance.
Their song was partial but the harmony
(What could it less when spirits immortal sing?)
Suspended Hell and took with ravishment
The thronging audience. In discourse more sweet
(For eloquence the soul, song charms the sense)
Others apart sat on a hill retired
In thoughts more elevate and reasoned high
Of providence, foreknowledge, will and fate,
Fixed fate, free will, foreknowledge absolute,

530. *Olympian . . . Pythian*: The devils take up heroic games (a staple of epic poetry) such as those held in Greece at Olympia and at Delphi. *Olympian* has three syllables: 'ol-imp-yan,' and *Pythian* has two syllables: 'pyth-yan.'

536. *Prick*: ride (while 'pricking' the sides of the horse with one's spurs). See Spenser, *Faerie Queene* 1.1.1: "A gentle knight was pricking on the plaine." The transition is from classical games to medieval jousts.

538. *heav'n*: the sky of hell, the *welkin*.

539. *Typhoean*: rage like that of the monster Typhon. See Glossary. Three syllables: 'ty-fee-an.'

542–46. *Alcides*: Hercules, who when returning from the conquest of Oechalia received from his wife a robe that she thought was infused with a love potion. It was infused with a poison, which caused Hercules the agony described, in the course of which he threw his friend Lichas into the sea.

550–51. *Free virtue* is the direct object of *fate*. The devils complain that free will is enthralled to fate. Milton's reply would be that freedom is never safe and never easy: freedom can be lost (by rebelling against God), and freedom demands discipline to resist the work of fate.

552. *partial*: sung in several different parts, perhaps with the suggestion of *prejudiced*.

And found no end in wand'ring mazes lost.
Of good and evil much they argued then,
Of happiness and final misery,
Passion and apathy, and glory and shame:
Vain wisdom all and false philosophy!
Yet with a pleasing sorcery could charm
Pain for a while, or anguish, and excite
Fallacious hope or arm th' obdurèd breast
With stubborn patience as with triple steel.
  Another part in squadrons and gross bands
On bold adventure to discover wide
That dismal world, if any clime perhaps
Might yield them easier habitation, bend
Four ways their flying march along the banks
Of four infernal rivers that disgorge
Into the burning lake their baleful streams:
Abhorrèd Styx, the flood of deadly hate,
Sad Acheron of sorrow black and deep,
Cocytus, named of lamentation loud
Heard on the rueful stream, fierce Phlegethon
Whose waves of torrent fire inflame with rage.
Far off from these a slow and silent stream,
Lethe the river of oblivion rolls
Her wat'ry labyrinth whereof who drinks
Forthwith his former state and being forgets,
Forgets both joy and grief, pleasure and pain.
Beyond this flood a frozen continent
Lies dark and wild, beat with perpetual storms
Of whirlwind and dire hail which on firm land
Thaws not but gathers heap and ruin seems
Of ancient pile. All else deep snow and ice,
A gulf profound as that Serbonian bog
Betwixt Damiata and Mount Casius old
Where armies whole have sunk. The parching air
Burns frore and cold performs th' effect of fire.
Thither by harpy-footed furies haled
At certain revolutions all the damned

564. *glory* and *and* are elided, with a total of two syllables: 'glor-yand.'
568. *obdurèd*: hardened.
570–76. *squadrons* and *bands* (not *part*) are the subject of *bend*: four squadrons bend, or turn, in four directions, to explore the four rivers of Hell.
583. *Lethe* has two syllables.
591. *pile*: castle or fortress.
593. *Damiata* has three syllables, *Casius* two.
595. *frore*: sea frost that forms on a ship's lines and cables. The sensation *frore* gives to the touch is of burning. See Spenser's Proteus, in *Faerie Queene* 3.8.30, whose beard is "frory hoar." The word is still used in Newfoundland.

Are brought and feel by turns the bitter change
Of fierce extremes. Extremes by change more fierce:
From beds of raging fire to starve in ice
Their soft ethereal warmth and there to pine
Immovable, infixed and frozen round,
Periods of time, thence hurried back to fire.
They ferry over this Lethéan sound
Both to and fro, their sorrow to augment,
And wish and struggle as they pass to reach
The tempting stream with one small drop to lose
In sweet forgetfulness all pain and woe
All in one moment, and so near the brink.
But fate withstands and to oppose th' attempt
Medusa with gorgonian terror guards
The ford and of itself the water flies
All taste of living wight as once it fled
The lip of Tantalus. Thus roving on
In cónfused march forlorn th' advent'rous bands
With shudd'ring horror pale and eyes aghast
Viewed first their lamentable lot and found
No rest. Through many a dark and dreary vale
They passed and many a region dolorous,
O'er many a frozen, many a fiery alp,
Rocks, caves, lakes, fens, bogs, dens, and shades of death,
A universe of death which God by curse
Created evil, for evil only good,
Where all life dies, death lives, and nature breeds
Perverse all monstrous, all prodigious things,
Abominable, inutt'rable, and worse
Than fables yet have feigned or fear conceived:
Gorgons and hydras and chimeras dire.
   Meanwhile the Adversary of God and Man,
Satan, with thoughts inflamed of high'st design
Puts on swift wings and towards the gates of Hell
Explores his solitary flight. Sometimes

600. *starve*: to perish.
607. *tempting stream*: Lethe.
619. *many* and *a* are elided, with a total of two syllables: 'man-ya.'
621. A line famous for the way its meter (especially in the first six syllables, up to the caesura) reproduces the feeling created by the landscape of Hell: of endlessness and sameness, even in variety.
623. The first *evil* has one syllable, the second *evil* two.
626. *Abominable* has three syllables: 'abominab.'
628. I.e., The monsters of Hell are far worse than anything the human imagination has conceived, such as gorgons, hydras, and chimeras, bad as these are.
629. See Glossary, SATAN.
631. *towards* is one syllable.
632. *Explores*. Milton intends the Latinate, military sense of *exploro*, "to spy, reconnoiter." Satan is spying out all the confines of Hell to find the way out.

He scours the right-hand coast, sometimes the left,
Now shaves with level wing the deep, then soars
Up to the fiery concave tow'ring high.
As when far off at sea a fleet descried
Hangs in the clouds by equinoctial winds
Close sailing from Bengala or the isles
Of Ternate and Tidore whence merchants bring
Their spicy drugs, they on the trading flood
Through the wide Ethiopian to the Cape
Ply stemming nightly toward the pole, so seemed
Far off the flying Fiend. At last appear
Hell bounds high reaching to the horrid roof
And thrice threefold the gates. Three folds were brass,
Three iron, three of adamantine rock
Impenetrable, impaled with circling fire
Yet unconsumed. Before the gates there sat
On either side a formidable shape:
The one seemed woman to the waist and fair
But ended foul in many a scaly fold
Voluminous and vast, a serpent armed
With mortal sting. About her middle round
A cry of hell-hounds never ceasing barked
With wide Cerberean mouths full loud and rung
A hideous peal. Yet when they list would creep
If aught disturbed their noise into her womb
And kennel there, yet there still barked and howled
Within unseen. Far less abhorred than these
Vexed Scylla bathing in the sea that parts
Calabria from the hoarse Trinacrian shore.
Nor uglier follow the night-hag when, called
In secret, riding through the air she comes

634. *shaves with level wing the deep*: glides along close to the floor of Hell, which is like the ocean bottom.

635. *concave*: adjective ("curving in," like the surface under a dome) used here as a noun. From the inside, the roof of Hell is concave, like a dome. The whole of Hell seems to be spherical, the better to focus its intense flames on those within.

640–42. *trading flood*: the trade route on the Indian Ocean between northwestern India and northeastern Africa (Ethiopia). Once returning ships (laden with Indian spices) reach Ethiopia, they sail south to the Cape of Good Hope, the southern tip of Africa, i.e., *toward the [south] pole*. *Stemming*: steering. Literally, directing the prow, the most forward point of a ship's bow, known as the *stem*, an upright timber to which the horizontal planks are joined at the bow.

647. *Impaled*: surrounded by a fence of pillars, or upright poles (pales). *Impenetrable* has four syllables: 'im-pent-rab-le'; *fire* has one syllable.

656. *list*: wish.

659–66. The sea dogs of Sicily that chewed Scylla's private parts were far less horrible than these dogs, which tormented their mother's womb from the inside. Their mother (Sin) is uglier than the hags who fly to Lapland for the pleasure of murdering children and drinking their blood. See Glossary, SCYLLA.

Lured with the smell of infant blood to dance
With Lapland witches while the laboring moon
Eclipses at their charms. The other shape
(If shape it might be called that shape had none
Distinguishable in member, joint, or limb,
Or substance might be called that shadow seemed,
For each seemed either): black it stood as night,
Fierce as ten furies, terrible as Hell
And shook a dreadful dart. What seemed his head
The likeness of a kingly crown had on.
Satan was now at hand and from his seat
The monster moving onward came as fast
With horrid strides. Hell trembled as he strode!
Th' undaunted Fiend what this might be admired,
Admired, not feared. God and his Son except,
Created thing naught valued he, nor shunned,
And with disdainful look thus first began:
  Whence and what art thou, execrable shape,
That dar'st though grim and terrible advance
Thy miscreated front athwart my way
To yonder gates? Through them I mean to pass,
That be assured, without leave asked of thee.
Retire, or taste thy folly and learn by proof,
Hell-born, not to contend with spirits of Heav'n!
  To whom the goblin full of wrath replied:
Art thou that traitor angel, art thou he
Who first broke peace in Heav'n and faith, till then
Unbroken, and in proud rebellious arms
Drew after him the third part of Heav'n's sons
Conjured against the High'st for which both thou
And they outcast from God are here condemned
To waste eternal days in woe and pain?
And reckon'st thou thyself with spirits of Heav'n,
Hell-doomed, and breath'st defiance here and scorn
Where I reign king, and to enrage thee more,
Thy king and lord? Back to thy punishment,
False fugitive, and to thy speed add wings
Lest with a whip of scorpions I pursue

665. *laboring moon*: the moon going into eclipse, struggling to survive.
669–70. I.e., If it can be called a substance, since it appeared instead to be a shadow, although its very shadowiness seemed substantial.
677. *admired*: wondered. Latin *admiror*, "to wonder at, to be astonished at."
679. *he*: Satan.
686. *folly* and *and* are elided, with a total of two syllables: 'foll-yand.'
691. *rebellious* has three syllables: 'ree-bell-yus.'

Thy ling'ring or with one stroke of this dart
Strange horror seize thee and pangs unfelt before!
  So spake the grisly terror and in shape,
So speaking and so threat'ning, grew tenfold
More dreadful and deform. On th' other side
Incensed with indignation Satan stood
Unterrified and like a comet burned
That fires the length of Ophiucus huge
In th' arctic sky and from his horrid hair
Shakes pestilence and war. Each at the head
Levelled his deadly aim: their fatal hands
No second stroke intend. And such a frown
Each cast at th' other as when two black clouds
With heav'n's artill'ry fraught come rattling on
Over the Caspian, then stand front to front
Hov'ring a space till winds the signal blow
To join their dark encounter in mid air.
So frowned the mighty cómbatants that Hell
Grew darker at their frown. So matched they stood,
For never but once more was either like
To meet so great a foe. And now great deeds
Had been achieved whereof all Hell had rung,
Had not the snaky sorceress that sat
Fast by Hell gate and kept the fatal key
Ris'n and with hideous outcry rushed between:
  O Father, what intends thy hand, she cried,
Against thy only son? What fury, O Son,
Possesses thee to bend that mortal dart
Against thy father's head? And know'st for whom?
For Him who sits above and laughs the while
At thee ordained His drudge to execute
Whate'er His wrath (which He calls "justice") bids,
His wrath which one day will destroy ye both!
  She spake and at her words the hellish pest
Forbore. Then these to her Satan returned:
  So strange thy outcry and thy words so strange

703. *seize*, *thee*, and *and* are elided: 'seas-thand.'
710. *horrid hair*: bristling like the hair of an enraged animal, such as a boar. The word *comet* is from Greek *komê*, "the hair," and *komêtês*, "long-haired." Comets were thought to be the portents or even the causes of disasters such as *pestilence* and *war*.
711–13. Satan and Death are at a Mexican standoff.
715. *artillery* has three syllables ('artill-ree'), and *rattling* has two.
722. *so great a foe*: the Son. "For he [Christ] must reign, till he hath put all enemies under his feet. And the last enemy that shall be destroyed is death" (1 Corinthians 15:25–26).
726. *hideous* has two syllables: 'hid-jus.'
735. *pest*: not Satan but his adversary.
737–40. I.e., Your words are so strange that they delay my (usually undelaying) hand from proclaiming, in the language of deeds, what it intends to do.

Thou interposest that my sudden hand
Prevented spares to tell thee yet by deeds
What it intends till first I know of thee
What thing thou art thus double-formed and why
In this infernal vale first met thou call'st
Me "father" and that phantasm call'st my son.
I know thee not nor ever saw till now
Sight more detestable than him and thee.
  T' whom thus the portress of Hell gate replied:
Hast thou forgot me then and do I seem
Now in thine eyes so foul, once deemed so fair
In Heav'n when at th' assembly and in sight
Of all the seraphim with thee combined
In bold conspiracy 'gainst Heaven's King?
All on a sudden miserable pain
Surprised thee: dim thine eyes and dizzy swum
In darkness while thy head flames thick and fast
Threw forth till on the left side op'ning wide,
Likest to thee in shape and count'nance bright
(Then shining Heav'nly fair) a goddess armed
Out of thy head I sprung! Amazement seized
All th' host of Heav'n. Back they recoiled afraid
At first and called me "Sin" and for a sign
Portentous held me. But familiar grown
I pleased and with attractive graces won
The most averse (thee chiefly) who full oft
Thyself in me thy perfect image viewing
Becam'st enamoured and such joy thou took'st
With me in secret that my womb conceived
A growing burden. Meanwhile war arose
And fields were fought in Heav'n wherein remained
(For what could else) to our almighty Foe
Clear victory, to our part loss and rout
Through all the empyréan. Down they fell
Driv'n headlong from the pitch of Heaven, down
Into this deep and in the general fall
I also, at which time this pow'rful key
Into my hand was giv'n with charge to keep
These gates for ever shut which none can pass
Without my op'ning. Pensive here I sat
Alone, but long I sat not till my womb—
Pregnant by thee and now excessive grown—

743. *phantasm* has two syllables: 'fan-tazm.'
755–58. Like Athena, goddess of wisdom, who burst out of Zeus's head.
773. *general* has two syllables: 'jen-ral.'

Prodigious motion felt and rueful throes.
At last this odious offspring whom thou seest,
Thine own begotten, breaking violent way
Tore through my entrails, that with fear and pain
Distorted all my nether shape thus grew
Transformed. But he my inbred enemy
Forth issued brandishing his fatal dart
Made to destroy. I fled and cried out "Death!"
Hell trembled at the hideous name and sighed
From all her caves and back resounded "Death!"
I fled but he pursued (though more, it seems,
Inflamed with lust than rage) and swifter far
Me overtook, his mother, all dismayed,
And in embraces forcible and foul
Engend'ring with me of that rape begot
These yelling monsters that with ceaseless cry
Surround me as thou saw'st, hourly conceived
And hourly born with sorrow infinite
To me. For when they list, into the womb
That bred them they return and howl and gnaw
My bowels, their repast, then bursting forth
Afresh with conscious terrors vex me round
That rest or intermission none I find.
Before mine eyes in opposition sits
Grim Death, my son and foe, who sets them on
And me his parent would full soon devour
For want of other prey but that he knows
His end with mine involved and knows that I
Should prove a bitter morsel and his bane
Whenever that shall be: so Fate pronounced.
But thou, O Father, I forewarn thee, shun
His deadly arrow. Neither vainly hope
To be invulnerable in those bright arms,
Though tempered Heav'nly, for that mortal dint,
Save He who reigns above, none can resist.
  She finished and the subtle Fiend his lore
Soon learned, now milder, and thus answered smooth:
  Dear Daughter, since thou claim'st me for thy sire
And my fair son here show'st me (the dear pledge
Of dalliance had with thee in Heav'n and joys
Then sweet, now sad to mention through dire change
Befall'n us unforeseen, unthought of), know
I come no enemy but to set free

782. *thine own begotten*: recalling the Son as the only begotten of the Father.
812. *invulnerable* has four syllables: 'in-vuln-rab-le.'

From out this dark and dismal house of pain
Both him and thee and all the Heav'nly host
Of spirits that in our just pretenses armed
Fell with us from on high. From them I go
This uncouth errand sole and one for all
Myself expose with lonely steps to tread
Th' unfounded deep and through the void immense
To search with wand'ring quest a place foretold
Should be (and by concurring signs, ere now
Created, vast and round) a place of bliss
In the purlieus of Heav'n and therein placed
A race of upstart creatures to supply
Perhaps our vacant room, though more removed,
Lest Heav'n surcharged with potent multitude
Might hap to move new broils. Be this or aught
Than this more secret now designed I haste
To know and this once known shall soon return
And bring ye to the place where thou and Death
Shall dwell at ease and up and down unseen
Wing silently the buxom air, embalmed
With odors. There ye shall be fed and filled
Immeasurably: all things shall be your prey!
  He ceased, for both seemed highly pleased, and Death
Grinned horrible a ghastly smile to hear
His famine should be filled and blest his maw
Destined to that good hour. No less rejoiced
His mother bad and thus bespake her sire:
  The key of this infernal pit by due
And by command of Heav'n's all-powerful King
I keep, by Him forbidden to unlock
These adamantine gates. Against all force
Death ready stands to interpose his dart,
Fearless to be o'ermatched by living might.
But what owe I to His commands above
Who hates me and hath hither thrust me down
Into this gloom of Tartarus profound
To sit in hateful office here confined,
Inhabitant of Heav'n and Heav'nly-born,

830–32. He seeks the created universe, which was foretold by prophecy in heaven, and which by reading other signs Satan knows has now been created.
833. *purlieus*: neighborhood. More precisely, a piece of land on the edge of a royal forest, which might be turned over to private use under some restrictions; a fairly precise word for the legal status of the world Adam and Eve are given.
842. *embalmed*: made odorous, as with balm. The practice of embalming corpses may also be suggested.
844. *immeasurably* has four syllables: 'imm-mesj-rab-ly.'

Here in perpetual agony and pain
With terrors and with clamors compassed round
Of mine own brood that on my bowels feed?
Thou art my father, thou my author, thou
My being gav'st me: whom should I obey
But thee, whom follow? Thou wilt bring me soon
To that new world of light and bliss among
The gods who live at ease, where I shall reign
At thy right hand voluptuous as beseems
Thy daughter and thy darling without end.
  Thus saying, from her side the fatal key,
Sad instrument of all our woe, she took
And towards the gate rolling her bestial train
Forthwith the huge portcullis high up drew
Which but herself not all the Stygian pow'rs
Could once have moved, then in the key-hole turns
Th' intrícate wards and every bolt and bar
Of massy iron or solid rock with ease
Unfastens. On a sudden open fly
With impetuous recoil and jarring sound
Th' infernal doors and on their hinges grate
Harsh thunder that the lowest bottom shook
Of Erebus. She opened, but to shut
Excelled her pow'r. The gates wide open stood
That with extended wings a bannered host
Under spread ensigns marching might pass through
With horse and chariots ranked in loose array.
So wide they stood and like a furnace mouth
Cast forth redounding smoke and ruddy flame.
Before their eyes in sudden view appear
The secrets of the hoary deep, a dark
Illimitable ocean without bound,
Without dimension, where length, breadth, and heighth,
And time and place are lost, where eldest Night
And Chaos, áncestors of Nature, hold
Eternal anarchy amidst the noise
Of endless wars and by confusion stand.
For Hot, Cold, Moist, and Dry, four champions fierce
Strive here for mast'ry and to battle bring
Their embryon atoms. They around the flag

869. *voluptuous*: an adverb modifying *reign*; "pleasure," Latin *voluptas*.
878. *iron* has one syllable.
879–83. The horrid sound made by the opening of Hell's gates imitates the grinding hinges of the gates of the temple of Mars, in *Aeneid* 6.573–74.
880. *impetuous* has three syllables: 'im-pet-chus.'
900. *they*: the *embryon atoms*. *Embryon* has two syllables: 'embr-yon.'

Of each his faction in their several clans,
Light-armed or heavy, sharp, smooth, swift or slow,
Swarm populous, unnumbered as the sands
Of Barca or Cyrenè's torrid soil,
Levied to side with warring winds and poise
Their lighter wings. To whom these most adhere,
He rules a moment. Chaos umpire sits
And by decision more embroils the fray
By which he reigns. Next him high arbiter
Chance governs all. Into this wild abyss
(The womb of Nature and perhaps her grave)
Of neither sea, nor shore, nor air, nor fire,
But all these in their pregnant causes mixed
Confus'dly, and which thus must ever fight
Unless th' Almighty Maker them ordain
His dark materials to create more worlds.
Into this wild abyss the wary Fiend
Stood on the brink of Hell and looked a while,
Pond'ring his voyage, for no narrow frith
He had to cross. Nor was his ear less pealed
With noises loud and ruinous (to compare
Great things with small) than when Bellona storms
With all her batt'ring engines bent to raze
Some capital city—or less than if this frame
Of Heav'n were falling and these elements
In mutiny had from her axle torn
The steadfast earth. At last his sail-broad vans
He spreads for flight and in the surging smoke
Uplifted spurns the ground, thence many a league
As in a cloudy chair ascending rides
Audacious but that seat soon failing meets
A vast vacuity. All unawares,
Flutt'ring his pennons vain, plumb down he drops
Ten thousand fathom deep and to this hour
Down had been falling had not by ill chance

904. *Cyrenè*: all vowels are long: 'sigh-ree-nee.'

910–20. The main structure of the sentence is "Into this wild abyss the Fiend looked a while." The opening prepositional phrase, *into this wild abyss*, is repeated at line 917 because of the heavy freight of descriptive ideas on the purpose and nature of chaos borne in lines 911–16.

912. *of*: composed of.

919. *frith*: firth, a long narrow arm of the sea, related to *fjord*.

920. *pealed*: battered with noise.

922. *Bellona*: goddess of war.

924–25. *capital* has two syllables: 'cap-tal,' and *city* and *or* are elided: 'cit-yor.' *or less*: picking up from line 920, *nor . . . less*: the sound of chaos was no less loud than if the earth imploded.

932. *unawares*: unexpectedly.

The strong rebuff of some tumultuous cloud
Instínct with fire and nitre hurried him
As many miles aloft. *That* fury stayed,
Quenched in a boggy Syrtis, neither sea
Nor good dry land, nigh foundered, on he fares
Treading the crude consistence half on foot,
Half flying: behooves him now both oar and sail!
As when a gryphon through the wilderness
With wingèd course o'er hill or moory dale
Pursues the Arimaspian who by stealth
Had from his wakeful custody purloined
The guarded gold, so eagerly the Fiend
O'er bog or steep, through strait, rough, dense, or rare,
With head, hands, wings, or feet pursues his way
And swims, or sinks, or wades, or creeps, or flies.
At length a universal hubbub wild
Of stunning sounds and voices all confused
Borne through the hollow dark assaults his ear
With loudest vehemence. Thither he plies
Undaunted to meet there whatever pow'r
Or spirit of the nethermost abyss
Might in that noise reside, of whom to ask
Which way the nearest coast of darkness lies,
Bord'ring on light, when straight, behold! the throne
Of Chaos and his dark pavilion spread
Wide on the wasteful deep. With him enthroned
Sat sable-vested Night, eldest of things,
The consort of his reign, and by them stood
Orcus and Ades and the dreaded name
Of Demogorgon, Rumor next and Chance
And Tumult and Confusion all embroiled
And Discord with a thousand various mouths.
T' whom Satan turning boldly, thus: Ye pow'rs
And spirits of the nethermost abyss,
Chaos and ancient Night, I come no spy
With purpose to explore or to disturb
The secrets of your realm but by constraint,
Wand'ring this darksome desert (as my way
Lies through your spacious empire up to light)

936. *tumultuous* has three syllables: 'tumul-chus.'
942. *flying* has one syllable.
943–47. The one-eyed Arimaspians like to steal gold from gryphons.
948–50. The onomatopoeic meter of lines 948–50 has been justly praised. Lines 948 and 949 move into irregular rhythm, imitating the difficulty of the passage through chaos. Line 950 falls into mechanically regular iambic pentameter (something Milton rarely does).

Alone and without guide, half lost, I seek
What readiest path leads where your gloomy bounds
Confine with Heav'n. Or if some other place
From your dominion won th' ethereal King
Possesses lately, thither to arrive
I travel this profound: direct my course!
Directed, no mean recompense it brings
To your behoof if I that region lost,
All usurpation thence expelled, reduce
To her original darkness and your sway
(Which is my present journey) and once more
Erect the standard there of ancient Night.
Yours be th' advantage all, mine the revenge!
  Thus Satan, and him thus the anarch old
With falt'ring speech and visage incomposed
Answered: I know thee, stranger, who thou art,
That mighty leading angel who of late
Made head against Heav'n's King, though overthrown.
I saw and heard, for such a num'rous host
Fled not in silence through the frighted deep
With ruin upon ruin, rout on rout,
Confusion worse confounded, and Heav'n gates
Poured out by millions her victorious bands
Pursuing. I upon my frontiers here
Keep residence. If all I can will serve
That little which is left so to defend,
Encroached on still through your intestine broils,
Weak'ning the scepter of old Night: first Hell,
Your dungeon stretching far and wide beneath,
Now lately Heav'n and Earth, another world
Hung o'er my realm, linked in a golden chain
To that side Heav'n from whence your legions fell.
If that way be your walk you have not far,
So much the nearer danger. Go and speed:
Havoc and spoil and ruin are my gain!
  He ceased and Satan stayed not to reply
But glad now that his sea should find a shore
With fresh alacrity and force renewed
Springs upward like a pyramid of fire
Into the wide expanse and through the shock
Of fighting elements on all sides round
Environed wins his way, harder beset

984. *original* has three syllables: 'or-ij-nal.'
1001. *your*: in the 1667 and 1674 printings: *our*.

And more endangered than when Argo passed
Through Bosphorus betwixt the justling rocks
Or when Ulysses on the larboard shunned
Charybdis and by th' other whirlpool steered,
So he with difficulty and labor hard
Moved on—with difficulty and labor he,
But he once passed, soon after when Man fell,
Strange alteration! Sin and Death amain
Following his track (such was the will of Heav'n)
Paved after him a broad and beaten way,
Over the dark abyss whose boiling gulf
Tamely endured a bridge of wondrous length
From Hell continued reaching th' utmost orb
Of this frail world, by which the spirits perverse
With easy intercourse pass to and fro
To tempt or punish mortals (except whom
God and good angels guard by special grace).
But now at last the sacred influence
Of light appears and from the walls of Heav'n
Shoots far into the bosom of dim night
A glimmering dawn. Here nature first begins
Her farthest verge and chaos to retire
As from her outmost works a broken foe
With tumult less and with less hostile din,
That Satan with less toil and now with ease
Wafts on the calmer wave by dubious light
And like a weather-beaten vessel holds
Gladly the port, though shrouds and tackle torn,
Or in the emptier waste resembling air
Weighs his spread wings, at leisure to behold
Far off th' empyreal Heav'n extended wide
In circuit, undetermined square or round,
With opal tow'rs and battlements adorned

1018. *justling*: jostling.
1021. *difficulty* and *and* are elided: 'difficult-yand.'
1021–26. *he*: Satan. Satan had difficulty but Sin and Death will make the way across Chaos easy for the devils after the fall of mankind.
1029–30. *utmost orb / Of this frail world*: the outside of the outermost sphere of the created universe.
1031. *intercourse*: passage back and forth. Latin *intercursus*, a running between.
1034. *influence*. Literally, a "flowing in." See 3.1–55.
1042. *Wafts*: floats gently, but moves.
1043. *holds*: heads for.
1048. *undetermined*. From Satan's viewpoint it is unclear whether heaven is square or round. The Bible (Revelation 21:16, based on Ezekiel 40) describes heaven as square. But Milton may be suggesting the form of heaven, which mystically unites the rationally incompatible shapes of the square and the circle.

Of living sapphire, once his native seat,
And fast by hanging in a golden chain
This pendent world in bigness as a star
Of smallest magnitude close by the moon.
Thither full fraught with mischievous revenge
Accurst, and in a cursèd hour, he hies.

Book Three

The Argument

God sitting on His throne sees Satan flying towards this world, then newly created, shows him to the Son who sat at His right hand, foretells the success of Satan in perverting Mankind, clears His own justice and wisdom from all imputation, having created Man free and able enough to have withstood his tempter, yet declares His purpose of grace towards him, in regard he fell not of his own malice as did Satan, but by him seduced. The Son of God renders praises to his Father for the manifestation of his gracious purpose towards Man but God again declares that grace cannot be extended towards Man without the satisfaction of divine justice. Man hath offended the majesty of God by aspiring to godhead and therefore, with all his progeny devoted to death, must die unless someone can be found sufficient to answer for his offence and undergo his punishment. The Son of God freely offers Himself a ransom for Man. The Father accepts Him, ordains His incarnation, pronounces His exaltation above all names in Heaven and Earth, commands all the angels to adore Him. They obey and, hymning to their harps in full choir, celebrate the Father and the Son. Meanwhile Satan alights upon the bare convex of this world's outermost orb where wand'ring he first finds a place since called the Limbo of Vanity. What persons and things fly up thither. Thence comes to the gate of Heaven, described ascending by stairs, and the waters above the firmament that flow about it. His passage thence to the orb of the sun: he finds there Uriel, the regent of that orb, but first changes himself into the shape of a meaner angel, pretending a zealous desire to behold the new Creation and Man whom God had placed here, inquires of him the place of his habitation and is directed, alights first on Mount Niphates.

1051. *in*: by. The golden chain mentioned in the *Iliad* (8.18–27) became, for later interpreters of the poem, a symbol of the unity and order of the universe on all its levels, leading up to God.
1052. *pendent*: hanging. *world*: universe.

Hail, holy Light, offspring of Heav'n, first-born,
Or of th' Eternal co-eternal beam
May I express thee unblamed? Since God is light
And never but in unapproachèd light
Dwelt from eternity, dwelt then in thee,
Bright effluence of bright essence increate.
Or hear'st thou rather pure ethereal stream
Whose fountain who shall tell? Before the sun,
Before the heavens thou wert and at the voice
Of God as with a mantle didst invest
The rising world of waters dark and deep,
Won from the void and formless infinite.
Thee I revisit now with bolder wing
Escaped the Stygian pool though long detained
In that obscure sojourn while in my flight
Through utter and through middle darkness borne
With other notes than to th' Orphéan lyre
I sung of Chaos and Eternal Night,
Taught by the Heav'nly Muse to venture down
The dark descent and up to reascend
Though hard and rare. Thee I revisit safe
And feel thy sovereign vital lamp but thou
Revisit'st not these eyes that roll in vain
To find thy piercing ray and find no dawn,

Book Three

1–55. This prayer to light is the most famous passage of *Paradise Lost* and the most personal. Its setting is the transition from the darkness of Hell and Chaos to the light of Heaven, first seen through Satan's eyes (2.1034–39). Now the light is greeted by the poet, who advances the startling claim that in making his poem he has flown to Hell and back, following Satan's track (lines 13–21). He then speaks of his blindness, which separates him from the beauty of nature but which no more stops him from making poetry than it did the poets and prophets of old. He asks the heavenly light to *shine inward* (line 52), and that request prepares for the main event of Book Three: the scene in heaven in which the Father reveals his plan for history and the Son offers himself as a sacrifice to rescue mankind.

1–8. Milton conjectures three things of light: (1) that light is the spontaneous growth, or "offspring," of heaven (line 1), (2) that light was never created because it has existed forever with God (lines 2–6), and (3) that light is mysterious in origin (lines 7–8). All three conflict with the Bible (Genesis 1:1–3), where light is created by God after the heaven and the earth. But see 3.6 n. See also 7.243–51.

6. *effluence*: flowing forth; two syllables: 'eff-lence.' *essence*: unchanging, inner being of something. *increate*: never created. Radiant light is a flowing forth out of what is also bright but does not flow forth: the uncreated essence of light. The word *increate* suggests that while the essence of light is eternally with God, the *effluence* of that essence is created in Genesis 1:3: "Let there be light: and there was light." With this distinction between essential and radiant light Milton reconciles his mystical vision of the eternity of light with the literal text of the Bible.

7. *Or hear'st thou*: 'or are you called.'

14. *Stygian*: of the infernal river Styx.

17. *Orphéan*: of Orpheus, alluding to an archaic Greek poem, "Hymn to Night," attributed to the legendary poet Orpheus, who, like the narrator of *Paradise Lost*, visited Hell.

19–21. See 2.432–33 and n.

So thick a drop serene hath quenched their orbs
Or dim suffusion veiled. Yet not the more
Cease I to wander where the muses haunt
Clear spring or shady grove or sunny hill,
Smit with the love of sacred song. But chief
Thee, Sion, and the flow'ry brooks beneath
That wash thy hallowed feet and warbling flow,
Nightly I visit nor sometimes forget
Those other two equaled with me in fate
(So were I equaled with them in renown)
Blind Thamyris and blind Maeonides,
And Tiresias and Phineus, prophets old.
Then feed on thoughts that voluntary move
Harmonious numbers as the wakeful bird
Sings darkling and in shadiest covert hid
Tunes her nocturnal note. Thus with the year
Seasons return but not to me returns
Day or the sweet approach of ev'n or morn
Or sight of vernal bloom or summer's rose
Or flocks or herds or human face divine
But cloud instead and ever-during dark
Surrounds me, from the cheerful ways of men
Cut off and, for the book of knowledge fair,
Presented with a universal blank
Of nature's works to me expunged and razed
And wisdom at one entrance quite shut out.
So much the rather thou, celestial Light,
Shine inward and the mind through all her powers
Irradiate. *There* plant eyes. All mist from thence
Purge and disperse, that I may see and tell
Of things invisible to mortal sight!
  Now had th' almighty Father from above,
From the pure empyréan where He sits
High throned above all heighth, bent down His eye
His own works and their works at once to view.

25–26. *drop serene . . . dim suffusion*: medical language of Milton's day that suggests he is uncertain whether he is permanently or temporarily blind, whether his sight is *quenched* or only *veiled*.

30. *Sion*: The mount of Jerusalem (Zion), associated with the Bible, especially the psalms.

33–35. The reference is to Homer (*Maeonides*) and a legendary blind poet, Thamyris; i.e., I am equal to them in blindness. So may I be equal to them in fame!

35. *Tiresias* and *Phineus* are blind prophets in Greek literature. In both figures, the power of prophecy and the affliction of blindness are linked.

37. *voluntary*: spontaneously.

38. *numbers*: metrical verse. *wakeful bird*: nightingale. Milton often composed at night.

47. *book of knowledge*: nature, traditionally regarded as a book in which the Creator's purpose can be read.

About Him all the sanctities of Heav'n
Stood thick as stars and from His sight received
Beatitude past utterance. On His right
The radiant image of His glory sat,
His only Son. On Earth He first beheld
Our two first parents, yet the only two
Of mankind, in the happy garden placed,
Reaping immortal fruits of joy and love,
Uninterrupted joy, unrivaled love
In blissful solitude. He then surveyed
Hell and the gulf between and Satan there
Coasting the wall of Heav'n on this side night
In the dun air sublime and ready now
To stoop with wearied wings and willing feet
On the bare outside of this world that seemed
Firm land embosomed without firmament—
Uncertain which, in ocean or in air.
Him God beholding from His prospect high
(Wherein past, present, future He beholds)
Thus to His only Son foreseeing spake:
  Only begotten Son, seest thou what rage
Transports our Adversary whom no bounds
Prescribed, no bars of Hell nor all the chains
Heaped on him there nor yet the main abyss
Wide interrupt can hold, so bent he seems
On desperate revenge that shall redound
Upon his own rebellious head? And now
Through all restraint broke loose he wings his way
Not far off Heav'n in the precincts of light
Directly towards the new created world
And Man there placed, with purpose to assay
If him by force he can destroy or worse
By some false guile pervert. And shall pervert,
For Man will hearken to his glozing lies
And easily transgress the sole command,
Sole pledge of his obedience. So will fall
He and his faithless progeny. Whose fault?

60. *sanctities*: blessed ones, angels.
64. *Son*. The Son of God, who will be incarnate as Jesus, is here the visible image of God's invisible glory. (See lines 139–40 and 6.680.)
73. *stoop*: descend. A term from hawking.
74. *world*: the entire created universe, not the earth. See lines 418–19.
75–76. *imbosomed . . . air*: The outer, convex surface of the universe is directly exposed to chaos, without any protective *firmament*, or upper sky. The universe is thus *embosomed* in the violence of chaos, which batters it like the ocean.
77. *Him*: Satan.
88. *precincts*: the outskirts.

Whose but his own? Ingrate! He had of Me
All he could have. I made him just and right,
Sufficient to have stood though free to fall.
Such I created all th' ethereal pow'rs
And spirits, both them who stood and them who failed:
Freely they stood who stood and fell who fell.
Not free, what proof could they have giv'n sincere
Of true allegiance, constant faith or love
Where only what they needs must do appeared,
Not what they would? What praise could they receive?
What pleasure I from such obedience paid
When will and reason (reason also is choice)
Useless and vain, of freedom both despoiled,
Made passive both, had served necessity,
Not Me? They therefore, as to right belonged,
So were created, nor can justly accuse
Their Maker or their making or their fate,
As if predestination overruled
Their will disposed by absolute decree
Or high foreknowledge. They themselves decreed
Their own revolt, not I. If I foreknew
Foreknowledge had no influence on their fault
Which had no less proved certain unforeknown.
So without least impúlse or shadow of fate
Or aught by me immutably foreseen
They trespass, authors to themselves in all
Both what they judge and what they choose, for so
I formed them free and free they must remain
Till they enthrall themselves. I else must change
Their nature and revoke the high decree,
Unchangeable, eternal, which ordained
Their freedom: they themselves ordained their Fall.
The first sort by their own suggestion fell
Self-tempted, self-depraved. Man falls deceived
By th' other first: Man therefore shall find grace,
The other none. In mercy and justice both

97. *Ingrate!* . . . *had*. Because God is in eternity he sees all events as present. This makes his use of tenses somewhat arbitrary. See argument to Book Three: "Man hath offended." But he hasn't, yet.

100–101. *powers / And spirits*: angels.

108. To make the most reasonable choice in any matter (e.g., whether to remain faithful to God) is still a free choice. See *Areopagitica*: "When God gave him reason he gave him freedom to choose, for reason is but choosing," (p. 354).

112. *so*: free.

120. *shadow* and *of* are elided: 'shad-wov.'

129. *first sort*: the rebel angels.

131. *other*: Satan, the head of the rebel angels.

132. *mercy* and *justice* are elided: 'merce-yand.'

Through Heav'n and Earth so shall my glory excel,
But mercy first and last shall brightest shine.
  Thus while God spake ambrosial fragrance filled
All Heav'n and in the blessèd spirits elect
Sense of new joy ineffable diffused.
Beyond compare the Son of God was seen
Most glorious. In Him all His Father shone
Substantially expressed and in His face
Divine compassion visibly appeared:
Love without end and without measure grace,
Which uttering thus He to His Father spake:
  O Father, gracious was that word which closed
Thy sov'reign sentence, that Man should find grace,
For which both Heav'n and Earth shall high extol
Thy praises with th' innumerable sound
Of hymns and sacred songs wherewith Thy throne
Encompassed shall resound Thee ever blest.
For should Man finally be lost? Should Man,
Thy creature late so loved, Thy youngest son,
Fall circumvented thus by fraud, though joined
With his own folly? That be from Thee far,
That far be from Thee, Father, who art judge
Of all things made and judgest only right.
Or shall the Adversary thus obtain
His end and frustrate Thine? Shall he fulfill
His malice and Thy goodness bring to naught
Or proud return (though to his heavier doom,
Yet with revenge accomplished) and to Hell
Draw after him the whole race of mankind
By him corrupted? Or wilt Thou thyself
Abolish Thy creation and unmake
For him what for Thy glory Thou hast made?
So should Thy goodness and Thy greatness both
Be questioned and blasphémed without defense.
  To whom the great Creator thus replied:
O Son in whom my soul hath chief delight,
Son of my bosom, Son who art alone
My Word, my wisdom, and effectual might,
All hast thou spoken as my thoughts are, all
As my eternal purpose hath decreed.
Man shall not quite be lost but saved who will,

133. *glory* and *excel* are elided: 'glor-yexcell.'
142. *grace*: salvation, forgiveness.
170. *effectual*: producing effects. The Father's power acts through the Son.
173. *who will*: whoever chooses. God's grace softens the hard heart and makes one capable of choosing to be saved. See 11.2–5.

Yet not of will in him but grace in me
Freely vouchsafed. Once more I will renew
His lapsèd pow'rs though forfeit and enthralled
By sin to foul exorbitant desires.
Upheld by me, yet once more he shall stand
On even ground against his mortal foe,
By me upheld that he may know how frail
His fall'n condition is and to me owe
All his deliv'rance, and to none but me.
Some I have chosen of peculiar grace
Elect above the rest: so is my will.
The rest shall hear me call and oft be warned
Their sinful state and to appease betimes
Th' incensèd Deity while offered grace
Invites, for I will clear their senses dark
What may suffice and soften stony hearts
To pray, repent, and bring obedience due.
To prayer, repentance, and obedience due,
Though but endeavored with sincere intent,
Mine ear shall not be slow, mine eyes not shut.
And I will place within them as a guide
My umpire conscience whom if they will hear
Light after light well used they shall attain
And to the end persisting safe arrive.
This my long suff'rance and my day of grace
They who neglect and scorn shall never taste
But hard be hardened, blind be blinded more,
That they may stumble on and deeper fall:
And none but such from mercy I exclude!
But yet all is not done: Man disobeying
Disloyal breaks his fealty and sins
Against the high supremacy of Heav'n,
Affecting godhead, and so, losing all,
To expiate his treason hath naught left
But to destruction sacred and devote
He with his whole posterity must die.

184. *elect*: chosen.
185. *The rest*: those of mankind who will be saved, but are not of the *elect*.
189. "I will take the stony heart out of their flesh, and will give them an heart of flesh" (Ezekiel 11:19).
196. *Light after light well used*: i.e., they shall attain the light of true repentance by using the light of conscience.
202. *such*: *they* (3.199) who scorn God's offered grace.
206. *Godhead*: the status of God. Man's crime is to intend to be like a god. *losing all*: having lost all goodness by this crime.
208. *sacred*: set apart and formally doomed. (One of the Latin senses of *sacer*.) *devote*: cursed formally and outlawed.
209. *whole posterity*: all his children.

Die he or justice must, unless for him
Some other able and as willing pay
The rigid satisfaction, death for death.
Say, Heavn'ly Pow'rs, where shall we find such love?
Which of ye will be mortal to redeem
Man's mortal crime and, just, th' unjust to save?
Dwells in all Heaven charity so dear?
  He asked, but all the Heavn'ly choir stood mute
And silence was in Heav'n. On Man's behalf
Patron or intercessor none appeared,
Much less that durst upon his own head draw
The deadly forfeiture and ransom set.
And now without redemption all mankind
Must have been lost, adjudged to death and Hell
By doom severe, had not the Son of God
In whom the fullness dwells of love divine
His dearest mediation thus renewed:
  Father, Thy word is past: Man shall find grace!
And shall Grace not find means that finds her way
The speediest of Thy wingèd messengers
To visit all Thy creatures and to all
Comes unprevented, unimplored, unsought?
Happy for Man, so coming. He her aid
Can never seek once dead in sins and lost:
Atonement for himself or offering meet,
Indebted and undone, hath none to bring.
Behold Me then, Me for him, life for life
I offer. On Me let thine anger fall.
Account Me Man. I for his sake will leave
Thy bosom and this glory next to Thee
Freely put off and for him lastly die
Well pleased. On Me let Death wreck all his rage!
Under his gloomy pow'r I shall not long
Lie vanquished. Thou hast giv'n me to possess
Life in myself for ever. By Thee I live
Though now to Death I yield and am his due:
All that of Me *can* die. Yet that debt paid

210. Man must die or justice will.

215. "For Christ also hath once suffered for sins, the just for the unjust" (1 Peter 3:18). The reference is to the Crucifixion.

216. *charity*: heavenly love (Latin *caritas*, trans. Greek *agapê*, disinterested, altruistic love, as opposed to *eros*, erotic love). See line 225: *love divine*.

231. *unprevented*: not preceded (by prayer) (Latin *praevenio*, "precede, anticipate"). Divine grace comes before Man knows he needs it, softening the heart, which has been hardened by sin.

232. *her*: grace's.

238–40. The Son will leave God's presence, become human, and die.

Thou wilt not leave me in the loathsome grave
His prey nor suffer my unspotted soul
For ever with corruption there to dwell
But I shall rise victorious and subdue
My vanquisher, spoiled of his vaunted spoil.
Death his death's wound shall then receive and stoop
Inglorious, of his mortal sting disarmed.
I through the ample air in triumph high
Shall lead Hell captive maugre Hell and show
The pow'rs of darkness bound. Thou at the sight
Pleased, out of Heaven shalt look down and smile
While by Thee raised I ruin all my foes,
Death last, and with his carcass glut the grave,
Then with the multitude of my redeemed
Shall enter Heav'n long absent and return,
Father, to see Thy face wherein no cloud
Of anger shall remain but peace assured
And reconcilement. Wrath shall be no more
Thenceforth but in Thy presence joy entire.
  His words here ended but his meek aspéct
Silent yet spake and breathed immortal love
To mortal men, above which only shone
Filial obedience. As a sacrifice,
Glad to be offered, He attends the will
Of his great Father. Admiration seized
All Heav'n, what this might mean and whither tend,
Wond'ring. But soon th' Almighty thus replied:
  O Thou in Heav'n and Earth the only peace
Found out for mankind under wrath, O Thou
My sole complacence! Well Thou know'st how dear
To me are all my works nor Man the least,
Though last created, that for him I spare
Thee from My bosom and right hand to save,
By losing Thee a while, the whole race lost.
Thou therefore whom Thou only canst redeem,
Their nature also to Thy nature join
And be Thyself man among men on Earth,
Made flesh (when time shall be) of virgin seed

247–49. "For thou wilt not leave my soul in hell; neither wilt thou suffer thine Holy One to see corruption" (Psalms 16:10).
252. "The last enemy that shall be destroyed is death" and "O death, where is thy sting? O grave, where is thy victory?" (1 Corinthians 15:26 and 55).
255. *maugre*: despite (French *malgré*). "Thou hast led captivity captive" (Psalms 68:18).
271. *Admiration*: wonder (Latinate sense: *admiror*, "to regard with wonder").
280. *lost*: which would otherwise be lost.
281–82. I.e., Join your nature to the nature of mankind, whom only you can redeem.
284. The Son will be Jesus Christ, who is born of the virgin Mary.

By wondrous birth. Be Thou in Adam's room
The head of all mankind though Adam's son.
As in him perish all men so in Thee
As from a second root shall be restored
As many as are restored, without Thee none.
His crime makes guilty all his sons. Thy merit
Imputed shall absolve them who renounce
Their own both righteous and unrighteous deeds
And live in Thee transplanted and from Thee
Receive new life. So Man, as is most just,
Shall satisfy for Man, be judged and die,
And dying rise and rising with Him raise
His brethren ransomed with His own dear life.
So heav'nly love shall outdo hellish hate,
Giving to death and dying to redeem
(So dearly to redeem) what hellish hate
So easily destroyed and still destroys
In those who, when they may, accept not grace.
Nor shalt Thou by descending to assume
Man's nature lessen or degrade thine own.
Because Thou hast, though throned in highest bliss
Equal to God and equally enjoying
God-like fruition, quitted all to save
A world from utter loss and hast been found
By merit more than birthright Son of God
(Found worthiest to be so by being good
Far more than great or high, because in Thee
Love hath abounded more than glory abounds)
Therefore thy humiliation shall exalt
With Thee thy manhood also to this throne.

285. *room*: place.
289. *many* and *as* are elided: 'men-yaz.'
291. *Imputed*: attributed. Because the Son becomes a man himself, before he pays for the sins of mankind, his sacrifice is imputed to humanity.
292–93. From the Calvinist perspective, it is not enough to renounce one's unrighteous deeds. One must also renounce any credit, or merit, for one's righteous deeds, since these can be performed only with Christ's help. One must therefore *transplant* (line 293) oneself in Christ.
295. *be judged*: The reference is to Christ's trial before he is crucified.
296–97. Christ's rising from the grave after the Crucifixion is an assurance that humanity will rise from the dead at the end of time.
299. Christ gives himself to death to redeem mankind.
301. *and still destroys*. None of this has occurred yet. See 3.97n.
303–4 and 313–14. By becoming incarnate and mortal, as a man, the Son does not bring down his divinity to the level of the human but raises the human to the divine.
305–12. By voluntarily quitting the status of equality with God in order to save mankind, the Son earns his title, "Son of God," which was his before only by birthright.
307. *fruition*: enjoyment (Latin *fructus*, "enjoyment, delight, satisfaction").
312. *glory* and *abounds* are elided: 'glor-yabounds.'
314–17. After the resurrection, the Son will ascend to heaven in his human body and will sit beside the Father in that body.

Here shalt Thou sit incarnate, here shalt reign
Both God and Man, Son both of God and Man,
Anointed universal King. All pow'r
I give Thee: reign for ever and assume
Thy merits! Under Thee as Head Supreme
Thrones, princedoms, pow'rs, dominions I reduce:
All knees to Thee shall bow of them that bide
In Heaven or Earth or under Earth in Hell,
When Thou attended gloriously from Heav'n
Shalt in the sky appear and from Thee send
The summoning archangels to proclaim
Thy dread tribunal. Forthwith from all winds
The living and forthwith the cited dead
Of all past ages to the general doom
Shall hasten, such a peal shall rouse their sleep.
Then all Thy saints assembled, Thou shalt judge
Bad men and angels: they arraigned shall sink
Beneath Thy sentence. Hell, her numbers full,
Thenceforth shall be for ever shut. Meanwhile
The world shall burn and from her ashes spring
New Heav'n and Earth wherein the just shall dwell
And after all their tribulations long
See golden days fruitful of golden deeds
With Joy and Love triúmphing and fair Truth.
Then Thou thy regal scepter shalt lay by,
For regal scepter then no more shall need:
God shall be All in all. But all ye gods
Adore Him who to compass all this dies!
Adore the Son and honor Him as Me!
  No sooner had th' Almighty ceased but all
The multitude of angels with a shout
Loud as from numbers without number, sweet

321–22. "At the name of Jesus every knee should bow, of things in heaven, and things in earth, and things under the earth" (Philippians 2:10). The entire second chapter of Philippians underlies God's discourse here.

323–29. The Son's return to earth at the Last Judgment: "And they shall see the Son of man coming in the clouds of heaven with power and great glory" (Matthew 24:30). All people who have died rise from the dead and, joined by those who are still living, go up to judgment in their bodies. "For the Lord himself shall descend from heaven . . . and the dead in Christ shall rise first. Then we which are alive . . . shall be caught up together with them in the clouds, to meet the Lord in the air" (1 Thessalonians 4:17). "For the trumpet shall sound, and the dead shall be raised incorruptible" (1 Corinthians 15:52).

330. *saints assembled*: The faithful angels and the humans who have been saved will be gathered together to watch the Son damn the wicked.

334–35. "And I saw a new heaven and a new earth: for the first heaven and the first earth were passed away; and there was no more sea" (Revelation 21:1).

341. *gods*: angels.

As from blest voices uttering joy, Heav'n rung
With jubilee and loud hosannas filled
Th' eternal regions. Lowly reverent
Towards either throne they bow and to the ground
With solemn adoration down they cast
Their crowns inwove with amarant and gold,
Immortal amarant, a flow'r which once
In Paradise fast by the Tree of Life
Began to bloom but soon for Man's offence
To Heav'n removed where first it grew, there grows
And flow'rs aloft, shading the Fount of Life
And where the river of bliss through midst of Heav'n
Rolls o'er Elysian flow'rs her amber stream.
With these that never fade the spirits elect
Bind their resplendent locks inwreathed with beams.
Now in loose garlands thick thrown off, the bright
Pavement, that like a sea of jasper shone,
Impurpled with celestial roses, smiled.
Then, crowned again, their golden harps they took
(Harps ever tuned that glittering by their side
Like quivers hung) and with preamble sweet
Of charming symphony they introduce
Their sacred song and waken raptures high.
No voice exempt, no voice but well could join
Melodious part, such concord is in Heav'n.
  Thee, Father, first they sung omnipotent,
Immutable, immortal, infinite,
Eternal King, Thee Author of all being,
Fountain of light, Thyself invisible
Admidst the glorious brightness where Thou sitt'st
Throned inaccessible. But when Thou shad'st
The full blaze of thy beams and through a cloud
Drawn round about Thee like a radiant shrine,
Dark with excessive bright thy skirts appear
Yet dazzle Heav'n that brightest seraphim
Approach not but with both wings veil their eyes!
Thee next they sang of all Creation first,

347. *rung*: rang. The syntax of lines 345–48 makes *Heav'n* the object, not the subject, of *rung*. I.e., With a shout, the angels made heaven ring with celebration.
353. *amarant*: the legendary, unfading flower, *amaranthus*, its name derived from the Greek *marainô*, "to wither, fade away." The Greek word is present in 1 Peter 5:4: "ye shall receive a crown of glory that fadeth not away."
360. *these*: their amaranthus crowns (line 252).
381–82. The seraphim, who contemplate God, must cover their faces with their wings (Isaiah 6:2).
383–84. *of all Creation first* suggests the Son has been created by the Father, after which the Son creates everything else: the angels, the universe, the earth, and humanity.

Begotten Son, divine similitude,
In whose conspicuous count'nance without cloud
Made visible th' almighty Father shines
Whom else no creature can behold. On Thee
Impressed th' effulgence of His glory abides;
Transfused on Thee his ample Spirit rests.
He Heav'n of heav'ns and all the pow'rs therein
By Thee created and by Thee threw down
Th' aspiring dominations. Thou that day
Thy Father's dreadful thunder didst not spare
Nor stop Thy flaming chariot wheels that shook
Heav'n's everlasting frame while o'er the necks
Thou drov'st of warring angels disarrayed.
Back from pursuit Thy pow'rs with loud acclaim
Thee only extolled, Son of thy Father's might,
To execute fierce vengeance on His foes.
Not so on Man! Him through their malice fall'n,
Father of mercy and grace, Thou didst not doom
So strictly but much more to pity incline.
No sooner did Thy dear and only Son
Perceive Thee purposed not to doom frail Man
So strictly, but much more to pity inclined,
He to appease Thy wrath and end the strife
Of Mercy and Justice in Thy face discerned,
Regardless of the bliss wherein He sat
Second to Thee, offered himself to die
For Man's offence. O unexampled love!
Love nowhere to be found less than divine!
Hail Son of God, Savior of men, thy name
Shall be the copious matter of my song
Henceforth and never shall my harp thy praise
Forget nor from thy Father's praise disjoin!
　Thus they in Heav'n above the starry sphere
Their happy hours in joy and hymning spent.
Meanwhile upon the firm opacous globe
Of this round world whose first convéx divides

390–92. *He*: God the Father. *thee* . . . *thee*: the Son. God created the heavens and the angels through, or by means of, the Son.
392–96. In the same way, through the Son, God defeated the rebel angels, *th' aspiring dominations*. The action described here will be seen in Book Six.
398. *Only* and *extolled* are elided: 'on-lextolled.'
401, 407. *mercy* and *and* are elided: 'merce-yand.'
402, 405. *pity* and *incline* are elided: 'pit-yincline.'
418: *opacous*: dark, opaque.
418–21: the outermost sphere of the universe encloses and protects the *inferior* (lower) *orbs* (the stars, the planets, the sun, the moon) from chaos.

The luminous inferior orbs enclosed
From chaos and th' inroad of darkness old
Satan alighted walks. A globe far off
It seemed, now seems a boundless continent
Dark, waste, and wild, under the frown of Night
Starless exposed and ever threat'ning storms
Of chaos blust'ring round, inclement sky
Save on that side which from the wall of Heav'n
Though distant far some small reflection gains
Of glimm'ring air less vexed with tempest loud.
Here walked the Fiend at large in spacious field.
As when a vulture on Imaüs bred,
Whose snowy ridge the roving Tartar bounds,
Dislodging from a region scarce of prey
To gorge the flesh lambs or yeanling kids
On hills where flocks are fed, flies toward the springs
Of Ganges or Hydaspes, Indian streams,
But in his way lights on the barren plains
Of Sericana where Chineses drive
With sails and wind their cany wagons light,
So on this windy sea of land the Fiend
Walked up and down alone, bent on his prey.
Alone, for other creature in this place
Living or lifeless to be found was none,
None yet, but store hereafter from the earth
Up hither like aerïal vapors flew
Of all things transitory and vain when sin
With vanity had filled the works of men:
Both all things vain and all who in vain things
Build their fond hopes of glory or lasting fame
Or happiness in this or th' other life,
All who have their reward on Earth, the fruits
Of painful superstition and blind zeal
(Naught seeking but the praise of men) here find
Fit retribution empty as their deeds.

422–23. See 2.1052–53, when Satan first catches sight of the universe, which seems no bigger than the smallest star.

431–41. Satan is compared to a vulture that flies in search of prey from northern Asia over the Himalayas to India, pausing in his flight on the high, arid plains of central China.

444–97. The Paradise of Fools, the chief anti-Catholic passage of the poem, is distantly inspired by the episode of Ariosto's *Orlando Furioso* (canto 34), in which the knight Astolfo visits the moon, where he finds all vain and forgotten things. See 3.459. Milton's tone is much more serious.

446. *transitory* has three syllables: 'tran-si-tree.' *vain*: empty, weightless (Latin *vanus*).

449. *glory* and *or* are elided: 'glor-yor.'

452. *painful*: laborious.

All th' unaccomplished works of Nature's hand,
Abortive, monstrous, or unkindly mixed,
Dissolved on Earth, fleet hither and in vain
Till final dissolution wander here,
Not in the neighb'ring moon as some have dreamed.
Those argent fields more likely habitants
Translated saints or middle spirits hold
Betwixt th' angelical and human kind.
Hither of ill-joined sons and daughters born
First from the ancient world those giants came
With many a vain explóit though then renowned.
The builders next of Babel on the plain
Of Sennaär and still with vain design
New Babels, had they wherewithal, would build.
Others came single: he who to be deemed
A god leaped fondly into Etna flames,
Empedocles, and he who to enjoy
Plato's Elysium leaped into the sea,
Cleombrotus, and many more too long:
Embryos and idiots, eremites and friars,
White, black and grey with all their trumpery.
Here pilgrims roam that strayed so far to seek
In Golgotha Him dead who lives in Heav'n,
And they who to be sure of Paradise
Dying put on the weeds of Dominic
Or in Franciscan think to pass disguised.
They pass the planets sev'n and pass the fixed
And that crystálline sphere whose balance weighs
The trepidation talked, and that first moved.

456. *unkindly*: unnaturally.
457. *fleet*: fly.
460. *argent*: silver.
461. *Translated saints*: those who have not died but have been carried off to heaven: Enoch (Genesis 5:24) and Elijah (2 Kings 2:11). *middle spirits*: beings between angels and humans. The plan for humans, before the Fall, is that they will gradually become like angels. The moon might be an intermediate place for such spirits to reside.
466–67. The tower of Babel (Genesis 11:1–9), built in the plain of Shinar (*Sennaär*), in Babylonia, was a type of human folly and of the aspiration to compete with God.
469–73. Both suicides, Empedocles and Cleombrotus, are mentioned by the Christian fathers as examples of the vanity of pagan wishes.
473. *too long*: too long to tell.
474. *eremites*: hermits.
474–80. Examples of empty forms of hope in Roman Catholicism: the three orders of friars, the institution of pilgrimage to Jerusalem, and the practice of worldly men being buried in friar's robes or donning them shortly before dying. All are to Milton external and mechanical substitutes for inward sincerity.
477. *Golgotha*: "place of the skull"; the hill on which Christ was crucified.
481–83. The ten translucent spheres enclosing the earth: the seven planetary spheres; the sphere of the fixed stars; the ninth, or crystalline sphere; and the outermost, tenth sphere, *primum mobile* ("first mover"), which imparts motion to all the others.
483. *trepidation*: trembling in the cosmic spheres is said to be the cause of anomalies in astronomical observations. The word *talked* suggests that Milton thought it mere jargon.

And now Saint Peter at Heav'n's wicket seems
To wait them with his keys and now at foot
Of Heav'n's ascent they lift their feet when, lo!
A violent crosswind from either coast
Blows them transverse ten thousand leagues awry
Into the devious air. Then might ye see
Cowls, hoods and habits with their wearers tossed
And fluttered into rags, then relics, beads,
Indulgences, dispenses, pardons, bulls,
The sport of winds. All these upwhirled aloft
Fly o'er the backside of the world far off
Into a limbo large and broad since called
The Paradise of Fools, to few unknown
Long after, now unpeopled and untrod.
  All this dark globe the Fiend found as he passed
And long he wandered till at last a gleam
Of dawning light turned thitherward in haste
His traveled steps. Far distant he descries
Ascending by degrees magnificent
Up to the wall of Heav'n a structure high
At top whereof, but far more rich, appeared
The work as of a kingly palace gate
With frontispiece of diamond and gold
Embellished thick. With sparkling orient gems
The portal shone, inimitable on Earth
By model or by shading pencil drawn.
The stairs were such as whereon Jacob saw
Angels ascending and descending, bands
Of guardians bright, when he from Esau fled
To Padan-Aram in the field of Luz,
Dreaming by night under the open sky,
And waking cried, "This is the gate of Heav'n!"
Each stair mysteriously was meant nor stood
There always but drawn up to Heav'n sometimes
Viewless, and underneath a bright sea flowed
Of jasper or of liquid pearl whereon

484. *wicket*: gate. As Milton did not believe that Saint Peter guards heaven's gate, this image too is an example of vanity. The ascent through the spheres and the arrival at Saint Peter's gate are what the fools think they see.
487. *violent* has three syllables.
490–92. Accoutrements of Roman Catholic devotion and papal arrogance.
494. *world*: universe.
506. *diamond* has three syllables.
508. *inimitable* and *on* are elided.
510–15. Jacob fled from his brother Esau, from whom he had stolen his birthright. One night on his journey, Jacob dreamed of a ladder extending from heaven to earth. He woke and said, "this is none other but the house of God, and this is the gate of heaven" (Genesis 28:17).

Who after came from Earth sailing arrived
Wafted by angels or flew o'er the lake
Rapt in a chariot drawn by fiery steeds.
The stairs were then let down, whether to dare
The Fiend by easy ascent or aggravate
His sad exclusion from the doors of bliss.
Direct against, which opened from beneath,
Just o'er the blissful seat of Paradise,
A passage down to th' earth, a passage wide,
Wider by far than that of aftertimes
Over Mount Sion and, though that were large,
Over the Promised Land to God so dear
By which to visit oft those happy tribes
On high behests, His angels, to and fro
Passed frequent, and His eye with choice regard
From Paneas, the fount of Jordan's flood,
To Beërsaba where the Holy Land
Borders on Egypt and th' Arabian shore.
So wide the op'ning seemed, where bounds were set
To darkness, such as bound the ocean wave.
Satan from hence now on the lower stair
That scaled by steps of gold to Heaven gate
Looks down with wonder at the sudden view
Of all this world at once, as when a scout
Through dark and desert ways with peril gone
All night at last by break of cheerful dawn
Obtains the brow of some high climbing hill
Which to his eye discovers unaware
The goodly prospect of some foreign land
First seen, or some renowned metropolis
With glistering spires and pinnacles adorned
Which now the rising sun gilds with his beams.
Such wonder seized (though after Heaven seen)
The spirit malign but much more envy seized
At sight of all this world beheld so fair.
Round he surveys (and well might where he stood
So high above the circling canopy
Of night's extended shade) from eastern point

520–22. *Who*: humans who go to heaven. This account of how humans are transported to heaven is in contrast with the false idea of Peter's gate (3.484). Arrival by ship recalls the beginning of Dante's *Purgatorio*.

524. *easy* and *ascent* are elided: 'eas-yassent.'

535–37. The opening in the globe of the universe is wide enough to give God a clear view of the entire holy land, from the north, where the Jordan rises, to the south, which borders on Egypt and the Red Sea. The eastern shore is the shore of Arabia.

557–65. From his position at the opening into the universe, Satan is directly above these constellations and is looking down through them at the earth. Before plunging into the

Of Libra to the fleecy star that bears
Andromeda far off Atlantic seas
Beyond th' horizon. Then from pole to pole
He views in breadth and without longer pause
Down right into the world's first region throws
His flight precipitant and winds with ease
Through the pure marble air his oblique way
Amongst innumerable stars that shone—
Stars distant, but nigh hand seemed other worlds.
Or other worlds they seemed or happy isles
Like those Hesperian gardens famed of old,
Fortunate fields and groves and flow'ry vales,
Thrice happy isles, but who dwelt happy there
He stayed not to inquire. Above them all
The golden sun in splendor likest Heaven
Allured his eye. Thither his course he bends
Through the calm firmament (but up or down
By center or eccentric, hard to tell,
Or longitude) where the great luminary
(Aloof the vulgar constellations thick
That from his lordly eye keep distance due)
Dispenses light from far. They as they move
Their starry dance in numbers that compute
Days, months and years, towards his all-cheering lamp
Turn swift their various motions or are turned
By his magnetic beam that gently warms
The universe and to each inward part
With gentle penetration, though unseen,
Shoots invisible virtue even to the deep:
So wondrously was set his station bright.
  There lands the Fiend: a spot like which perhaps
Astronomer in the sun's lucent orb
Through his glazed optic tube yet never saw.
The place he found beyond expression bright
Compared with aught on earth, metal or stone.
Not all parts like but all alike informed

---

universe (the *world*, line 562) and descending through the *first region* (line 562) of liquid (*marble*, line 564) air, Satan views the interior of the entire universe, scanning *from pole to pole* (line 560).

567. *Or . . . or*: either . . . or. A Latin construction.

568–70. The western paradise, the garden of the Hesperides, can no longer be thought in Milton's day to be beyond the ocean, where the sun sets. Milton suggests that the myth may still be true, but in other worlds, in space. Milton thinks the stars could be distant worlds, like earth, but not distant suns.

572–87. Despite his expanded cosmic vision, Milton still thinks there is only one sun, which turns the constellations and dispenses light and life (*virtue*, line 586) throughout the universe.

With radiant light as glowing iron with fire.
If metal, part seemed gold, part silver clear.
If stone, carbuncle most or chrysolite,
Ruby or topaz, to the twelve that shone
In Aaron's breastplate and a stone besides
Imagined rather oft than elsewhere seen.
That stone, or like to that, which here below
Philosophers in vain so long have sought,
In vain though by their powerful art they bind
Volatile Hermes and call up unbound
In various shapes old Proteus from the sea,
Drained through a limbec to his native form.
What wonder then if fields and regions here
Breathe forth elixir pure and rivers run
Potable gold when with one virtuous touch
Th' arch-chemic sun so far from us remote
Produces with terrestrial humor mixed
Here in the dark so many precious things
Of color glorious and effect so rare?
Here matter new to gaze the Devil met
Undazzled. Far and wide his eye commands,
For sight no obstacle found here nor shade
But all sunshine (as when his beams at noon
Culminate from th' equator, as they now
Shot upward still direct, whence no way round
Shadow from body opaque can fall) and th' air,
Nowhere so clear, sharpened his visual ray
To objects distant far, whereby he soon
Saw within ken a glorious angel stand,
The same whom John saw also in the sun.
His back was turned but not his brightness hid
Of beaming sunny rays, a golden tiar
Circled his head, nor less his locks behind
Illustrious on his shoulders (fledge with wings)

598. The life-giving stones in the sun are like those in the high priest Aaron's breastplate in Exodus 28:17–20. *stone besides*: the "philosopher's stone" of the alchemists, which transforms ordinary metals into gold. Milton does not believe in the philosopher's stone, but he likens what is claimed for it to the real life-giving power of the sun. See lines 609–12.

601. *Philosophers*: alchemists.

603. *Hermes*: mercury, which vaporizes readily, is used in alchemical research.

604. *Proteus*: the shape-shifter god is the symbol of the central idea of alchemy: that metals are convertible into one another.

605. *limbec*: alembic, glass instrument used in distilling and refining.

609–12. The sun's rays were thought to create precious stones in the earth, just as they bring living plants out of the earth.

615–19. As the sun's rays fall from directly overhead at the equator, leaving no shadow, so here the rays fly straight up and leave no shadow.

623. "And I saw an angel standing in the sun" (Revelation 19:17).

625. *tiar*: *tiara*, crown, or *coronet* (line 640).

Lay waving round. On some great charge employed
He seemed or fixed in cogitation deep.
Glad was the spirit impure as now in hope
To find who might direct his wand'ring flight
To Paradise, the happy seat of Man,
His journey's end and our beginning woe.
But first he casts to change his proper shape
Which else might work him danger or delay:
And now a stripling cherub he appears,
Not of the prime yet such as in his face
Youth smiled celestial and to every limb
Suitable grace diffused, so well he feigned.
Under a coronet his flowing hair
In curls on either cheek played. Wings he wore
Of many a colored plume sprinkled with gold,
His habit fit for speed succinct, and held
Before his decent steps a silver wand.
He drew not nigh unheard: the angel bright
Ere he drew nigh his radiant visage turned
(Admonished by his ear) and straight was known
Th' Archangel Uriel, one of the sev'n
Who in God's presence nearest to His throne
Stand ready at command and are His eyes
That run through all the heav'ns or down to th' earth
Bear his swift errands over moist and dry,
O'er sea and land. Him Satan thus accosts:
  Uriel, for thou of those sev'n spirits that stand
In sight of God's high throne, gloriously bright,
The first art wont His great authentic will,
Interpreter, through highest Heav'n to bring
Where all His sons thy embassy attend
And here art likeliest by supreme decree
Like honor to obtain and as His eye
To visit oft this new Creation round.
Unspeakable desire to see and know
All these His wondrous works (but chiefly Man,
His chief delight and favor, him for whom
All these His works so wondrous He ordained)
Hath brought me from the choirs of cherubim
Alone thus wand'ring. Brightest Seraph, tell,
In which of all these shining orbs hath Man
His fixèd seat, or fixèd seat hath none
But all these shining orbs his choice to dwell,

643. *succinct*: drawn up and secured (Latin).

That I may find him and with secret gaze
Or open admiration him behold
On whom the great Creator hath bestowed
Worlds and on whom hath all these graces poured,
That both in him and all things, as is meet,
The Universal Maker we may praise,
Who justly hath driv'n out His rebel foes
To deepest Hell and to repair that loss
Created this new happy race of men
To serve Him better: wise are all His ways.
  So spake the false dissembler unperceived,
For neither man nor angel can discern
Hypocrisy, the only evil that walks
Invisible except to God alone
By His permissive will through Heav'n and Earth.
And oft, though Wisdom wake, Suspicion sleeps
At Wisdom's gate and to Simplicity
Resigns her charge while Goodness thinks no ill
Where no ill seems, which now for once beguiled
Uriel, though regent of the sun and held
The sharpest sighted spirit of all in Heav'n,
Who to the fraudulent impostor foul
In his uprightness answer thus returned:
  Fair angel, thy desire which tends to know
The works of God thereby to glorify
The great Work-Master leads to no excess
That reaches blame but rather merits praise
The more it seems excess that led thee hither
From thy empyreal mansion thus alone
To witness with thine eyes what some perhaps
Contented with report hear only in Heav'n.
For wonderful indeed are all His works,
Pleasant to know and worthiest to be all
Had in remembrance, always with delight.
But what created mind can comprehend
Their number or the wisdom infinite
That brought them forth but hid their causes deep?
I saw when at His Word the formless mass,
This world's material mold, came to a heap.
Confusion heard His voice and Wild Uproar
Stood ruled, stood Vast Infinitude confined,

675. *him*: Man.
689. *which*: Hypocrisy, which beguiled Uriel.
701. *only* and *in* are elided: 'on-lin.'
710–13. Vestigial personifications in 710–11 fade into abstractions in 712–13.

Till at His second bidding darkness fled,
Light shone, and order from disorder sprung.
Swift to their several quarters hasted then
The cumbrous elements, earth, flood, air, fire,
And this ethereal quíntessence of Heav'n
Flew upward, spirited with various forms
That rolled orbicular and turned to stars
Numberless, as thou seest, and how they move.
Each had his place appointed, each his course,
The rest in circuit walls this universe.
Look downward on that globe whose hither side
With light from hence though but reflected shines.
That place is Earth, the seat of Man, that light
His day, which else as th' other hemisphere
Night would invade. But there the neighboring Moon
(So call that opposite fair star) her aid
Timely interposes and her monthly round
Still ending, still renewing, through mid heav'n
With borrowed light her countenance triform,
Hence fills and empties to enlighten th' earth
And in her pale dominion checks the night.
That spot to which I point is Paradise,
Adam's abode, those lofty shades his bower.
Thy way thou canst not miss, me mine requires.
  Thus said he turned and Satan, bowing low
As to superior spirits is wont in Heav'n
(Where honor due and reverence none neglects),
Took leave and toward the coast of Earth beneath,
Down from th' ecliptic, sped with hoped success,
Throws his steep flight in many an airy wheel,
Nor stayed till on Niphates' top he lights.

721. A reference to the sphere of the fixed stars, as opposed to those (actually planets and the moon) that wander in the heavens.
723. *light from hence*: light from here, on the sun.
726. *there*: on the dark side of the earth.
730. *triform*: the three phases of the moon.
732. *checks*: prevents from becoming total.
740. *ecliptic*: here, the orbit of the sun around the earth and therefore the point of departure for Satan's flight downward to earth. Satan flies down *from* the ecliptic. But this point of departure is moving along the arc of the ecliptic, meaning that Satan's flight will not be direct but must adjust to the altering positions of the sun and the earth. Hence the splendid phrase describing Satan's devious flight, "with many an airy wheel" (line 741). Milton is perhaps remembering Ariosto's sinister enchanter, Atlante, who when flying the winged Hippogriff soars "with large circles" ("*con large ruote*") before he lands. Cf. 9.62–66 and n. *sped*: impelled.
742. *Niphates*, a mountain in Assyria, near Eden, its name suggesting that its peak is snow-covered, an appropriate backdrop for Satan's soliloquy there (4.32–113).

Book Four

The Argument

Satan, now in prospect of Eden, and nigh the place where he must now attempt the bold enterprise which he undertook alone against God and Man, falls into many doubts with himself and many passions—fear, envy, and despair—but at length confirms himself in evil, journeys on to Paradise (whose outward prospect and situation is described), overleaps the bounds, sits in the shape of a cormorant on the Tree of Life (as highest in the garden) to look about him. The garden described; Satan's first sight of Adam and Eve; his wonder at their excellent form and happy state, but with resolution to work their Fall; overhears their discourse; thence gathers that the Tree of Knowledge was forbidden them to eat of, under penalty of death; and thereon intends to found his temptation, by seducing them to transgress. Then leaves them a while, to know further of their state by some other means. Meanwhile Uriel, descending on a sunbeam, warns Gabriel, who had in charge the gate of Paradise, that some evil spirit had escaped the deep and passed at noon by his sphere in the shape of a good angel down to Paradise, discovered after by his furious gestures in the mount. Gabriel promises to find him out ere morning. Night coming on, Adam and Eve discourse of going to their rest; their bower described; their evening worship. Gabriel, drawing forth his bands of night-watch to walk the round of Paradise, appoints two strong angels to Adam's bower, lest the evil spirit should be there doing some harm to Adam or Eve sleeping. There they find him at the ear of Eve, tempting her in a dream, and bring him, though unwilling, to Gabriel; by whom questioned, he scornfully answers, prepares resistance, but hindered by a sign from Heaven, flies out of Paradise.

O! for that warning voice which he who saw
Th' Apocalypse heard cry in Heav'n aloud
Then when the Dragon, put to second rout,
Came furious down to be revenged on men:
"Woe to the inhabitants on Earth!" That now,
While time was, our first parents had been warned
The coming of their secret foe and 'scaped,

Book Four

1. *he*: John, author of the Book of Revelation, which recounts the visions he saw of the end of the world.
2. *Apocalypse*: "unveiling"; the Greek title of the Book of Revelation.
3. *Dragon*: Satan. Revelation 12:3–9.
5. Revelation 12:12: "Woe to the inhabiters of the earth and of the sea! for the devil is come down unto you, having great wrath, because he knoweth that he hath but a short time."

Haply so 'scaped, his mortal snare. For now
Satan, now first inflamed with rage, came down
The tempter ere th' accuser of mankind
To wreck on innocent frail Man his loss
Of that first battle and his flight to Hell.
Yet not rejoicing in his speed, though bold,
Far off and fearless, nor with cause to boast
Begins his dire attempt which, nigh the birth,
Now rolling boils in his tumultuous breast
And like a dev'lish engine back recoils
Upon himself. Horror and doubt distract
His troubled thoughts and from the bottom stir
The Hell within him, for within him Hell
He brings and round about him, nor from Hell
One step no more than from himself can fly
By change of place. Now conscience wakes despair
That slumbered, wakes the bitter memory
Of what he was, what is, and what must be
Worse: of worse deeds worse sufferings must ensue.
Sometimes towards Eden which now in his view
Lay pleasant his grieved look he fixes sad,
Sometimes towards Heav'n and the full-blazing sun
Which now sat high in his meridian tower.
Then much revolving thus in sighs began:
  O thou that with surpassing glory crowned
Look'st from thy sole dominion like the god
Of this new world, at whose sight all the stars
Hide their diminished heads, to thee I call
But with no friendly voice and add thy name,
O Sun, to tell thee how I hate thy beams
That bring to my remembrance from what state
I fell, how glorious once above thy sphere
Till pride and worse ambition threw me down,
Warring in Heav'n against Heav'n's matchless King.

8. *Haply*: perhaps; also: happily.
10. *accuser*: one of the meanings of the name *Satan*, in the sense of being God's prosecuting attorney, a role Satan performs in the first two chapters of the Book of Job.
11. *his*: Satan's.
20–21. A famous borrowing from Marlowe's *Doctor Faustus*, lines 311–12: "*Faustus*. How comes it then that thou art out of hell? / *Mephistophilis*. Why this is hell, nor am I out of it."
26. *sufferings* has two syllables.
31. *revolving*: turning over in himself many thoughts and many strong emotions.
32. *thou*: the sun, to whom the first part of this speech is addressed, as if the sun were a god himself and not something created by God.
32–41. According to Milton's nephew, Edward Phillips, Milton composed these lines when he was still thinking of making a tragedy, *Adam Unparadised*, rather than an epic. The lines recall addresses to the sun in two ancient tragedies: Aeschylus's *Prometheus Bound* (91) and Euripides' *Phoenissae* (1–3).

Ah wherefore! He deserved no such return
From me, whom He created what I was
In that bright eminence and with His good
Upbraided none. Nor was His service hard:
What could be less than to afford Him praise,
The easiest recompense, and pay Him thanks?
How due! Yet all His good proved ill in me
And wrought but malice. Lifted up so high
I 'sdeigned subjection and thought one step higher
Would set me high'st and in a moment quit
The debt immense of endless gratitude
So burdensome—still paying! still to owe!—
Forgetful what from Him I still received
And understood not that a grateful mind
By owing owes not but still pays, at once
Indebted and discharged. What burden then?
O had His pow'rful destiny ordained
Me some inferior angel! I had stood
Then happy: no unbounded hope had raised
Ambition. Yet why not? Some other pow'r
As great might have aspired and me, though mean,
Drawn to his part. But other pow'rs as great
Fell not but stand unshaken from within
Or from without to all temptations armed.
Hadst thou the same free will and pow'r to stand?
Thou hadst. Whom hast thou then or what t' accuse
But Heav'n's free love dealt equally to all?
Be then His love accursed, since love or hate
To me alike it deals eternal woe!
Nay cursed be thou since against His thy will
Chose freely what it now so justly rues.
Me miserable! Which way shall I fly
Infinite wrath and infinite despair?
Which way I fly is Hell, myself am Hell,
And in the lowest deep a lower deep

50. *'sdeigned*: disdained.
53–54. *still*: always, perpetually.
55–57. In the economy of heaven the debt one owes God for one's creation is discharged by gratitude, which, paradoxically, recognizes the continuing nature of the debt even as it pays it off.
58–60. I.e., If *only* God had made me a lower-ranking angel! It is, however, possible to read the sentence as the first term of a proposition in the form "if . . . then": If God had made me a low-ranking angel, then I would not have rebelled.
62. *mean*: low-ranking.
63. *as great*: as eminent as Satan was. For Milton, Lucifer before his fall was among the highest angels but was not the highest. See 5.659–60.
66. *thou*: you. Satan is speaking to himself.
74. *wrath* and *despair* are direct objects of *fly*.

Still threat'ning to devour me opens wide,
To which the Hell I suffer seems a Heav'n.
O then at last relent! Is there no place
Left for repentance, none for pardon left?
None left but by submission and that word
Disdain forbids me and my dread of shame
Among the spirits beneath whom I seduced
With other promises and other vaunts
Than to submit, boasting I could subdue
Th' Omnipotent. Ay me! they little know
How dearly I abide that boast so vain,
Under what torments inwardly I groan
While they adore me on the throne of Hell
With diadem and scepter high advanced
The lower still I fall, only supreme
In misery. Such joy ambition finds.
But say I could repent and could obtain
By act of grace my former state. How soon
Would heighth recall high thoughts? How soon unsay
What feigned submission swore? Ease would recant
Vows made in pain as violent and void
(For never can true reconcilement grow
Where wounds of deadly hate have pierced so deep)
Which would but lead me to a worse relapse
And heavier fall. So should I purchase dear
Short intermission bought with double smart.
This knows my punisher. Therefore as far
From granting He as I from begging peace.
All hope excluded thus, behold instead
Of us outcast, exiled, His new delight:
Mankind created and for him this world.
So farewell hope and with hope farewell fear!
Farewell remorse! All good to me is lost.
Evil, be thou my good. By thee at least
Divided empire with Heav'n's King I hold
By thee, and more than half perhaps will reign,

88–92. An example of Milton's compressed syntax, where two distinct sentences coincide in one: 'I groan while they adore me with my diadem and scepter raised' and 'the higher my diadem and scepter are raised the lower I fall.'

90. *diadem*: crown. *scepter*: a rod borne in the hand as an emblem of royal authority.

96–97. Once restored to blessedness, I would recant my vow of faith as invalid, since it was made under duress.

102. *double smart*: redoubled agony.

110. Isaiah 5:20: "Woe unto them that call evil good, and good evil!"

110 and 112. *By thee*: by evil. The ungrammatical repetition of the phrase *by thee* perhaps indicates a minor lapse in transmission: the poet began the sentence with "By thee" and then moved the phrase behind the principal clause without eliminating the first appearance.

As man ere long and this new world shall know.
  Thus while he spake each passion dimmed his face
Thrice changed with pale ire, envy and despair,
Which marred his borrowed visage and betrayed
Him counterfeit if any eye beheld,
For Heav'nly minds from such distempers foul
Are ever clear. Whereof he soon aware
Each perturbation smoothed with outward calm,
Artíficer of fraud, and was the first
That practiced falsehood: under saintly show
Deep malice to conceal couched with revenge.
Yet not enough had practiced to deceive
Uriel once warned, whose eye pursued him down
The way he went and on th' Assyrian mount
Saw him disfigured more than could befall
Spirit of happy sort. His gestures fierce
He marked and mad demeanor, then alone,
As he supposed, all unobserved, unseen.
So on he fares and to the border comes
Of Eden where delicious Paradise,
Now nearer, crowns with her enclosure green
As with a rural mound the champaign head
Of a steep wilderness whose hairy sides
With thicket overgrown, grotesque and wild,
Access denied. And overhead up grew
Insuperable heighth of loftiest shade,
Cedar and pine and fir and branching palm,
A sylvan scene, and as the ranks ascend
Shade above shade, a woody theater
Of stateliest view. Yet higher than their tops
The verdurous wall of Paradise up sprung
Which to our gen'ral sire gave prospect large

116. *borrowed visage*: Satan is still disguised as the *stripling cherub* of 3.636.
126. *Assyrian mount*: Niphates (3.742).
129. *He*: Uriel.
130. *he*: Satan.
131. *he*: Satan.
132. *Eden* and *Paradise*: see Glossary.
132–35. I.e., The garden, *Paradise*, enclosed with trees, lies on the broad plain (*champaign*) that surmounts a steep hill overgrown with thickets.
136. *grotesque*: full of caves (grottos) as well as like the decorative, tangled growth depicted on Roman wall paintings.
137. *Access* is the direct object of *wilderness*. The wilderness on the side of the paradisal mountain denied access to Paradise at the top.
137–42. *overhead*: As ranks of trees *ascend* the mountainside, each rank overshadows the last (*shade above shade*) so that the trees appear to form a kind of theater. Milton follows closely a description of trees in the *Aeneid* 1.164–65, capturing the phrase *silvis scaena* in *sylvan scene* (line 140).
143. *verdurous*: green. The wall is overgrown with plants.
144. *our general sire*: the father of us all, Adam. *general* has two syllables: 'gen-ral.'

Into his nether empire neighboring round.
And higher than that wall a circling row
Of goodliest trees loaden with fairest fruit
Blossoms, and fruits at once of golden hue
Appeared with gay enameled colors mixed,
On which the sun more glad impressed his beams
Than in fair evening cloud or humid bow
When God hath show'red the earth, so lovely seemed
That landscip. And of pure now purer air
Meets his approach and to the heart inspires
Vernal delight and joy, able to drive
All sadness but despair. Now gentle gales
Fanning their odoriferous wings dispense
Native perfumes and whisper whence they stole
Those balmy spoils. As when to them who sail
Beyond the Cape of Hope and now are passed
Mozámbique, off at sea, northeast winds blow
Sabean odors from the spicy shore
Of Araby the blest—with such delay
Well pleased they slack their course and many a league
Cheered with the grateful smell old Ocean smiles—
So entertained those odorous sweets the Fiend
Who came their bane, though with them better pleased
Than Asmodeus with the fishy fume
That drove him, though enamored, from the spouse
Of Tobit's son and with a vengeance sent
From Media post to Egypt, there fast bound.
  Now to th' ascent of that steep savage hill
Satan had journeyed on, pensive and slow,
But further way found none, so thick entwined
As one continued brake the undergrowth
Of shrubs and tangling bushes had perplexed
All path of man or beast that passed that way.
One gate there only was and that looked east
On th' other side. Which when th' arch-felon saw
Due entrance he disdained and in contempt

146. *circling row*: fruit trees within the encircling wall of Paradise, rising above that wall so that their tops are visible from without.

153. *landscip*: land view. The Dutch word for "landscape," a new, fashionable term in Milton's day.

154. *his*: Satan's. This entire description of Eden as we first see it, up to line 356, is seen, with impressive irony, through Satan's eyes. See lines 194–207.

157. *odoriferous*: odor bearing; four syllables: 'odorif-rous.'

166. *odorous* has two syllables: 'od'rous.'

170 and 171. *sent* and *bound*: the object of these verbs is *Asmodeus*. The smell drives him from Persia to Egypt, where he is bound.

179. *other side*. Satan approaches Paradise from the west, in the direction opposite to that of the sun.

At one slight bound high overleaped all bound
Of hill or highest wall and sheer within
Lights on his feet. As when a prowling wolf
Whom hunger drives to seek new haunt for prey,
Watching where shepherds pen their flocks at eve
In hurdled cotes amid the field secure,
Leaps o'er the fence with ease into the fold,
Or as a thief bent to unhoard the cash
Of some rich burgher, whose substantial doors
Cross-barred and bolted fast fear no assault,
In at the window climbs or o'er the tiles:
So clomb this first grand thief into God's fold.
So since into His Church lewd hirelings climb!
Thence up he flew and on the Tree of Life,
The middle tree and highest there that grew,
Sat like a cormorant. Yet not true life
Thereby regained but sat devising death
To them who lived. Nor on the virtue thought
Of that life-giving plant but only used
For prospect what well used had been the pledge
Of immortality. So little knows
Any but God alone to value right
The good before him but perverts best things
To worst abuse or to their meanest use.
Beneath him with new wonder now he views
To all delight of human sense exposed
In narrow room Nature's whole wealth, yea more,
A Heav'n on Earth, for blissful Paradise
Of God the garden was by Him in th' east
Of Eden planted. Eden stretched her line
From Auran eastward to the royal towers
Of great Seleucia built by Grecian kings
Or where the sons of Eden long before
Dwelt in Telassar. In this pleasant soil
His far more pleasant garden God ordained.
Out of the fertile ground He caused to grow

186. *hurdled*: made of interlaced branches. *cotes*: moveable pens in which sheep are kept at night.
187. *fold*: an enclosure for sheep.
189. *burgher*: town dweller.
193. *hirelings*: priests, such as those in the Church of England, who accept pay or other emolument for their pastoral work. As Milton notes in "Lycidas," wolves climb into the fold to snatch their prey. The image is biblical, John 10:1–11.
195. *middle*: in the center of the garden.
196. *cormorant*: large, ugly, voracious sea bird.
198–201. Satan uses the tree only to get a good view (*prospect*) of the garden, not for its power to confer immortality. But immortality is Satan's biggest problem.

All trees of noblest kind for sight, smell, taste
And all amid them stood the Tree of Life
High eminent blooming ambrosial fruit
Of vegetable gold. And next to Life
Our death, the Tree of Knowledge, grew fast by:
Knowledge of good bought dear by knowing ill.
Southward through Eden went a river large
Nor changed his course but through the shaggy hill
Passed underneath engulfed, for God had thrown
That mountain as His garden mold high raised
Upon the rapid current which through veins
Of porous earth with kindly thirst up drawn
Rose a fresh fountain and with many a rill
Watered the garden; thence united fell
Down the steep glade and met the nether flood
Which from his darksome passage now appears,
And now divided into four main streams
Runs diverse wand'ring many a famous realm
And country. Whereof here needs no account
But rather to tell how, if art could tell,
How from that sapphire fount the crispèd brooks
Rolling on orient pearl and sands of gold
With mazy error under pendent shades
Ran nectar, visiting each plant, and fed
Flow'rs worthy of Paradise which not nice art
In beds and curious knots, but Nature boon
Poured forth profuse on hill and dale and plain,
Both where the morning sun first warmly smote
The open field and where th' unpiercèd shade
Embrowned the noontide bowers. Thus was this place
A happy rural seat of various view,
Groves whose rich trees wept odorous gums and balm,
Others whose fruit, burnished with golden rind,

219. A hypermetrical line (if *ambrosial* is not elided to three syllables) with three dactyls in the middle: *éminent blóoming ambrósial* (/ ˘˘ / ˘˘ / ˘˘). The rhythm of the full line is audaciously ornate, as befits its subject, the Tree of Life, and this rhythm flows into the next line for its completion: *Of végetable góld* (˘ / ˘˘˘ /).
221. *our death*: the cause of our death.
222. This formulation Milton worked out many years before in *Areopagitica*: "this is that doom which Adam fell into of knowing good and evil, that is to say of knowing good by evil" (p. 349).
223–35. I.e., The streams of Paradise are fed by a river that flows under the mount. They flow together again south of the garden and become a waterfall, the source of the major rivers of the world.
237. *crispèd*: Latin *crispus*, "curled, waving, trembling," often of hair.
238. *orient*: irridescent, lustrous, like the dawn in the eastern sky.
239. *error*: wandering, meandering (Latin).
241. *worthy* and *of* are elided: 'worth-yov.' *nice art*: fussy calculation, by which flowers would be planted in carefully arranged beds and entangling designs (*curious knots*, line 242).

Hung amiable: Hesperian fables true,
If true, here only, and of delicious taste.
Betwixt them lawns or level downs and flocks
Grazing the tender herb were interposed
Or palmy hillock or the flow'ry lap
Of some irriguous valley spread her store—
Flow'rs of all hue and without thorn the rose.
Another side umbrageous grots and caves
Of cool recéss o'er which the mantling vine
Lays forth her purple grape and gently creeps
Luxuriant. Meanwhile murmuring waters fall
Down the slope hills, dispersed, or in a lake
That to the fringèd bank with myrtle crowned
Her crystal mirror holds unite their streams.
The birds their choir apply. Airs, vernal airs,
Breathing the smell of field and grove attune
The trembling leaves while universal Pan
Knit with the Graces and the Hours in dance
Led on th' eternal spring. Not that fair field
Of Enna where Prosérpine gath'ring flow'rs,
Herself a fairer flow'r, by gloomy Dis
Was gathered, which cost Ceres all that pain
To seek her through the world, nor that sweet grove
Of Daphne by Orontes and th' inspired
Castalian spring might with this paradise
Of Eden strive, nor that Nyseian isle
Girt with the river Triton where old Cham
(Whom Gentiles Ammon call and Libyan Jove)

250. *amiable* has three syllables: 'aim-ya-bull.' *Hesperian* has three syllables: 'Hes-pair-yan.'

250–51. I.e., If the classical fables of the magical fruit of the Hesperides are true, they are true only because they refer to this place, Paradise.

251. *only* and *and* are elided.

252. *them*: the groves.

255. *irriguous*: well-watered.

260. *Luxuriant* has three syllables. *Murmuring* has two syllables.

260–63. *waters* is the subject of two successive principal clauses, the main verbs of which are *fall* and *unite*; i.e., Waters falling downhill either disperse in various directions or they flow together (*unite their streams*) in a lake, a calm lake that holds its mirror up to the bank, which is fringed with myrtle.

264. *apply*: add to the scene or fold into the scene, with the suggestion that the birds' choral singing is not in unison but folded together in several parts, like counterpoint.

266. *Pan*: the goat god and a symbol of the totality of nature (since his name in Greek means "all").

268–87. A series of four mythical paradises negatively compared with the Paradise Milton describes. The main verb with its auxiliary, *might . . . strive* (lines 274–75), is set in the middle, with two comparisons before it (*Not . . . nor*, lines 268 and 274) and two after (*nor . . . Nor*, lines 275 and 280). The symmetrical structure of the sentence is then given over to the forward movement of the action by the clause beginning *but wide remote* and by the sudden reappearance of Satan as observer; i.e., the mythical paradises, which cannot compare with this Paradise, are all far distant from this garden in Assyria, where the Fiend saw all delight and all the new creatures. At this moment, Adam and Eve are introduced (line 288).

Hid Amalthéa and her florid son,
Young Bacchus, from his stepdame Rhea's eye,
Nor where Abássin kings their issue guard,
Mount Amara, though this by some supposed
True Paradise, under the Ethiop line
By Nilus' head, enclosed with shining rock
A whole day's journey high, but wide remote
From this Assyrian garden where the Fiend
Saw undelighted all delight, all kind
Of living creatures new to sight and strange.
  Two of far nobler shape erect and tall,
Godlike erect with native honor clad
In naked majesty, seemed lords of all.
And worthy seemed for in their looks divine
The image of their glorious Maker shone:
Truth, wisdom, sanctitude severe and pure,
Severe, but in true filial freedom placed,
Whence true authority in men. Though both
Not equal as their sex not equal seemed:
For contemplation he and valor formed,
For softness she and sweet attractive grace:
He for God only, she for God in him.
His fair large front and eye sublime declared
Absolute rule, and hyacinthine locks
Round from his parted forelock manly hung
Clust'ring but not beneath his shoulders broad.
She as a veil down to the slender waist
Her unadornèd golden tresses wore
Dishevelled but in wanton ringlets waved
As the vine curls her tendrils, which implied
Subjection, but required with gentle sway
And by her yielded, by him best received,
Yielded with coy submission, modest pride,
And sweet reluctant amorous delay.
Nor those mysterious parts were then concealed:
Then was not guilty shame, dishonest shame

278. *florid*: red-complexioned, flushed with wine; associated with blooming flowers.

292. *image*: "So God created man in his own image, in the image of God created he him; male and female created he them" (Genesis 1:27).

301. *hyacinthine locks*: rich, dark hair. See *Odyssey* 6.230–31. A Homeric expression. Odysseus's hair, improved by Athena.

308. *subjection*: Eve's long, beautiful hair is a sign of her submission to Adam's authority. Adam and Eve are not equals but exist, like everything else in Milton's idea of divine Creation, in hierarchy. "Doth not even nature itself teach you, that, if a man have long hair, it is a shame unto him? But if a woman have long hair, it is a glory to her: for her hair is given her for a covering" (Corinthians 11:14–15). *sway*: rule.

Of nature's works, honor dishonorable,
Sin-bred. How have ye troubled all mankind
With shows instead—mere shows of seeming pure!—
And banished from Man's life his happiest life:
Simplicity and spotless innocence.
So passed they naked on nor shunned the sight
Of God or angel, for they thought no ill.
So hand in hand they passed, the loveliest pair
That ever since in love's embraces met:
Adam the goodliest man of men since born
His sons, the fairest of her daughters Eve.
Under a tuft of shade that on a green
Stood whispering soft by a fresh fountain side
They sat them down and after no more toil
Of their sweet gard'ning labor than sufficed
To recommend cool Zephyr and made ease
More easy, wholesome thirst and appetite
More grateful, to their supper fruits they fell:
Nectarine fruits which the compliant boughs
Yielded them sidelong as they sat recline
On the soft downy bank, damasked with flowers.
The savory pulp they chew and in the rind
Still as they thirsted scoop the brimming stream.
Nor gentle purpose nor endearing smiles
Wanted, nor youthful dalliance as beseems
Fair couple linked in happy nuptial league,
Alone as they. About them frisking played
All beasts of th' earth, since wild, and of all chase
In wood or wilderness, forest or den.
Sporting the lion ramped and in his paw
Dandled the kid. Bears, tigers, ounces, pards
Gamboled before them. Th' unwieldy elephant
To make them mirth used all his might and wreathed
His lithe proboscis. Close the serpent sly
Insinuating wove with Gordian twine
His braided train and of his fatal guile

314. *honor dishonorable*: A tedious paradox: decently covering one's genitals is indecent because doing so acknowledges the shame that came in with the Fall.
315. *ye*: i.e., *shame* and *honor*.
323–24. *goodliest . . . fairest*: Adam and Eve are the best physical specimens of humanity that ever were.
338. *dalliance*: flirtation. *wanted*: lacked.
341. *chase*: a game preserve. Every habitat, as in a wildlife preserve.
344. *pards*: leopards.
347. *lithe proboscis*: flexible snout, i.e., trunk.
348. *Insinuating*: winding, with a suggestion of our sense of the word. The serpent must be seen here as innocent because it is uninhabited by Satan. But the serpent's naturally subtle character makes it the perfect vessel for Satan's fraud.

Gave proof unheeded. Others on the grass
Couched and now filled with pasture gazing sat
Or bedward ruminating, for the sun,
Declined, was hasting now with prone career
To th' ocean isles and in th' ascending scale
Of Heav'n the stars that usher evening rose.
When Satan, still in gaze as first he stood,
Scarce thus at length failed speech recovered sad:
  O Hell! What do mine eyes with grief behold?
Into our room of bliss thus high advanced
Creatures of other mold, earth-born perhaps,
Not spirits, yet to Heav'nly spirits bright
Little inferior, whom my thoughts pursue
With wonder and could love, so lively shines
In them divine resemblance and such grace
The hand that formed them on their shape hath poured.
Ah, gentle pair, ye little think how nigh
Your change approaches when all these delights
Will vanish and deliver ye to woe,
More woe the more your taste is now of joy!
Happy, but for so happy ill secured
Long to continue and this high seat, your Heav'n,
Ill fenced for Heav'n to keep out such a foe
As now is entered! Yet no purposed foe
To you whom I could pity, thus forlorn,
Though I unpitied. League with you I seek
And mutual amity so strait, so close,
That I with you must dwell or you with me
Henceforth. My dwelling haply may not please,
Like this fair Paradise, your sense, yet such
Accept your Maker's work. He gave it me
Which I as freely give. Hell shall unfold
To entertain you two her widest gates
And send forth all her kings. There will be room
Not like these narrow limits to receive
Your numerous offspring. If no better place,

351. *pasture*: food.
353. *prone career*: headfirst, downward course.
359. *room*: place.
370. *Happy*: i.e., you are happy.
371. *continue* and *and* are elided.
374. *thus forlorn*: i.e., I could pity you, Adam and Eve, since you are abandoned here without protection from me.
380. *your Maker's work*: Hell.
385. *numerous* has two syllables. *no better place*: no place better than Hell.
385–87. i.e., If you do not like Hell, blame (*Thank*) God, who forces me unwillingly to take revenge on you, who never wronged me, instead of on God, who did wrong me.

Thank Him who puts me, loath to this revenge,
On you who wrong me not for Him who wronged.
And should I at your harmless innocence
Melt, as I do, yet public reason just,
Honor and empire with revenge enlarged
By conquering this new world compels me now
To do what else, though damned, I should abhor.
So spake the Fiend and with necessity,
The tyrant's plea, excused his dev'lish deeds.
Then from his lofty stand on that high tree
Down he alights among the sportful herd
Of those four-footed kinds, himself now one,
Now other, as their shape served best his end
Nearer to view his prey and unespied
To mark what of their state he more might learn
By word or action marked. About them round
A lion now he stalks with fiery glare,
Then as a tiger who by chance hath spied
In some purlieu two gentle fawns at play,
Straight couches close, then rising changes oft
His couchant watch as one who chose his ground
Whence rushing he might surest seize them both
Gripped in each paw, when Adam, first of men,
To first of women, Eve, thus moving speech
Turned him all ear to hear new utterance flow:
Sole partner and sole part of all these joys,
Dearer thyself than all, needs must the Power
That made us and for us this ample world
Be infinitely good. And of His good
As liberal and free as infinite
That raised us from the dust and placed us here
In all this happiness who at His hand
Have nothing merited nor can perform
Aught whereof He hath need, He who requires
From us no other service than to keep
This one, this easy charge, of all the trees
In Paradise that bear delicious fruit
So various, not to taste that only Tree
Of Knowledge planted by the Tree of Life.
So near grows death to life, whate'er death is,
Some dreadful thing no doubt, for well thou know'st

389. *Melt*: weep.
404. *purlieu*: land on the skirts of the forest.
406. *couchant*: lying close to the ground, ready to pounce. When Satan is inside them, the animals become more like the predators they will be after the Fall.

God hath pronounced it death to taste that tree,
The only sign of our obedience left
Among so many signs of pow'r and rule
Conferred upon us, and dominion giv'n
Over all other creatures that possess
Earth, air, and sea. Then let us not think hard
One easy prohibition who enjoy
Free leave so large to all things else and choice
Unlimited of manifold delights.
But let us ever praise Him and extol
His bounty, following our delightful task
To prune these growing plants and tend these flowers
Which, were it toilsome, yet with thee were sweet.
  To whom thus Eve replied: O thou for whom
And from whom I was formed flesh of thy flesh
And without whom am to no end, my guide
And head, what thou hast said is just and right.
For we to Him indeed all praises owe
And daily thanks, I chiefly who enjoy
So far the happier lot, enjoying thee
Preëminent by so much odds while thou
Like consort to thyself canst nowhere find.
That day I oft remember when from sleep
I first awaked and found myself reposed
Under a shade on flow'rs, much wond'ring where
And what I was, whence thither brought and how.
Not distant far from thence a murmuring sound
Of waters issued from a cave and spread
Into a liquid plain, then stood unmoved
Pure as th' expanse of heav'n. I thither went
With unexperienced thought and laid me down
On the green bank to look into the clear
Smooth lake that to me seemed another sky.
As I bent down to look, just opposite
A shape within the wat'ry gleam appeared
Bending to look on me. I started back,
It started back, but pleased I soon returned,
Pleased *it* returned as soon with answering looks
Of sympathy and love. There I had fixed

442. *am to no end*: without whom my being has no purpose.
443. *head*. "The head of every man is Christ; and the head of the woman is the man; and the head of Christ is God" (1 Corinthians 11:3).
457. *unexperienced* has four syllables: 'unex-spear-yenced.'
465–66. The episode closely follows that of Narcissus, in Ovid, *Metamorphoses* 3.407–36, the crucial difference being that Eve is rescued and does not *pine with vain desire* for herself.

Mine eyes till now and pined with vain desire
Had not a Voice thus warned me: "What thou seest,
What there thou seest, fair creature, is thyself:
With thee it came and goes. But follow me
And I will bring thee where no shadow stays
Thy coming and thy soft embraces. He
Whose image thou art, him thou shalt enjoy
Inseparably thine. To him shalt bear
Multitudes like thyself and thence be called
Mother of human race." What could I do
But follow straight, invisibly thus led?
Till I espied thee (fair indeed, and tall!)
Under a platan. Yet methought less fair,
Less winning soft, less amiably mild
Than that smooth wat'ry image: back I turned.
Thou following cried'st aloud: "Return, fair Eve!
Whom fli'st thou? Whom thou fli'st, of him thou art,
His flesh, his bone. To give thee being I lent
Out of my side to thee, nearest my heart,
Substantial life to have thee by my side
Henceforth an individual solace dear.
Part of my soul I seek thee and thee claim
My other half." With that thy gentle hand
Seized mine, I yielded, and from that time see
How beauty is excelled by manly grace
And wisdom which alone is truly fair.
  So spake our gen'ral mother and with eyes
Of conjugal attraction unreproved
And meek surrender half embracing leaned
On our first father. Half her swelling breast
Naked met his under the flowing gold
Of her loose tresses hid. He in delight
Both of her beauty and submissive charms
Smiled with superior love as Jupiter
On Juno smiles when he impregns the clouds
That shed May flow'rs, and pressed her matron lip
With kisses pure. Aside the Devil turned
For envy, yet with jealous leer malign
Eyed them askance and to himself thus plained:

478. *platan*: a stately near-eastern fruit tree, *platanus orientalis*, related to the plane trees Milton would have seen in Europe.
486. *individual* has four syllables: 'indivi-djal.'
492. *our general mother*: the mother of us all.
499. *superior*: from above.
499–501. *Jupiter . . . flowers*: an example of the rationalizing interpretation of classical myth: Jupiter impregnates the clouds with the seeds of the flowers that grow after rain.

Sight hateful! sight tormenting! Thus these two
Imparadised in one another's arms,
The happier Eden, shall enjoy their fill
Of bliss on bliss while I to Hell am thrust
Where neither joy nor love but fierce desire
(Among our other torments not the least)
Still unfulfilled with pain of longing pines.
Yet let me not forget what I have gained
From their own mouths. All is not theirs it seems.
One fatal Tree there stands of Knowledge called
Forbidden them to taste. Knowledge forbidden?
Suspicious, reasonless. Why should their Lord
Envy them that? Can it be sin to know?
Can it be death? And do they only stand
By ignorance? Is that their happy state,
The proof of their obedience and their faith?
O fair foundation laid whereon to build
Their ruin! Hence I will excite their minds
With more desire to know and to reject
Envious commands invented with design
To keep them low whom knowledge might exalt
Equal with gods. Aspiring to be such,
They taste and die: what likelier can ensue?
But first with narrow search I must walk round
This garden and no corner leave unspied.
A chance but chance may lead where I may meet
Some wand'ring spirit of Heav'n by fountain side
Or in thick shade retired from him to draw
What further would be learnt. Live while ye may
Yet happy pair! Enjoy, till I return,
Short pleasures, for long woes are to succeed!
So saying his proud step he scornful turned
But with sly circumspection and began
Through wood, through waste, o'er hill, o'er dale his roam.
Meanwhile in utmost longitude, where heav'n
With earth and ocean meets, the setting sun
Slowly descended and with right aspect
Against the eastern gate of Paradise
Leveled his evening rays. It was a rock
Of alabaster piled up to the clouds,
Conspicuous far, winding with one ascent

509. *fierce desire*: sexual desire, one of the torments of the devils.
530. *A chance but chance*: "by chance, with luck."
539–43. As the sun set in the west, its rays passed level through Paradise to strike (and cause to glow) the white, eastern gate of Paradise.
544. *alabaster*: smooth, white stone.

Accessible from earth, one entrance high.
The rest was craggy cliff that overhung
Still as it rose, impossible to climb.
Betwixt these rocky pillars Gabriel sat,
Chief of th' angelic guards, awaiting night.
About him exercised heroic games
The unarmed youth of Heav'n but nigh at hand
Celestial armory, shields, helms and spears
Hung high with diamond flaming and with gold.
Thither came Uriel gliding through the even
On a sunbeam, swift as a shooting star
In autumn thwarts the night when vapors fired
Impress the air and shows the mariner
From what point of his compass to beware
Impetuous winds. He thus began in haste:
  Gabriel, to thee thy course by lot hath giv'n
Charge and strict watch that to this happy place
No evil thing approach or enter in.
This day at heighth of noon came to my sphere
A spirit zealous as he seemed to know
More of th' Almighty's works, and chiefly Man,
God's latest image. I descried his way
Bent on all speed and marked his airy gait
But in the mount that lies from Eden north
Where he first lighted soon discerned his looks
Alien from Heav'n with passions foul obscured.
Mine eye pursued him still but under shade
Lost sight of him. One of the banished crew
I fear hath ventured from the deep to raise
New troubles: him thy care must be to find!
  To whom the wingèd warrior thus returned:
Uriel, no wonder if thy perfect sight
Amid the sun's bright circle where thou sitt'st
See far and wide. In at this gate none pass
The vigilance here placed but such as come
Well known from Heav'n and since meridian hour
No creature thence. If spirit of other sort
So minded have o'erleaped these earthy bounds
On purpose, hard thou know'st it to exclude
Spiritual substance with corporeal bar.

549. *rocky pillars*: the alabaster gate posts.
555. *Uriel* has two syllables: 'Yur-yell.' *even*: evening, pronounced with one syllable: 'een.'
557. *thwarts*: cuts across.
558. *Impress*: compress.
560. *Impetuous* has three syllables: 'impet-chus.'
567. *latest*: The angels are also made in God's image. *Described*: descried, carefully noted.

But if within the circuit of these walks,
In whatsoever shape he lurk of whom
Thou tell'st, by morrow dawning I shall know.
  So promised he, and Uriel to his charge
Returned on that bright beam whose point now raised
Bore him slope downward to the sun now fall'n
Beneath the Azores. Whether the prime orb,
Incredible how swift, had thither rolled
Diurnal or this less voluble earth
By shorter flight to th' east had left him there
Arraying with reflected purpl' and gold
The clouds that on his western throne attend.
Now came still evening on and twilight grey
Had in her sober livery all things clad.
Silence accompanied, for beast and bird,
They to their grassy couch, these to their nests
Were slunk—all but the wakeful nightingale.
She all night long her amorous descant sung:
Silence was pleased. Now glowed the firmament
With living sapphires. Hesperus that led
The starry host rode brightest till the Moon,
Rising in clouded majesty, at length
Apparent queen, unveiled her peerless light
And o'er the dark her silver mantle threw.
  When Adam thus to Eve: Fair consort, th' hour
Of night and all things now retired to rest
Mind us of like repose since God hath set
Labor and rest as day and night to men
Successive. And the timely dew of sleep
Now falling with soft slumberous weight inclines
Our eyelids. Other creatures all day long
Rove idle unemployed and less need rest.
Man hath his daily work of body or mind
Appointed which declares his dignity
And the regard of Heav'n on all his ways
While other animals unactive range
And of their doings God takes no account.
Tomorrow ere fresh morning streak the east
With first approach of light we must be ris'n

590–95. Uriel must tilt his sunbeam so that it will carry him to the west, where the sun now sets. Either the sun rolled around the earth to the west or the earth itself rotated to the east, leaving the stationary sun behind, in the west. In Milton's eyes one point in favor of the latter, Copernican system is that it does not require the celestial orbs to move with *incredible* (line 593) swiftness.

603. *amorous* has two syllables: 'am-rous.' *Descant*: melody.

618. *body or* is elided: 'bod-yor.'

And at our pleasant labor to reform
Yon flow'ry arbors, yonder alleys green,
Our walk at noon with branches overgrown
That mock our scant manuring and require
More hands than ours to lop their wanton growth.
Those blossoms also and those dropping gums
That lie bestrewn unsightly and unsmooth
Ask riddance if we mean to tread with ease.
Meanwhile as nature wills night bids us rest.
  To whom thus Eve with perfect beauty adorned:
My author and disposer, what thou bidst
Unargued I obey: so God ordains.
God is thy law, thou mine. To know no more
Is woman's happiest knowledge and her praise.
With thee conversing I forget all time,
All seasons and their change all please alike.
Sweet is the breath of morn, her rising sweet
With charm of earliest birds. Pleasant the sun
When first on this delightful land he spreads
His orient beams on herb, tree, fruit and flower
Glist'ring with dew. Fragrant the fertile earth
After soft showers and sweet the coming on
Of grateful evening mild, then silent night
With this her solemn bird and this fair moon
And these, the gems of heav'n, her starry train!
But neither breath of morn when she ascends
With charm of earliest birds, nor rising sun
On this delightful land, nor herb, fruit, flower
Glist'ring with dew, nor fragrance after showers,
Nor grateful evening mild, nor silent night
With this her solemn bird, nor walk by moon
Or glitt'ring starlight without thee is sweet.
But wherefore all night long shine these? For whom
This glorious sight when sleep hath shut all eyes?
  To whom our gen'ral ancestor replied:
Daughter of God and Man, accomplished Eve,

628. *manuring*: manual labor. Old French *manoeuvrer*, "to work with the hands"; Latin *manus*, "hand." The etymological reference is picked up in the verse following: *More hands than ours*.

634. *beauty* and *adorned* are elided: 'beut-yadorned.'

635. *author and disposer*: origin and commander, arranger.

639–56. The last seven lines of this elaborate poem (lines 650–56), beginning *But neither* . . . , gather up in summary the things and events Eve has described as *sweet*.

657. *these*: the stars.

657–58. Although the suddenness of this question is jarring, it follows logically from the statement Eve has made in her poem: that things are not of value in themselves but only as they are perceived and shared.

Those have their course to finish round the Earth
By morrow evening and from land to land
In order, though to nations yet unborn,
Minist'ring light prepared they set and rise
Lest total darkness should by night regain
Her old possession and extinguish life
In nature and all things which these soft fires
Not only enlighten but with kindly heat
Of various influence foment and warm,
Temper or nourish, or in part shed down
Their stellar virtue on all kinds that grow
On Earth, made hereby apter to receive
Perfection from the Sun's more potent ray.
These then though unbeheld in deep of night
Shine not in vain. Nor think, though men were none,
That Heav'n would want spectators, God want praise!
Millions of spiritual creatures walk the earth
Unseen both when we wake and when we sleep.
All these with ceaseless praise His works behold
Both day and night. How often from the steep
Of echoing hill or thicket have we heard
Celestial voices to the midnight air,
Sole or responsive each to other's note,
Singing their great Creator. Oft in bands,
While they keep watch or nightly rounding walk,
With Heav'nly touch of instrumental sounds
In full harmonic number joined their songs
Divide the night and lift our thoughts to Heav'n.
  Thus talking hand in hand alone they passed
On to their blissful bow'r. It was a place
Chos'n by the sov'reign planter when He framed
All things to Man's delightful use. The roof
Of thickest covert was inwoven shade,
Laurel and myrtle, and what higher grew
Of firm and fragrant leaf. On either side
Acanthus and each odorous bushy shrub
Fenced up the verdant wall. Each beauteous flower,
Iris all hues, roses and jessamine
Reared high their flourished heads between and wrought
Mosaic. Underfoot the violet,
Crocus and hyacinth with rich inlay

661–73. The stars shine on countries where humans will live in the future. The stars also shed their invisible streams, their influences (Latin *in* + *fluo*, "to flow in"), to nourish plants and prepare them to receive the light of the sun.

675. *though men were none*: even if there were no humans.

677. spiritual has two syllables: 'spear-chal.'

Broidered the ground more colored than with stone
Of costliest emblem. Other creature here
Beast, bird, insect or worm durst enter none,
Such was their awe of Man. In shadier bow'r
More sacred and sequestered, though but feigned,
Pan or Silvanus never slept nor nymph
Nor Faunus haunted. Here in close recess
With flowers, garlands and sweet-smelling herbs
Espousèd Eve decked first her nuptial bed
And Heav'nly choirs the hymenéan sung,
What day the genial angel to our sire
Brought her in naked beauty more adorned,
More lovely than Pandora whom the gods
Endowed with all their gifts—and O! too like
In sad event when to th' unwiser son
Of Japhet, brought by Hermes, she ensnared
Mankind with her fair looks to be avenged
On him who had stole Jove's authentic fire.
  Thus at their shady lodge arrived both stood,
Both turned, and under open sky adored
The God who made both sky, air, earth and heav'n
Which they beheld, the moon's resplendent globe
And starry pole: Thou also mad'st the night,
Maker Omnipotent, and Thou the day
Which we in our appointed work employed
Have finished happy in our mutual help
And mutual love, the crown of all our bliss
Ordained by Thee, and this delicious place
For us too large where Thy abundance wants
Partakers and uncropped falls to the ground.

703. *emblem*: inlay.

706. *though but feigned*. Another reference to classical myth as untrue except as it dimly recalls the truth of Paradise.

711. *hymenean*: marriage song, after the Roman god of marriage, Hymen.

712. *genial angel*: procreative messenger. In Adam's later account of Eve's creation, it is the Creator who leads Eve to Adam. See 8.484–85. But in the Hebrew scriptures God sometimes appears as an angel, or as three angels.

714. *Pandora*: meaning "gifts from all [the gods]." To avenge the theft of fire from the gods, Zeus sends Pandora to earth. She is a beautiful virgin endowed with gifts from all the gods, e.g., beauty, given by Aphrodite, and skill at lying, given by Hermes. She is also provided with a jar containing all the evils that assail mankind. She opens it and the evils escape. The story is told in Hesiod, *Works and Days* 70–104.

715. *too like*. As events will show, Eve proves to be *too like* Pandora.

716–17. *unwiser son*: Epimetheus ("after-thought"), as opposed to his wiser brother, Prometheus ("fore-thought"). *Japhet*, one of the three sons of Noah, thought to be the father of the Greeks and other non-Semitic and non-African peoples, has a name similar to that of the father of Prometheus and Epimetheus: Iapetos. Zeus calls Prometheus "son of Iapetos" (Hesiod, *Works and Days* 54).

719. *him*: Prometheus, who in pity for mankind stole fire from Heaven.

724–35. Adam and Eve's evening prayer, in which they praise the Creator and recall that their own progeny will fill the earth and praise the Creator too.

But Thou hast promised from us two a race
To fill the earth who shall with us extol
Thy goodness infinite both when we wake
And when we seek, as now, Thy gift of sleep.
  This said unanimous and other rites
Observing none but adoration pure
Which God likes best into their inmost bower
Handed they went and, eased the putting off
These troublesome disguises which we wear,
Straight side by side were laid. Nor turned I ween
Adam from his fair spouse nor Eve the rites
Mysterious of connubial love refused,
Whatever hypocrites austerely talk
Of purity and place and innocence,
Defaming as impure what God declares
Pure and commands to some, leaves free to all.
Our Maker bids increase. Who bids abstain
But our destroyer, foe to God and Man?
Hail wedded love, mysterious law, true source
Of human offspring, sole propriety
In Paradise, of all things common else!
By thee adult'rous lust was driv'n from men
Among the bestial herds to range. By thee
Founded in reason, loyal, just and pure,
Relations dear and all the charities
Of father, son and brother first were known.
Far be it that I should write thee sin or blame
Or think thee unbefitting holiest place,
Perpetual fountain of domestic sweets
Whose bed is undefiled and chaste pronounced,
Present or past, as saints and patriarchs used.
Here Love his golden shaft employs, here lights
His constant lamp and waves his purple wings,
Reigns here and revels, not in the bought smile
Of harlots, loveless, joyless, unendeared,
Casual fruition, nor in court amours,

739. *eased*: a participle; i.e., and being eased of the burden of removing their clothes, since they wore none, they lay down side by side.
741. *ween*: expect, suppose.
743. *connubial*: conjugal, married.
748. "And God blessed them, and God said unto them, Be fruitful and multiply, and replenish the earth" Genesis 1:28.
758. *be* and *it* are elided: 'beet.'
761. "Marriage is honourable in all, and the bed undefiled: but whoremongers and adulterers God will judge" (Hebrews 13:4).
763. *shaft*: arrow (of Cupid).
767. *amours*: affairs at the royal court.

Mixed dance or wanton masque or midnight ball
Or serenade which the starved lover sings
To his proud fair, best quitted with disdain.
These lulled by nightingales embracing slept
And on their naked limbs the flow'ry roof
Show'red roses which the morn repaired. Sleep on
Blest pair and O yet happiest if ye seek
No happier state and know to know no more!
  Now had night measured with her shadowy cone
Half way up hill this vast sublunar vault
And from their ivory port the cherubim
Forth issuing at th' accustomed hour stood armed
To their night watches in warlíke parade
When Gabriel to his next in pow'r thus spake:
  Uzziel, half these draw off and coast the south
With strictest watch, these other wheel the north!
Our circuit meets full west. As flame they part,
Half wheeling to the shield half to the spear.
From these two strong and subtle spirits he called
That near him stood and gave them thus in charge:
  Ithuriel and Zephon, with winged speed
Search through this garden! Leave unsearched no nook
But chiefly where those two fair creatures lodge,
Now laid perhaps asleep secure of harm.
This evening from the sun's decline arrived
Who tells of some infernal spirit seen
Hitherward bent (who could have thought?) escaped
The bars of Hell, on errand bad, no doubt.
Such where ye find, seize fast and hither bring!
  So saying, on he led his radiant files,
Dazzling the moon, these to the bow'r direct

768. *Mixed dance*: dance in which partners are frequently changed, giving opportunity for assignations. *wanton masque*: theatrical performance at court in which courtiers (often in masks) participated.

771. *These*: Adam and Eve.

775. *know no more*: The knowledge referred to here is knowledge of the sexual pleasures and stimulants described in the previous lines.

776–77. The vault of the sky under the moon has been half darkened (in the east) by night. The shadow of night, which is cast by the earth, is cone-shaped.

778. *ivory port*: the eastern gate of Paradise, which, whether made of ivory or *alabaster* (line 544), is white.

782. *Uzziel* has two syllables: 'Uz-yell.' Uzziel is commanded to draw off half the troop of angels and lead it round the garden to the south, meeting the other half of the troop, led by Gabriel, in the west, opposite their point of departure.

786. *he*: Gabriel.

791. *secure*: unaware.

793. *Who*: Uriel.

798. *These*: Ithuriel and Zephon. The verb *went* is understood. Or "direct" can be taken as a verb, not an adverb: they *direct* their course.

In search of whom they sought. Him there they found
Squat like a toad close at the ear of Eve
Assaying by his dev'lish art to reach
The organs of her fancy and with them forge
Illusions as he list, phantasms and dreams,
Or if inspiring venom he might taint
Th' animal spirits that from pure blood arise
Like gentle breaths from rivers pure, thence raise
At least distempered, discontented thoughts,
Vain hopes, vain aims, inordinate desires
Blown up with high conceits engend'ring pride.
Him thus intent Ithuriel with his spear
Touched lightly, for no falsehood can endure
Touch of celestial temper but returns
Of force to its own likeness. Up he starts
Discovered and surprised. As when a spark
Lights on a heap of nitrous powder laid
Fit for the tun (some magazine to store
Against a rumored war) the smutty grain
With sudden blaze diffused inflames the air,
So started up in his own shape the Fiend.
Back stepped those two fair angels half amazed
So sudden to behold the grisly king
Yet thus unmoved with fear accost him soon:
  Which of those rebel spirits adjudged to Hell
Com'st thou, escaped thy prison and transformed?
Why sat'st thou like an enemy in wait
Here watching at the head of these that sleep?
  Know ye not then, said Satan, filled with scorn,
Know ye not me? Ye knew me once no mate
For you, there sitting where ye durst not soar.
Not to know me argues yourselves unknown:
The lowest of your throng! Or if ye know
Why ask ye and superfluous begin
Your message, like to end as much in vain?
  To whom thus Zephon answering scorn with scorn:
Think not, revolted spirit, thy shape the same
Or undiminished brightness to be known
As when thou stood'st in Heav'n upright and pure!
That glory then when thou no more wast good

799. *whom* and *Him*: the infernal spirit (Satan).
802. *fancy* and *and* are elided: 'fanc-yand.'
803. *phantasms* and *and* can be elided: 'fantas-mand.'
816. *tun*: cask. *magazine*: a secure place for storing weapons and ammunition.
829. *durst*: dared.
834. *answering* has two syllables.

Departed from thee and thou resemblest now
Thy sin and place of doom obscure and foul.
But come! For thou, be sure, shalt give account
To him who sent us, whose charge is to keep
This place inviolable and these from harm.
So spake the cherub and his grave rebuke
Severe in youthful beauty added grace
Invincible. Abashed the devil stood
And felt how awful goodness is and saw
Virtue in her shape how lovely, saw and pined
His loss, but chiefly to find here observed
His luster visibly impaired. Yet seemed
Undaunted: If I must contend, said he,
Best with the best, the sender not the sent,
Or all at once, more glory will be won
Or less be lost. Thy fear, said Zephon bold,
Will save us trial what the least can do
Single against thee wicked and thence weak.
The Fiend replied not, overcome with rage,
But like a proud steed reined went haughty on
Champing his iron curb. To strive or fly
He held it vain. Awe from above had quelled
His heart not else dismayed. Now drew they nigh
The western point where those half-rounding guards
Just met and closing stood in squadron joined
Awaiting next command. To whom their chief,
Gabriel, from the front thus called aloud:
O friends, I hear the tread of nimble feet
Hasting this way and now by glimpse discern
Ithuriel and Zephon through the shade
And with them comes a third of regal port
But faded splendor wan who by his gait
And fierce demeanor seems the Prince of Hell,
Not likely to part hence without contést.
Stand firm, for in his look defiance lours!
He scarce had ended when those two approached
And brief related whom they brought, where found,
How busied, in what form and posture couched.
To whom with stern regard thus Gabriel spake:
Why hast thou, Satan, broke the bounds prescribed

855. *the least*: the weakest (i.e., as you account me). *trial* has two syllables.

856. *Single*: alone, in single combat.

862. *The western point*: Gabriel has divided the force of angels into two wings, one led by him, one by Uzziel (see 4.782n). Starting in the east of Paradise, they encircle the garden on either side and meet again in the extreme west, where Ithuriel and Zephon conduct Satan.

To thy transgressions and disturbed the charge
Of others who approve not to transgress
By thy example but have pow'r and right
To question thy bold entrance on this place,
Employed, it seems, to violate sleep and those
Whose dwelling God hath planted here in bliss?
  To whom thus Satan with contemptuous brow:
Gabriel, thou had'st in Heav'n th' esteem of wise
And such I held thee, but this question asked
Puts me in doubt. Lives there who loves his pain?
Who would not, finding way, break loose from Hell
Though thither doomed? Thou wouldst thyself, no doubt,
And boldly venture to whatever place
Farthest from pain where thou might'st hope to change
Torment with ease and soonest recompense
Dole with delight, which in this place I sought.
To thee no reason, who knowst only good
But evil hast not tried. And wilt object
His will who bound us? Let Him surer bar
His iron gates if He intends our stay
In that dark durance: thus much what was asked.
The rest is true, they found me where they say.
But that implies not violence or harm.
  Thus he in scorn. The warlike angel, moved
Disdainfuly, half smiling thus replied:
O loss of one in Heav'n to judge of wise
Since Satan fell, whom folly overthrew!
And now returns him from his prison 'scaped
Gravely in doubt whether to hold them wise
Or not who ask what boldness brought him hither
Unlicensed from his bounds in Hell prescribed?
So wise he judges it to fly from pain,
However, and to 'scape his punishment.
So judge thou still, presumptuous, till the wrath
Which thou incurr'st by flying meet that flight
Sevenfold and scourge that wisdom back to Hell
Which taught thee yet no better that no pain
Can equal anger infinite provoked!
But wherefore thou alone? Wherefore with thee

883. *it*: Satan's escape from Hell and intrusion in Paradise.
899. *durance*: imprisonment. *thus much*: so much for what you asked.
902. *moved*: being moved (to anger).
904–5. Gabriel's reply is ironical: What a pity we have lost from Heaven one who is as good a judge of wisdom as you are. The irony continues in the repetition of *wise* (lines 907, 910, and 914).
908. A feminine line. See 2.27n.

Came not all Hell broke loose? Is pain to them
Less pain, less to be fled, or thou than they
Less hardy to endure? Courageous chief:
The first in flight from pain! Hadst thou alleged
To thy deserted host this cause of flight
Thou surely hadst not come sole fugitive.
   To which the Fiend thus answered frowning stern:
Not that I less endure or shrink from pain,
Insulting angel, well thou know'st I stood
Thy fiercest when in battle to thy aid
The blasting volleyed thunder made all speed
And seconded thy else not dreaded spear.
But still thy words at random, as before,
Argue thy inexperience what behooves
From hard assays and ill successes past
A faithful leader, not to hazard all
Through ways of danger by himself untried.
I therefore, I alone first undertook
To wing the desolate abyss and spy
This new-created world whereof in Hell
Fame is not silent, here in hope to find
Better abode and my afflicted powers
To settle here on earth or in mid air,
Though for possession put to try once more
What thou and thy gay legions dare against,
Whose easier business were to serve their Lord
High up in Heav'n with songs to hymn His throne
And practiced distances to cringe, not fight.
   To whom the warrior angel soon replied:
To say and straight unsay—pretending first
Wise to fly pain, professing next the spy—
Argues no leader but a liar traced,
Satan. And couldst thou "faithful" add? O name,
O sacred name of *faithfulness* profaned!
Faithful to whom? to thy rebellious crew,
Army of fiends? Fit body to fit head!
Was this your discipline and faith engaged,
Your military obedience, to dissolve
Allegiance to th' acknowledged Power Supreme?
And thou, sly hypocrite, who now wouldst seem
Patron of liberty, who more than thou

928. I.e., The Son's thunderbolts drove us all to flight.
941. *possession* of the earth and middle air.
945. *practiced distances*: courtly bows.
950. *faithful*. See line 933.
955. *military* and *obedience* have three syllables each.

Once fawned, and cringed, and servilely adored
Heav'n's awful Monarch? Wherefore but in hope
To dispossess Him and thyself to reign?
But mark what I aread thee now: avaunt!
Fly thither whence thou fledst! If from this hour
Within these hallowed limits thou appear,
Back to th' infernal pit I drag thee chained
And seal thee so as henceforth not to scorn
The facile gates of Hell too slightly barred!
  So threatened he but Satan to no threats
Gave heed but waxing more in rage replied:
  Then when I *am* thy captive talk of chains,
Proud limitary cherub! But ere then
Far heavier load thyself expect to feel
From my prevailing arm though Heaven's King
Ride on thy wings and thou with thy compeers,
Used to the yoke, draw'st his triumphant wheels
In progress through the road of Heav'n star-paved!
  While thus he spake th' angelic squadron bright
Turned fiery red, sharp'ning in moonèd horns
Their phalanx and began to hem him round
With ported spears as thick as when a field
Of Ceres ripe for harvest waving bends
Her bearded grove of ears which way the wind
Sways them. The careful ploughman doubting stands
Lest on the threshing floor his hopeful sheaves
Prove chaff. On th' other side Satan alarmed,
Collecting all his might, dilated stood
Like Teneriffe or Atlas unremoved.
His stature reached the sky and on his crest
Sat Horror plumed. Nor wanted in his grasp
What seemed both spear and shield. Now dreadful deeds
Might have ensued. Nor only Paradise
In this commotion but the starry cope
Of heav'n perhaps or all the elements
At least had gone to wrack, disturbed and torn

962. *avaunt!*: away!
971. *limitary*: guarding the frontier.
979. *phalanx*: a tight formation of heavily armed infantry (Greek). See 1.549–55 n.
980. *ported*: held up and forward at an angle, in the ready position.
983–85. *careful*: full of care. The ploughman worries that in the strong wind the kernels will be blown out of the husks so that when the sheaves are brought in to be threshed there will be nothing but chaff.
986. *dilated*: expanded. See 1.429.
987. *Teneriffe* and *Atlas* are mountains.
989. From Latin *horror*, frequently used to describe "bristling," dreadful arms. See line 996 and 1.563 n.

With violence of this conflict, had not soon
Th' Eternal to prevent such horrid fray
Hung forth in heav'n His golden scales, yet seen
Betwixt Astraea and the Scorpion sign,
Wherein all things created first He weighed
(The pendulous round earth with balanced air
In counterpoise), now ponders all events,
Battles and realms. In these He put two weights,
The sequel each of parting and of fight.
The latter quick up flew and kicked the beam
Which Gabriel spying thus bespake the Fiend:
  Satan, I know thy strength and thou know'st mine:
Neither our own, but giv'n. What folly then
To boast what arms can do since thine no more
Than Heav'n permits—nor mine, though doubled now
To trample thee as mire. For proof look up
And read thy lot in yon celestial sign
Where thou art weighed and shown how light, how weak,
If thou resist. The Fiend looked up and knew
His mounted scale aloft. Nor more, but fled
Murmuring, and with him fled the shades of night.

Book Five

The Argument

Morning approached, Eve relates to Adam her troublesome dream. He likes it not, yet comforts her. They come forth to their day labors: their morning hymn at the door of their bower. God, to render man inexcusable, sends Raphael to admonish him of his obedience, of his free state, of his enemy near at hand, who he is, and why his enemy, and whatever else may avail Adam to know. Raphael comes down to Paradise, his appearance described, his coming discerned by Adam afar off, sitting at the door of his bower. He goes out to meet him, brings him to his lodge, entertains him with the choicest fruits of

997–1014. *golden scales*. See *Iliad* 22.209–13, where Zeus weighs the fates of Hector and Achilles in his golden scales (cf. 8.69–77), and *Aeneid* 12.725–27, where Jove weighs the fates of Turnus and Aeneas. In the classical epics, the sinking scale means death, and the rising scale victory. In Milton, the rising scale indicates weakness (line 1012) and certain defeat. In the Hebrew tradition, the scales are implied in the Creation, when God weighs "the mountains in scales, and the hills in a balance" (Isaiah 40:12). Milton says that God first used the scales in the work of Creation and now uses them to weigh events in human history (line 1002). *ponders*: weighs (Latin *pondus*, "weight").

1007. Neither your strength nor mine is owned by us but is given from God.

1013–14. Satan knew that it was his side of the scales that had risen aloft, thus showing him to be weaker than Gabriel.

1014. *Nor more*: he said no more.

Paradise got together by Eve. Their discourse at table. Raphael performs his message, minds Adam of his state and of his enemy, relates at Adam's request who that enemy is and how he came to be so, beginning from his first revolt in Heaven and the occasion thereof. How he drew his legions after him to the parts of the North and there incited them to rebel with him, persuading all but only Abdiel, a seraph, who in argument dissuades and opposes him, then forsakes him.

Now Morn her rosy steps in th' eastern clime
Advancing sowed the earth with orient pearl
When Adam waked, so customed, for his sleep
Was airy light from pure digestion bred
And temperate vapors bland which th' only sound
Of leaves and fuming rills, Aurora's fan,
Lightly dispersed and the shrill matin song
Of birds on every bough. So much the more
His wonder was to find unwakened Eve
With tresses discomposed and glowing cheek
As through unquiet rest. He on his side
Leaning half-raised with looks of cordial love
Hung over her enamored and beheld
Beauty which whether waking or asleep
Shot forth peculiar graces. Then with voice
Mild as when Zephyrus on Flora breathes
Her hand soft touching whispered thus: Awake,
My fairest, my espoused, my latest found,
Heav'n's last best gift, my ever new delight,
Awake! The morning shines and the fresh field
Calls us. We lose the prime to mark how spring
Our tended plants, how blows the citron grove,
What drops the myrrh and what the balmy reed,
How Nature paints her colors, how the bee
Sits on the bloom extracting liquid sweet.
  Such whispering waked her, but with startled eye
On Adam, whom embracing, thus she spake:
  O sole in whom my thoughts find all repose,
My glory, my perfection, glad I see
Thy face and morn returned, for I this night
(Such night till this I never passed) have dreamed,

Book Five

1–2. A Homeric description of dawn. But see Psalm 97:11: "light is sown for the righteous."

5. *vapors bland*: mild exhalations. A discreet answer to the perennial question of Edenic excretion. Adam's sleep is light because his digestion is so efficient that nothing is left over as waste except mild vapors emitted through the pores, which the goddess of the dawn, Aurora, disperses with her fan. Aurora's fan is the mere sound of leaves, rushing streams, and bird song.

16. I.e., As when the west wind blows on the flowers.

If dreamed, not as I oft am wont, of thee,
Works of day past or morrow's next design
But of offense and trouble which my mind
Knew never till this irksome night. Methought
Close at mine ear one called me forth to walk
With gentle voice. I thought it thine. It said,
"Why sleep'st thou, Eve? Now is the pleasant time,
The cool, the silent, save where silence yields
To the night-warbling bird that now awake
Tunes sweetest his love-labored song. Now reigns
Full orbed the moon and with more pleasing light
Shadowy sets off the face of things—in vain
If none regard! Heav'n wakes with all his eyes
Whom to behold but thee, Nature's desire,
In whose sight all things joy with ravishment,
Attracted by thy beauty still to gaze."
I rose as at thy call but found thee not.
To find thee I directed then my walk
And on methought alone I passed through ways
That brought me on a sudden to the Tree
Of interdicted Knowledge. Fair it seemed,
Much fairer to my fancy than by day.
And as I wond'ring looked, beside it stood
One shaped and winged like one of those from Heav'n
By us oft seen. His dewy locks distilled
Ambrosia. On that tree he also gazed
And "O fair plant," said he, "with fruit surcharged,
Deigns none to ease thy load and taste thy sweet,
Nor god, nor man? Is knowledge so despised?
Or envy or what reserve forbids to taste?
Forbid who will, none shall from me withhold
Longer thy offered good: why else set here?"
This said, he paused not but with vent'rous arm
He plucked, he tasted. Me damp horror chilled
At such bold words vouched with a deed so bold.
But he thus overjoyed, "O fruit divine,
Sweet of thyself but much more sweet thus cropped,
Forbidden here, it seems, as only fit
For gods yet able to make gods of men.
And why not gods of men since good the more

44–47. I.e., The voice says, Whom does Heaven stay awake to see, if not you, on whom all things gaze with joy at your beauty?

61. *envy* and *or* are elided: 'env-yor.'

71–72. I.e., Since goodness increases the more it is shared, why should not this good, the fruit, make gods of men? The unstated assumption of the last clause is that to make gods of men—in our terms, to increase human power indefinitely—is in itself a good thing.

Communicated more abundant grows,
The Author not impaired but honored more?
Here, happy creature, fair angelic Eve,
Partake thou also! Happy though thou art,
Happier thou may'st be, worthier canst not be.
Taste this and be henceforth among the gods
Thyself a goddess, not to earth confined
But sometimes in the air as we! Sometimes
Ascend to Heav'n, by merit thine, and see
What life the gods live there—and such live thou!"
So saying he drew nigh and to me held,
E'en to my mouth, of that same fruit held part
Which he had plucked. The pleasant savory smell
So quickened appetite that I, methought,
Could not but taste. Forthwith up to the clouds
With him I flew and underneath beheld
The earth outstretched immense, a prospect wide
And various, wond'ring at my flight and change
To this high exaltation. Suddenly
My guide was gone and I, methought, sunk down
And fell asleep. But O how glad I waked
To find this but a dream! Thus Eve her night
Related and thus Adam answered sad:
  Best image of myself and dearer half,
The trouble of thy thoughts this night in sleep
Affects me equally. Nor can I like
This uncouth dream, of evil sprung I fear.
Yet evil whence? In thee can harbor none,
Created pure. But know that in the soul
Are many lesser faculties that serve
Reason as chief. Among these Fancy next
Her office holds. Of all external things
Which the five watchful senses represent
She forms imaginations, airy shapes

81. I.e., See what kind of life the gods live in heaven, which is where *you* should be, and live that life yourself. Note the subtle appeal to envy.
82–83. *held . . . held*: either the verb *held* is being repeated for dramatic emphasis or the second *held* means "deemed," "supposed." The latter alternative deftly captures the quality of dreams: Eve says she *supposed* the fruit held to her mouth was a piece of the fruit the speaker had plucked. She wasn't sure. See lines 85–86.
84. *savory* has two syllables: "sav'ry."
85–86. Eve does not taste the fruit in her dream. There is a break in her consciousness between the moment when she feels she can do nothing other than taste and the moment when she finds herself soaring to the clouds. This break is important.
94. *sad* (adverb): seriously.
102. *next*: beneath.
105. *she*: fancy. *imaginations*: mental images.

Which Reason joining or disjoining frames
All what we affirm or what deny and call
Our knowledge or opinion, then retires
Into her private cell when nature rests.
Oft in her absence mimic Fancy wakes
To imitate her but misjoining shapes
Wild work produces oft, and most in dreams,
Ill matching words and deeds long past or late.
Some such resemblances methinks I find
Of our last evening's talk in this thy dream
But with addition strange. Yet be not sad:
Evil into the mind of god or man
May come and go, so unapproved, and leave
No spot or blame behind. Which gives me hope
That what in sleep thou didst abhor to dream
Waking thou never wilt consent to do.
Be not disheartened then nor cloud those looks
That wont to be more cheerful and serene
Than when fair morning first smiles on the world!
And let us to our fresh employments rise
Among the groves, the fountains and the flow'rs
That open now their choicest bosomed smells
Reserved from night and kept for thee in store.
  So cheered he his fair spouse and she was cheered
But silently a gentle tear let fall
From either eye and wiped them with her hair.
Two other precious drops that ready stood
Each in their crystal sluice he ere they fell
Kissed as the gracious signs of sweet remorse
And pious awe that feared to have offended.
  So all was cleared and to the field they haste.
But first from under shady arborous roof
Soon as they forth were come to open sight
Of day-spring and the sun (who scarce up risen

106. *frames*: makes, fashions.
108–12. *retires*: the subject of this verb is *reason* (line 106), not *She* (line 105). Reason *retires* when we go to sleep, i.e., *when [human] nature rests*. Fancy, like the sorcerer's apprentice, then imitates Reason but misjoins the mental images.
113. *late*: recent.
114–16. *last evening's talk*, in which Adam spoke of *spiritual creatures* (4.677), angels, who walk the earth at night, keeping watch and making music in praise of the Creator. Yet the spiritual creatures show no interest in the tree with the forbidden fruit; that is the *addition strange* that Adam discerns in Eve's dream and that cannot be explained psychologically.
117. *god*: angel.
128. *reserved from night*: the flowers close at night to hold in their smells and open in the day to release them for Eve. Elsewhere (9.193–97), the smell of the opening flowers is directed to God in *silent praise*, filling his nostrils with *grateful [welcome] smell*.

With wheels yet hov'ring o'er the ocean brim
Shot parallel to th' earth his dewy ray,
Discov'ring in wide landscape all the east
Of Paradise and Eden's happy plains)
Lowly they bowed adoring and began
Their orisons, each morning duly paid
In various style. For neither various style
Nor holy rapture wanted they to praise
Their Maker in fit strains pronounced or sung
Unmeditated. Such prompt eloquence
Flowed from their lips in prose or num'rous verse
More tuneable than needed lute or harp
To add more sweetness. And they thus began:
  These are thy glorious works, Parent of Good
Almighty, thine this universal frame
Thus wondrous fair. Thyself how wondrous then,
Unspeakable, who sitt'st above these heavens
To us invisible or dimly seen
In these Thy lowest works! Yet these declare
Thy goodness beyond thought and power divine.
Speak ye who best can tell, ye sons of light,
Angels, for ye behold Him and with songs
And choral symphonies day without night
Circle His throne rejoicing, ye in Heav'n!
On earth join all ye creatures to extol
Him first, Him last, Him midst and without end!
Fairest of stars, last in the train of night
(If better thou belong not to the dawn,
Sure pledge of day) that crown'st the smiling Morn
With thy bright circlet, praise Him in thy sphere
While day arises, that sweet hour of prime!
Thou, Sun, of this great World both eye and soul,
Acknowledge Him thy greater, sound His praise
In thy eternal course both when thou climb'st
And when high noon hast gained and when thou fall'st!

147. *wanted*: lacked.

149. *Unmeditated*: spontaneous, improvised. Adam and Eve are natural poets: they do spontaneously what later poets, however talented, must study long and labor hard to do.

153–208. For Milton, the deepest impulse for poetry is not imitation but praise, praise of the Creator of the world. Adam and Eve's morning hymn is based on the language of praise in the Psalms (e.g., 19, 194, and 148). Milton regards the psalms as humanity's highest achievement in poetry and as the actual (though "ill imitated") source of classical poetry. See *Paradise Regained* 4.337–38 and 347.

166. *Fairest of stars*: Hesperus (*Iliad* 22.318), or the planet Venus, seen in the evening as the first "star" to appear, and at dawn, as the last "star" to disappear. Adam and Eve say that this star may be better called the first light of the day rather than the last light of the night.

170. *prime*: first light.

Moon that now meet'st the orient sun, now fli'st
With the fixed stars fixed in their orb that flies
And ye five other wand'ring fires that move
In mystic dance, not without song, resound
His praise who out of darkness called up light!
Air and ye elements, the eldest birth
Of Nature's womb that in quaternion run
Perpetual circle multiform and mix
And nourish all things, let your ceaseless change
Vary to our Great Maker still new praise!
Ye mists and exhalations that now rise
From hill or steaming lake, dusky or grey,
Till the sun paint your fleecy skirts with gold
In honor to the world's Great Author, rise!
Whether to deck with clouds th' uncolored sky
Or wet the thirsty Earth with falling showers:
Rising or falling, still advance His praise!
His praise ye winds that from four quarters blow
Breathe soft or loud! And wave your tops, ye pines,
With every plant: in sign of worship wave!
Fountains, and ye that warble as ye flow
Melodious murmurs, warbling tune His praise!
Join voices all ye living souls, ye birds
That singing up to Heaven gate ascend
Bear on your wings and in your notes His praise!
Ye that in waters glide and ye that walk
The earth and stately tread or lowly creep
Witness if I be silent, morn or ev'n,
To hill or valley, fountain or fresh shade
Made vocal by my song and taught His praise!
Hail Universal Lord! Be bounteous still
To give us only good! And if the night
Have gathered aught of evil or concealed,
Disperse it as now light dispels the dark!
So prayed they innocent and to their thoughts
Firm peace recovered soon and wonted calm.

175. *orient*: in the east. As the sun rises in the east, the moon, which faces (*meets*) the sun in the west, retreats over the western horizon, followed by the stars, which do not change position with respect to each other but are *fixed* on their crystal *orb*. Milton no longer believes this ancient and medieval cosmology, but it seems reasonable to him that Adam and Eve would.

177. *wand'ring fires*: planets, or "wanderers," from Greek *planaô*, "to wander."

181–82. *quaternion*: fourfold intercombination. The four elements of medieval and Renaissance science—air, water, earth, and fire—are combined in all things in nature and are continually mixing and adjusting their balance.

196. *warbling*: singing.

197. *living souls*: animate creatures (Genesis 2:7)

203. *valley* and *or* are elided: 'val-yor.'

On to their morning's rural work they haste
Among sweet dews and flow'rs where any row
Of fruit-trees over-woody reached too far
Their pampered boughs and needed hands to check
Fruitless embraces. Or they led the vine
To wed her elm: she spoused about him twines
Her marriageable arms and with her brings
Her dow'r, th' adopted clusters, to adorn
His barren leaves. Them thus employed beheld
With pity Heav'n's high King and to Him called
Raphael the sociable spirit that deigned
To travel with Tobias and secured
His marriage with the sev'n-times-wedded maid.
Raphael, said He, thou hear'st what stir on Earth
Satan from Hell 'scaped through the darksome gulf
Hath raised in Paradise and how disturbed
This night the human pair, how he designs
In them at once to ruin all mankind.
Go therefore: half this day as friend with friend
Converse with Adam in what bow'r or shade
Thou find'st him from the heat of noon retired
To respite his day-labor with repast
Or with repose and such discourse bring on
As may advise him of his happy state—
Happiness in his pow'r left free to will,
Left to his own free will, his will though free
Yet mutable. Whence warn him to beware
He swerve not too secure. Tell him withal
His danger and from whom, what enemy
Late fall'n himself from Heav'n is plotting now
The fall of others from like state of bliss:
By violence, no, for that shall be withstood,
But by deceit and lies. This let him know
Lest willfully transgressing he pretend
Surprisal unadmonished, unforewarned.
So spake th' eternal Father and fulfilled

215–19. The ancient practice of winding grape vines around and up the trunks of elms was a commonplace in Roman literature. See Virgil, *Georgics* 1.2; 2.221, 360–61, 367; Horace, *Odes* 4.5.30, *Epodes* 2.9–10.

216. *she*: the grape vine.

221. *sociable* has three syllables, *spirit* has two.

222–23. See Glossary, *Asmodeus*. A romantic story from the biblical Apocrypha, in which the young Tobias is aided by the angel Raphael against a demon who has killed Sarah's seven successive husbands (Tobit 7:11). See 4.167–71.

235–37. Happiness depends on freedom of the will. But free will is not free from the danger of changing into something less than free.

All justice. Nor delayed the wingèd saint
After his charge received but from among
Thousand celestial ardors where he stood
Veiled with his gorgeous wings up springing light
Flew through the midst of Heav'n. Th' angelic choirs
On each hand parting to his speed gave way
Through all th' empyreal road till at the gate
Of Heav'n arrived. The gate self-opened wide
On golden hinges turning as by work
Divine the Sov'reign Architect had framed.
From hence (no cloud or to obstruct his sight
Star interposed, however small) he sees,
Not unconform to other shining globes,
Earth and the gard'n of God with cedars crowned
Above all hills, as when by night the glass
Of Galileo, less assured, observes
Imagined lands and regions in the moon,
Or pilot from amidst the Cyladës,
Delos or Samos, first appearing kens
A cloudy spot. Down thither prone in flight
He speeds and through the vast ethereal sky
Sails between worlds and worlds with steady wing
Now on the polar winds, then with quick fan
Winnows the buxom air till, within soar
Of tow'ring eagles, to all fowls he seems
A phoenix: gazed by all as that sole bird
When to enshrine his relics in the Sun's
Bright temple to Egyptian Thebes he flies.
At once on th' eastern cliff of Paradise
He lights and to his proper shape returns
A seraph winged. Six wings he wore to shade
His lineaments divine: the pair that clad
Each shoulder broad came mantling o'er his breast

249. *ardors*: flames, angels aflame with divine love.
253. *empyreal* has three syllables.
256. *Sovereign Architect*: the Son, who puts the Father's will into effect.
262. *less assured*: less clear sight. Across a "distance inexpressible / By numbers that have name" (8.113–14), Raphael's angelic vision gives perfect knowledge of whatever it is focused on. The comparisons that follow—to Galileo's telescope and to the keen-eyed Aegean sailor—are examples of imperfect vision.
269–70. *polar winds . . . buxom air*: These are the contrasting conditions through which Raphael flies. He needs both great strength and delicacy of touch, strength for steering on the high winds blowing down from chaos (see 3.425–26) and delicacy of touch for rapidly fanning the more rarefied, "flexible" (the old sense of *buxom*) air above the earth. *winnows*: verb; a fanning action used to separate chaff from grain. The principles of flight were poorly understood in Milton's day. This passage, which works by analogy to propulsion through water, shows remarkable powers of hypothesis.
270. *within soar*: descended to the height which the highest soaring eagles attain.

With regal ornament. The middle pair
Girt like a starry zone his waist and round
Skirted his loins and thighs with downy gold
And colors dipped in Heav'n. The third his feet
Shadowed from either heel with feathered mail,
Sky-tinctured grain. Like Maia's son he stood
And shook his plumes that Heav'nly fragrance filled
The circuit wide. Straight knew him all the bands
Of angels under watch and to his state
And to his message high in honor rise,
For on some message high they guessed him bound.
Their glitt'ring tents he passed and now is come
Into the blissful field through groves of myrrh
And flow'ring odors, cassia, nard and balm,
A wilderness of sweets, for Nature here
Wantoned as in her prime and played at will
Her virgin fancies pouring forth more sweet,
Wild above rule or art, enormous bliss.
Him through the spicy forest onward come
Adam discerned as in the door he sat
Of his cool bow'r while now the mounted sun
Shot down direct his fervid rays to warm
Earth's inmost womb, more warmth than Adam needs.
And Eve within, due at her hour, prepared
For dinner savory fruits of taste to please
True appetite and not disrelish thirst
Of nectarous draughts between from milky stream,
Berry or grape. To whom thus Adam called:
  Haste hither Eve and worth thy sight behold
Eastward among those trees what glorious shape
Comes this way moving! Seems another morn
Ris'n on mid-noon. Some great behest from Heav'n
To us perhaps he brings and will vouchsafe
This day to be our guest. But go with speed
And what thy stores contain bring forth and pour
Abundance fit to honor and receive
Our Heav'nly stranger. Well we may afford
Our givers their own gifts and large bestow

281. *zone*: belt.
287–88. *bands of angels*: these are the troops of angels, under Gabriel's command, guarding Paradise at its eastern gate (4.541–54).
295. *Wantoned*: played. *prime*: beginning, dawn.
298. *Him . . . come*: I.e., Raphael, having come onward through the forest. *Spicy*: aromatic.
299. Abraham is visited by the divine presence when "he sat in the tent door in the heat of the day" (Genesis 18:1).
306. *draughts between*: drinks taken between courses of fruit. *Nectarous* has two syllables: 'nec-trous.'

From large bestowed where nature multiplies
Her fertile growth and by disburd'ning grows
More fruitful, which instructs us not to spare.
  To whom thus Eve: Adam, earth's hallowed mold,
Of God inspired, small store will serve where store
All seasons ripe for use hangs on the stalk,
Save what by frugal storing firmness gains
To nourish and superfluous moist consumes.
But I will haste and from each bough and brake,
Each plant and juiciest gourd, will pluck such choice
To entertain our angel guest as he
Beholding shall confess that here on Earth
God hath dispensed His bounties as in Heav'n.
  So saying with dispatchful looks in haste
She turns, on hóspitable thoughts intent
What choice to choose for delicacy best,
What order so contrived as not to mix
Tastes not well joined, inelegant, but bring
Taste after taste upheld with kindliest change.
Bestirs her then and from each tender stalk
Whatever Earth all-bearing mother yields
In India east or west, or middle shore
In Pontus or the Punic coast, or where
Alcinous reigned, fruit of all kinds in coat
(Rough or smooth rined or bearded husk or shell)
She gathers tribute large and on the board
Heaps with unsparing hand. For drink the grape
She crushes, inoffensive must, and meaths
From many a berry, and from sweet kernels pressed
She tempers dulcet creams nor these to hold
Wants her fit vessels pure, then strews the ground
With rose and odors from the shrub unfumed.
Meanwhile our primitive great sire to meet
His godlike guest walks forth without more train
Accompanied than with his own complete
Perfections. In himself was all his state
More solemn than the tedious pomp that waits
On princes when their rich retínue long

321–22. *hallowed mold / Of God inspired*. I.e., you who are formed of the sacred earth and animated by God's breath.
325. *superfluous* has three syllables.
339. *middle shore*: the shores of the Mediterranean, situated on the globe between the east and west Indies, India, and North America.
345. *inoffensive must*: unfermented wine and so not intoxicating. *meaths*: sweet drinks.
349. *unfumed*: not burned, as an incense, since Adam and Eve have no fire. In Eden the twigs of shrubs give odors as rich as burning incense.
350. *primitive*: original, first (Latin *prima*, "first").

Of horses led and grooms besmeared with gold
Dazzles the crowd and sets them all agape.
Nearer his presence Adam, though not awed,
Yet with submiss approach and reverence meek
As to a superior nature bowing low
Thus said: Native of Heav'n, for other place
None can than Heav'n such glorious shape contain,
Since by descending from the thrones above
Those happy places thou hast deigned a while
To want, and honor these, vouchsafe with us
Two only who yet by sov'reign gift possess
This spacious ground in yonder shady bow'r
To rest and what the garden choicest bears
To sit and taste till this meridian heat
Be over and the sun more cool decline.
  Whom thus th' angelic virtue answered mild:
Adam, I therefore came, nor art thou such
Created or such place hast here to dwell
As may not oft invite, though spirits of Heav'n,
To visit thee. Lead on then where thy bow'r
O'ershades, for these mid-hours till evening rise
I have at will. So to the sylvan lodge
They came that like Pomona's arbor smiled
With flow'rets decked and fragrant smells. But Eve
(Undecked save with herself, more lovely fair
Than wood-nymph or the fairest goddess feigned
Of three that in Mount Ida naked strove)
Stood to entertain her guest from Heav'n. No veil
She needed, virtue-proof, no thought infirm
Altered her cheek. On whom the angel Hail
Bestowed, the holy salutation used
Long after to blest Mary, second Eve:
  Hail Mother of Mankind whose fruitful womb
Shall fill the world more numerous with thy sons

360. *superior* has three syllables: 'sup-eeryor.' The line is hypermetrical. The *a*, which might be dropped, is in both 1667 and 1674.
365. *to want*: to be absent from. *these*: places on earth.
369. *meridian*: midday.
372. *therefore*: for that purpose (to socialize with you).
372–75. *Spirits*: a good example of Milton's compressed syntax; i.e., "Although they are spirits of heaven, you, Adam, are created so nobly that it is suitable for you to invite spirits of heaven to visit."
378. *Pomona*: goddess of fruit trees.
380. *Undecked*: unclothed.
381. *feigned*: pretended by the classical poets. Aphrodite, Athena, and Hera strove for the prize of beauty on Mount Ida, where the Trojan prince Paris awarded the prize to Aphrodite in return for the love of Helen, an event that caused the Trojan War.
384. *virtue-proof*: being guarded by her virtue.

Than with these various fruits the trees of God
Have heaped this table! Raised of grassy turf
Their table was and mossy seats had round
And on her ample square from side to side
All autumn piled, though spring and autumn here
Danced hand in hand. A while discourse they hold
(No fear lest dinner cool) when thus began
Our author: Heav'nly stranger, please to taste
These bounties which our Nourisher (from whom
All perfect good unmeasured out descends
To us for food and for delight) hath caused
The earth to yield. Unsavory food perhaps
To spiritual natures. Only this I know:
That one celestial Father gives to all.
  To whom the angel: Therefore what He gives
(Whose praise be ever sung) to Man in part
Spiritual may of purest spirits be found
No ingrateful food. And food alike those pure
Intelligential substances require
As doth your rational, and both contain
Within them every lower faculty
Of sense whereby they hear, see, smell, touch, taste,
Tasting concoct, digest, assimilate,
And corporeal to incorporeal turn.
For know whatever was created needs
To be sustained and fed. Of elements
The grosser feeds the purer: Earth the Sea,
Earth and the Sea feed Air, the Air those Fires
Ethereal and as lowest first the Moon,
Whence in her visage round those spots unpurged,
Vapors not yet into her substance turned.
Nor doth the Moon no nourishment exhale

393. *her*: the table's.
397. *our author*: our first father.
404–7. The food God gives to humans, who are partly spiritual beings, is welcome to the purest spirits as well.
407. A hypermetrical line.
408. *Intelligential substances*: angels' bodies, which, being material (though the highest degree of matter), need food.
409. *both*: *Intelligential* and *rational* substances: angelic and human bodies.
413. *incorporeal*: material, or substantial, but in a higher degree of existence than body, *corpus*, which has fixed boundaries and specialized parts. Through digestion the corporeal matter of fruits is refined into the incorporeal substance of angelic bodies and, in humans, into the reasoning power.
416. *grosser*: denser.
417–20. *Fires / Ethereal*: the liquid fire of the upper air, the empyrean, as well as the planets and stars. The lowest of these fires, the moon, is between the cool air of the upper atmosphere and the empyrean. Because the moon is on the border between the two realms, we can see in her face (*visage*) the as yet undigested vapors of the air being assimilated to her. The dark spots in the moon are the moon's food: atmospheric vapors.

From her moist continent to higher orbs.
The Sun that light imparts to all receives
From all his alimental recompense
In humid exhalations and at ev'n
Sups with the Ocean. Though in Heav'n the trees
Of life ambrosial fruitage bear and vines
Yield nectar, though from off the boughs each morn
We brush mellifluous dews and find the ground
Covered with pearly grain, yet God hath here
Varied His bounty so with new delights
As may compare with Heaven—and to taste
Think not I shall be nice! So down they sat
And to their viands fell, nor seemingly
The angel nor in mist (the common gloss
Of theologians) but with keen dispatch
Of real hunger and concoctive heat
To transubstantiate. What redounds transpires
Through spirits with ease. Nor wonder if by fire
Of sooty coal th' empiric alchemist
Can turn, or holds it possible to turn,
Metals of drossiest ore to perfect gold
As from the mine. Meanwhile at table Eve
Ministered naked and their flowing cups
With pleasant liquors crowned. O innocence
Deserving Paradise! If ever, then,
Then had the sons of God excuse t' have been
Enamoured at that sight. But in those hearts
Love unlibidinous reigned nor jealousy

423–26. The sun is sustained by vapors from all things, to which it gives nourishing light.
430. *here*: on earth.
433. *nice*: disinclined and fussy.
434. *viands*: food.
435. *in mist*: symbolically.
437. *concoctive*: cooking. The angel cooks his meal inside him.
438. *transubstantiate*: turn one substance into another, in this case a higher. A loaded term in Milton's day, denoting for Roman Catholics the changing of the bread and wine of the mass into Christ's body and blood. For Milton, true transubstantiation exists in the natural world, in the processes of digestion and in the entire movement of creatures upward on the scale of being toward their Creator. *redounds*: is in excess. *transpires*: is breathed or radiated out. See line 5 n.
440. *empiric alchemist*: one who attempts by trial and error to convert supposedly lower metals, such as lead, into supposedly higher metals, ultimately gold. Many alchemists were charlatans, as in Jonson's play *The Alchemist*, and Milton at the very least doubts what they claim.
445. *crowned*: cups filled with noble drink.
447. *Sons of God*: rogue angels who became enamored of human women—"the sons of God saw the daughters of men that they were fair" (Genesis 6:2)—and mated with them, bringing forth a race of mighty men, which was destroyed in the Flood. Milton's point here is that if ever the Sons of God (e.g., Raphael) had excuse for being attracted to human women it was here, where Eve *ministered naked*. See Glossary, *Ramiel*.
448. *those*: Adam and Eve's.
449. *unlibidinous*: not lustful. Four syllables.

Was understood, the injured lover's Hell.
  Thus when with meats and drinks they had sufficed,
Not burdened nature, sudden mind arose
In Adam not to let th' occasion pass
Giv'n him by this great conference to know
Of things above his world and of their being
Who dwell in Heav'n whose excellence he saw
Transcend his own so far, whose radiant forms'
Divine effulgence, whose high pow'r so far
Exceeded human, and his wary speech
Thus to th' empyreal minister he framed:
  Inhabitant with God, now know I well
Thy favor in this honor done to Man
Under whose lowly roof thou hast vouchsafed
To enter and these earthly fruits to taste,
Food not of angels yet accepted so
As that more willingly thou couldst not seem
At Heav'n's high feasts t' have fed, yet what compare?
  To whom the wingèd hierarch replied:
O Adam! one Almighty is, from whom
All things proceed and up to Him return
If not depraved from good, created all
Such to perfection, one first matter all
Endued with various forms, various degrees
Of substance and in things that live of life,
But more refined, more spiritous and pure
As nearer to Him placed or nearer tending,
Each in their several active spheres assigned
Till body up to spirit work in bounds
Proportioned to each kind. So from the root
Springs lighter the green stalk, from thence the leaves
More airy, last the bright consummate flower
Spirits odorous breathes: flow'rs and their fruit,
Man's nourishment, by gradual scale sublimed
To vital spirits aspire, to animal,
To intellectual, give both life and sense,
Fancy and understanding, whence the soul
Reason receives, and reason is her being,
Discursive or intuitive: discourse
Is oftest yours, the latter most is ours,
Differing but in degree, of kind the same.
Wonder not then what God for you saw good

455. *their*: the angels'.
465. *accepted so*: i.e., you accepted and enjoyed our lower, human food as willingly as you would the food served at heaven's feasts.

If I refuse not but convert as you
To proper substance. Time may come when men
With angels may participate and find
No inconvenient diet nor too light fare.
And from these corporal nutriments perhaps
Your bodies may at last turn all to spirit,
Improved by tract of time, and winged ascend
Ethereal as we, or may at choice
Here or in Heav'nly paradises dwell—
If ye be found obedient and retain
Unalterably firm His love entire
Whose progeny you are. Meanwhile enjoy
Your fill what happiness this happy state
Can comprehend, incapable of more.
  To whom the patriarch of mankind replied:
O favorable Spirit, propitious guest,
Well hast thou taught the way that might direct
Our knowledge and the scale of nature set
From center to circumference whereon
In contemplation of created things
By steps we may ascend to God. But say,
What meant that caution joined, "if ye be found
Obedient"? Can we want obedience then
To Him or possibly His love desert
Who formed us from the dust and placed us here
Full to the utmost measure of what bliss
Human desires can seek or apprehend?
  To whom the angel: Son of Heav'n and Earth,
Attend! That thou art happy owe to God.
That thou continuest such owe to thyself,
That is, to thy obedience: therein stand!
This was that caution giv'n thee. Be advised!
God made thee perfect, not immutable,
And good He made thee. But to persevere

493. *to proper substance*: to my own (Latin *proprius*) body.
494. *participate*: a learned pun: "to share meals with" or "to be of like substance with."
495. *inconvenient*: inappropriate. *diet* has one syllable.
496. *corporal* has two syllables: 'corp-ral.'
497. *spirit*: highest, most refined degree of substance.
498–99. *winged*: being winged. *ascend / Ethereal as we*: ascend so high as to become ethereal, as we are.
503. *Whose progeny you are*. Strictly speaking, Adam and Eve are not God's offspring (only the Son is) but His creatures: they are beings God has made. Raphael's phrase is meant figuratively, as it is in its source, Saint Paul's sermon to the Athenians, on "Mars' hill," the Areopagus; Acts 17:28: "For in him we live, and move, and have our being; as certain also of your own poets have said, For we are also his offspring."
505. *incapable*: unable, given your present bodily structure, to be happier than you now are.
509. *scale*: Latin *scala*, "ladder."

He left it in thy pow'r, ordained thy will
By nature free, not overruled by fate
Inextricáble or strict necessity.
Our voluntary service He requires,
Not our necessitated: such with Him
Finds no acceptance, nor *can* find. For how
Can hearts, not free, be tried whether they serve
Willing or no, who will but what they must
By destiny and can no other choose?
Myself and all th' angelic host that stand
In sight of God enthroned our happy state
Hold as you yours while our obedience holds,
On other surety none. Freely we serve
Because we freely love as in our will
To love or not: in this we stand or fall.
And some are fall'n, to disobedience fall'n
And so from Heav'n to deepest Hell. O fall
From what high state of bliss into what woe!
  To whom our great progenitor: Thy words
Attentive and with more delighted ear,
Divine instructor, I have heard than when
Cherubic songs by night from neighboring hills
Aerïal music send. Nor knew I not
To be both will and deed created free.
Yet that we never shall forget to love
Our Maker and obey Him whose command
Single is yet so just, my constant thoughts
Assured me and still assure, though what thou tell'st
Hath passed in Heav'n some doubt within me move
But more desire to hear, if thou consent,
The full relation which must needs be strange,
Worthy of sacred silence to be heard!
And we have yet large day, for scarce the Sun
Hath finished half his journey and scarce begins
His other half in the great zone of Heav'n.
  Thus Adam made request and Raphael

528. *Inextricable* and *or* are elided: 'inextricáb-lor.'

538–40. Raphael says that the angels, like mankind, serve God freely because they love God. Angels are free to choose to love God. They are not compelled to do so either by God or by their own nature.

546. *than when*: "as when."

553. *me* and *and* are elided: 'm' and.'

557. An expression from Horace, *Odes* 2.13.29, describing songs worthy of being heard in sacred silence, *sacro digna silentio*. Another indication that poetry is the natural speech of Eden. See line 149 and n, and 4. 639–56 and n.

559. *journey* and *and* are elided: 'journ-yand.'

560. *great zone*: belt of the zodiac, through whose signs the sun travels through the day.

After short pause assenting thus began:
  High matter thou enjoin'st me O Prime of Men,
Sad task and hard, for how shall I relate
To human sense th' invisible explóits
Of warring spirits, how without remorse
The ruin of so many glorious once
And perfect while they stood, how last unfold
The secrets of another world perhaps
Not lawful to reveal? Yet for thy good
This is dispensed, and what surmounts the reach
Of human sense I shall delineate so
By lik'ning spiritual to corporal forms
As may express them best. Though what if Earth
Be but the shadow of Heav'n and things therein
Each to other like more than on Earth is thought?
  As yet this world was not and chaos wild
Reigned where these heav'ns now roll, where Earth now rests
Upon her center poised, when on a day
(For time, though in eternity, applied
To motion measures all things durable
By present, past and future) on such day
As Heav'n's Great Year brings forth th' empyreal host
Of angels, by imperial summons called,
Innum'rable before th' Almighty's throne,
Forthwith from all the ends of Heav'n appeared
Under their hierarchs in orders bright,
Ten thousand thousand ensigns high advanced,
Standards and gonfalons 'twixt van and rear
Stream in the air and for distinction serve
Of hierarchies, of orders and degrees
Or in their glittering tissues bear imblazed
Holy memorials, acts of zeal and love
Recorded eminent. Thus when in orbs
Of circuit inexpressible they stood,

564. *Sad task*: Raphael's preface recalls Aeneas's words to Dido before recounting, at her request, the fall of Troy. *Aeneid* 2.3: "Unspeakable, O queen, is the grief you command me to revive."

571–73. The war in heaven will be recounted in terms that are at once figurative and literal: figurative because the events described entirely exceed anything on the level of the human senses, literal because the events as described cannot be translated into other terms (such as concepts) or apprehended by the human mind in any other way.

573. *spiritual* has two syllables, *corporal* has three.

575. *shadow* and *of* are elided.

581. *durable*: having extension in time.

583. *Great Year*: A period of 36,000 earth years, when the stars return to their original positions. Plato, *Timaeus* 37–39 and *Republic* 546.

589. *gonfalons*: banners suspended from crossbars. *Van*: the front line of troops.

591. *hierarchies* has three syllables.

592. *tissues*: woven fabrics.

Orb within orb, the Father Infinite,
By whom in bliss embosomed sat the Son,
Amidst as from a flaming mount whose top
Brightness had made invisible, thus spake:
  "Hear all ye angels, progeny of light,
Thrones, Dominations, Princedoms, Virtues, Powers,
Hear My decree, which unrevoked shall stand!
This day I have begot whom I declare
My only Son and on this holy hill
Him have anointed whom ye now behold
At My right hand. Your head I Him appoint
And by Myself have sworn to Him shall bow
All knees in Heav'n and shall confess Him Lord.
Under His great vicegerent reign abide
United as one individual soul
For ever happy. Him who disobeys
Me disobeys, breaks union, and that day,
Cast out from God and blessèd vision, falls
Into utter darkness, deep engulfed, his place
Ordained without redemption, without end."
  So spake th' Omnipotent and with His words
All seemed well pleased: all seemed but were not all.
That day as other solemn days they spent
In song and dance about the sacred hill,
Mystical dance which yonder starry sphere
Of planets and of fixed in all her wheels
Resembles nearest, mazes intricate,
Eccentric, intervolved, yet regular
Then most when most irregular they seem
And in their motions harmony divine
So smooths her charming tones that God's own ear
Listens delighted. Evening now approached
(For we have also our evening and our morn,
We ours for change delectable, not need),

598–99. *flaming mount . . . invisible*: recalls Mount Sinai, where Moses received the Hebrew Law (Exodus 19:19–20).

603. "The Lord hath said unto me, Thou art my Son; this day I have begotten thee" (Psalm 2:7). This event, the proclamation of the Son as Messiah and king over the angels, is the earliest in the action of the poem. The Son is not literally begotten by the Father at this time but is revealed to the angels as such. In fact, the Son created the angels, acting as the Father's instrument, or Word, when doing so (lines 835–37).

607–8. "I have sworn by myself . . . that unto me every knee shall bow" (Isaiah 45:23). "God also hath highly exalted him, and given him a name which is above every name: That at the name of Jesus every knee should bow" (Philippians 2:9–10).

610. *individual* has four syllables: 'individ-jal.'

621. *fixed*: stars fixed on their crystal sphere. They do not change position with respect to each other.

628. *also* and *our* are elided.

Forthwith from dance to sweet repast they turn
Desirous. All in circles as they stood
Tables are set and on a sudden piled
With angels' food and rubied nectar flows
In pearl, in diamond and massy gold,
Fruit of delicious vines, the growth of Heav'n.
On flow'rs reposed and with fresh flow'rets crowned
They eat, they drink, and in communion sweet
Quaff immortality and joy (secure
Of surfeit where full measure only bounds
Excess) before th' all-bounteous King, who show'red
With copious hand, rejoicing in their joy.
  Now when ambrosial night with clouds exhaled
From that high Mount of God (whence light and shade
Spring both) the face of brightest Heav'n had changed
To grateful twilight (for night comes not there
In darker veil) and roseate dews disposed
All but th' unsleeping eyes of God to rest,
Wide over all the plain and wider far
Than all the globous Earth in plain outspread
(Such are the courts of God) th' angelic throng,
Dispersed in bands and files, their camp extend
By living streams among the trees of life,
Pavilions numberless and sudden reared,
Celestial tabernacles where they slept
Fanned with cool winds, save those who in their course
Melodious hymns about the sov'reign throne
Alternate all night long. But not so waked
Satan (so call him now: his former name
Is heard no more in Heav'n). He of the first
If not the first archangel great in pow'r,
In favor, and preëminence, yet fraught
With envy against the Son of God that day

633. *nectar*: in Homer the drink of the gods. The epithet *rubied* is close in sound to Homer's *eruthros*, "red."

638–40. *secure / of surfeit . . . Excess*: in no danger of eating or drinking too much because the glasses and plates, when full, hold just enough to satisfy.

640. *Bounteous* has two syllables.

642–44. The direct object of *night* is *face*; i.e., when night changed the face of heaven.

642–57. This sentence opens with a complex subordinate clause (governed by *when*) extending from line 642 to line 647. The subject is *throng* (line 650), the main verb *reared* (line 653), and the direct object *Pavilions*: 'the angelic throng reared their pavilions.' (The force of *extend*, line 651, is participial: 'their camp being extended.')

658. *his former name*: *Lucifer*, "light-bearer": "How art thou fallen from heaven, O Lucifer, son of the morning!" (Isaiah 14:12). But Raphael may mean another, more mysterious name as well. See lines 760–62.

659–60. Milton's Satan is not necessarily as in Christian tradition the head of the angels before his fall. But he is one of the archangels.

662. *envy* and *against* are elided: 'env-yagainst.'

Honored by His great Father and proclaimed
Messiah, King Anointed, could not bear
Through pride that sight and thought himself impaired.
Deep malice thence conceiving and disdain,
Soon as midnight brought on the dusky hour
Friendliest to sleep and silence, he resolved
With all his legions to dislodge and leave
Unworshipped, unobeyed, the throne supreme,
Contemptuous, and his next subordinate
Awak'ning, thus to him in secret spake:
"Sleep'st thou, companion dear? What sleep can close
Thy eyelids? And remember'st what decree
Of yesterday so late hath passed the lips
Of Heav'n's Almighty? Thou to me thy thoughts
Wast wont, I mine to thee was wont t' impart:
Both waking we were one. How then can now
Thy sleep dissent? New laws thou seest imposed,
New laws from Him who reigns new minds may raise
In us who serve, new counsels, to debate
What doubtful may ensue. More in this place
To utter is not safe. Assemble thou
Of all those myriads which we lead the chief.
Tell them that by command ere yet dim night
Her shadowy cloud withdraws I am to haste,
And all who under me their banners wave,
Homeward with flying march where we possess
The quarters of the north, there to prepare
Fit entertainment to receive our King
The great Messiah and His new commands,
Who speedily through all the hierarchies
Intends to pass triumphant and give laws."
So spake the false archangel and infused
Bad influence into th' unwary breast

664. *King Anointed* is the meaning of *Messiah*.

671. *Contemptuous*: either an adjective modifying *he* (line 668) or an adverb modifying *leave* (line 669): 'he, being contemptuous, left' or 'he left, contemptuously.' *next subordinate*: Beëlzebub.

680–81. I.e., New laws will raise new ways of thinking (*minds*) in us who serve. (We may, for example, think of serving no more).

689. *north*: "For thou hast said in thine heart . . . I will exalt my throne above the stars of God: I will sit also upon the mount of the congregation, in the sides of the north" (Isaiah 14:13).

690. *fit entertainment*: suitable greeting, whether peaceful or warlike. An example of Satan's ambiguous way of speaking.

692. *hierarchies*: orders of angels.

693. *give laws*: a classical expression, evoking the image of a Roman general conquering new territories and imposing laws (and taxes).

Of his associate. He together calls,
Or several one by one, the regent powers,
Under him regent, tells as he was taught
That the Most High Commanding now ere night,
Now ere dim night had disencumbered Heav'n,
The great hierarchal standard was to move,
Tells the suggested cause and casts between
Ambiguous words and jealousies to sound
Or taint integrity. But all obeyed
The wonted signal and superior voice
Of their great potentate. For great indeed
His name and high was his degree in Heav'n!
His count'nance as the morning star that guides
The starry flock allured them and with lies
Drew after him the third part of Heav'n's host.
Meanwhile th' Eternal Eye whose sight discerns
Abstrusest thoughts from forth His holy mount
And from within the golden lamps that burn
Nightly before Him saw without their light
Rebellion rising, saw in whom, how spread
Among the sons of morn, what multitudes
Were banded to oppose His high decree
And smiling to His only Son thus said:
"Son, Thou in whom My glory I behold
In full resplendence, heir of all My might,
Nearly it now concerns us to be sure
Of our omnipotence and with what arms
We mean to hold what anciently we claim
Of deity or empire, such a foe
Is rising who intends t' erect his throne
Equal to ours throughout the spacious north!
Nor so content hath in his thought to try
In battle what our pow'r is or our right.

696–98. *He . . . him . . . he*: Beëlzebub, who is *regent* (one who rules in another's name) under Satan.

699. *the Most High Commanding*: tendentious title of Satan.

703. *Ambiguous* has three syllables: 'ambig-yus.'

707. *His name*: Satan's name, Lucifer. See 658 n.

708. *morning star*: Hesperus, the planet Venus, which in the morning appears to lead the stars from the sky. See "On the Morning of Christ's Nativity," stanza 6.

710. *third part*: "and [the dragon's] tail drew the third part of the stars of heaven, and did cast them to the earth" (Revelation 12:4). See 2.692.

714. *their*: the lamps'.

727–28. *Nor so content . . . right*: 'and not being content with having his own empire in the north (which he has not yet achieved), intends to fight us here.' That God says this *smiling* (line 718) shows that he holds Satan's plans in derision. See also the Son's reply at lines 735–37. That there is any real danger God does not for a moment suppose. Yet for dramatic purposes Milton must give the impression that some danger exists, that Satan's powers are real.

Let us advise and to this hazard draw
With speed what force is left and all employ
In our defense, lest unawares we lose
This our high place, our sanctuary, our hill."
   To whom the Son with calm aspéct and clear,
Lightning divine, ineffable, serene,
Made answer: "Mighty Father, thou thy foes
Justly hast in derision and, secure,
Laugh'st at their vain designs and tumults vain,
Matter to Me of glory whom their hate
Illústrates when they see all regal power
Giv'n Me to quell their pride and in event
Know whether I be dextrous to subdue
Thy rebels or be found the worst in Heav'n."
   So spake the Son. But Satan with his pow'rs
Far was advanced on wingèd speed, an host
Innumerable as the stars of night
Or stars of morning, dew-drops which the sun
Impearls on every leaf and every flower.
Regions they passed, the mighty regencies
Of seraphim and potentates and thrones
In their triple degrees, regions to which
All thy dominion, Adam, is no more
Than what this garden is to all the Earth
And all the sea from one entire globose
Stretched into longitude! Which having passed
At length into the limits of the north
They came and Satan to his royal seat
(High on a hill far blazing as a mount
Raised on a mount with pyramids and tow'rs
From diamond quarries hewn and rocks of gold)
The palace of great Lucifer (so call
That structure in the dialect of men
Interpreted) which not long after he
(Affecting all equality with God

729–32. There is an unavoidable contradiction between what God is as a character in a story and what God must be theologically. Is God truly worried about the safety of "our hill"? If he is worried, then he is not omnipotent. If he is not worried, then his irony (unlike, e.g., Gabriel's at 4.904–11) is unpleasant. The Son takes the latter view, that God is not worried, and the Son is, of course, theologically correct (5.735–37). But we cannot so easily dispel this apparition of a God who laughs at the weakness of his foes.

740. *in event*: when the issue is put to the test.

741. *be dextrous*: have the power (Latin *dextera* or *dextra*, "the right hand," metaphorically applied to military force).

753–54. *one entire globose . . . into longitude*: the sea from an entire globe (like this earth) stretched out flat.

754–71. Satan came to his royal seat, the palace of Lucifer. Not long after, Satan called it the Mountain of the Congregation.

In imitation of that mount whereon
Messiah was declared in sight of Heav'n)
The Mountain of the Congregation called;
For thither he assembled all his train
(Pretending so commanded to consult
About the great reception of their King
Thither to come) and with calumnious art
Of counterfeited truth thus held their ears:
"Thrones, Dominations, Princedoms, Virtues, Powers,
If these magnific titles yet remain
Not merely titular since by decree
Another now hath to himself engrossed
All power and us eclipsed under the name
Of King Anointed for whom all this haste
Of midnight march and hurried meeting here,
This only to consult how we may best
With what may be devised of honors new
Receive Him coming to receive from us
Knee-tribute yet unpaid—prostration vile!
Too much to one but double how endured,
To one and to His image now proclaimed!
But what if better counsels might erect
Our minds and teach us to cast off this yoke?
Will ye submit your necks and choose to bend
The supple knee? Ye will not if I trust
To know ye right or if ye know yourselves
Natives and sons of Heav'n possessed before
By none, and if not equal all, yet free,
Equally free, for orders and degrees
Jar not with liberty but well consist.
Who can in reason then or right assume
Monarchy over such as live by right
His equals if, in power and splendor less,
In freedom equal? Or can introduce
Law and edíct on us who without law
Err not, much less for this to be our lord

777. *King Anointed*: Messiah.

777–78. *for whom . . . meeting here*. This is a lie: Satan has commanded the haste, the march, and the meeting. See 754–71 n.

783–84. *one*: God the Father. *double*: the Father and the Son. *his image*: the Son.

792–97. Satan attempts to conceal a contradiction in what he says. Because he intends to preserve his ascendancy over the rebel angels, Satan says that hierarchy is not inconsistent with freedom. Yet he also says that it is unjust for the Son to assume monarchy over those who are his equals. Abdiel catches this contradiction at line 812.

796–98. I.e., 'Who can in reason impose laws and commands on us when we do nothing wrong, nothing such laws would forbid?' Cf. Adam's remark to Michael at 12.283: "So many laws argue so many sins."

797. *Or can*: the implied subject is *who*.

And look for adoration to th' abuse
Of those imperial titles which assert
Our being ordained to govern, not to serve?"
  Thus far his bold discourse without control
Had audience when among the seraphim
Abdiel (than whom none with more zeal adored
The Deity and divine commands obeyed)
Stood up and in a flame of zeal severe
The current of his fury thus opposed:
  "O argument blasphémous, false and proud!
Words which no ear ever to hear in Heav'n
Expected, least of all from thee, ingrate,
In place thyself so high above thy peers!
Canst thou with impious obloquy condemn
The just decree of God pronounced and sworn
That to His only Son by right endued
With regal scepter every soul in Heav'n
Shall bend the knee and in that honor due
Confess Him rightful King? Unjust thou say'st,
Flatly unjust, to bind with laws the free
And equal over equals to let reign,
One over all with unsucceeded pow'r.
Shalt thou give law to God, shalt thou dispute
With Him the points of liberty who made
Thee what thou art and formed the pow'rs of Heav'n
Such as He pleased and circumscribed their being?
Yet by experience taught we know how good
And of our good and of our dignity
How provident He is, how far from thought
To make us less, bent rather to exalt
Our happy state under one head more near
United. But to grant it thee unjust
That equal over equals monarch reign:
Thyself though great and glorious dost thou count,
Or all angelic nature joined in one,
Equal to him, begotten Son, by whom

800. *And look*: the implied subject is *who* and the implied auxiliary verb is *can*: 'who can look?'
802. *to govern, not to serve*: But this is not an either/or choice: the disjunction is false.
806. *Deity* has two syllables.
808. *his*: Satan's.
813. *obloquy*: abusive language.
821. *unsucceeded*: not supplanted by another, a successor, and not nearly approached by any other.
822–25. Romans 9:20: "Shall the thing formed say to him that formed it, Why hast thou made me thus?"
825. *circumscribed*: established the limits to.

As by His Word the mighty Father made
All things, ev'n thee, and all the spirits of Heav'n
By Him created in their bright degrees,
Crowned them with glory and to their glory named
Thrones, Dominations, Princedoms, Virtues, Powers,
Essential Powers, nor by His reign obscured
But more illustrious made since He, the Head,
One of our number thus reduced becomes,
His laws our laws: all honor to Him done
Returns our own. Cease then this impious rage
And tempt not these but hasten to appease
Th' incensèd Father and th' incensèd Son
While pardon may be found in time besought!"
  So spake the fervent angel but his zeal
None seconded as out of season judged
Or singular and rash, whereat rejoiced
Th' Apostate and more haughty thus replied:
"That we were formed then say'st thou? And the work
Of secondary hands by task transferred
From Father to His Son? Strange point and new!
Doctrine which we would know whence learnt: who saw
When this Creation was? Remember'st thou
Thy making while the Maker gave thee being?
We know no time when we were not as now,
Know none before us, self-begot, self-raised
By our own quick'ning power when fatal course
Had circled his full orb, the birth mature
Of this our native Heav'n, ethereal sons.
Our puissance is our own. Our own right hand
Shall teach us highest deeds by proof to try
Who is our equal. Then thou shalt behold
Whether by supplication we intend
Address and to begirt th' almighty throne
Beseeching or besieging! This report,
These tidings carry to th' Anointed King—
And fly, ere evil intercept thy flight!"
  He said, and as the sound of waters deep

841. *Essential*: constituting the very being of those powers.

853–63. With some justice Satan points out that there is no evidence for, because no angelic witness of, what Abdiel affirms: the Son's creation of the angels. But such evidence is by definition impossible to obtain: Abdiel cannot witness his own creation because he isn't there to be a witness until he is made, when it's too late. Satan's objection to Abdiel's statement recoils on his own: if direct witness is the only valid evidence, Satan can have no evidence for his claim about his own generation, *self-begot . . . By . . . quick'ning power*.

869. *Beseeching or besieging*: a rhetorical effect typical of Satan's ambiguous language: the two words sound almost identical but are opposite in meaning. Cf. *entertainment* (line 690).

Hoarse murmur echoed to his words applause
Through the infinite host. Nor less for that
The flaming seraph fearless though alone,
Encompassed round with foes, thus answered bold:
"O alienate from God! O spirit accurst,
Forsaken of all good! I see thy fall
Determined and thy hapless crew involved
In this perfidious fraud, contagion spread
Both of thy crime and punishment! Henceforth
No more be troubled how to quit the yoke
Of God's Messiah: those indulgent laws
Will not be now vouchsafed! Other decrees
Against thee are gone forth without recall.
That golden scepter which thou didst reject
Is now an iron rod to bruise and break
Thy disobedience. Well thou didst advise,
Yet not for thy advice or threats I fly
These wicked tents devoted, lest the wrath
Impendent raging into sudden flame
Distinguish not. For soon expect to feel
His thunder on thy head, devouring fire!
Then who created thee lamenting learn
When who can uncreate thee thou shalt know!"
So spake the seraph Abdiel faithful found
Among the faithless, faithful only he
Among innumerable false. Unmoved,
Unshaken, unseduced, unterrified
His loyalty he kept, his love, his zeal.
Nor number nor example with him wrought
To swerve from truth or change his constant mind
Though single. From amidst them forth he passed
Long way through hostile scorn which he sustained
Superior, nor of violence feared aught

880. *contagion*: Satan's fraud is like a disease that will be rapidly spread by the crimes to follow (rebellion against God, destruction of Man) and even by the punishment of those crimes.

884–88. Abdiel here speaks as a prophet. He has no direct information on what he says (*Other decrees / Against thee are gone forth*) but is inspired to knowledge.

887. *iron rod*: Psalm 2:9: "Thou shalt break them with a rod of iron; thou shalt dash them in pieces."

890. *wicked tents*: Moses' words to the Hebrews in the wilderness when rebellion rose among them: "Depart, I pray you, from the tents of these wicked men, and touch nothing of theirs, lest ye be consumed in all their sins" (Numbers 16:26). See Psalms (84:10): "I had rather be a doorkeeper in the house of my God than to dwell in the tents of wickedness."

901. *nor . . . nor*: neither . . . nor. Neither the quantity of those rebelling nor their example affected Abdiel's judgment.

903. *though single*: although he was alone.

905. *Superior* has three syllables. *violence* has three syllables. *feared* has one syllable.

And with retorted scorn his back he turned
On those proud tow'rs to swift destruction doomed.

Book Six

The Argument

Raphael continues to relate how Michael and Gabriel were sent forth to battle against Satan and his angels. The first fight described. Satan and his powers retire under night, he calls a council, invents devilish engines which in the second day's fight put Michael and his angels to some disorder. But they at length pulling up mountains overwhelmed both the force and machines of Satan. Yet the tumult not so ending, God on the third day sends Messiah his Son for whom He had reserved the glory of that victory. He in the power of his Father coming to the place and causing all His legions to stand still on either side, with His chariot and thunder driving into the midst of his enemies, pursues them unable to resist towards the wall of Heaven. Which opening, they leap down with horror and confusion into the place of punishment prepared for them in the deep. Messiah returns with triumph to his Father.

All night the dreadless angel unpursued
Through Heav'n's wide champaign held his way till Morn,
Waked by the circling Hours, with rosy hand
Unbarred the gates of light. There is a cave
Within the Mount of God fast by His throne
Where light and darkness in perpetual round
Lodge and dislodge by turns which makes through Heaven
Grateful vicissitude like day and night:
Light issues forth and at the other door
Obsequious darkness enters till her hour
To veil the Heav'n, though darkness there might well
Seem twilight here. And now went forth the Morn
Such as in highest Heav'n, arrayed in gold

906. *retorted*: Latin *retorqueo*, "to turn back, to throw back." This word can refer either to Abdiel's verbal response, which has been thrown back at Satan, or to Abdiel's physical gesture of turning his back in scorn, or to both. I incline to the latter without turning my back on the former.

907. *proud tow'rs*: one of the boldest metaphors in the epic. As Abdiel departs, the rebel angels are seen as gigantic, sinister towers, recalling the Tower of Babel (Genesis 11:1–9). See also 2 Peter 2:1 "false prophets [and] false teachers . . . who . . . bring upon themselves swift destruction." To Milton, false teaching is even worse than open war, to which it leads. Although the rebel angels will conduct an actual war against God, the root cause of their destruction is not that they rebel but that they succumb to Satan's false arguments.

Book Six

8. *Grateful vicissitude*: welcome change.

Empyreal. From before her vanished Night,
Shot through with orient beams, when all the plain,
Covered with thick embattled squadrons bright,
Chariots and flaming arms and fiery steeds
Reflecting blaze on blaze, first met his view.
War he perceived, war in procinct, and found
Already known what he for news had thought
To have reported. Gladly then he mixed
Among those friendly pow'rs who him received
With joy and acclamations loud, that one
That of so many myriads fall'n—yet one!—
Returned not lost. Onto the sacred hill
They led him high applauded and present
Before the Seat Supreme, from whence a Voice
From midst a golden cloud thus mild was heard:
"Servant of God, well done, well hast thou fought
The better fight, who single hast maintained
Against revolted multitudes the cause
Of truth, in word mightier than they in arms,
And for the testimony of truth hast borne
Universal reproach, far worse to bear
Than violence. For this was all thy care:
To stand approved in sight of God though worlds
Judged thee perverse. The easier conquest now
Remains thee, aided by this host of friends:
Back on thy foes more glorious to return
Than scorned thou didst depart and to subdue
By force who reason for their law refuse,
Right reason for their law and for their King
Messiah who by right of merit reigns.
Go, Michael, of celestial armies prince
And thou in military prowess next,
Gabriel, lead forth to battle these my sons
Invincible, lead forth my armèd saints
By thousands and by millions ranged for fight
Equal in number to that godless crew
Rebellious! Them with fire and hostile arms
Fearless assault and to the brow of Heaven
Pursuing drive them out from God and bliss
Into their place of punishment, the gulf
Of Tartarus which ready opens wide

18. *his*: Abdiel's.
19. *in procinct*: Latin *in procinctus*, girded up in readiness for battle.
32. *mightier* has two syllables.
41. *their*: the rebel angels'.

His fiery chaos to receive their fall!"
  So spake the Sov'reign Voice and clouds began
To darken all the hill and smoke to roll
In dusky wreaths, reluctant flames, the sign
Of wrath awaked. Nor with less dread the loud
Ethereal trumpet from on high gan blow,
At which command the powers militant
That stood for Heav'n, in mighty quadrate joined
Of union irresistible, moved on
In silence their bright legions to the sound
Of instrumental harmony that breathed
Heroic ardor to advent'rous deeds
Under their godlike leaders in the cause
Of God and His Messiah. On they move
Indíssolubly firm, nor obvious hill,
Nor strait'ning vale, nor wood nor stream divides
Their perfect ranks. For high above the ground
Their march was and the passive air upbore
Their nimble tread as when the total kind
Of birds in orderly array on wing
Came summoned over Eden to receive
Their names of thee. So over many a tract
Of Heav'n they marched and many a province wide
Tenfold the length of this terrene. At last
Far in th' horizon to the north appeared
From skirt to skirt a fiery region stretched
In battailous aspéct and, nearer view,
Bristled with upright beams innumerable
Of rigid spears and helmets thronged and shields
Various with boastful argument portrayed,
The banded powers of Satan hasting on
With furious expedition. For they weened
That selfsame day by fight or by surprise
To win the Mount of God and on His throne
To set the envier of His state, the proud

58. *reluctant*: Latin *reluceo*, "to blaze, shine, glow," as in Livy, "relucens flamma," but also the Latin deponent verb *reluctor*, "to struggle against," i.e., the brightness of the flames struggles against the darkness of the smoke. Cf. 2.337.

60. *gan*: began.

62. *quadrate*: square, a Roman formation.

64. The angels advance silently to martial music, like Homer's Achaeans in contrast to the Trojans and their confederates, who advance making a loud noise, like flocks of cranes (*Iliad* 3.1–9).

69. *obvious* has two syllables.

76. *thee*: Adam, to whom Raphael is speaking.

78. *this terrene*: this earth. I.e., The provinces of Heaven which the angels cross are ten times wider than this earth.

80. *from skirt to skirt*: from one edge to the other.

Aspirer, but their thoughts proved fond and vain
In the mid way, though strange to us it seemed
At first that angel should with angel war
And in fierce hosting meet who wont to meet
So oft in festivals of joy and love
Unanimous as sons of one great Sire,
Hymning th' Eternal Father. But the shout
Of battle now began and rushing sound
Of onset ended soon each milder thought.
High in the midst exalted as a god
Th' Apostate in his sun-bright chariot sat,
Idol of majesty divine, enclosed
With flaming cherubim and golden shields,
Then lighted from his gorgeous throne, for now
'Twixt host and host but narrow space was left,
A dreadful interval, and front to front
Presented stood in terrible array
Of hideous length. Before the cloudy van
On the rough edge of battle ere it joined
Satan, with vast and haughty strides advanced,
Came tow'ring armed in adamant and gold.
Abdiel that sight endured not where he stood
Among the mightiest bent on highest deeds
And thus his own undaunted heart explores:
  "O Heav'n! That such resemblance of the Highest
Should yet remain where faith and fealty
Remain not! Wherefore should not strength and might
There fail where virtue fails or weakest prove
Where boldest, though to sight unconqu'rable?
His puissance, trusting in th' Almighty's aid,
I mean to try whose reason I have tried
Unsound and false. Nor is it aught but just
That he who in debate of truth hath won
Should win in arms, in both disputes alike
Victor, though brutish that contést and foul
When reason hath to deal with force, yet so
Most reason is that reason overcome."

91. *mid way*: The rebel angels' intentions proved to be empty before their attempt to fulfill those intentions was half complete.

93. *hosting*: as in *hostile*, playing on the ambiguity in many languages, e.g., Old English (*gæst*) and Latin (*hospes*), by which the same word is used for *enemy*, *guest*, and *host*. See also the archaic word for an army, *host*, line 104. *wont*: were accustomed.

100. *Apostate*: Satan, "he who stands apart."

113. *explores*: pours forth.

119. *His*: Satan's.

120–26. Abdiel is saying, since conflict in arms is inferior to conflict by reason, he who wins by force of reason should also win by force of arms.

So pondering and from his armèd peers
Forth stepping opposite half way he met
His daring foe, at this prevention more
Incensed, and thus securely him defied:
"Proud, art thou met? Thy hope was to have reached
The heighth of thy aspiring unopposed,
The Throne of God unguarded and His side
Abandoned at the terror of thy power
Or potent tongue. Fool! Not to think how vain
Against th' Omnipotent to rise in arms
Who out of smallest things could without end
Have raised incessant armies to defeat
Thy folly or with solitary hand,
Reaching beyond all limit, at one blow
Unaided could have finished thee and whelmed
Thy legions under darkness! But thou seest
All are not of thy train: there be who faith
Prefer and piety to God though then
To thee not visible when I alone
Seemed in thy world erroneous to dissent
From all. My sect thou seest: now learn too late
How few sometimes may know when thousands err!"
Whom the grand Foe with scornful eye askance
Thus answered: "Ill for thee, but in wished hour
Of my revenge first sought, for thou return'st
From flight, seditious angel, to receive
Thy merited reward, the first assay
Of this right hand provoked since first that tongue
Inspired with contradiction durst oppose
A third part of the gods in synod met
Their deities to assert who while they feel
Vigor divine within them can allow
Omnipotence to none! But well thou com'st
Before thy fellows ámbitious to win
From me some plume that thy success may show
Destruction to the rest. This pause between
(Unanswered lest thou boast) to let thee know:

129. *prevention*: coming foremost, beforehand. Abdiel is incensed at Satan's boldness in stepping forward between the armies before the fight begins.

147. *sect*: adherents to a party or a cause, especially, in Milton's day, in religion.

150–56. I.e., That you should be the first enemy I meet is unlucky for you, Abdiel, but happy for me, for I will punish you for daring to contradict me and my confederates during our meeting last night.

160. *ámbitious* is an adverb modifying *com'st* (line 159), not an adjective modifying *fellows*. Abdiel comes ambitious for success.

At first I thought that liberty and Heaven
To heav'nly souls had been all one but now
I see that most through sloth had rather serve,
Minist'ring spirits trained up in feast and song.
Such hast thou armed—the minstrelsy of Heaven!—
Servility with freedom to contend,
As both their deeds compared this day shall prove."
  To whom in brief thus Abdiel stern replied:
"Apostate, still thou err'st nor end wilt find
Of erring, from the path of truth remote!
Unjustly thou deprav'st it with the name
Of servitude to serve whom God ordains
Or Nature: God and Nature bid the same
When he who rules is worthiest and excels
Them whom he governs. This is servitude:
To serve th' unwise or him who hath rebelled
Against his worthier as thine now serve thee,
Thyself not free but to thyself enthralled,
Yet lewdly dar'st our minist'ring upbraid.
Reign thou in Hell thy kingdom, let me serve
In Heav'n God ever blest and His divine
Behests obey, worthiest to be obeyed.
Yet chains in Hell, not realms, expect! Meanwhile
From me returned, as erst thou saidst, from flight,
This greeting on thy impious crest receive!"
  So saying, a noble stoke he lifted high
Which hung not but so swift with tempest fell
On the proud crest of Satan that no sight
Nor motion of swift thought (less could his shield)
Such ruin intercept. Ten paces huge
He back recoiled, the tenth on bended knee
His massy spear upstayed, as if on Earth
Winds under ground or waters forcing way
Sidelong had pushed a mountain from his seat
Half sunk with all his pines. Amazement seized
The rebel thrones but greater rage to see
Thus foiled their mightiest. Ours joy filled and shout,
Presage of victory and fierce desire
Of battle, whereat Michaël bid sound

164–70. I.e., I once thought that for angels freedom and being in Heaven were one and the same. Now I see that for some angels Heaven is making music (and eating feasts) to flatter God. These are the sort you have now placed in arms—musicians, not soldiers! You have armed them for the war between the cause of servility, which you champion, and the cause of freedom, which we champion: we shall see today which cause makes better fighters.

177. *He*: God, although the principle expressed is a general one: it is only natural that the best should govern.

Th' archangel trumpet. Through the vast of Heav'n
It sounded and the faithful armies rung
Hosanna to the Highest. Nor stood at gaze
Th' adverse legions nor less hideous joined
The horrid shock. Now storming fury rose
And clamor such as heard in Heav'n till now
Was never: arms on armor clashing brayed
Horrible discord and the madding wheels
Of brazen chariots raged. Dire was the noise
Of conflict. Overhead the dismal hiss
Of fiery darts in flaming volleys flew
And flying vaulted either host with fire.
So under fiery cope together rushed
Both battles main with ruinous assault
And inextinguishable rage. All Heav'n
Resounded and had earth been then, all earth
Had to her center shook. What wonder? When
Millions of fierce encount'ring angels fought
On either side the least of whom could wield
These elements and arm him with the force
Of all their regions. How much more of power
Army against army numberless to raise
Dreadful combustion warring and disturb,
Though not destroy, their happy native seat,
Had not th' Eternal King Omnipotent
From His stronghóld of Heav'n high overruled
And limited their might, though numbered such
As each divided legion might have seemed
A num'rous host, in strength each armèd hand
A legion. Led in fight, yet leader seemed
Each warrior, single as in chief, expért
When to advance or stand or turn the sway
Of battle, open when and when to close
The ridges of grim war: no thought of flight,
None of retreat, no unbecoming deed
That argued fear. Each on himself relied
As only in his arm the moment lay
Of victory. Deeds of eternal fame
Were done, but infinite, for wide was spread
That war and various. Sometimes on firm ground
A standing fight, then soaring on main wing
Tormented all the air: all air seemed then

210. *madding*: whirling, furious, maddening.
221–23. Even the least of the angels could wield the elements of the cosmos, such as stars, for weapons.

Conflicting fire. Long time in even scale
The battle hung till Satan, who that day
Prodigious power had shown and met in arms
No equal, ranging through the dire attack
Of fighting seraphim confused at length,
Saw where the sword of Michael smote and felled
Squadrons at once with huge two-handed sway:
Brandished aloft the horrid edge came down
Wide wasting. Such destruction to withstand
He hasted and opposed the rocky orb
Of tenfold adamant, his ample shield,
A vast circumference. At his approach
The great archangel from his warlike toil
Surceased and glad as hoping here to end
Intestine war in Heav'n, th' arch-foe subdued
Or captive dragged in chains, with hostile frown
And visage all inflamed first thus began:
"Author of evil unknown till thy revolt,
Unnamed in Heav'n, now plenteous, as thou seest:
These acts of hateful strife, hateful to all
Though heaviest by just measure on thyself
And thy adherents. How hast thou disturbed
Heav'n's blessèd peace and into nature brought
Misery uncreated till the crime
Of thy rebellion! How hast thou instilled
Thy malice into thousands once upright
And faithful, now proved false! But think not here
To trouble holy rest: Heav'n casts thee out
From all her confines. Heav'n the seat of bliss
Brooks not the works of violence and war.
Hence then, and evil go with thee along,
Thy offspring, to the place of evil, Hell,
Thou and thy wicked crew! There mingle broils
Ere this avenging sword begin thy doom
Or some more sudden vengeance winged from God
Precipitate thee with augmented pain!"
So spake the Prince of Angels. To whom thus
The Adversary: "Nor think thou with wind
Of airy threats to awe whom yet with deeds
Thou canst not! Hast thou turned the least of these
To flight or, if to fall, but that they rise

254. *He*: Satan. *rocky orb*: Satan's shield, made of adamant; see 1.48.
262. *evil* has one syllable.
263. The subject of *Unnamed* and *plenteous* is *evil*.

Unvanquished, easier to transact with me
That thou shouldst hope, imperious, and with threats
To chase me hence? Err not that so shall end
The strife which thou call'st evil but we style
The strife of glory, which we mean to win
Or turn this Heav'n itself into the Hell
Thou fablest, here however to dwell free,
If not to reign. Meanwhile thy utmost force—
And join Him named Almighty to thy aid—
I fly not but have sought thee far and nigh."
  They ended parley and both addressed for fight
Unspeakable. For who though with the tongue
Of angels can relate or to what things
Liken on Earth conspicuous that may lift
Human imagination to such heighth
Of godlike pow'r! For likest gods they seemed,
Stood they or moved, in stature, motion, arms,
Fit to decide the empire of great Heaven.
Now waved their fiery swords and in the air
Made horrid circles. Two broad suns their shields
Blazed opposite while Expectation stood
In horror. From each hand with speed retired
Where erst was thickest fight th' angelic throng
And left large field, unsafe within the wind
Of such commotion, such as (to set forth
Great things by small) if, nature's concord broke,
Among the constellations war were sprung,
Two planets rushing from aspéct malign
Of fiercest opposition in mid sky
Should combat and their jarring spheres confound.
Together both with next t' almighty arm
Uplifted imminent one stroke they aimed
That might determine and not need repeat
As not of power at once, nor odds appeared
In might or swift prevention. But the sword
Of Michael from the armory of God
Was giv'n him tempered so that neither keen
Nor solid might resist that edge. It met

286. *easier to transact with me*: do you think it easier to fight me?
289. *style*: call; literally "write" (Latin *stilus*, "pen").
296. *parley*: discussion or negotiation before battle (like most military terms, French). Elided with *and*. *addressed*: prepared.
310–15. The syntax of the two complete clauses—*war were sprung* and *planets should combat*—will be clearer if one imagines an *or* between them.
319. *As not of power at once*: as not having any power if not victorious in one stroke.
323. *It*: the sword's edge.

The sword of Satan with steep force to smite
Descending and in half cut sheer, nor stayed
But with swift wheel reverse deep ent'ring sheared
All his right side. Then Satan first knew pain
And writhed him to and fro convolved, so sore
The griding sword with discontinuous wound
Passed through him. But th' ethereal substance closed,
Not long divisible, and from the gash
A stream of nectarous humor issuing flowed
Sanguine, such as celestial spirits may bleed,
And all his armor stained, erewhile so bright.
Forthwith on all sides to his aid was run
By angels many and strong who interposed
Defense while others bore him on their shields
Back to his chariot where it stood retired
From off the files of war. There they him laid
Gnashing for anguish and despite and shame
To find himself not matchless and his pride
Humbled by such rebuke so far beneath
His confidence to equal God in power.
Yet soon he healed, for spirits that live throughout
Vital in every part—not as frail man
In entrails, heart or head, liver or reins—
Cannot but by annihilating die
Nor in their liquid texture mortal wound
Receive no more than can the fluid air:
All heart they live, all head, all eye, all ear,
All intellect, all sense, and as they please
They limn themselves and color, shape or size

325–27. With a downstroke Michael cuts Satan's sword in half. Then with an upstroke, he cuts open Satan's right side.

329. *discontinuous*: breaking the unity of the body.

332. *nectarous humor*: the blood of angels, from Homeric *ichor*, the blood of the gods, and *nectar*, the drink of the gods. *Nectarous* and *issuing* have each two syllables.

333. *Sanguine*: blood red.

344–53. Spiritual beings are material, and *Vital*, but they are not *organic* in the sense of having parts specialized for various functions, such as seeing. All functions are performable everywhere in them. They can, moreover, alter their entire appearance into any form they choose: *They limn themselves*. They are like *liquid* in being able to take any shape. But spiritual beings are like *air* in being able to be compressed into small space or spread out thinly over a large area: *condense* or *rare*.

346. *reins*: kidneys.

352. *limn*, an emendation of *limb* (1667, 1674; Shawcross, 2002, p. 392). The angels can refashion their total appearance, as when a pliable substance is modeled. Milton uses the word in this sense in *Reason of Church Government* (*YP* 1.777–78) when he speaks of the prelates, who would "frame of their own heads as it were with wax a kinde of Mimic Bishop limm'd out to the life." The primary sense of *limn* is from painting, but its broader, metaphorical sense, "to bring to life and to refashion by conscious art," was current, as when Thomas Nashe speaks of the essence of writing being the ability "with life and spirit to limn deadness itself" (*Four Letters Confuted*, in *Works*, ed. McKerrow and Wilson, 1958, I.282.33).

Assume as likes them best, condense or rare.
   Meanwhile in other parts like deeds deserved
Memorial: where the might of Gabriel fought
And with fierce ensigns pierced the deep array
Of Moloch furious king who him defied
And at his chariot wheels to drag him bound
Threatened, nor from the Holy One of Heaven
Refrained his tongue blasphémous, but anon
Down cloven to the waist with shattered arms
And uncouth pain fled bellowing. On each wing
Uriel and Raphael his vaunting foe—
Though huge and in a rock of diamond armed—
Vanquished Adramelech and Asmadai,
Two potent thrones that to be less than gods
Disdained but meaner thoughts learned in their flight,
Mangled with ghastly wounds through plate and mail.
Nor stood unmindful Abdiel to annoy
The atheist crew but with redoubled blow
Ariel and Arioch and the violence
Of Ramiel, scorched and blasted, overthrew.
I might relate of thousands and their names
Eternize here on Earth but those elect
Angels, contented with their fame in Heaven,
Seek not the praise of men. The other sort,
In might though wondrous and in acts of war,
Nor of renown less eager, yet by doom
Cancelled from Heav'n and sacred memory,
Nameless in dark oblivion let them dwell.
For strength, from truth divided and from just,
Illaudable, naught merits but dispraise
And ignominy, yet to glory aspires
Vainglorious and through infamy seeks fame:
Therefore eternal silence be their doom.
   And now their mightiest quelled, the battle swerved

356. *ensigns*: military banners. Gabriel's powers, marked by their several banners, cut through Moloch's troop formations.
358. *chariot wheels*: In the *Iliad*, Achilles drags the dead Hector behind his chariot.
360. *anon*: soon.
363–65. Uriel and Raphael each vanquished his vaunting foe: Uriel beat Adramelech and Raphael beat Asmadai.
369. *Abdiel* has two syllables.
376. *other sort*: the rebel angels, now devils in Hell.
382. *Illaudable*: unworthy of praise, a predicate of *strength*. I.e., strength divided from truth and justice merits no praise.
383. *glory* and *aspires* are elided (*ignominy* and *yet* are not).
386. *Their*: the devils'.
386–99. This passage contrasts the disarray of the rebel angels' formations, and their shameful flight, with the aggressive order of the faithful angels' army.

With many an inroad gored. Deformèd rout
Entered and foul disorder. All the ground
With shivered armor strewn and on a heap
Chariot and charioteer lay overturned
And fiery foaming steeds. What stood, recoiled
O'er-wearied, through the faint Satanic host
Defensive scarce or with pale fear surprised,
Then first with fear surprised and sense of pain
Fled ignominious, to such evil brought
By sin of disobedience, till that hour
Not liable to fear or flight or pain.
Far otherwise th' inviolable saints
In cubic phalanx firm advanced entire,
Invulnerable, impenetrably armed,
Such high advantages their innocence
Gave them above their foes not to have sinned,
Not to have disobeyed. In fight they stood
Unwearied, unobnoxious to be pained
By wound though from their place by violence moved.
Now Night her course began and over Heaven
Inducing darkness grateful truce imposed
And silence on the odious din of war.
Under her cloudy covert both retired,
Victor and vanquished. On the foughten field
Michaël and his angels prevalent
Encamping placed in guard their watches round,
Cherubic waving fires. On th' other part
Satan with his rebellious disappeared
Far in the dark, dislodged and void of rest,

387–88. *inroad*: area into which the faithful angels have penetrated the rebel angels' formations, as a bull gores with its horns. *Rout*: defeat, causing deformity and disorder in the rebel angels' formations.

391–97. *What stood*: those rebel angels left standing fled, exhausted, through the troops behind them. And even these troops, who had not yet been in the battle, were scarcely able to mount any defense, being surprised with fear. For their sin of disobedience to God, giving them guilty consciences, makes them susceptible to fear.

395. *Ignominious*: four syllables, 'ignomin-yus.'

398. *inviolable*: five syllables, "th' inviolable."

399 *cubic*: because angels are airborne when they fight, their military formations can improve by one dimension on the Roman square, or *quadrate* (see line 62 and n.). *phalanx*: an ancient Greek formation of heavily armed, closely ranked infantry. Cf. 1.549–55 and n.

400 *Invulnerable*: four syllables (dropping the last): 'invulnerab.' *Impenetrably*: five syllables.

404. *Unobnoxious*: unable. The faithful angels experience the force (*violence*) of blows but not the pain such blows cause the rebel angels.

409. *her*: Night's.

414–16. The principal verb following *Satan* is *called*, not *disappeared*. The force of *disappeared* is adjectival. I.e., Satan, having disappeared into the dark with his rebellious troops, called his potentates. It is possible, however, that Milton intends the reader first to take *disappeared* as the main verb ("Satan disappeared") and then to take *called* as the main verb ("Satan called"), thus condensing two actions into one sentence.

His potentates to council called by night
And in the midst thus undismayed began:
"O now in danger tried, now known in arms
Not to be overpow'red, companions dear,
Found worthy not of liberty alone,
Too mean pretense, but what we more affect,
Honor, dominion, glory and renown
Who have sustained one day in doubtful fight
(And if one day, why not eternal days?)
What Heaven's Lord had pow'rfullest to send
Against us from about His throne and judged
Sufficient to subdue us to His will,
But proves not so! Then fallible it seems
Of future we may deem Him though till now
Omniscient thought. True is, less firmly armed,
Some disadvantage we endured and pain
Till now not known, but known as soon contemned
Since now we find this our empyreal form
Incapable of mortal injury,
Imperishable, and though pierced with wound
Soon closing and by native vigor healed.
Of evil then so small as easy think
The remedy! Perhaps more valid arms,
Weapons more violent when next we meet,
May serve to better us and worse our foes
Or equal what between us made the odds—
In nature none. If other hidden cause
Left them superior, while we can preserve
Unhurt our minds and understanding sound,
Due search and consultation will disclose."
He sat and in th' assembly next upstood
Nisroch of principalities the prime.
As one he stood escaped from cruel fight
Sore toiled, his riven arms to havoc hewn
And cloudy in aspéct, thus answering spake:
"Deliv'rer from new lords, leader to free
Enjoyment of our right as gods, yet hard

428–29. *fallible . . . of future*: because God couldn't predict our having survived today, He is shown to be capable of error.
432. *contemned*: despised.
433. *empyreal*: of the sky, the empyrean. Three syllables: 'empir-yal.'
439. *when next we meet*: when our armies fight next.
441–42. *what between us made the odds in nature none*: whatever it was that gave them the advantage today, since they don't have any natural advantage over us.
451. *new lords*: referring to the Son, whose proclamation as the angels' "Lord" occasioned the rebellion. Nisroch makes it seem as if many lords, rather than one, have been placed over the angels.

For gods and too unequal work we find
Against unequal arms to fight in pain
Against unpained, impassive, from which evil
Ruin must needs ensue. For what avails
Valor or strength, though matchless, quelled with pain
Which all subdues and makes remiss the hands
Of mightiest? Sense of pleasure we may well
Spare out of life perhaps and not repine
But live content, which is the calmest life.
But pain is perfect misery, the worst
Of evils, and, excessive, overturns
All patience. He who therefore can invent
With what more forcible we may offend
Our yet unwounded enemies or arm
Ourselves with like defense to me deserves
No less than for deliverance what we owe."
  Whereto with look composed Satan replied:
"Not uninvented that which thou aright
Believ'st so main to our success I bring.
Which of us who beholds the bright surface
Of this ethereous mold whereon we stand,
This continent of spacious Heav'n adorned
With plant, fruit, flow'r ambrosial, gems and gold,
Whose eye so superficially surveys
These things as not to mind from whence they grow
Deep under ground, materials dark and crude
Of spiritous and fiery spume, till touched
With Heaven's ray and tempered they shoot forth
So beauteous, op'ning to the ambient light?
These in their dark nativity the deep
Shall yield us pregnant with infernal flame
Which into hollow engines long and round
Thick-rammed, at th' other bore with touch of fire
Dilated and infuriate shall send forth
From far with thund'ring noise among our foes
Such implements of mischief as shall dash
To pieces and o'erwhelm whatever stands

458. *remiss*: slack, slow, incapable of action.
459–60. The first indication that the rebel angels can no longer experience pleasure.
482. *These*: the fiery spirits (related to asphalt) underground, which the sun warms gently, causing plants to grow. Satan proposes to mine them and make them into gunpowder for cannon.
482–91. The cannon, invented in the Renaissance, was widely regarded as a diabolic invention and as marking the end of chivalric martial values. See Ariosto's *Orlando Furioso* 9.91, where the paragon of chivalric martial valor, Orlando, delivers an oration against the cannon and sinks one in the ocean.
486. *Dilated*: expanding with explosive force.

Adverse, that they shall fear we have disarmed
The Thund'rer of His only dreaded bolt.
Nor long shall be our labor yet: ere dawn
Effect shall end our wish. Meanwhile, revive!
Abandon fear! To strength and counsel joined
Think nothing hard, much less to be despaired!"
  He ended, and his words their drooping cheer
Enlightened and their languished hope revived.
Th' invention all admired and each how he
To be th' inventor missed, so easy it seemed
Once found which yet unfound most would have thought
Impossible. Yet haply of thy race
In future days if malice should abound
Someone intent on mischief or inspired
With dev'lish machination might devise
Like instrument to plague the sons of men
For sin, on war and mutual slaughter bent.
  Forthwith from council to the work they flew:
None arguing stood! Innumerable hands
Were ready. In a moment up they turned
Wide the celestial soil and saw beneath
Th' originals of nature in their crude
Conception: sulfurous and nitrous foam
They found, they mingled, and with subtle art
Concocted and adusted they reduced
To blackest grain and into store conveyed.
Part hidden veins digged up (nor hath this Earth
Entrails unlike) of mineral and stone
Whereof to found their engines and their balls
Of missive ruin, part incentive reed
Provide pernicious with one touch to fire.
So all ere day-spring under conscious night
Secret they finished and in order set
With silent circumspection unespied.
  Now when fair morn orient in Heav'n appeared

493. *Effect*: comes about, arrives (Latin *efficio*).
496. *their*: the rebel angels'.
499. *easy* and *it* are elided.
501. *thy*: Adam's. Raphael now speculates on the future of the human race, should it fall into sin: someone will invent a weapon like the cannon.
516–19. *Part . . . part*: "some [do this] . . . some [do that]," a Virgilianism.
518. *engines*: "ingenious constructions," here cannons.
519. *missive*: missile. *incentive*: flammable. A tar-soaked reed is used to ignite the charge in the cannon.
521. *day-spring*: dawn. *conscious night*: night witnessing their work, an expression from Ovid, *Metamorphoses* 13.15: "of which night alone is witness" (*quorum nox conscia sola est*).
524. *orient* has two syllables: 'or-yént.'

Up rose the victor angels and to arms
The matin trumpet sung. In arms they stood
Of golden panoply, refulgent host
Soon banded. Others from the dawning hills
Looked round and scouts each coast light-armèd scour,
Each quarter, to descry the distant foe
Where lodged or whither fled or if for fight
In motion or in halt. Him soon they met
Under spread ensigns moving nigh in slow
But firm battalion. Back with speediest sail
Zophiel of Cherubim the swiftest wing
Came flying and in mid air aloud thus cried:
"Arm, warriors, arm for fight! The foe at hand
Whom fled we thought will save us long pursuit
This day. Fear not his flight! So thick a cloud
He comes and settled in his face I see
Sad resolution and secure. Let each
His adamantine coat gird well and each
Fit well his helm, grip fast his orbèd shield
Borne ev'n or high! For this day will pour down,
If I conjecture aught, no drizzling show'r
But rattling storm of arrows barbed with fire!"
So warned he them aware themselves and soon
In order, quit of all impediment,
Instant without disturb they took alarm
And onward move embattled when, behold!
Not distant far with heavy pace the foe
Approaching gross and huge in hollow cube
Training his dev'lish engin'ry impaled
On every side with shadowing squadrons deep
To hide the fraud. At interview both stood
A while but suddenly at head appeared
Satan and thus was heard commanding loud:

525. *victor angels*: the army of the faithful angels.
532. *Him*: the enemy army, the rebel angels.
535. *Zophiel* has two syllables: 'zoph-yel.'
541. *sad*: sober, grim.
544. *ev'n or high*: held directly in front (even) or over the head, to protect against missiles. In the Roman formation, the *testudo* (tortoise), shields were held overhead by tightly packed formations, making a roof against missiles.
548. *impediment*: military baggage and supplies, a term much used in Caesar's accounts of his wars.
552. *hollow cube*: a formation imitating the *cubic phalanx* (line 399) of the faithful angels, but hollow within, where the cannons are concealed.
553. *impaled*: surrounded, as by a fence, with troops.
554. *shadowing* has two syllables: 'shad-wing.'
555. *interview*: within sight of each other.

"Vanguard to right and left the front unfold
That all may see who hate us how we seek
Peace and composure and with open breast
Stand ready to receive them if they like
Our overture and turn not back perverse!
But that I doubt. However, witness Heaven,
Heav'n witness thou anon while we discharge
Freely our part! Ye who appointed stand
Do as ye have in charge and briefly touch
What we propound—and loud, that all may hear!"
So scoffing in ambiguous words he scarce
Had ended when to right and left the front
Divided and to either flank retired,
Which to our eyes discovered new and strange,
A triple-mounted row of pillars laid
On wheels (for like to pillars most they seemed
Or hollowed bodies made of oak or fir
With branches lopped in wood or mountain felled),
Brass, iron, stony mold, had not their mouths
With hideous orifice gaped on us wide,
Portending hollow truce. At each behind
A seraph stood and in his hand a reed
Stood waving tipped with fire while we suspense
Collected stood within our thoughts amused
Not long, for sudden all at once their reeds
Put forth and to a narrow vent applied
With nicest touch. Immediate in a flame,
But soon obscured with smoke, all Heav'n appeared
From those deep-throated engines belched, whose roar
Embowelled with outrageous noise the air

558. *Vanguard*: advance guard, or front rank, of an army.

559–67. *how we seek peace . . . overture . . . turn not back . . . discharge . . . touch . . . propound . . . loud*: with somewhat laborious irony, Satan speaks the language of negotiation and peace while his meaning is violent. The rebel angels seek peace, but peace by victory, via cannon. Their opening bombardment is an *overture*, though not to negotiation but to battle. If the faithful angels like this overture, they will not *turn back* (i.e., be driven back) by cannon balls. The rebel angels will *discharge* not their part in a negotiation but their cannons. The rebel angels' artillery officers are told to *briefly touch* not on the conditions for peace but to touch, with their flaming reeds, the fuses at the bases of the cannons. What the rebel angels *propound* (Latin, "to put forward") is not the terms of peace but a hail of cannonballs, and these propositions will be *loud*. See Landor (p. 396).

571. *our*: Raphael was among the armies of the faithful angels and a participant in the events he describes. The plural possessive pronoun reminds us of this fact, since Raphael, being like the other angels "contented with [his] fame in Heav'n" (line 375), will recount none of his own deeds in the war.

578. *hollow truce*: Raphael here catches the infection of Satan's verbal play. The cannons are literally hollow, like the truce Satan speaks of.

581. *amused*: puzzled.

585. *all Heav'n appeared*: an angelic version of the expression "all Hell broke loose."

And all her entrails tore disgorging foul
Their dev'lish glut: chained thunderbolts and hail
Of iron globes which on the victor host
Leveled with such impetuous fury smote
That whom they hit none on their feet might stand
Though standing else as rocks. But down they fell
By thousands, angel on archangel rolled
The sooner for their arms. Unarmed they might
Have easily as spirits evaded swift
By quick contraction or remove but now
Foul dissipation followed and forced rout—
Nor served it to relax their serried files!
What should they do? If on they rushed repulse
Repeated and indecent overthrow
Doubled would render them yet more despised
And to their foes a laughter, for in view
Stood ranked of seraphim another row
In posture to displode their second tire
Of thunder. Back defeated to return
They worse abhorred. Satan beheld their plight
And to his mates thus in derision called:
"O friends! why come not on these victors proud?
Erewhile they fierce were coming and when we
To entertain them fair with open front
And breast (what could we more?) propounded terms
Of composition, straight they changed their minds,
Flew off, and into strange vagaries fell
As they would dance! Yet for a dance they seemed
Somewhat extravagant and wild, perhaps
For joy of offered peace. But I suppose
If our proposals once again were heard
We should compel them to a quick result!"
To whom thus Belial in like gamesome mood:
"Leader, the terms we sent were terms of weight,

589. *glut*: contents of the cannons. *chained*: an allusion to chain shot: missiles joined by chains so as to cut a swath through the enemy's formations.

598. *dissipation*: scattering.

599. *relax their serried files*: allow the ranks of the faithful angels to spread out, thus presenting a less concentrated target to the rebel angels' artillery. This is another shaft of angelic wit.

604. *seraphim*: rebel seraphim, not the faithful ones.

605. *displode*: explode, fire. *Tire*: volley.

614. *vagaries*: wanderings.

621–27. Belial continues Satan's jest, comparing the artillery assault to a verbal statement of terms of truce. The terms were hard to understand and forcefully presented. The terms therefore confused (*amused*) their recipients and caused many to misconstrue them (*stumbled many*). Whoever correctly understands the terms of truce (i.e., *receives* a direct hit)

Of hard conténts and full of force urged home
Such as we might perceive amused them all
And stumbled many. Who receives them right
Had need from head to foot well understand.
Not understood, this gift they have besides:
They show us when our foes walk not upright."
   So they among themselves in pleasant vein
Stood scoffing, heightened in their thoughts beyond
All doubt of victory. Eternal Might
To match with their inventions they presumed
So easy and of His thunder made a scorn
And all His host derided while they stood
Awhile in trouble. But they stood not long.
Rage prompted them at length and found them arms
Against such hellish mischief fit t' oppose.
Forthwith—behold the excellence, the power
Which God hath in His mighty angels placed!—
Their arms away they threw and to the hills
(For Earth hath this variety from Heaven,
Of pleasure situate in hill and dale)
Light as the lightning glimpse they ran, they flew:
From their foundations loos'ning to and fro
They plucked the seated hills with all their load,
Rocks, waters, woods, and by the shaggy tops
Uplifting bore them in their hands. Amaze,
Be sure, and terror seized the rebel host
When coming tówards them so dread they saw
The bottom of the mountains upward turned
Till on those cursèd engines' triple row
They saw them whelmed and all their confidence
Under the weight of mountains buried deep,
Themselves invaded next and on their heads
Main promontories flung which in the air
Came shadowing and oppressed whole legions armed.
Their armor helped their harm, crushed in and bruised
Into their substance pent which wrought them pain
Implacable and many a dolorous groan

must understand them from beginning to end (*from head to foot*). Then he will *well understand* (i.e., be overthrown and no longer stand). The truce terms have, however, another benefit for us. When the terms are not understood, they show us when our foes are not dealing honestly with us (*walk not upright*) in negotiation—for they have fallen down.

632. *easy* and *and* are elided.

640. The pleasant variety of hills and valleys on earth is derived from Heaven, where it existed first.

651. *them*: the cannons.

653–54. *Themselves invaded* and *promontories flung* are objects of *saw* (line 651). I.e., the rebel angels next saw themselves invaded and saw promontories flung on them.

Long struggling underneath ere they could wind
Out of such prison though spirits of purest light,
Purest at first, now gross by sinning grown.
The rest in imitation to like arms
Betook them and the neighboring hills uptore:
So hills amid the air encountered hills
Hurled to and fro with jaculation dire
That under ground they fought in dismal shade,
Infernal noise. War seemed a civil game
To this uproar. Horrid confusion heaped
Upon confusion rose and now all Heav'n
Had gone to wrack with ruin overspread
Had not th' Almighty Father where He sits
Shrined in His sanctuary of Heav'n secure
Consulting on the sum of things forseen
This tumult and permitted all advised,
That His great purpose He might so fulfill
To honor his Anointed Son avenged
Upon His enemies and to declare
All power on Him transferred, whence to his Son,
Th' assessor of his throne, He thus began:
"Effulgence of my glory, Son beloved,
Son in whose face invisible is beheld
Visibly what by deity I am
And in whose hand what by decree I do,
Second Omnipotence, two days are passed,
Two days as we compute the days of Heav'n,
Since Michael and his powers went forth to tame
These disobedient. Sore hath been their fight
As likeliest was when two such foes met armed,
For to themselves I left them and thou know'st
Equal in their creation they were formed
Save what sin hath impaired which yet hath wrought
Insensibly, for I suspend their doom
Whence in perpetual fight they needs must last
Endless and no solution will be found.

660. *prison* has one syllable.

661. *gross*: densely material. The rebel angels have already become more *condense*, as opposed to *rare* (line 353). They therefore not only suffer more when crushed in their armor but have a harder time squeezing out.

665. *jaculation*: throwing (Latin *iacio*). In classical authors, hills are used as missiles in the wars between the Olympians and the giants and between the Olympians and the titans.

666. *under ground*: the fighting continues beneath the hills that have been thrown, in darkness and amid terrible noise. Milton may intend this detail to be understood as the source of the later notion that Hell is deep within the earth.

679. *Assessor*: "he who sits beside."

691–92. *impaired*: changed for the worse. *Insensibly*: without being noticed.

War, wearied, hath performed what war can do
And to disordered rage let loose the reins
With mountains as with weapons armed which makes
Wild work in Heav'n and dangerous to the main.
Two days are therefore passed, the third is thine.
For Thee I have ordained it and thus far
Have suffered that the glory may be thine
Of ending this great war since none but Thou
Can end it. Into Thee such virtue and grace
Immense I have transfused that all may know
In Heav'n and Hell thy pow'r above compare
And this perverse commotion governed thus
To manifest Thee worthiest to be Heir
Of all things, to be Heir and to be King
By sacred unction, thy deservèd right.
Go then Thou, mightiest in thy Father's might!
Ascend My chariot, guide the rapid wheels
That shake Heav'n's basis! Bring forth all my war,
My bow and thunder, my almighty arms
Gird on, and sword upon thy puissant thigh!
Pursue these sons of darkness, drive them out
From all Heav'n's bounds into the utter deep!
There let them learn as likes them to despise
God and Messiah, his Anointed King."
  He said, and on his Son with rays direct
Shone full: he all his Father full expressed,
Ineffably into his face received,
And thus the Filial Godhead answering spake:
  "O Father, O Supreme of Heav'nly thrones,
First, highest, holiest, best, Thou always seek'st
To glorify thy Son, I always Thee,
As is most just. This I my glory account,
My exaltation and my whole delight,
That Thou in Me well pleased declar'st thy will
Fulfilled which to fulfil is all my bliss.
Scepter and pow'r, thy giving, I assume
And gladlier shall resign when in the end

698. *main*: the whole (structure of Heaven). God observes that a continued rumpus will destroy not only things in Heaven but the very walls and foundations of Heaven.
701. *suffered*: put up with [the war].
703. *virtue* and *and* are elided.
709. *sacred unction*: anointing with oil, the biblical act of creating a king. The Hebrew word *messiah* and the Greek word *christos* both mean "anointed one."
720–22. I.e., The Father cannot be perceived in himself. But when the Father shines on the Son, the Son's face becomes the full expression of the Father's nature.
726. *glory* and *account* are elided.
728. *well pleased*: the gospel phrase with which the Father acknowledges Jesus as His son (Matthew 3:17 and 17:5; Mark 1:11).

Thou shalt be all in all and I in Thee
For ever, and in Me all whom Thou lov'st.
But whom Thou hat'st I hate and can put on
Thy terrors as I put thy mildness on,
Image of Thee in all things, and shall soon,
Armed with thy might, rid Heav'n of these rebelled
To their prepared ill mansion driven down,
To chains of darkness and th' undying worm,
That from thy just obedience could revolt
Whom to obey is happiness entire.
Then shall thy saints unmixed and from th' impure
Far separate, circling thy Holy Mount,
Unfeignèd hallelujahs to Thee sing,
Hymns of high praise, and I among them chief."
  So said, He o'er his scepter bowing rose
From the right hand of glory where He sat
And the third sacred morn began to shine,
Dawning through Heav'n. Forth rushed with whirlwind sound
The Chariot of Paternal Deity
Flashing thick flames, wheel within wheel undrawn,
Itself instínct with spirit but convoyed
By four cherubic shapes. Four faces each
Had wondrous. As with stars their bodies all
And wings were set with eyes, with eyes the wheels
Of beryl and careering fires between.
Over their heads a crystal firmament
Whereon a sapphire throne inlaid with pure

730–33. In the Son's words Milton sets forth his mystical vision of the end of time, his *eschatology* (reasoning about the highest, or last, things), and his theory of the relation of the Son to the Father. At the end of time, and for eternity thereafter, God will encompass all Being, for all beings will have returned to God as their Creator. Conscious beings, however, angels and humans, will have returned to God by entering the Son, who will himself enter God. That the Son will be in God, rather than the two being somehow inside each other (together with the third, the Holy Ghost), is a mildly subordinationist, or non-trinitarian position. In Milton's theodicy, the Son is not quite the equal of God. But God promotes the Son to equality with him, by giving the Son power over all beings. But after the Last Judgment, the Son will willingly relinquish this power and "be subject unto him that put all things under him" (1 Corinthians 15:28).

739. Mark 9:48. Hell, "where their worm dieth not."

742. *saints*: literally, "sanctified ones," all the conscious beings in heaven who are not God, or the Son, or the Holy Ghost: the faithful angels and all humans who have been saved.

749–59. The description of the chariot is based on the visions in Ezekiel 1 and 10. "And when I looked, behold the four wheels by the cherubims, one wheel by one cherub, and another wheel by another cherub: and the appearance of the wheels was as the colour of a beryl stone. And as for their appearances, they four had one likeness, as if a wheel had been in the midst of a wheel" (Ezekiel 10:9–10).

751. *undrawn*: not pulled by horses but powered from within by *spirit* (line 752).

752. *instínct*: "standing within." *convoyed*: "accompanied."

754–56. the verb *set* has three parallel objects: *stars*, *eyes*, and again *eyes*, the subjects being *bodies*, *wings*, and *wheels*. I.e., their bodies "were set" with stars; their wings "were set" with eyes; the wheels "were set" with eyes.

757–59. The understood verb is *was*.

Amber and colors of the show'ry arch.
He in celestial panoply all armed
Of radiant Urim, work divinely wrought,
Ascended. At his right hand Victory
Sat eagle-winged, beside Him hung his bow
And quiver with three-bolted thunder stored
And from about Him fierce effusion rolled
Of smoke and bickering flame and sparkles dire.
Attended with ten thousand thousand saints
He onward came. Far off his coming shone
And twenty thousand (I their number heard)
Chariots of God half on each hand were seen.
He on the wings of cherub rode sublime
On the crystálline sky in sapphire throned,
Illustrious far and wide but by his own
First seen. Them unexpected joy surprised
When the great ensign of Messiah blazed
Aloft by angels borne, his sign in Heav'n,
Under whose conduct Michael soon reduced
His army circumfused on either wing
Under their Head embodied all in one.
Before Him pow'r divine his way prepared.
At his command th' uprooted hills retired
Each to his place: they heard his voice and went
Obsequious. Heav'n his wonted face renewed
And with fresh flow'rets hill and valley smiled.
This saw his hapless foes but stood obdured
And to rebellious fight rallied their powers
Insensate, hope conceiving from despair.
In Heav'nly spirits could such perverseness dwell?
But to convince the proud what signs avail
Or wonders move th' obdúrate to relent?
They, hardened more by what might most reclaim,
Grieving to see his glory, at the sight
Took envy and aspiring to his heighth

762–66. After the biblical imagery of the chariot, Milton adds to his depiction of the Son the imagery of the classical Jove, attended by the eagle and armed with thunderbolts.

769. *I*: Raphael, a reminder that what we see is being related by the angel to Adam.

773. *his own*: the faithful angels.

777. *reduced*: led back (Latin *reducio*).

778–79. *circumfused*: joined together in a great circle so that the army is now like one body, with the Son, like a head, at its center and above the mass.

785. *obdured*: hardened.

788. A famous epic phrase, derived from Virgil, *Aeneid* 1.11: "in heavenly beings [gods] can so much anger dwell?"

791. *what might most reclaim*: the Son, submission to whom is their only chance of being restored from sin to faithfulness.

Stood re-embattled fierce by force or fraud
Weening to prosper and at length prevail
Against God and Messiah or to fall
In universal ruin last. And now
To final battle drew, disdaining flight
Or faint retreat, when the great Son of God
To all his host on either hand thus spake:
  "Stand still in bright array, ye saints, here stand
Ye angels armed, this day from battle rest!
Faithful hath been your warfare and of God
Accepted, fearless in his righteous cause,
And as ye have received so have ye done
Invincibly. But of this cursèd crew
The punishment to other hand belongs.
Vengeance is his or whose He sole appoints.
Number to this day's work is not ordained
Nor multitude: stand only and behold
God's indignation on these godless poured
By Me! Not you but Me they have despised,
Yet envied. Against Me is all their rage
Because the Father, t' whom in Heav'n supreme
Kingdom and pow'r and glory appertains,
Hath honored Me according to his will.
Therefore to Me their doom He hath assigned
That they may have their wish to try with Me
In battle which the stronger proves, they all
Or I alone against them, since by strength
They measure all, of other excellence
Not emulous, nor care who them excels—
Nor other strife with them do I vouchsafe."
  So spake the Son and into terror changed
His count'nance too severe to be beheld
And full of wrath bent on his enemies.
At once the four spread out their starry wings
With dreadful shade contiguous and the orbs
Of his fierce chariot rolled as with the sound
Of torrent floods or of a num'rous host.

794. *re-embattled*: returned to their ranks.
795. *weening*: imagining, hoping.
808. *Vengeance*: "vengeance is mine" (Romans 12:19, Deuteronomy 32–35; Psalms 94:1).
818–23. I.e., Since the rebel angels value only physical power and care nothing for other (and higher) forms of excellence, such as wisdom, they shall have what they desire: a physical contest of power with me. Nor would I allow them to strive with me in any other way (such as in debate).
827. *four*: cherubim.

He on his impious foes right onward drove
Gloomy as night. Under his burning wheels
The steadfast empyréan shook throughout
All but the throne itself of God. Full soon
Among them He arrived, in his right hand
Grasping ten thousand thunders which He sent
Before Him such as in their souls infixed
Plagues. They, astonished, all resistance lost,
All courage: down their idle weapons dropped.
O'er shields and helms and helmèd heads He rode
Of thrones and mighty seraphim prostrate
That wished the mountains now might be again
Thrown on them as a shelter from his ire.
Nor less on either side tempestuous fell
His arrows from the fourfold-visaged four
Distinct with eyes and from the living wheels
Distinct alike with multitude of eyes.
One spirit in them ruled and every eye
Glared lightning and shot forth pernicious fire
Among th' accurst that withered all their strength
And of their wonted vigor left them drained,
Exhausted, spiritless, afflicted, fall'n.
Yet half his strength he put not forth but checked
His thunder in mid volley for He meant
Not to destroy but root them out of Heav'n.
The overthrown He raised and as a herd
Of goats or timorous flock together thronged
Drove them before him thunderstruck, pursued
With terrors and with furies to the bounds
And crystal wall of Heav'n which op'ning wide
Rolled inward and a spacious gap disclosed
Into the wasteful deep. The monstrous sight
Strook them with horror backward but far worse
Urged them behind: headlong themselves they threw
Down from the verge of Heav'n. Eternal wrath
Burnt after them to the bottomless pit.
  Hell heard th' unsufferable noise. Hell saw
Heav'n ruining from Heav'n and would have fled
Affrighted but strict Fate had cast too deep
Her dark foundations and too fast had bound.
Nine days they fell. Confounded, Chaos roared

833. *steadfast empyréan*: the solid foundation of heaven, as opposed to the fiery region of the upper air.
852. *afflicted*: cast down.

And felt tenfold confusion in their fall
Through his wild anarchy, so huge a rout
Encumbered him with ruin. Hell at last
Yawning received them whole and on them closed,
Hell their fit habitation fraught with fire
Unquenchable, the house of woe and pain.
Disburdened, Heav'n rejoiced and soon repaired
Her mural breach returning whence it rolled.
Sole Victor, from th' expulsion of his foes
Messiah his triumphal chariot turned.
To meet him all his saints who silent stood
Eye witnesses of his almighty acts
With jubilee advancèd as they went
Shaded with branching palm. Each order bright
Sung triumph and Him sung Victorious King,
Son, Heir and Lord, to him dominion giv'n,
Worthiest to reign. He, celebrated, rode
Triumphant through mid Heav'n into the courts
And temple of his mighty Father throned
On high who into glory Him received
Where now He sits at the right hand of bliss.
  Thus measuring things in Heav'n by things on Earth,
At thy request, and that thou may'st beware
By what is past to thee I have revealed
What might have else to human race been hid:
The discord which befell and war in Heav'n
Among th' angelic pow'rs and the deep fall
Of those too high aspiring who rebelled
With Satan, he who envies now thy state,
Who now is plotting how he may seduce
Thee also from obedience, that with him
Bereaved of happiness thou may'st partake
His punishment eternal misery,
Which would be all his solace and revenge
As a despite done against the Most High,
Thee once to gain companion of his woe.
But listen not to his temptations! Warn
Thy weaker! Let it profit thee t' have heard
By terrible example the reward

873–74. *his* and *him*: Chaos.
879. *mural breach*: hole in the wall. Part of the wall rolled out; now that part rolls back.
884. *jubilee*: a song calling for rejoicing.
885. *palm*: the procession is meant to recall Christ's entry into Jerusalem.
892. *He*: the Son.
909. *Thy weaker*: Eve, Adam's weaker half.

Of disobedience! Firm they might have stood
Yet fell. Remember, and fear to transgress!

Book Seven

The Argument

Raphael, at the request of Adam, relates how and wherefore this world was first created: that God, after the expelling of Satan and his angels out of Heaven, declared his pleasure to create another world and other creatures to dwell therein; sends his Son with glory and attendance of angels to perform the work of Creation in six days; the angels celebrate with hymns the performance thereof, and His reascension into Heaven.

Descend from Heav'n, Urania, by that name
If rightly thou art called, whose voice divine
Following above th' Olympian hill I soar,
Above the flight of Pegaséan wing.
The meaning not the name I call for thou
Nor of the Muses nine nor on the top
Of old Olympus dwell'st but Heav'nly born.
Before the hills appeared or fountain flowed
Thou with eternal Wisdom didst converse,
Wisdom thy sister, and with her didst play
In presence of th' Almighty Father, pleased
With thy celestial song. Up led by thee
Into the Heav'n of Heav'ns I have presumed
An earthly guest and drawn empyreal air,

911. *they*: the rebel angels.

Book Seven

1. Changing the name of the muse from Calliope to Urania, the opening half verse translates Horace's invocation in *Odes* 3.4.1–2: *Descende caelo . . . Calliope*. The theme of Horace's ode, the power of wisdom and learning in subduing violence, is also Milton's theme.

1–12. The poet questions the appropriateness of the name by which he calls his muse: *Urania*, meaning "skylike one" (Greek *ouraniê*). She is higher than the classical muses on Olympus and older than the sky after which she is named.

1–39. Reaching the halfway point in his epic, the poet re-invokes his muse, Urania, declaring that the rest of the poem will be sung by him *standing on earth* (line 23), not while in flight to heaven or to hell. Raphael's narrative now moves from destruction to creation, from the war in heaven to the creation of the universe and of Adam and Eve.

4. *Pegasus*, the winged horse, was a traditional figure of poetic flight but also of hubris.

7–12. In the Bible, Wisdom says, "Before the mountains were settled, before the hills was I brought forth . . . When he prepared the heavens, I was there: when he set a compass upon the face of the depth . . . I was daily his delight, rejoicing always before him" (Proverbs 8: 25–30).

14–15. The poet has breathed the fiery air of empyrean, which has been tempered for him by the muse.

Thy temp'ring. With like safety guided down
Return me to my native element
Lest from this flying steed unreined (as once
Bellerophon, though from a lower clime)
Dismounted on th' Aleian field I fall
Erroneous there to wander and forlorn.
Half yet remains unsung but narrower bound
Within the visible diurnal sphere:
Standing on earth, not rapt above the pole,
More safe I sing with mortal voice unchanged
To hoarse or mute though fall'n on evil days,
On evil days though fall'n and evil tongues,
In darkness and with dangers compassed round
And solitude. Yet not alone while thou
Visit'st my slumbers nightly or when morn
Purples the east. Still govern thou my song,
Urania, and fit audience find, though few!
But drive far off the barbarous dissonance
Of Bacchus and his revelers, the race
Of that wild rout that tore the Thracian bard
In Rhodopè where woods and rocks had ears
To rapture till the savage clamor drowned
Both harp and voice, nor could the Muse defend
Her son. So fail not thou who thee implores,
For thou art Heav'nly, she an empty dream.
   Say, Goddess, what ensued when Raphaël
The affable archangel had forewarned
Adam by dire example to beware
Apostasy by what befell in Heaven
To those apostates lest the like befall
In Paradise to Adam or his race,

15–20. Resuming the Pegasus reference of line 4, the poet's flight beyond the confines of the world is now seen as a dangerous undertaking unless guided by the heavenly muse. The hero Bellerophon was thrown from Pegasus (Zeus sent a gadfly to sting the flying horse) and after falling to earth wandered on the Aleian plain.

22. *visible diurnal sphere*: the sphere of the heavens that is visible from earth.

23. *rapt*: caught up. *pole*: the pole of the universe, not of the earth. To be above the pole is to be in hell, chaos, or heaven.

25–28. *evil days . . . evil tongues . . . darkness . . . solitude*. After the Restoration (the return of Charles II, which Milton publicly opposed) the blind poet spent a period of time in hiding and, later, several weeks in prison. After his release, his blindness rendered him vulnerable to assassination, which was not unreasonably feared.

29. *nightly . . . morn*. New verses often came to Milton at night or in the early morning.

30. *govern*: guide, steer, as a ship (Greek *kubernaô*).

32–38. As in "Lycidas," Milton fears sharing the fate of Orpheus. Orpheus was torn to pieces by the bacchantes, Thracian worshippers of Bacchus (Dionysus).

39. *thou*: the heavenly muse. *she*: the muse of epic poetry, Calliope, the mother of Orpheus.

43. *Apostasy*: literally, "standing apart," but implying also betrayal.

Charged not to touch the interdicted tree
If they transgress and slight that sole command
So easily obeyed amid the choice
Of all tastes else to please their appetite,
Though wand'ring. He with his consorted Eve
The story heard attentive and was filled
With admiration and deep muse to hear
Of things so high and strange, things to their thought
So unimaginable as hate in Heav'n
And war so near the peace of God in bliss
With such confusion. But the evil soon
Driv'n back redounded as a flood on those
From whom it sprung, impossible to mix
With blessedness, whence Adam soon repealed
The doubts that in his heart arose and now
Led on, yet sinless, with desire to know
What nearer might concern him: how this world
Of Heav'n and Earth conspicuous first began,
When and whereof created, for what cause,
What within Eden or without was done
Before his memory. As one whose drouth
Yet scarce allayed still eyes the current stream
Whose liquid murmur heard new thirst excites
Proceeded thus to ask his Heav'nly guest:
  Great things and full of wonder in our ears
Far differing from this world thou hast revealed,
Divine Interpreter, by favor sent
Down from the empyréan to forewarn
Us timely of what might else have been our loss,
Unknown, which human knowledge could not reach,
For which to th' Infinitely Good we owe
Immortal thanks and His admonishment
Receive with solemn purpose to observe
Immutably His sov'reign will, the end
Of what we are. But since thou hast vouchsafed
Gently for our instruction to impart
Things above earthly thought (which yet concerned

50. *wand'ring*: seeking variety.
62–63. *world . . . conspicuous*: the visible world of the sky and the earth. *conspicuous*: seen together. See 22 n.
66. *drouth*: thirst.
67. *current*: adj. "running."
69. *proceeded*. The subject is *Adam*, line 59.
72. *Interpreter*: mediator, messagebearer.
74. *timely* and *of* are elided.
79. *end*. Greek *telos*, "ultimate purpose."

Our knowing, as to Highest Wisdom seemed)
Deign to descend now lower and relate
What may no less perhaps avail us known:
How first began this heav'n which we behold
Distant so high with moving fires adorned
Innumerable and this which yields or fills
All space, the ambient air wide interfused
Embracing round this florid earth? What cause
Moved the Creator in His holy rest
Through all eternity so late to build
In chaos and, the work begun, how soon
Absolved? If unforbid thou may'st unfold
What we, not to explore the secrets ask
Of His eternal empire but the more
To magnify His works the more we know,
And the great light of day yet wants to run
Much of his race, though steep, suspense in heav'n
Held by thy voice: thy potent voice he hears
And longer will delay to hear thee tell
His generation and the rising birth
Of Nature from the unapparent deep.
Or if the star of evening and the Moon
Haste to thy audience Night with her will bring
Silence; and Sleep, list'ning to thee, will watch,
Or we can bid his absence till thy song
End and dismiss thee ere the morning shine.
  Thus Adam his illustrious guest besought
And thus the godlike angel answered mild:
This also thy request with caution asked
Obtain, though to recount almighty works
What words or tongue of seraph can suffice
Or heart of man suffice to comprehend?
Yet what thou canst attain which best may serve

83. *as to Highest Wisdom seemed*: i.e., It seemed to God that it is not only instructive but necessary for us to know what we could not apprehend by our unaided intellectual powers (e.g., Satan's revolt).
88. The air *yields* to physical objects, which take up space within it, and the air *fills* the space between those objects. *innumerable* and *and* are elided.
89. *interfused*. Latin *interfusus*, "poured between."
90. *florid*: blooming.
94. *absolved*: completed.
98–101. The sun has begun his *steep* descent from his noonday height but delays his course (*suspense in heav'n*) to hear Raphael speak.
103. *unapparent*: invisible. *deep*: chaos.
104. *star of evening*: Hesperus.
106. *watch*: remain awake.
107. *his*: Sleep's.
115. *attain*: understand.

To glorify the Maker and infer
Thee also happier shall not be withheld
Thy hearing, such commission from above
I have received to answer thy desire
Of knowledge within bounds. Beyond abstain
To ask nor let thine own inventions hope
Things not revealed which the invisible King
Only omniscient hath suppressed in night,
To none communicable in Earth or Heaven:
Enough is left besides to search and know.
But knowledge is as food and needs no less
Her temperance over appetite to know
In measure what the mind may well contain,
Oppresses else with surfeit and soon turns
Wisdom to folly as nourishment to wind.
  Know then that after Lucifer from Heaven
(So call him, brighter once amidst the host
Of angels than that star the stars among)
Fell with his flaming legions through the deep
Into his place and the great Son returned
Victorious with His saints, th' Omnipotent
Eternal Father from His throne beheld
Their multitude and to his Son thus spake:
  "At least our envious foe hath failed who thought
All like himself rebellious, by whose aid
This inaccessible high strength, the seat
Of Deity supreme, us dispossessed,
He trusted to have seized and into fraud
Drew many whom their place knows here no more.
Yet far the greater part have kept, I see,
Their station. Heav'n yet populous retains
Number sufficient to possess her realms,
Though wide, and this high temple to frequént

116–17. *infer / Thee also happier*: lead you to conclude that you are happier than you now know.

121. *inventions*: speculations. *hope*, with the implied verb, "to grasp." I.e., neither ask to know nor hope to grasp by your own intellectual powers what God has hid.

122. *invisible* has three syllables: 'in-viz-ble.'

129–30. As eating too much results in flatulence, so knowing too much results in folly. The subject of *Oppresses* is *knowledge* (line 126). *folly* and *as* are elided.

131. *Lucifer*: "light bearer"; the name of Satan before his fall. "How art thou fallen from heaven, O Lucifer, son of the morning!" (Isaiah 14:12). See 5.708 and n.

136. *saints*: "sacred ones," the angels in Heaven. (Human saints are so called because they are deemed to be among the angels in heaven.)

139. *at least*. An ironical understatement: at the very least, Satan failed in his plan to rule Heaven. But Satan's failure was much greater than that, having been expelled from Heaven into Hell.

142. *us dispossessed*: once we had been dispossessed (of heaven). God is saying (with continuing irony), 'as if dispossessing us were a foregone conclusion.'

148. *this high temple*. The place of the presence of God, where the angels worship Him.

With ministéries due and solemn rites.
But lest his heart exalt him in the harm
Already done to have dispeopled Heav'n
(My damage fondly deemed) I can repair
That detriment (if such it be to lose
Self-lost) and in a moment will create
Another world, out of one man a race
Of men innumerable there to dwell,
Not here, till by degrees of merit raised
They open to themselves at length the way
Up hither, under long obedience tried,
And Earth be changed to Heav'n and Heav'n to Earth,
One Kingdom, joy and union without end.
Meanwhile inhabit lax, ye pow'rs of Heaven,
And Thou my Word, begotten Son, by Thee
This I perform: speak Thou and be it done!
My overshadowing Spirit and might with Thee
I send along: ride forth and bid the deep
Within appointed bounds be Heav'n and Earth!
Boundless the deep because I am who fill
Infinitude, nor vacuous the space
(Though I uncircumscribed Myself retire
And put not forth My goodness which is free
To act or not): necessity and chance
Approach not Me, and what I will is fate."

150–61. A third of the angels joined Satan and fell. The remaining angels are sufficient in number to occupy heaven. But lest Satan boast the contrary, God will create humans, who will eventually rise up to heaven and replace the precise number of angels who fell. The earth will become more like Heaven, until the two places are united. See lines 188–90 and 5.493–503.

152. *fondly*: foolishly.

153–54. I.e. If the loss of those who have lost themselves can be counted a loss to me too, which it can't.

162. *inhabit lax*: spread out. (To fill the space formerly occupied by the angels who rebelled.)

163. The Creation now begins. It is performed by God's Son, who is also the *Word*, the power of command by which God brings his creatures into being. "In the beginning was the Word. . . . All things were made by him [the Word]; and without him was not any thing made that was made" (John 1:1–3).

165. *spirit*: God's creative power, which the poet invokes to his aid at the beginning of *Paradise Lost* (1.17). Milton means the power named in Genesis 1:2: "And the Spirit of God moved upon the face of the waters," which in orthodox Christian doctrine is the Holy Ghost, the third person of the trinity.

168–73. These verses contain the only truly metaphysical statement in *Paradise Lost*. In the beginning, God is totality and fills, to infinity, all space. Space is therefore not empty (*vacuous*) but filled with the substance of God, his essential being. God withdraws from totality to the place of his presence in Heaven, *this high temple* (line 148), leaving a residue, which was formerly (but is no longer) God's substance. The residue is instead the substance of chaos, which is ruled by *necessity* (compulsion, force) and *chance*. God now confronts this chaos of substance and may (or may not) *put forth [his] goodness* by creating new beings and even giving them freedom.

173. *fate*: Fate, which includes the laws of the universe and the more inscrutable laws governing human actions, is not prior to God's will but is the expression of God's will. Richard Hooker (*The Laws of Ecclesiastical Polity* 1.2.6) describes fate as "that order which God before all ages hath set down with himself, for himself to do all things by."

So spake th' Almighty and to what He spake
His Word, the Filial Godhead, gave effect.
Immediate are the acts of God, more swift
Than time or motion but to human ears
Cannot without procéss of speech be told
(So told as earthly notion can receive).
Great triumph and rejoicing was in Heaven
When such was heard declared th' Almighty's will.
Glory they sung to the Most High, good will
To future men and in their dwellings peace,
Glory to Him whose just avenging ire
Had driven out th' ungodly from His sight
And th' habitations of the just, to Him
Glory and praise whose wisdom had ordained
Good out of evil to create: instead
Of spirits malign a better race to bring
Into their vacant room and thence diffuse
His good to worlds and ages infinite.
So sang the hierarchies. Meanwhile the Son
On his great expedition now appeared
Girt with omnipotence, with radiance crowned
Of majesty divine, sapience and love
Immense, and all his Father in him shone.
About his chariot numberless were poured
Cherub and seraph, potentates and thrones,
And virtues, wingèd spirits, and chariots winged
From th' armory of God where stand of old
Myriads between two brazen mountains lodged
Against a solemn day, harnessed at hand,
Celestial equipage, and now came forth
Spontaneous (for within them Spirit lived)
Attendant on their Lord. Heav'n opened wide
Her ever-during gates, harmonious sound
On golden hinges moving, to let forth
The King of Glory in his powerful Word
And Spirit coming to create new worlds.
On Heav'nly ground they stood and from the shore
They viewed the vast immeasurable abyss

175. *His Word, the filial Godhead*: the Son.
176–79. The Creation, which is now to be described, happened in an instant but will be told in a narrative so that it may be grasped by Adam's human mind.
189–90. See lines 150–61 n.
203. *equipage*: chariots with horses. "Behold, there came four chariots out from between two mountains; and the mountains were mountains of brass" (Zechariah 6:1).
208. *King of Glory*: the Father. *Word*: the Son.
209. *Spirit*: creative power of God. See line 165 and n.
211. *immeasurable* has four syllables.

Outrageous as a sea, dark, wasteful, wild,
Up from the bottom turned by furious winds
And surging waves as mountains to assault
Heav'n's heighth and with the center mix the pole.
  "Silence, ye troubled waves and thou, deep, peace!"
Said then th' Omnific Word, "Your discord end!"
  Nor stayed but on the wings of cherubim
Uplifted in paternal glory rode
Far into chaos and the world unborn.
For chaos heard his voice. Him all his train
Followed in bright procession to behold
Creation and the wonders of his might.
Then stayed the fervid wheels and in his hand
He took the golden compasses prepared
In God's eternal store to circumscribe
This universe and all created things.
One foot He centered and the other turned
Round through the vast profundity obscure
And said, "Thus far extend, thus far thy bounds,
This be thy just circumference, O world!"
Thus God the heav'n created, thus the earth,
Matter unformed and void. Darkness profound
Covered th' abyss but on the wat'ry calm
His brooding wings the Spirit of God outspread
And vital virtue infused and vital warmth
Throughout the fluid mass but downward purged
The black tartareous cold infernal dregs
Adverse to life, then founded, then conglobed
Like things to like, the rest to several place
Disparted and between spun out the air,
And Earth self-balanced on her center hung.
  "Let there be light," said God, and forthwith light
Ethereal, first of things, quintessence pure,
Sprung from the deep and from her native east
To journey through the airy gloom began,

216. "And he arose, and rebuked the wind, and said unto the sea, Peace, be still. And the wind ceased, and there was a great calm" (Mark 4:39).
221. *Him*: the Son, probably.
224. *fervid*: burning.
224–550. The account of creation that follows is a vast imaginative amplification of the first two chapters of Genesis.
225. See lines 7–12 n.
233. *Matter*: out of matter.
236. *virtue* and *infused* are elided: 'virch-infused.'
242. "He . . . hangeth the earth upon nothing" (Job 26:7). Earth is balanced around a vertical axis, as a standing person is balanced. But earth is balanced laterally as well, so that it can be suspended in space without support from below. Milton still thinks of space as having an "up" and a "down."

Sphered in a radiant cloud, for yet the sun
Was not: she in a cloudy tabernacle
Sojourned the while. God saw the light was good
And light from darkness by the hemisphere
Divided: light the "day" and darkness "night"
He named. Thus was the first day, ev'n and morn.
Nor passed uncelebrated nor unsung
By the celestial choirs when orient light
Exhaling first from darkness they beheld,
Birthday of Heav'n and Earth. With joy and shout
The hollow universal orb they filled
And touched their golden harps and hymning praised
God and His works: "Creator" him they sung
Both when first evening was and when first morn.
  Again God said: "Let there be firmament
Amid the waters and let it divide
The waters from the waters. And God made
The firmament, expanse of liquid, pure,
Transparent, elemental air diffused
In circuit to the uttermost convéx
Of this great round, partition firm and sure,
The waters underneath from those above
Dividing. For as earth, so he the world
Built on circumfluous waters calm in wide
Crystálline ocean and the loud misrule
Of chaos far removed lest fierce extremes
Contiguous might distemper the whole frame.
And heav'n he named the "firmament." So ev'n
And morning chorus sung the second day.
  The Earth was formed but in the womb as yet
Of waters—embryon immature, involved—
Appeared not. Over all the face of Earth
Main ocean flowed not idle but with warm
Prolific humor, soft'ning all her globe,
Fermented the Great Mother to conceive,
Satiate with genial moisture, when God said,
"Be gathered now, ye waters under heav'n,

248. *she*: the sun.
263. *the waters from the waters*: the waters on the earth from the waters supposed to be above the sky, making the sky appear blue.
267. *great round*: the sphere of the universe, which is supposed to be filled with liquid air.
270–73. Just as the continents on the earth rest on the surrounding seas, so the universe (*world*) rests on liquid air, which functions as a buffer between creation and chaos.
276–77. The earth, like a human embryo, was formed but still immature, and still sunk (*involved*) within the waters.
280. *prolific humor*: life-giving liquid.
282. *satiate* and *genial* are two syllables each.

Into one place and let dry land appear!"
Immediately the mountains huge appear
Emergent and their broad bare backs upheave
Into the clouds, their tops ascend the sky.
So high as heaved the tumid hills, so low
Down sunk a hollow bottom broad and deep,
Capacious bed of waters. Thither they
Hasted with glad precipitance, uprolled
As drops on dust conglobing from the dry.
Part rise in crystal wall or ridge direct
For haste, such flight the great command impressed
On the swift floods. As armies at the call
Of trumpet (for of armies thou hast heard)
Troop to their standard, so the wat'ry throng,
Wave rolling after wave, where way they found:
If steep, with torrent rapture, if through plain,
Soft ebbing. Nor withstood them rock or hill
But they or under ground or circuit wide
With serpent error wand'ring found their way
And on the washy ooze deep channels wore
Easy ere God had bid the ground be dry,
All but within those banks where rivers now
Stream and perpetual draw their humid train.
The dry land, earth, and the great receptácle
Of congregated waters he called "seas"
And saw that it was good and said, "Let th' earth
Put forth the verdant grass, herb yielding seed
And fruit tree yielding fruit after her kind
Whose seed is in herself upon the earth!"
He scarce had said when the bare earth till then
Desert and bare, unsightly, unadorned,
Brought forth the tender grass whose verdure clad
Her universal face with pleasant green,
Then herbs of every leaf that sudden flow'red
Op'ning their various colors and made gay
Her bosom smelling sweet. And these scarce blown
Forth flourished thick the clust'ring vine, forth crept
The swelling gourd, up stood the corny reed

291. *precipitance*: rushing headlong.

292. The waters roll up into huge balls resembling water drops. These balls roll down into the ocean beds and fill the oceans. "[The waters] go down by the valleys unto the place which thou hast founded for them" (Psalm 104:8).

296. *thou hast heard*: One of the moments when the poet reminds us we are hearing a narrative spoken by Raphael to Adam. Adam first heard of armies when Raphael told him of the war in heaven.

306. *perpetual* has three syllables.

Embattled in her field and th' humble shrub
And bush with frizzled hair implicit. Last
Rose as in dance the stately trees and spread
Their branches hung with copious fruit or gemmed
Their blossoms. With high woods the hills were crowned,
With tufts the valleys and each fountain side,
With borders long the rivers, that Earth now
Seemed like to Heav'n, a seat where gods might dwell
Or wander with delight and love to haunt
Her sacred shades, though God had not yet rained
Upon the earth and man to till the ground
None was, but from the earth a dewy mist
Went up and watered all the ground and each
Plant of the field which ere 't was in the earth
God made and every herb before it grew
On the green stem. God saw that it was good.
So ev'n and morn recorded the third day.
  Again th' Almighty spake: "Let there be lights
High in th' expanse of heaven to divide
The day from night and let them be for signs,
For seasons, and for days and circling years,
And let them be for lights as I ordain
Their office in the firmament of heaven
To give light on the earth!" And it was so.
And God made two great lights, great for their use
To Man, the greater to have rule by day,
The less by night altern, and made the stars
And set them in the firmament of heav'n
T' illuminate the earth and rule the day
In their vicissitude and rule the night
And light from darkness to divide. God saw,
Surveying his great work, that it was good.
For of celestial bodies first the sun
A mighty sphere he framed, unlightsome first
Though of ethereal mold, then formed the moon
Globose and every magnitude of stars
And sowed with stars the heav'n thick as a field.
Of light by far the greater part he took
Transplanted from her cloudy shrine and placed

325. *gemmed*: budded.
348. *altern*: The sun and moon rule day and night alternately.
355. *unlightsome*: not yet giving off light.
358. "All sowd with glistring stars more thicke than grasse" (Spenser, *Hymn to Heavenly Beauty*, line 53).

In the sun's orb, made porous to receive
And drink the liquid light, firm to retain
Her gathered beams, great palace now of light.
Hither as to their fountain other stars
Repairing in their golden urns draw light
And hence the morning planet gilds her horns.
By tincture or reflection they augment
Their small peculiar though from human sight
So far remote with diminution seen.
First in his east the glorious lamp was seen,
Regent of day and all th' horizon round
Invested with bright rays, jocund to run
His longitude through heav'n's high road. The grey
Dawn and the Pleiades before him danced
Shedding sweet influence. Less bright the moon
(But opposite in leveled west was set)
His mirror with full face borrowing her light
From him, for other light she needed none
In that aspéct and still that distance keeps
Till night. Then in the east her turn she shines
Revolved on heav'n's great axle and her reign
With thousand lesser lights dividual holds,
With thousand thousand stars that then appeared
Spangling the hemisphere. Then first adorned
With their bright luminaries that set and rose,
Glad Evening and glad Morn crowned the fourth day.
  And God said, "Let the waters generate
Reptile with spawn abundant, living soul,

361–62. *porous . . . firm*: The sun is porous so that it can soak up light, which Milton conceives of as a liquid. Through these pores light will radiate out in controlled amounts. The sun is also firm so that all the light will not escape it at once.

364–66. The stars come to the palace of the sun to obtain light, just as the moon receives light from the sun. Galileo discovered that Venus, the *morning planet*, has moonlike phases, hence golden *horns*.

367–69. Each star has a little light of its own (its small portion, or *peculiar*). But each star increases this amount by borrowing light from the sun. This light is borrowed either by reflection, as with the moon, or by direct infusion (*tincture*).

370. *lamp*: the sun.

376. *leveled west*: due west.

377. *His mirror* modifies *moon* (line 375): the moon is the sun's mirror because she reflects his light.

379. *in that aspéct*: from that angle.

381. *axle*: a reference to the great but invisible whorl to which all the celestial bodies are fixed and by which their movements are governed (Plato, *Republic*, 616 e–d).

382. *dividual*: shared, modifying *reign* (line 381).

384–86. When they crown the fourth day, evening and morning are adorned with stars and celestial bodies that rise and set.

385. *luminaries* has three syllables: either 'lumin-ries' or 'luminaires.'

388. *living soul*: principle of life in beings, whether reptiles and fish or humans, that move and make decisions.

And let fowl fly above the earth with wings
Displayed on th' open firmament of heav'n!"
And God created the great whales and each
Soul living, each that crept, which plenteously
The waters generated by their kinds,
And every bird of wing after his kind,
And saw that it was good and blessed them saying,
"Be fruitful, multiply, and in the seas
And lakes and running streams the waters fill!
And let the fowl be multiplied on th' earth!"
Forthwith the sounds and seas, each creek and bay,
With fry innumerable swarm and shoals
Of fish that with their fins and shining scales
Glide under the green wave in schools that oft
Bank the mid sea. Part single or with mate
Graze the seaweed their pasture and through groves
Of coral stray or sporting with quick glance
Show to the sun their waved coats dropped with gold
Or in their pearly shells at ease attend
Moist nutriment or under rocks their food
In jointed armor watch. On smooth, the seal
And bended dolphins play, part huge of bulk
Wallowing unwieldy, enormous in their gait,
Tempest the ocean. There Leviathan,
Hugest of living creatures, on the deep
Stretched like a promontory sleeps or swims
And seems a moving land and at his gills
Draws in and at his trunk spouts out a sea.
Meanwhile the tepid caves and fens and shores
Their brood as num'rous hatch from th' egg that soon
Bursting with kindly rupture forth disclosed
Their callow young, but feathered soon and fledge
They summed their pens and soaring th' air sublime
With clang despised the ground under a cloud
In prospect. There the eagle and the stork

400. *fry*: hatchling fish.
409. *on smooth*: on the calm surface. *jointed armor*: shellfish.
411. For the line to scan regularly, *wallowing* would have two syllables and *unwieldy* and *enormous* would be elided. But note how well the line sounds when *unwieldy* and *wallowing* are given three syllables and there is a strong pause in the caesura, after *unwieldy*.
412. *Leviathan*: whale.
417. *tepid*: moist.
419. *kindly*: natural.
420. *callow*: immature. *fledge*: able to fly.
421. *summed their pens*: their pinions reached full growth.
422. *clang*: noise (Greek *klangê*, loud sharp sound, associated with the screeching of birds).
422–23. *despised*: looked down upon. *under a cloud*: The birds are above a cloud, looking down at the earth below it. Despite the cloud, the earth remains in view (*in prospect*).

On cliffs and cedar tops their aeries build.
Part loosely wing the region, part, more wise,
In common ranged, in figure wedge their way
Intelligent of seasons and set forth
Their airy caravan high over seas
Flying and over lands with mutual wing
Easing their flight. So steers the prudent crane
Her annual voyage, borne on winds. The air
Floats as they pass, fanned with unnumbered plumes.
From branch to branch the smaller birds with song
Solaced the woods and spread their painted wings
Till ev'n, nor then the solemn nightingale
Ceased warbling but all night tuned her soft lays.
Others on silver lakes and rivers bathed
Their downy breast: the swan with archèd neck
Between her white wings mantling proudly rows
Her state with oary feet. Yet oft they quit
The dank, and rising on still pennons tow'r
The mid aerïal sky. Others on ground
Walked firm: the crested cock whose clarion sounds
The silent hours and th' other whose gay train
Adorns him colored with the florid hue
Of rainbows and starry eyes. The waters thus
With fish replenished and the air with fowl,
Evening and Morn solémnized the fifth day.
  The sixth and of Creation last arose
With evening harps and matin when God said,
"Let th' Earth bring forth soul living in her kind,
Cattle and creeping things and beast of th' earth
Each in their kind. The Earth obeyed and straight,
Op'ning her fertile womb, teemed at a birth
Innumerous living creatures, perfect forms,
Limbed and full-grown. Out of the ground uprose
As from his lair the wild beast where he wons
In forest wild, in thicket, brake or den.
Among the trees in pairs they rose, they walked,
The cattle in the fields and meadows green,
Those rare and solitary, these in flocks
Pasturing at once and in broad herds upsprung.

426. They travel in flocks and in wedge formations.
429–30. *mutual wing*: flying together and beating the air in time with one another.
441. *dank*: water. *pennons*: wings, pinions.
446. The final syllable of *starry* elides with *eyes*, though not easily.
450. *matin*: morning song of angels.
451. *soul*] 1667 *Fowle*] 1674 *Foul*. See line 388 and n.
457. *wons*: dwells.

The grassy clods now calved, now half appeared
The tawny lion pawing to get free
His hinder parts, then springs as broke from bonds
And rampant shakes his brinded mane. The ounce,
The libbard and the tiger, as the mole
Rising, the crumbled earth above them threw
In hillocks. The swift stag from under ground
Bore up his branching head. Scarce from his mold
Behemoth, biggest born of earth, upheaved
His vastness. Fleeced the flocks and bleating rose,
As plants. Ambiguous between sea and land
The river horse and scaly crocodile.
At once came forth whatever creeps the ground,
Insect or worm. Those waved their limber fans
For wings and smallest lineaments exact
In all the liveries decked of summer's pride
With spots of gold and purple, azure and green.
These as a line their long dimension drew
Streaking the ground with sinuous trace. Not all
Minims of nature: some of serpent kind
Wondrous in length and corpulence involved
Their snaky folds and added wings. First crept
The parsimonious emmet, provident
Of future, in small room large heart enclosed,
Pattern of just equality perhaps
Hereafter, joined in her popular tribes
Of commonalty. Swarming next appeared
The female bee that feeds her husband drone
Deliciously and builds her waxen cells
With honey stored. The rest are numberless
And thou their natures know'st and gav'st them names,
Needless to thee repeated. Nor unknown

466. *ounce*: snow leopard. *rampant*: on hind legs (heraldic term).
467. *libbard*: leopard.
471. *Behemoth*: an imaginary biblical land beast. "Behold now behemoth, which I made with thee . . . his strength is in his loins, and his force is in the navel of his belly. He moveth his tail like a cedar: the sinews of his stones are wrapped together . . . his bones are like bars of iron. He is the chief of the ways of God" (Job 40:15–19).
473. *Ambiguous* has three syllables. Unclear whether these beasts are sea or land creatures, since they inhabit both.
474. *river horse*: a literal translation of the Greek word *hippopotamus*.
476. *those*: the insects.
479. *purple* has one syllable.
480. *these*: the worms.
481. *sinuous* has two syllables.
481–82. Not all the worms were minute creatures (*minims*). Some were big snakes.
485. *emmet*: ant.

The serpent, subtlest beast of all the field,
Of huge extent sometimes with brazen eyes
And hairy mane terrific though to thee
Not noxious but obedient at thy call.
Now heav'n in all her glory shone and rolled
Her motions as the great First Mover's hand
First wheeled their course. Earth in her rich attire
Consúmmate lovely smiled. Air, water, earth,
By fowl, fish, beast, was flown, was swum, was walked
Frequent. And of the sixth day yet remained
There wanted yet the master work, the end
Of all yet done: a creature who not prone
And brute as other creatures but endued
With sanctity of reason might erect
His stature and, upright with front serene,
Govern the rest, self-knowing, and from thence
Magnanimous to correspond with Heaven,
But grateful to acknowledge whence his good
Descends, thither with heart and voice and eyes
Directed in devotion to adore
And worship God supreme who made him chief
Of all His works. Therefore th' Omnipotent
Eternal Father (for where is not He
Present?) thus to his Son audibly spake:
"Let us now make Man in our image, Man
In our similitude, and let them rule
Over the fish and fowl of sea and air,
Beast of the field and over all the earth
And every creeping thing that creeps the ground."
This said, He formed thee, Adam, thee O Man,
Dust of the ground, and in thy nostrils breathed
The breath of life. In His own image He
Created thee, in the image of God

495. The last of the animals mentioned by Raphael is the serpent. The serpent is *subtle* (intelligent) but not harmful (*noxious*), despite its brassy eyes and its frightening (*terrific*) hairy mane. See *Aeneid* 2.206–7.

504–5. *yet remained . . . wanted yet*. In the time remaining on the sixth day, the creation of the *master work*, humans, remained to be done.

508. The subject of *erect* is *creature* (line 506), i.e., Man.

509. *front*: forehead.

511. *Magnanimous*: of great and noble mind. *correspond*: to be in regular communication with, and eventually to be like.

512. *grateful* modifies *creature*.

515. *him*: the *creature* (line 506), Man.

516–19. Although in Book 7 generally it is the Son who performs the Creation while the Father remains in Heaven (see lines 163–64), Milton here makes the Father present, on the scene of Creation, at the crucial moment when Man is created. Doing so allows Milton to be more faithful to the literal text of Genesis, in which God alone creates the world and mankind.

Express, and thou becam'st a living soul.
Male He created thee but thy consort
Female for race, then blessed mankind and said,
"Be fruitful, multiply, and fill the earth,
Subdue it and throughout dominion hold
Over fish of the sea and fowl of th' air
And every living thing that moves on th' earth!"
Wherever thus created, for no place
Is yet distinct by name, thence as thou know'st
He brought thee into this delicious grove,
This garden planted with the trees of God
Delectable both to behold and taste,
And freely all their pleasant fruit for food
Gave thee. All sorts are here that all th' earth yields,
Variety without end, but of the tree
Which tasted works knowledge of good and evil
Thou may'st not. In the day thou eat'st, thou diest:
Death is the penalty imposed. Beware!
And govern well thy appetite lest Sin
Surprise thee and her black attendant Death.
  Here finished He and all that he had made
Viewed and, behold! all was entirely good.
So ev'n and morn accomplished the sixth day,
Yet not till the Creator from his work
Desisting, though unwearied, up returned,
Up to the Heav'n of Heav'ns his high abode
Thence to behold this new created world,
Th' addition of his empire, how it showed
In prospect from his throne, how good, how fair,
Answering his great idea. Up He rode
Followed with acclamation and the sound
Symphonious of ten thousand harps that tuned
Angelic harmonies. The earth, the air
Resounded (thou remember'st, for thou heard'st),

528. *Express*: represented.

535–37. Adam is not made in the garden, Paradise, but somewhere else on the earth. After Adam is made, he is transported to the garden. See 8.295–306. Milton follows the second creation account in Genesis, where only after God has created Man does God plant the garden and place Man in it: "And the Lord God planted a garden eastward in Eden; and there he put the man whom he had formed" (2:8).

542. *Variety* has three syllables: 'vari-ty.'

544. *diest* has one syllable.

556. *In prospect*: in view. Cf. line 423.

557. *idea*: a thing that is seen before the mind's eye, the Platonic form. This is the only occurrence of the word in Milton's English poetry. (He did write a Latin poem called "On the Platonic Idea as Aristotle Understood It.") Milton uses the term here in a very un-Platonic sense: the created world, far from being a poor copy of the realm of ideas, is a perfect material realization of the mental plan the Son formed beforehand. And the created world is more excellent than the plan.

The heav'ns and all the constellations rung,
The planets in their stations list'ning stood
While the bright pomp ascended jubilant.
"Open, ye everlasting gates!" they sung,
"Open, ye Heav'ns, your living doors! Let in
The great Creator from his work returned
Magnificent, his six days' work, a world!
Open, and henceforth oft! For God will deign
To visit oft the dwellings of just men
Delighted and with frequent intercourse
Thither will send his wingèd messengers
On errands of supernal grace." So sung
The glorious train ascending. He through Heav'n
That opened wide her blazing portals led
To God's eternal house direct the way,
A broad and ample road whose dust is gold
And pavement stars as stars to thee appear
Seen in the galaxy, that Milky Way
Which nightly as a circling zone thou seest
Powdered with stars. And now on earth the seventh
Evening arose in Eden for the sun
Was set and twilight from the east came on
Forerunning night when at the holy mount
Of Heav'n's high-seated top, th' imperial throne
Of Godhead fixed for ever firm and sure,
The Filial Pow'r arrived and sat Him down
With his great Father (for He also went
Invisible, yet stayed—such privilege
Hath omnipresence—and the work ordained,
Author and end of all things) and from work
Now resting blessed and hallowed the sev'nth day
As resting on that day from all his work.
But not in silence holy kept: the harp
Had work and rested not, the solemn pipe,
And dulcimer, all organs of sweet stop,
All sounds on fret by string or golden wire

565. *they*: the angels. The angels sing; the constellations resonate to the song, like instruments; and the planets stop to listen.

565–67. "Lift up your heads, O ye gates; and be ye lift up, ye everlasting doors; and the King of glory shall come in" (Psalm 24:7).

571. *intercourse*: going (running) back and forth (Latin *intercursus*). The word suggests mutual visiting between heaven and earth but also the eventual sharing of natures, a blending of the human and divine.

580. *zone*: belt.

590. The Father *ordains* (commands) the work that the Son has performed: Creation.

592. The subject of *resting*, *blessed*, and *hallowed* is the Son.

594. The Sabbath in Heaven is a day of rest, but the angels make music, for making music is not work.

Tempered soft tunings intermixed with voice
Choral or unison. Of incense clouds
Fuming from golden censers hid the Mount.
Creation and the six days' acts they sung:
"Great are thy works, Jehovah, infinite
Thy pow'r! What thought can measure Thee or tongue
Relate Thee? greater now in thy return
Than from the giant angels! Thee that day
Thy thunders magnified! But to create
Is greater than created to destroy.
Who can impair Thee, Mighty King, or bound
Thy empire? Easily the proud attempt
Of spirits apostate and their counsels vain
Thou hast repelled while impiously they thought
Thee to diminish and from Thee withdraw
The number of thy worshippers. Who seeks
To lessen Thee against his purpose serves
To manifest the more thy might, his evil
Thou usest and from thence creat'st more good.
Witness this new-made world, another Heav'n
From Heaven gate not far, founded in view
On the clear hyaline, the glassy sea
Of amplitude almost immense, with stars
Numerous and every star perhaps a world
Of destined habitation. But Thou know'st
Their seasons. Among these the seat of men,
Earth, with her nether ocean circumfused,
Their pleasant dwelling place. Thrice happy men
And sons of men whom God hath thus advanced,
Created in His image there to dwell
And worship Him and in reward to rule
Over his works on earth, in sea, or air,
And multiply a race of worshippers
Holy and just! Thrice happy if they know
Their happiness and persevere upright!"
So sung they and the empyréan rung

600. *censers*: holders for burning incense.
605. *giant angels*: rebel angels, with an allusion to the titans and giants of classical myth who warred against the Olympians. See 1.573–87 and n.
606. *magnified*: praised. On the day the Son defeated the rebel angels, his own thunderbolts spoke his, the Son's, praise. But on this day our song praises him.
608. *impair*: diminish.
613. *who*: whoever.
619. *hyaline*: the cosmic sea of liquid air, the waters above the firmament. Cf. *crystalline ocean*, 271 and n. and 624 and n. Greek *hyalinos*, "made of glass"; Latin *hyalus*, "glass." Glass in antiquity was green; hence the use of this word for the sea when calm.
624. *nether ocean*: lower terrestrial ocean, as distinct from the "upper" ocean of the waters above the firmament.

With hallelujahs. Thus was Sabbath kept.
And thy request think now fulfilled that asked
How first this world and face of things began
And what before thy memory was done
From the beginning, that posterity
Informed by thee might know. If else thou seek'st
Aught not surpassing human measure, say.

Book Eight

The Argument

Adam inquires concerning celestial motions, is doubtfully answered and exhorted to search rather things more worthy of knowledge. Adam assents and, still desirous to detain Raphael, relates to him what he remembered since his own creation, his placing in Paradise, his talk with God concerning solitude and fit society, his first meeting and nuptials with Eve, his discourse with the angel thereupon who, after admonitions repeated, departs.

The angel ended and in Adam's ear
So charming left his voice that he a while
Thought him still speaking, still stood fixed to hear,
Then as new waked thus gratefully replied:
What thanks sufficient or what recompense
Equal have I to render thee, divine
Historian, who thus largely hast allayed
The thirst I had of knowledge and vouchsafed
This friendly condescension to relate
Things else by me unsearchable, now heard
With wonder, but delight, and, as is due,
With glory attribúted to the High
Creator. Something yet of doubt remains
Which only thy solution can resolve:

Book Eight

2. *charming*: spellbinding. *he*: Adam.
3. *him*: Raphael.
13–38. The question Adam now puts to Raphael implies a *doubt* (line 13) of the efficiency of divine creation. Why should the heavenly bodies be compelled to circle the earth, at vast distances and unimaginable speeds, merely to bring light to this one tiny spot? Would it not be more *frugal* (line 25) and less *superfluous* (line 26) for the earth to move instead? Eve has already raised essentially the same doubt (4.657–58), asking why the stars shine at night when there is no one to see them, since she and Adam are asleep. But perhaps God has created the universe on such a vast scale to teach mankind humility: "that Man may know he dwells not in his own, / An edifice too large for him to fill" (line 103–4). This, of course, would mean the universe was created for mankind after all, but as a lesson in human limits rather than as a thing for human use.

When I behold this goodly frame, this world
Of heav'n and earth consisting and compute
Their magnitudes, this earth a spot, a grain,
An atom with the firmament compared
And all her numbered stars that seem to roll
Spaces incomprehensible (for such
Their distance argues and their swift return
Diurnal) merely to officiate light
Round this opacous earth, this punctual spot
One day and night, in all their vast survéy
Useless besides, reasoning I oft admire
How Nature wise and frugal could commit
Such disproportions with superfluous hand:
So many nobler bodies to create
Greater so manifold to this one use
(For aught appears) and on their orbs impose
Such restless revolution day by day
Repeated while the sedentary earth
(That better might with far less compass move,
Served by more noble than herself) attains
Her end without least motion and receives
As tribute (such a sumless journey brought
Of incorporeal speed) her warmth and light—
Speed to describe whose swiftness number fails!
  So spake our sire and by his count'nance seemed
Ent'ring on studious thoughts abstruse, which Eve
Perceiving where she sat retired in sight
With lowliness majestic from her seat
And grace that won who saw to wish her stay,
Rose and went forth among her fruits and flow'rs
To visit how they prospered, bud and bloom,
Her nursery. They at her coming sprung
And touched by her fair tendance gladlier grew.
Yet went she not as not with such discourse
Delighted or not capable her ear
Of what was high. Such pleasure she reserved,
Adam relating, she sole auditress:
Her husband the relater she preferred

15. *goodly frame*: cf. Spenser, *Faerie Queene* 2.11.1: "Now gins this goodly frame of Temperance / Fairly to rise." *frame*: constructed thing. *world*: universe.
19. *her*: the firmament's.
23. *opacous*: opaque.
24. *vast survéy*: nonearthly regions over which the stars look.
28. *nobler* than the earth.
29. *Greater so manifold*: capable of so much more. *this one use*: to serve the earth.
36. *sumless*: incalculable.
37. *incorporeal speed*: speed greater than would seem possible to bodies with mass.

Before the angel and of him to ask
Chose rather. He, she knew, would intermix
Grateful digressions and solve high dispute
With conjugal caresses (from his lip
Not words alone pleased her). O when meet now
Such pairs in love and mutual honor joined?
With goddess-like demeanor forth she went,
Not unattended for on her as queen
A pomp of winning graces waited still
And from about her shot darts of desire
Into all eyes to wish her still in sight.
And Raphael now to Adam's doubt proposed
Benevolent and facile thus replied:
  To ask or search I blame thee not for heav'n
Is as the book of God before thee set
Wherein to read his wondrous works and learn
His seasons, hours or days or months or years.
This to attain, whether heav'n move or earth,
Imports not if thou reckon right. The rest
From man or angel the Great Architect
Did wisely to conceal and not divulge
His secrets to be scanned by them who ought
Rather admire. Or if they list to try
Conjecture He his fabric of the heav'ns
Hath left to their disputes perhaps to move
His laughter at their quaint opinions wide
Hereafter when they come to model heav'n
And calculate the stars, how they will wield
The mighty frame, how build, unbuild, contrive
To save appearances, how gird the sphere
With centric and eccentric scribbled o'er

61. *pomp*: formal procession. In classical mythology the *graces*, daughters of Zeus, are goddesses of beauty and attendants of Venus. *waited*: attended.
62. The subject of *shot* is *graces* (line 61).
65. *facile*: friendly, easygoing.
70. *attain*: know.
79. *Hereafter*: In the future, i.e., in Milton's day, when many scientific conjectures about the universe and the stars will be ventured.
80. *wield*: an ironical choice of verb; i.e., in speculating about the universe, men will reveal their desire to master it for their use, to wield it like a tool.
81. *build, unbuild* continues the irony of *wield* (line 80).
82. *save appearances*: a technical term from ancient Greek science (*sôzein ta phainomena*); to reconcile new observations with an existing theoretical model. Raphael now describes the increasingly desperate attempts of astronomers in later times to reconcile new observations with the earth-centered, Ptolemaic system.
82. *gird the sphere*: add to the cosmic sphere.
83. *centric*: a sphere centered on the earth. *eccentric*: a sphere enclosing the earth but not centered on the earth.

Cycle and epicycle, orb in orb.
Already by thy reasoning this I guess,
Who art to lead thy offspring, and supposest
That bodies bright and greater should not serve
The less not bright nor heav'n such journeys run,
Earth sitting still when she alone receives
The benefit. Consider first that great
Or bright infers not excellence: the earth
Though in comparison of heav'n so small,
Nor glistering, may of solid good contain
More plenty than the sun that barren shines
Whose virtue on itself works no effect
But in the fruitful earth. There first received
His beams, unactive else, their vigor find.
Yet not to earth are those bright luminaries
Officious but to thee earth's habitant.
And for the heav'n's wide circuit: let it speak
The Maker's high magnificence who built
So spacious and His line stretched out so far
That Man may know he dwells not in his own,
An edifice too large for him to fill,
Lodged in a small partition and the rest
Ordained for uses to his Lord best known.
The swiftness of those circles áttribute,
Though numberless, to His omnipotence,
That to corporeal substances could add
Speed almost spiritual. Me thou think'st not slow
Who since the morning hour set out from Heav'n
Where God resides and ere mid-day arrived
In Eden, distance inexpressible
By numbers that have name. But this I urge,
Admitting motion in the heav'ns, to show
Invalid that which thee to doubt it moved,
Not that I so affirm, though so it seem
To thee who hast thy dwelling here on earth.
God to remove His ways from human sense

84. *cycle*: orbit of a planet. *epicycle*: orbit of a planet (such as Mars) that has its center not on the earth but on the circumference of another orbit that *is* centered on the earth. An epicycle is like the circle partly described by the swinging of a chair on a Ferris wheel.
96. *There*: on earth.
97. *His*: the sun's.
105. *small partition*: the earth.
109. *corporeal*. See line 37 n.
114–18. I.e., For the sake of argument, let us suppose that the heavenly bodies actually do move, rather than seeming to move because the earth does. Even if your assumption of such motion is true, your conclusion, that nature is wasteful, does not follow.
116. *it*: read "has." I.e., to show that what has moved you to doubt is an invalid proposition.

Placed heav'n from earth so far that earthly sight
If it presume might err in things too high
And no advantage gain. What if the sun
Be center to the world and other stars
By his attractive virtue and their own
Incited dance about him various rounds?
Their wand'ring course now high, now low, then hid,
Progressive, retrograde or standing still
In six thou seest. And what if seventh to these
The planet earth, so steadfast though she seem,
Insensibly three different motions move,
Which else to several spheres thou must ascribe,
Moved contrary with thwart obliquities
Or save the sun his labor and that swift
Nocturnal and diurnal rhomb supposed,
Invisible else above all stars, the wheel
Of day and night, which needs not thy belief
If Earth industrious of herself fetch day
Traveling east and with her part averse
From the sun's beam meet night, her other part
Still luminous by his ray. What if that light
Sent from her through the wide transpicuous air
To the terrestrial moon be as a star
Enlight'ning her by day as she by night
This earth reciprocal if land be there,
Fields and inhabitants? Her spots thou seest
As clouds and clouds may rain and rain produce

122–58. After showing that the geocentric system is consistent with God's creative wisdom, Raphael expounds the heliocentric system to show that it too is consistent with God's creative wisdom.

126. *Their* now means planets, not stars, as the phrase "wand'ring course" indicates. See 5.177n.

128–29. *six*: Moon, Mercury, Venus, Mars, Jupiter, Saturn. I.e., What if earth is the seventh planet, instead of the sun, around which all the planets revolve?

130. *three different motions*: daily rotation around the earth's axis, annual orbiting of the sun, and seasonal rotation of the ends of the earth's axis. The earth spins, travels, and wobbles. That this third motion does not begin until after the Fall (10.668–71), making it meaningless for Raphael to mention it here, should not be taken as a mistake on Milton's part but rather as a fold in the poem's frames of reference. Raphael is indeed speaking to Adam, before the Fall, but Milton is also in these passages speaking to his contemporaries, who were as concerned about the consequences for Christian faith of the struggle between the Ptolemaic and Copernican systems as, two centuries later, people would be about the struggle between biblical Genesis and Darwinian evolution.

131–40. *several spheres*: different spherical structures beyond the earth, providing an alternative (but overelaborate) explanation for the three motions of the earth. Such motion would *save the sun his labor* by not requiring the sun to move at all. *rhomb*: Greek *rhombos*, anything that spins, like a top. The *wheel of day and night* (lines 135–36) need not be believed in if the earth is understood simply to rotate to the east: by rotating, the earth moves toward day, rather than day moving toward the earth. Night would then fall on the side of the earth (*her part averse*) that is shielded from the sun.

144. *reciprocal*: i.e., as the moon gives light to the inhabitants of the earth, so the earth may give light to the inhabitants of the moon.

Fruits in her softened soil for some to eat
Allotted there. And other suns perhaps
With their attendant moons thou wilt descry
Communicating male and female light
(Which two great sexes animate the world)
Stored in each orb perhaps with some that live.
For such vast room in nature unpossessed
By living soul, desért and desolate,
Only to shine yet scarce to cóntribute
Each orb a glimpse of light conveyed so far
Down to this habitable, which returns
Light back to them, is obvious to dispute.
But whether thus these things or whether not,
Whether the sun predominant in heav'n
Rise on the earth or earth rise on the sun,
He from the east his flaming road begin
Or she from west her silent course advance
With inoffensive pace that spinning sleeps
On her soft axle while she paces ev'n
And bears thee soft with the smooth air along,
Solicit not thy thoughts with matters hid.
Leave them to God above. Him serve and fear!
Of other creatures as Him pleases best,
Wherever placed, let Him dispose. Joy thou
In what He gives to thee: this Paradise
And thy fair Eve. Heav'n is for thee too high
To know what passes there. Be lowly wise:
Think only what concerns thee and thy being.
Dream not of other worlds, what creatures there
Live in what state, condition or degree,
Contented that thus far hath been revealed
Not of earth only but of highest Heav'n.
   To whom thus Adam cleared of doubt replied:
How fully hast thou satisfied me, pure
Intelligence of Heav'n, angel serene,
And freed from intricacies, taught to live
The easiest way nor with perplexing thoughts
To interrupt the sweet of life from which

148–49. An allusion to the moons of Jupiter, discovered by Galileo.

150. *male and female light*: direct and reflected light, as with the light of the sun and the moon.

153–58. Raphael here allows some validity to Adam's doubt: 'It would indeed be strange if the vast universe has no life in it and its innumerable stars exist only to afford a glimpse of their light here, on earth. But in that case it is more reasonable to suppose that there are inhabitants of other planets than to suppose that nature is wasteful.'

158. *obvious*: open.

God hath bid dwell far off all anxious cares
And not molest us, unless we ourselves
Seek them with wand'ring thoughts and notions vain.
But apt the mind or fancy is to rove
Unchecked and of her roving is no end
Till warned or by experience taught she learn
That not to know at large of things remote
From use, obscure and subtle, but to know
That which before us lies in daily life
Is the prime wisdom. What is more is fume
Or emptiness or fond impertinence
And renders us in things that most concern
Unpracticed, unprepared and still to seek.
Therefore from this high pitch let us descend
A lower flight and speak of things at hand
Useful, whence haply mention may arise
Of something not unseasonable to ask
By sufferance and thy wonted favor deigned.
Thee I have heard relating what was done
Ere my remembrance. Now hear me relate
My story which perhaps thou hast not heard,
And day is yet not spent. Till then thou seest
How subtly to detain thee I devise,
Inviting thee to hear while I relate—
Fond, were it not in hope of thy reply!
For while I sit with thee I seem in Heav'n
And sweeter thy discourse is to my ear
Than fruits of palm tree pleasantest to thirst
And hunger both from labor at the hour
Of sweet repast: they satiate and soon fill,
Though pleasant, but thy words with grace divine
Imbued bring to their sweetness no satiety.
To whom thus Raphael answered Heav'nly meek:
Nor are thy lips ungraceful, Sire of Men,
Nor tongue ineloquent. For God on thee
Abundantly His gifts hath also poured
Inward and outward both, His image fair.
Speaking or mute, all comeliness and grace

195. *fond*: foolish. *impertinence*: irrelevance.
201. *unseasonable* has four syllables: 'unseas-nable.'
209. *Fond*: to no purpose.
214. *they*: the fruits (line 212). *satiate* has two syllables: 'say-shut.'
216. A twelve-syllable line, the last two syllables of *satiety* unaccented: ⏑ / ⏑⏑. (The *i* of *satiety* is long: 'sat-I-etee.')
221. Adam is the image of God not only outwardly, in his appearance, but inwardly too, in his reason and eloquence.

Attends thee and each word, each motion forms.
Nor less think we in Heav'n of thee on Earth
Than of our fellow servant and inquire
Gladly into the ways of God with Man:
For God we see hath honored thee and set
On Man His equal love. Say therefore on!
For I that day was absent, as befell,
Bound on a voyage uncouth and obscure
Far on excursion toward the gates of Hell.
Squared in full legion such command we had
To see that none thence issued forth a spy
Or enemy while God was in His work
Lest He incensed at such eruption bold
Destruction with Creation might have mixed.
Not that they durst without His leave attempt,
But us He sends upon His high behests
For state, as Sov'reign King, and to inure
Our prompt obedience. Fast we found, fast shut
The dismal gates and barricadoed strong.
But long ere our approaching heard within
Noise other than the sound of dance or song,
Torment and loud lament and furious rage.
Glad we returned up to the coasts of light
Ere Sabbath evening, so we had in charge.
But thy relation now! For I attend
Pleased with thy words no less than thou with mine.
  So spake the godlike pow'r. And thus our sire:
For Man to tell how human life began
Is hard: for who himself beginning knew?
Desire with thee still longer to converse
Induced me. As new waked from soundest sleep
Soft on the flow'ry herb I found me laid
In balmy sweat which with his beams the sun
Soon dried and on the reeking moisture fed.
Straight toward heav'n my wond'ring eyes I turned
And gazed a while the ample sky till raised
By quick instinctive motion up I sprung
As thitherward endeavoring and upright
Stood on my feet. About me round I saw
Hill, dale, and shady woods and sunny plains

232. *Squared in full legion*: Raphael was part of a full legion (an army division) formed in a square.
254. *herb*: grass.
255. *balmy*: sweet-smelling.
256. *reeking*: evaporating. The word does not have the negative sense it now has.
260. *thitherward*: toward heaven. *endeavoring* has three syllables: 'endeav-ring.'

And liquid lapse of murmuring streams; by these,
Creatures that lived and moved and walked or flew,
Birds on the branches warbling. All things smiled.
With fragrance and with joy my heart o'erflowed!
Myself I then perused and limb by limb
Surveyed and sometimes went and sometimes ran
With supple joints as lively vigor led.
But who I was, or where, or from what cause
Knew not. To speak I tried and forthwith spake:
My tongue obeyed and readily could name
Whate'er I saw. "Thou Sun," said I, "fair light,
And thou enlightened Earth so fresh and gay,
Ye hills and dales, ye rivers, woods and plains,
And ye that live and move, fair creatures, tell,
Tell if ye saw how came I thus, how here.
Not of myself: by some great Maker, then,
In goodness and in pow'r preëminent.
Tell me how may I know Him, how adore,
From whom I have that thus I move and live
And feel that I am happier than I know!"
While thus I called and strayed I knew not whither
From where I first drew air and first beheld
This happy light, when answer none returned,
On a green shady bank profuse of flowers
Pensive I sat me down. There gentle sleep
First found me and with soft oppression seized
My drowsèd sense untroubled, though I thought
I then was passing to my former state
Insensible and forthwith to dissolve.
When suddenly stood at my head a dream
Whose inward apparition gently moved
My fancy to believe I yet had being
And lived. One came, methought, of shape divine
And said, "Thy mansion wants thee, Adam. Rise,
First man of men innum'rable ordained,
First father! Called by thee I come thy guide
To the garden of bliss, thy seat prepared."
So saying by the hand He took me raised
And over fields and waters as in air
Smooth sliding without step, last led me up
A woody mountain whose high top was plain,

267. *perused*: considered, looked at.
268. *went*: walked.
297. Two things are *ordained* (commanded): that Adam shall be the first man, and that men, Adam's sons, shall be innumerable.

A circuit wide enclosed, with goodliest trees
Planted, with walks and bow'rs, that what I saw
Of earth before scarce pleasant seemed! Each tree
Loaden with fairest fruit that hung to th' eye
Tempting stirred in me sudden appetite
To pluck and eat, whereat I waked and found
Before mine eyes all real as the dream
Had lively shadowed. Here had new begun
My wand'ring had not He who was my guide
Up hither from among the trees appeared,
Presence Divine. Rejoicing, but with awe
In adoration, at His feet I fell
Submiss. He reared me and, "Whom thou sought'st I am,"
Said mildly, "Author of all this thou seest
Above or round about thee or beneath.
This Paradise I give thee, count it thine
To till and keep and of the fruit to eat.
Of every tree that in the garden grows
Eat freely with glad heart: fear here no dearth!
But of the tree whose operation brings
Knowledge of good and ill (which I have set
The pledge of thy obedience and thy faith
Amid the garden by the Tree of Life)
Remember what I warn thee: shun to taste
And shun the bitter consequence! For know,
The day thou eat'st thereof, my sole command
Transgressed, inevitably thou shalt die,
From that day mortal and this happy state
Shalt lose, expelled from hence into a world
Of woe and sorrow." Sternly He pronounced
The rigid interdiction which resounds
Yet dreadful in mine ear, though in my choice
Not to incur. But soon His clear aspéct
Returned and gracious purpose thus renewed:
"Not only these fair bounds but all the Earth
To thee and to thy race I give. As lords
Possess it and all things that therein live,
Or live in sea or air, beast, fish and fowl,
In sign whereof each bird and beast behold
After their kinds. I bring them to receive

310. *real* is pronounced here with two syllables.
329–32. Adam will not die on the very day he eats the fruit. But on that day he will become mortal and his death inevitable.
341. *Or live in*: whether they live in.

From thee their names and pay thee fealty
With low subjection. Understand the same
Of fish within their wat'ry residence,
Not hither summoned since they cannot change
Their element to draw the thinner air."
As thus He spake each bird and beast behold!
Approaching two and two, these cow'ring low
With blandishment, each bird stooped on his wing.
I named them as they passed and understood
Their nature: with such knowledge God endued
My sudden apprehension. But in these
I found not what methought I wanted still
And to the Heav'nly Vision thus presumed:
  "O by what name (for Thou above all these,
Above mankind or aught than mankind higher,
Surpassest far my naming) how may I
Adore Thee, Author of this universe
And all this good to Man for whose well being
So amply and with hands so liberal
Thou hast provided all things? But with me
I see not who partakes. In solitude
What happiness? Who can enjoy alone
Or all enjoying what contentment find?"
Thus I presumptuous, and the Vision bright
As with a smile more brightened thus replied:
  "What call'st thou solitude? Is not the earth
With various living creatures and the air
Replenished? And all these at thy command
To come and play before thee? Know'st thou not
Their language and their ways? They also know
And reason not contemptibly. With these
Find pastime and bear rule: thy realm is large!"
So spake the Universal Lord and seemed
So ordering. I with leave of speech implored
And humble deprecation thus replied:
  "Let not my words offend Thee, Heav'nly Power,
My Maker, be propitious while I speak.

345–48. It is typical of Milton's love of complete explanations that he should have God explain to Adam why the fish are not being summoned into Adam's presence to be given their names.
350. *these*: the beasts.
351. *stooped*: descended, or dove. A term from hawking.
355. *wanted*: lacked.
358. *aught than Mankind higher*. I.e., angels.
371. *Replenished*: filled.
380. *propitious*: favorable.

Hast Thou not made me here Thy substitute
And these inferior far beneath me set?
Among unequals what society
Can sort, what harmony or true delight,
Which must be mutual in proportion due
Given and received? But in disparity—
The one intense, the other still remiss—
Cannot well suit with either but soon prove
Tedious alike. Of fellowship I speak
Such as I seek, fit to participate
All rational delight wherein the brute
Cannot be human consort. They rejoice
Each with their kind, lion with lioness,
So fitly them in pairs thou hast combined.
Much less can bird with beast or fish with fowl
So well converse, nor with the ox the ape,
Worse then can Man with beast, and least of all!"
  Whereto th' Almighty answered not displeased:
"A nice and subtle happiness I see
Thou to thyself proposest in the choice
Of thy associates, Adam, and wilt taste
No pleasure, though in pleasure, solitary.
What think'st thou then of Me and this My state?
Seem I to thee sufficiently possessed
Of happiness, or not, who am alone
From all eternity? For none I know
Second to Me or like, equal much less.
How have I then with whom to hold converse

382. *these*: the animals.

383. *unequals*. A passage important for what it says about Milton's idealized vision of marriage. The inequality referred to here is between animals and humans, which is so great that it is impossible for animals and humans to engage in harmonious, music-like interactions. Animals and humans, Milton holds, cannot be *mutual* (line 385). Adam and Eve, however, will be *equals* in Milton's musical but nonmathematical sense of the word. They can engage in *mutual* interactions in which the differences between them complement one another, as harmonious differences of pitch in music (*proportion due*, line 385) are complementary and may be said, in a loose sense, to be *equal*. But Adam and Eve are not *equal* in the stricter sense of the word, which is identity.

386. A feminine line. See 2.27 n. Neither *given* nor *disparity* is shortened.

387. *intense*: in tune, like the taut string of an instrument. *remiss*: out of tune, like a string that has gone slack. In addition to the organ, Milton played the viola da gamba, a forerunner of the modern 'cello, and when he was a boy his family made music together.

395–97. Conversation between Man and beast is even more absurd than social interaction between beasts of different kind, such as birds and fish.

401–2. I.e., You will taste no pleasure alone (*solitary*), although you are in the place of pleasure itself. The name *Eden* was interpreted by allegorical commentators to mean *pleasure* (Greek *hêdonê*).

403. The Son, not the Father, is present to Adam, but the Son speaks as the Father. Milton is keeping to the account of Creation in Genesis, in which the Father creates. That the Father creates through the person of the Son is the later, Christian interpretation of the Creation in Genesis.

Save with the creatures which I made, and those
To me inferior, infinite descents
Beneath what other creatures are to thee?"
  He ceased, I lowly answered: "To attain
The heighth and depth of Thy eternal ways
All human thoughts come short, Supreme of Things.
Thou in Thyself art perfect and in Thee
Is no deficience found. Not so is Man
But in degree, the cause of his desire
By conversation with his like to help
Or solace his defects. No need that Thou
Shouldst propagate, already infinite
And through all numbers absolute, though One.
But Man by number is to manifest
His single imperfection and beget
Like of his like, his image multiplied
In unity defective which requires
Collateral love and dearest amity.
Thou in Thy secrecy, although alone,
Best with Thyself accompanied, seek'st not
Social communication. Yet, so pleased,
Canst raise Thy creature to what heighth Thou wilt
Of union or communion deified.
I by conversing cannot these erect
From prone, nor in their ways complacence find."
Thus I emboldened spake and freedom used
Permissive and acceptance found which gained
This answer from the gracious Voice Divine:
  "Thus far to try thee, Adam, I was pleased
And find thee knowing not of beasts alone
Which thou hast rightly named but of thyself,
Expressing well the spirit within thee free,
My image, not imparted to the brute
Whose fellowship therefore unmeet for thee

416–19. *in degree*: Adam argues that Man, unlike God, is in the hierarchy of created beings and is, therefore, open to improvement. Married persons can help each other improve while accepting, with mutual love, the *defects* they have in respect of higher beings, such as angels.

419–21. God is already infinite in number, although each of these numbers is itself perfect, a totality. Although he encloses these totalities, God remains a *one*.

422–26. Having children shows that man is incomplete (*imperfect*) as an individual. The individual man is like an integer in pre-Cartesian mathematics, containing a sort of desire in itself to go beyond itself by combination with other numbers. Adam likens this desire in numbers to human sexual desire.

432. *these*: animals.

440–41. Adam's inner freedom, which permits him to reason and to question, is God's image in him, an image not imparted to the animals, which are therefore unsuitable company for Adam.

Good reason was thou freely shouldst dislike:
And be so minded still! I, ere thou spak'st,
Knew it not good for Man to be alone
And no such company as then thou saw'st
Intended thee—for trial only brought
To see how thou could'st judge of fit and meet.
What next I bring shall please thee, be assured,
Thy likeness, thy fit help, thy other self,
Thy wish exactly to thy heart's desire."
He ended or I heard no more for now
My earthly by His Heav'nly overpowered
Which it had long stood under, strained to th' heighth
In that celestial colloquy sublime
As with an object that excels the sense,
Dazzled and spent, sunk down, and sought repair
Of sleep which instantly fell on me, called
By nature as in aid, and closed mine eyes.
Mine eyes He closed but open left the cell
Of fancy my internal sight by which
Abstráct as in a trance methought I saw
(Though sleeping where I lay) and saw the Shape
Still glorious before whom awake I stood,
Who stooping opened my left side and took
From thence a rib with cordial spirits warm
And life-blood streaming fresh. Wide was the wound
But suddenly with flesh filled up and healed.
The rib He formed and fashioned with His hands,
Under His forming hands a creature grew,
Manlike but different sex, so lovely fair
That what seemed fair in all the world seemed now
Mean—or in her summed up, in her contained,
And in her looks, which from that time infused
Sweetness into my heart, unfelt before,
And into all things from her air inspired
The spirit of love and amorous delight.
She disappeared and left me dark. I waked
To find her or for ever to deplore
Her loss and other pleasures all abjure
When out of hope behold her not far off
Such as I saw her in my dream, adorned

455. *colloquy*: conversation.
466. *cordial*: of the heart, life-giving.
471–77. The syntax, imitating the dream state, is vague. All that is fair is summed up in Eve's person and also in her *looks*, which go out from her as a *sweetness* that is poured into Adam's heart.

With what all Earth or Heaven could bestow
To make her amiable. On she came
Led by her Heav'nly Maker, though unseen,
And guided by His voice nor uninformed
Of nuptial sanctity and marriage rites.
Grace was in all her steps, Heav'n in her eye,
In every gesture dignity and love.
I overjoyed could not forbear aloud:
"This turn hath made amends, thou hast fulfilled
Thy words, Creator bounteous and benign,
Giver of all things fair but fairest this
Of all Thy gifts, nor enviest. I now see
Bone of my bone, flesh of my flesh, my self
Before me: *Woman* is her name, of Man
Extracted. For this cause he shall forgo
Father and mother and to his wife adhere
And they shall be one flesh, one heart, one soul."
She heard me thus and though divinely brought
Yet innocence and virgin modesty,
Her virtue and the conscience of her worth
That would be wooed and not unsought be won,
Not obvious, not obtrusive, but retired
The more desirable, or to say all,
Nature herself though pure of sinful thought
Wrought in her so that seeing me she turned.
I followed her: she what was honor knew
And with obsequious majesty approved
My pleaded reason. To the nuptial bow'r
I led her blushing like the morn. All heav'n
And happy constellations on that hour
Shed their selectest influence. The earth
Gave sign of gratulation, and each hill.
Joyous the birds, fresh gales and gentle airs
Whispered it to the woods and from their wings
Flung rose, flung odors from the spicy shrub

486–87. *nor uninformed . . . marriage rites*: See 4.470–75.
492. *bounteous* has two syllables.
496–97. *Woman* means "of Man."
500–507. Compare Adam's speculation on Eve's motive for turning away from him with Eve's account of this moment (4.477–80).
509. *obsequious*: accommodating. The Latin sense of the word (*obsequor*, "to accommodate oneself to another's will") is not negative, as it is in English. Since *sequor* means "to follow," we picture Eve following, or going along with Adam, but majestically.
510. *pleaded* has here the sense of arguing a case, as in court. For what Adam says, see 4.481–88.
516. *it*: news of the marriage.

Disporting till the amorous bird of night
Sung spousal and bid haste the evening star
On his hill top to light the bridal lamp.
  Thus I have told thee all my state and brought
My story to the sum of earthly bliss
Which I enjoy and must confess to find
In all things else delight indeed but such
As, used or not, works in the mind no change
Nor vehement desire. These delicacies
I mean of taste, sight, smell, herbs, fruits and flowers,
Walks, and the melody of birds. But here
Far otherwise: transported I behold,
Transported touch. Here passion first I felt,
Commotion strange! In all enjoyments else
Superior and unmoved, here only weak
Against the charm of beauty's powerful glance.
Or nature failed in me and left some part
Not proof enough such object to sustain
Or from my side subducting took perhaps
More than enough, at least on her bestowed
Too much of ornament, in outward show
Elaborate, of inward less exact.
For well I understand in the prime end
Of nature her th' inferior in the mind
And inward faculties which most excel,
In outward also her resembling less
His image who made both and less expressing
The character of that dominion giv'n
O'er other creatures. Yet when I approach
Her loveliness so absolute she seems
And in herself complete so well to know
Her own that what she wills to do or say

518. *bird*: the nightingale.

519. *evening star*: Venus, the goddess of love.

520. *his*: the nightingale's.

528. *here*: in this pleasure, love.

529. *transported*: carried out of himself.

531–33. Adam is superior to all other pleasures (which he names in lines 527–28) and not carried away by them, but not to the pleasure of beauty's glance. See 471–77 n.

534–36. *Or . . . Or . . .* : Following Latin usage, Milton expresses disjunctive propositions not in the form "Either . . . or . . ." but in the form "Or . . . or . . ." I.e., Either Nature left me internally weak in some part (we may guess which), or Nature took more than was necessary out of my side, which made Eve's beauty overwhelming.

536. *subducting*: drawing out, from under.

539. *exact*: The word is used in the broader Latin sense (formed from *exigo*, "to put in order, to complete"): "well-ordered, complete." The same meaning as *absolute* (line 547) and *complete* (line 548). Compare Adam's use of *exact* at 9.1017.

544. *His*: God's.

545. *character*: visual appearance, as of a mask. I.e., Adam's face, less beautiful than Eve's, is more excellent because it has on it the look of command and royal authority.

Seems wisest, virtuousest, discreetest, best.
All higher knowledge in her presence falls
Degraded. Wisdom in discourse with her
Loses discount'nanced and like folly shows.
Authority and Reason on her wait
As one intended first, not after made
Occasionally. And to consúmmate all,
Greatness of mind and nobleness their seat
Build in her loveliest and create an awe
About her as a guard angelic placed.
To whom the angel with contracted brow:
  Accuse not Nature: she hath done her part,
Do thou but thine and be not diffident
Of Wisdom! She deserts thee not if thou
Dismiss not her when most thou need'st her nigh
By áttributing overmuch to things
Less excellent as thou thyself perceiv'st.
For what admir'st thou, what transports thee so,
An outside? Fair no doubt and worthy well
Thy cherishing, thy honoring, and thy love,
Not thy subjection. Weigh with her thyself,
Then value. Oft times nothing profits more
Than self-esteem grounded on just and right
Well managed. Of that skill the more thou know'st
The more she will acknowledge thee her head
And to realities yield all her shows
Made so adorn for thy delight the more,
So awful that with honor thou may'st love
Thy mate, who sees when thou art seen least wise.
But if the sense of touch whereby mankind
Is propagated seem such dear delight
Beyond all other, think the same vouchsafed
To cattle and each beast, which would not be
To them made common and divulged if aught

550. *virtuousest*: most virtuous; pronounced in three syllables, the first and last accented: 'vírchus-ést.' Milton makes Adam inelegantly hiss to indicate a slight moral deviation, which the following lines (lines 551–59) show.

552. *Degraded*. The word is placed at the beginning of the line, after an enjambment, for a more shocking effect.

554–56. Divine *Authority* and natural *Reason* are prior conditions of Eve's being. Adam is troubled because he knows that the opposite can't be true, yet his senses tell him otherwise. We know what he means.

557. *seat*: Latin *sedes*, "dwelling place, throne."

563. *She*: wisdom.

569. *honoring* has two syllables: 'hon-ring.'

577. *awful*: awe-inspiring.

583. *made common*: made available to all equally. *Divulged* (Latin *divolgo*) has the same meaning, "to spread among all."

Therein enjoyed were worthy to subdue
The soul of Man or passion in him move.
What higher in her society thou find'st
Attractive, human, rational, love still.
In loving thou dost well, in passion not,
Wherein true love consists not. Love refines
The thoughts and heart enlarges, hath his seat
In reason and is judicious, is the scale
By which to Heav'nly love thou may'st ascend,
Not sunk in carnal pleasure, for which cause
Among the beasts no mate for thee was found.
  To whom thus half abashed Adam replied:
Neither her outside formed so fair nor aught
In procreation common to all kinds
(Though higher of the genial bed by far
And with mysterious reverence I deem)
So much delights me as those graceful acts,
Those thousand decencies that daily flow
From all her words and actions mixed with love
And sweet compliance, which declare unfeigned
Union of mind or in us both one soul.
Harmony to behold in wedded pair
More grateful than harmonious sound to th' ear,
Yet these subject not. I to thee disclose
What inward thence I feel: not therefore foiled
Who meet with various objects from the sense
Variously representing, yet still free
Approve the best and follow what I approve.
To love thou blam'st me not for love thou say'st
Leads up to Heav'n, is both the way and guide.
Bear with me then if lawful what I ask:
Love not the Heav'nly spirits? And how their love
Express they? By looks only or do they mix
Irradiance? Virtual or immediate touch?
  To whom the angel with a smile that glowed
Celestial rosy red, love's proper hue,
Answered: Let it suffice thee that thou know'st

585. Raphael says sex is not supposed to cause passion. See line 588. Milton portrays sex before the Fall, but not excitement, which Raphael condemns as beastly (line 594). See 4.741–70. At lines 598–99 we learn that Adam does not agree with Raphael's condemnation of sexual excitement as beastly.

608–11. We remain free to choose among our mental representations, according to reason.

611. *follow* has one syllable, elided with *what*: 'foll-what.'

617. *virtual or immediate*: i.e., Do angels when they love touch each other only virtually—for example, by looks—or do they touch each other directly, without intermediary—for example, by mixing their *Irradiance[s]*, their bodies of light?

Us happy and without love no happiness.
Whatever pure thou in the body enjoy'st
(And pure thou wert created) we enjoy
In eminence and obstacle find none
Of membrane, joint or limb, exclusive bars.
Easier than air with air, if spirits embrace,
Total they mix, union of pure with pure
Desiring, nor restrained conveyance need
As flesh to mix with flesh or soul with soul.
But I can now no more: the parting sun
Beyond the earth's green cape and verdant isles
Hesperian sets, my signal to depart.
Be strong, live happy and love, but first of all
Him whom to love is to obey, and keep
His great command! Take heed lest passion sway
Thy judgement to do aught which else free will
Would not admit! Thine and of all thy sons
The weal or woe in thee is placed: beware!
I in thy persevering shall rejoice
And all the blest. Stand fast! To stand or fall
Free in thine own arbitrement it lies.
Perfect within, no outward aid require
And all temptation to transgress repel.
  So saying he arose, whom Adam thus
Followed with benediction: Since to part,
Go Heav'nly guest, ethereal messenger,
Sent from whose sov'reign goodness I adore.
Gentle to me and affable hath been
Thy condescension and shall be honored ever
With grateful memory. Thou to mankind
Be good and friendly still, and oft return!
  So parted they, the angel up to Heaven
From the thick shade and Adam to his bower.

628. *restrained conveyance*: sexual organs for conducting a part of one body into a part of another. This is a restraint in comparison with angels, who mix totally (line 627).
633. *happy* and *and* are elided.
634. *Him*: love Him; i.e., Love each other, but first love God.
640. *all the blest*: all the other angels.
641. *arbitrement*: choice.
642. I.e., Since you are perfect in yourselves, you need nothing from without.
645. *benediction*: farewell blessing.
649. A feminine line, the final syllable of *ever* being unstressed. *Condescension* and *and* are elided. See 2.27 n.
653. *thick shade*: a foreboding image of the evening coming on.

Book Nine

The Argument

Satan, having compassed the earth with meditated guile, returns as a mist by night into Paradise, enters into the serpent sleeping. Adam and Eve in the morning go forth to their labors, which Eve proposes to divide in several places, each laboring apart. Adam consents not, alleging the danger lest that enemy of whom they were forewarned should attempt her, found alone. Eve, loath to be thought not circumspect or firm enough, urges her going apart, the rather desirous to make trial of her strength. Adam at last yields; the serpent finds her alone; his subtle approach, first gazing then speaking with much flattery, extolling Eve above all other creatures. Eve, wondering to hear the serpent speak, asks how he attained to human speech and such understanding not till now. The serpent answers that by tasting of a certain tree in the garden he attained both to speech and reason, till then void of both. Eve requires him to bring her to that tree and finds it to be the Tree of Knowledge forbidden. The serpent, now grown bolder, with many wiles and arguments induces her at length to eat. She, pleased with the taste, deliberates a while whether to impart thereof to Adam or not, at last brings him of the fruit, relates what persuaded her to eat thereof. Adam, at first amazed but perceiving her lost, resolves through vehemence of love to perish with her and extenuating the trespass eats also of the fruit. The effects thereof in them both. They seek to cover their nakedness, then fall to variance and accusation of one another.

No more of talk where God or angel guest
With Man as with his friend familiar used
To sit indulgent and with him partake
Rural repast, permitting him the while
Venial discourse unblamed. I now must change
Those notes to tragic: foul distrust and breach
Disloyal on the part of Man, revolt
And disobedience. On the part of Heaven,
Now alienated, distance and distaste,
Anger and just rebuke and judgment given
That brought into this world a world of woe,
Sin and her shadow Death, and Misery,
Death's harbinger. Sad task! Yet argument

Book Nine
4. *him*: Man.
5. *Venial discourse*: talk that is graciously permitted to range freely (Latin *venia*, "grace, favor, indulgence").
13. *harbinger*: a servant who goes before to prepare the way for his master.

Not less but more heroic than the wrath
Of stern Achilles on his foe pursued
Thrice fugitive about Troy wall or rage
Of Turnus for Lavinia disespoused,
Or Neptune's ire or Juno's that so long
Perplexed the Greek and Cytherea's son,
If answerable style I can obtain
Of my celestial patroness who deigns
Her nightly visitation unimplored
And díctates to me slumb'ring or inspires
Easy my unpremeditated verse,
Since first this subject for heroic song
Pleased me, long choosing and beginning late,
Not sedulous by nature to indite
Wars, hitherto the only argument
Heroic deemed, chief mast'ry to dissect
With long and tedious havoc fabled knights
In battles feigned, the better fortitude
Of patience and heroic martyrdom
Unsung. Or to describe races and games
Or tilting furniture, emblazoned shields,
Impreses quaint, caparisons and steeds,
Bases and tinsel trappings, gorgeous knights
At joust and tournament, then marshaled feast
Served up in hall with sewers and seneschals:
The skill of artifice or office mean,
Not that which justly gives heroic name

14–19. The epic poems referred to by these names are the *Iliad*, in which Hector is pursued about the walls of Troy and killed; the *Aeneid*, in the second half of which Turnus leads an Italian alliance against Aeneas and the Trojans; the *Odyssey*, in which Poseidon (in Latin, *Neptune*) is angry at Odysseus (*the Greek*); and the *Aeneid* again, in the first half of which Juno opposes Aeneas's efforts to reach Italy. (Aeneas is the son of Venus, or *Cytherea.*)

21. *celestial patroness*: Urania, Milton's muse. See 7.1–8 and 28–30.

26. Milton did not begin *Paradise Lost* until he was in his late forties.

27. *sedulous*: diligent, busy. The word is used here mockingly.

34. *tilting furniture*: equipment for jousting. *emblazoned*: decorated with heraldic imagery.

34–39. Milton moves from ancient epic to medieval and Renaissance romances: very long, elaborate tales of knights, ladies, tournaments and feasts.

35. *Impreses*: Italian *imprese* (heraldic devices). *quaint*: strange, riddling; the word is used here mockingly, dismissing such devices as trivial. *caparisons*: decorative coverings for a horse's harness.

36. *Bases*: decorated coverings for the body of a horse, complementing the *caparisons* above.

37. *marshaled feast*: a very large, highly organized feast, with marshals to seat guests in their assigned places.

38. *sewers*: a steward overseeing waiters at a feast (Anglo-French *asseour*, "seater"). *seneschal*: a head servant (like a head butler) in a medieval household.

39. I.e., To describe such things requires only technical skill or personal experience as a waiter, a low occupation (*office mean*).

To person or to poem. Me of these
Nor skilled nor studious, higher argument
Remains sufficient of itself to raise
That name unless an age too late or cold
Climate or years damp my intended wing
Depressed, and much they may if all be mine,
Not hers who brings it nightly to my ear.
  The sun was sunk and after him the star
Of Hesperus whose office is to bring
Twilight upon the earth, short arbiter
'Twixt day and night. And now from end to end
Night's hemisphere had veiled th' horizon round
When Satan who late fled before the threats
Of Gabriel out of Eden, now improved
In meditated fraud and malice bent
On Man's destruction, maugre what might hap
Of heavier on himself, fearless returned.
By night he fled and at midníght returned
From compassing the Earth, cautious of day
Since Uriel regent of the sun descried
His entrance and forewarned the cherubim
That kept their watch. Thence full of anguish driv'n
The space of seven continued nights he rode
With darkness, thrice the equinoctial line

41–44. I.e., A higher subject remains for me to take up, since I am unskilled in these lower, trivial things; and that subject is sufficient in itself, even if I were not particularly skilled, to deserve the name *heroic*.

44. *that name*: *heroic* (line 40).

44–45. Three things may weigh Milton down and keep him from completing his heroic poem: (1) he lives too late in history for such a poem to succeed; (2) he lives too far north, in a cold climate, rather than near the warm Mediterranean sea, where all great epics have hitherto been written; and (3) he is himself too old.

46. *Depressed*: pushed down (to earth).

50. *arbiter*. One who decides, in this case when day shall end and night officially begin.

54. *improved*: concealed, unseen.

56. *maugre*: despite. French *malgré*.

63–66. *rode / With darkness*. Over a week, Satan directs his flight around the earth to remain, as much as is possible, in darkness, within the cone-shaped shadow of the earth. In the *space* (line 63) of time occupied by the first three nights, Satan flies along the equator, which is (before the Fall) the *equinoctial line* (line 64), keeping just ahead of the advancing light. On the next four nights, altering his course ninety degrees, Satan flies longitudinally, around the earth's poles. He stays just within the dark by veering continuously away from the advancing edge of light, on what becomes a spiral course around the globe. (Such a course transposes the sinuous movement of a serpent in two dimensions, on a flat plane, into the third dimension, turning always to the left, or sinister.) On this latter course, however, Satan would flash into view momentarily as he passed over each pole, when traversing the *colure[s]* (longitudinal circles around the earth which intersect at right angles at the poles). Although the latter course therefore risks observation at the poles (if Uriel happens to be looking in that direction at that instant), it is much less obvious than the simple tactic of concealment on the former course. That is why Satan changes course and is willing to accept the slight risk of being glimpsed at the poles. *car* (line 65): chariot. If *Night* is imagined as a mythological figure driving a chariot around the earth, Satan crosses the path of the chariot (always just after it has passed) four times.

He circled, four times crossed the car of Night
From pole to pole traversing each colure,
On th' eighth returned and on the coast averse
From entrance or cherubic watch by stealth
Found unsuspected way. There was a place,
Now not (though sin, not time, first wrought the change)
Where Tigris at the foot of Paradise
Into a gulf shot underground till part
Rose up a fountain by the Tree of Life.
In with the river sunk and with it rose
Satan involved in rising mist, then sought
Where to lie hid. Sea he had searched and land
From Eden over Pontus and the pool
Maeotis up beyond the river Ob,
Downward as far Antarctic and in length
West from Orontes to the ocean barred
At Darien, thence to the land where flows
Ganges and Indus. Thus the orb he roamed
With narrow search and with inspection deep
Considered every creature: which of all
Most opportune might serve his wiles and found
The serpent subtlest beast of all the field.
Him after long debate irresolute
Of thoughts revolved his final sentence chose
Fit vessel, fittest imp of fraud in whom
To enter and his dark suggestions hide
From sharpest sight for in the wily snake
Whatever sleights none would suspicious mark,
As from his wit and native subtlety
Proceeding which in other beasts observed
Doubt might beget of diabolic pow'r
Active within beyond the sense of brute.
Thus he resolved but first from inward grief
His bursting passion into plaints thus poured:
  O Earth! how like to Heav'n if not preferred
More justly, seat worthier of gods as built
With second thoughts reforming what was old!
For what god after better worse would build?

67. *coast averse*: the western side of the garden, farthest from the eastern gate where Gabriel and his troop of cherubs are on watch.

87. *Him*: the serpent.

88. *final sentence*: concluding decision.

89. *imp*: not a devil but the archaic sense of the word as "offspring, shoot, or graft" (Old English *impian*, "to graft"). Spenser, *Faerie Queene* 4.9.4: "That headlesse tyrants tronke he reard from ground, / And having ympt the head to it agayne, / Vpon his vsuall beast it firmely bound." The serpent is the fittest shoot for Satan to graft his fraud with. Because the serpent is grafted to fraud it is "vitiated in nature" (10.169).

Terrestrial heav'n danced round by other heav'ns
That shine yet bear their bright officious lamps,
Light above light for thee alone, as seems
In thee concent'ring all their precious beams
Of sacred influence! As God in Heav'n
Is center yet extends to all, so thou
Cent'ring receiv'st from all those orbs. In thee,
Not in themselves, all their known virtue appears
Productive in herb, plant, and nobler birth
Of creatures animate with gradual life
Of growth, sense, reason: all summed up in Man!
With what delight could I have walked thee round
(If I could joy in aught) sweet interchange
Of hill and valley, rivers, woods and plains,
Now land, now sea and shores with forest crowned,
Rocks, dens and caves! But I in none of these
Find place or refuge and the more I see
Pleasures about me so much more I feel
Torment within me as from the hateful siege
Of cóntraries: all good to me becomes
Bane, and in Heav'n much worse would be my state.
But neither here seek I, no, nor in Heav'n
To dwell (unless by mast'ring Heav'n's Supreme),
Nor hope to be myself less miserable
By what I seek but others to make such
As I, though thereby worse to me redound.
For only in destroying I find ease
To my relentless thoughts. And him destroyed
Or won to what may work his utter loss
For whom all this was made, all this will soon
Follow as to him linked in weal or woe:
In woe then, that destruction wide may range!
To me shall be the glory sole among
Th' infernal pow'rs in one day to have marred
What He, "Almighty" styled, six nights and days
Continued making. And who knows how long
Before had been contriving? Though perhaps
Not longer than since I in one night freed

105. *thee*: Earth.
110. *virtue appears*: pronounced as three syllables: 'virch-wo-pears.'
112. *gradual* has two syllables: 'gra-jal.'
121. *me* and *as* are elided: 'm-as from.'
130. *him*: Man, "for whom all this was made" (line 132).
133. *weal*: happiness.
137. *styled*: titled.

From servitude inglorious well nigh half
Th' angelic name and thinner left the throng
Of His adorers. He to be avenged
And to repair His numbers thus impaired,
Whether such virtue, spent of old, now failed
More angels to create (if they at least
Are His created), or to spite us more
Determined to advance into our room
A creature formed of earth and him endow,
Exalted from so base original,
With Heav'nly spoils—*our* spoils! What He decreed
He effected: Man He made and for him built
Magnificent this world and Earth his seat,
Him "Lord" pronounced and (O indignity!)
Subjected to his service angel wings
And flaming ministers to watch and tend
Their earthy charge. Of these the vigilance
I dread and to elude thus wrapped in mist
Of midnight vapor glide obscure and pry
In every bush and brake where hap may find
The serpent sleeping in whose mazy folds
To hide me and the dark intent I bring.
O foul descent! That I who erst contended
With gods to sit the high'st am now constrained
Into a beast and mixed with bestial slime
This essence to incarnate and imbrute
That to the heighth of deity aspired!
But what will not ambition and revenge
Descend to? Who aspires must down as low
As high he soared, obnoxious first or last
To basest things. Revenge at first though sweet
Bitter ere long back on itself recoils.
Let it! I reck not, so it light well aimed
(Since higher I fall short) on him who next

141. *half*: in fact, one-third.
142. *angelic name*: those named "angels."
145. *virtue*: creative power.
146–47. See 5.857–61, where Satan questions whether God made the angels. *They* likely refers to humans, whom Satan does not doubt God created. But if emphasis is placed on *Are*, then *they* could refer to the angels whom Satan has just now, inadvertently, referred to as created. In the parenthesis, Satan catches himself and puts the matter back into question.
153–54. *his . . . Him*: Man.
156. *flaming ministers*: "Who maketh his angels spirits; his ministers a flaming fire" (Psalm 104:4).
163. *erst*: erstwhile, formerly.
170. *obnoxious*: exposed, subject to.
174. *Since higher I fall short*: i.e., since his revenge on God is unsuccessful.

Provokes my envy: this new favorite
Of Heav'n, this man of clay, son of despite
Whom us the more to spite his Maker raised
From dust. Spite then with spite is best repaid!
So saying through each thicket dank or dry
Like a black mist low creeping he held on
His midnight search where soonest he might find
The serpent. Him fast sleeping soon he found
In labyrinth of many a round self-rolled,
His head the midst well stored with subtle wiles.
Not yet in horrid shade or dismal den
Nor nocent yet but on the grassy herb
Fearless unfeared he slept. In at his mouth
The Devil entered and his brutal sense
In heart or head possessing soon inspired
With act intelligential, but his sleep
Disturbed not, waiting close th' approach of morn.
Now when as sacred light began to dawn
In Eden on the humid flow'rs that breathed
Their morning incense, when all things that breathe
From th' Earth's great altar send up silent praise
To the Creator and His nostrils fill
With grateful smell, forth came the human pair
And joined their vocal worship to the choir
Of creatures wanting voice; that done, partake
The season prime for sweetest scents and airs;
Then cómmune how that day they best may ply
Their growing work. For much their work outgrew
The hands' dispatch of two, gardening so wide,
And Eve first to her husband thus began:
Adam, well may we labor still to dress
This garden, still to tend plant, herb and flow'r,
Our pleasant task enjoined, but till more hands
Aid us, the work under our labor grows
Luxurious by restraint: what we by day
Lop overgrown or prune or prop or bind
One night or two with wanton growth derides,
Tending to wild. Thou therefore now advise
Or hear what to my mind first thoughts present:
Let us divide our labors, thou where choice
Leads thee or where most needs, whether to wind

186. *nocent*: harmful (Latin *noceo*, "to injure, harm").
187–90. *his*: All three occurrences of *his* refer to the serpent.
198–99. *choir / Of creatures*: the flowers. *wanting*: lacking. The smell of the flowers is "silent praise" (line 195).

The woodbine round this arbor or direct
The clasping ivy where to climb, while I
In yonder spring of roses intermixed
With myrtle find what to redress till noon.
For while so near each other thus all day
Our task we choose what wonder if, so near,
Looks intervene and smiles or object new
Casual discóurse draw on which intermits
Our day's work brought to little, though begun
Early, and th' hour of supper come unearned.
  To whom mild answer Adam thus returned:
Sole Eve, associate soul, to me beyond
Compare above all living creatures dear,
Well hast thou motioned, well thy thoughts employed
How we might best fulfil the work which here
God hath assigned us, nor of me shalt pass
Unpraised, for nothing lovelier can be found
In woman than to study household good
And good works in her husband to promote.
Yet not so strictly hath our Lord imposed
Labor as to debar us when we need
Refreshment, whether food or talk between,
Food of the mind or this sweet intercourse
Of looks and smiles, for smiles from reason flow,
To brute denied, and are of love the food,
Love not the lowest end of human life.
For not to irksome toil but to delight
He made us and delight to reason joined.
These paths and bow'rs, doubt not but our joint hands
Will keep from wilderness with ease as wide
As we need walk till younger hands ere long
Assist us. But if much convérse perhaps
Thee satiate, to short absence I could yield,
For solitude sometimes is best society
And short retirement urges sweet return.
But other doubt possesses me lest harm
Befall thee severed from me for thou know'st
What hath been warned us, what malicious foe,
Envying our happiness and of his own
Despairing, seeks to work us woe and shame
By sly assault and somewhere nigh at hand

232–34. "She looketh well to the ways of her household, and eateth not the bread of idleness" (Proverbs 31:27).

238. *intercourse*: exchange; literally "running between" (Latin).

246. *younger hands*: those of their children.

248. *satiate* has two syllables: 'say-shut.'

Watches no doubt with greedy hope to find
His wish and best advantage: us asunder,
Hopeless to circumvent us joined where each
To other speedy aid might lend at need,
Whether his first design be to withdraw
Our fealty from God or to disturb
Conjugal love, than which perhaps no bliss
Enjoyed by us excites his envy more.
Or this or worse, leave not the faithful side
That gave thee being, still shades thee and protects!
The wife where danger or dishonor lurks
Safest and seemliest by her husband stays
Who guards her or with her the worst endures.
 To whom the virgin majesty of Eve
As one who loves and some unkindness meets
With sweet austere composure thus replied:
 Offspring of Heav'n and Earth and all Earth's lord,
That such an enemy we have who seeks
Our ruin both by thee informed I learn
And from the parting angel overheard
As in a shady nook I stood behind
Just then returned at shut of evening flow'rs.
But that thou shouldst my firmness therefore doubt
To God or thee because we have a foe
May tempt it I expected not to hear.
His violence thou fear'st not, being such
As we, not capable of death or pain
Can either not receive or can repel.
His fraud is then thy fear, which plain infers
Thy equal fear that my firm faith and love
Can by his fraud be shaken or seduced!—
Thoughts which, how found they harbor in thy breast,
Adam, misthought of her to thee so dear.
 To whom with healing words Adam replied:
Daughter of God and Man, immortal Eve,
For such thou art, from sin and blame entire:
Not diffident of thee do I dissuade
Thy absence from my sight but to avoid

262–64. Adam guesses correctly. Satan envies Adam and Eve's physical love and mentions that relentless "fierce desire" is one of the torments of Hell (4.509–11).
282–83. The implied subject of *being* is *we*. I.e., We, being as we are incapable of death or pain.
284. The object of *receive* and *repel* is *violence* (line 282).
288–89. I.e., However those thoughts came into your breast, Adam, they are *misthought* of me, who am to you so dear.
292. *entire*: untouched.
293. *diffident*: distrusting.

Th' attempt itself intended by our foe.
For he who tempts, though in vain, at least asperses
The tempted with dishonor foul, supposed
Not incorruptible of faith, not proof
Against temptation. Thou thyself with scorn
And anger would'st resent the offered wrong
Though ineffectual found. Misdeem not then
If such affront I labor to avert
From thee alone which on us both at once
The enemy, though bold, will hardly dare
Or, daring, first on me th' assault shall light.
Nor thou his malice and false guile condemn:
Subtle he needs must be who could seduce
Angels. Nor think superfluous others' aid:
I from the influence of thy looks receive
Accés in every virtue, in thy sight
More wise, more watchful, stronger if need were
Of outward strength while Shame, thou looking on
(Shame to be overcome or overreached)
Would utmost vigor raise and, raised, unite.
Why shouldst not thou like sense within thee feel
When I am present and thy trial choose
With me, best witness of thy virtue tried?
So spake domestic Adam in his care
And matrimonial love. But Eve who thought
Less áttributed to her faith sincere
Thus her reply with accent sweet renewed:
  If this be our condition thus to dwell
In narrow circuit straitened by a foe
Subtle or violent, we not endued
Single with like defence wherever met,
How are we happy, still in fear of harm?
But harm precedes not sin: only our foe
Tempting affronts us with his foul esteem
Of our integrity. His foul esteem
Sticks no dishonor on our front but turns

306. *condemn*: despise, underestimate.
309. *influence* has two syllables: 'in-flence.' Alternatively, *the* and *influence* are elided: 'th'inflúence.'
310. *Accés*: increased power.
312–14. Adam's personified Shame would arouse his, Adam's, greatest reserves of strength. His shame would then join forces with his strength to defeat the enemy. *Shame* at line 313 can be read as a verb ('is ashamed'), the subject of which is *Shame* (line 312); i.e., Shame is ashamed to be overcome. But this would detract from the force of the main verb *raise* (line 314). The sentence works better if line 313 is a restrictive clause modifying *Shame* in line 312—hence the parentheses.
319. *matrimonial* has four syllables: 'matrimon-yal.'
326. *still*: always.

Foul on himself! Then wherefore shunned or feared
By us who rather double honor gain
From his surmise proved false, find peace within,
Favor from Heav'n, our witness, from th' event?
And what is faith, love, virtue unassayed,
Alone, without exterior help sustained?
Let us not then suspect our happy state
Left so imperfect by the Maker wise
As not secure to single or combined.
Frail is our happiness if this be so
And Eden were no Eden thus exposed!
To whom thus Adam fervently replied:
O Woman! best are all things as the will
Of God ordained them. His creating hand
Nothing imperfect or deficient left
Of all that He created, much less Man
Or aught that might his happy state secure,
Secure from outward force. Within himself
The danger lies, yet lies within his power:
Against his will he can receive no harm.
But God left free the will, for what obeys
Reason is free, and reason he made right
But bid her well beware and still erect
Lest by some fair appearing good surprised
She díctate false and misinform the will
To do what God expressly hath forbid.
Not then mistrust but tender love enjoins
That I should mind thee oft—and mind thou me!
Firm we subsist, yet possible to swerve
Since reason not impossibly may meet
Some specious object by the foe suborned
And fall into deception unaware,
Not keeping strictest watch as she was warned.
Seek not temptation, then, which to avoid
Were better and most likely if from me
Thou sever not: trial will come unsought.
Wouldst thou approve thy constancy? Approve
First thy obedience! Th' other who can know

335–36. I.e., Of what value are faith, love, and virtue if they remain alone and are not put to the test by what is outside them? Whatever tempts virtue helps virtue to be more clearly what it is. This statement, the argument of Milton's *Areopagitica*, describes the dialectical conditions in which virtue operates after the Fall, but not before. (See pp. 349–50.)

341. *exposed*: to danger.

348. *Secure*: God has secured them against any direct violence (*outward force*). But because they are free, they are not secure against inward treason (lines 351–52).

363. *she*: reason.

368. *th'other*: constancy.

Not seeing thee attempted, who attest?
But if thou think trial unsought may find
Us both securer than thus warned thou seem'st,
Go, for thy stay, not free, absents thee more.
Go in thy native innocence, rely
On what thou hast of virtue, summon all,
For God towards thee hath done his part: do thine!
So spake the patriarch of mankind. But Eve
Persisted, yet submiss, though last, replied:
With thy permission then and thus forewarned
Chiefly by what thy own last reasoning words
Touched only, that our trial when least sought
May find us both perhaps far less prepared,
The willinger I go, nor much expect
A foe so proud will first the weaker seek:
So bent, the more shall shame him his repulse.
Thus saying, from her husband's hand her hand
Soft she withdrew and like a wood-nymph light,
Oread or Dryad, or of Delia's train,
Betook her to the groves, but Delia's self
In gait surpassed and goddess-like deport,
Though not, as she, with bow and quiver armed
But with such gard'ning tools as art yet rude,
Guiltless of fire, had formed, or angels brought.
To Pales or Pomona thus adorned
Likest she seemed (Pomona when she fled
Vertumnus) or to Ceres in her prime
Yet virgin of Prosérpina from Jove.
Her long with ardent look his eye pursued
Delighted but desiring more her stay.
Oft he to her his charge of quick return
Repeated, she to him as oft engaged

372. *thy stay . . . more*. The truest thing said in this poem.

377. I.e., Although she continued verbally to express submission to Adam, Eve spoke last. Milton implies that Eve's verbal submission to Adam is not borne out by her insistence on going. Milton offers the subtle thought that it is possible, even in the state of innocence, to make a mistake. (It is also possible to lose your temper, as Adam does at line 342, when he replies *fervently*.) The difference is that in the state of innocence no mistake has necessary or irreversible consequences. After the Fall, mistakes are irreversible and cannot be set right.

390. *she*: Delia.

391–92. A good example of Milton's wish to leave no practical detail unexplained. Since there was no fire in Eden, there was no forge to make iron tools. Therefore Adam and Eve either made *rude* stone tools themselves or the angels brought them rather better ones from heaven.

392. *Guiltless*: Iron tools were made in the forge, but so were weapons. Fire is therefore seen as a symptom of the Fall, of human guilt.

393–96. Goddesses associated with fertility.

396. *Yet virgin*: before Persephone was born, and therefore before winter.

To be returned by noon amid the bow'r
And all things in best order to invite
Noontide repast or afternoon's repose.
O much deceived, much failing, hapless Eve,
Of thy presumed return! Event perverse!
Thou never from that hour in Paradise
Found'st either sweet repast or sound repose,
Such ambush hid among sweet flow'rs and shades,
Waited with hellish rancor imminent
To intercept thy way or send thee back
Despoiled of innocence, of faith, of bliss.
  For now and since first break of dawn the Fiend,
Mere serpent in appearance, forth was come
And on his quest where likeliest he might find
The only two of mankind (but in them
The whole included race) his purposed prey.
In bow'r and field he sought where any tuft
Of grove or garden plot more pleasant lay
Their tendance or plantation for delight.
By fountain or by shady rivulet
He sought them both but wished his hap might find
Eve separate. He wished, but not with hope
Of what so seldom chanced when to his wish
Beyond his hope Eve separate he spies
Veiled in a cloud of fragrance where she stood,
Half spied, so thick the roses bushing round
About her glowed, oft stooping to support
Each flow'r of slender stalk whose head, though gay
Carnation, purple, azure or specked with gold
Hung drooping unsustained. Them she upstays
Gently with myrtle band, mindless the while
Herself though fairest unsupported flow'r
From her best prop so far and storm so nigh.
Nearer he drew and many a walk traversed
Of stateliest covert, cedar, pine or palm,
Then voluble and bold, now hid, now seen,
Among thick-woven arborets and flow'rs
Embordered on each bank, the hand of Eve,
Spot more delicious than those gardens feigned
Or of revived Adonis or renowned

417. *bow'r*: overhanging wood (not Adam and Eve's nuptial bower).
417–18. *tuft of grove*: cluster of trees.
421. *wished his hap*: wished he would have the luck.
431. *myrtle band*: rods from the myrtle bush, which, like the roses these myrtles support, are sacred to Venus, the goddess of love.
438. *the hand of Eve*: done by Eve's hand.

Alcinous host of old Laertes' son
Or that, not mystic, where the sapient king
Held dalliance with his fair Egyptian spouse.
Much he the place admired, the person more.
As one who long in populous city pent
Where houses thick and sewers annoy the air
Forth issuing on a summer's morn to breathe
Among the pleasant villages and farms
Adjoined, from each thing met conceives delight—
The smell of grain or tedded grass, or kine
Or dairy, each rural sight, each rural sound—
If chance with nymph-like step fair virgin pass
What pleasing seemed, for her now pleases more,
She most, and in her look sums all delight.
Such pleasure took the serpent to behold
This flow'ry plat the sweet recess of Eve,
Thus early, thus alone. Her Heav'nly form
Angelic but more soft and feminine,
Her graceful innocence, her every air
Of gesture or least action overawed
His malice and with rapine sweet bereaved
His fierceness of the fierce intent it brought.
That space the evil one abstracted stood
From his own evil and for the time remained
Stupidly good, of enmity disarmed,
Of guile, of hate, of envy, of revenge.
But the hot Hell that always in him burns,
Though in mid-Heav'n, soon ended his delight
And tortures him now more the more he sees
Of pleasure not for him ordained. Then soon
Fierce hate he recollects and all his thoughts
Of mischief gratulating thus excites:
  Thoughts, whither have ye led me, with what sweet
Compulsion thus transported to forget
What hither brought us? Hate, not love! Nor hope
Of Paradise for Hell, hope here to taste

442. *not mystic*: not imagined ("feigned," line 439), like the gardens just mentioned, but real, because biblical.

442–43. *sapient king*: Solomon, legendary for his wisdom and also for his many wives, one of whom was an Egyptian princess.

444. *he*: Satan. *the person*: Eve.

450. *tedded grass*: hay spread out to dry before storage.

451. *dairy* and *each* are elided.

461. *rapine*: a seizing, a rapture.

465. *stupidly good*: good because he is in a stupor. *Stupid* here does not mean "unintelligent"; it means "stunned."

472. *gratulating*: taking pleasure in. The object of *excites* (Latin *excito*, "to wake, rouse, call forth") is *thoughts* (line 471).

Of pleasure, but all pleasure to destroy
Save what is in destroying! Other joy
To me is lost. Then let me not let pass
Occasion which now smiles: behold alone
The woman opportune to all attempts,
Her husband (for I view far round) not nigh,
Whose higher intellectual more I shun
And strength of courage haughty and of limb
Heroic built though of terrestrial mould,
Foe not informidable, exempt from wound,
I not, so much hath Hell debased and pain
Enfeebled me to what I was in Heav'n.
She fair, divinely fair, fit love for gods,
Not terrible, though terror be in love
And beauty not approached by stronger hate,
Hate stronger under show of love well-feigned,
The way which to her ruin now I tend.
  So spake the enemy of mankind, enclosed
In serpent, inmate bad, and toward Eve
Addressed his way not with indented wave
Prone on the ground, as since, but on his rear,
Circular base of rising folds that towered
Fold above fold, a surging maze. His head
Crested aloft and carbuncle his eyes
With burnished neck of verdant gold erect
Amidst his circling spires that on the grass
Floated redundant. Pleasing was his shape
And lovely, never since of serpent kind
Lovelier, not those that in Illyria changed
Hermione and Cadmus or the god
In Epidaurus, nor to which transformed
Ammonian Jove or Capitoline was seen,
He with Olympias this with her who bore

480. *Occasion*: opportunity.
490–92. Love (and beauty) can inspire a kind of terror in the lover, unless the lover secretly hates whom he merely pretends to love.
494. *Enemy* has two syllables: 'en-my.'
498–99. *surging maze*: This picture of the rising, moving, complicatedly twisting loops of the serpent's body is among the finest poetic images in the poem.
500. *carbuncle*: red, like burning coals (Latin *carbo*, "a coal").
501. *verdant*: green. A greenish tint to the serpent's lustrous, gold neck.
502. The head is in the center of a circle of folds, which rise like spires. The architectural image suggests a moving castle.
503. *redundant*: pour over one another.
505–10. A passage of virtuosic classical allusion. The stories are about serpents that were not what they seemed. In the serpents were concealed a king and his queen, the god of healing, and the king of the gods, who as a serpent begot (on separate occasions) Alexander the Great and Scipio, Rome's greatest military hero.

Scipio the heighth of Rome. With tract oblique,
At first as one who sought accéss but feared
To interrupt, sidelong he works his way.
As when a ship by skilful steersman wrought
Nigh river's mouth or foreland where the wind
Veers oft, as oft so steers and shifts her sail,
So varied he and of his tortuous train
Curled many a wanton wreath in sight of Eve
To lure her eye. She, busied, heard the sound
Of rustling leaves but minded not as used
To such disport before her through the field
From every beast more duteous at her call
Than at Circean call the herd disguised.
He bolder now uncalled before her stood
But as in gaze admiring. Oft he bowed
His turret crest and sleek enamelled neck,
Fawning, and licked the ground whereon she trod.
His gentle dumb expression turned at length
The eye of Eve to mark his play. He, glad
Of her attention gained, with serpent tongue
Organic or impúlse of vocal air
His fraudulent temptation thus began:
  Wonder not, Sovereign Mistress, if perhaps
Thou canst, who art sole wonder, much less arm
Thy looks, the heav'n of mildness, with disdain,
Displeased that I approach thee thus and gaze
Insatiate, I thus single, nor have feared
Thy awful brow, more awful thus retired!
Fairest resemblance of thy Maker fair,
Thee all things living gaze on (all things thine
By gift) and thy celestial beauty adore
With ravishment beheld, there best beheld
Where universally admired. But here
In this enclosure wild these beasts among
(Beholders rude and shallow to discern
Half what in thee is fair), one man except,
Who sees thee? (and what is one?), who shouldst be seen
A goddess among gods adored and served

519. *minded not*: paid no attention.

529–30. Satan emits sound through the serpent either by using the serpent's tongue or by emitting pulses of air, which make sound by vibrating in the elongated tube of the serpent's body.

538. We are to recall that Adam, not Eve, is made in God's image. Eve is made in the image of Adam's desire.

540. *beauty* and *adore* are elided: 'beaut-yadore.'

By angels numberless thy daily train!
  So glozed the Tempter and his proem tuned.
Into the heart of Eve his words made way
Though at the voice much marveling. At length
Not unamazed she thus in answer spake:
  What may this mean? Language of man pronounced
By tongue of brute and human sense expressed?
The first at least of these I thought denied
To beasts whom God on their creation-day
Created mute to all articulate sound,
The latter I demur for in their looks
Much reason and in their actions oft appears.
Thee, Serpent, subtlest beast of all the field
I knew, but not with human voice endued.
Redouble then this miracle and say
How cam'st thou speakable of mute and how
To me so friendly grown above the rest
Of brutal kind that daily are in sight?
Say, for such wonder claims attention due.
  To whom the guileful Tempter thus replied:
Empress of this fair world, resplendent Eve,
Easy to me it is to tell thee all
What thou command'st and right thou shouldst be obeyed.
I was at first as other beasts that graze
The trodden herb: of abject thoughts and low,
As was my food, nor aught but food discerned,
Or sex, and apprehended nothing high.
Till on a day roving the field I chanced
A goodly tree far distant to behold
Loaden with fruit of fairest colors mixed,
Ruddy and gold. I nearer drew to gaze
When from the boughs a savory odor blown,
Grateful to appetite, more pleased my sense
Than smell of sweetest fennel or the teats
Of ewe or goat dropping with milk at ev'n
Unsucked of lamb or kid that tend their play.
To satisfy the sharp desire I had
Of tasting those fair apples I resolved
Not to defer. Hunger and thirst at once,

549. *glozed*: spoke deceitfully. *proem*: prelude, introduction.
555. *first*: language.
558. *latter*: *human sense* (line 554), meaning.
570. A hypermetrical line. *thou* and *shouldst* are elided: 'thou'lst.'
581–82. Snakes were popularly supposed to suck milk from sheep and goats.
585. The forbidden fruit is here for the first time referred to as *apples*. Satan will do so again at 10.487.

Powerful persuaders, quickened by the scent
Of that alluring fruit, urged me so keen.
About the mossy trunk I wound me soon
For high from ground the branches would require
Thy utmost reach or Adam's. Round the tree
All other beasts that saw with like desire
Longing and envying stood but could not reach.
Amid the tree now got, where plenty hung
Tempting so nigh, to pluck and eat my fill
I spared not, for such pleasure till that hour
At feed or fountain never had I found.
Sated at length ere long I might perceive
Strange alteration in me to degree
Of reason in my inward pow'rs, and speech
Wanted not long though to this shape retained.
Thenceforth to speculations high or deep
I turned my thoughts and with capacious mind
Considered all things visible in heav'n
Or earth or middle, all things fair and good.
But all that fair and good in thy divine
Semblance and in thy beauty's heav'nly ray
United I beheld, no fair to thine
Equivalent or second, which compelled
Me thus though importune perhaps to come
And gaze and worship thee, of right declared
Sovereign of creatures, universal dame!
   So talked the spirited sly snake and Eve
Yet more amazed unwary thus replied:
   Serpent, thy overpraising leaves in doubt
The virtue of that fruit in thee first proved.
But say, where grows that tree, from hence how far?
For many are the trees of God that grow
In Paradise and various yet unknown
To us: in such abundance lies our choice
As leaves a greater store of fruit untouched,
Still hanging incorruptible till men
Grow up to their provision and more hands
Help to disburden Nature of her birth.
   To whom the wily adder blithe and glad:
Empress, the way is ready and not long:
Beyond a row of myrtles on a flat

593. Satan introduces Eve to the pleasure of hoarding what others desire.
601. Although he gained the power of speech, that power remained confined to the form (*shape*) of a serpent.
605. *Middle*: the air between earth and heaven.
612. *universal dame*: lady, and ruler of the universe.

Fast by a fountain, one small thicket past
Of blowing myrrh and balm. If thou accept
My conduct I can bring thee thither soon.
  Lead then, said Eve. He leading swiftly rolled
In tangles and made intricate seem straight
To mischief swift. Hope elevates and joy
Brightens his crest. As when a wand'ring fire,
Compact of unctuous vapor which the night
Condenses and the cold environs round,
Kindled through agitation to a flame
Which oft, they say, some evil spirit attends,
Hovering and blazing with delusive light,
Misleads th' amazed night-wanderer from his way
To bogs and mires and oft through pond or pool,
There swallowed up and lost from succor far,
So glistered the dire snake and into fraud
Led Eve our credulous mother to the Tree
Of Prohibition, root of all our woe.
Which when she saw thus to her guide she spake:
  Serpent, we might have spared our coming hither,
Fruitless to me though fruit be here t' excess,
The credit of whose virtue rest with thee,
Wondrous indeed if cause of such effects.
But of this tree we may not taste nor touch:
God so commanded and left that command
Sole daughter of His voice. The rest we live
Law to ourselves: our reason is our law.
  To whom the Tempter guilefully replied:
Indeed? Hath God then said that of the fruit
Of all these garden trees ye shall not eat
Yet lords declared of all in earth or air?
To whom thus Eve yet sinless: Of the fruit
Of each tree in the garden we may eat
But of the fruit of this fair tree amidst
The garden God hath said, "Ye shall not eat
Thereof nor shall ye touch it, lest ye die."
  She scarce had said, though brief, when now more bold
The Tempter but with show of zeal and love

634–42. *wand'ring fire*: Fairy light: phosphorescent swamp gas that misleads travelers at night, thought to be the malicious work of fairies. Typically, Milton gives a scientific account of the phenomenon before mentioning the folkloric account, which he then darkens by making an "evil spirit" responsible.

653–54. *The rest*: I.e., As to the rest of the natural world, we do as we please, governed by our own reason, which is our only law. "For when the Gentiles, which have not the law, do by nature the things contained in the law, these, having not the law, are a law unto themselves: Which show the work of the law written in their hearts" (Romans 2:14–15).

To man and indignation at his wrong
New part puts on and as to passion moved
Fluctuates disturbed, yet comely, and in act
Raised as of some great matter to begin.
As when of old some orator renowned
In Athens or free Rome where eloquence
Flourished (since mute) to some great cause addressed
Stood in himself collected while each part,
Motion, each act won audience ere the tongue,
Sometimes in heighth began as no delay
Of preface brooking through his zeal of right,
So standing, moving, or to heighth upgrown
The Tempter all impassioned thus began:
  O sacred, wise, and wisdom-giving plant,
Mother of science, now I feel thy pow'r
Within me clear not only to discern
Things in their causes but to trace the ways
Of highest agents deemed however wise!
Queen of this universe, do not believe
Those rigid threats of death! Ye shall not die.
How should ye? By the fruit? It gives you life
To knowledge. By the Threat'ner? Look on me!
Me who have touched and tasted yet both live
And life more perfect have attained than fate
Meant me by vent'ring higher than my lot.
Shall that be shut to Man which to the beast
Is open? Or will God incense His ire
For such a petty trespass and not praise
Rather your dauntless virtue whom the pain
Of death denounced (whatever thing death be)
Deterred not from achieving what might lead
To happier life, knowledge of good and evil?
Of good, how just? Of evil (if what is evil
Be real) why not known since easier shunned?
God therefore cannot hurt ye and be just:
Not just, not God! Not feared then, nor obeyed.
Your fear itself of death removes the fear!

668. *in act*: by his actions seemed.

671. *free Rome*: Rome of the Republic, before the emperors.

683. *highest agents*: God, whom Satan refers to in the plural, the first of Satan's efforts to instill polytheism and idolatry in the human mind. See line 709 and n. and lines 716–19. We see Satan's success at line 804.

698. *evil*: The first occurrence of this word in this line should be pronounced with one syllable, 'eel.'

702. What appears to be a chain of necessary consequences is drawn into a circle: i.e., God would not allow anything fearful to exist. Because you fear death, death must not exist: your fear therefore proves that there is nothing to fear.

Why then was this forbid? Why but to awe,
Why but to keep ye low and ignorant,
His worshippers? He knows that in the day
Ye eat thereof your eyes, that seem so clear
Yet are but dim, shall perfectly be then
Opened and cleared and ye shall be as gods
Knowing both good and evil as they know.
That ye should be as gods since I as Man,
Internal Man, is but proportion meet:
I of brute human, ye of human gods.
So ye shall die perhaps by putting off
Human to put on gods: death to be wished,
Though threatened, which no worse than this can bring!
And what are gods that Man may not become
As they, participating godlike food?
The gods are first and that advantage use
On our belief that all from them proceeds.
I question it, for this fair earth I see
Warmed by the sun producing every kind,
Them nothing. If they all things, who enclosed
Knowledge of good and evil in this tree
That whoso eats thereof forthwith attains
Wisdom without their leave? And wherein lies
Th' offence that Man should thus attain to know?
What can your knowledge hurt Him or this tree
Impart against His will if all be His?
Or is it envy? And can envy dwell
In Heav'nly breasts? These, these and many more
Causes import your need of this fair fruit.
Goddess humane, reach then and freely taste!

709. *they*: God and the angels. The plural is biblical: "And the Lord God said, Behold, the man is become as one of us, to know good and evil" (Genesis 3:22). But Satan's aim is to suggest multiplicity in God, in order to make it easier for the rebel angels to present themselves on earth as gods. See lines 716–19.

712. *of*: from. The understood verbs are *was made* and *shall be made*: 'As I was made human from an animal, so you shall be made gods from humans.'

713–14. "For this corruptible matter must put on incorruption, and this mortal must put on immortality" (1 Corinthians 15:53).

716–19. The earlier suggestion that God is plural becomes explicit in these lines.

718–19. This is essentially the same argument Satan uses at 5.856–60, where he suggests that the idea that God created the angels is a fiction devised by God to get an advantage over the angels.

722–30. The insinuation in these lines is that the gods enclosed knowledge of good and evil in the tree, and forbade eating its fruit, to conceal the lie that all things proceed from the gods. If Eve were to eat the fruit, she would see the lie of Creation exposed.

729–30. *can envy . . . breasts?* A conspicuous allusion to the question of Virgil's *Aeneid* (1.11). The poet tells of Juno's hostility to Aeneas and asks, "Can so much anger dwell in heavenly breasts?"

731. *need*: a telling word. Temptation always works like advertising: by persuading the tempted that she or he has a need not recognized before. See line 755: *our want*.

732. *humane*: human, and humane. Satan says Eve is a human goddess, and a gracious one.

He ended and his words replete with guile
Into her heart too easy entrance won.
Fixed on the fruit she gazed which to behold
Might tempt alone and in her ears the sound
Yet rung of his persuasive words impregned
With reason (to her seeming) and with truth.
Meanwhile the hour of noon drew on and waked
An eager appetite raised by the smell
So savory of that fruit which with desire
Inclinable now grown to touch or taste
Solicited her longing eye. Yet first
Pausing a while thus to herself she mused:
Great are thy virtues doubtless, best of fruits,
Though kept from Man, and worthy to be admired,
Whose taste too long forborne at first assay
Gave elocution to the mute and taught
The tongue not made for speech to speak thy praise.
Thy praise He also who forbids thy use
Conceals not from us, naming thee the Tree
Of Knowledge, knowledge both of good and evil,
Forbids us then to taste, but His forbidding
Commends thee more while it infers the good
By thee communicated and our want.
For good unknown sure is not had or had
And yet unknown is as not had at all!
In plain then what forbids He but to know,
Forbids us good, forbids us to be wise?
Such prohibitions bind not! But if death
Bind us with after-bands what profits then
Our inward freedom? In the day we eat
Of this fair fruit our doom is we shall die.
How dies the serpent? He hath eat'n and lives
And knows, and speaks, and reasons and discerns,
Irrational till then. For us alone
Was death invented? Or to us denied
This intellectual food for beasts reserved?
For beasts it seems: yet that one beast which first
Hath tasted envies not but brings with joy
The good befall'n him, author unsuspect,
Friendly to man, far from deceit or guile.
What fear I then, rather what know to fear

737. *impregned*: filled with, impregnated with.
741. *savory* has two syllables: 'save-ry.'
771. *author*: authority (the serpent).
773–75. I.e., Since I do not know the difference between good and evil, it can't be evil of me to eat the fruit. And I can't possibly fear death when I don't know what it is.

Under this ignorance of good and evil,
Of God or death, of law or penalty?
Here grows the cure of all: this fruit divine,
Fair to the eye, inviting to the taste,
Of virtue to make wise. What hinders then
To reach and feed at once both body and mind?
So saying, her rash hand in evil hour
Forth reaching to the fruit, she plucked, she eat:
Earth felt the wound and Nature from her seat
Sighing through all her works gave signs of woe
That all was lost. Back to the thicket slunk
The guilty serpent and well might for Eve
Intent now wholly on her taste naught else
Regarded, such delight till then as seemed
In fruit she never tasted whether true
Or fancied so, through expectation high
Of knowledge, nor was godhead from her thought.
Greedily she engorged without restraint
And knew not eating death. Satiate at length
And heightened as with wine, jocund and boon,
Thus to herself she pleasingly began:
O sovereign, virtuous, precious of all trees
In Paradise, of operation blest
To sapience, hitherto obscured, infamed,
And thy fair fruit let hang as to no end
Created! But henceforth my early care,
Not without song each morning and due praise,
Shall tend thee and the fertile burden ease
Of thy full branches offered free to all
Till dieted by thee I grow mature
In knowledge as the gods who all things know,
Though others envy what they cannot give,
For had the gift been theirs it had not here
Thus grown. Experience next, to thee I owe,
Best guide. Not foll'wing thee, I had remained
In ignorance. Thou open'st wisdom's way
And giv'st accéss though secret she retire.
And I perhaps am secret: Heav'n is high,

778. *Of virtue*: having the power.
779. *body* and *and* are elided: 'bod-yand.'
792. *Satiate* has two syllables.
793. *jocund and boon*: cheerful, gay, convivial.
805. *others*: the gods.
807. *next*. Eve thanks the tree first and experience (as opposed to reason, or precept) next. She knows the fruit is good because she has experienced its goodness in herself. Milton takes a dim view of empiricism.

High and remote to see from thence distinct
Each thing on Earth and other care perhaps
May have diverted from continual watch
Our great Forbidder, safe with all His spies
About Him. But to Adam in what sort
Shall I appear? Shall I to him make known
As yet my change and give him to partake
Full happiness with me? Or rather not,
But keep the odds of knowledge in my pow'r
Without copartner so to add what wants
In female sex, the more to draw his love
And render me more equal and, perhaps,
A thing not undesirable, sometime
Superior: for inferior who is free?
This may be well. But what if God have seen
And death ensue? Then I shall be no more
And Adam wedded to another Eve
Shall live with her enjoying, I extinct:
A death to think! Confirmed then I resolve
Adam shall share with me in bliss or woe.
So dear I love him that with him all deaths
I could endure, without him live no life.
  So saying from the tree her step she turned,
But first low reverence done as to the pow'r
That dwelt within whose presence had infused
Into the plant sciential sap derived
From nectar, drink of gods. Adam the while
Waiting desirous her return had wove
Of choicest flow'rs a garland to adorn
Her tresses and her rural labors crown

814. *continual* has three syllables: 'contin-yal.'

815. The shock given by Eve's language—God is a *Forbidder*, the angels are his *spies*—is greater for being the delayed subject of lines 813–14 and for being placed at the head of the line after an enjambment.

816–17. *But to Adam . . . appear*. The influence of the English stage, especially of Shakespeare, becomes clearer as this speech proceeds. Eve gives a soliloquy, calculating how she will appear to and manipulate others.

822. *the more to draw his love*. Eve shows the beginnings of insecurity in marriage, wishing to improve herself in some way to draw more love from her husband, suspecting that he doesn't love her enough.

826–27. Eve's hope of being superior to Adam depends on God's not seeing her take the fruit. For if God does, she will die.

830. *A death to think!* I.e., It is as horrible as death merely to think of Adam with another wife. (It is not.)

835. The first formal act of idolatry: Eve worships the tree, supposing there to be a godlike *power* within it.

835–38. *as to the pow'r . . . gods*: these lines reflect how Eve understands the tree, supposing divine and magical properties dwell in it. They are intended to show where and how false ideas in religion (especially in Roman Catholic notions of the real presence of Christ in the eucharist) get started.

As reapers oft are wont their harvest queen.
Great joy he promised to his thoughts and new
Solace in her return so long delayed.
Yet oft his heart, divine of something ill,
Misgave him: he the falt'ring measure felt
And forth to meet her went the way she took
That morn when first they parted. By the Tree
Of Knowledge he must pass. There he her met
Scarce from the tree returning, in her hand
A bough of fairest fruit that downy smiled
New gathered and ambrosial smell diffused.
To him she hasted. In her face excuse
Came prologue and apology too prompt
Which with bland words at will she thus addressed:
  Hast thou not wondered, Adam, at my stay?
Thee I have missed and thought it long, deprived
Thy presence, agony of love till now
Not felt, nor shall be twice, for never more
Mean I to try what rash untried I sought:
The pain of absence from thy sight. But strange
Hath been the cause and wonderful to hear!
This tree is not as we are told a tree
Of danger tasted nor to evil unknown
Op'ning the way but of divine effect
To open eyes and make them gods who taste,
And hath been tasted such! The serpent wise,
Or not restrained as we or not obeying,
Hath eaten of the fruit and is become
Not dead, as we are threatened, but thenceforth
Endued with human voice and human sense
Reasoning to admiration and with me
Persuasively hath so prevailed that I
Have also tasted and have also found
Th' effects to correspond: opener mine eyes,
Dim erst, dilated spirits, ampler heart
And growing up to godhead which for thee

845. *divine*: divining.
846. *Misgave him*: caused him misgivings. *falt'ring measure*: irregular heartbeat.
852. *ambrosial smell*: smell of the food of the gods, ambrosia.
856. Eve immediately attacks Adam with a vulgar question that is meant to put him off balance with the implied accusation that he doesn't love her enough. See line 895 and n.
857–58. *long* modifies *agony*. I.e., it was a long agony of sexual desire to be deprived Adam's presence.
864. *evil* and *unknown* are elided: 'ev-lun-known.'
876. *erst*: formerly. *dilated*: expanded, increased. *ampler heart*: more courageous, generous.
877. *godhead*: divine status.

Chiefly I sought, without thee can despise.
For bliss as thou hast part to me is bliss,
Tedious unshared with thee and odious soon.
Thou therefore also taste that equal lot
May join us, equal joy as equal love,
Lest thou not tasting, different degree
Disjoin us and I then too late renounce
Deity for thee when fate will not permit.
  Thus Eve with count'nance blithe her story told
But in her cheek distemper flushing glowed.
On th' other side Adam, soon as he heard
The fatal trespass done by Eve, amazed,
Astonied stood and blank while horror chill
Ran through his veins and all his joints relaxed.
From his slack hand the garland wreathed for Eve
Down dropped and all the faded roses shed.
Speechless he stood and pale till thus at length
First to himself he inward silence broke:
  O fairest of Creation, last and best
Of all God's works, creature in whom excelled
Whatever can to sight or thought be formed,
Holy, divine, good, amiable or sweet!
How art thou lost, how on a sudden lost,
Defaced, deflow'red, and now to death devote?
Rather how hast thou yielded to transgress
The strict forbiddance, how to violate
The sacred fruit forbidd'n? Some cursèd fraud
Of enemy hath beguiled thee, yet unknown,
And me with thee hath ruined, for with thee
Certain my resolution is to die!
How can I live without thee, how forgo
Thy sweet convérse and love so dearly joined
To live again in these wild woods forlorn?
Should God create another Eve and I

885. *Deity* has two syllables: 'dee-tee.'

887. *distemper*: imbalance of elements in the body.

890–91. See *Aeneid* 1.92: "Immediately Aeneas's limbs were dissolved with cold" (*Extemplo Aeneae solvuntur frigora membra*).

895. *to himself*. A new phenomenon in marriage enters here: Adam thinks one thing to himself and says another to his wife.

896–97. Eve is the *last* of all God's works, but not the *best*. Adam is the best of God's works, but Adam is about to change that.

905. *yet unknown* can refer to the *fraud*, or trick, which is not yet known; to the *enemy*, whose identity is not yet known for certain; or to *thee*, Eve: that you have been deceived is as yet unknown to you. *enemy* has two syllables: 'en-my.'

910. *these wild woods*. Adam's weakness is to think the Fall has already occurred, that there is no point in resistance or in seeking higher aid. He thinks of himself as already fallen, and so thinks of the garden as already a wilderness. In other words, he thinks here like a loser.

Another rib afford, yet loss of thee
Would never from my heart. No! No! I feel
The link of nature draw me, flesh of flesh,
Bone of my bone thou art and from thy state
Mine never shall be parted, bliss or woe.
  So having said as one from sad dismay
Recomforted and after thoughts disturbed
Submitting to what seemed remédiless
Thus in calm mood his words to Eve he turned:
  Bold deed thou hast presumed, advent'rous Eve,
And peril great provoked who thus hast dared,
Had it been only coveting, to eye
That sacred fruit, sacred to abstinence,
Much more to taste it under ban to touch.
But past who can recall or done undo?
Not God omnipotent nor fate. Yet so
Perhaps thou shalt not die. Perhaps the fact
Is not so heinous now: foretasted fruit,
Profaned first by the serpent, by him first
Made common and unhallowed ere our taste,
Nor yet on him found deadly—he yet lives,
Lives as thou saidst and gains to live as man
Higher degree of life, inducement strong
To us as likely tasting to attain
Proportional ascent which cannot be
But to be gods or angels, demigods.
Nor can I think that God, creator wise,
Though threat'ning, will in earnest so destroy
Us His prime creatures, dignified so high,
Set over all His works which in our Fall
For us created needs with us must fail,
Dependent made: so God shall uncreate,
Be frustrate, do, undo, and labor lose.
Not well conceived of God who though His power
Creation could repeat yet would be loath
Us to abolish lest the Adversary
Triumph and say, "Fickle their state whom God
Most favors! Who can please Him long? Me first
He ruined, now mankind! Whom will He next?"
Matter of scorn not to be giv'n the foe.

914–15. "And Adam said, This is now bone of my bones, and flesh of my flesh: she shall be called Woman, because she was taken out of Man. Therefore shall a man leave his father and mother, and shall cleave unto his wife: and they shall be one flesh" (Genesis 2:23).

926–27. While it is true that God himself cannot undo what has been done, God can, and will, overcome what has been done.

928. *fact*: deed (substantive of Latin *facio*, "to make, do").

However, I with thee have fixed my lot
Certain to undergo like doom. If death
Consort with thee death is to me as life,
So forcible within my heart I feel
The bond of nature draw me to my own,
My own in thee, for what thou art is mine.
Our state cannot be severed. We are one,
One flesh: to lose thee were to lose myself.
  So Adam, and thus Eve to him replied:
O glorious trial of exceeding love,
Illustrious evidence, example high,
Engaging me to emulate! But short
Of thy perfection how shall I attain,
Adam, from whose dear side I boast me sprung
And gladly of our union hear thee speak,
One heart, one soul in both whereof good proof
This day affords, declaring thee resolved
Rather than death or aught than death more dread
Shall separate us, linked in love so dear,
To undergo with me one guilt, one crime
(If any be) of tasting this fair fruit
Whose virtue (for of good still good proceeds)
Direct or by occasion hath presented
This happy trial of thy love which else
So eminently never had been known.
Were it I thought death menaced would ensue
This my attempt I would sustain alone
The worst and not persuade thee, rather die
Deserted than oblige thee with a fact
Pernicious to thy peace, chiefly assured
Remarkably so late of thy so true,
So faithful love unequaled. But I feel
Far otherwise th' event: not death but life
Augmented, opened eyes, new hopes, new joys,
Taste so divine that what of sweet before

959. *one flesh*: see lines 914–15 n.
962. *Illustrious* has three syllables: 'Illus-trous.'
963–64. I.e., How shall I attain to a degree of nobility even close to yours, which is perfect.
973–76. I.e., Because good comes out of good, the power of the goodness (*virtue*, line 973) in this fruit either has directly caused this trial of your love or has indirectly been the occasion for that trial. In either case, the height of your love would never have been known if the fruit had not been eaten.
977–83. I.e., If I really believed eating the fruit would cause us to die, I would die alone rather than make you die with me, and I would be comforted for the loss of my life by the assurance of your unequaled love and faith. Lines 826–31 show that Eve decides to compel Adam to eat the fruit precisely when she fears death may indeed result.
980. *oblige thee with a fact*: use my own action to oblige you to act.
984. *event*: consequence.

Hath touched my sense flat seems to this and harsh.
On my experience, Adam, freely taste
And fear of death deliver to the winds!
  So saying she embraced him and for joy
Tenderly wept, much won that he his love
Had so ennobled as of choice t' incur
Divine displeasure for her sake, or death.
In recompense (for such compliance bad
Such recompense best merits) from the bough
She gave him of that fair enticing fruit
With liberal hand. He scrupled not to eat,
Against his better knowledge, not deceived
But fondly overcome with female charm.
Earth trembled from her entrails as again
In pangs and Nature gave a second groan.
Sky loured and mutt'ring thunder some sad drops
Wept at completing of the mortal sin
Original while Adam took no thought,
Eating his fill. Nor Eve to iterate
Her former trespass feared, the more to soothe
Him with her loved society that now
As with new wine intoxicated both
They swim in mirth and fancy that they feel
Divinity within them breeding wings
Wherewith to scorn the earth. But that false fruit
Far other operation first displayed,
Carnal desire inflaming. He on Eve
Began to cast lascivious eyes, she him
As wantonly repaid: in lust they burn
Till Adam thus gan Eve to dalliance move:
  Eve, now I see thou art exact of taste
And elegant of sapience no small part
Since to each meaning savor we apply
And palate call judicious. I the praise
Yield thee, so well this day thou hast purveyed.
Much pleasure we have lost while we abstained
From this delightful fruit, nor known till now
True relish tasting. If such pleasure be
In things to us forbidd'n it might be wished
For this one tree had been forbidden ten!

992. *ennobled*. This is from Eve's point of view. The poet means us to hear the word ironically.
1016. *dalliance*: erotic play; it has two syllables: 'dall-yance.'
1018. *sapience*: a play on the double meaning of the Latin *sapientia*, "good taste, knowledge."
1024–26. *relish* and *pleasure* refer to enjoyment of food, but the underlying suggestion is that they also refer to enjoyment of sex. The confusion of appetites is one of the signs of the Fall.

But come, so well refreshed now let us play
As meet is after such delicious fare,
For never did thy beauty since the day
I saw thee first and wedded thee adorned
With all perfections so inflame my sense
With ardor to enjoy thee, fairer now
Than ever, bounty of this virtuous tree!
  So said he and forbore not glance or toy
Of amorous intent, well understood
Of Eve whose eye darted contagious fire.
Her hand he seized and to a shady bank
Thick overhead with verdant roof embow'red
He led her nothing loath. Flow'rs were the couch,
Pansies and violets and asphodel
And hyacinth, Earth's freshest softest lap.
There they their fill of love and love's disport
Took largely, of their mutual guilt the seal,
The solace of their sin, till dewy sleep
Oppressed them, wearied with their am'rous play.
Soon as the force of that fallacious fruit
That with exhilarating vapor bland
About their spirits had played and inmost pow'rs
Made err was now exhaled and grosser sleep
Bred of unkindly fumes with conscious dreams
Encumbered now had left them, up they rose
As from unrest and each the other viewing
Soon found their eyes how opened and their minds
How darkened. Innocence that as a veil
Had shadowed them from knowing ill was gone,
Just Confidence and Native Righteousness
And Honor from about them, naked left
To guilty Shame: he covered but his robe
Uncovered more. So rose the Danite strong,

1027. *play*: have sex; meant to recall the Hebrews when, after they worshipped the golden calf, they "sat down to eat and to drink, and rose up to play" (Exodus 32:6).

1027–33. The language of Adam's proposal echoes Paris's words to Helen in the *Iliad* 3.441–42: "For never before has eros so entangled and veiled my mind, not even when I first seized you and carried you away from Sparta."

1039–41. This scene, with its flowers, is similar to the *Iliad* 14.346–52, when the earth pushes up flowers beneath Zeus and Hera as they make love.

1042. *fill of love*: In Proverbs 7:18 the harlot entices the young man to his death with the words "Come, let us take our fill of love until the morning."

1054–59. *Confidence*, *Righteousness*, and *Honor* share with *Innocence* the predicate *was gone* (line 1055). These good things were *about* (line 1057) Adam and Eve like a garment. With the garment gone, Adam and Eve are morally naked and so exposed to *Shame* (line 1058). It is *Shame*'s robe that still covers Adam and Eve, since it would be morally worse for them if they felt no shame at their moral nakedness. But *Shame*'s robe also leaves Adam and Eve's depravity more exposed. "Let mine adversaries be clothed with shame" (Psalms 109: 29).

Herculean Samson, from the harlot-lap
Of Philistéan Dálilah and waked
Shorn of his strength, they destitute and bare
Of all their virtue. Silent and in face
Confounded long they sat as strucken mute
Till Adam though not less than Eve abashed
At length gave utterance to these words constrained:
O Eve, in evil hour thou didst give ear
To that false worm of whomsoever taught
To counterfeit man's voice, true in our Fall,
False in our promised rising, since our eyes
Opened we find indeed and find we know
Both good and evil: good lost, and evil got!
Bad fruit of knowledge if this be to know
Which leaves us naked thus, of honor void,
Of innocence, of faith, of purity,
Our wonted ornaments now soiled and stained
And in our faces evident the signs
Of foul concupiscence, whence evil store,
Ev'n shame the last of evils—of the first
Be sure then! How shall I behold the face
Henceforth of God or angel, erst with joy
And rapture so oft beheld? Those Heav'nly shapes
Will dazzle now this earthly with their blaze
Insufferably bright. O might I here
In solitude live savage in some glade
Obscured where highest woods impenetrable
To star or sunlight spread their umbrage broad
And brown as evening! Cover me ye pines,
Ye cedars, with innumerable boughs
Hide me where I may never see them more!
But let us now as in bad plight devise
What best may for the present serve to hide
The parts of each from other that seem most
To shame obnoxious and unseemliest seen:
Some tree whose broad smooth leaves together sewed

1061. Dalilah, Samson's lover, has a servant shave off the seven locks of Samson's hair, in which Samson's great strength resided. (Judges 16:19).
1062. *they*: so rose they.
1078. *concupiscence*: lust.
1079–80. Shame is the last of evils because it comes only after one has committed crimes. But it is among the first of evils because it is involved in crimes as the effect is involved in its cause.
1086. *Impenetrable* has four syllables.
1086–87. *Faerie Queene* 1.i.7.6: "Not perceable with power of any starre."
1088–90. "They shall say to the mountains, Cover us; and to the hills, Fall on us" (Hosea 10:8). Echoed in Luke 23:30 and in Revelation 6:16.

And girded on our loins may cover round
Those middle parts that this newcomer, Shame,
There sit not and reproach us as unclean.
 So counseled he and both together went
Into the thickest wood, there soon they chose
The fig-tree: not that kind for fruit renowned
But such as at this day to Indians known
In Malabar or Deccan spreads her arms
Branching so broad and long that in the ground
The bended twigs take root and daughters grow
About the mother tree, a pillared shade
High overarched and echoing walks between.
There oft the Indian herdsman shunning heat
Shelters in cool and tends his pasturing herds
At loopholes cut through thickest shade. Those leaves
They gathered broad as Amazonian targe
And with what skill they had together sewed
To gird their waist, vain covering if to hide
Their guilt and dreaded shame. O how unlike
To that first naked glory! Such of late
Columbus found th' American so girt
With feathered cincture, naked else and wild
Among the trees on isles and woody shores.
Thus fenced and, as they thought, their shame in part
Covered, but not at rest or ease of mind
They sat them down to weep. Nor only tears
Rained at their eyes but high winds worse within
Began to rise, high passions—anger, hate,
Mistrust, suspicion, discord—and shook sore
Their inward state of mind, calm region once
And full of peace, now tossed and turbulent:
For Understanding ruled not and the Will
Heard not her lore, both in subjection now
To sensual Appetite who from beneath
Usurping over sov'reign Reason claimed
Superior sway. From thus distempered breast
Adam estranged in look and altered style
Speech intermitted thus to Eve renewed:

1111. The leaves are as broad as the shields of Amazons, female warriors of Greek legend.

1117. *cincture*: belt around the waist, with feathers concealing the genitals.

1121. "By the rivers of Babylon, there we sat down, yea, we wept, when we remembered Zion" (Psalms 137:1).

1127–31. In the proper hierarchy of the faculties, reason is at the top, governing the will, which in turn governs the appetites. When the hierarchy is upset, when a lower faculty gains control over a higher, the passions are roused and the balance of the whole constitution—the body, its faculties, and its passions—is *distempered* (line 1131). See line 887 and n.

Would thou hadst hearkened to my words and stayed
With me as I besought thee when that strange
Desire of wandering this unhappy morn
(I know not whence) possessed thee! We had then
Remained still happy, not as now despoiled
Of all our good, shamed, naked, miserable!
Let none henceforth seek needless cause t' approve
The faith they owe. When earnestly they seek
Such proof, conclude they then begin to fail.
To whom soon moved with touch of blame thus Eve:
What words have passed thy lips, Adam severe?
Imput'st thou that to my default (or will
Of wandering as thou call'st it) which who knows
But might as ill have happened thou being by
Or to thyself perhaps? Hadst thou been there,
Or here th' attempt, thou couldst not have discerned
Fraud in the serpent, speaking as he spake,
No ground of enmity between us known,
Why he should mean me ill or seek to harm.
Was I t' have never parted from thy side?
As good have grown there still a lifeless rib!
Being as I am, why didst not thou, the head,
Command me absolutely not to go,
Going into such danger as thou saidst?
Too facile then thou didst not much gainsay,
Nay, didst permit, approve, and fair dismiss!
Hadst thou been firm and fixed in thy dissent
Neither had I transgressed nor thou with me.
To whom then first incensed Adam replied:
Is this the love, is this the recompense
Of mine to thee, ingrateful Eve, expressed
Immutable when *thou* wert lost, not I,
Who might have lived and joyed immortal bliss
Yet willingly chose rather death with thee?
And am I now upbraided as the cause
Of thy transgressing, not enough severe
It seems in thy restraint? What could I more?
I warned thee, I admonished thee, foretold
The danger and the lurking Enemy
That lay in wait. Beyond this had been force
And force upon free will hath here no place.
But confidence then bore thee on secure
Either to meet no danger or to find

1144. *What words* . . . : a Homeric formula.
1158. *facile*: easygoing.

Matter of glorious trial. And perhaps
I also erred in overmuch admiring
What seem'd in thee so perfect that I thought
No evil durst attempt thee. But I rue
That error now which is become my crime
And thou th' accuser. Thus it shall befall
Him who to worth in women overtrusting
Lets her will rule! Restraint she will not brook
And left t' herself if evil thence ensue
She first his weak indulgence will accuse.
  Thus they in mutual accusation spent
The fruitless hours, but neither self-condemning,
And of their vain contést appeared no end.

Book Ten

The Argument

Man's transgression known, the guardian angels forsake Paradise and return up to Heaven to approve their vigilance, and are approved, God declaring that the entrance of Satan could not be by them prevented. He sends his Son to judge the transgressors, who descends and gives sentence accordingly; then, in pity, clothes them both and reascends. Sin and Death, sitting till then at the gates of Hell, by wondrous sympathy feeling the success of Satan in this new world, and the sin by man there committed, resolve to sit no longer confined in Hell but to follow Satan their sire up to the place of Man. To make the way easier from Hell to and fro, they pave a broad highway or bridge over chaos according to the track that Satan first made. Then, preparing for Earth, they meet him, proud of his success, returning to Hell; their mutual gratulation. Satan arrives at Pandemonium, in full assembly relates with boasting his success against Man; instead of applause is entertained with a general hiss by all his audience, transformed with himself also suddenly into serpents, according to his doom, given in Paradise. Then, deluded with a show of the Forbidden Tree springing up before them, they greedily reaching to take of the fruit, chew dust and bitter ashes. The proceedings of Sin and Death. God foretells the final victory of his Son over them and the renewing of all things; but for the present commands his angels to make several alterations in the heavens and elements. Adam more and more perceiving his fallen condition, heavily bewails, rejects the condolement of Eve; she persists and at length appeases him; then to evade the curse likely to fall on their offspring, proposes to Adam violent ways which he approves not, but conceiving better hope, puts her in mind of the late promise made them that her seed should be revenged on the serpent, and exhorts her with him to seek peace of the offended Deity by repentance and supplication.

Meanwhile the heinous and despiteful act
Of Satan done in Paradise and how
He in the serpent had perverted Eve,
Her husband she, to taste the fatal fruit
Was known in Heav'n. For what can 'scape the eye
Of God all-seeing or deceive His heart
Omniscient who, in all things wise and just,
Hindered not Satan to attempt the mind
Of Man with strength entire and free will armed
Complete to have discovered and repulsed
Whatever wiles of foe or seeming friend.
For still they knew and ought t' have still remembered
The high injunction not to taste that fruit,
Whoever tempted, which they not obeying
Incurred (what could they less?) the penalty
And, manifold in sin, deserved to fall.
Up into Heav'n from Paradise in haste
Th' angelic guards ascended mute and sad
For Man, for of his state by this they knew,
Much wond'ring how the subtle Fiend had stolen
Entrance unseen. Soon as th' unwelcome news
From Earth arrived at Heaven gate, displeased
All were who heard: dim sadness did not spare
That time celestial visages, yet mixed
With pity violated not their bliss.
About the new-arrived in multitudes
Th' ethereal people ran to hear and know
How all befell. They towards the throne supreme
Accountable made haste to make appear
With righteous plea their utmost vigilance,
And easily approved when the Most High
Eternal Father from His secret cloud
Amidst in thunder uttered thus His voice:
Assembled angels and ye pow'rs returned
From unsuccessful charge, be not dismayed
Nor troubled at these tidings from the Earth
Which your sincerest care could not prevent,
Foretold so lately what would come to pass

Book Ten
27. *ethereal people*: angels.
31. *approved*: vindicated.

When first this Tempter crossed the gulf from Hell.
I told ye then he should prevail and speed
On his bad errand, Man should be seduced
And flattered out of all, believing lies
Against his Maker, no decree of mine
Concurring to necessitate his Fall
Or touch with lightest moment of impulse
His free will, to her own inclining left
In even scale. But fall'n he is. And now
What rests but that the mortal sentence pass
On his transgression: death denounced that day
Which he presumes already vain and void
Because not yet inflicted as he feared
By some immediate stroke but soon shall find
Forbearance no acquittance ere day end.
Justice shall not return as bounty, scorned.
But whom send I to judge them? Whom but thee
Vicegerent Son, to thee I have transferred
All judgement whether in Heav'n, or Earth, or Hell.
Easy it may be seen that I intend
Mercy colléague with justice, sending thee
Man's friend, his Mediator, his designed
Both ransom and Redeemer voluntary
And destined man himself to judge Man fallen.
  So spake the Father and unfolding bright
Toward the right hand his glory on the Son
Blazed forth unclouded deity. He full
Resplendent all his Father manifest
Expressed, and thus divinely answered mild:
  Father Eternal, Thine is to decree,
Mine both in Heav'n and Earth to do Thy will
Supreme, that Thou in Me thy Son beloved
May'st ever rest well pleased. I go to judge
On Earth these Thy transgressors but Thou know'st,
Whoever judged, the worst on Me must light
When time shall be, for so I undertook
Before Thee and, not repenting, this obtain
Of right: that I may mitigate their doom
On Me derived. Yet I shall temper so
Justice with mercy as may illústrate most

54. I.e., I sent my bounty to earth and it was scorned, and so returned to heaven. Now I will send my justice: let's see them try send *that* back!
56. *Vicegerent*: officer appointed as assistant to a supreme commander.
62. I.e., the Son is destined to be a man, Jesus.
77. *derived*: diverted.

Them fully satisfied and Thee appease.
Attendance none shall need, nor train, where none
Are to behold the judgement but the judged,
Those two. The third, best absent, is condemned,
Convict by flight and rebel to all law.
Conviction to the serpent none belongs.
  Thus saying from his radiant seat he rose
Of high collateral glory. Him thrones and powers,
Princedoms and dominations ministrant
Accompanied to Heaven gate from whence
Eden and all the coast in prospect lay.
Down he descended straight. The speed of gods
Time counts not though with swiftest minutes winged.
Now was the sun in western cadence low
From noon and gentle airs due at their hour
To fan the earth now waked and usher in
The evening cool when he, from wrath more cool,
Came the mild Judge and Intercessor both
To sentence Man. The voice of God they heard
Now walking in the garden by soft winds
Brought to their ears while day declined. They heard
And from his presence hid themselves among
The thickest trees, both man and wife, till God
Approaching thus to Adam called aloud:
  Where art thou, Adam, wont with joy to meet
My coming seen far off? I miss thee here,
Not pleased thus entertained with solitude
Where obvious duty erewhile appeared unsought.
Or come I less conspicuous or what change
Absents thee or what chance detains? Come forth!
He came and with him Eve more loath, though first
T' offend, discount'nanced both and discomposed.
Love was not in their looks either to God
Or to each other but apparent guilt
And shame and perturbation and despair,
Anger and obstinacy and hate and guile.
Whence Adam falt'ring long thus answered brief:
  I heard Thee in the garden and of Thy voice
Afraid, being naked, hid myself. To whom
The gracious Judge without revile replied:
  My voice thou oft hast heard and hast not feared

82. *third*: Satan.

84. I.e., The serpent, being merely Satan's instrument, is not convicted of any crime. But see lines 164–69 and n.

106. *obvious*: coming in the way, to meet. *duty* and *erewhile* are elided: 'dut-yerwhile.'

116. *garden* and *and* are elided: 'gard-nand.'

But still rejoiced. How is it now become
So dreadful to thee? That thou art naked, who
Hath told thee? Hast thou eaten of the tree
Whereof I gave thee charge thou shouldst not eat?
  To whom thus Adam sore beset replied:
O Heav'n! in evil straight this day I stand
Before my Judge, either to undergo
Myself the total crime or to accuse
My other self, the partner of my life,
Whose failing while her faith to me remains
I should conceal and not expose to blame
By my complaint! But strict necessity
Subdues me and calamitous constraint
Lest on my head both sin and punishment
However insupportable be all
Devolved, though should I hold my peace yet Thou
Wouldst easily detect what I conceal.
This woman whom Thou mad'st to be my help
And gav'st me as Thy perfect gift so good,
So fit, so acceptáble, so divine
That from her hand I could suspect no ill,
And what she did, whatever in itself,
Her doing seemed to justify the deed,
She gave me of the tree and I did eat.
  To whom the sov'reign Presence thus replied:
Was she thy God that her thou didst obey
Before His voice? Or was she made thy guide
Superior, or but equal, that to her
Thou didst resign thy manhood and the place
Wherein God set thee 'bove her, made of thee
And for thee, whose perfection far excelled
Hers in all real dignity? Adorned
She was indeed and lovely to attract
Thy love, not thy subjection, and her gifts
Were such as under government well seemed,
Unseemly to bear rule, which was thy part
And person hadst thou known thyself aright.
  So having said, he thus to Eve in few:
Say, woman, what is this which thou hast done?
  To whom sad Eve with shame nigh overwhelmed
Confessing soon, yet not before her Judge
Bold or loquacious, thus abashed replied:

150. *whose*: Adam's.

153–55. Eve's gifts, though good in themselves, were such that it would be unseemly for them to be seen in a ruler.

The serpent me beguiled and I did eat.
  Which when the Lord God heard without delay
To judgement he proceeded on th' accused
Serpent, though brute, unable to transfer
The guilt on him who made him instrument
Of mischief and polluted from the end
Of his creation: justly then accurst
As vitiated in nature. More to know
Concerned not Man (since he no further knew)
Nor altered his offence. Yet God at last
To Satan, first in sin, His doom applied,
Though in mysterious terms judged as then best
And on the serpent thus His curse let fall:
  Because thou hast done this thou art accurst
Above all cattle, each beast of the field.
Upon thy belly groveling thou shalt go
And dust shalt eat all the days of thy life.
Between thee and the woman I will put
Enmity and between thine and her seed:
Her seed shall bruise thy head, thou bruise his heel.
  So spake this oracle, then verified
When Jesus son of Mary, second Eve,
Saw Satan fall like lightning down from Heav'n,
Prince of the Air; then rising from His grave
Spoiled principalities and pow'rs, triúmphed
In open show, and with ascension bright
Captivity led captive through the air,
The realm itself of Satan long usurped,
Whom he shall tread at last under our feet,
Ev'n he who now foretold his fatal bruise,
And to the woman thus his sentence turned:

164–69. Although God said the serpent is not liable to conviction (line 84), the Son is unable to transfer from the serpent to Satan the guilt for having tempted Eve. The serpent is *vitiated* (line 169) not only by having been Satan's *instrument* (line 166) but also by having been grafted to Satan. See 9.89 and n. Satan is condemned, *in mysterious terms* (line 173), as Satan confirms: "True is, me also He hath judged or rather / Me not but the brute serpent in whose shape / Man I deceived" (lines 494–96). This is Milton's somewhat contorted but stubbornly honest effort to come to terms with a major discrepancy between the Christian story and the account in Genesis (3:14–15), where the serpent alone is condemned. The tension between the simple tale of Genesis and the later, Jewish and Christian interpretation of it continues in lines 182–91.

166. The first *him* is Satan, the second the serpent.

170. *no further knew*: did not know that the serpent was inhabited by Satan.

184. "And he said unto them, I beheld Satan as lightning fall from heaven" (Luke 10:18). A prophecy of the apocalypse, when Satan will lose his power in the air and be driven into Hell forever. See lines 188–89.

188. "Thou hast ascended on high, thou hast led captivity captive" (Psalms 68:18).

190. Since the Son retains his human nature, when he treads Satan under his feet it is our feet as well that do so. "And the God of peace shall bruise Satan under your feet shortly" (Romans 16:20).

Thy sorrow I will greatly multiply
By thy conception: children thou shalt bring
In sorrow forth and to thy husband's will
Thine shall submit: he over thee shall rule.
On Adam last thus judgment he pronounced:
Because thou hast harkened to the voice of thy wife
And eaten of the tree concerning which
I charged thee saying, "Thou shalt not eat thereof,"
Cursed is the ground for thy sake, thou in sorrow
Shalt eat thereof all the days of thy life.
Thorns also and thistles it shall bring thee forth
Unbid and thou shalt eat th' herb of the field.
In the sweat of thy face shalt thou eat bread
Till thou return unto the ground for thou
Out of the ground wast taken. Know thy birth,
For dust thou art and shalt to dust return.
So judged he Man, both Judge and Savior sent
And th' instant stroke of death, denounced that day,
Removed far off. Then, pitying how they stood
Before him naked to the air that now
Must suffer change disdained not to begin
Thenceforth the form of Servant to assume
As when he washed his servants' feet, so now
As father of his family he clad
Their nakedness with skins of beasts, or slain
Or as the snake with youthful coat repaid,
And thought not much to clothe his enemies.
Nor he their outward only with the skins
Of beasts but inward nakedness much more
Opprobrious with his robe of righteousness
Arraying covered from his Father's sight.
To Him with swift ascent he up returned,
Into His blissful bosom reassumed
In glory as of old. To Him, appeased,
All, though all-knowing, what had passed with Man
Recounted, mixing intercession sweet.

204. *herb of the field*: grass, wheat made into bread.
210. *denounced*: pronounced.
217–18. *or slain / Or as the snake*: The Son either kills some beasts to make garments for Adam and Eve or picks up skins that have been shed, like a snake's skin. "Unto Adam also and to his wife did the Lord God make coats of skins, and clothed them" (Genesis 3:21).
222. "He hath covered me with the robe of righteousness" (Isaiah 61:10).
224–28. After the Son has ascended to the Father and resumed his place of glory in the Father's bosom, he tells the Father, whose justice is now appeased, what occurred during the judgment of Man.
226–28. The direct object of *Recounted* (line 228) is *All* (line 227) and the indirect object is *Him* (line 226): i.e., The Son recounted all to the all-knowing Father. *appeased* modifies *Him* (line 226), the Father, not *All* (line 227).

Meanwhile, ere thus was sinned and judged on Earth,
Within the gates of Hell sat Sin and Death,
In counterview, within the gates that now
Stood open wide, belching outrageous flame
Far into chaos since the Fiend passed through,
Sin op'ning, who thus now to Death began:
O son, why sit we here each other viewing
Idly while Satan our great author thrives
In other worlds and happier seat provides
For us his offspring dear? It cannot be
But that success attends him. If mishap,
Ere this he had returned with fury driv'n
By his avengers since no place like this
Can fit his punishment or their revenge.
Methinks I feel new strength within me rise,
Wings growing and dominion giv'n me large
Beyond this deep, whatever draws me on,
Or sympathy or some connatural force
Pow'rful at greatest distance to unite
With secret amity things of like kind
By secretest conveyance. Thou my shade
Inseparable must with me along,
For Death from Sin no pow'r can separate.
But lest the difficulty of passing back
Stay his return perhaps over this gulf
Impassable, impervious, let us try
Advent'rous work yet to thy pow'r and mine
Not unagreeable: to found a path
Over this main from Hell to that new world
Where Satan now prevails, a monument
Of merit high to all th' infernal host,
Easing their passage hence for intercourse
Or transmigration as their lot shall lead.
Nor can I miss the way so strongly drawn
By this new felt attraction and instínct.
Whom thus the meagre shadow answered soon:
Go whither fate and inclination strong
Leads thee! I shall not lag behind nor err
The way, thou leading, such a scent I draw
Of carnage, prey innumerable, and taste
The savor of death from all things there that live.
Nor shall I to the work thou enterprisest
Be wanting but afford thee equal aid.

250. *Inseparable* has five syllables.
254. *impervious* has three syllables.

So saying with delight he snuffed the smell
Of mortal change on Earth. As when a flock
Of rav'nous fowl though many a league remote
Against the day of battle to a field
Where armies lie encamped come flying, lured
With scent of living carcasses designed
For death the following day in bloody fight,
So scented the grim feature and upturned
His nostril wide into the murky air,
Sagacious of his quarry from so far.
Then both from out Hell gates into the waste
Wide anarchy of chaos damp and dark
Flew diverse and with pow'r (their pow'r was great)
Hov'ring upon the waters. What they met
Solid or slimy as in raging sea
Tossed up and down together crowded drove
From each side shoaling towards the mouth of Hell,
As when two polar winds blowing adverse
Upon the Cronian Sea together drive
Mountains of ice that stop th' imagined way
Beyond Petsora eastward to the rich
Cathayan coast. The aggregated soil
Death with his mace petrific, cold and dry,
As with a trident smote and fixed as firm
As Delos floating once. The rest his look
Bound with Gorgonian rigor not to move
And with asphaltic slime. Broad as the gate,
Deep to the roots of Hell, the gathered beach
They fastened and the mole immense wrought on
Over the foaming deep, high arched a bridge
Of length prodigious joining to the wall
Immovable of this now fenceless world
Forfeit to Death. From hence a passage broad,
Smooth, easy, inoffensive down to Hell.

281. *Sagacious*: knowing, sensing.

290. *Cronian Sea*: Arctic Ocean, named after Cronus, who fled there. The ice blocks the northwest passage (which was not yet discovered, though eagerly sought) westward to Russia, with the river Petsora (see Glossary) and eventually China (Cathay).

294. *petrific*: turning to stone.

296. *Delos*: a floating island, which Zeus anchored with chains to the bottom of the sea.

297. *Gorgonian*: like the gorgon, whose face turned whoever saw it to stone.

299. *roots*: echoing Aeschylus's "pressed down with crushing weight by the roots of Etna" (*Prometheus Bound*, line 365).

300. *mole*: a massive, solid structure built in the water, a sea wall.

300–303. I.e., They *wrought* the *mole* onwards *and* (understood) they joined a high-arching bridge to the outer wall of the universe. We are to imagine a gigantic sea wall extending outward into Chaos from the gate of Hell and providing the footing for one end of the bridge, the other end being fixed to the universe with *pins* of *adamant* (line 318).

305. *inoffensive*: having no obstacles.

So if great things to small may be compared
Xerxes the liberty of Greece to yoke
From Susa his Memnonian palace high
Came to the sea and over Hellespont
Bridging his way Europe with Asia joined
And scourged with many a stroke th' indignant waves.
  Now had they brought the work by wondrous art
Pontifical, a ridge of pendent rock
Over the vexed abyss following the track
Of Satan to the selfsame place where he
First lighted from his wing and landed safe
From out of chaos to the outside bare
Of this round world. With pins of adamant
And chains they made all fast: too fast they made,
And durable! And now in little space
The confines met of empyréan Heav'n
And of this world, and on the left hand Hell
With long reach interposed: three several ways
In sight to each of these three places led.
And now their way to Earth they had descried,
To Paradise first tending when, behold!
Satan in likeness of an angel bright
Betwixt the Centaur and the Scorpion steering
His zenith while the sun in Aries rose.
  Disguised he came but those his children dear
Their parent soon discerned though in disguise.
He, after Eve seduced, unminded slunk
Into the wood fast by and changing shape
T' observe the sequel saw his guileful act
By Eve, though all unweeting, seconded
Upon her husband, saw their shame that sought
Vain covertures. But when he saw descend
The Son of God to judge them, terrified
He fled, not hoping to escape but shun
The present, fearing, guilty, what His wrath
Might suddenly inflict. That past, returned
By night and list'ning where the hapless pair
Sat in their sad discourse and various plaint,

306–11. The Persian king Xerxes, angry at the destruction of his bridge of ships over the Hellespont, commanded that the waves be flogged. A traditional example of hubris.

313. *Pontifical*: having to do with a bridge, Latin *pons*. A Roman high priest was called a *pontifex*, or "bridge maker," and the title was assumed by the bishop of Rome, as *pontif*.

328–29. Between the two constellations Satan steers his course from a mark taken above him on the stellar sphere. This places him in the constellation Anguis, the serpent. See Fowler, 2nd ed. (1998). See 2.709 and Glossary, OPHIUCHUS.

332. *unminded*: not paid attention to any longer by Adam and Eve.

Thence gathered his own doom, which understood
Not instant but of future time. With joy
And tidings fraught to Hell he now returned
And at the brink of chaos near the foot
Of this new wondrous pontifice unhoped
Met who to meet him came, his offspring dear.
Great joy was at their meeting and at sight
Of that stupendious bridge his joy increased.
Long he admiring stood till Sin his fair
Enchanting daughter thus the silence broke:
  O parent, these are thy magnific deeds,
Thy trophies which thou view'st as not thine own:
Thou art their author and prime architect,
For I no sooner in my heart divined
(My heart which by a secret harmony
Still moves with thine joined in connection sweet)
That thou on Earth hadst prospered (which thy looks
Now also evidence) but straight I felt,
Though distant from thee worlds between, yet felt
That I must after thee with this thy son,
Such fatal consequence unites us three.
Hell could no longer hold us in her bounds,
Nor this unvoyageable gulf obscure
Detain from following thy illustrious track.
Thou hast achieved our liberty, confined
Within Hell gates till now, thou us empow'red
To fortify thus far and overlay
With this portentous bridge the dark abyss.
Thine now is all this world, thy virtue hath won
That thy hands builded not, thy wisdom gained
With odds what war hath lost and fully avenged
Our foil in Heav'n. Here thou shalt monarch reign,
There didst not. There let Him still victor sway
As battle hath adjudged, from this new world
Retiring by His own doom alienated,
And henceforth monarchy with thee divide
Of all things parted by th' empyreal bounds,
His quadrature from thy orbicular world,

344. The subject of *understood* is Satan. Satan understands his doom to be reserved for a future time. This is the understanding that torments him in *Paradise Regained*.

372. *virtue* and *hath* are elided: 'virch-ath.'

375. *our foil*: He who foiled us.

378. I.e., the Son has withdrawn from this world, which has been further separated from him by his judgment on it.

381. *quadrature*: square-shaped heaven. *orbicular world*: the created universe. *orbicular* has three syllables: 'or-bi-clar.'

Or try thee now more dangrous to his throne.
  Whom thus the Prince of Darkness answered glad:
Fair daughter and thou son and grandchild both,
High proof ye now have giv'n to be the race
Of Satan (for I glory in the name
"Antagonist of Heav'n's Almighty King"),
Amply have merited of me, of all
Th' infernal empire, that so near Heav'n's door
Triumphal with triumphal act have met
Mine with this glorious work and made one realm
Hell and this world, one realm, one continent
Of easy thoroughfare. Therefore while I
Descend through darkness on your road with ease
To my associate pow'rs, them to acquaint
With these successes and with them rejoice,
You two this way among these numerous orbs
All yours right down to Paradise descend.
There dwell and reign in bliss! Thence on the earth
Dominion exercise and in the air,
Chiefly on Man, sole lord of all declared:
Him first make sure your thrall and lastly kill.
My substitutes I send ye and create
Plenipotent on Earth, of matchless might
Issuing from me. On your joint vigor now
My hold of this new kingdom all depends
Through Sin to Death exposed by my explóit.
If your joint pow'r prevail th' affairs of Hell
No detriment need fear. Go, and be strong!
  So saying he dismissed them. They with speed
Their course through thickest constellations held
Spreading their bane. The blasted stars looked wan
And planets, planet-strook, real eclipse
Then suffered. Th' other way Satan went down
The causey to Hell gate. On either side
Disparted Chaos overbuilt exclaimed
And with rebounding surge the bars assailed

382. I.e., Either accept a divided hegemony, God ruling in heaven and you here in the universe, or attempt something that will threaten God's throne.
387. See 1.82 and n.
391. *this glorious work*: the bridge.
397. *these numerous orbs*: the heavenly bodies inside the globe of the universe which are visible through the aperture mentioned at 3.525–28 and 542.
413. *planet-strook*: struck by the invisible influence, or "flowing-in," of a planet. Diseases and other catastrophes were thought to be caused by planetary influences. See lines 660–62 n. Now the planets themselves are stricken.
415. *causey*: causeway, bridge.
416–18. Chaos assails the bars of the bridge. The bars scorn Chaos's indignation. Chaos is here only vestigially identified.

That scorned his indignation. Through the gate
Wide open and unguarded Satan passed
And all about found desolate, for those
Appointed to sit there had left their charge,
Flown to the upper world. The rest were all
Far to th' inlánd retired about the walls
Of Pandemonium, city and proud seat
Of Lucifer (so by allusion called
Of that bright star to Satan paragoned).
There kept their watch the legions while the grand
In council sat, solicitous what chance
Might intercept their emperor sent: so he
Departing gave command and they observed.
As when the Tartar from his Russian foe
By Astracan over the snowy plains
Retires, or Bactrian Sophy from the horns
Of Turkish crescent leaves all waste beyond
The realm of Aladule in his retreat
To Tauris or Casbeen, so these the late
Heav'n-banished host left desert utmost Hell
Many a dark league reduced in careful watch
Round their metropolis, and now expecting
Each hour their great adventurer from the search
Of foreign worlds. He through the midst unmarked
In show plebeian angel militant
Of lowest order passed and from the door
Of that Plutonian hall invisible
Ascended his high throne which under state
Of richest texture spread at th' upper end
Was placed in regal luster. Down a while
He sat and round about him saw unseen.
At last as from a cloud his fulgent head
And shape star-bright appeared, or brighter, clad
With what permissive glory since his fall
Was left him, or false glitter. All amazed
At that so sudden blaze the Stygian throng
Bent their aspéct and whom they wished beheld:
Their mighty chief returned. Loud was th' acclaim.

431–36. Examples of barbaric warfare carried out in Asia.

432. *Astracan*: Astrakhan. City near the mouth of the Volga, on the Caspian Sea.

433–34. *Bactrian . . . crescent*: Persian king, from the crescent moon emblem on the Turkish flag.

435–36. *Aladule . . . Casbeen*: places in central Asia.

438. The subject of *reduced* is *these* (line 436). The devils are "drawn back" (the Latinate sense of *reduced*) around Pandemonium.

444. *Plutonian*: of Hell.

454. *Bent their aspéct*: turned their gaze.

Forth rushed in haste the great consulting peers
Raised from their dark divan and with like joy
Congratulant approached him who with hand
Silence and with these words attention won:
   Thrones, Dominations, Princedoms, Virtues, Powers!
For in possession such, not only of right,
I call ye and declare ye now, returned
Successful beyond hope to lead ye forth
Triumphant out of this infernal pit
Abominable, accurst, the house of woe
And dungeon of our Tyrant. Now possess
As lords a spacious world to our native Heaven
Little inferior, by my adventure hard
With peril great achieved. Long were to tell
What I have done, what suffered, with what pain
Voyaged th' unreal, vast, unbounded deep
Of horrible confusion over which
By Sin and Death a broad way now is paved
To expedite your glorious march. But I
Toiled out my uncouth passage, forced to ride
Th' intractable abyss, plunged in the womb
Of unoriginal Night and Chaos wild
That jealous of their secrets fiercely opposed
My journey strange with clamorous uproar
Protesting fate supreme. Thence how I found
The new created world which fame in Heav'n
Long had foretold, a fabric wonderful
Of absolute perfection, therein Man
Placed in a Paradise, by our exíle
Made happy. Him by fraud I have seduced
From his Creator and the more t' increase
Your wonder, with an apple! He thereat
Offended, worth your laughter, hath giv'n up
Both his beloved Man and all his world
To Sin and Death a prey and so to us
Without our hazard, labor, or alarm
To range in and to dwell and over Man

457. *divan* denotes both a council of state held by Turkish leaders and the long, low, cushioned seat on which such a council is held.
461. *only* and *of* are elided: 'on-lov.'
461–62. I.e., I call you by these titles not just because you have a right to them but because you now possess the realms they signify.
475. *uncouth*: unknown.
478. *fiercely* and *opposed* are elided: 'fierce-lopposed.'
482. *fabric*: construction.
487. *He*: God. *apple*: See 9.585 n.

To rule as over all he should have ruled.
True is, me also he hath judged or rather
Me not—but the brute serpent in whose shape
Man I deceived. That which to me belongs
Is enmity which he will put between
Me and mankind: I am to bruise his heel;
His Seed (when is not set) shall bruise my head.
A world who would not purchase with a bruise
Or much more grievous pain? Ye have th' account
Of my performance: what remains, ye gods,
But up and enter now into full bliss!
  So having said, a while he stood expecting
Their universal shout and high applause
To fill his ear when cóntrary he hears
On all sides from innumerable tongues
A dismal universal hiss, the sound
Of public scorn. He wondered but not long
Had leisure, wond'ring at himself now more:
His visage drawn he felt to sharp and spare,
His arms clung to his ribs, his legs entwining
Each other till supplanted down he fell
A monstrous serpent on his belly prone
Reluctant but in vain: a greater pow'r
Now ruled him, punished in the shape he sinned
According to his doom. He would have spoke
But hiss for hiss returned with forkèd tongue
To forkèd tongue, for now were all transformed
Alike to serpents, all as accessories
To his bold riot. Dreadful was the din
Of hissing through the hall thick swarming now
With complicated monsters, head and tail,

493. *he*: Man.

498–99. In both lines *his* refers to Man.

500–501. Satan speaks here of a literal *bruise*, knowing, as he shows in *Paradise Regained*, that the bruise is a prophetic figure of something much more serious.

511–15. Satan's transformation closely follows that of Cadmus in Ovid's *Metamorphoses* (4.576–89).

514. *on his belly prone* translates Ovid's *in pectusque cadit pronus* (4.579).

517–18. The shock experienced when trying to speak and hissing instead is also in Ovid's transformation of Cadmus (4.587–89).

521. *riot*: rebellion.

521–28. The catalog of serpents, many of them fabulous, is inspired by a much longer catalog in Lucan's *Pharsalia* (9.696–733). In Lucan, the snakes spring from the drops of blood that fall in the Libyan desert when Perseus flies over, bearing Medusa's severed head. Another important source for this passage is Phineas Fletcher's *Purple Island*, book 7, stanza 11, in which it is Adam and Eve who are turned into serpents by their tempter, a "dragon fell": "thus while the snake they heare they turn to snakes: / To make them gods he boasts, but beasts, and devils makes."

Scorpion and asp and amphisbaena dire,
Cerastes horned, hydrus and ellops drear
And dipsas. (Not so thick swarmed once the soil
Bedropped with blood of Gorgon or the isle
Ophiusa.) But still greatest he the midst
Now dragon grown larger than whom the sun
Engendered in the Pythian vale on slime,
Huge Python, and his pow'r no less he seemed
Above the rest still to retain. They all
Him followed issuing forth to th' open field
Where all yet left of that revolted rout,
Heav'n-fall'n, in station stood or just array
Sublime with expectation when to see
In triumph issuing forth their glorious chief.
They saw, but other sight instead: a crowd
Of ugly serpents. Horror on them fell
And horrid sympathy for what they saw
They felt themselves now changing: down their arms,
Down fell both spear and shield, down they as fast
And the dire hiss renewed and the dire form
Catched by contagion, like in punishment
As in their crime. Thus was th' applause they meant
Turned to exploding hiss, triumph to shame
Cast on themselves from their own mouths. There stood
A grove hard by sprung up with this their change
(His will who reigns above to aggravate
Their penance) laden with fair fruit like that
Which grew in Paradise, the bait of Eve
Used by the Tempter. On that prospect strange
Their earnest eyes they fixed, imagining
For one forbidden tree a multitude
Now ris'n to work them further woe or shame.
Yet parched with scalding thirst and hunger fierce,
Though to delude them sent, could not abstain,
But on they rolled in heaps and up the trees

527–28. Snakes sprang from the drops of blood that fell on the Libyan desert as Perseus flew by bearing Medusa's severed head.

528. *Ophiusa*: "serpent isle" (Greek *ophis*, "snake").

529–31. The great serpent, Python, engendered by Earth, was killed by the arrows of the sun god, Apollo: "You also, great Python, Earth then generated, an unknown serpent and a terror to recently-created humans, being as huge as a mountain. You the god who bears the bow . . . killed with a thousand arrows, nearly emptying his quiver, until the poison blood flowed from a thousand black wounds" (Ovid, *Metamorphoses* 1.438–44).

536. *Sublime*: raised up, exalted. They are both physically raised up and emotionally exalted, a prelude to their ignominious collapse.

545–46. *applause . . . exploding hiss*. In Latin the theater word *explodo* ("to hiss away") is the opposite of *plaudo* ("to applaud"): *explodo*: *ex*+*plaudo*.

Climbing sat thicker than the snaky locks
That curled Megaera. Greedily they plucked
The fruitage fair to sight like that which grew
Near that bituminous lake where Sodom flamed.
This, more delusive, not the touch but taste
Deceived. They, fondly thinking to allay
Their appetite with gust, instead of fruit
Chewed bitter ashes which th' offended taste
With spattering noise rejected. Oft they assayed,
Hunger and thirst constraining, drugged as oft
With hatefullest disrelish writhed their jaws
With soot and cinders filled: so oft they fell
Into the same illusion, not as Man,
Whom they triúmphed, once lapsed. Thus were they plagued
And worn with famine long and ceaseless hiss
Till their lost shape permitted they resumed,
Yearly enjoined, some say, to undergo
This annual humbling certain numbered days
To dash their pride and joy for Man seduced.
However some tradition they dispersed
Among the heathen of their purchase got
And fabled how the serpent whom they called
Ophion with Eurynome the wide-
Encroaching, Eve perhaps, had first the rule
Of high Olympus, thence by Saturn driv'n
And Ops ere yet Dictaean Jove was born.
  Meanwhile in Paradise the hellish pair
Too soon arrived, Sin there in pow'r before,
Once actual, now in body, and to dwell
Habitual habitant. Behind her Death
Close following pace for pace, not mounted yet

560. *That curled Megaera*: that curled about the head of the fury Megaera.

562. Near the shore of the Dead Sea, where Sodom stood before it was destroyed by fire from heaven (Genesis 19:24), a fruit was said to grow that when touched turned to ashes.

565. *gust*: taste.

568. *drugged*: made dry (Dutch *droog*).

572. *triúmphed*: exulted over.

577. *for Man seduced*: for having seduced Man.

578. *some tradition*: some have said. Parallel with *some say* (line 575). *dispersed*: spread the story.

579–84. *their purchase got*: their return for seducing Adam and Eve, i.e., their punishment. I.e., Some have said the devils spread among the pagans a lying fable about what was, in truth, their punishment for seducing Adam and Eve. Their story was that before Saturn and Ops (Rhea) ruled Olympus, and before Jove was born, a primordial serpent, Ophion, ruled Olympus with his consort, Eurynome, whose name means 'wide-ruling,' but who is perhaps Eve. The devils exploit their humiliating punishment to suggest that they are the oldest, most legitimate, gods.

587. *actual*: in action. Sin's power was in Paradise before, in the act committed by Adam and Eve. Now Sin is there in her own body.

On his pale horse, to whom Sin thus began:
  Second of Satan sprung, all-conquering Death,
What think'st thou of our empire now, though earned
With travail difficult? Not better far
Than still at Hell's dark threshold t' have sat watch,
Unnamed, undreaded, and thyself half-starved?
  Whom thus the Sin-born monster answered soon:
To me who with eternal famine pine
Alike is Hell or Paradise or Heav'n,
There best where most with ravin I may meet,
Which here though plenteous all too little seems
To stuff this maw, this vast unhidebound corpse.
  To whom th' incestuous mother thus replied:
Now therefore on these herbs and fruits and flow'rs
Feed first, on each beast next and fish and fowl,
No homely morsels, and whatever thing
The scythe of Time mows down devour unspared
Till I in Man residing through the race,
His thoughts, his looks, words, actions all infect
And season him thy last and sweetest prey.
  This said they both betook them several ways,
Both to destroy or unimmortal make
All kinds and for destruction to mature
Sooner or later, which th' Almighty seeing
From His transcendent seat the saints among
To those bright orders uttered thus His voice:
  See with what heat these dogs of Hell advance
To waste and havoc yonder world which I
So fair and good created and had still
Kept in that state had not the folly of Man
Let in these wasteful furies who impute
Folly to me! So doth the Prince of Hell
And his adherents that with so much ease
I suffer them to enter and possess
A place so Heav'nly, and conniving seem
To gratify my scornful enemies
That laugh, as if transported with some fit

590. "And I looked, and behold a pale horse: and his name that sat on him was Death, and Hell followed with him" (Revelation 6:8).
601. *unhidebound*: loose-skinned.
607. *race*: species.
609. *season*: to prepare game meat by hanging for a period of time, during which it dries and partly decays. Cf. Shakespeare, *Measure for Measure* (2.2.172): "corrupt with virtuous season."
615. *orders*: ranks of angels.
623. *them*: Sin and Death. Also lines 627 and 629.

Of passion I to them had quitted all,
At random yielded up to their misrule,
And know not that I called and drew them thither,
My Hell-hounds, to lick up the draff and filth
Which man's polluting sin with taint hath shed
On what was pure, till crammed and gorged, nigh burst
With sucked and glutted offal, at one sling
Of thy victorious arm, well-pleasing Son,
Both Sin and Death and yawning grave at last
Through chaos hurled obstruct the mouth of Hell
For ever and seal up his ravenous jaws.
Then Heav'n and Earth renewed shall be made pure
To sanctity that shall receive no stain.
Till then the curse pronounced on both precedes.
  He ended and the Heav'nly audience loud
Sung hallelujah as the sound of seas
Through multitude that sung: Just are Thy ways,
Righteous are Thy decrees on all Thy works!
Who can extenuate Thee? Next, to the Son,
Destined restorer of mankind by whom
New Heav'n and Earth shall to the ages rise
Or down from Heav'n descend. Such was their song
While the Creator calling forth by name
His mighty angels gave them several charge
As sorted best with present things. The sun
Had first his precept so to move, so shine
As might affect the Earth with cold and heat
Scarce tolerable and from the north to call
Decrepit winter, from the south to bring
Solstitial summer's heat. To the blank moon
Her office they prescribed, to th' other five
Their planetary motions and aspécts

630. *draff*: lees or refuse from brewing.
633. *offal*: inedible parts of a butchered animal.
637. *his*: Hell's. At the end of time, when the Son blocks the mouth of Hell with the bodies of Sin and Death (and the grave), the jaws of Hell will no longer be open to receive damned people. (The damned will be already in Hell.)
638. "We, according to his promise, look for new heavens and a new earth, wherein dwelleth righteousness" (2 Peter 3:13). "And I saw a new heaven and a new earth: for the first heaven and the first earth were passed away; and there was no more sea" (Revelation 21:1).
640. *both*: earth and the heavens, skies, within the universe, not heaven, the home of God. *precedes*: remains in effect.
645. *extenuate*: diminish.
645–48. The second part of the song appears to be indirect discourse rather than quotation. I.e., Next, they sang to the Son, praising him as the savior of mankind and as the creator of a new heaven and a new earth at the end of time.
647–48. See line 638 n.
654. *tolerable* has three syllables: 'tol-rable.'
656. *Solstitial*: of the solstice, when the sun has traveled to the farthest point north.

In sextile, square and trine and opposite
Of noxious efficacy and when to join
In synod unbenign, and taught the fixed
Their influence malignant when to show'r,
Which of them rising with the sun or falling
Should prove tempestuous. To the winds they set
Their corners, when with bluster to confound
Sea, air and shore, the thunder when to roll
With terror through the dark aerïal hall.
  Some say He bid his angels turn askance
The poles of earth twice ten degrees and more
From the sun's axle: they with labor pushed
Oblique the centric globe. Some say the sun
Was bid turn reins from th' equinoctial road
Like distant breadth to Taurus with the sev'n
Atlantic Sisters and the Spartan Twins
Up to the tropic Crab, thence down amain
By Leo and the Virgin and the Scales
As deep as Capricorn to bring in change
Of seasons to each clime. Else had the spring
Perpetual smiled on earth with vernant flowers
Equal in days and nights except to those
Beyond the polar circles. To them day
Had unbenighted shone while the low sun
To recompense his distance in their sight
Had rounded still th' horizon and not known
Or east or west, which had forbid the snow
From cold Estótiland and south as far
Beneath Magellan. At that tasted fruit
The sun as from Thyéstean banquet turned
His course intended, else how had the world
Inhabited, though sinless, more than now
Avoided pinching cold and scorching heat?
These changes in the heav'ns, though slow, produced

659. Astrological jargon concerning the angular positions of the planets as seen from the earth.

662. *influence malignant*: adjustments in the heavenly bodies, both wandering planets and stars fixed on the stellar sphere, causing bad influences on earth, such as diseases. Hence the word *influenza*, from stellar *influence* (Latin *in* + *fluo*, "to flow in").

668–78. Milton presents both the post-Copernican and the outdated (but more poetic) Ptolemaic accounts of the seasons, the former supposing the earth's axis to wobble, the latter supposing the sun to deviate in its course through the signs of the zodiac (*th' equinoctial road*) between the signs, Cancer and Capricorn.

679. *vernant*: vernal.

686–87. *Estótiland*: northern Canada. *Magellan*: the strait of Magellan, which rounds the tip of the South American mainland.

Like change on sea and land, sideral blast,
Vapor and mist and exhalation hot,
Corrupt and pestilent. Now from the north
Of Norumbega and the Samoed shore,
Bursting their brazen dungeon armed with ice
And snow and hail and stormy gust and flaw,
Boreas and Cacias and Argestes loud
And Thrascias rend the woods and seas upturn.
With adverse blast upturns them from the south
Notus and Afer black with thund'rous clouds
From Serraliona. Thwart of these as fierce
Forth rush the Lévant and the Pónent winds,
Eurus and Zephyr with their lateral noise,
Sirocco and Libecchio. Thus began
Outrage from lifeless things. But Discord, first
Daughter of Sin, among th' irrational
Death introduced through fierce antipathy:
Beast now with beast gan war and fowl with fowl
And fish with fish. To graze the herb all leaving
Devoured each other, nor stood much in awe
Of Man but fled him or with count'nance grim
Glared on him passing. These were from without
The growing miseries which Adam saw
Already in part though hid in gloomiest shade,
To sorrow abandoned, but worse felt within
And in a troubled sea of passion tossed
Thus to disburden sought with sad complaint:
  O miserable of happy! Is this the end
Of this new glorious world and me so late
The glory of that glory, who now, become
Accurst of blessèd, hide me from the face
Of God whom to behold was then my heighth
Of happiness? Yet well if here would end
The misery: I deserved it and would bear
My own deservings. But this will not serve:
All that I eat or drink or shall beget
Is propagated curse. O voice once heard
Delightfully, "increase and multiply,"

693. *sideral blast*: maleficent influence of stars. (Latin *sideralis*, "of or belonging to stars"). See line 662 n.
696. *Norumbega . . . Samoed shore*: northern Canada and northern Russia, Siberia.
699–706. A catalog of violent and maleficent winds.
703. *thwart of*: across.
704. *Levant*: from the east. *Ponent*: from the west.
707–9. Death introduces discord first among irrational beings, animals.
716. *Already* and *in* are elided. *gloomiest* has two syllables.

Now death to hear! For what can I increase
Or multiply but curses on my head?
Who of all ages to succeed but, feeling
The evil on him brought by me, will curse
My head: "ill fare our ancestor impure,
For this we may thank Adam." But his thanks
Shall be the execration. So besides
Mine own that bide upon me, all from me
Shall with a fierce reflux on me redound,
On me as on their natural center light,
Heavy though in their place. O fleeting joys
Of Paradise dear bought with lasting woes!
Did I request Thee, Maker, from my clay
To mold me Man? Did I solicit Thee
From darkness to promote me or here place
In this delicious garden? As my will
Concurred not to my being it were but right
And equal to reduce me to my dust,
Desirous to resign and render back
All I received, unable to perform
Thy terms too hard by which I was to hold
The good I sought not. To the loss of that,
Sufficient penalty, why hast thou added
The sense of endless woes? Inexplicable
Thy justice seems! Yet to say truth too late
I thus contést. Then should have been refused
Those terms whatever when they were proposed.
Thou didst accept them: wilt thou enjoy the good,
Then cavil the conditions? And though God
Made thee without thy leave, what if thy son
Prove disobedient and, reproved, retort
"Wherefore didst thou beget me? I sought it not."
Wouldst thou admit for his contempt of thee
That proud excuse? Yet him not thy election
But natural necessity begot.
God made thee of choice His own and of His own

738. *Mine own*: evils, curses.

741. *Heavy though in their place*: In pre-Newtonian physics objects are not moved by external forces but are drawn to their natural places, where they are at rest. Fire rises, seeking its home above the air, and earth sinks, seeking its home beneath the water. The principle has been invoked by Moloch: "in our proper motion we ascend / Up to our native seat. Descent and fall / To us is adverse" (2.75–77). The evils and curses find their natural place in Adam, their origin and center, but they are still heavy, crushing him with their weight.

762. A hypermetrical line.

766. *thee* and *of* are elided.

766–68. I.e., Because God made you, you owe him absolute service (as an implement is made only for the use of its maker). But God gave you a reward for your service: your freedom. Your punishment, therefore, is entirely up to him.

To serve Him. Thy reward was of His grace:
Thy punishment then justly is at His will.
Be it so, for I submit, His doom is fair:
That dust I am and shall to dust return.
O welcome hour whenever! Why delays
His hand to execute what His decree
Fixed on this day? Why do I overlive?
Why am I mocked with death and lengthened out
To deathless pain? How gladly would I meet
Mortality my sentence and be earth
Insensible, how glad would lay me down
As in my mother's lap! There I should rest
And sleep secure. His dreadful voice no more
Would thunder in my ears. No fear of worse
To me and to my offspring would torment me
With cruel expectation. Yet one doubt
Pursues me still: lest all I cannot die,
Lest that pure breath of life, the spirit of Man
Which God inspired cannot together perish
With this corporeal clod. Then in the grave
Or in some other dismal place, who knows
But I shall die a living death? O thought
Horrid if true! Yet why? It was but breath
Of life that sinned: what dies but what had life
And sin? The body properly hath neither.
All of me then shall die. Let this appease
The doubt since human reach no further knows.
For though the Lord of All be infinite,
Is His wrath also? Be it, Man is not so
But mortal doomed. How can He exercise
Wrath without end on Man whom death must end?
Can He make deathless death? That were to make

768. *justly* and *is* are elided.

773. *this day*: "For in the day that thou eatest thereof thou shalt surely die" (Genesis 2:17). See 7.544; 8.329–30.

782–93. Milton held that when we die we are entirely dead and remain so until the resurrection and last judgment. (For the resurrection of the body, see 1 Corinthians 15.) There is no place, such as purgatory, where a disembodied soul might live out the time in between, a thought that fills Adam with horror (line 783–89). (Milton's denial that any part of us lives after we die, until the resurrection, is the so-called mortalist heresy. See Milton's *On Christian Doctrine*, book 1, chapter 13; *YP* 6:399–414.) Adam reasons that because it is the soul, not the body, that sins ("It was but breath of life / That sinned," lines 789–90), the soul must bear the punishment, which is death: "All of me then shall die" (line 792). Adam has no idea that death is anything but final until Michael alludes to the resurrection: "well may then thy Lord appeased / Redeem thee quite from Death's rapacious claim" (11.257–58).

785. *inspired*: breathed in to me.

796–98. Having reached the conclusion that all of him will die, Adam wonders how God's wrath, which like everything in God is infinite, could possibly extend beyond his, Adam's, death. See lines 806–8 n.

Strange contradiction, which to God himself
Impossible is held, as argument
Of weakness not of pow'r. Will He draw out
For anger's sake finite to infinite
In punished Man to satisfy His rigor,
Satisfied never? That were to extend
His sentence beyond dust and nature's law
By which all causes else, according still
To the reception of their matter, act,
Not to th' extent of their own sphere. But say
That death be not one stroke as I supposed
Bereaving sense but endless misery
From this day onward which I feel begun
Both in me and without me, and so last
To perpetuity. Ay me! that fear
Comes thund'ring back with dreadful revolution
On my defenseless head! Both Death and I
Am found eternal and incorporate both,
Nor I on my part single: in me all
Posterity stands cursed. Fair patrimony
That I must leave ye, sons! O were I able
To waste it all myself and leave ye none!
So disinherited, how would ye bless
Me now your curse! Ah, why should all mankind
For one man's fault thus guiltless be condemned
If guiltless? But from me what can proceed
But all corrupt, both mind and will depraved,
Not to do only but to will the same
With me? How can they then acquitted stand
In sight of God? Him after all disputes
Forced I absolve: all my evasions vain
And reasonings, though through mazes, lead me still
But to my own conviction. First and last
On me, me only, as the source and spring
Of all corruption, all the blame lights due.
So might the wrath. Fond wish! Couldst thou support
That burden heavier than the earth to bear,

806–8. *causes else*: causes other than God's wrath. These causes must accord not only with their own *sphere* but with the nature of the matter they act in. Death may be infinite, but once death has killed you, it can no longer act on you.

808–13. Adam intuits eternal punishment in Hell.

816. *Am*: the singular verb expresses the unity of Adam and Death, since Adam is to die eternally. The grammatical distortion illustrates the point, as in Rimbaud's *Je est un autre* ("I is another").

820. *waste*: continues the irony of *patrimony*, inheritance. Adam wishes he could spend all the guilt himself, instead of passing it on to his children.

826. Adam's descendants will not only do evil but will wish to do evil.

Than all the world much heavier, though divided
With that bad woman? Thus what thou desir'st
And what thou fear'st alike destroys all hope
Of refuge and concludes thee miserable
Beyond all past example and futúre,
To Satan only like both crime and doom.
O conscience, into what abyss of fears
And horrors hast thou driv'n me, out of which
I find no way, from deep to deeper plunged!
  Thus Adam to himself lamented loud
Through the still night, not now as ere Man fell,
Wholesome and cool and mild, but with black air
Accompanied, with damps and dreadful gloom
Which to his evil conscience represented
All things with double terror. On the ground
Outstretched he lay, on the cold ground, and oft
Cursed his creation, Death as oft accused
Of tardy execution since denounced
The day of his offence: Why comes not Death,
Said he, with one thrice-acceptable stroke
To end me? Shall Truth fail to keep her word,
Justice divine not hasten to be just?
But Death comes not at call, Justice divine
Mends not her slowest pace for prayers or cries.
O woods, O fountains, hillocks, dales and bow'rs,
With other echo late I taught your shades
To answer and resound far other song!
  Whom thus afflicted when sad Eve beheld,
Desolate where she sat, approaching nigh,
Soft words to his fierce passion she assayed.
But her with stern regard he thus repelled:
  Out of my sight, thou serpent! That name best
Befits thee with him leagued, thyself as false
And hateful! Nothing wants but that thy shape
Like his and color serpentine may show
Thy inward fraud to warn all creatures from thee
Henceforth, lest that too Heav'nly form pretended
To Hellish falsehood snare them! But for thee

837–38. Adam both desires the wrath to fall on him alone and fears it absolutely. The contradiction within himself leaves him abject.

841–44. *To Satan only like*. The inner contradiction makes Adam like Satan. In the lines following (842–44), Adam's cry is strikingly like Satan's at 4.73–78.

854–56. Sophocles, *Philoctetes*, lines 797–98: "O Death! Death! How is it that I call you every day and yet you cannot come?"

861–62. Milton evokes the echoing songs of the pastoral landscape of Virgil's *Eclogues* (1.1–5), songs that are interrupted by the lamentations of those who are exiled.

I had persisted happy, had not thy pride
And wand'ring vanity when least was safe
Rejected my forewarning and disdained
Not to be trusted, longing to be seen,
Though by the Devil himself, him overweening
To overreach, but with the serpent meeting
Fooled and beguiled: by him thou, I by thee,
To trust thee from my side, imagined wise,
Constant, mature, proof against all assaults,
And understood not all was but a show
Rather than solid virtue, all but a rib
Crooked by nature, bent, as now appears
More to the part sinister from me drawn,
Well if thrown out as supernumerary
To my just number found. O why did God,
Creator wise, that peopled highest Heav'n
With spirits masculine, create at last
This novelty on earth, this fair defect
Of nature, and not fill the world at once
With men as angels, without feminine,
Or find some other way to generate
Mankind? This mischief had not then befall'n
And more that shall befall: innumerable
Disturbances on earth through female snares
And strait conjunction with this sex. For either
He never shall find out fit mate but such
As some misfortune brings him, or mistake,
Or whom he wishes most shall seldom gain
Through her perverseness but shall see her gained
By a far worse or, if she love, withheld
By parents, or his happiest choice too late
Shall meet already linked and wedlock-bound
To a fell advérsary, his hate or shame,
Which infinite calamity shall cause
To human life and household peace confound.
  He added not and from her turned, but Eve,
Not so repulsed, with tears that ceased not flowing
And tresses all disordered at his feet
Fell humble and embracing them besought

884–88. In post-biblical tradition Adam was supposed to have had an extra rib on the left (*sinister*) side, from which Eve was made.
898. *strait conjunction*: forced union.
906. *To* and *a* are elided.
910–12. "A woman in the city . . . stood at his feet behind him weeping, and began to wash his feet with tears, and did wipe them with the hairs of her head, and kissed his feet, and anointed them with the ointment" (Luke 7:37–38).

His peace and thus proceeded in her plaint:
  Forsake me not thus, Adam, witness Heaven,
What love sincere and reverence in my heart
I bear thee, and unweeting have offended,
Unhappily deceived. Thy suppliant,
I beg and clasp thy knees. Bereave me not
Whereon I live: thy gentle looks, thy aid,
Thy counsel, in this uttermost distress
My only strength and stay! Forlorn of thee,
Whither shall I betake me, where subsist?
While yet we live scarce one short hour perhaps
Between us two let there be peace, both joining,
As joined in injuries, one enmity
Against a foe by doom express assigned us,
That cruel serpent. On me exercise not
Thy hatred for this misery befall'n
On me, already lost, me than thyself
More miserable! Both have sinned, but thou
Against God only, I against God and thee,
And to the place of judgement will return,
There with my cries importune Heav'n that all
The sentence from thy head removed may light
On me, sole cause to thee of all this woe,
Me, me only just object of his ire!
  She ended weeping and her lowly plight,
Immovable till peace obtained from fault
Acknowledged and deplored, in Adam wrought
Commiseration. Soon his heart relented
Towards her, His life so late and sole delight
Now at his feet submissive in distress,
Creature so fair his reconcilement seeking,
His counsel whom she had displeased, his aid.
As one disarmed his anger all he lost
And thus with peaceful words upraised her soon:
  Unwary, and too desirous as before,
So now, of what thou know'st not, who desir'st
The punishment all on thyself; Alas!
Bear thine own first, ill able to sustain
His full wrath whose thou feel'st as yet least part
And my displeasure bear'st so ill. If prayers
Could alter high decrees I to that place
Would speed before thee and be louder heard

924–26. I.e., They *join enmity* against their *foe*, as armies join battle.
943–44. I.e., Eve seeks Adam's *reconcilement*, *counsel*, and *aid*.
951. *whose*: which.

That on my head all might be visited,
Thy frailty and infirmer sex forgiven,
To me committed and by me exposed.
But rise, let us no more contend, nor blame
Each other, blamed enough elsewhere, but strive
In offices of love how we may light'n
Each other's burden in our share of woe
Since this day's death denounced, if aught I see,
Will prove no sudden but a slow-paced evil,
A long day's dying to augment our pain
And to our seed (O hapless seed!) derived.
  To whom thus Eve recovering heart replied:
Adam, by sad experiment I know
How little weight my words with thee can find,
Found so erroneous, thence by just event
Found so unfortunate. Nevertheless,
Restored by thee, vile as I am, to place
Of new acceptance hopeful to regain
Thy love, the sole contentment of my heart,
Living or dying, from thee I will not hide
What thoughts in my unquiet breast are risen,
Tending to some relief of our extremes,
Or end, though sharp and sad, yet tolerable,
As in our evils and of easier choice.
If care of our descent perplex us most
Which must be born to certain woe, devoured
By Death at last (and miserable it is
To be to others cause of misery),
Our own begotten, and of our loins to bring
Into this cursèd world a woeful race
That after wretched life must be at last
Food for so foul a monster, in thy power
It lies yet ere conception to prevent
The race unblest, to being yet unbegot.
Childless thou art, childless remain! So Death
Shall be deceived his glut and with us two
Be forced to satisfy his rav'nous maw.
But if thou judge it hard and difficult,
Conversing, looking, loving to abstain
From love's due rites, nuptial embraces sweet,
And with desire to languish without hope

961. "Bear ye one another's burdens, and so fulfill the law of Christ" (Galatians 6:2).
977. *tolerable* has three syllables: 'tol-rable.'
978. *in our evils*: among our evils. She is referring to death and contemplating suicide, an *easier choice* than living to bear cursed offspring.
988. *to being yet unbegot*: not yet conceived, not yet destined to exist.

Before the present object languishing
With like desire, which would be misery
And torment less than none of what we dread,
Then, both ourselves and seed at once to free
From what we fear for both, let us make short,
Let us seek Death, or, he not found, supply
With our own hands his office on ourselves.
Why stand we longer shivering under fears
That show no end but death and have the pow'r
Of many ways to die, the shortest choosing,
Destruction with destruction to destroy?
  She ended here or vehement despair
Broke off the rest. So much of death her thoughts
Had entertained as dyed her cheeks with pale.
But Adam with such counsel nothing swayed
To better hopes his more attentive mind
Laboring had raised and thus to Eve replied:
  Eve, thy contempt of life and pleasure seems
To argue in thee something more sublime
And excellent than what thy mind contemns.
But self-destruction therefore sought refutes
That excellence thought in thee and implies
Not thy contempt but anguish and regret
For loss of life and pleasure overloved.
Or if thou covet death as utmost end
Of misery, so thinking to evade
The penalty pronounced, doubt not but God
Hath wiselier armed His vengeful ire than so
To be forestalled. Much more I fear lest death
So snatched will not exempt us from the pain
We are by doom to pay. Rather such acts
Of cóntumacy will provoke the High'st
To make Death in us live. Then let us seek
Some safer resolution which methinks
I have in view, calling to mind with heed
Part of our sentence, that thy Seed shall bruise
The serpent's head, piteous amends unless
Be meant whom I conjecture, our grand foe
Satan, who in the serpent hath contrived

1004. *and have*: when we have.

1013–19. A seemingly paradoxical but in fact sound argument: Eve's courage in rejecting pleasure and life itself shows that there is something in life, in human nature, worth preserving: nobility.

1015. *contemns*: condemns. The older form is kept because of the play of words with *contempt* (line 1013).

1033–35. This is the first indication that Adam knows Satan was hidden in the serpent.

Against us this deceit. To crush *his* head
Would be revenge indeed, which will be lost
By death brought on our selves or childless days
Resolved as thou proposest. So our foe
Shall 'scape his punishment ordained and we
Instead shall double ours upon our heads.
No more be mentioned then of violence
Against ourselves and willful barrenness
That cuts us off from hope and savors only
Rancor and pride, impatience and despite,
Reluctance against God and His just yoke
Laid on our necks. Remember with what mild
And gracious temper He both heard and judged
Without wrath or reviling. We expected
Immediate dissolution which we thought
Was meant by death that day when, lo! to thee
Pains only in childbearing were foretold
And bringing forth soon recompensed with joy,
Fruit of thy womb. On me the curse aslope
Glanced on the ground: with labor I must earn
My bread. What harm? Idleness had been worse.
My labor will sustain me and lest cold
Or heat should injure us His timely care
Hath unbesought provided and His hands
Clothed us unworthy, pitying while He judged.
How much more if we pray Him will His ear
Be open and His heart to pity incline
And teach us further by what means to shun
Th' inclément seasons, rain, ice, hail and snow,
Which now the sky with various face begins
To show us in this mountain while the winds
Blow moist and keen, shattering the graceful locks
Of these fair spreading trees, which bids us seek
Some better shroud, some better warmth to cherish
Our limbs benumbed ere this diurnal star
Leave cold the night, how we his gathered beams
Reflected may with matter sere foment,
Or by collision of two bodies grind

1052. "A woman when she is in travail hath sorrow . . . but as soon as she is delivered of the child, she remembereth no more the anguish, for joy that a man is born into the world" (John 16:21).
1061. *pity* and *incline* are elided.
1069. *diurnal star*: the sun.
1070–73. Adam conceives the two means by which fire can be kindled: focusing of sun's beams through a lens and friction to produce sparks.
1071. *foment*: grow or keep warm (Latin *foveo*).

The air attrite to fire, as late the clouds
Justling or pushed with winds rude in their shock
Tine the slant lightning whose thwart flame, driv'n down,
Kindles the gummy bark of fir or pine
And sends a comfortable heat from far
Which might supply the sun. Such fire to use
And what may else be remedy or cure
To evils which our own misdeeds have wrought
He will instruct us praying and of grace
Beseeching Him so as we need not fear
To pass commodiously this life, sustained
By Him with many comforts till we end
In dust, our final rest and native home.
What better can we do than to the place
Repairing where He judged us prostrate fall
Before Him reverent and there confess
Humbly our faults and pardon beg, with tears
Watering the ground and with our sighs the air
Frequenting, sent from hearts contrite in sign
Of sorrow unfeigned and humiliation meek?
Undoubtedly He will relent and turn
From His displeasure, in whose look serene
When angry most He seemed and most severe
What else but favor, grace and mercy shown?
  So spake our father penitent, nor Eve
Felt less remorse. They forthwith to the place
Repairing where He judged them prostrate fell
Before Him reverent and both confessed
Humbly their faults and pardon begged, with tears
Watering the ground and with their sighs the air
Frequenting, sent from hearts contrite in sign
Of sorrow unfeigned and humiliation meek.

1073. *attrite*: rubbed.

1075. *tine*: the prong of a fork, here used as a verb—"to make pronged." *thwart*: moving across [the sky]. Whereas fire on earth naturally flies up, in the sky fire naturally moves sideways, as lightning. But lightning can be *driv'n down* to strike a tree. See line 741 n.

1078. *supply the sun*: take the place of sun (at night) by giving heat.

1083. *commodiously*: suitably, in due measure, decently. The word is carefully chosen as a step below *happily*.

1091. *Frequenting*: crowding, assiduously attending. The Latin usage implies repeated appearance of the retainer or follower (*cliens*) at a great person's house, to show respect and be of service.

1092. *sorrow unfeigned*: *sorrow* has one syllable, 'soar,' but recovers a little of its second syllable in the elision with *unfeigned*: 'soar-wunfeigned.'

1098–1104. The repetition of lines 1086–92 is Homeric. It also emphasizes the ritual nature of prayer in the future and contrasts with the easy eloquence of the prayers that Adam and Eve sing before the Fall: the evening prayer at 4.720–35 and the morning prayer at 5.153–208.

Book Eleven

The Argument

The Son of God presents to his Father the prayers of our first parents, now repenting, and intercedes for them. God accepts them, but declares that they must no longer abide in Paradise, sends Michael with a band of cherubim to dispossess them, but first to reveal to Adam future things. Michael's coming down. Adam shows to Eve certain ominous signs; he discerns Michael's approach, goes out to meet him. The angel denounces their departure. Eve's lamentation. Adam pleads, but submits. The angel leads him up to a high hill, sets before him in vision what shall happen till the Flood.

Thus they in lowliest plight repentant stood
Praying for from the mercy-seat above
Prevenient grace descending had removed
The stony from their hearts and made new flesh
Regenerate grow instead that sighs now breathed
Unutterable which the spirit of prayer
Inspired and winged for Heav'n with speedier flight
Than loudest oratory. Yet their port
Not of mean suitors nor important less
Seemed their petition than when th' ancient pair
In fables old, less ancient yet than these,
Deucalion and chaste Pyrrha, to restore
The race of mankind drowned before the shrine
Of Themis stood devout. To Heav'n their prayers
Flew up nor missed the way by envious winds
Blown vagabond or frustrate. In they passed
Dimensionless through Heav'nly doors, then clad
With incense where the golden altar fumed
By their great Intercessor came in sight
Before the Father's throne. Them the glad Son

Book Eleven

1. *stood*. Adam and Eve were last seen *prostrate* (10.1099).
2. *mercy-seat*: throne of God. See Exodus 25:17.
3. *Prevenient grace*: the grace that is sent beforehand from God to soften the heart and make the sinner capable of repentance. *Prevenient*: that which comes before.
4. "A new heart also will I give you, and a new spirit will I put within you: and I will take away the stony heart out of your flesh, and I will give you an heart of flesh" (Ezekiel 36:26).
5. *Regenerate*: an adjective modifying *flesh*.
8. *their*: the prayers of Adam and Eve, personified as ambassadors. *port*: bearing.
12. *Deucalion and Pyrrha* repopulated the world after the Flood by casting stones over their shoulders. The stones became men and women.
14. *Themis*: goddess of justice.
17. *Dimensionless*: the Prayers have no bodies and so occupy no space.
19. *Intercessor*: the Son clothes the prayers in incense, as he clothed Adam and Eve in skins. In both instances the Son confers dignity on the abject.

Presenting thus to intercede began:
  See, Father, what first fruits on Earth are sprung
From Thy implanted grace in Man, these sighs
And prayers which in this golden censer mixed
With incense I Thy priest before Thee bring,
Fruits of more pleasing savor from Thy seed
Sown with contrition in his heart than those
Which his own hand manuring all the trees
Of Paradise could have produced ere fall'n
From innocence. Now therefore bend Thine ear
To supplication, hear his sighs though mute,
Unskillful with what words to pray. Let me
Interpret for him, me his advocate
And propitiation, all his works on me
Good or not good ingraft: my merit those
Shall perfect and for these my death shall pay.
Accept me and in me from these receive
The smell of peace toward mankind! Let him live
Before Thee reconciled at least his days
Numbered, though sad, till death his doom (which I
To mitigate thus plead, not to reverse)
To better life shall yield him where with me
All my redeemed may dwell in joy and bliss,
Made one with me as I with Thee am one.
  To whom the Father without cloud, serene:
All thy request for Man, accepted Son,
Obtain: all thy request was my decree.
But longer in that Paradise to dwell
The law I gave to nature him forbids:
Those pure immortal elements that know
No gross, no unharmonious mixture foul
Eject him tainted now and purge him off
As a distemper gross to air as gross
And mortal food as may dispose him best
For dissolution wrought by sin, that first
Distempered all things and of incorrupt
Corrupted. I at first with two fair gifts
Created him, endowed with happiness
And immortality. That fondly lost,

28. *manuring*: working by hand, fertilizing (French *manoeuvrer*). In his prose works Milton uses this word to signify careful diligence.
34. *propitiation* has four syllables.
37. *these*: the Prayers.
51. *gross*: thickened, unrefined, impure.
53. *to air as gross*: as gross as he is.
59. *That*: happiness.

This other served but to eternize woe
Till I provided death. So death becomes
His final remedy and after life,
Tried in sharp tribulation and refined
By faith and faithful works, to second life,
Waked in the renovation of the just,
Resigns him up with Heav'n and Earth renewed.
But let us call to synod all the blest
Through Heav'n's wide bounds. From them I will not hide
My judgments, how with mankind I proceed
As how with peccant angels late they saw
And in their state, though firm, stood more confirmed.
He ended and the Son gave signal high
To the bright minister that watched. He blew
His trumpet, heard in Oreb since perhaps
When God descended and perhaps once more
To sound at gen'ral doom. Th' angelic blast
Filled all the regions. From their blissful bow'rs
Of amarantine shade, fountain or spring,
By the waters of life where'er they sat
In fellowships of joy, the sons of light
Hasted resorting to the summons high
And took their seats, till from His throne supreme
Th' Almighty thus pronounced His sov'reign will:
O sons! like one of us Man is become
To know both good and evil since his taste
Of that defended fruit. But let him boast
His knowledge of good lost and evil got,
Happier had it sufficed him to have known
Good by itself and evil not at all!
He sorrows now, repents and prays contrite,
My motions in him. Longer than they move

60. *This*: immortality.
66. the subject of *Resigns* is *death* (line 61).
68. *them*: the loyal angels.
70. *peccant*: sinning.
71. *their*: the loyal angels'.
74. *Oreb*: Sinai. "There were thunders and lightnings, and a thick cloud upon the mount . . . And when the voice of the trumpet sounded long, and waxed louder and louder, Moses spake, and God answered him by a voice. And the Lord came down upon Mount Sinai" (Exodus 19:16, 20–21). *since*: formerly.
76. *general doom*: last judgment (Old English *dôm*, "judgment, law").
78. *amarantine*. See 3.353 n.
86. *defended*: forbidden (cf. French *défendu*; Latin *defenso*, "to protect diligently").
88. *Happier* has two syllables: 'hap-yer.'
91. *My motions*: prevenient grace. See line 3 and n.
91–93. *Longer than they move . . . Self-left*: I.e., I know how much longer repentance will move Man: not much longer. Left to himself, without my grace to help him, Man's heart is variable and vain.

His heart I know, how variable and vain
Self-left. Lest therefore his now bolder hand
Reach also of the Tree of Life and eat
And live for ever, dream at least to live
For ever, to remove him I decree
And send him from the garden forth to till
The ground whence he was taken, fitter soil.
  Michael, this my behest have thou in charge:
Take to thee from among the cherubim
Thy choice of flaming warriors lest the Fiend
Or in behalf of Man or to invade
Vacant possession some new trouble raise.
Haste thee and from the Paradise of God
Without remorse drive out the sinful pair,
From hallowed ground th' unholy, and denounce
To them and to their progeny from thence
Perpetual banishment. Yet lest they faint
At the sad sentence rigorously urged
(For I behold them softened and with tears
Bewailing their excess) all terror hide.
If patiently thy bidding they obey,
Dismiss them not disconsolate. Reveal
To Adam what shall come in future days
As I shall thee enlighten. Intermix
My covenant in the woman's seed renewed.
So send them forth—though sorrowing, yet in peace—
And on the east side of the garden place,
Where entrance up from Eden easiest climbs,
Cherubic watch and of a sword the flame
Wide waving all approach far off to fright
And guard all passage to the Tree of Life
Lest Paradise a receptacle prove
To spirits foul and all my trees their prey
With whose stol'n fruit Man once more to delude.
  He ceased and th' archangelic pow'r prepared

93–98. "And the Lord God said, Behold, the man is become as one of us, to know good and evil: and now, lest he put forth his hand, and take also of the tree of life, and eat, and live for ever: Therefore the Lord God sent him forth from the garden of Eden, to till the ground from whence he was taken. So he drove out the man; and he placed at the east of the garden of Eden Cherubims, and a flaming sword which turned every way, to keep the way of the tree of life" (Genesis 3:22–24).

116. *covenant*: a formal relationship between Man and God (also *testament*). The vision of history in books Eleven and Twelve is that of a progression of covenants. The forbidden fruit, although it was not called that, was the first covenant. Others are the rainbow, the promised land, the law given to Moses, and the new covenant in Jesus Christ, which replaces that of the law. This last is the covenant *in the woman's seed*.

119. *from Eden*: Eden is a large country in which the garden on the mountain top, Paradise, is only one place.

For swift descent, with him the cohort bright
Of watchful cherubim. Four faces each
Had like a double Janus, all their shape
Spangled with eyes more numerous than those
Of Argus and more wakeful than to drowse,
Charmed with Arcadian pipe, the pastoral reed
Of Hermes or his opiate rod. Meanwhile
To resalute the world with sacred light
Leucothea waked and with fresh dews embalmed
The earth when Adam and first matron Eve
Had ended now their orisons and found
Strength added from above, new hope to spring
Out of despair, joy but with fear yet linked,
Which thus to Eve his welcome words renewed:
  Eve, easily may faith admit that all
The good which we enjoy from Heav'n descends
But that from us aught should ascend to Heav'n
So prevalent as to concern the mind
Of God high-blest or to incline His will
Hard to belief may seem. Yet this will prayer
Or one short sigh of human breath upborn
Ev'n to the seat of God. For since I sought
By prayer th' offended Deity to appease,
Kneeled and before Him humbled all my heart,
Methought I saw Him placable and mild
Bending His ear. Persuasion in me grew
That I was heard with favor. Peace returned
Home to my breast and to my memory
His promise that thy Seed shall bruise our foe,
Which then not minded in dismay yet now
Assures me that the bitterness of death
Is past and we shall live. Whence hail to thee,
Eve, rightly called *Mother of all Mankind*,
Mother of all things living, since by thee
Man is to live and all things live for Man.
  To whom thus Eve with sad demeanor meek:

129. *Janus*, the Roman god of doorways, has two faces.
131. *Argus*: a giant with one hundred eyes who was charmed to sleep and killed by Hermes. The cherubim, as guardians, have more eyes than Argus does and cannot be put to sleep.
135. *Leucothea* has three syllables: 'lew-coath-ya.' She is the Roman goddess of the dawn. Her name means "White Goddess"; but Greek *leukos* also means "joyful."
146. *this will prayer*: The understood verb is *do*—prayer will incline God's will to do what we ask.
149. *Deity* has two syllables.
151. *placable*: inclined to peace.

Ill worthy, I, such title should belong
To me transgressor who for thee ordained
A help became thy snare. To me reproach
Rather belongs, distrust and all dispraise.
But infinite in pardon was my Judge,
That I who first brought death on all am graced
The source of life. Next favorable thou
Who highly thus t' entitle me vouchsaf'st,
Far other name deserving. But the field
To labor calls us now with sweat imposed
Though after sleepless night. For see! the Morn,
All unconcerned with our unrest begins
Her rosy progress smiling. Let us forth,
I never from thy side henceforth to stray,
Where'er our day's work lies, though now enjoined
Laborious till day droop. While here we dwell
What can be toilsome in these pleasant walks?
Here let us live, though in fall'n state, content.
  So spake, so wished much-humbled Eve, but Fate
Subscribed not: Nature first gave signs impressed
On bird, beast, air, air suddenly eclipsed
After short blush of morn. Nigh in her sight
The bird of Jove, stooped from his airy tow'r,
Two birds of gayest plume before him drove.
Down from a hill the beast that reigns in woods,
First hunter then, pursued a gentle brace,
Goodliest of all the forest, hart and hind:
Direct to th' eastern gate was bent their flight.
Adam observed and with his eye the chase
Pursuing not unmoved to Eve thus spake:
  O Eve, some further change awaits us nigh
Which Heav'n by these mute signs in nature shows
Forerunners of his purpose or to warn
Us, haply too secure of our discharge
From penalty because from death released
Some days. How long and what till then our life
Who knows, or more than this: that we are dust

163–65. I.e., I am unworthy of such an exalted title, having been made to help you and having snared you instead.

177. *though now enjoined*: work is now required.

185. *bird of Jove*: the eagle. *stooped*: plunged. *airy tow'r*: highest point to which he soars before plunging.

188. *brace*: pair.

198. *what till then our life*: I.e., what our life will be like until we die. Observing the animals beginning to prey on one another, Adam suggests that Eve's imagining a life of pastoral contentment in the garden is *too secure* (line 196): this life will be worse than they can imagine.

And thither must return and be no more.
Why else this double object in our sight
Of flight pursued in th' air and o'er the ground
One way the self-same hour? Why in the east
Darkness ere day's mid course and morning light
More orient in yon western cloud that draws
O'er the blue firmament a radiant white
And slow descends with something Heav'nly fraught?
He erred not, for by this the Heav'nly bands
Down from a sky of jasper lighted now
In Paradise and on a hill made halt,
A glorious apparition, had not doubt
And carnal fear that day dimmed Adam's eye.
Not that more glorious when the angels met
Jacob in Mahanaïm where he saw
The field pavilioned with his guardians bright,
Nor that which on the flaming mount appeared
In Dothan covered with a camp of fire
Against the Syrian king who to surprise
One man assassin-like had levied war,
War unproclaimed. The princely hierarch
In their bright stand there left his pow'rs to seize
Possession of the garden. He alone
To find where Adam sheltered took his way
Not unperceived of Adam who to Eve,
While the great visitant approached, thus spake:
Eve, now expect great tidings which perhaps
Of us will soon determine or impose
New laws to be observed, for I descry
From yonder blazing cloud that veils the hill
One of the Heav'nly host and by his gait
None of the meanest, some great potentate
Or of the thrones above, such majesty
Invests him coming. Yet not terrible
That I should fear nor sociably mild
As Raphael that I should much confide,
But solemn and sublime, whom not t' offend,

203–7. While cloud darkens the dawn in the east, a white light appears in the west: the descending troop of cherubim, under Michael's command.

213–15. Jacob meets God's army of angels, which will protect him: "And when Jacob saw them, he said, This is God's host: and he called the name of that place Mahanaim [two camps]" (Genesis 32:2). *pavilioned*: encamped with military tents erected.

216–20. When the Syrian king sent an army to Dothan to capture the prophet Elisha, God sent an army for Elisha's protection: "and behold, the mountain was full of horses and chariots of fire round about Elisha" (2 Kings 6:17).

220. *princely hierarch*: Michael.

233: *invests him*: surrounds him.

With reverence I must meet and thou retire.
He ended and th' archangel soon drew nigh,
Not in his shape celestial but as man
Clad to meet man: over his lucid arms
A military vest of purple flowed
Livelier than Meliboean or the grain
Of Sarra worn by kings and heroes old
In time of truce. Iris had dipped the woof.
His starry helm unbuckled showed him prime
In manhood where youth ended. By his side
As in a glist'ring zodiac hung the sword,
Satan's dire dread, and in his hand the spear.
Adam bowed low. He kingly from his state
Inclined not but his coming thus declared:
  Adam, Heaven's high behest no preface needs:
Sufficient that thy prayers are heard and death
Then due by sentence when thou didst transgress
Defeated of his seizure many days
Giv'n thee of grace wherein thou may'st repent
And one bad act with many deeds well done
May'st cover. Well may then thy Lord appeased
Redeem thee quite from Death's rapacious claim.
But longer in this Paradise to dwell
Permits not. To remove thee I am come
And send thee from the garden forth to till
The ground whence thou wast taken, fitter soil.
  He added not, for Adam at the news
Heart-strook with chilling gripe of sorrow stood
That all his senses bound. Eve who unseen
Yet all had heard with audible lament
Discovered soon the place of her retire:
  O! unexpected stroke worse than of death!
Must I thus leave thee, Paradise? Thus leave
Thee, native soil, these happy walks and shades,
Fit haunt of gods, where I had hope to spend
Quiet though sad the respite of that day
That must be mortal to us both? O flowers,
That never will in other climate grow,

242–43. The places named are famous for their fine purple dye, which was exceedingly rare. See Glossary.

244. *Iris*: goddess of the rainbow and, in the *Iliad*, a messenger of Zeus who repeats Zeus's messages verbatim. See lines 261–62 n. *woof*: woven fabric.

254. *his*: Death's. *seizure*: a legal term for taking possession of property.

257–58. An important moment: the first indication to Adam that death may not be final.

261–62. Cf. lines 97–98. The repetition of the exact words of the divine command is a Homeric effect. See line 244 n.

My early visitation and my last
At ev'n which I bred up with tender hand
From the first op'ning bud and gave ye names,
Who now shall rear ye to the sun or rank
Your tribes and water from th' ambrosial fount?
Thee lastly, nuptial bow'r, by me adorned
With what to sight or smell was sweet, from thee
How shall I part and whither wander down
Into a lower world, to this obscure
And wild? How shall we breath in other air
Less pure, accustomed to immortal fruits?
  Whom thus the angel interrupted mild:
Lament not, Eve, but patiently resign
What justly thou hast lost nor set thy heart
Thus over-fond on that which is not thine.
Thy going is not lonely: with thee goes
Thy husband. Him to follow thou art bound.
Where he abides think there thy native soil.
  Adam, by this from the cold sudden damp
Recovering and his scattered spirits returned,
To Michael thus his humble words addressed:
  Celestial, whether 'mong the thrones or named
Of them the high'st, for such of shape may seem
Prince above princes, gently hast thou told
Thy message which might else in telling wound
And in performing end us. What besides
Of sorrow and dejection and despair
Our frailty can sustain thy tidings bring:
Departure from this happy place, our sweet
Recess and only consolation left
Familiar to our eyes. All places else
Inhóspitable appear and desolate,
Nor knowing us nor known. And if by prayer
Incessant I could hope to change the will
Of Him who all things can I would not cease
To weary Him with my assiduous cries.
But prayer against His absolute decree
No more avails than breath against the wind
Blown stifling back on him that breathes it forth.
Therefore to His great bidding I submit.
This most afflicts me: that departing hence

283. *to this*: compared to this.
296. *thrones*: the order of angels beneath the cherubim.
297. *the high'st*: seraphim, the order of angels above the cherubim.
306. *Inhóspitable* and *appear* are elided: 'inhospitab-lappear.'

As from His face I shall be hid, deprived
His blessèd countenance. Here I could frequent
With worship place by place where He vouchsafed
Presence divine and to my sons relate,
"On this mount He appeared, under this tree
Stood visible, among these pines His voice
I heard, here with Him at this fountain talked."
So many grateful altars I would rear
Of grassy turf and pile up every stone
Of luster from the brook in memory
Or monument to ages and thereon
Offer sweet-smelling gums and fruits and flow'rs.
In yonder nether world where shall I seek
His bright appearances or footstep trace?
For though I fled him angry, yet recalled
To life prolonged and promised race I now
Gladly behold though but His utmost skirts
Of glory, and far off His steps adore.
To whom thus Michael with regard benign:
Adam, thou know'st Heav'n His and all the Earth,
Not this rock only: His omnipresence fills
Land, sea, and air and every kind that lives,
Fomented by His virtual pow'r and warmed.
All th' Earth He gave thee to possess and rule,
No despicable gift. Surmise not then
His presence to these narrow bounds confined
Of Paradise or Eden. This had been
Perhaps thy capital seat from whence had spread
All generations and had hither come
From all the ends of th' earth to celebrate
And reverence thee their great progenitor.
But this preëminence thou hast lost, brought down
To dwell on even ground now with thy sons.
Yet doubt not but in valley and in plain
God is as here and will be found alike
Present and of His presence many a sign
Still following thee, still compassing thee round
With goodness and paternal love, His face

333. *far off His steps adore*: a phrase from the conclusion of the Statius's epic poem the *Thebaid*, in which the poet instructs his poem not to rival the *Aeneid* but to follow its example from afar and always to adore its steps: *sed longe sequere et vestigia semper adora* (12.817).

340. *No despicable gift*: a nice understatement, considering that much of history will be a violent, unsuccessful struggle for world domination.

342–46. An intriguing glimpse into what might have been had Adam and Eve not fallen.

353–54. *His face/ Express*: natural signs that will express, though indirectly, the face of God.

Express, and of His steps the track divine.
Which that thou may'st believe and be confirmed
Ere thou from hence depart, know I am sent
To show thee what shall come in future days
To thee and to thy offspring. Good with bad
Expect to hear, supernal grace contending
With sinfulness of men thereby to learn
True patience and to temper joy with fear
And pious sorrow, equally inured
By moderation either state to bear,
Prosperous or adverse. So shalt thou lead
Safest thy life and best prepared endure
Thy mortal passage when it comes. Ascend
This hill. Let Eve (for I have drenched her eyes)
Here sleep below while thou to foresight wak'st,
As once thou slept'st while she to life was formed.
  To whom thus Adam gratefully replied:
Ascend! I follow thee, safe guide, the path
Thou lead'st me, and to the hand of Heav'n submit
However chast'ning, to the evil turn
My obvious breast, arming to overcome
By suffering and earn rest from labor won
If I may so attain. So both ascend
In the visions of God. It was a hill
Of Paradise the highest from whose top
The hemisphere of Earth in clearest ken
Stretched out to th' amplest reach of prospect lay.
Not higher that hill nor wider looking round
Whereon for different cause the Tempter set
Our Second Adam in the wilderness
To show him all Earth's kingdoms and their glory.
His eye might there command wherever stood
City of old or modern fame, the seat
Of mightiest empire from the destined walls
Of Cambalu, seat of Cathaian Khan,
And Samarkand by Oxus, Temir's throne,
To Paquin of Sinaean kings and thence

374. *obvious*: exposed, in the path of the approaching evil. In the sentence spanning the lines 371 to 376, *My obvious breast* can be the object of *turn* (line 373) or the object of a participle *arming* (line 374). He turns his exposed breast to the coming evil, or he arms his exposed breast with suffering. Cf. 12.569–570: "suffering for Truth's sake / Is fortitude." I have punctuated to favor the former reading, taking the understood object of *arming* to be *myself*.

377. *In the visions of God*: "In the visions of God brought he me into the land of Israel, and set me upon a very high mountain" (Ezekiel 40:2).

377–80. The hill is so high that fully half the earth can be seen from its top, the other half falling beneath the horizon.

383. *Second Adam*: Jesus Christ, so called because he undoes the effects of Adam's sin.

388–96. Virtuosic catalog of kingdoms in Asia, from China in the far east to the region, bordering Europe, around the Hellespont and Bosphorus.

To Agra and Lahore of Great Mogul
Down to the golden Chersonese, or where
The Persian in Ecbátan sat or since
In Hispahan, or where the Russian Czar
In Moscow or the Sultan in Bizance,
Turkestan-born. Nor could his eye not ken
Th' empire of Negus to his utmost port,
Ercoco, and the less maritime kings,
Mombaza and Quiloa and Melind,
And Sofala, thought Ophir, to the realm
Of Congo and Angola farthest south.
Or thence from Niger flood to Atlas mount
The kingdoms of Almansor, Fez and Sus,
Morocco and Algiers and Tremisen,
On Europe thence and where Rome was to sway
The world. In spirit perhaps he also saw
Rich Mexico, the seat of Montezume,
And Cusco in Peru, the richer seat
Of Atabálipa and yet unspoiled
Guiana whose great city Geryon's sons
Call El Dorado. But to nobler sights
Michael from Adam's eyes the film removed
Which that false fruit that promised clearer sight
Had bred, then purged with euphrasy and rue
The visual nerve (for he had much to see)
And from the Well of Life three drops instilled.
So deep the power of these ingredients pierced
Even to the inmost seat of mental sight
That Adam now enforced to close his eyes
Sunk down and all his spirits became entranced.
But him the gentle angel by the hand
Soon raised and his attention thus recalled:
  Adam, now ope thine eyes and first behold
Th' effects which thy original crime hath wrought
In some to spring from thee who never touched
Th' excepted tree nor with the snake conspired
Nor sinned thy sin, yet from that sin derive
Corruption to bring forth more violent deeds.
  His eyes he opened and beheld a field

397–404. Moving from Asia to the southwest, the catalog continues with kingdoms in Africa, from the Red Sea facing the Arabian peninsula to the Atlas mountains across from Gibraltar, the nearest point to Europe.

398. *kings*: kingdoms.

405–11. After the mention of Rome, Adam is then shown the great kingdoms of North and South America that were destroyed by the Spaniards (*Geryon's sons*). But because these would have been over the horizon from the point where Adam stands, they were seen, if seen, *in spirit* (line 406).

414–15. *euphrasy and rue*: herbs medicinal to the sight.

Part arable and tilth whereon were sheaves
New-reaped, the other part sheep-walks and folds.
I' th' midst an altar as the landmark stood
Rustic of grassy sward. Thither anon
A sweaty reaper from his tillage brought
First fruits, the green ear and the yellow sheaf
Unculled as came to hand. A shepherd next
More meek came with the firstlings of his flock
Choicest and best, then sacrificing laid
The innards and their fat with incense strewed
On the cleft wood and all due rites performed.
His off'ring soon propitious fire from Heav'n
Consumed with nimble glance and grateful steam,
The other's not for his was not sincere,
Whereat he inly raged and as they talked
Smote him into the midriff with a stone
That beat out life: he fell and deadly pale
Groaned out his soul with gushing blood effused.
Much at that sight was Adam in his heart
Dismayed and thus in haste to th' angel cried:
  O teacher! some great mischief hath befall'n
To that meek man who well had sacrificed.
Is piety thus and pure devotion paid?
  To whom Michael thus, he also moved, replied:
These two are brethren, Adam, and to come
Out of thy loins. Th' unjust the just hath slain
For envy that his brother's off'ring found
From Heav'n acceptance. But the bloody fact
Will be avenged and th' other's faith, approved,
Lose no reward though here thou see him die,
Rolling in dust and gore. To which our sire:
  Alas, both for the deed and for the cause!
But have I now seen death? Is this the way
I must return to native dust? O sight
Of terror foul and ugly to behold,
Horrid to think, how horrible to feel!

430. *tilth*: cultivated land.
433. *sward*: turf.
434. *tillage*: harvest from cultivated land. *reaper*: Cain, the first murderer, represented in the Bible as an agriculturalist. As a pastoral people, the early Hebrews were at odds with the large, powerful, agricultural civilizations to the east and southwest, Babylon and Egypt.
436. *Unculled*: the grain has not been winnowed and separated from the chaff. This is Milton's rationalization for God's finding Cain's sacrifice unacceptable (Genesis 4:3–7). In the Bible, no reason is given. See line 434 n. *shepherd*: Abel, Cain's brother.
442. *glance*: flame. *steam*: smoke.
445. *him*: Abel.
459. *Lose no reward*. Another indication that death is not final.

To whom thus Michaël: Death thou hast seen
In his first shape on Man. But many shapes
Of Death and many are the ways that lead
To his grim cave, all dismal, yet to sense
More terrible at the entrance than within.
Some as thou saw'st by violent stroke shall die,
By fire, flood, famine; by intemp'rance more
In meats and drinks which on the earth shall bring
Diseases dire, of which a monstrous crew
Before thee shall appear that thou may'st know
What misery th' inabstinence of Eve
Shall bring on men. Immediately a place
Before his eyes appeared, sad, noisome, dark.
A lazar-house it seemed wherein were laid
Numbers of all diseased, all maladies
Of ghastly spasm or racking torture, qualms
Of heart-sick agony, all feverous kinds,
Convulsions, epilepsies, fierce catarrhs,
Intestine stone and ulcer, colic pangs,
Demoniac frenzy, moping melancholy
And moon-struck madness, pining atrophy,
Marasmus and wide-wasting pestilence,
Dropsies and asthmas and joint-racking rheums.
Dire was the tossing, deep the groans. Despair
Tended the sick busiest from couch to couch
And over them triumphant Death his dart
Shook, but delayed to strike though oft invoked
With vows as their chief good and final hope.
Sight so deform what heart of rock could long
Dry-eyed behold? Adam could not but wept,
Though not of woman born. Compassion quelled
His best of man and gave him up to tears
A space till firmer thoughts restrained excess,
And scarce recovering words his plaint renewed:
O miserable mankind! To what fall
Degraded, to what wretched state reserved!
Better end here unborn. Why is life giv'n
To be thus wrested from us? Rather why
Obtruded on us thus? who if we knew
What we receive would either not accept

470. *terrible* has two syllables.
472. *fire* has one syllable: 'faar.' *intemperance* has three syllables: 'intem-prance.'
479. *lazar-house*: place of confinement for victims of leprosy.
480–88. A virtuosic catalog of diseases. Lines 485–87 were added in 1674.
496. *not of woman born*: because Adam is the only man without a mother, he is supposed to be less inclined to weep than other men.

Life offered or soon beg to lay it down,
Glad to be so dismissed in peace. Can thus
The image of God in Man created once
So goodly and erect, though faulty since,
To such unsightly sufferings be debased
Under inhuman pains? Why should not Man
Retaining still divine similitude
In part from such deformities be free
And for his Maker's image sake exempt?
  Their Maker's image, answered Michael, then
Forsook them when themselves they vilified
To serve ungoverned appetite and took
His image whom they served, a brutish vice,
Inductive mainly to the sin of Eve.
Therefore so abject is their punishment,
Disfiguring not God's likeness but their own,
Or *if* His likeness, by themselves defaced
While they pervert pure nature's healthful rules
To loathsome sickness—worthily, since they
God's image did not reverence in themselves.
  I yield it just, said Adam, and submit.
But is there yet no other way besides
These painful passages how we may come
To death and mix with our connatural dust?
  There is, said Michael, if thou well observe
The rule of not too much by temp'rance taught
In what thou eat'st and drink'st, seeking from thence
Due nourishment, not gluttonous delight,
Till many years over thy head return.
So may'st thou live till like ripe fruit thou drop
Into thy mother's lap or be with ease
Gathered, not harshly plucked, for Death mature.
This is old age, but then thou must outlive
Thy youth, thy strength, thy beauty which will change
To withered, weak and grey. Thy senses, then
Obtuse, all taste of pleasure must forgo
To what thou hast. And for the air of youth,
Hopeful and cheerful, in thy blood will reign
A melancholy damp of cold and dry
To weigh thy spirits down and last consume
The balm of life. To whom our ancestor:
  Henceforth I fly not death nor would prolong

518. *His image*: of Gluttony.
519. *Inductive . . . to*: brought in from.
542. I.e., In comparison with what you know of pleasure now.

Life much, bent rather how I may be quit
Fairest and easiest of this cumbrous charge
Which I must keep till my appointed day
Of rend'ring up, and patiently attend
My dissolution. Michaël replied:
  Nor love thy life nor hate but what thou liv'st
Live well, how long or short permit to Heav'n.
And now prepare thee for another sight.
  He looked and saw a spacious plain whereon
Were tents of various hue. By some were herds
Of cattle grazing, others whence the sound
Of instruments that made melodious chime
Was heard of harp and organ and who moved
Their stops and chords was seen: his volant touch
Instínct through all proportions low and high
Fled and pursued transverse the resonant fugue.
In other part stood one who at the forge
Laboring two massy clods of iron and brass
Had melted, whether found where casual fire
Had wasted woods on mountain or in vale
Down to the veins of earth, thence gliding hot
To some cave's mouth or whether washed by stream
From underground. The liquid ore he drained
Into fit molds prepared from which he formed
First his own tools, then what might else be wrought
Fusile or grav'n in metal. After these
But on the hither side, a different sort
From the high neighb'ring hills which was their seat
Down to the plain descended. By their guise
Just men they seemed and all their study bent
To worship God aright and know his works
Not hid, nor those things last which might preserve
Freedom and peace to men. They on the plain
Long had not walked when from the tents behold
A bevy of fair women richly gay
In gems and wanton dress. To the harp they sung

549. *cumbrous charge*: the body. 'This bothersome responsibility.'
556–73. The beginnings of the arts and sciences, of music, and of the work of the forge, useful for peace and war.
574. *a different sort*: the sons of Cain.
577. *study*: effort, concentration.
579–80. *nor those things last . . . men*: Nor did they neglect the study of political wisdom.
582. *bevy*: a group, usually of women.
582–92. Loosely based on Genesis 6:1–2, where angels ("sons of God"), seeing how attractive women are, beget giants on them (line 642). Milton takes the "sons of God" as men, descendants of Cain (line 609). The offspring of these amours are the first tyrants, figuratively represented as giants (line 642). For Milton, the inward tyranny of vice leads inevitably to outward, political tyranny. See lines 714–18 and 12.83–101. See Glossary, RAMIEL.

Soft amorous ditties and in dance came on.
The men, though grave, eyed them and let their eyes
Rove without rein till in the amorous net
Fast caught they like and each his liking chose.
And now of love they treat till th' evening star,
Love's harbinger, appeared; then all in heat
They light the nuptial torch and bid invoke
Hymen, then first to marriage rites invoked:
With feast and music all the tents resound.
Such happy interview and fair event
Of love and youth not lost, songs, garlands, flow'rs,
And charming symphonies attached the heart
Of Adam soon inclined t' admit delight,
The bent of nature, which he thus expressed:
  True opener of mine eyes, prime angel blest,
Much better seems this vision and more hope
Of peaceful days portends than those two past:
Those were of hate and death or pain much worse,
Here Nature seems fulfilled in all her ends.
  To whom thus Michael: Judge not what is best
By pleasure though to nature seeming meet,
Created as thou art to nobler end
Holy and pure, conformity divine.
Those tents thou saw'st so pleasant were the tents
Of wickedness wherein shall dwell his race
Who slew his brother. Studious they appear
Of arts that polish life, inventors rare,
Unmindful of their Maker though his Spirit
Taught them. But they his gifts acknowledged none.
Yet they a beauteous offspring shall beget,
For that fair female troop thou saw'st that seemed
Of goddesses so blithe, so smooth, so gay,
Yet empty of all good wherein consists
Woman's domestic honor and chief praise,
Bred only and completed to the taste
Of lustful áppetence: to sing, to dance,
To dress and troll the tongue and roll the eye.
To these that sober race of men whose lives
Religious titled them the sons of God
Shall yield up all their virtue, all their fame
Ignobly to the trains and to the smiles

606. *conformity divine*: i.e., you are like God in nobility and purity, not in pleasure.
612. *acknowledged none*. This is arguably inconsistent with lines 577–78.
619. *áppetence*: desire.

Of these fair atheists, and now swim in joy
(Erelong to swim at large) and laugh, for which
The world erelong a world of tears must weep.
  To whom thus Adam of short joy bereft:
O pity and shame that they who to live well
Entered so fair should turn aside to tread
Paths indirect or in the mid-way faint!
But still I see the tenor of man's woe
Holds on the same from woman to begin.
  From man's effeminate slackness it begins,
Said th' angel, who should better hold his place
By wisdom and superior gifts received.
But now prepare thee for another scene.
  He looked and saw wide territory spread
Before him, towns and rural works between,
Cities of men with lofty gates and tow'rs,
Concourse in arms, fierce faces threat'ning war,
Giants of mighty bone and bold emprise.
Part wield their arms, part curb the foaming steed
Single or in array of battle ranged
Both horse and foot, nor idly must'ring stood.
One way a band select from forage drives
A herd of beeves, fair oxen and fair kine
From a fat meadow ground, or fleecy flock,
Ewes and their bleating lambs, over the plain,
Their booty. Scarce with life the shepherds fly
But call in aid which tacks a bloody fray.
With cruel tournament the squadrons join.
Where cattle pastured late now scattered lies
With carcasses and arms th' ensanguined field
Deserted. Others to a city strong
Lay siege encamped, by batt'ry, scale and mine
Assaulting. Others from the wall defend
With dart and javelin, stones and sulph'rous fire.
On each hand slaughter and gigantic deeds.

625. *atheists* has two syllables: 'ath-yests.'

626. *Erelong to swim at large*: a grim foreboding of the Flood, in which they will all drown.

645. *mus'tring*: assembling (of troops). Latin *monstro*, "to show."

651. *tacks* 1667] *makes* 1674. The change from the technical *tacks* ("joins in battle") to the more banal *makes* may or may not have been Milton's decision, prompted by complaint against the more obscure word. But the common word *makes*, in contrast to the technical word *tacks*, suggests a disorganized brawl rather than an engagement between trained soldiers, which is what the following line suggests. In *Of Reformation* Milton uses *tack* as a noun: "holding tack against two of the king's generals" (*YP* 1.530).

654. *ensanguined*: soaked with blood.

656. *batt'ry, scale and mine*: battering ram, scaling ladders, and tunnels under the walls.

In other part the sceptred heralds call
To council in the city gates. Anon
Grey-headed men and grave with warriors mixed
Assemble and harangues are heard, but soon
In factious opposition, till at last
Of middle age one rising, eminent
In wise deport, spake much of right and wrong,
Of justice, of religion, truth and peace,
And judgment from above. Him old and young
Exploded and had seized with violent hands
Had not a cloud descending snatched him thence
Unseen amid the throng. So violence
Proceeded and oppression and sword-law
Through all the plain, and refuge none was found.
Adam was all in tears and to his guide
Lamenting turned full sad: O what are these,
Death's ministers not men who thus deal death
Inhumanly to men and multiply
Ten thousandfold the sin of him who slew
His brother? For of whom such massacre
Make they but of their brethren, men of men?
But who was that just man whom had not Heav'n
Rescued had in his righteousness been lost?
  To whom thus Michael: These are the product
Of those ill-mated marriages thou saw'st,
Where good with bad were matched, who of themselves
Abhor to join and by imprudence mixed
Produce prodigious births of body or mind.
Such were these giants, men of high renown,
For in those days might only shall be admired
And "valor" and "heroic virtue" called.
To overcome in battle and subdue
Nations and bring home spoils with infinite
Manslaughter shall be held the highest pitch
Of human glory and for glory done
Of triumph to be styled great conquerors,
Patrons of mankind, gods, and sons of gods:
Destroyers rightlier called and plagues of men!
Thus fame shall be achieved, renown on earth,

665. Enoch, whom, like Elijah, God raised to Heaven without his having first to suffer death (Genesis 5:21–24). Without biblical precedent Milton makes Enoch a figure of political courage not unlike Abdiel and not unlike himself. See lines 700–710.

669. *Exploded*: hissed out (Latin *explodo*, a theater term, opposite of *plaudo*, "to applaud"). See 10.546 n.

685–86. *of themselves / Abhor to join*: abhor to marry their own kind but mix with women of foreign race.

And what most merits fame in silence hid.
But he the seventh from thee, whom thou beheld'st,
The only righteous in a world perverse
And therefore hated, therefore so beset
With foes for daring single to be just
And utter odious truth that God would come
To judge them with his saints, him the Most High
Rapt in a balmy cloud with wingèd steeds
Did, as thou saw'st, receive to walk with God
High in salvation and the climes of bliss
Exempt from death, to show thee what reward
Awaits the good, the rest what punishment,
Which now direct thine eyes and soon behold.
  He looked and saw the face of things quite changed:
The brazen throat of war had ceased to roar.
All now was turned to jollity and game,
To luxury and riot, feast and dance,
Marrying or prostituting as befell,
Rape or adultery where passing fair
Allured them: thence from cups to civil broils.
At length a reverend sire among them came
And of their doings great dislike declared
And testified against their ways. He oft
Frequented their assemblies whereso met,
Triumphs or festivals, and to them preached
Conversion and repentance as to souls
In prison under judgments imminent.
But all in vain, which when he saw he ceased
Contending and removed his tents far off.
Then from the mountain hewing timber tall
Began to build a vessel of huge bulk
Measured by cubit, length and breadth and heighth,
Smeared round with pitch and in the side a door
Contrived, and of provisions laid in large
For man and beast, when, lo, a wonder strange!
Of every beast and bird and insect small
Came sevens and pairs and entered in as taught
Their order, last the sire and his three sons
With their four wives, and God made fast the door.
Meanwhile the south wind rose and with black wings
Wide hovering all the clouds together drove
From under heav'n. The hills to their supply
Vapor and exhalation, dusk and moist

700–710. Enoch. See line 665.
719. *reverend sire*: Noah (Genesis 6:9 to 9:18).

Sent up amain. And now the thickened sky
Like a dark ceiling stood. Down rushed the rain
Impetuous and continued till the earth
No more was seen. The floating vessel swum
Uplifted and secure with beakèd prow
Rode tilting o'er the waves. All dwellings else
Flood overwhelmed and them with all their pomp
Deep under water rolled. Sea covered sea,
Sea without shore, and in their palaces
Where luxury late reigned sea-monsters whelped
And stabled. Of mankind, so numerous late,
All left in one small bottom swum embarked.
How didst thou grieve then, Adam, to behold
The end of all thy offspring, end so sad,
Depopulation! Thee another flood
Of tears and sorrow, a flood thee also drowned
And sunk thee as thy sons, till gently reared
By th' angel on thy feet thou stood'st at last,
Though comfortless as when a father mourns
His children all in view destroyed at once,
And scarce to th' angel utter'dst thus thy plaint:
  O visions ill foreseen! Better had I
Lived ignorant of future, so had borne
My part of evil only, each day's lot
Enough to bear! Those now that were dispensed,
The burden of many ages, on me light
At once, by my foreknowledge gaining birth
Abortive to torment me, ere their being,
With thought that they must be! Let no man seek
Henceforth to be foretold what shall befall
Him or his children: evil he may be sure,
Which neither his foreknowing can prevent
And he the future evil shall no less
In apprehension than in substance feel
Grievous to bear. But that care now is past:
Man is not whom to warn. Those few escaped
Famine and anguish will at last consume
Wand'ring that wat'ry desert! I had hope
When violence was ceased and war on earth,
All would have then gone well: peace would have crowned
With length of happy days the race of Man.

753. *bottom*: ship's hull.
766. *dispensed*: killed.
773. *neither*: not a disjunctive *neither* . . . *nor* construction, but a simple negative.
777. *Man* . . . *warn*: No man now lives who can be warned of this calamity, the Flood.

But I was far deceived, for now I see
Peace to corrupt no less than war to waste.
How comes it thus? Unfold, celestial guide,
And whether here the race of Man will end.
  To whom thus Michael: Those whom last thou saw'st
In triumph and luxurious wealth are they
First seen in acts of prowess eminent
And great exploits but of true virtue void,
Who having spilt much blood and done much waste
Subduing nations and achieved thereby
Fame in the world, high titles and rich prey,
Shall change their course to pleasure, ease and sloth,
Surfeit and lust till wantonness and pride
Raise out of friendship hostile deeds in peace.
The conquered also and enslaved by war
Shall with their freedom lost all virtue lose
And fear of God from whom their piety feigned
In sharp contést of battle found no aid
Against invaders. Therefore cooled in zeal
Thenceforth shall practice how to live secure,
Worldly or dissolute on what their lords
Shall leave them to enjoy, for th' earth shall bear
More than enough that temp'rance may be tried.
So all shall turn degenerate, all depraved,
Justice and temp'rance, truth and faith forgot,
One man except, the only son of light
In a dark age against example good,
Against allurement, custom and a world
Offended, fearless of reproach and scorn
Or violence. He of their wicked ways
Shall them admonish and before them set
The paths of righteousness, how much more safe
And full of peace, denouncing wrath to come
On their impenitence, and shall return,
Of them derided but of God observed,
The one just man alive. By His command
Shall build a wondrous ark as thou beheld'st
To save himself and household from amidst
A world devote to universal wrack.
No sooner he with them of man and beast
Select for life shall in the ark be lodged
And sheltered round but all the cataracts

797–801. *The conquered*: an anticipation of Israel's subjection to foreign powers in the period covered by the book of Judges.
808. *One man*: Noah. Michael gives Noah's story in more clearly moral terms.

Of heav'n set open on the earth shall pour
Rain day and night, all fountains of the deep
Broke up shall heave the ocean to usurp
Beyond all bounds till inundation rise
Above the highest hills. Then shall this mount
Of Paradise by might of waves be moved
Out of his place, pushed by the hornèd Flood
With all his verdure spoiled and trees adrift
Down the great river to the op'ning gulf
And there take root an island salt and bare,
The haunt of seals and orcs and sea-mews' clang,
To teach thee that God attributes to place
No sanctity if none be thither brought
By men who there frequent or therein dwell.
And now what further shall ensue, behold.
He looked and saw the ark hull on the Flood
Which now abated for the clouds were fled
Driv'n by a keen north wind that blowing dry
Wrinkled the face of Deluge, as decayed,
And the clear sun on his wide wat'ry glass
Gazed hot and of the fresh wave largely drew
As after thirst, which made their flowing shrink
From standing lake to tripping ebb that stole
With soft foot towards the deep who now had stopped
His sluices as the heav'n his windows shut.
The ark no more now floats but seems on ground
Fast on the top of some high mountain fixed.
And now the tops of hills as rocks appear.
With clamor thence the rapid currents drive
Towards the retreating sea their furious tide.
Forthwith from out the ark a raven flies
And after him the surer messenger:
A dove sent forth once and again to spy
Green tree or ground whereon his foot may light.
The second time returning, in his bill

831–35. *hornèd flood*: rushing waters that divide in two courses around the mount of Paradise, tearing it from its foundations. The mount is driven down the swollen Euphrates River into the Arabian gulf, where it is reduced to a bare rock. *orcs*: sea monsters, whales. *sea-mews*: seagulls. *clang*: noise made by a multitude, often used of birds (Greek *klangê*). See 7.422 n.

843. A drying north wind wrinkles the surface of the Flood, as if the Flood were aging and close to its death, which it is. Milton admired the Metaphysical poet Cowley, and this image, though it is untypical of Milton, is a typical Metaphysical "conceit."

844. *glass*: the Flood is the sun's mirror.

846. *their*: the waters of the Flood.

847. *tripping*: with quick steps and pleasant rhythm, the waters slip back toward the ocean.

854. *Towards* has one syllable: 'tords.'

An olive leaf he brings, pacific sign.
Anon dry ground appears and from his ark
The ancient sire descends with all his train.
Then with uplifted hands and eyes devout,
Grateful to Heav'n, over his head beholds
A dewy cloud and in the cloud a bow
Conspicuous with three listed colors gay
Betok'ning peace from God and cov'nant new.
Whereat the heart of Adam erst so sad
Greatly rejoiced and thus his joy broke forth:
O thou who future things canst represent
As present, Heav'nly instructor, I revive
At this last sight, assured that Man shall live
With all the creatures and their seed preserve.
Far less I now lament for one whole world
Of wicked sons destroyed than I rejoice
For one man found so perfect and so just
That God vouchsafes to raise another world
From him and all His anger to forget.
But say, what mean those colored streaks in heav'n
Distended as the brow of God appeased,
Or serve they as a flow'ry verge to bind
The fluid skirts of that same wat'ry cloud
Lest it again dissolve and show'r the Earth?
To whom th' Archangel: Dexterously thou aim'st.
So willingly doth God remit His ire,
Though late repenting Him of man depraved,
Grieved at His heart when looking down He saw
The whole Earth filled with violence and all flesh
Corrupting each their way. Yet those removed,
Such grace shall one just man find in His sight
That He relents, not to blot out mankind,
And makes a cov'nant never to destroy
The Earth again by flood nor let the sea
Surpass his bounds nor rain to drown the world
With Man therein or beast; but when He brings
Over the Earth a cloud will therein set
His triple-colored bow whereon to look
And call to mind His cov'nant: day and night,

860. *pacific sign*: the sign of peace.
862. *train*: followers.
866. *Conspicuous* has three syllables: 'conspic-yus.'
874–78. Adam's language, applied to Noah, anticipates Christ's establishing of "a new heaven and a new earth" (Revelation 21:1). Likewise, the covenant of the rainbow anticipates the better covenant of the new testament in Christ. See lines 890–98.

Seed time and harvest, heat and hoary frost
Shall hold their course till fire purge all things new,
Both Heav'n and Earth, wherein the just shall dwell.

Book Twelve

The Argument

The angel Michael continues from the Flood to relate what shall succeed. Then, in the mention of Abraham, comes by degrees to explain who that Seed of the woman shall be which was promised Adam and Eve in the Fall: His Incarnation, Death, Resurrection, and Ascension, the state of the Church till His Second Coming. Adam, greatly satisfied and recomforted by these relations and promises, descends the hill with Michael, wakens Eve who all this while had slept, but with gentle dreams composed to quietness of mind and submission. Michael in either hand leads them out of Paradise, the fiery sword waving behind them and the cherubim taking their stations to guard the place.

As one who in his journey bates at noon,
Though bent on speed, so here th' archangel paused
Betwixt the world destroyed and world restored
If Adam aught perhaps might interpose,
Then with transition sweet new speech resumes:
  Thus thou hast seen one world begin and end
And Man as from a second stock proceed.
Much thou hast yet to see, but I perceive
Thy mortal sight to fail: objects divine
Must needs impair and weary human sense.
Henceforth what is to come I will relate:
Thou therefore give due audience and attend!
  This second source of men while yet but few
And while the dread of judgement past remains
Fresh in their minds, fearing the Deity
With some regard to what is just and right,
Shall lead their lives and multiply apace,
Laboring the soil and reaping plenteous crop,
Corn, wine, and oil, and from the herd or flock

900. *till fire . . . new*: "Looking for and hasting unto the coming of the day of God, wherein the heavens being on fire shall be dissolved, and the elements shall melt with fervent heat . . . we, according to his promise, look for new heavens and a new earth, wherein dwelleth righteousness" (2 Peter 3:12–13).

Book Twelve

1. *bates*: halts.

11. *relate*: narrate, instead of show in visions.

Oft sacrificing bullock, lamb or kid
With large wine off'rings poured and sacred feast,
Shall spend their days in joy unblamed and dwell
Long time in peace by families and tribes
Under paternal rule. Till one shall rise
Of proud ambitious heart who not content
With fair equality, fraternal state,
Will arrogate dominion undeserved
Over his brethren and quite dispossess
Concord and law of Nature from the Earth,
Hunting (and men not beasts shall be his game)
With war and hostile snare such as refuse
Subjection to his empire tyrannous.
"A mighty hunter" thence shall he be styled
"Before the Lord" as in despite of Heav'n
Or from Heav'n claiming second sovereignty,
And from rebellion shall derive his name
Though of rebellion others he accuse.
He with a crew whom like ambition joins
With him or under him to tyrannize,
Marching from Eden towards the west shall find
The plain wherein a black bituminous gurge
Boils out from underground, the mouth of Hell.
Of brick and of that stuff they cast to build
A city and tow'r whose top may reach to Heav'n
And get themselves a name, lest far dispersed
In foreign lands their memory be lost,
Regardless whether good or evil fame.
But God, who oft descends to visit men
Unseen and through their habitations walks
To mark their doings, them beholding soon,
Comes down to see their city ere the tow'r
Obstruct Heav'n's tow'rs and in derision sets
Upon their tongues a various spirit to raze
Quite out their native language and instead
To sow a jangling noise of words unknown.
Forthwith a hideous gabble rises loud

24. *one*: Nimrod. By legend the first warrior-tyrant after the flood and the first builder of great cities in Babylonia (Shinar): "And Cush begat Nimrod: he began to be a mighty one in the earth. He was a mighty hunter before the Lord . . . And the beginning of his kingdom was Babel, and Erech, and Accad, and Caineh, in the land of Shinar" (Genesis 10:8–10).

36. *Nimrod* was supposed to derive from a Hebrew verb meaning "to rebel."

38–62. The story of the tower of Babel: "And they said, Go to, let us build a city and a tower, whose top may reach unto heaven; and let us make us a name, lest we be scattered abroad upon the face of the whole earth" (Genesis 11:4). Although Nimrod is not named in the story, Milton identifies those who *found a plain in the land of Shinar* with Nimrod's founding his kingdom *in the land of Shinar* (10:10).

Among the builders: each to other calls
Not understood, till hoarse and all in rage,
As mocked, they storm. Great laughter was in Heav'n
And looking down to see the hubbub strange
And hear the din, thus was the building left
Ridiculous and the work "Confusion" named.
  Whereto thus Adam fatherly displeased:
O execrable son so to aspire
Above his brethren, to himself assuming
Authority usurped from God not giv'n:
He gave us only over beast, fish, fowl
Dominion absolute. That right we hold
By His donation. But man over men
He made not lord, such title to himself
Reserving, human left from human free.
But this usurper his encroachment proud
Stays not on Man: to God his tow'r intends
Siege and defiance. Wretched man! what food
Will he convey up thither to sustain
Himself and his rash army where thin air
Above the clouds will pine his entrails gross
And famish him of breath if not bread?
  To whom thus Michael: Justly thou abhorr'st
That son who on the quiet state of men
Such trouble brought, affecting to subdue
Rational liberty. Yet know withal,
Since thy original lapse true liberty
Is lost which always with right reason dwells
Twinned and from her hath no dividual being.
Reason in man obscured or not obeyed
Immediately inordinate desires
And upstart passions catch the government
From reason and to servitude reduce
Man till then free. Therefore since he permits
Within himself unworthy pow'rs to reign
Over free reason God in judgement just

62. *Confusion named*: "Therefore is the name of it called Babel; because the Lord did there confound the language of all the earth: and from thence did the Lord scatter them abroad upon the face of all the earth" (Genesis 11:9).

83–101. These lines state the principal lesson of *Paradise Lost* (but see lines 561–73): that outward political liberty and inward moral self-command are reciprocal, and that both are under reason. When inward moral self command is lost, outward political liberty is too. See 9.1127–31 and the opening of *Tenure of Kings and Magistrates*: "If men within themselves would be governed by reason, and not generally give up their understanding to a double tyranny, of custom from without and blind affections [passions] within, they would discern better what it is to favor and uphold the tyrant of a nation . . . For indeed none can love freedom heartily but good men" (*YP* 3.190).

84. *right reason*: the philosophic conscience, implanted in us by God.

Subjects him from without to violent lords
Who oft as undeservedly enthrall
His outward freedom. Tyranny must be,
Though to the tyrant thereby no excuse.
Yet sometimes nations will decline so low
From virtue, which is reason, that no wrong
But justice and some fatal curse annexed
Deprives them of their outward liberty,
Their inward lost: witness th' irreverent son
Of him who built the ark who for the shame
Done to his father heard this heavy curse,
"Servant of servants," on his vicious race.
Thus will this latter as the former world
Still tend from bad to worse till God at last
Wearied with their iniquities withdraw
His presence from among them and avert
His holy eyes, resolving from thenceforth
To leave them to their own polluted ways
And one peculiar nation to select
From all the rest of whom to be invoked,
A nation from one faithful man to spring,
Him on this side Euphrates yet residing,
Bred up in idol worship. Oh! that men
(Canst thou believe?) should be so stupid grown
While yet the patriarch lived who 'scaped the flood
As to forsake the living God and fall
To worship their own work in wood and stone
For gods! Yet him God the Most High vouchsafes
To call by vision from his father's house,

101–4. Noah's son Ham saw his drunken father naked and asleep. Ham's brothers, Japhet and Shem, placed a covering on their shoulders, walked backward into the tent so that they would not see Noah naked, and laid the covering on him. "And Noah woke from his wine, and knew what his younger son [Ham] had done unto him. And he said, Cursed be Canaan; a servant of servants shall he be unto his brethren. And he said, Blessed be the Lord God of Shem; and Canaan shall be his servant" (Genesis 9:24–26). The Canaanites are the inhabitants of the Promised Land, which is conquered by the Hebrews in the Book of Judges. See lines 260–62 n.

105. *latter . . . former world*: the world after and before the Flood.

111. *nation*: the Hebrews. *Nation* here does not mean a political but a familial entity: the seed of Abraham.

113. *one faithful man*: Abraham, who lives in Ur on the lower Euphrates, below Babylon, near the Arabian Gulf. He is called *Abram* until God re-names him *Abraham* "father of many nations" (Genesis 17:5). See line 152.

120–37. Milton skillfully compresses the biblical tale. In the Bible, Abram's father, Terah, travels from Ur up the Euphrates valley to Haran, north of Canaan, taking his son, Abram, and his grandson, Lot. Called thence by God into "a land that I will show thee" (Genesis 12:2), Abram travels south into Canaan, making camp at Sichem, where God promises the land to him and his descendants: "Unto thy seed will I give this land" (Genesis 12:7). The promise is later renewed as a formal covenant: "In the same day the Lord made a covenant with Abram, saying, Unto thy seed have I given this land, from the river of Egypt unto the great river, the river Euphrates" (Genesis 15:18).

His kindred and false gods, into a land
Which he will show him and from him will raise
A mighty nation and upon him show'r
His benediction so that in his seed
All nations shall be blest. He straight obeys,
Not knowing to what land, yet firm believes.
I see him (but thou canst not) with what faith
He leaves his gods, his friends, and native soil,
Ur of Chaldea, passing now the ford
To Haran, after him a cumbrous train
Of herds and flocks and numerous servitude,
Not wand'ring poor but trusting all his wealth
With God who called him in a land unknown.
Canaan he now attains: I see his tents
Pitched about Sechem and the neighb'ring plain
Of Moreh. There by promise he receives
Gift to his progeny of all that land:
From Hamath northward to the desert south
(Things by their names I call, though yet unnamed)
From Hermon east to the great western sea.
Mount Hermon, yonder sea, each place behold
In prospect as I point them: on the shore
Mount Carmel, here the double-founted stream
Jordan, true limit eastward, but his sons
Shall dwell to Senir, that long ridge of hills.
This ponder: that all nations of the earth
Shall in his seed be blessèd. (By that seed
Is meant thy great Deliverer who shall bruise
The Serpent's head, whereof to thee anon
Plainlier shall be revealed.) This patriarch blest,
Whom faithful Abraham due time shall call,
A son and of his son a grandchild leaves
Like him in faith, in wisdom and renown.

139–46. The holy land, Palestine, is delineated, extending from Syria (Hamath) in the north to the Sinai desert bordering Egypt in the south, and from Mount Hermon, which Milton (following his sources) supposed was in the east, to the Mediterranean Sea in the west. (Hermon, the highest peak in Palestine, is in the north.) Mount Carmel, on the Mediterranean, is the promontory near modern Haifa. The eastern boundary, the Jordan River, flows south into the Dead Sea. The Hebrews will inhabit the hill country (*that long ridge of hills*) to the west of the Jordan, in the heart of ancient Judea.

147–51. After Abraham has shown his willingness to sacrifice his son Isaac (an episode Milton omits), God blesses Abraham again and says that not only Abraham's children but all the nations of the earth will be blessed: "I will multiply thy seed as the stars of the heaven, and as the sand which is upon the sea shore . . . and in thy seed shall all the nations of the earth be blessed" (Genesis 22:17–18). Christians interpreted the second use of *thy seed* in this passage as Jesus Christ, who will extend God's blessing from Israel to all nations. "Now to Abraham and his seed were the promises made. He saith not, And to seeds, as of many; but as of one, And to thy seed, which is Christ" (Galatians 3:16).

153. *son*: Isaac. *grandchild*: Jacob.

The grandchild with twelve sons increased departs
From Canaan to a land hereafter called
Egypt, divided by the river Nile.
See where it flows disgorging at sev'n mouths
Into the sea! To sojourn in that land
He comes invited by a younger son
In time of dearth, a son whose worthy deeds
Raise him to be the second in that realm
Of Pharaoh. There he dies and leaves his race
Growing into a nation and, now grown,
Suspected to a sequent king who seeks
To stop their overgrowth, as inmate guests
Too num'rous, whence of guests he makes them slaves,
Inhospitably, and kills their infant males,
Till by two brethren (those two brethren call
Moses and Aaron) sent from God to claim
His people from enthrallment they return
With glory and spoil back to their promised land.
But first the lawless tyrant who denies
To know their God or message to regard
Must be compelled by signs and judgements dire:
To blood unshed the rivers must be turned;
Frogs, lice and flies must all his palace fill
With loathed intrusion and fill all the land;
His cattle must of rot and murrain die;
Botches and blains must all his flesh emboss
And all his people; thunder mixed with hail,
Hail mixed with fire must rend th' Egyptian sky
And wheel on th' earth devouring where it rolls;
What it devours not, herb or fruit or grain,
A darksome cloud of locusts swarming down
Must eat and on the ground leave nothing green;
Darkness must overshadow all his bounds,
Palpable darkness, and blot out three days;
Last with one midnight stroke all the first-born
Of Egypt must lie dead. Thus with ten wounds

160. *younger son*: Joseph.
163. *he*: Joseph.
165. *sequent king*: later pharaoh.
168. *Inhospitably* and *and* are elided: 'Inhospitab-land.'
172. *spoil*: "and they borrowed of the Egyptians jewels of silver, and jewels of gold, and raiment. . . . And they spoiled the Egyptians" (Exodus 12:35–36).
173. *tyrant*: Pharaoh.
175–90. The plagues of Egypt, recounted in Exodus 7–12, by which Pharaoh was at last compelled to let the Israelites leave Egypt for the Promised Land.

The river-dragon tamed at length submits
To let his sojourners depart and oft
Humbles his stubborn heart, but still as ice
More hardened after thaw till in his rage,
Pursuing whom he late dismissed, the sea
Swallows him with his host but *them* lets pass
As on dry land between two crystal walls,
Awed by the rod of Moses so to stand
Divided till his rescued gain their shore.
Such wondrous pow'r God to His saint will lend,
Though present in His angel, who shall go
Before them in a cloud and pillar of fire,
By day a cloud, by night a pillar of fire
To guide them in their journey and remove
Behind them while th' obdúrate king pursues.
All night he will pursue but his approach
Darkness defends between till morning watch.
Then through the fiery pillar and the cloud
God looking forth will trouble all his host
And craze their chariot wheels when by command
Moses once more his potent rod extends
Over the sea. The sea his rod obeys:
On their embattled ranks the waves return
And overwhelm their war. The race elect
Safe towards Canaan from the shore advance
Through the wild desert, not the readiest way,
Lest ent'ring on the Canaanite alarmed
War terrify them inexpért and fear
Return them back to Egypt, choosing rather
Inglorious life with servitude, for life
To noble and ignoble is more sweet
Untrained in arms where rashness leads not on.
This also shall they gain by their delay
In the wide wilderness: there they shall found

191. *river-dragon*: Pharaoh. "I am against thee, Pharaoh king of Egypt, the great dragon that lieth in the midst of his rivers, which hath said, My river is mine own, and I have made it for myself" (Ezekiel 29:3).

194–214. In Exodus 14, the Israelites, pursued by Pharaoh and his army, cross the Red sea, which at Moses' signal, the extending of his *potent rod* (line 211), divides for them. Once the Israelites have crossed, Moses causes the sea to close again over Pharaoh's pursuing army. Cf. 1.306–11.

215–16. The Israelites begin their forty years' journey in the wilderness.

216–26. By taking the more indirect and extremely harsh route to Canaan, through Sinai and the country to the east of the Dead Sea, the Israelites become tough and warlike. But they also become a nation governed by laws delivered to Moses on Mount Sinai, where God descends (Exodus 19–23). Milton places more emphasis on their political organization than on their religious rites.

Their government and their great senate choose
Through the twelve tribes to rule by laws ordained.
God from the Mount of Sinai, whose grey top
Shall tremble, He descending will himself
In thunder, lightning and loud trumpet's sound
Ordain them laws, part such as appertain
To civil justice, part religious rites
Of sacrifice, informing them by types
And shadows of that destined Seed to bruise
The Serpent, by what means He shall achieve
Mankind's deliv'rance. But the voice of God
To mortal ear is dreadful: they beseech
That Moses might report to them His will
And terror cease. He grants what they besought,
Instructed that to God is no accéss
Without Mediator, whose high office now
Moses in figure bears to introduce
One greater, of whose day he shall foretell,
And all the prophets in their age the times
Of great Messiah shall sing. Thus laws and rites
Established, such delight hath God in men
Obedient to His will that He vouchsafes
Among them to set up His tabernacle,
The Holy One with mortal men to dwell.
By His prescript a sanctuary is framed
Of cedar overlaid with gold, therein
An ark and in the ark his testimony,
The records of His cov'nant. Over these
A mercy-seat of gold between the wings
Of two bright cherubim. Before Him burn
Sev'n lamps as in a zodiac representing
The heav'nly fires. Over the tent a cloud
Shall rest by day, a fiery gleam by night,
Save when they journey, and at length they come

231–35. The religious rites given to the Israelites in the law are seen by Christians as mysterious types (historical symbols) of the new covenant to come in Jesus Christ, the *destined Seed* (line 233), who will deliver humanity from the power of Satan.

235–44. Moses' ascending Mount Sinai alone, because God is too dreadful for the people to encounter directly, is a type of Christ's being a mediator between God and Man. Moses bears Christ's *high office* (line 240) symbolically (*in figure* [line 241]).

242. *he*: Moses.

243. *in their age*. The age of the prophets, who will foretell the Messiah more openly than do the *types and shadows* (lines 232–33) of the ritual law, is much later. The suggestion is that as history goes forward, God's purpose for history becomes increasingly clear.

247. *tabernacle*: the enclosure for the ark of the covenant, the box in which the tablets of the law were carried. The ark is kept in the sanctuary and is considered to be the presence of God, who has come down from heaven to live among his people (Exodus 24–27).

Conducted by His angel to the land
Promised to Abraham and his seed. The rest
Were long to tell: how many battles fought,
How many kings destroyed and kingdoms won,
Or how the sun shall in mid heav'n stand still
A day entire and night's due course adjourn,
Man's voice commanding, "Sun in Gibeon stand
And thou, Moon, in the vale of Aialon
Till Israel overcome." So call the third
From Abraham son of Isaac and from him
His whole descent, who thus shall Canaan win.
  Here Adam interposed: O sent from Heav'n,
Enlight'ner of my darkness, gracious things
Thou hast revealed, those chiefly which concern
Just Abraham and his seed. Now first I find
Mine eyes true op'ning and my heart much eased,
Erewhile perplexed with thoughts what would become
Of me and all mankind, but now I see
His Day in whom all nations shall be blest,
Favor unmerited by me who sought
Forbidden knowledge by forbidden means.
This yet I apprehend not, why to those
Among whom God will deign to dwell on Earth
So many and so various laws are giv'n?
So many laws argue so many sins
Among them: how can God with such reside?
  To whom thus Michael: Doubt not but that sin
Will reign among them as of thee begot
And therefore was Law giv'n them to evince
Their natural pravity by stirring up
Sin against Law to fight that when they see
Law can discover sin but not remove
Save by those shadowy expiations weak,
The blood of bulls and goats, they may conclude

260. *Abraham* is pronounced with two syllables here and hereafter.

260–62. The Israelites cross the Jordan into the Promised Land, led by Joshua (see lines 307–14 and n.), and conquer the people there, the Canaanites, who have been cursed by Noah.

265–67. "Then spake Joshua to the Lord in the day when the Lord delivered up the Amorites before the children of Israel, and he said in the sight of Israel, Sun, stand thou still upon Gibeon; and thou, Moon, in the valley of Ajalon" (Joshua 10:12).

267–69. *So call the third*: Jacob is the son of Isaac and is later called *Israel*. His twelve sons are the children of Israel.

277. *His Day*: the Day of the Lord, the Last Judgment.

287–88. The Law was given to the Hebrews not with the expectation that it could be obeyed but with the aim of convincing the Hebrews of their sinfulness. See lines 300–302.

Some blood more precious must be paid for Man,
Just for unjust, that in such righteousness,
To them by faith imputed, they may find
Justification towards God and peace
Of conscience, which the Law by ceremonies
Cannot appease nor Man the moral part
Perform and, not performing, cannot live.
So Law appears imperfect and but giv'n
With purpose to resign them in full time
Up to a better covenant, disciplined
From shadowy types to truth, from flesh to spirit,
From imposition of strict laws to free
Acceptance of large grace, from servile fear
To filial, works of law to works of faith.
And therefore shall not Moses, though of God
Highly beloved, being but the minister
Of Law, his people into Canaan lead,
But Joshua, whom the Gentiles "Jesus" call,
His name and office bearing who shall quell
The Adversary Serpent and bring back
Through the world's wilderness long wandered Man
Safe to Eternal Paradise of rest.
Meanwhile they in their earthly Canaan placed
Long time shall dwell and prosper, but when sins

293. *blood more precious*: Christ's blood shed on the Cross. The repetitive nature of animal sacrifice shows that the expiation of sin is never complete. But Christ's sacrifice need occur only once: "For if the blood of bulls and of goats, and of the ashes of an heifer sprinkling the unclean, sanctifieth to the purifying of the flesh: How much more shall the blood of Christ, who through the eternal Spirit offered himself without spot to God, purge your conscience from dead works to serve the living God?" (Hebrews 9:13–14).

294–98. Christ's righteousness is attributed (*imputed*) to Man, who will be saved through faith in Christ rather than by obedience to the law. Justification by faith is the great theme of Paul's epistle to the Romans and of the Protestant Reformation.

300–302. *Law appears imperfect*: Because the Law cannot be obeyed, it is an incomplete covenant, given only to be replaced by a *better* (line 302) covenant, that of Christ's sacrifice. See lines 287–88 n.

303–6. *From . . . to*. Each of these five transitions contrasts the old covenant, under Moses, with the new covenant, under Christ.

306. *servile . . . filial*: the transition from slaves to sons.

307–14. Moses is not allowed to lead the people into the Promised Land because he is a symbol of the Law, which can only condemn. Instead, Joshua leads the Hebrews into the Promised Land. Joshua's name, *Yeshua*, is *Iesous* in Greek and *Jesus* in Latin. Joshua's leading the Hebrews into Canaan is therefore a type, a historical symbol, of Jesus leading humanity into heaven.

311. *His name*: Jesus' name. *who*: Jesus.

313. *wilderness*: the wilderness of human history from the Fall to the apocalypse. History is symbolized by the wilderness through which the Israelites wander for forty years.

315. *earthly Canaan*. See lines 307–10 n.

316–17. *sins / National*: sins committed by the entire nation, worshipping the idols and false gods of the surrounding peoples. "If they break my statutes, and keep not my commandments; Then I will visit their transgression with the rod, and their iniquity with stripes. Nevertheless my lovingkindness will I not utterly take from him, nor suffer my faithfulness to fail" (Psalms 89:31–34).

National interrupt their public peace,
Provoking God to raise them enemies,
From whom as oft He saves them penitent,
By judges first, then under kings, of whom
The second both for piety renowned
And puissant deeds a promise shall receive
Irrevocable: that his regal throne
For ever shall endure. The like shall sing
All prophecy: that of the royal stock
Of David (so I name this king) shall rise
A son, the woman's Seed to thee foretold,
Foretold to Abraham, as in whom shall trust
All nations, and to kings foretold—of kings
The last, for of his reign shall be no end.
But first a long succession must ensue
And his next son, for wealth and wisdom famed,
The clouded ark of God till then in tents,
Wand'ring, shall in a glorious temple enshrine.
Such follow him as shall be registered
Part good, part bad, of bad the longer scroll
Whose foul idolatries and other faults
Heaped to the popular sum will so incense
God as to leave them and expose their land,
Their city, His temple and His holy ark
With all His sacred things a scorn and prey
To that proud city whose high walls thou saw'st
Left in confusion, Babylon thence called.
There in captivity He lets them dwell
The space of seventy years, then brings them back,
Rememb'ring mercy and His cov'nant sworn

320. *judges*: In the biblical book of that name, judges are military leaders (one of whom is Samson) who in time of crisis unite the tribes and lead them as a nation. *kings*: The people ask the prophet Samuel to give them a king, and the first king chosen is Saul. Milton follows the history of the kingdom of Israel (later, of the two kingdoms, Israel and Judea) until the conquest of Jerusalem by the king of Babylon, Nebuchadnezzar, and the carrying away of the Hebrews into captivity in Babylon.

321. *second*: David, who comes to the throne after Saul. Jesus will be a king in David's line.

323–27. "For unto us a child is born . . . of the increase of his government and peace there shall be no end, upon the throne of David" (Isaiah 9:6–7). "I saw in the night visions, and, behold, one like the Son of man came with the clouds of heaven. . . . And there was given him dominion, and glory, and a kingdom, that all people, nations, and languages should serve him: his dominion is an everlasting dominion, which shall not pass away" (Daniel 7:13–14).

327–28. *Seed . . . Abraham*: see lines 147–51 n.

329–30. *of kings / The last*. For Milton, who defended the execution of King Charles I, Jesus is the last legitimate king. All subsequent kings are usurpers of Jesus' right.

332. *next son*: Solomon, who built the temple to house the ark of the covenant.

335–36. *Such follow him*: the kings that come after Solomon.

340–43. The conquest of Jerusalem by the king of Babylon, Nebuchadnezzar, who carries the Hebrews into captivity.

To David, 'stablished as the days of Heav'n.
Returned from Babylon by leave of kings
Their lords (whom God disposed) the house of God
They first re-edify and for a while
In mean estate live moderate, till grown
In wealth and multitude, factious they grow.
But first among the priests dissension springs,
Men who attend the altar and should most
Endeavor peace. Their strife pollution brings
Upon the temple itself. At last they seize
The scepter and regard not David's sons,
Then lose it to a stranger, that the true
Anointed King, Messiah, might be born
Barred of His right. Yet at His birth a star
Unseen before in Heav'n proclaims Him come
And guides the eastern sages who inquire
His place to offer incense, myrrh and gold.
His place of birth a solemn angel tells
To simple shepherds keeping watch by night.
They gladly thither haste and by a choir
Of squadroned angels hear His carol sung.
A virgin is His mother but His sire
The Pow'r of the Most High. He shall ascend
The throne hereditary and bound His reign
With earth's wide bounds, His glory with the heav'ns.
  He ceased, discerning Adam with such joy
Surcharged as had like grief been dewed in tears
Without the vent of words, which these he breathed:
  O prophet of glad tidings, finisher
Of utmost hope! Now clear I understand
What oft my steadiest thoughts have searched in vain,
Why our great expectation should be called
The Seed of woman: Virgin Mother, hail!
High in the love of Heav'n, yet from my loins

348. *kings*: Cyrus, king of Persia, who conquers Babylon and allows the Hebrews to return to Jerusalem. Cyrus is succeeded by Darius and Artaxerxes. ". . . The Lord stirred up the spirit of Cyrus king of Persia, that he made a proclamation. . . . All the kingdoms of the earth hath the Lord God of heaven given me; and he hath charged me to build him an house in Jerusalem, which is in Judah. Who is there among you of all his people? The Lord his God be with him, and let him go up" (2 Chronicles 36:22–23).

359. *Messiah*: anointed one, king, although in David's royal line, Jesus is born in humble circumstances under the Roman domination of Palestine.

360–67. The story of Jesus' birth, summarized here, is told in Matthew 2 and Luke 2.

379–80. "And the angel came in unto her, and said, Hail, thou that art highly favoured, the Lord is with thee: blessed art thou among women. . . . Behold, thou shalt conceive in thy womb, and bring forth a son, and shalt call his name JESUS. He shall be great, and shall be called the Son of the Highest: and the Lord God shall give unto him the throne of his father David . . . and of his kingdom there shall be no end" (Luke 1:28–33).

Thou shalt proceed and from thy womb the Son
Of God Most High: so God with Man unites!
Needs must the serpent now his capital bruise
Expect with mortal pain. Say where and when
Their fight! What stroke shall bruise the Victor's heel?
  To whom thus Michael: Dream not of their fight
As of a duel or the local wounds
Of head or heel. Not therefore joins the Son
Manhood to Godhead with more strength to foil
Thy enemy nor so is overcome
Satan, whose fall from Heav'n—a deadlier bruise—
Disabled not to give thee thy death's wound,
Which he who comes thy Savior shall recure
Not by destroying Satan but his works
In thee and in thy seed. Nor can this be
But by fulfilling that which thou didst want:
Obedience to the Law of God imposed
On penalty of death, and suffering death,
The penalty to thy transgression due,
And due to theirs which out of thine will grow—
So only can high justice rest apaid.
The Law of God exact He shall fulfill
Both by obedience and by love, though love
Alone fulfill the Law. Thy punishment
He shall endure by coming in the flesh
To a reproachful life and cursèd death,
Proclaiming life to all who shall believe
In his Redemption and that his obedience
Imputed becomes theirs by faith, his merits
To save them, not their own, though Legal works.
For this he shall live hated, be blasphemed,
Seized on by force, judged and to death condemned,
A shameful and accurst, nailed to the cross
By his own nation, slain for bringing life.

383. *capital*: of the head (Latin *caput*, "head").

394–401: The Son will defeat Satan's works in human beings by being perfectly obedient to God (as no other human can) and by taking on himself the punishment for disobedience, death.

396. *want*: lack, fail.

397–401. Justice can be fulfilled because the Son will do two things: he will obey the law of God (which Adam failed to do) and he will suffer death to pay for the crime of Adam and the crimes of humanity.

407–10. We cannot obey God on our own, but if we believe in Christ his obedience will be attributed (imputed) to us. Christians are saved by Christ's obedience and love, not by *legal works* (obedience either to the law or to ordinances of the Church). Milton saw Roman Catholic and Anglican formalities as outward, legal works of the same kind as the Hebrew law. See line 512 n.

But to the cross he nails thy enemies:
The Law that is against thee and the sins
Of all mankind with him there crucified,
Never to hurt them more who rightly trust
In this his satisfaction. So he dies
But soon revives: Death over him no pow'r
Shall long usurp. Ere the third dawning light
Return the stars of morn shall see him rise
Out of his grave, fresh as the dawning light,
Thy ransom paid which Man from death redeems,
His death for Man: as many as offered life
Neglect not and the benefit embrace
By faith not void of works. This godlike act
Annuls thy doom, the death thou shouldst have died
In sin for ever lost from life. This act
Shall bruise the head of Satan, crush his strength,
Defeating Sin and Death, his two main arms,
And fix far deeper in his head their stings
Than temporal death shall bruise the Victor's heel
Or theirs whom he redeems, a death like sleep,
A gentle wafting to immortal life.
Nor after Resurrection shall he stay
Longer on Earth than certain times t' appear
To his disciples, men who in his life
Still followed him. To them shall leave in charge
To teach all nations what of him they learned
And his salvation, them who shall believe
Baptizing in the profluent stream, the sign
Of washing them from guilt of sin to life
Pure, and in mind prepared, if so befall,
For death like that which the Redeemer died.
All nations they shall teach, for from that day
Not only to the sons of Abraham's loins
Salvation shall be preached but to the sons
Of Abraham's faith wherever through the world:
So in his Seed all nations shall be blest.

415–17. "Blotting out the handwriting of the ordinances that was against us, which was contrary to us, and took it out of the way, nailing it to his cross" (Colossians 2:14).

432–33. I.e., the stings of Sin and Death shall strike Satan's head, a more serious and permanent wound than will be the temporary death of Jesus or of those whom Jesus has redeemed from death.

439–45. The ministry of the apostles, who establish the Church and spread it throughout the nations.

447–49. The Christian Church will be open not only to the descendants of Abraham through his son Isaac but to all people who have Abraham's faith. But that faith is now faith in Jesus' sacrifice of himself for the salvation of humanity.

450. *his*: Abraham's. *seed*: Jesus.

Then to the Heav'n of Heav'ns he shall ascend
With victory triúmphing through the air
Over his foes and thine; there shall surprise
The Serpent, Prince of Air, and drag in chains
Through all his realm and there confounded leave,
Then enter into glory and resume
His seat at God's right hand, exalted high
Above all names in Heav'n, and thence shall come
When this world's dissolution shall be ripe
With glory and pow'r to judge both quick and dead:
To judge th' unfaithful dead but to reward
His faithful and receive them into bliss,
Whether in Heav'n or Earth, for then the Earth
Shall all be Paradise, far happier place
Than this of Eden, and far happier days.
  So spake th' archangel Michaël, then paused
As at the world's great period, and our sire
Replete with joy and wonder thus replied:
  O goodness infinite, goodness immense!
That all this good of evil shall produce
And evil turn to good more wonderful
Than that which by Creation first brought forth
Light out of darkness! Full of doubt I stand,
Whether I should repent me now of sin
By me done and occasioned or rejoice
Much more that much more good thereof shall spring,
To God more glory, more good will to men
From God, and over wrath grace shall abound!
But say, if our Deliverer up to Heav'n
Must reascend, what will betide the few
His faithful left among th' unfaithful herd,
The enemies of truth? Who then shall guide
His people, who defend? Will they not deal
Worse with his followers than with him they dealt?
  Be sure they will, said th' angel, but from Heav'n
He to his own a Comforter will send,

453–55. I.e., after his resurrection and ascension Christ will banish Satan and the devils from their kingdom in the air and drag them to Hell.

458–60. The last judgment.

473–78. A version of the medieval idea of a "fortunate fall." Milton doesn't take the idea seriously but uses it to express how Adam feels at this moment.

478. "Moreover the law entered, that the offence might abound. But where sin abounded, grace did much more abound" (Romans 5:20).

484. *followers*: has two syllables.

486–92. *Comforter*: the Paraclete, Holy Spirit, which comes from the Father and is sent by the Son. (John 14:16–17, 15:26–27). Milton understands the Paraclete to be the source of our conscience, the law of God written in the heart, and of the fortitude to hold to what

The promise of his Father, who shall dwell
His Spirit within them and the Law of Faith,
Working through love, upon their hearts shall write
To guide them in all truth and also arm
With spiritual armor able to resist
Satan's assaults and quench his fiery darts,
What Man can do against them, not afraid,
Though to the death, against such cruelties
With inward consolations recompensed
And oft supported so as shall amaze
Their proudest persecutors. For the Spirit
Poured first on his apostles whom he sends
T' evangelize the nations, then on all
Baptized, shall them with wondrous gifts endue
To speak all tongues and do all miracles
As did their Lord before them. Thus they win
Great numbers of each nation to receive
With joy the tidings brought from Heav'n. At length,
Their ministry performed and race well run,
Their doctrine and their story written left,
They die, but in their room, as they forewarn,
Wolves shall succeed for teachers, grievous wolves
Who all the sacred mysteries of Heav'n
To their own vile advantages shall turn
Of lucre and ambition and the truth
With superstitions and traditions taint,
Left only in those written records pure
Though not but by the Spirit understood.
Then shall they seek t' avail themselves of names,
Places and titles and with these to join
Secular power though feigning still to act

---

is right. "I will put my laws into their mind, and write them in their hearts" (Hebrews 8: 10).

492. Satan's *assaults* and *fiery darts* are the cruelties and persecutions brought upon Christians in this world.

497–502. "And when the day of Pentecost was come . . . there appeared unto them cloven tongues like as of fire, and it sat upon each of them. And they were all filled with the Holy Ghost, and began to speak with other tongues, as the Spirit gave them utterance" (Acts 2:1–4). The apostles are given the power to speak all languages in order to bring the good news to all nations.

499. *evangelize*: convert to Christ by bringing the "good news" (Greek *eu* "good" and *angelia* "message").

508. *Wolves*: corrupt churchmen, who will devour the flock rather than feeding it. St. Paul, who organized the church in its early years, settling its doctrine and bringing the gospel to the gentiles, said, "For I know this, that after my departing shall grievous wolves enter in amongst you, not sparing the flock" (Acts 20:29).

512. In addition to enriching themselves, the wolves will introduce into the church practices that are merely external and formal, polluting the only legitimate traditions, those left to us in the Bible. See lines 408–9 n.

By spiritual, to themselves appropriating
The Spirit of God promised alike and giv'n
To all believers and from that pretense
Spiritual laws by carnal pow'r shall force
On every conscience, laws which none shall find
Left them enrolled or what the Spirit within
Shall on the heart engrave. What will they then
But force the Spirit of Grace itself and bind
His consort Liberty? What but unbuild
His living temples built by faith to stand,
Their own faith not another's? For on Earth
Who against faith and conscience can be heard
Infallible? Yet many will presume,
Whence heavy persecution shall arise
On all who in the worship persevere
Of Spirit and Truth. The rest, far greater part,
Will deem in outward rites and specious forms
Religion satisfied. Truth shall retire
Bestuck with sland'rous darts and works of faith
Rarely to be found. So shall the world go on,
To good malignant, to bad men benign,
Under her own weight groaning till the day
Appear of respiration to the just
And vengeance to the wicked at return
Of Him so lately promised to thy aid,
The woman's Seed, obscurely then foretold,
Now amplier known thy Savior and thy Lord,
Last in the clouds from Heav'n to be revealed
In glory of the Father to dissolve
Satan with his perverted world, then raise
From the conflagrant mass, purged and refined,
New Heav'ns, new Earth, ages of endless date
Founded in righteousness and peace and love
To bring forth fruits' joy and eternal bliss.

521–24. The wolves will use physical force—war, the Inquisition—to impose spiritual laws on others. These new laws will be neither in the scriptures nor in the human conscience.

527. Each Christian is a *living temple*, surpassing the temple at Jerusalem (which was destroyed by the Romans in 70 A.D.). "For the temple of God is holy, which temple ye are" (1 Corinthians 3:17).

545–51. The apocalypse, from the book of Revelation, which describes the final events in the world.

551. What is brought forth in these "ages of endless date" is slightly unclear as to number, or at least it is so if *fruits* is taken as possessive, *fruits'*, which slightly improves the sense. If three things are referred to, as the unpunctuated line in the 1667 and 1674 texts suggests, they are *fruits*, *joy*, and *eternal bliss*. But in that case, what is the difference between joy and bliss? If two things are referred to, they are *joy of fruits* and *eternal bliss*, e.g., joyful recompense for good deeds (*fruits*) and the bliss that is experienced simply by being in the presence of God. I have punctuated the line in favor of the latter meaning.

He ended, and thus Adam last replied:
How soon hath thy prediction, seer blest,
Measured this transient world, the race of time
Till time stand fixed. Beyond all is abyss,
Eternity, whose end no eye can reach.
Greatly instructed I shall hence depart,
Greatly in peace of thought and have my fill
Of knowledge, what this vessel can contain,
Beyond which was my folly to aspire.
Henceforth I learn that to obey is best,
And love with fear the only God, to walk
As in His presence, ever to observe
His providence and on Him sole depend,
Merciful over all His works, with good
Still overcoming evil and by small
Accomplishing great things, by things deemed weak
Subverting worldly strong, and worldly wise
By simply meek, that suffering for Truth's sake
Is fortitude to highest victory
And to the faithful death the gate of life:
Taught this by His example whom I now
Acknowledge my Redeemer ever blest.
To whom thus also th' angel last replied:
This having learned thou hast attained the sum
Of wisdom. Hope no higher, though all the stars
Thou knew'st by name and all th' ethereal powers,
All secrets of the deep, all nature's works
Or works of God in Heav'n, air, earth or sea,
And all the riches of this world enjoy'dst
And all the rule, one empire. Only add
Deeds to thy knowledge answerable, add faith,
Add virtue, patience, temperance, add love,
By name to come called charity, the soul
Of all the rest. Then wilt thou not be loath
To leave this Paradise but shalt possess
A paradise within thee, happier far.

559. *this vessel*: the body and mind, the container of the soul.

567–68. "God hath chosen the weak things of the world to confound the things which are mighty" (1 Corinthians 1:27).

581–84. "Add to your faith virtue; and to virtue add knowledge; and to knowledge temperance; and to temperance patience; and to patience godliness; and to godliness brotherly kindness; and to brotherly kindness charity" (2 Peter 5–7).

584–85. *charity*, Latin *caritas*, in the biblical Greek, *agapê*, often rendered in English as *love*, i.e., caring for and kindness toward others. "Though I speak with the tongues of men and of angels, and have not charity, I am become as sounding brass, or a tinkling cymbal"; "And now abideth faith, hope, charity, these three; but the greatest of these is charity" (1 Corinthians 13:1 and 13).

Let us descend now therefore from this top
Of speculation for the hour precise
Exacts our parting hence. And see! the guards
By me encamped on yonder hill expect
Their motion, at whose front a flaming sword
In signal of remove waves fiercely round:
We may no longer stay. Go, waken Eve.
Her also I with gentle dreams have calmed
Portending good and all her spirits composed
To meek submission. Thou at season fit
Let her with thee partake what thou hast heard,
Chiefly what may concern her faith to know:
The great deliv'rance by her Seed to come
(For by the woman's Seed) on all mankind,
That ye may live, which will be many days,
Both in one faith unanimous, though sad
With cause for evils past, yet much more cheered
With meditation on the happy end.
  He ended, and they both descend the hill.
Descended, Adam to the bow'r where Eve
Lay sleeping ran before but found her waked,
And thus with words not sad she him received:
  Whence thou return'st and whither went'st I know,
For God is also in sleep and dreams advise
Which he hath sent propitious, some great good
Presaging, since with sorrow and heart's distress
Wearied I fell asleep. But now lead on.
In me is no delay. With thee to go
Is to stay here; without thee here to stay
Is to go hence unwilling. Thou to me
Art all things under Heav'n, all places thou,

588–89. *top / Of speculation*: high place for viewing. The word *speculation* here implies prophetic vision but not theoretical reflection (Latin *specula*, "watchtower").

592–93. "And he placed at the east of the garden of Eden Cherubims, and a flaming sword which turned every way" (Genesis 3:24).

601. It is possible that during composition Milton closed a phrase with *by her seed to come* and began a new phrase with *For by the woman's Seed.* He then cancelled *For by the woman's Seed* and made *on all Mankind* a continuation of the first phrase, as direct object of *to come.* The cancelled phrase may have survived because the line left half empty was never filled in. The best way to understand the parenthetical phrase "*For by the woman's seed*" is to suppose that "deliverance will call" is understood.

611. "I the Lord . . . will speak unto him in a dream" (Numbers 12:6). A closer echo is the *Iliad* 1.63, where Achilles says, "for a dream also is from Zeus."

615. *In me is no delay* translates (changing only the tense) Virgil's *in me mora non erit ulla*" (Eclogues 3.53).

615–18. Eve's words recall Ruth's to Naomi: "Intreat me not to leave thee, or to return from following after thee: for whither thou goest, I will go; and where thou lodgest, I will lodge: thy people shall be my people, and thy God my God" (Ruth 1:16). In the *Iliad*, Andromache says to her husband, Hector, "You are to me father and mother and brother, you who are my young husband" (6.429–30).

Who for my willful crime art banished hence.
This further consolation yet secure
I carry hence: though all by me is lost,
Such favor I unworthy am vouchsafed,
By me the promised Seed shall all restore.
  So spake our mother Eve and Adam heard
Well pleased but answered not. For now too nigh
Th' archangel stood and from the other hill
To their fixed station all in bright array
The cherubim descended, on the ground
Gliding meteorous as evening mist
Ris'n from a river o'er the marish glides
And gathers ground fast at the laborer's heel
Homeward returning. High in front advanced,
The brandished sword of God before them blazed
Fierce as a comet which with torrid heat
And vapor as the Libyan air adust
Began to parch that temperate clime. Whereat
In either hand the hast'ning angel caught
Our ling'ring parents and to the eastern gate
Led them direct and down the cliff as fast
To the subjected plain, then disappeared.
They, looking back, all th' eastern side beheld
Of Paradise, so late their happy seat,
Waved over by that flaming brand. The gate
With dreadful faces thronged and fiery arms.
Some natural tears they dropped but wiped them soon.
The world was all before them, where to choose
Their place of rest, and Providence their guide.
They hand in hand with wand'ring steps and slow
Through Eden took their solitary way.

629. *meteorous*: in midair (the Greek etymological sense of the word). It is possible but not necessary to accent the second syllable, *metéorous*. Doing so gives the interesting rhythm of two dactyls opening the line (/˘˘/˘˘) and improves an otherwise abrupt caesura. Accenting the first and third syllables gives a more regular rhythm of three trochees (/˘/˘/˘).

632–34. See lines 592–93 n.

635. *adust*: dry from having been burned by the sun.

640. *subjected*: lying below.

649. *through Eden*: Eden is not the garden paradise but the large country in which that paradise is contained. Outside the garden, on the plain beneath it, Adam and Eve move through the country of Eden. See Glossary, EDEN and PARADISE.

SOURCES AND BACKGROUNDS

Selections from the Bible

Genesis

1

In the beginning God created the heaven and the earth.
2 And the earth was without form, and void; and darkness was upon
the face of the deep. And the Spirit of God moved upon the face of
the waters.
3 And God said, Let there be light: and there was light.
4 And God saw the light, that it was good: and God divided the light
from the darkness.
5 And God called the light Day, and the darkness he called Night.
And the evening and the morning were the first day.
6 And God said, Let there be a firmament in the midst of the
waters, and let it divide the waters from the waters.
7 And God made the firmament, and divided the waters which were
under the firmament from the waters which were above the firma-
ment: and it was so.
8 And God called the firmament Heaven. And the evening and the
morning were the second day.
9 And God said, Let the waters under the heaven be gathered
together unto one place, and let the dry land appear: and it was so.
10 And God called the dry land Earth; and the gathering together
of the waters called he Seas: and God saw that it was good.
11 And God said, Let the earth bring forth grass, the herb yielding
seed, and the fruit tree yielding fruit after his kind, whose seed is in
itself, upon the earth: and it was so.
12 And the earth brought forth grass, and herb yielding seed after
his kind, and the tree yielding fruit, whose seed was in itself, after
his kind: and God saw that it was good.
13 And the evening and the morning were the third day.
14 And God said, Let there be lights in the firmament of the
heaven to divide the day from the night; and let them be for signs,
and for seasons, and for days, and years:
15 And let them be for lights in the firmament of the heaven to give
light upon the earth: and it was so.

16 And God made two great lights; the greater light to rule the day,
and the lesser light to rule the night: he made the stars also.
17 And God set them in the firmament of the heaven to give light
upon the earth,
18 And to rule over the day and over the night, and to divide the
light from the darkness: and God saw that it was good.
19 And the evening and the morning were the fourth day.
20 And God said, Let the waters bring forth abundantly the moving
creature that hath life, and fowl that may fly above the earth in the
open firmament of heaven.
21 And God created great whales, and every living creature that
moveth, which the waters brought forth abundantly, after their kind,
and every winged fowl after his kind: and God saw that it was good.
22 And God blessed them, saying, Be fruitful, and multiply, and fill
the waters in the seas, and let fowl multiply in the earth.
23 And the evening and the morning were the fifth day.

24 And God said, Let the earth bring forth the living creature
after his kind, cattle, and creeping thing, and beast of the earth after
his kind; and it was so.
25 And God made the beast of the earth after his kind, and cattle
after their kind, and every thing that creepeth upon the earth after
his kind: and God saw that it was good.

26 And God said, Let us make man in our image, after our like-
ness: and let them have dominion over the fish of the sea, and over
the fowl of the air, and over the cattle, and over all the earth, and
over every creeping thing that creepeth upon the earth.
27 So God created man in his own image, in the image of God
created he him; male and female created he them.
28 And God blessed them, and God said unto them, Be fruitful, and
multiply, and replenish the earth, and subdue it: and have dominion
over the fish of the sea, and over the fowl of the air, and over every
living thing that moveth upon the earth.

29 And God said, Behold, I have given you every herb bearing
seed, which is upon the face of all the earth, and every tree, in the
which is the fruit of a tree yielding seed; to you it shall be for meat.
30 And to every beast of the earth, and to every fowl of the air, and
to every thing that creepeth upon the earth, wherein there is life, I
have given every green herb for meat: and it was so.
31 And God saw every thing that he had made, and, behold, it was
very good. And the evening and the morning were the sixth day.

2

Thus the heavens and the earth were finished, and all the host of
them.
2 And on the seventh day God ended his work which he had made;
and he rested on the seventh day from all his work which he had
made.
3 And God blessed the seventh day, and sanctified it: because that
in it he had rested from all his work which God created and made.
4 These are the generations of the heavens and of the earth when
they were created, in the day that the LORD God made the earth and
the heavens,
5 And every plant of the field before it was in the earth, and every
herb of the field before it grew: for the LORD God had not caused it
to rain upon the earth, and there was not a man to till the ground.
6 But there went up a mist from the earth, and watered the whole
face of the ground.
7 And the LORD God formed man of the dust of the ground, and
breathed into his nostrils the breath of life; and man became a living
soul.
8 And the LORD God planted a garden eastward in Eden; and
there he put the man whom he had formed.
9 And out of the ground made the LORD God to grow every tree that
is pleasant to the sight, and good for food; the tree of life also in the
midst of the garden, and the tree of knowledge of good and evil.
10 And a river went out of Eden to water the garden; and from
thence it was parted, and became into four heads.
11 The name of the first is Pison: that is it which compasseth the
whole land of Havilah, where there is gold;
12 And the gold of that land is good; there is bdellium and the onyx
stone.
13 And the name of the second river is Gihon: the same is it that
compasseth the whole land of Ethiopia.
14 And the name of the third river is Hiddekel: that is it which goeth
toward the east of Assyria. And the fourth river is Euphrates.
15 And the LORD God took the man, and put him into the garden
of Eden to dress it and to keep it.
16 And the LORD God commanded the man, saying, Of every tree
of the garden thou mayest freely eat.
17 But of the tree of the knowledge of good and evil, thou shalt not
eat of it: for in the day that thou eatest thereof thou shalt surely die.
18 And the LORD God said, It is not good that the man should be
alone; I will make him an help meet for him.
19 And out of the ground the LORD God formed every beast of the
field, and every fowl of the air; and brought them unto Adam to see

what he would call them: and whatsoever Adam called every living
creature, that was the name thereof.
20 And Adam gave names to all cattle, and to the fowl of the air,
and to every beast of the field; but for Adam there was not found an
help meet for him.
21 And the LORD God caused a deep sleep to fall upon Adam, and
he slept: and he took one of his ribs, and closed up the flesh instead
thereof;
22 And the rib, which the LORD God had taken from man, made he
a woman, and brought her unto the man.
23 And Adam said, This is now bone of my bones, and flesh of my
flesh: she shall be called Woman, because she was taken out of Man.
24 Therefore shall a man leave his father and his mother, and shall
cleave unto his wife: and they shall be one flesh.
25 And they were both naked, the man and his wife, and were not
ashamed.

3

Now the serpent was more subtil than any beast of the field which
the LORD God had made. And he said unto the woman, Yea, hath
God said, Ye shall not eat of every tree of the garden?
2 And the woman said unto the serpent, We may eat of the fruit of
the trees of the garden:
3 But of the fruit of the tree which is in the midst of the garden,
God hath said, Ye shall not eat of it, neither shall ye touch it, lest ye
die.
4 And the serpent said unto the woman, Ye shall not surely die:
5 For God doth know that in the day ye eat thereof, then your eyes
shall be opened, and ye shall be as gods, knowing good and evil.
6 And when the woman saw that the tree was good for food, and
that it was pleasant to the eyes, and a tree to be desired to make one
wise, she took of the fruit thereof, and did eat, and gave also unto
her husband with her; and he did eat.
7 And the eyes of them both were opened, and they knew that they
were naked; and they sewed fig leaves together, and made themselves
aprons.
8 And they heard the voice of the LORD God walking in the garden
in the cool of the day: and Adam and his wife hid themselves from
the presence of the LORD God amongst the trees of the garden.
9 And the LORD God called unto Adam, and said unto him, Where
art thou?
10 And he said, I heard thy voice in the garden, and I was afraid,
because I was naked; and I hid myself.
11 And he said, Who told thee that thou wast naked? Hast thou

eaten of the tree, whereof I commanded thee that thou shouldest
not eat?
12 And the man said, The woman whom thou gavest to be with me,
she gave me of the tree, and I did eat.
13 And the LORD God said unto the woman, What is this that thou
hast done? And the woman said, The serpent beguiled me, and I did
eat.
14 And the LORD God said unto the serpent, Because thou hast
done this, thou art cursed above all cattle, and above every beast of
the field; upon thy belly shalt thou go, and dust shalt thou eat all
the days of thy life:
15 And I will put enmity between thee and the woman, and between
thy seed and her seed; it shall bruise thy head, and thou shalt bruise
his heel.
16 Unto the woman he said, I will greatly multiply thy sorrow and
thy conception; in sorrow thou shalt bring forth children; and thy
desire shall be to thy husband, and he shall rule over thee.
17 And unto Adam he said, Because thou hast hearkened unto the
voice of thy wife, and hast eaten of the tree, of which I commanded
thee, saying, Thou shalt not eat of it: cursed is the ground for thy
sake; in sorrow shalt thou eat of it all the days of thy life;
18 Thorns also and thistles shall it bring forth to thee; and thou
shalt eat the herb of the field;
19 In the sweat of thy face shalt thou eat bread, till thou return
unto the ground; for out of it wast thou taken: for dust thou art, and
unto dust shalt thou return.
20 And Adam called his wife's name Eve; because she was the
mother of all living.
21 Unto Adam also and to his wife did the LORD God make coats
of skins, and clothed them.
22 And the LORD God said, Behold, the man is become as one of
us, to know good and evil: and now, lest he put forth his hand, and
take also of the tree of life, and eat, and live for ever:
23 Therefore the LORD God sent him forth from the garden of Eden,
to till the ground from whence he was taken.
24 So he drove out the man; and he placed at the east of the garden
of Eden Cherubims, and a flaming sword which turned every way,
to keep the way of the tree of life.

* * *

11

And the whole earth was of one language, and of one speech.
2 And it came to pass, as they journeyed from the east, that they
found a plain in the land of Shinar; and they dwelt there.

3 And they said one to another, Go to, let us make brick, and burn
them throughly. And they had brick for stone, and slime had they
for morter.
4 And they said, Go to, let us build us a city and a tower, whose top
may reach unto heaven; and let us make us a name, lest we be scat-
tered abroad upon the face of the whole earth.
5 And the LORD came down to see the city and the tower, which
the children of men builded.
6 And the LORD said, Behold, the people is one, and they have all
one language; and this they begin to do: and now nothing will be
restrained from them, which they have imagined to do.
7 Go to, let us go down, and there confound their language, that
they may not understand one another's speech.
8 So the LORD scattered them abroad from thence upon the face of
all the earth: and they left off to build the city.
9 Therefore is the name of it called Babel; because the LORD did
there confound the language of all the earth: and from thence did
the LORD scatter them abroad upon the face of all the earth.

* * *

12

Now the LORD had said unto Abram, Get thee out of thy country,
and from thy kindred, and from thy father's house, unto a land that
I will shew thee:
2 And I will make of thee a great nation, and I will bless thee, and
make thy name great; and thou shalt be a blessing:
3 And I will bless them that bless thee, and curse him that curseth
thee: and in thee shall all families of the earth be blessed.
4 So Abraham departed, as the LORD had spoken unto him; and Lot
went with him: and Abram was seventy and five years old when he
departed out of Haran.
5 And Abram took Sarai his wife, and Lot his brother's son, and all
their substance that they had gathered, and the souls that they had
gotten in Haran; and they went forth to go into the land of Canaan;
and into the land of Canaan they came.
6 And Abram passed through the land unto the place of Sichem,
unto the plain of Moreh. And the Canaanite was then in the land.
7 And the LORD appeared unto Abram, and said, Unto thy seed will
I give this land: and there builded he an altar unto the LORD, who
appeared unto him.

* * *

Exodus

14

And the LORD spake unto Moses, saying,
2 Speak unto the children of Israel, that they turn and encamp
before Pi-hahiroth, between Migdol and the sea, over against Baal-
zephon: before it shall ye encamp by the sea.
3 For Pharaoh will say of the children of Israel, They are entangled
in the land, the wilderness hath shut them in.
4 And I will harden Pharaoh's heart, that he shall follow after them;
and I will be honoured upon Pharaoh, and upon all his host; that
the Egyptians may know that I am the LORD. And they did so.
5 And it was told the king of Egypt that the people fled: and the
heart of Pharaoh and of his servants was turned against the people,
and they said, Why have we done this, that we have let Israel go from
serving us?
6 And he made ready his chariot, and took his people with him:
7 And he took six hundred chosen chariots, and all the chariots of
Egypt, and captains over every one of them.
8 And the LORD hardened the heart of Pharaoh king of Egypt, and
he pursued after the children of Israel: and the children of Israel
went out with an high hand.
9 But the Egyptians pursued after them, all the horses and chariots
of Pharaoh, and his horsemen, and his army, and overtook them
encamping by the sea, beside Pi-hahiroth, before Baal-zephon.
10 And when Pharaoh drew nigh, the children of Israel lifted
up their eyes, and, behold, the Egyptians marched after them; and
they were sore afraid; and the children of Israel cried out unto the
LORD.
11 And they said unto Moses, Because there were no graves in
Egypt, hast thou taken us away to die in the wilderness? wherefore
hast thou dealt thus with us, to carry us forth out of Egypt?
12 Is not this the word that we did tell thee in Egypt, saying, Let us
alone, that we may serve the Egyptians? For it had been better for
us to serve the Egyptians, than that we should die in the wilderness.
13 And Moses said unto the people, Fear ye not, stand still, and
see the salvation of the LORD, which he will shew to you to day: for
the Egyptians whom ye have seen to day, ye shall see them again no
more for ever.
14 The LORD shall fight for you, and ye shall hold your peace.
15 And the LORD said unto Moses, Wherefore criest thou unto
me? speak unto the children of Israel, that they go forward:
16 But lift thou up thy rod, and stretch out thine hand over the sea,

and divide it: and the children of Israel shall go on dry ground
through the midst of the sea.
17 And I, behold, I will harden the hearts of the Egyptians, and they
shall follow them: and I will get me honour upon Pharaoh, and upon
all his host, upon his chariots, and upon his horsemen.
18 And the Egyptians shall know that I am the LORD, when I have
gotten me honour upon Pharaoh, upon his chariots, and upon his
horsemen.

19 And the angel of God, which went before the camp of Israel,
removed and went behind them; and the pillar of the cloud went
from before their face, and stood behind them:
20 And it came between the camp of the Egyptians and the camp
of Israel; and it was a cloud and darkness to them, but it gave light
by night to these: so that the one came not near the other all the
night.
21 And Moses stretched out his hand over the sea; and the LORD
caused the sea to go back by a strong east wind all that night, and
made the sea dry land, and the waters were divided.
22 And the children of Israel went into the midst of the sea upon
the dry ground: and the waters were a wall unto them on their right
hand, and on their left.

23 And the Egyptians pursued, and went in after them to the
midst of the sea, even all Pharaoh's horses, his chariots, and his
horsemen.
24 And it came to pass, that in the morning watch the LORD looked
unto the host of the Egyptians through the pillar of fire and of the
cloud, and troubled the host of the Egyptians,
25 And took off their chariot wheels, that they drave them heavily;
so that the Egyptians said, Let us flee from the face of Israel: for the
LORD fighteth for them against the Egyptians.

26 And the LORD said unto Moses, Stretch out thine hand over
the sea that the waters may come again upon the Egyptians, upon
their chariots, and upon their horsemen.
27 And Moses stretched forth his hand over the sea, and the sea
returned to his strength when the morning appeared; and the Egyp-
tians fled against it; and the LORD overthrew the Egyptians in the
midst of the sea.
28 And the waters returned, and covered the chariots, and the
horsemen, and all the host of Pharaoh that came into the sea after
them; there remained not so much as one of them.
29 But the children of Israel walked upon dry land in the midst of
the sea; and the waters were a wall unto them on their right hand,
and on their left
30 Thus the LORD saved Israel that day out of the hand of the Egyp-
tians, and Israel saw the Egyptians dead upon the sea shore.

31 And Israel saw that great work which the LORD did upon the
Egyptians: and the people feared the LORD and believed the LORD,
and his servant Moses.

Psalms

104

Bless the LORD, O my soul. O LORD my God, thou art very great;
thou art clothed with honour and majesty.
2 Who coverest thyself with light as with a garment: who stretchest
out the heavens like a curtain:
3 Who layeth the beams of his chambers in the waters: who maketh
the clouds his chariot: who walketh upon the wings of the wind:
4 Who maketh his angels spirits; his ministers a flaming fire:
5 Who laid the foundations of the earth, that it should not be
removed for ever.
6 Thou coveredst it with the deep as with a garment: the waters
stood above the mountains.
7 At thy rebuke they fled; at the voice of thy thunder they hasted
away.
8 They go up by the mountains; they go down by the valleys unto
the place which thou hast founded for them.
9 Thou hast set a bound that they may not pass over; that they turn
not again to cover the earth.
10 He sendeth the springs into the valleys, which run among the hills.
11 They give drink to every beast of the field: the wild asses quench
their thirst.
12 By them shall the fowls of the heaven have their habitation,
which sing among the branches.
13 He watereth the hills from his chambers: the earth is satisfied
with the fruit of thy works.
14 He causeth the grass to grow for the cattle, and herb for the
service of man: that he may bring forth food out of the earth;
15 And wine that maketh glad the heart of man, and oil to make his
face to shine, and bread which strengtheneth man's heart.
16 The trees of the LORD are full of sap; the cedars of Lebanon,
which he hath planted;
17 Where the birds make their nests: as for the stork, the fir trees
are her house.
18 The high hills are a refuge for the wild goats; and the rocks for
the conies.
19 He appointed the moon for seasons: the sun knoweth his going
down.

20 Thou makest darkness, and it is night: wherein all the beasts of the forest do creep forth.
21 The young lions roar after their prey, and seek their meat from God.
22 The sun ariseth, they gather themselves together, and lay them down in their dens.
23 Man goeth forth unto his work and to his labour until the evening.
24 O LORD, how manifold are thy works! in wisdom hast thou made them all: the earth is full of thy riches.
25 So is this great and wide sea, wherein are things creeping innumerable, both small and great beasts.
26 There go the ships: there is that leviathan, whom thou hast made to play therein.
27 These wait all upon thee; that thou mayest give them their meat in due season.
28 That thou givest them they gather. thou openest thine hand, they are filled with good.
29 Thou hidest thy face, they are troubled: thou takest away their breath, they die, and return to their dust.
30 Thou sendest forth thy spirit, they are created: and thou renewest the face of the earth.
31 The glory of the LORD shall endure for ever: the LORD shall rejoice in his works.
32 He looketh on the earth, and it trembleth: he toucheth the hills, and they smoke.
33 I will sing unto the LORD as long as I live: I will sing praise to my God while I have my being.
34 My meditation of him shall be sweet: I will be glad in the LORD.
35 Let the sinners be consumed out of the earth, and let the wicked be no more. Bless thou the LORD, O my soul. Praise ye the LORD.

114

When Israel went out of Egypt, the house of Jacob from a people of strange language;
2 Judah was his sanctuary, and Israel his dominion.
3 The sea saw it, and fled: Jordan was driven back.
4 The mountains skipped like rams, and the little hills like lambs.
5 What ailed thee, O thou sea, that thou fleddest? thou Jordan, that thou wast driven back?
6 Ye mountains, that ye skipped like rams; and ye little hills, like lambs?
7 Tremble, thou earth, at the presence of the Lord, at the presence of the God of Jacob;

8 Which turned the rock into a standing water, the flint into a fountain of waters.

148

Praise ye the Lord. Praise ye the Lord from the heavens: praise him in the heights.
2 Praise ye him, all his angels: praise ye him, all his hosts.
3 Praise ye him, sun and moon: praise him, all ye stars of light.
4 Praise him, ye heavens of heavens, and ye waters that be above the heavens.
5 Let them praise the name of the Lord: for he commanded, and they were created.
6 He hath also stablished them for ever and ever: he hath made a decree which shall not pass.
7 Praise the Lord from the earth, ye dragons, and all deeps:
8 Fire, and hail; snow, and vapour; stormy wind fulfilling his word:
9 Mountains, and all hills; fruitful trees, and all cedars:
10 Beasts, and all cattle; creeping things, and flying fowl:
11 Kings of the earth, and all people; princes, and all judges of the earth:
12 Both young men, and maidens; old men, and children:
13 Let them praise the name of the Lord: for his name alone is excellent; his glory is above the earth and heaven.
14 He also exalteth the horn of his people, the praise of all his saints; even of the children of Israel, a people near unto him. Praise ye the Lord.

Isaiah

6

In the year that king Uzziah died I saw also the Lord sitting upon a throne, high and lifted up, and his train filled the temple.
2 Above it stood the seraphims: each one had six wings; with twain he covered his face, and with twain he covered his feet, and with twain he did fly.
3 And one cried unto another, and said, Holy, holy, holy, is the Lord of hosts: the whole earth is full of his glory.
4 And the posts of the door moved at the voice of him that cried, and the house was filled with smoke.
5 Then said I, Woe is me! for I am undone; because I am a man of unclean lips, and I dwell in the midst of a people of unclean lips: for mine eyes have seen the King, the Lord of hosts.

6 Then flew one of the seraphims unto me, having a live coal in his
hand, which he had taken with the tongs from off the altar:
7 And he laid it upon my mouth, and said, Lo, this hath touched
thy lips; and thine iniquity is taken away, and thy sin purged.
8 Also I heard the voice of the Lord, saying, Whom shall I send, and
who will go for us? Then said I, Here am I: send me.

* * *

9

* * *

6 For unto us a child is born, unto us a son is given: and the gov-
ernment shall be upon his shoulder: and his name shall be called
Wonderful, Counsellor, The mighty God. The everlasting Father,
The Prince of Peace.
7 Of the increase of his government and peace there shall be no
end, upon the throne of David, and upon his kingdom, to order it,
and to establish it with judgment and with justice from henceforth
even for ever. The zeal of the LORD of hosts will perform this.

* * *

40

Comfort ye, comfort ye my people, saith your God.
2 Speak ye comfortably to Jerusalem, and cry unto her, that her
warfare is accomplished, that her iniquity is pardoned: for she hath
received of the LORD's hand double for all her sins.
3 The voice of him that crieth in the wilderness, Prepare ye the
way of the LORD, make straight in the desert a highway for our God.
4 Every valley shall be exalted, and every mountain and hill shall be
made low: and the crooked shall be made straight, and the rough
places plain:
5 And the glory of the LORD shall be revealed, and all flesh shall see
it together: for the mouth of the LORD hath spoken it.
6 The voice said. Cry. And he said, What shall I cry? All flesh is
grass, and all the goodliness thereof is as the flower of the field:
7 The grass withereth, the flower fadeth: because the spirit of the
LORD bloweth upon it: surely the people is grass.
8 The grass withereth, the flower fadeth: but the word of our God
shall stand for ever.

* * *

Ezekiel

1

Now it came to pass in the thirtieth year, in the fourth month, in
the fifth day of the month, as I was among the captives by the river
of Chebar, that the heavens were opened, and I saw visions of God.
2 In the fifth day of the month, which was the fifth year of king
Jehoiachin's captivity.
3 The word of the LORD came expressly unto Ezekiel the priest, the
son of Buzi, in the land of the Chaldeans by the river Chebar; and
the hand of the LORD was there upon him.
4 And I looked, and, behold, a whirlwind came out of the north,
a great cloud, and a fire infolding itself, and a brightness was about
it, and out of the midst thereof as the colour of amber, out of the
midst of the fire.
5 Also out of the midst thereof came the likeness of four living crea-
tures. And this was their appearance; they had the likeness of a man.
6 And every one had four faces, and every one had four wings.
7 And their feet were straight feet; and the sole of their feet was like
the sole of a calf's foot: and they sparkled like the colour of burnished
brass.
8 And they had the hands of a man under their wings on their four
sides; and they four had their faces and their wings.
9 Their wings were joined one to another; they turned not when
they went; they went every one straight forward.
10 As for the likeness of their faces, they four had the face of a man,
and the face of a lion, on the right side: and they four had the face
of an ox on the left side; they four also had the face of an eagle.
11 Thus were their faces: and their wings were stretched upward;
two wings of every one were joined one to another, and two covered
their bodies.
12 And they went every one straight forward: whither the spirit was
to go, they went; and they turned not when they went.
13 As for the likeness of the living creatures, their appearance was
like burning coals of fire, and like the appearance of lamps: it went
up and down among the living creatures; and the fire was bright, and
out of the fire went forth lightning.
14 And the living creatures ran and returned as the appearance of
a flash of lightning.
15 Now as I beheld the living creatures, behold one wheel upon
the earth by the living creatures, with his four faces.
16 The appearance of the wheels and their work was like unto
the colour of a beryl: and they four had one likeness: and their

appearance and their work was as it were a wheel in the middle of a
wheel.
17 When they went, they went upon their four sides: and they
turned not when they went.
18 As for their rings, they were so high that they were dreadful; and
their rings were full of eyes round about them four.
19 And when the living creatures went, the wheels went by them:
and when the living creatures were lifted up from the earth, the
wheels were lifted up.
20 Whithersoever the spirit was to go, they went, thither was their
spirit to go; and the wheels were lifted up over against them: for the
spirit of the living creature was in the wheels.
21 When those went, these went; and when those stood, these
stood; and when those were lifted up from the earth, the wheels were
lifted up over against them: for the spirit of the living creature was
in the wheels.
22 And the likeness of the firmament upon the heads of the living
creature was as the colour of the terrible crystal, stretched forth over
their heads above.
23 And under the firmament were their wings straight, the one
toward the other: every one had two, which covered on this side, and
every one had two, which covered on that side, their bodies.
24 And when they went, I heard the noise of their wings, like the
noise of great waters, as the voice of the Almighty, the voice of
speech, as the noise of an host: when they stood, they let down their
wings.
25 And there was a voice from the firmament that was over their
heads, when they stood, and had let down their wings.

26 And above the firmament that was over their heads was the
likeness of a throne, as the appearance of a sapphire stone: and upon
the likeness of the throne was the likeness as the appearance of a
man above upon it.
27 And I saw as the colour of amber, as the appearance of fire round
about within it, from the appearance of his loins even upward, and
from the appearance of his loins even downward, I saw as it were
the appearance of fire and it had brightness round about.
28 As the appearance of the bow that is in the cloud in the day
of rain, so was the appearance of the brightness round about. This
was the appearance of the likeness of the glory of the LORD. And
when I saw it, I fell upon my face, and I heard a voice of one that
spake.

Mark

13

* * *

24 But in those days, after that tribulation, the sun shall be dark-
ened, and the moon shall not give her light.
25 And the stars of heaven shall fall, and the powers that are in
heaven shall be shaken.
26 And then shall they see the Son of man coming in the clouds
with great power and glory.
27 And then shall he send his angels, and shall gather together his
elect from the four winds, from the uttermost part of the earth to
the uttermost part of heaven.
28 Now learn a parable of the fig tree; When her branch is yet
tender, and putteth forth leaves, ye know that summer is near:
29 So ye in like manner, when ye shall see these things come to
pass, know that it is nigh, even at the doors.
30 Verily I say unto you, that this generation shall not pass, till all
these things be done.
31 Heaven and earth shall pass away: but my words shall not pass
away.

* * *

Acts

13

* * *

16 Then Paul stood up, and beckoning with his hand said, Men of
Israel, and ye that fear God, give audience.
17 The God of this people of Israel chose our fathers, and exalted
the people when they dwelt as strangers in the land of Egypt, and
with an high arm brought he them out of it.
18 And about the time of forty years suffered he their manners in
the wilderness.
19 And when he had destroyed seven nations in the land of Cha-
naan, he divided their land to them by lot.
20 And after that he gave unto them judges about the space of four
hundred and fifty years, until Samuel the prophet.
21 And afterward they desired a king: and God gave unto them Saul

the son of Cis, a man of the tribe of Benjamin, by the space of forty
years.
22 And when he had removed him, he raised up onto them David
to be their king; to whom also he gave testimony, and said, I have
found David the son of Jesse, a man after mine own heart, which
shall fulfil all my will.
23 Of this man's seed hath God according to his promise raised unto
Israel a Saviour, Jesus:
24 When John had first preached before his coming the baptism of
repentance to all the people of Israel.
25 And as John fulfilled his course, he said, Whom think ye that I
am? I am not he. But, behold, there cometh one after me, whose
shoes of his feet I am not worthy to loose.
26 Men and brethren, children of the stock of Abraham, and who-
soever among you feareth God, to you is the word of this salvation
sent.
27 For they that dwell at Jerusalem, and their rulers, because they
knew him not, nor yet the voices of the prophets which are read
every sabbath day, they have fulfilled them in condemning him.
28 And though they found no cause of death in him, yet desired
they Pilate that he should be slain.
29 And when they had fulfilled all that was written of him, they took
him down from the tree, and laid him in a sepulchre.
30 But God raised him from the dead:
31 And he was seen many days of them which came up with him
from Galilee to Jerusalem, who are his witnesses unto the people.
32 And we declare unto you glad tidings, how that the promise
which was made unto the fathers.
33 God hath fulfilled the same unto us their children, in that he
hath raised up Jesus again; as it is also written in the second psalm,
Thou art my Son, this day have I begotten thee.
34 And as concerning that he raised him up from the dead, now no
more to return to corruption, he said on this wise, I will give you the
sure mercies of David.
35 Wherefore he saith also in another psalm, Thou shalt not suffer
thine Holy One to see corruption.
36 For David, after he had served his own generation by the will of
God, fell on sleep, and was laid unto his fathers, and saw corrup-
tion:
37 But he, whom God raised again, saw no corruption.

* * *

1 Corinthians

15

Moreover, brethren, I declare unto you the gospel which I preached
unto you, which also ye have received, and wherein ye stand;
2 By which also ye are saved, if ye keep in memory what I preached
unto you, unless ye have believed in vain.
3 For I delivered unto you first of all that which I also received, how
that Christ died for our sins according to the scriptures;
4 And that he was buried, and that he rose again the third day
according to the scriptures:
5 And that he was seen of Cephas, then of the twelve:
6 After that, he was seen of above five hundred brethren at once;
of whom the greater part remain unto this present, but some are
fallen asleep.
7 After that, he was seen of James; then of all the apostles.
8 And last of all he was seen of me also, as of one born out of due
time.
9 For I am the least of the apostles, that am not meet to be called
an apostle, because I persecuted the church of God.
10 But by the grace of God I am what I am: and his grace which
was bestowed upon me was not in vain; but I laboured more abun-
dantly than they all: yet not I, but the grace of God which was with
me.
11 Therefore whether it were I or they, so we preach, and so ye
believed.
12 Now if Christ be preached that he rose from the dead, how say
some among you that there is no resurrection of the dead?
13 But if there be no resurrection of the dead, then is Christ not
risen:
14 And if Christ be not risen, then is our preaching vain, and your
faith is also vain.
15 Yea, and we are found false witnesses of God; because we have
testified of God that he raised up Christ: whom he raised not up, if
so be that the dead rise not.
16 For if the dead rise not, then is not Christ raised:
17 And if Christ be not raised, your faith is vain; ye are yet in your
sins.
18 Then they also which are fallen asleep in Christ are perished.
19 If in this life only we have hope in Christ, we are of all men most
miserable.
20 But now is Christ risen from the dead, and become the firstfruits
of them that slept.

21 For since by man came death, by man came also the resurrection
of the dead.
22 For as in Adam all die, even so in Christ shall all be made alive.
23 But every man in his own order: Christ the firstfruits; afterward
they that are Christ's at his coming.
24 Then cometh the end, when he shall have delivered up the king-
dom to God, even the Father; when he shall have put down all rule
and all authority and power.
25 For he must reign, till he hath put all enemies under his feet.
26 The last enemy that shall be destroyed is death.
27 For he hath put all things under his feet. But when he saith all
things are put under him, it is manifest that he is excepted, which
did put all things under him.
28 And when all things shall be subdued unto him, then shall the
Son also himself be subject unto him that put all things under him,
that God may be all in all.
29 Else what shall they do which are baptized for the dead, if the
dead rise not at all? why are they then baptized for the dead?
30 And why stand we in jeopardy every hour?
31 I protest by your rejoicing which I have in Christ Jesus our Lord,
I die daily.
32 If after the manner of men I have fought with beasts at Ephesus,
what advantageth it me, if the dead rise not? let us eat and drink;
for to morrow we die.
33 Be not deceived: evil communications corrupt good manners.
34 Awake to righteousness, and sin not; for some have not the
knowledge of God: I speak this to your shame.
35 But some man will say, How are the dead raised up? and with
what body do they come?
36 Thou fool, that which thou sowest is not quickened, except it
die:
37 And that which thou sowest, thou sowest not that body that shall
be, but bare grain, it may chance of wheat, or of some other grain:
38 But God giveth it a body as it hath pleased him, and to every
seed his own body.
39 All flesh is not the same flesh: but there is one kind of flesh of
men, another flesh of beasts, another of fishes, and another of birds.
40 There are also celestial bodies, and bodies terrestrial: but the
glory of the celestial is one, and the glory of the terrestrial is another.
41 There is one glory of the sun, and another glory of the moon,
and another glory of the stars: for one star differeth from another
star in glory.
42 So also is the resurrection of the dead. It is sown in corruption;
it is raised in incorruption:

43 It is sown in dishonour; it is raised in glory: it is sown in weak-
ness; it is raised in power:
44 It is sown a natural body; it is raised a spiritual body. There is a
natural body, and there is a spiritual body.
45 And so it is written, The first man Adam was made a living soul;
the last Adam was made a quickening spirit.
46 Howbeit that was not first which is spiritual, but that which is
natural; and afterward that which is spiritual.
47 The first man is of the earth, earthy: the second man is the Lord
from heaven.
48 As is the earthy, such are they also that are earthy: and as is the
heavenly, such are they also that are heavenly.
49 And as we have borne the image of the earthy, we shall also bear
the image of the heavenly.
50 Now this I say, brethren, that flesh and blood cannot inherit the
kingdom of God; neither doth corruption inherit incorruption.
51 Behold, I shew you a mystery; We shall not all sleep, but we shall
all be changed,
52 In a moment, in the twinkling of an eye, at the last trump: for
the trumpet shall sound, and the dead shall be raised incorruptible,
and we shall be changed.
53 For this corruptible must put on incorruption, and this mortal
must put on immortality.
54 So when this corruptible shall have put on incorruption, and this
mortal shall have put on immortality, then shall be brought to pass
the saying that is written, Death is swallowed up in victory.
55 O death, where is thy sting? O grave, where is thy victory?
56 The sting of death is sin; and the strength of sin is the law.
57 But thanks be to God, which giveth us the victory through our
Lord Jesus Christ.
58 Therefore, my beloved brethren, be ye stedfast, unmoveable,
always abounding in the work of the Lord, forasmuch as ye know
that your labour is not in vain in the Lord.

Revelation

12

And there appeared a great wonder in heaven; a woman clothed with
the sun, and the moon under her feet, and upon her head a crown
of twelve stars:
2 And she being with child cried, travailing in birth, and pained to
be delivered.

3 And there appeared another wonder in heaven; and behold a great
red dragon, having seven heads and ten horns, and seven crowns
upon his heads.
4 And his tail drew the third part of the stars of heaven, and did cast
them to the earth: and the dragon stood before the woman which
was ready to be delivered, for to devour her child as soon as it was
born.
5 And she brought forth a man child, who was to rule all nations
with a rod of iron: and her child was caught up unto God, and to his
throne.
6 And the woman fled into the wilderness, where she hath a place
prepared of God, that they should feed her there a thousand two
hundred and threescore days.
7 And there was war in heaven: Michael and his angels fought
against the dragon; and the dragon fought and his angels.
8 And prevailed not; neither was their place found any more in
heaven.
9 And the great dragon was cast out, that old serpent, called the
Devil, and Satan, which deceiveth the whole world: he was cast out
into the earth, and his angels were cast out with him.
10 And I heard a loud voice saying in heaven, Now is come salvation,
and strength, and the kingdom of our God, and the power of his
Christ: for the accuser of our brethren is cast down, which accused
them before our God day and night.
11 And they overcame him by the blood of the Lamb, and by the
word of their testimony; and they loved not their lives unto the death.
12 Therefore rejoice, ye heavens, and ye that dwell in them. Woe
to the inhabiters of the earth and of the sea! for the devil is come
down unto you, having great wrath, because he knoweth that he hath
but a short time.
13 And when the dragon saw that he was cast unto the earth, he
persecuted the woman which brought forth the man child.
14 And to the woman were given two wings of a great eagle, that
she might fly into the wilderness, into her place, where she is nour-
ished for a time, and times, and half a time, from the face of the
serpent.
15 And the serpent cast out of his mouth water as a flood after the
woman, that he might cause her to be carried away of the flood.
16 And the earth helped the woman, and the earth opened her
mouth, and swallowed up the flood which the dragon cast out of his
mouth.
17 And the dragon was wroth with the woman, and went to make
war with the remnant of her seed, which keep the commandments
of God, and have the testimony of Jesus Christ.

20

And I saw an angel come down from heaven, having the key of the
bottomless pit and a great chain in his hand.
2 And he laid hold on the dragon, that old serpent, which is the
Devil, and Satan, and bound him a thousand years.
3 And cast him into the bottomless pit, and shut him up, and set a
seal upon him, that he should deceive the nations no more, till the
thousand years should be fulfilled: and after that he must be loosed
a little season.
4 And I saw thrones, and they sat upon them, and judgment was
given unto them: and I saw the souls of them that were beheaded
for the witness of Jesus, and for the word of God, and which had not
worshipped the beast, neither his image, neither had received his
mark upon their foreheads, or in their hands; and they lived and
reigned with Christ a thousand years.
5 But the rest of the dead lived not again until the thousand years
were finished. This is the first resurrection.
6 Blessed and holy is he that hath part in the first resurrection: on
such the second death hath no power, but they shall be priests of
God and of Christ, and shall reign with him a thousand years.
7 And when the thousand years are expired, Satan shall be loosed
out of his prison.
8 And shall go out to deceive the nations which are in the four
quarters of the earth, Gog and Magog, to gather them together to
battle: the number of whom is as the sand of the sea.
9 And they went up on the breadth of the earth, and compassed the
camp of the saints about, and the beloved city: and fire came down
from God out of heaven, and devoured them.
10 And the devil that deceived them was cast into the lake of fire
and brimstone, where the beast and the false prophet are, and shall
be tormented day and night for ever and ever.
11 And I saw a great white throne, and him that sat on it, from
whose face the earth and the heaven fled away; and there was found
no place for them.
12 And I saw the dead, small and great, stand before God; and the
books were opened: and another book was opened, which is the book
of life: and the dead were judged out of those things which were
written in the books, according to their works.
13 And the sea gave up the dead which were in it; and death and
hell delivered up the dead which were in them: and they were judged
every man according to their works.
14 And death and hell were cast into the lake of fire. This is the
second death.

15 And whosoever was not found written in the book of life was cast
into the lake of fire.

21

And I saw a new heaven and a new earth: for the first heaven and
the first earth were passed away; and there was no more sea.
2 And I John saw the holy city, new Jerusalem, coming down from
God out of heaven, prepared as a bride adorned for her husband.
3 And I heard a great voice out of heaven saying, Behold, the tab-
ernacle of God is with men, and he will dwell with them, and they
shall be his people, and God himself shall be with them, and be their
God.
4 And God shall wipe away all tears from their eyes; and there shall
be no more death, neither sorrow, nor crying, neither shall there be
any more pain: for the former things are passed away.
5 And he that sat upon the throne said, Behold, I make all things
new. And he said unto me, Write: for these words are true and faith-
ful.
6 And he said unto me, It is done. I am Alpha and Omega, the
beginning and the end. I will give unto him that is athirst of the
fountain of the water of life freely.
7 He that overcometh shall inherit all things; and I will be his God,
and he shall be my son.
8 But the fearful, and unbelieving, and the abominable, and mur-
derers, and whoremongers, and sorcerers, and idolaters, and all liars,
shall have their part in the lake which burneth with fire and brim-
stone: which is the second death.
9 And there came unto me one of the seven angels which had the
seven vials full of the seven last plagues, and talked with me, saying,
Come hither, I will shew thee the bride, the Lamb's wife.
10 And he carried me away in the spirit to a great and high moun-
tain, and shewed me that great city, the holy Jerusalem, descending
out of heaven from God,
11 Having the glory of God: and her light was like unto a stone most
precious, even like a jasper stone, clear as crystal;
12 And had a wall great and high, and had twelve gates, and at the
gates twelve angels, and names written thereon, which are the names
of the twelve tribes of the children of Israel:
13 On the east three gates; on the north three gates; on the south
three gates; and on the west three gates.
14 And the wall of the city had twelve foundations, and in them the
names of the twelve apostles of the Lamb.
15 And he that talked with me had a golden reed to measure the
city, and the gates thereof, and the wall thereof.

16 And the city lieth foursquare, and the length is as large as the
breadth: and he measured the city with the reed, twelve thousand
furlongs. The length and the breadth and the height of it are equal.
17 And he measured the wall thereof, an hundred and forty and
four cubits, according to the measure of a man, that is, of the angel.
18 And the building of the wall of it was of jasper: and the city was
pure gold, like unto clear glass.
19 And the foundations of the wall of the city were garnished
with all manner of precious stones. The first foundation was jas-
per; the second, sapphire; the third, a chalcedony; the fourth, an
emerald;
20 The fifth, sardonyx; the sixth, sardius; the seventh; chrysolite;
the eighth, beryl; the ninth, a topaz; the tenth, a chrysoprasus; the
eleventh, a jacinth; the twelfth, an amethyst.
21 And the twelve gates were twelve pearls; every several gate was
of one pearl: and the street of the city was pure gold, as it were
transparent glass.
22 And I saw no temple therein: for the Lord God Almighty and the
Lamb are the temple of it.
23 And the city had no need of the sun, neither of the moon, to
shine in it: for the glory of God did lighten it, and the Lamb is the
light thereof.
24 And the nations of them which are saved shall walk in the light
of it: and the kings of the earth do bring their glory and honour into
it.
25 And the gates of it shall not be shut at all by day: for there shall
be no night there.
26 And they shall bring the glory and honour of the nations into it.
27 And there shall in no wise enter into it any thing that defileth,
neither whatsoever worketh abomination, or maketh a lie: but they
which are written in the Lamb's book of life.

22

And he shewed me a pure river of water of life, clear as crystal,
proceeding out of the throne of God and of the Lamb.
2 In the midst of the street of it, and on either side of the river, was
there the tree of life, which bare twelve manner of fruits, and yielded
her fruit every month: and the leaves of the tree were for the healing
of the nations.
3 And there shall be no more curse: but the throne of God and of
the Lamb shall be in it; and his servants shall serve him:
4 And they shall see his face; and his name shall be in their fore-
heads.
5 And there shall be no night there; and they need no candle,

neither light of the sun; for the Lord God giveth them light: and they
shall reign for ever and ever.
6 And he said unto me, These sayings are faithful and true: and the
Lord God of the holy prophets sent his angel to shew unto his ser-
vants the things which must shortly be done.
7 Behold, I come quickly: blessed is he that keepeth the sayings of
the prophecy of this book.
8 And I John saw these things, and heard them. And when I had
heard and seen, I fell down to worship before the feet of the angel
which shewed me these things.
9 Then saith he unto me, See thou do it not: for I am thy fellow-
servant, and of thy brethren the prophets, and of them which keep
the sayings of this book: worship God.
10 And he saith unto me, Seal not the sayings of the prophecy of
this book: for the time is at hand.
11 He that is unjust, let him be unjust still: and he which is filthy,
let him be filthy still: and he that is righteous, let him be righteous
still: and he that is holy, let him be holy still.
12 And, behold, I come quickly; and my reward is with me, to give
every man according as his work shall be.
13 I am Alpha and Omega, the beginning and the end, the first and
the last.
14 Blessed are they that do his commandments, that they may have
right to the tree of life, and may enter in through the gates into the
city.
15 For without are dogs, and sorcerers, and whoremongers, and
murderers, and idolaters, and whosoever loveth and maketh a lie.
16 I Jesus have sent mine angel to testify unto you these things in
the churches. I am the root and the offspring of David, and the bright
and morning star.
17 And the Spirit and the bride say, Come. And let him that heareth
say, Come. And let him that is athirst come. And whosoever will, let
him take the water of life freely.
18 For I testify unto every man that heareth the words of the proph-
ecy of this book, If any man shall add unto these things, God shall
add unto him the plagues that are written in this book:
19 And if any man shall take away from the words of the book of
this prophecy, God shall take away his part out of the book of life,
and out of the holy city, and from the things which are written in
this book.
20 He which testifieth these things saith, Surely I come quickly.
Amen. Even so, come, Lord Jesus.
21 The grace of our Lord Jesus Christ be with you all. Amen.

Selections from Milton's Prose

From The Reason of Church Government Urged against Prelaty

(*Introduction to Book II*)

How happy were it for this frail, and as it may be truly called mortal life of man, since all earthly things, which have the name of good and convenient in our daily use, are withal so cumbersome and full of trouble, if knowledge, yet which is the best and lightsomest possession of the mind, were, as the common saying is, no burden; and that what it wanted of being a load to any part of the body, it did not with a heavy advantage overlay upon the spirit! For not to speak of that knowledge that rests in the contemplation of natural causes and dimensions, which must needs be a lower wisdom, as the object is low, certain it is that he who hath obtained in more than the scantiest measure to know anything distinctly of God, and of his true worship; and what is infallibly good and happy in the state of man's life, what in itself evil and miserable, though vulgarly not so esteemed; he that hath obtained to know this, the only high valuable wisdom indeed, remembering also that God, even to a strictness, requires the improvement of these his entrusted gifts, cannot but sustain a sorer burden of mind, and more pressing, than any supportable toil or weight which the body can labour under; how and in what manner he shall dispose and employ those sums of knowledge and illumination, which God hath sent him into this world to trade with.

And that which aggravates the burden more is, that, having received amongst his allotted parcels certain precious truths, of such an orient lustre as no diamond can equal, which nevertheless he has in charge to put off at any cheap rate, yea for nothing to them that will; the great merchants of this world, fearing that this course would soon discover and disgrace the false glitter of their deceitful wares, wherewith they abuse the people, like poor Indians with beads and glasses, practise by all means how they may suppress the vending of such rarities, and at such a cheapness as would undo them, and turn their trash upon their hands. Therefore, by gratifying the corrupt desires of men in fleshly doctrines, they stir them up to persecute with hatred and contempt all those that seek to bear themselves uprightly in this their spiritual factory: which they foreseeing, though they cannot but testify of truth, and the excellence of that heavenly traffic which they bring, against what opposition or danger soever, yet needs must it sit heavily upon their spirits, that being, in God's prime intention and their own, selected heralds of peace and dispensers of treasure inestimable, without price, to them that have no pence, they find in the discharge of their commission, that they are made the greatest variance and offence, a very sword and fire both in house and city over the whole earth.

This is that which the sad prophet Jeremiah laments: *Woe is me, my mother, that thou hast borne me, a man of strife and contention!* And although divine inspiration must certainly have been sweet to those ancient prophets, yet the irksomeness of that truth which they brought was so unpleasant to them, that everywhere they call it a burden. Yea, that mysterious book of Revelation, which the great Evangelist was bid to eat, as it had been some eye-brightening electuary of knowledge and foresight, though it were sweet in his mouth and in the learning, it was bitter in his belly, bitter in the denouncing. Nor was this hid from the wise poet Sophocles, who in that place of his tragedy where Tiresias is called to resolve King Oedipus in a matter which he knew would be grievous, brings him in bemoaning his lot, that he knew more than other men. For surely to every good and peaceable man, it must in nature needs be a hateful thing to be the displeaser and molester of thousands; much better would it like him doubtless to be the messenger of gladness and contentment, which is his chief intended business to all mankind, but that they resist and oppose their own true happiness.

But when God commands to take the trumpet, and blow a dolorous or a jarring blast, it lies not in man's will what he shall say, or what he shall conceal. If he shall think to be silent, as Jeremiah did, because of the reproach and derision he met with daily, *And all his familiar friends watched for his halting,* to be revenged on him for speaking the truth, he would be forced to confess as he confessed: *His word was in my heart as a burning fire shut up in my bones; I was weary with forbearing, and could not stay.* Which might teach these times not suddenly to condemn all things that are sharply spoken or vehemently written as proceeding out of stomach, virulence, and ill-nature; but to consider rather that, if the prelates have leave to say the worst that can be said, or do the worst that can be done, while they strive to keep to themselves, to their great pleasure and commodity, those things which they ought to render up no man can be justly offended with him that shall endeavour to impart and bestow, without any gain to himself, those sharp but saving words which would be a terror and a torment in him to keep back.

For me, I have determined to lay up as the best treasure and solace of a good old age, if God vouchsafe it me, the honest liberty of free speech from my youth, where I shall think it available in so dear a concernment as the Church's good. For if I be, either by disposition or what other cause, too inquisitive, or suspicious of myself and mine own doings, who can help it? But this I foresee, that should the Church be brought under heavy oppression, and God have given me ability the while to reason against that man that should be the author of so foul a deed; or should she, by blessing from above on the industry and courage of faithful men, change this her distracted estate into better days, without the least furtherance or contribution of those few talents which God at that present had lent me; I foresee what stories I should hear within myself, all my life after, of discourage and reproach.

"Timorous and ungrateful, the Church of God is now again at the foot of her insulting enemies, and thou bewailest. What matters it for thee, or thy bewailing? When time was, thou couldst not find a syllable of all that thou hadst read, or studied, to utter in her behalf. Yet ease and leisure was given thee for thy retired thoughts, out of the sweat of other men. Thou hadst the diligence, the parts, the language of a man, if a vain subject were to be adorned or beautified; but when the cause of God and his Church was to be pleaded, for which purpose that tongue was given thee which thou hast, God listened if he could hear thy voice among his zealous servants, but thou wert dumb as a beast: from henceforward be that which thine own brutish silence hath made thee."

Or else I should have heard on the other ear: "Slothful, and ever to be set light by, the Church hath now overcome her late distresses after the unwearied labours of many her true servants that stood up in her defence; thou also wouldst take upon thee to share amongst them of their joy: but wherefore thou? Where canst thou show any word or deed of thine which might have hastened her peace? Whatever thou dost now talk, or write, or look, is the alms of other men's active prudence and zeal. Dare not now to say or do anything better than thy former sloth and infancy; or if thou darest, thou dost impudently to make a thrifty purchase of boldness to thyself out of the painful merits of other men; what before was thy sin is now thy duty, to be abject and worthless."

These, and such like lessons as these, I know would have been my matins duly, and my evensong. But now by this little diligence, mark what a privilege I have gained with good men and saints, to claim my right of lamenting the tribulations of the Church, if she should suffer, when others, that have ventured nothing for her sake, have not the honour to be admitted mourners. But if she lift up her drooping head and prosper, among those that have something more than wished her welfare, I have my charter and freehold of rejoicing to me and my heirs. Concerning therefore this wayward subject against prelaty, the touching whereof is so distasteful and disquietous to a number of men, as by what hath been said I may deserve of charitable readers to be credited, that neither envy nor gall hath entered me upon this controversy, but the enforcement of conscience only, and a preventive fear lest the omitting of this duty should be against me, when I would store up to myself the good provision of peaceful hours: so, lest it be still imputed to me, as I have found it hath been, that some self-pleasing humour of vainglory hath incited me to contest with men of high estimation, now while green years are upon my head; from this needless surmisal I shall hope to dissuade the intelligent and equal auditor, if I can but say successfully that which in this exigent behooves me; although I would be heard only, if it might be, by the elegant and learned reader, to whom principally for a while I shall beg leave I may address myself.

To him it will be no new thing, though I tell him that if I hunted after praise, by the ostentation of wit and learning, I should not write thus out of mine own season when I have neither yet completed to my mind the full circle of my private studies, although I complain not of any insufficiency to the matter in hand; or were I ready to my wishes, it were a folly to commit anything elaborately composed to the careless and interrupted listening of these tumultuous times. Next, if I were wise only to my own ends, I would certainly take such a subject as of itself might catch applause, whereas this hath all the disadvantages on the contrary; and such a subject as the publishing whereof might be delayed at pleasure, and time enough to pencil it over with all the curious touches of art, even to the perfection of a faultless picture; whenas in this argument the not deferring is of great moment to the good speeding, that, if solidity have leisure to do her office, art cannot have much. Lastly, I should not choose this manner of writing, wherein knowing myself inferior to myself, led by the genial power of nature to another task, I have the use, as I may account it, but of my left hand.

And though I shall be foolish in saying more to this purpose, yet, since it will be such a folly as wisest men go about to commit, having only confessed and so committed, I may trust with more reason, because with more folly, to have courteous pardon. For although a poet, soaring in the high region of his fancies with his garland and singing robes about him, might, without apology, speak more of himself than I mean to do; yet for me sitting here below in the cool element of prose, a mortal thing among many readers of no empyreal conceit, to venture and divulge unusual things of myself, I shall petition to the gentler sort, it may not be envy to me.

I must say, therefore, that after I had for my first years, by the ceaseless diligence and care of my father (whom God recompense!), been exercised to the tongues and some sciences, as my age would suffer, by sundry masters and teachers, both at home and at the schools, it was found that whether aught was imposed me by them that had the overlooking, or betaken to of mine own choice in English, or other tongue, prosing or versing, but chiefly this latter, the style, by certain vital signs it had, was likely to live. But much latelier in the private academies of Italy, whither I was favoured to resort, perceiving that some trifles which I had in memory, composed at under twenty or thereabout (for the manner is, that everyone must give some proof of his wit and reading there), met with acceptance above what was looked for; and other things, which I had shifted in scarcity of books and conveniences to patch up amongst them, were received with written encomiums, which the Italian is not forward to bestow on men of this side the Alps; I began thus far to assent both to them and divers of my friends here at home, and not less to an inward prompting which now grew daily upon me, that by labour and intense study (which I take to be my portion in this life), joined with the strong propensity of nature, I might perhaps leave something so written to aftertimes, as they should not willingly let it die.

These thoughts at once possessed me, and these other; that if I were certain to write as men buy leases, for three lives and downward, there ought no regard be sooner had than to God's glory, by the honour and instruction of my country. For which cause, and not only for that I knew it would he hard to arrive at the second rank among the Latins, I applied myself to that resolution, which Ariosto followed against the persuasions of Bembo, to fix all the industry and art I could unite to the adorning of my native tongue; not to make verbal curiosities the end (that were a toilsome vanity), but to be an interpreter and relater of the best and sagest things among mine own citizens throughout this island in the mother dialect. That, what the greatest and choicest wits of Athens, Rome, or modern Italy, and those Hebrews of old did for their country, I, in my proportion, with this over and above, of being a Christian, might do for mine, not caring to be once named abroad, though perhaps I could attain to that, but content with these British islands as my world; whose fortune hath hitherto been that, if the Athenians, as some say, made their small deeds great and renowned by their eloquent writers, England hath had her noble achievements made small by the unskilful handling of monks and mechanics.

Time serves not now, and perhaps I might seem too profuse, to give any certain account of what the mind at home, in the spacious circuits of her musing, hath liberty to propose to herself, though of highest hope and hardest attempting; whether that epic form whereof the two poems of Homer, and those other two of Virgil and

Tasso, are a diffuse, and the book of Job a brief model: or whether the rules of Aristotle herein are strictly to be kept, or nature to be followed, which in them that know art, and use judgment, is no transgression, but an enriching of art; and lastly, what king or knight, before the conquest, might be chosen in whom to lay the pattern of a Christian hero. And as Tasso gave to a prince of Italy his choice whether he would command him to write of Godfrey's expedition against the Infidels, or Belisarius against the Goths, or Charlemain against the Lombards; if to the instinct of nature and the emboldening of art aught may be trusted, and that there be nothing adverse in our climate, or the fate of this age, it haply would be no rashness, from an equal diligence and inclination, to present the like offer in our own ancient stories; or whether those dramatic constitutions, wherein Sophocles and Euripides reign, shall be found more doctrinal and exemplary to a nation.

The scripture also affords us a divine pastoral drama in the Song of Solomon, consisting of two persons, and a double chorus, as Origen rightly judges. And the Apocalypse of St. John is the majestic image of a high and stately tragedy, shutting up and intermingling her solemn scenes and acts with a sevenfold chorus of hallelujahs and harping symphonies: and this my opinion the grave authority of Paraeus, commenting that book, is sufficient to confirm. Or if occasion shall lead, to imitate those magnific odes and hymns, wherein Pindarus and Callinachus are in most things worthy, some others in their frame judicious, in their matter most an end faulty. But those frequent songs throughout the law and prophets beyond all these, not in their divine argument alone, but in the very critical art of composition, may be easily made appear over all the kinds of lyric poesy to be incomparable.

These abilities, wheresoever they be found, are the inspired gift of God, rarely bestowed, but yet to some (though most abuse) in every nation; and are of power, beside the office of a pulpit, to imbreed and cherish in a great people the seeds of virtue and public civility, to allay the perturbations of the mind, and set the affections in right tune; to celebrate in glorious and lofty hymns the throne and equipage of Gods' almightiness, and what he works, and what he suffers to be wrought with high providence in his Church; to sing victorious agonies of martyrs and saints, the deeds and triumphs of just and pious nations, doing valiantly through faith against the enemies of Christ; to deplore the general relapses of kingdoms and states from justice and God's true worship.

Lastly, whatsoever in religion is holy and sublime, in virtue amiable or grave, whatsoever hath passion or admiration in all the changes of that which is called fortune from without, or the wily subtleties and refluxes of man's thoughts from within; all these things with a solid and treatable smoothness to paint out and describe. Teaching over the whole book of sanctity and virtue, through all the instances of example, with such delight to those especially of soft and delicious temper, who will not so much as look upon Truth herself, unless they see her elegantly dressed, that whereas the paths of honesty and good life appear now rugged and difficult, though they be indeed easy and pleasant, they will then appear to all men both easy and pleasant, though they were rugged and difficult indeed. And what a benefit this would be to our youth and gentry, may be soon guessed by what we know of the corruption and bane which they suck in daily from the writings and interludes of libidinous and ignorant poetasters; who, having scarce ever heard of that which is the main consistence of a true poem, the choice of such persons as they ought to introduce, and what is moral and decent to each one, do for the most part lap up vicious principles in sweet pills to be swallowed down, and make the taste of virtuous documents harsh and sour.

But because the spirit of man cannot demean itself lively in this body, without some recreating intermission of labour and serious things, it were happy for the Commonwealth, if our magistrates, as in those famous governments of old, would take into their care, not only the deciding of our contentious law-cases and brawls, but the managing of our public sports and festival pastimes; that they might be, not such as were authorized a while since, the provocations of drunkenness and lust, but such as may inure and harden our bodies by martial exercises to all warlike skill and performance°d may civilize, adorn, and make discreet our minds by the learned and affable meeting of frequent Academies, and the procurement of wise and artful recitations, sweetened with eloquent and graceful enticements to the love and practice of justice, temperance, and fortitude, instructing and bettering the nation at all opportunities, that the call of wisdom and virtue may be heard everywhere, as Solomon saith: *She crieth without, she uttereth her voice in the streets, in the top of high places, in the chief concourse, and in the openings of the gates.* Whether this may not be, not only in pulpits, but after another persuasive method, at set and solemn paneguries, in theatres, porches, or what other place or way may win most upon the people to receive at once both recreation and instruction, let them in authority consult.

The thing which I had to say, and those intentions which have lived within me ever since I could conceive myself anything worth to my country, I return to crave excuse that urgent reason hath plucked from me, by an abortive and foredated discovery. And the accomplishment of them lies not but in a power above man's to promise, but that none hath by more studious ways endeavoured, and with more unwearied spirit that none shall, that I dare almost aver of myself, as far as life and free leisure will extend; and that the land had once enfranchised herself from this impertinent yoke of prelaty, under whose inquisitorious and tyrannical duncery no free and splendid wit can flourish.

Neither do I think it shame to covenant with any knowing reader, that for some few years yet I may go on trust with him toward the payment of what I am now indebted, as being a work not to be raised from the heat of youth, or the vapours of wine; like that which flows at waste from the pen of some vulgar amorist, or the trencher fury of a rhyming parasite; nor to be obtained by the invocation of Dame Memory and her siren daughters, but by devout prayer to that eternal Spirit, who can enrich with all utterance and knowledge, and sends out his Seraphim, with the hallowed fire of his altar, to touch and purify the lips of whom he pleases: to this must be added industrious and select reading, steady observation, insight into all seemly and generous arts and affairs; till which in some measure be compassed, at mine own peril and cost, I refuse not to sustain this expectation from as many as are not loath to hazard so much credulity upon the best pledges that I can give them.

Although it nothing content me to have disclosed thus much beforehand, but that I trust hereby to make it manifest with what small willingness I endure to interrupt the pursuit of no less hopes than these, and leave a calm and pleasing solitariness, fed with cheerful and confident thoughts, to embark in a troubled sea of noises and hoarse disputes, put from beholding the bright countenance of Truth in the quiet and still air of delightful studies, to come into the dim reflection of hollow antiquities sold by the seeming bulk, and there be fain to club quotations with men whose learning and belief lies in marginal stuffings; who, when they have, like good sumpters, laid ye down their horse-loads of citations and fathers at your door with a rhapsody of who and who were bishops here or there, ye may take off their pack-saddles, their day's work is done, and episcopacy, as they think, stoutly vindicated. Let any gentle apprehension, that can distinguish learned pains from unlearned drudgery, imagine what pleasure or profoundness can be in this, or what honour to deal against such adversaries.

But were it the meanest under-service, if God by his secretary Conscience enjoin it, it were sad for me if I should draw back; for me especially, now when all men offer their aid to help, ease, and lighten the difficult labours of the Church, to whose service, by the intentions of my parents and friends, I was destined of a child, and in mine own resolutions: till coming to some maturity of years, and perceiving what tyranny had invaded the Church, that he who would take orders must subscribe slave, and take an oath withal, which unless he took with a conscience that would retch, he must either straight perjure, or split his faith, I thought it better to prefer a blameless silence before the sacred office of speaking, bought and begun with servitude and forswearing. Howsoever, thus Church-outed by the prelates, hence may appear the right I have to meddle in these matters, as before the necessity and constraint appeared.

Areopagitica

A Speech for the Liberty of Unlicensed Printing to the Parliament of England

Τοὐλεύθερον δ'ἐκεῖνο, εἰ τις θέλει πόλει
Χρηστόν τι βούλευμ' εἰς μέσον φέρειν, ἔχων.
Καὶ ταῦθ' ὁ χρῄζων, λαμπρὸς ἐσθ', ὁ μὴ θέλων,
Σιγᾷ, τι τούτων ἐστιν ἰσαίτερον πόλει;
Euripdes. Hicetides.

This is true liberty, when free-born men,
Having to advise the public, may speak free,
Which he who can, and will, deserves high praise;
Who neither can, nor will, may hold his peace:
What can be juster in a state than this?
Euripides. *Suppliant Women.*

They, who to states and governors of the Commonwealth direct their speech, High Court of Parliament, or, wanting such access in a private condition, write that which they foresee may advance the public good; I suppose them, as at the beginning of no mean endeavour, not a little altered and moved inwardly in their minds: some with doubt of what will be the success, others with fear of what will be the censure, some with hope, others with confidence of what they have to speak. And me perhaps each of these dispositions, as the subject was whereon I entered, may have at other times variously affected, and likely might in these foremost expressions now also disclose which of them swayed most, but that the very attempt of this address thus made, and the thought of whom it hath recourse to, hath got the power within me to a passion, far more welcome than incidental to a preface.

Which though I stay not to confess ere any ask, I shall be blameless, if it be no other than the joy and gratulation which it brings to all who wish and promote their country's liberty; whereof this whole discourse proposed will be a certain testimony, if not a trophy. For this is not the liberty which we can hope, that no grievance ever should arise in the Commonwealth—that let no man in this world expect; but when complaints are freely heard, deeply considered and speedily reformed, then is the utmost bound of civil liberty attained that wise men look for. To which if I now manifest by the very sound of this which I shall utter, that we are already in good part arrived, and yet from such a steep disadvantage of tyranny and superstition grounded into our principles as was beyond the manhood of a Roman recovery, it will be attributed first, as is most due, to the strong assistance of God our deliverer, next to your faithful guidance and undaunted wisdom, Lords and Commons of England. Neither is it in God's esteem the diminution of his glory, when honourable things are spoken of good men and worthy magistrates; which if I now first should begin to do, after so fair a progress of your laudable deeds, and such a long obligement upon the whole realm to your indefatigable virtues, I might be justly reckoned among the tardiest, and the unwillingest of them that praise ye.

Nevertheless there being three principal things, without which all praising is but courtship and flattery: First, when that only is praised which is solidly worth praise: next, when greatest likelihoods are brought that such things are truly and really in those persons to whom they are ascribed: the other, when he who praises, by showing that such his actual persuasion is of whom he writes, can demonstrate that he flatters not; the former two of these I have heretofore endeavoured, rescuing the employment from him who went about to impair your merits with a trivial and malignant encomium; the latter as belonging chiefly to mine own acquittal, that whom I so extolled I did not flatter, hath been reserved opportunely to this occasion.

For he who freely magnifies what hath been nobly done, and fears not to declare as freely what might be done better, gives ye the best covenant of his fidelity; and that his loyalest affection and his hope waits on your proceedings. His highest praising is not flattery, and his plainest advice is a kind of praising. For though I should affirm and hold by argument, that it would fare better with truth, with learning and the Commonwealth, if one of your published Orders, which I should name, were called in; yet at the same time it could not but much redound to the lustre of your mild and equal government, whenas private persons are hereby animated to think ye better pleased with public advice, than other statists have been delighted heretofore with public flattery. And men will then see what difference there is between the magnanimity of a triennial Parliament, and that jealous haughtiness of prelates and cabin counsellors that usurped of late, whenas they shall observe ye in the midst of your victories and successes more gently brooking written exceptions against a voted Order than other courts, which had produced nothing worth memory but the weak ostentation of wealth, would have endured the least signified dislike at any sudden proclamation.

If I should thus far presume upon the meek demeanour of your civil and gentle greatness, Lords and Commons, as what your published Order hath directly said, that to gainsay, I might defend myself with ease, if any should accuse me of being new or insolent, did they but know how much better I find ye esteem it to imitate the old and elegant humanity of Greece, than the barbaric pride of a Hunnish and Norwegian stateliness. And out of those ages, to whose polite wisdom and letters we owe that we are not yet Goths and Jutlanders, I could name him who from his private house wrote that discourse to the Parliament of Athens, that persuades them to change the form of democracy which was then established. Such honour was done in those days to men who professed the study of wisdom and eloquence, not only in their own country, but in other lands, that cities and signiories heard them gladly, and with great respect, if they had aught in public to admonish the state. Thus did Dion Prusaeus, a stranger and a private orator, counsel the Rhodians against a former edict; and I abound with other like examples, which to set here would be superfluous.

But if from the industry of a life wholly dedicated to studious labours, and those natural endowments haply not the worst for two and fifty degrees of northern latitude, so much must be derogated, as to count me not equal to any of those who had this privilege, I would obtain to be thought not so inferior, as yourselves are superior to the most of them who received their counsel: and how far you excel them, be assured, Lords and Commons, there can no greater testimony appear, than when your prudent spirit acknowledges and obeys the voice of reason from what quarter soever it be heard speaking; and renders ye as willing to repeal any Act of your own setting forth, as any set forth by your predecessors.

If ye be thus resolved, as it were injury to think ye were not, I know not what should withhold me from presenting ye with a fit instance wherein to show both that love of truth which ye eminently profess, and that uprightness of your judgment which is not wont to be partial to yourselves; by judging over again that Order which ye have ordained to regulate printing:—that no book, pamphlet, or paper shall be henceforth printed, unless the same be first approved and licensed by such, or at least one of such, as shall be thereto appointed. For that part which preserves justly every man's copy to himself, or provides for the poor, I touch not, only wish they be not made pretences to abuse and persecute honest and painful men, who offend not in either of these particulars. But that other clause of licensing books, which we thought had died with his brother quadragesimal and matrimonial when the prelates expired, I shall now attend with such a homily, as shall lay before ye, first the inventors of it to be those whom ye will be loath to own; next what is to be thought in general of reading, whatever sort the books be; and that this Order avails nothing to the suppressing of scandalous, seditious, and libellous books, which were mainly intended to be suppressed. Last, that it will be primely to the discouragement of all learning, and the stop of truth, not only by disexercising and blunting our abilities in what we know already, but by hindering and cropping the discovery that might be yet further made both in religious and civil wisdom.

I deny not, but that it is of greatest concernment in the Church and Commonwealth, to have a vigilant eye how books demean themselves as well as men; and thereafter to confine, imprison, and do sharpest justice on them as malefactors. For books are not absolutely dead things, but do contain a potency of life in them to be as active as that soul was whose progeny they are; nay, they do preserve as in a vial the purest efficacy and extraction of that living intellect that bred them. I know they are as lively, and as vigorously productive, as those fabulous dragon's teeth; and being sown up and down, may chance to spring up armed men. And yet, on the other hand, unless wariness be used, as good almost kill a man as kill a good book. Who kills a man kills a reasonable creature, God's image; but he who destroys a good book, kills reason itself, kills the image of God, as it were in the eye. Many a man lives a burden to the earth; but a good book is the precious life-blood of a master spirit, embalmed and treasured up on purpose to a life beyond life. 'Tis true, no age can restore a life, whereof perhaps there is no great loss; and revolutions of ages do not oft recover the loss of a rejected truth, for the want of which whole nations fare the worse.

We should be wary therefore what persecution we raise against the living labours of public men, how we spill that seasoned life of man, preserved and stored up in books; since we see a kind of homicide may be thus committed, sometimes a martyrdom, and if it extend to the whole impression, a kind of massacre; whereof the execution ends not in the slaying of an elemental life, but strikes at that ethereal and fifth essence, the breath of reason itself, slays an immortality rather than a life. But lest I should be condemned of introducing licence, while I oppose licensing, I refuse not the pains to be so much historical, as will serve to show what hath been done by ancient and famous commonwealths against this disorder, till the very time that this project of licensing crept out of the Inquisition, was catched up by our prelates, and hath caught some of our presbyters.

In Athens, where books and wits were ever busier than in any other part of Greece, I find but only two sorts of writings which the magistrate cared to take notice of; those either blasphemous and atheistical, or libellous. Thus the books of Protagoras were by the judges of Areopagus commanded to be burnt, and himself banished the territory for a discourse begun with his confessing not to know *whether there were gods, or whether not*. And against defaming, it was decreed that none should be traduced by name, as was the manner of Vetus Comoedia, whereby we may guess how they censured libelling. And this course was quick enough, as Cicero writes, to quell both the desperate wits of other atheists, and the open way of defaming, as the event showed. Of other sects and opinions, though tending to voluptuousness, and the denying of divine Providence, they took no heed.

Therefore we do not read that either Epicurus, or that libertine school of Cyrene, or what the Cynic impudence uttered, was ever questioned by the laws. Neither is it recorded that the writings of those old comedians were suppressed, though the acting of them were forbid; and that Plato commended the reading of Aristophanes, the loosest of them all, to his royal scholar Dionysius, is commonly known, and may be excused, if holy Chrysostom, as is reported, nightly studied so much the same author and had the art to cleanse a scurrilous vehemence into the style of a rousing sermon.

That other leading city of Greece, Lacedaemon, considering that Lycurgus their lawgiver was so addicted to elegant learning, as to have been the first that brought out of Ionia the scattered works of Homer, and sent the poet Thales from Crete to prepare and mollify the Spartan surliness with his smooth songs and odes, the better to plant among them law and civility, it is to be wondered how museless and unbookish they were, minding nought but the feats of war. There needed no licensing of books among them, for they disliked all but their own laconic apophthegms, and took a slight occasion to chase Archilochus out of their city, perhaps for composing in a higher strain than their own soldierly ballads and roundels could reach to. Or if it were for his broad verses, they were not therein so cautious but they were as dissolute in their promiscuous conversing; whence Euripides affirms in *Andromache*, that their women were all unchaste. Thus much may give us light after what sort of books were prohibited among the Greeks.

The Romans also, for many ages trained up only to a military roughness resembling most the Lacedaemonian guise, knew of learning little but what their twelve Tables, and the Pontific College with their augurs and flamens taught them in religion and law; so unacquainted with other learning, that when Carneades and Critolaus, with the Stoic Diogenes, coming ambassadors to Rome, took thereby occasion to give the city a taste of their philosophy, they were suspected for seducers by no less a man than Cato the Censor, who moved it in the Senate to dismiss them speedily, and to banish all such Attic babblers out of Italy. But Scipio and others of the noblest senators withstood him and his old Sabine austerity; honoured and admired the men; and the censor himself at last, in his old age, fell to the study of that whereof before he was so scrupulous. And yet at the same time Naevius and Plautus, the first Latin comedians, had filled the city with all the borrowed scenes of Menander and Philemon. Then began to be considered there also what was to be done to libellous books and authors; for Naevius was quickly cast into prison for his unbridled pen, and released by the tribunes upon his recantation; we read also that libels were burnt, and the makers punished by Augustus. The like severity, no doubt, was used, if aught were impiously written against their esteemed gods. Except in these two points, how the world went in books, the magistrate kept no reckoning.

And therefore Lucretius without impeachment versifies his Epicurism to Memmius, and had the honour to be set forth the second time by Cicero, so great a father of the Commonwealth; although himself disputes against that opinion in his own writings. Nor was the satirical sharpness or naked plainness of Lucilius, or Catullus, or Flaccus, by any order prohibited. And for matters of state, the story of Titus Livius, though it extolled that part which Pompey held, was not therefore suppressed by Octavius Caesar of the other faction. But that Naso was by him banished in his old age, for the wanton poems of his youth, was but a mere covert of state over some secret cause: and besides, the books were neither banished nor called in. From hence we shall meet with little else but tyranny in the Roman empire, that we may not marvel, if not so often bad as good books were silenced. I shall therefore deem to have been large enough, in producing what among the ancients was punishable to write; save only which, all other arguments were free to treat on.

By this time the emperors were become Christians, whose discipline in this point I do not find to have been more severe than what was formerly in practice. The books of those whom they took to be grand heretics were examined, refuted, and condemned in the general Councils; and not till then were prohibited, or burnt, by authority of the emperor. As for the writings of heathen authors, unless they were plain invectives against Christianity, as those of Porphyrius and Proclus, they met with no interdict that can be cited, till about the year 400, in a Carthaginian Council, wherein bishops themselves were forbid to read the books of Gentiles, but heresies they might read: while others long before them, on the contrary, scrupled more the books of heretics than of Gentiles. And that the primitive Councils and bishops were wont only to declare what books were not commendable, passing no further, but leaving it to each one's conscience to read or to lay by, till after the year 800, is observed already by Padre Paolo, the great unmasker of the Trentine Council.

After which time the Popes of Rome, engrossing what they pleased of political rule into their own hands, extended their dominion over men's eyes, as they had before over their judgments, burning and prohibiting to be read what they fancied not; yet sparing in their censures, and the books not many which they so dealt with: till Martin V., by his bull, not only prohibited, but was the first that excommunicated the reading of heretical books; for about that time Wickliffe and Huss, growing terrible, were they who first drove the Papal Court to a stricter policy of prohibiting. Which course Leo X. and his successors followed, until the Council of Trent and the Spanish Inquisition engendering together brought forth, or perfected, those Catalogues and expurging Indexes, that rake through the entrails of many an old good author, with a violation worse than any could be offered to his tomb. Nor did they stay in matters heretical, but any subject that was not to their palate, they either condemned in a Prohibition, or had it straight into the new purgatory of an index.

To fill up the measure of encroachment, their last invention was to ordain that no book, pamphlet, or paper should be printed (as if St. Peter had bequeathed them the keys of the press also out of Paradise) unless it were approved and licensed under the hands of two or three glutton friars. For example:

> Let the Chancellor Cini be pleased to see if in this present work be contained aught that may withstand the printing.
>
> VINCENT RABBATTA, *Vicar of Florence.*

> I have seen this present work, and find nothing athwart the Catholic faith and good manners: in witness whoreof I have given, etc.
>
> NICOLO CINI, *Chancellor of Florence.*

> Attending the precedent relation, it is allowed that this present work of Davanzati may be printed.
>
> VINCENT RABBATTA, *etc.*

> It may be printed, July 15.
>
> FRIAR SIMON MOMPEI D'AMELIA, *Chancellor of the Holy Office in Florence.*

Sure they have a conceit, if he of the bottomless pit had not long since broke prison, that this quadruple exorcism would bar him down. I fear their next design will be to get into their custody the licensing of that which they say Claudius intended, but went not through with. Vouchsafe: to see another of their forms, the Roman stamp:

> Imprimatur, If it seem good to the reverend Master of the Holy Palace.
>
> BELCASTRO, *Vicegerent. Imprimatur, Friar Nicolo Rodolphi, Master of the Holy Palace.*

Sometimes five Imprimaturs are seen together dialogue-wise in the piazza of one title-page, complimenting and ducking each to other with their shaven reverences, whether the author, who stands by in perplexity at the foot of his epistle, shall to the press or to the sponge. These are the pretty responsories, these are the dear antiphonies, that so bewitched of late our prelates and their chaplains with the goodly echo they made; and besotted us to the gay imitation of a lordly Imprimatur, one from Lambeth House, another from the west end of Paul's; so apishly Romanizing, that the word of command still was set down in Latin; as if the learned grammatical pen that wrote it would cast no ink without Latin; or perhaps, as they thought, because no vulgar tongue was worthy to express the pure conceit of an Imprimatur, but rather, as I hope, for that our English, the language of men ever famous and foremost in the achievements of liberty, will not easily find servile letters enow to spell such a dictatory presumption English.

And thus ye have the inventors and the original of book-licensing ripped up and drawn as lineally as any pedigree. We have it not, that can be heard of, from any ancient state, or polity or church; nor by any statute left us by our ancestors elder or later; nor from the modern custom of any reformed city or church abroad, but from the most anti-christian council and the most tyrannous inquisition that ever inquired. Till then books were ever as freely admitted into the world as any other birth; the issue of the brain was no more stifled than the issue of the womb: no envious Juno sat cross-legged over the nativity of any man's intellectual offspring; but if it proved a monster, who denies, but that it was justly burnt, or sunk into the sea? But that a book, in worse condition than a peccant soul, should be to stand before a jury ere it be born to the world, and undergo yet in darkness the judgment of Radamanth and his colleagues, ere it can pass the ferry backward into light, was never heard before, till that mysterious iniquity, provoked and troubled at the first entrance of Reformation, sought out new limbos and new hells wherein they might include our books also within the number of their damned. And this was the rare morsel so officiously snatched up, and so ill-favouredly imitated by our inquisiturient bishops, and the attendant minorites their chaplains. That ye like not now these most certain authors of this licensing order, and that all sinister intention was far distant from your thoughts, when ye were importuned the passing it, all men who know the integrity of your actions, and how ye honour truth, will clear ye readily.

But some will say, what though the inventors were bad, the thing for all that may be good? It may so; yet if that thing be no such deep invention, but obvious, and easy for any man to light on, and yet best and wisest commonwealths through all ages and occasions have forborne to use it, and falsest seducers and oppressors of men were the first who took it up, and to no other purpose but to obstruct and hinder the first approach of Reformation; I am of those who believe it will be a harder alchemy than Lullius ever knew, to sublimate any good use out of such an invention. Yet this only is what I request to gain from this reason, that it may be held a dangerous and suspicious fruit, as certainly it deserves, for the tree that bore it, until I can dissect one by one the properties it has. But I have first to finish, as was propounded, what is to be thought in general of reading books, whatever sort they be, and whether be more the benefit or the harm that thence proceeds.

Not to insist upon the examples of Moses, Daniel, and Paul, who were skilful in all the learning of the Egyptians, Chaldeans, and Greeks, which could not probably be without reading their books of all sorts; in Paul especially, who thought it no defilement to insert into Holy Scripture the sentences of three Greek poets, and one of them a tragedian; the question was notwithstanding sometimes controverted among the primitive doctors, but with great odds on that side which affirmed it both lawful and profitable; as was then evidently perceived, when Julian the Apostate and subtlest enemy to our faith made a decree forbidding Christians the study of heathen learning: for, said he, they wound us with our own weapons, and with our own arts and sciences they overcome us. And indeed the Christians were put so to their shifts by this crafty means, and so much in danger to decline into all ignorance, that the two Apollinarii were fain, as a man may say, to coin all the seven liberal sciences out of the Bible, reducing it into divers forms of orations, poems, dialogues, even to the calculating of a new Christian grammar. But, saith the historian Socrates, the providence of God provided better than the industry of Apollinarius and his son, by taking away that illiterate law with the life of him who devised it. So great an injury they then held it to be deprived of Hellenic learning; and thought it a persecution more undermining, and secretly decaying the Church, than the open cruelty of Decius or Diocletian.

And perhaps it was the same politic drift that the devil whipped St. Jerome in a Lenten dream, for reading Cicero; or else it was a phantasm bred by the fever which had then seized him. For had an angel been his discipliner, unless it were for dwelling too much upon

Ciceronianisms, and had chastised the reading, not the vanity, it had been plainly partial; first to correct him for grave Cicero, and not for scurril Plautus, whom he confesses to have been reading, not long before; next to correct him only, and let so many more ancient fathers wax old in those pleasant and florid studies without the lash of such a tutoring apparition; insomuch that Basil teaches how some good use may be made of *Margites*, a sportful poem, not now extant, writ by Homer; and why not then of *Morgante*, an Italian romance much to the same purpose?

But if it be agreed we shall be tried by visions, there is a vision recorded by Eusebius, far ancienter than this tale of Jerome, to the nun Eustochium, and, besides, has nothing of a fever in it. Dionysius Alexandrinus was about the year 240 a person of great name in the Church for piety and learning, who had wont to avail himself much against heretics by being conversant in their books; until a certain presbyter laid it scrupulously to his conscience, how he durst venture himself among those defiling volumes. The worthy man, loath to give offence, fell into a new debate with himself what was to be thought; when suddenly a vision sent from God (it is his own epistle that so avers it) confirmed him in these words: *Read any books whatever come to thy hands, for thou art sufficient both to judge aright, and to examine each matter*. To this revelation he assented the sooner, as he confesses, because it was answerable to that of the Apostle to the Thessalonians, *Prove all things, hold fast that which is good*. And he might have added another remarkable saying of the same author: *To the pure, all things are pure*; not only meats and drinks, but all kind of knowledge whether of good or evil; the knowledge cannot defile, nor consequently the books, if the will and conscience be not defiled.

For books are as meats and viands are; some of good, some of evil substance; and yet God, in that unapocryphal vision, said without exception, *Rise, Peter, kill and eat*, leaving the choice to each man's discretion. Wholesome meats to a vitiated stomach differ little or nothing from unwholesome; and best books to a naughty mind are not unappliable to occasions of evil. Bad meats will scarce breed good nourishment in the healthiest concoction; but herein the difference is of bad books, that they to a discreet and judicious reader serve in many respects to discover, to confute, to forewarn, and to illustrate. Whereof what better witness can ye expect I should produce, than one of your own now sitting in Parliament, the chief of learned men reputed in this land, Mr. Selden; whose volume of natural and national laws proves, not only by great authorities brought together, but by exquisite reasons and theorems almost mathematically demonstrative, that all opinions, yea errors, known, read, and collated, are of main service and assistance toward the speedy attainment of what is truest. I conceive, therefore, that when God did enlarge the universal diet of man's body, saving ever the rules of temperance, he then also, as before, left arbitrary the dieting and repasting of our minds; as wherein every mature man might have to exercise his own leading capacity.

How great a virtue is temperance, how much of moment through the whole life of man! Yet God commits the managing so great a trust, without particular law or prescription, wholly to the demeanour of every grown man. And therefore when he himself tabled the Jews from heaven, that omer, which was every man's daily portion of manna, is computed to have been more than might have well sufficed the heartiest feeder thrice as many meals. For those actions which enter into a man, rather than issue out of him, and therefore defile not, God uses not to captivate under a perpetual childhood of prescription, but trusts him with the gift of reason to be his own chooser; there were but little work left for preaching, if law and compulsion should grow so fast upon those things which heretofore were governed only by exhortation. Solomon informs us, that much reading is a weariness to the flesh; but neither he nor other inspired author tells us that such or such reading is unlawful: yet certainly had God thought good to limit us herein, it had been much more expedient to have told us what was unlawful than what was wearisome. As for the burning of those Ephesian books by St. Paul's converts; 'tis replied the books were magic, the Syriac so renders them. It was a private act, a voluntary act, and leaves us to a voluntary imitation: the men in remorse burnt those books which were their own; the magistrate by this example is not appointed; these men practised the books, another might perhaps have read them in some sort usefully.

Good and evil we know in the field of this world grow up together almost inseparably; and the knowledge of good is so involved and interwoven with the knowledge of evil, and in so many cunning resemblances hardly to be discerned, that those confused seeds which were imposed upon Psyche as an incessant labour to cull out, and sort asunder, were not more intermixed. It was from out the rind of one apple tasted, that the knowledge of good and evil, as two twins cleaving together, leaped forth into the world. And perhaps this is that doom which Adam fell into of knowing good and evil, that is to say of knowing good by evil. As therefore the state of man now is; what wisdom can there be to choose, what continence to forbear without the knowledge of evil? He that can apprehend and consider vice with all her baits and seeming pleasures, and yet abstain, and yet distinguish, and yet prefer that which is truly better, he is the true warfaring Christian.

I cannot praise a fugitive and cloistered virtue, unexercised and unbreathed, that never sallies out and sees her adversary, but slinks out of the race, where that immortal garland is to be run for, not without dust and heat. Assuredly we bring not innocence into the world, we bring impurity much rather; that which purifies us is trial, and trial is by what is contrary. That virtue therefore which is but a youngling in the contemplation of evil, and knows not the utmost that vice promises to her followers, and rejects it, is but a blank virtue, not a pure; her whiteness is but an excremental whiteness. Which was the reason why our sage and serious poet Spenser, whom I dare be known to think a better teacher than Scotus or Aquinas, describing true temperance under the person of Guion, brings him in with his palmer through the cave of Mammon, and the bower of earthly bliss, that he might see and know, and yet abstain. Since therefore the knowledge and survey of vice is in this world so necessary to the constituting of human virtue, and the scanning of error to the confirmation of truth, how can we more safely, and with less danger, scout into the regions of sin and falsity than by reading all manner of tractates and hearing all manner of reason? And this is the benefit which may be had of books promiscuously read.

But of the harm that may result hence three kinds are usually reckoned. First, is feared the infection that may spread; but then all human learning and controversy in religious points must remove out of the world, yea the Bible itself; for that ofttimes relates blasphemy not nicely, it describes the carnal sense of wicked men not unelegantly, it brings in holiest men passionately murmuring against Providence through all the arguments of Epicurus: in other great disputes it answers dubiously and darkly to the common reader. And ask a Talmudist what ails the modesty of his marginal Keri, that Moses and all the prophets cannot persuade him to pronounce the textual Chetiv. For these causes we all know the Bible itself put by the Papist into the first rank of prohibited books. The ancientest fathers must be next removed, as Clement of Alexandria, and that Eusebian book of Evangelic preparation, transmitting our ears through a hoard of heathenish obscenities to receive the Gospel. Who finds not that Irenaeus, Epiphanius, Jerome, and others discover more heresies than they well confute, and that oft for heresy which is the truer opinion?

Nor boots it to say for these, and all the heathen writers of greatest infection, if it must be thought so, with whom is bound up the life of human learning, that they writ in an unknown tongue, so long as we are sure those languages are known as well to the worst of men, who are both most able and most diligent to instil the poison they suck, first into the courts of princes, acquainting them with the choicest delights and criticisms of sin. As perhaps did that Petronius whom Nero called his Arbiter, the master of his revels; and the notorious ribald of Arezzo, dreaded and yet dear to the Italian courtiers.

I name not him for posterity's sake, whom Henry VIII. named in merriment his vicar of hell. By which compendious way all the contagion that foreign books can infuse will find a passage to the people far easier and shorter than an Indian voyage, though it could be sailed either by the north of Cataio eastward, or of Canada westward, while our Spanish licensing gags the English press never so severely.

But on the other side that infection which is from books of controversy in religion is more doubtful and dangerous to the learned than to the ignorant; and yet those books must be permitted untouched by the licenser. It will be hard to instance where any ignorant man hath been ever seduced by papistical book in English, unless it were commended and expounded to him by some of that clergy: and indeed all such tractates, whether false or true, are as the prophecy of Isaiah was to the eunuch, not to be *understood without a guide*. But of our priests and doctors how many have been corrupted by studying the comments of Jesuits and Sorbonists, and how fast they could transfuse that corruption into the people, our experience is both late and sad. It is not forgot, since the acute and distinct Arminius was perverted merely by the perusing of a nameless discourse written at Delft, which at first he took in hand to confute.

Seeing, therefore, that those books, and those in great abundance, which are likeliest to taint both life and doctrine, cannot be suppressed without the fall of learning and of all ability in disputation, and that these books of either sort are most and soonest catching to the learned, from whom to the common people whatever is heretical or dissolute may quickly be conveyed, and that evil manners are as perfectly learnt without books a thousand other ways which cannot be stopped, and evil doctrine not with books can propagate, except a teacher guide, which he might also do without writing, and so beyond prohibiting, I am not able to unfold, how this cautelous enterprise of licensing can be exempted from the number of vain and impossible attempts. And he who were pleasantly disposed could not well avoid to liken it to the exploit of that gallant man who thought to pound up the crows by shutting his park gate.

Besides another inconvenience, if learned men be the first receivers out of books and dispreaders both of vice and error, how shall the licensers themselves be confided in, unless we can confer upon them, or they assume to themselves above all others in the land, the grace of infallibility and uncorruptedness? And again, if it be true that a wise man, like a good refiner, can gather gold out of the drossiest volume, and that a fool will be a fool with the best book, yea or without book; there is no reason that we should deprive a wise man of any advantage to his wisdom, while we seek to restrain from a fool, that which being restrained will be no hindrance to his folly. For if there should be so much exactness always used to keep that from him which is unfit for his reading, we should in the judgment of Aristotle not only, but of Solomon and of our Saviour, not vouchsafe him good precepts, and by consequence not willingly admit him to good books; as being certain that a wise man will make better use of an idle pamphlet, than a fool will do of sacred Scripture.

'Tis next alleged we must not expose ourselves to temptations without necessity, and next to that, not employ our time in vain things. To both these objections one answer will serve, out of the grounds already laid, that to all men such books are not temptations, nor vanities, but useful drugs and materials wherewith to temper and compose effective and strong medicines, which man's life cannot want. The rest, as children and childish men, who have not the art to qualify and prepare these working minerals, well may be exhorted to forbear, but hindered forcibly they cannot be by all the licensing that Sainted Inquisition could ever yet contrive. Which is what I promised to deliver next: that this order of licensing conduces nothing to the end for which it was framed; and hath almost prevented me by being clear already while thus much hath been explaining. See the ingenuity of Truth, who, when she gets a free and willing hand, opens herself faster than the pace of method and discourse can overtake her.

It was the task which I began with, to show that no nation, or well-instituted state, if they valued books at all, did ever use this way of licensing; and it might be answered, that this is a piece of prudence lately discovered. To which I return, that as it was a thing slight and obvious to think on, so if it had been difficult to find out, there wanted not among them long since who suggested such a course; which they not following, leave us a pattern of their judgment that it was not the not knowing, but the not approving, which was the cause of their not using it.

Plato, a man of high authority, indeed, but least of all for his Commonwealth, in the book of his Laws, which no city ever yet received, fed his fancy by making many edicts to his airy burgomasters, which they who otherwise admire him wish had been rather buried and excused in the genial cups of an Academic night sitting. By which laws he seems to tolerate no kind of learning but by unalterable decree, consisting most of practical traditions, to the attainment whereof a library of smaller bulk than his own Dialogues would be abundant. And there also enacts, that no poet should so much as read to any private man what he had written, until the judges and law-keepers had seen it, and allowed it. But that Plato meant this law peculiarly to that commonwealth which he had imagined, and to no other, is evident. Why was he not else a lawgiver to himself, but a transgressor, and to be expelled by his own magistrates; both for the wanton epigrams and dialogues which he made, and his perpetual reading of Sophron Mimus and Aristophanes, books of grossest infamy, and also for commending the latter of them, though he were the malicious libeller of his chief friends, to be read by the tyrant Dionysius, who had little need of such trash to spend his time on? But that he knew this licensing of poems had reference and dependence to many other provisos there set down in his fancied republic, which in this world could have no place: and so neither he himself, nor any magistrate or city, ever imitated that course, which, taken apart from those other collateral injunctions, must needs be vain and fruitless. For if they fell upon one kind of strictness, unless their care were equal to regulate all other things of like aptness to corrupt the mind, that single endeavour they knew would be but a fond labour; to shut and fortify one gate against corruption, and be necessitated to leave others round about wide open.

If we think to regulate printing, thereby to rectify manners, we must regulate all recreations and pastimes, all that is delightful to man. No music must be heard, no song be set or sung, but what is grave and Doric. There must be licensing dancers, that no gesture, motion, or deportment be taught our youth but what by their allowance shall be thought honest; for such Plato was provided of. It will ask more than the work of twenty licensers to examine all the lutes, the violins, and the guitars in every house; they must not be suffered to prattle as they do, but must be licensed what they may say. And who shall silence all the airs and madrigals that whisper softness in chambers? The windows also, and the balconies must be thought on; there are shrewd books, with dangerous frontispieces, set to sale; who shall prohibit them, shall twenty licensers? The villages also must have their visitors to inquire what lectures the bagpipe and the rebeck reads, even to the ballatry and the gamut of every municipal fiddler, for these are the countryman's Arcadias, and his Monte Mayors.

Next, what more national corruption, for which England hears ill abroad, than household gluttony: who shall be the rectors of our daily rioting? And what shall be done to inhibit the multitudes that frequent those houses where drunkenness is sold and harboured? Our garments also should be referred to the licensing of some more sober workmasters to see them cut into a less wanton garb. Who shall regulate all the mixed conversation of our youth, male and female together, as is the fashion of this country? Who shall still appoint what shall be discoursed, what presumed, and no further? Lastly, who shall forbid and separate all idle resort, all evil company? These things will be, and must be; but how they shall be least hurtful, how least enticing, herein consists the grave and governing wisdom of a state.

To sequester out of the world into Atlantic and Utopian polities, which never can be drawn into use, will not mend our condition; but to ordain wisely as in this world of evil, in the midst whereof God hath placed us unavoidably. Nor is it Plato's licensing of books will do this, which necessarily pulls along with it so many other kinds of licensing, as will make us all both ridiculous and weary, and yet frustrate; but those unwritten, or at least unconstraining, laws of virtuous education, religious and civil nurture, which Plato there mentions as the bonds and ligaments of the commonwealth, the pillars and the sustainers of every written statute; these they be which will bear chief sway in such matters as these, when all licensing will be easily eluded. Impunity and remissness, for certain, are the bane of a commonwealth; but here the great art lies, to discern in what the law is to bid restraint and punishment, and in what things persuasion only is to work.

If every action, which is good or evil in man at ripe years, were to be under pittance and prescription and compulsion, what were virtue but a name, what praise could be then due to well-doing, what gramercy to be sober, just, or continent? Many there be that complain of divine Providence for suffering Adam to transgress; foolish tongues! When God gave him reason, he gave him freedom to choose, for reason is but choosing; he had been else a mere artificial Adam, such an Adam as he is in the motions. We ourselves esteem not of that obedience, or love, or gift, which is of force: God therefore left him free, set before him a provoking object, ever almost in his eyes; herein consisted his merit, herein the right of his reward, the praise of his abstinence. Wherefore did he create passions within us, pleasures round about us, but that these rightly tempered are the very ingredients of virtue?

They are not skilful considerers of human things, who imagine to remove sin by removing the matter of sin; for, besides that it is a huge heap increasing under the very act of diminishing, though some part of it may for a time be withdrawn from some persons, it cannot from all, in such a universal thing as books are; and when this is done, yet the sin remains entire. Though ye take from a covetous man all his treasure, he has yet one jewel left, ye cannot bereave him of his covetousness. Banish all objects of lust, shut up all youth into the severest discipline that can be exercised in any hermitage, ye cannot make them chaste, that came not thither so; such great care and wisdom is required to the right managing of this point. Suppose we could expel sin by this means; look how much we thus expel of sin, so much we expel of virtue: for the matter of them both is the same; remove that, and ye remove them both alike.

This justifies the high providence of God, who, though he command us temperance, justice, continence, yet pours out before us, even to a profuseness, all desirable things, and gives us minds that can wander beyond all limit and satiety. Why should we then affect a rigour contrary to the manner of God and of nature, by abridging or scanting those means, which books freely permitted are, both to the trial of virtue and the exercise of truth? It would be better done, to learn that the law must needs be frivolous, which goes to restrain things, uncertainly and yet equally working to good and to evil. And were I the chooser, a dram of well-doing should be preferred before many times as much the forcible hindrance of evil-doing. For God sure esteems the growth and completing of one virtuous person more than the restraint of ten vicious.

And albeit whatever thing we hear or see, sitting, walking, ravelling, or conversing, may be fitly called our book, and is of the same effect that writings are, yet grant the thing to be prohibited were only books, it appears that this Order hitherto is far insufficient to the end which it intends. Do we not see, not once or oftener, but weekly, that continued court-libel against the Parliament and City, printed, as the wet sheets can witness, and dispersed among us, for all that licensing can do? Yet this is the prime service a man would think, wherein this Order should give proof of itself. If it were executed, you'll say. But certain, if execution be remiss or blindfold now, and in this particular, what will it be hereafter and in other books? If then the Order shall not be vain and frustrate, behold a new labour, Lords and Commons, ye must repeal and proscribe all scandalous and unlicensed books already printed and divulged; after ye have drawn them up into a list, that all may know which are condemned, and which not; and ordain that no foreign books be delivered out of custody, till they have been read over. This office will require the whole time of not a few overseers, and those no vulgar men. There be also books which are partly useful and excellent, partly culpable and pernicious; this work will ask as many more officials, to make expurgations and expunctions, that the commonwealth of learning be not damnified. In fine, when the multitude of books increase upon their hands, ye must be fain to catalogue all those printers who are found frequently offending, and forbid the importation of their whole suspected typography. In a word, that this your Order may be exact and not deficient, ye must reform it perfectly according to the model of Trent and Seville, which I know ye abhor to do.

Yet though ye should condescend to this, which God forbid, the Order still would be but fruitless and defective to that end whereto ye meant it. If to prevent sects and schisms, who is so unread or so uncatechized in story, that hath not heard of many sects refusing books as a hindrance, and preserving their doctrine unmixed for many ages, only by unwritten traditions? The Christian faith, for that was once a schism, is not unknown to have spread all over Asia ere any Gospel or Epistle was seen in writing. If the amendment of manners be aimed at, look into Italy and Spain, whether those places be one scruple the better, the honester, the wiser, the chaster, since all the inquisitional rigour that hath been executed upon books.

Another reason, whereby to make it plain that this Order will miss the end it seeks, consider by the quality which ought to be in every licenser. It cannot be denied but that he who is made judge to sit upon the birth or death of books, whether they may be wafted into this world or not, had need to be a man above the common measure, both studious, learned, and judicious; there may be else no mean mistakes in the censure of what is passable or not; which is also no mean injury. If he be of such worth as behooves him, there cannot be a more tedious and unpleasing journey-work, a greater loss of time levied upon his head, than to be made the perpetual reader of unchosen books and pamphlets, ofttimes huge volumes. There is no book that is acceptable unless at certain seasons; but to be enjoined the reading of that at all times, and in a hand scarce legible, whereof three pages would not down at any time in the fairest print, is an imposition which I cannot believe how he that values time and his own studies, or is but of a sensible nostril, should be able to endure. In this one thing I crave leave of the present licensers to be pardoned for so thinking; who doubtless took this office up, looking on it through their obedience to the Parliament, whose command perhaps made all things seem easy and unlaborious to them; but that this short trial hath wearied them out already, their own expressions and excuses to them who make so many journeys to solicit their licence are testimony enough. Seeing therefore those who now possess the employment by all evident signs wish themselves well rid of it; and that no man of worth, none that is not a plain unthrift of his own hours, is ever likely to succeed them, except he mean to put himself to the salary of a press corrector; we may easily foresee what kind of licensers we are to expect hereafter, either ignorant, imperious, and remiss, or basely pecuniary. This is what I had to show, wherein this Order cannot conduce to that end whereof it bears the intention.

I lastly proceed from the no good it can do, to the manifest hurt it causes, in being first the greatest discouragement and affront that can be offered to learning, and to learned men.

It was the complaint and lamentation of prelates, upon every least breath of a motion to remove pluralities, and distribute more equally Church revenues, that then all learning would be for ever dashed and discouraged. But as for that opinion, I never found cause to think that the tenth part of learning stood or fell with the clergy: nor could I ever but hold it for a sordid and unworthy speech of any churchman who had a competency left him. If therefore ye be loath to dishearten utterly and discontent, not the mercenary crew of false pretenders to learning, but the free and ingenuous sort of such as evidently were born to study, and love learning for itself, not for lucre or any other end but the service of God and of truth, and perhaps that lasting fame and perpetuity of praise which God and good men have consented shall be the reward of those whose published labours advance the good of mankind; then know that, so far to distrust the judgment and the honesty of one who hath but a common repute in learning, and never yet offended, as not to count him fit to print his mind without a tutor and examiner, lest he should drop a schism, or something of corruption, is the greatest displeasure and indignity to a free and knowing spirit that can be put upon him.

What advantage is it to be a man, over it is to be a boy at school, if we have only escaped the ferula to come under the fescue of an Imprimatur; if serious and elaborate writings, as if they were no more than the theme of a grammar-lad under his pedagogue, must not be uttered without the cursory eyes of a temporizing and extemporizing licenser? He who is not trusted with his own actions, his drift not being known to be evil, and standing to the hazard of law and penalty, has no great argument to think himself reputed in the Commonwealth wherein he was born for other than a fool or a foreigner. When a man writes to the world, he summons up all his reason and deliberation to assist him; he searches, meditates, is industrious, and likely consults and confers with his judicious friends; after all which done he takes himself to be informed in what he writes, as well as any that writ before him. If, in this the most consummate act of his fidelity and ripeness, no years, no industry, no former proof of his abilities can bring him to that state of maturity, as not to be still mistrusted and suspected, unless he carry all his considerate diligence, all his midnight watchings and expense of Palladian oil, to the hasty view of an unleisured licenser, perhaps much his younger, perhaps far his inferior in judgment, perhaps one who never knew the labour of book-writing, and if he be not repulsed or slighted, must appear in print like a puny with his guardian, and his censor's hand on the back of his title to be his bail and surety that he is no idiot or seducer, it cannot be but a dishonour and derogation to the author, to the book, to the privilege and dignity of learning.

And what if the author shall be one so copious of fancy, as to have many things well worth the adding come into his mind after licensing, while the book is yet under the press, which not seldom happens to the best and diligentest writers, and that perhaps a dozen times in one book? The printer dares not go beyond his licensed copy, so often then must the author trudge to his leave-giver that those his new insertions may be viewed; and many a jaunt will be made, ere that licenser, for it must be the same man, can either be found, or found at leisure; meanwhile either the press must stand still, which is no small damage, or the author lose his accuratest thoughts, and send the book forth worse than he had made it, which to a diligent writer is the greatest melancholy and vexation that can befall.

And how can a man teach with authority, which is the life of teaching; how can he be a doctor in his book as he ought to be, or else had better be silent, whenas all he teaches, all he delivers, is but under the tuition, under the correction of his patriarchal licenser to blot or alter what precisely accords not with the hidebound humour which he calls his judgment? When every acute reader, upon the first sight of a pedantic licence, will be ready with these like words to ding the book a quoit's distance from him. I hate a pupil teacher, I endure not an instructor that comes to me under the wardship of an overseeing fist. I know nothing of the licenser, but that I have his own hand here for his arrogance; who shall warrant me his judgment? The State, sir, replies the stationer, but has a quick return: The State shall be my governors, but not my critics; they may be mistaken in the choice of a licenser, as easily as this licenser may be mistaken in an author; this is some common stuff; and he might add from Sir Francis Bacon, *That such authorized books are but the language of the times.* For though a licenser should happen to be judicious more than ordinary, which will be a great jeopardy of the next succession, yet his very office and his commission enjoins him to let pass nothing but what is vulgarly received already.

Nay, which is more lamentable, if the work of any deceased author, though never so famous in his lifetime and even to this day, come to their hands for licence to be printed, or reprinted, if there be found in his book one sentence of a venturous edge, uttered in the height of zeal (and who knows whether it might not be the dictate of a divine spirit?) yet not suiting with every low decrepit humour of their own, though it were Knox himself, the reformer of a kingdom, that spake it, they will not pardon him their dash: the sense of that great man shall to all posterity be lost, for the fearfulness or the presumptuous rashness of a perfunctory licenser. And to what an author this violence hath been lately done, and in what book of greatest consequence to be faithfully published, I could now instance, but shall forbear till a more convenient season.

Yet if these things be not resented seriously and timely by them who have the remedy in their power, but that such iron-moulds as these shall have authority to gnaw out the choicest periods of exquisitest books, and to commit such a treacherous fraud against the orphan remainders of worthiest men after death, the more sorrow will belong to that hapless race of men, whose misfortune it is to have understanding. Henceforth let no man care to learn, or care to be more than worldly-wise; for certainly in higher matters to be ignorant and slothful, to be a common steadfast dunce, will be the only pleasant life, and only in request.

And as it is a particular disesteem of every knowing person alive, and most injurious to the written labours and monuments of the dead, so to me it seems an undervaluing and vilifying of the whole nation. I cannot set so light by all the invention, the art, the wit, the grave and solid judgment which is in England, as that it can be comprehended in any twenty capacities how good soever, much less that it should not pass except their superintendence be over it, except it be sifted and strained with their strainers, that it should be uncurrent without their manual stamp. Truth and understanding are not such wares as to be monopolized and traded in by tickets and statutes and standards. We must not think to make a staple commodity of all the knowledge in the land, to mark and licence it like our broadcloth and our woolpacks. What is it but a servitude like that imposed by the Philistines, not to be allowed the sharpening of our own axes and coulters, but we must repair from all quarters to twenty licensing forges? Had anyone written and divulged erroneous things and scandalous to honest life, misusing and forfeiting the esteem had of his reason among men, if after conviction this only censure were adjudged him that he should never henceforth write but what were first examined by an appointed officer, whose hand should be annexed to pass his credit for him that now he might be safely read; it could not be apprehended less than a disgraceful punishment. Whence to include the whole nation, and those that never yet thus offended, under such a diffident and suspectful prohibition, may plainly be understood what a disparagement it is. So much the more, whenas debtors and delinquents may walk abroad without a keeper, but unoffensive books must not stir forth without a visible jailer in their title.

Nor is it to the common people less than a reproach; for if we be so jealous over them, as that we dare not trust them with an English pamphlet, what do we but censure them for a giddy, vicious, and ungrounded people; in such a sick and weak state of faith and discretion, as to be able to take nothing down but through the pipe of a licenser? That this is care or love of them, we cannot pretend, whenas, in those popish places where the laity are most hated and despised, the same strictness is used over them. Wisdom we cannot call it, because it stops but one breach of licence, nor that neither: whenas those corruptions, which it seeks to prevent, break in faster at other doors which cannot be shut.

And in conclusion it reflects to the disrepute of our ministers also, of whose labours we should hope better, and of the proficiency which their flock reaps by them, than that after all this light of the Gospel which is, and is to be, and all this continual preaching, they should still be frequented with such an unprincipled, unedified and laic rabble, as that the whiff of every new pamphlet should stagger them out of their catechism and Christian walking. This may have much reason to discourage the ministers when such a low conceit is had of all their exhortations, and the benefiting of their hearers, as that they are not thought fit to be turned loose to three sheets of paper without a licenser; that all the sermons, all the lectures preached, printed, vented in such numbers, and such volumes, as have now well nigh made all other books unsaleable, should not be armour enough against one single Enchiridion, without the castle of St. Angelo of an Imprimatur.

And lest some should persuade ye, Lords and Commons, that these arguments of learned men's discouragement at this your Order are mere flourishes, and not real, I could recount what I have seen and heard in other countries, where this kind of inquisition tyrannizes; when I have sat among their learned men, for that honour I had, and been counted happy to be born in such a place of philosophic freedom, as they supposed England was, while themselves did nothing but bemoan the servile condition into which learning amongst them was brought; that this was it which had damped the glory of Italian wits; that nothing had been there written now these many years but flattery and fustian. There it was that I found and visited the famous Galileo, grown old, a prisoner to the Inquisition, for thinking in astronomy otherwise than the Franciscan and Dominican licensers thought. And though I knew that England then was groaning loudest under the prelatical yoke, nevertheless I took it as a pledge of future happiness, that other nations were so persuaded of her liberty. Yet was it beyond my hope that those worthies were then breathing in her air, who should be her leaders to such a deliverance, as shall never be forgotten by any revolution of time that this world hath to finish. When that was once begun, it was as little in my fear that what words of complaint I heard among learned men of other parts uttered against the Inquisition, the same I should hear by as learned men at home, uttered in time of Parliament against an order of licensing; and that so generally that, when I had disclosed myself a companion of their discontent, I might say, if without envy, that he whom an honest quaestorship had endeared to the Sicilians was not more by them importuned against Verres, than the favourable opinion which I had among many who honour ye, and are known and respected by ye, loaded me with entreaties and persuasions, that I would not despair to lay together that which just reason should bring into my mind, toward the removal of an undeserved thraldom upon learning. That this is not therefore the disburdening of a particular fancy, but the common grievance of all those who had prepared their minds and studies above the vulgar pitch to advance truth in others, and from others to entertain it, thus much may satisfy.

And in their name I shall for neither friend nor foe conceal what the general murmur is; that if it come to inquisitioning again and licensing, and that we are so timorous of ourselves, and so suspicious of all men, as to fear each book and the shaking of every leaf, before we know what the contents are; if some who but of late were little better than silenced from preaching shall come now to silence us from reading, except what they please, it cannot be guessed what is intended by some but a second tyranny over learning: and will soon put it out of controversy, that bishops and presbyters are the same to us, both name and thing. That those evils of prelaty, which before from five or six and twenty sees were distributively charged upon the whole people, will now light wholly upon learning, is not obscure to us: whenas now the pastor of a small unlearned parish on the sudden shall be exalted archbishop over a large diocese of books, and yet not remove, but keep his other cure too, a mystical pluralist. He who but of late cried down the sole ordination of every novice Bachelor of Art, and denied sole jurisdiction over the simplest parishioner, shall now at home in his private chair assume both these over worthiest and excellentest books and ablest authors that write them.

This is not, ye Covenants and Protestations that we have made! this is not to put down prelaty; this is but to chop an episcopacy; this is but to translate the Palace Metropolitan from one kind of dominion into another; this is but an old canonical sleight of commuting our penance. To startle thus betimes at a mere unlicensed pamphlet will after a while be afraid of every conventicle, and a while after will make a conventicle of every Christian meeting. But I am certain that a State governed by the rules of justice and fortitude, or a Church built and founded upon the rock of faith and true knowledge, cannot be so pusillanimous. While things are yet not constituted in religion, that freedom of writing should be restrained by a discipline imitated from the prelates and learnt by them from the Inquisition, to shut us up all again into the breast of a licenser, must needs give cause of doubt and discouragement to all learned and religious men.

Who cannot but discern the fineness of this politic drift, and who are the contrivers; that while bishops were to be baited down, then all presses might be open; it was the people's birthright and privilege in time of Parliament, it was the breaking forth of light. But now, the bishops abrogated and voided out of the Church, as if our Reformation sought no more but to make room for others into their seats under another name, the episcopal arts begin to bud again, the cruse of truth must run no more oil, liberty of printing must be enthralled again under a prelatical commission of twenty, the privilege of the people nullified, and, which is worse, the freedom of learning must groan again, and to her old fetters: all this the Parliament yet sitting. Although their own late arguments and defences against the prelates might remember them, that this obstructing violence meets for the most part with an event utterly opposite to the end which it drives at: instead of suppressing sects and schisms, it raises them and invests them with a reputation. *The punishing of wits enhances their authority*, saith the Viscount St. Albans; *and a forbidden writing is thought to be a certain spark of truth that flies up in the faces of them who seek to tread it out*. This Order, therefore, may prove a nursing-mother to sects, but I shall easily show how it will be a step-dame to Truth: and first by disenabling us to the maintenance of what is known already.

Well knows he who uses to consider, that our faith and knowledge thrives by exercise, as well as our limbs and complexion. Truth is compared in Scripture to a streaming fountain; if her waters flow not in a perpetual progression, they sicken into a muddy pool of conformity and tradition. A man may be a heretic in the truth; and if he believe things only because his pastor says so, or the Assembly so determines, without knowing other reason, though his belief be true, yet the very truth he holds becomes his heresy.

There is not any burden that some would gladlier post off to another than the charge and care of their religion. There be—who knows not that there be?—of Protestants and professors who live and die in as arrant an implicit faith as any lay Papist of Loretto. A wealthy man, addicted to his pleasure and to his profits, finds religion to be a traffic so entangled, and of so many piddling accounts, that of all mysteries he cannot skill to keep a stock going upon that trade. What should he do? fain he would have the name to be religious, fain he would bear up with his neighbours in that. What does he therefore, but resolves to give over toiling, and to find himself out some factor, to whose care and credit he may commit the whole managing of his religious affairs; some divine of note and estimation that must be. To him he adheres, resigns the whole warehouse of his religion, with all the locks and keys, into his custody; and indeed makes the very person of that man his religion; esteems his associating with him a sufficient evidence and commendatory of his own piety. So that a man may say his religion is now no more within himself, but is become a dividual movable, and goes and comes near him, according as that good man frequents the house. He entertains him, gives him gifts, feasts him, lodges him; his religion comes home at night, prays, is liberally supped, and sumptuously laid to sleep; rises, is saluted, and after the malmsey, or some well-spiced brewage, and better breakfasted than he whose morning appetite would have gladly fed on green figs between Bethany and Jerusalem, his religion walks abroad at eight, and leaves his kind entertainer in the shop trading all day without his religion.

Another sort there be who, when they hear that all things shall be ordered, all things regulated and settled, nothing written but what passes through the custom-house of certain publicans that have the tonnaging and poundaging of all free-spoken truth, will straight give themselves up into your hands, make 'em and cut 'em out what religion ye please: there be delights, there be recreations and jolly pastimes that will fetch the day about from sun to sun, and rock the tedious year as in a delightful dream. What need they torture their heads with that which others have taken so strictly and so unalterably into their own purveying? These are the fruits which a dull ease and cessation of our knowledge will bring forth among the people. How goodly and how to be wished were such an obedient unanimity as this, what a fine conformity would it starch us all into! Doubtless a staunch and solid piece of framework, as any January could freeze together.

Nor much better will be the consequence even among the clergy themselves. It is no new thing never heard of before, for a parochial minister, who has his reward and is at his Hercules' pillars in a warm benefice, to be easily inclinable, if he have nothing else that may rouse up his studies, to finish his circuit in an English Concordance and a topic folio, the gatherings and savings of a sober graduateship, a Harmony and a Catena; treading the constant round of certain common doctrinal heads, attended with their uses, motives, marks, and means, out of which, as out of an alphabet, or sol-fa, by forming and transforming, joining and disjoining variously, a little bookcraft, and two hours' meditation, might furnish him unspeakably to the performance of more than a weekly charge of sermoning: not to reckon up the infinite helps of interlinearies, breviaries, synopses, and other loitering gear. But as for the multitude of sermons ready printed and piled up, on every text that is not difficult, our London trading St. Thomas in his vestry, and add to boot St. Martin and St. Hugh, have not within their hallowed limits more vendible ware of all sorts ready made: so that penury he never need fear of pulpit provision, having where so plenteously to refresh his magazine. But if his rear and flanks be not impaled, if his back door be not secured by the rigid licenser, but that a bold book may now and then issue forth and give the assault to some of his old collections in their trenches, it will concern him then to keep waking, to stand in watch, to set good guards and sentinels about his received opinions, to walk the round and counter-round with his fellow inspectors, fearing lest any of his flock be seduced, who also then would be better instructed, better exercised and disciplined. And God send that the fear of this diligence, which must then be used, do not make us affect the laziness of a licensing Church.

For if we be sure we are in the right, and do not hold the truth guiltily, which becomes not, if we ourselves condemn not our own weak and frivolous teaching, and the people for an untaught and irreligious gadding rout, what can be more fair than when a man judicious, learned, and of a conscience, for aught we know, as good as theirs that taught us what we know, shall not privily from house to house, which is more dangerous, but openly by writing publish to the world what his opinion is, what his reasons, and wherefore that which is now thought cannot be sound? Christ urged it as wherewith to justify himself, that he preached in public; yet writing is more public than preaching; and more easy to refutation, if need be, there being so many whose business and profession merely it is to be the champions of truth; which if they neglect, what can be imputed but their sloth, or unability?

Thus much we are hindered and disinured by this course of licensing, toward the true knowledge of what we seem to know. For how much it hurts and hinders the licensers themselves in the calling of their ministry, more than any secular employment, if they will discharge that office as they ought, so that of necessity they must neglect either the one duty or the other, I insist not, because it is a particular, but leave it to their own conscience, how they will decide it there.

There is yet behind of what I purposed to lay open, the incredible loss and detriment that this plot of licensing puts us to; more than if some enemy at sea should stop up all our havens and ports and creeks, it hinders and retards the importation of our richest merchandise, truth; nay, it was first established and put in practice by Antichristian malice and mystery on set purpose to extinguish, if it were possible, the light of Reformation, and to settle falsehood; little differing from that policy wherewith the Turk upholds his Alcoran, by the prohibition of printing. 'Tis not denied, but gladly confessed, we are to send our thanks and vows to Heaven louder than most of nations, for that great measure of truth which we enjoy, especially in those main points between us and the Pope, with his appurtenances the prelates: but he who thinks we are to pitch our tent here, and have attained the utmost prospect of reformation that the mortal glass wherein we contemplate can show us, till we come to beatific vision, that man by this very opinion declares that he is yet far short of truth.

Truth indeed came once into the world with her divine Master, and was a perfect shape most glorious to look on: but when he ascended, and his Apostles after him were laid asleep, then straight arose a wicked race of deceivers, who, as that story goes of the Egyptian Typhon with his conspirators, how they dealt with the good Osiris, took the virgin Truth, hewed her lovely form into a thousand pieces, and scattered them to the four winds. From that time ever since, the sad friends of Truth, such as durst appear, imitating the careful search that Isis made for the mangled body of Osiris, went up and down gathering up limb by limb, still as they could find them. We have not yet found them all, Lords and Commons, nor ever shall do, till her Master's second coming; he shall bring together every joint and member, and shall mould them into an immortal feature of loveliness and perfection. Suffer not these licensing prohibitions to stand at every place of opportunity, forbidding and disturbing them that continue seeking, that continue to do our obsequies to the torn body of our martyred saint.

We boast our light; but if we look not wisely on the sun itself, it smites us into darkness. Who can discern those planets that are oft combust, and those stars of brightest magnitude that rise and set with the sun, until the opposite motion of their orbs bring them to such a place in the firmament, where they may be seen evening or morning? The light which we have gained was given us, not to be ever staring on, but by it to discover onward things more remote from our knowledge. It is not the unfrocking of a priest, the unmitring of a bishop, and the removing him from off the presbyterian shoulders, that will make us a happy nation. No, if other things as great in the Church, and in the rule of life both economical and political, be not looked into and reformed, we have looked so long upon the blaze that Zuinglius and Calvin hath beaconed up to us, that we are stark blind. There be who perpetually complain of schisms and sects, and make it such a calamity that any man dissents from their maxims. 'Tis their own pride and ignorance which causes the disturbing, who neither will hear with meekness, nor can convince; yet all must be suppressed which is not found in their Syntagma. They are the troublers, they are the dividers of unity, who neglect and permit not others to unite those dissevered pieces which are yet wanting to the body of Truth. To be still searching what we know not by what we know, still closing up truth to truth as we find it (for all her body is homogeneal and proportional), this is the golden rule in theology as well as in arithmetic, and makes up the best harmony in a Church; not the forced and outward union of cold, and neutral, and inwardly divided minds.

Lords and Commons of England! consider what nation it is whereof ye are, and whereof ye are the governors: a nation not slow and dull, but of a quick, ingenious and piercing spirit, acute to invent, subtle and sinewy to discourse, not beneath the reach of any point the highest that human capacity can soar to. Therefore the studies of learning in her deepest sciences have been so ancient and so eminent among us, that writers of good antiquity and ablest judgment have been persuaded that even the school of Pythagoras and the Persian wisdom took beginning from the old philosophy of this island. And that wise and civil Roman, Julius Agricola, who governed once here for Caesar, preferred the natural wits of Britain before the laboured studies of the French. Nor is it for nothing that the grave and frugal Transylvanian sends out yearly from as far as the mountainous borders of Russia, and beyond the Hercynian wilderness, not their youth, but their staid men, to learn our language and our theologic arts.

Yet that which is above all this, the favour and the love of Heaven, we have great argument to think in a peculiar manner propitious and propending towards us. Why else was this nation chosen before any other, that out of her, as out of Sion, should be proclaimed and sounded forth the first tidings and trumpet of Reformation to all Europe? And had it not been the obstinate perverseness of our prelates against the divine and admirable spirit of Wickliff, to suppress him as a schismatic and innovator, perhaps neither the Bohemian Huss and Jerome, no nor the name of Luther or of Calvin, had been ever known: the glory of reforming all our neighbours had been completely ours. But now, as our obdurate clergy have with violence demeaned the matter, we are become hitherto the latest and the backwardest scholars, of whom God offered to have made us the teachers. Now once again by all concurrence of signs, and by the general instinct of holy and devout men, as they daily and solemnly express their thoughts, God is decreeing to begin some new and great period in his Church, even to the reforming of Reformation itself: what does he then but reveal himself to his servants, and as his manner is, first to his Englishmen? I say, as his manner is, first to us, though we mark not the method of his counsels, and are unworthy.

Behold now this vast city: a city of refuge, the mansion house of liberty, encompassed and surrounded with his protection; the shop of war hath not there more anvils and hammers waking, to fashion out the plates and instruments of armed justice in defence of beleaguered truth, than there be pens and heads there, sitting by their studious lamps, musing, searching, revolving new notions and ideas wherewith to present, as with their homage and their fealty, the approaching Reformation: others as fast reading, trying all things, assenting to the force of reason and convincement. What could a man require more from a nation so pliant and so prone to seek after knowledge? What wants there to such a towardly and pregnant soil, but wise and faithful labourers, to make a knowing people, a nation of prophets, of sages, and of worthies? We reckon more than five months yet to harvest; there need not be five weeks; had we but eyes to lift up, the fields are white already.

Where there is much desire to learn, there of necessity will be much arguing, much writing, many opinions; for opinion in good men is but knowledge in the making. Under these fantastic terrors of sect and schism, we wrong the earnest and zealous thirst after knowledge and understanding which God hath stirred up in this city. What some lament of, we rather should rejoice at, should rather praise this pious forwardness among men, to reassume the ill-deputed care of their religion into their own hands again. A little generous prudence, a little forbearance of one another, and some grain of charity might win all these diligences to join, and unite in one general and brotherly search after truth; could we but forgo this prelatical tradition of crowding free consciences and Christian liberties into canons and precepts of men. I doubt not, if some great and worthy stranger should come among us, wise to discern the mould and temper of a people, and how to govern it, observing the high hopes and aims, the diligent alacrity of our extended thoughts and reasonings in the pursuance of truth and freedom, but that he would cry out as Pyrrhus did, admiring the Roman docility and courage: If such were my Epirots, I would not despair the greatest design that could be attempted, to make a Church or kingdom happy.

Yet these are the men cried out against for schismatics and sectaries; as if, while the temple of the Lord was building, some cutting, some squaring the marble, others hewing the cedars, there should be a sort of irrational men who could not consider there must be many schisms and many dissections made in the quarry and in the timber, ere the house of God can be built. And when every stone is laid artfully together, it cannot be united into a continuity, it can but be contiguous in this world; neither can every piece of the building be of one form; nay rather the perfection consists in this, that, out of many moderate varieties and brotherly dissimilitudes that are not vastly disproportional, arises the goodly and the graceful symmetry that commends the whole pile and structure.

Let us therefore be more considerate builders, more wise in spiritual architecture, when great reformation is expected. For now the time seems come, wherein Moses the great prophet may sit in heaven rejoicing to see that memorable and glorious wish of his fulfilled, when not only our seventy elders, but all the Lord's people, are become prophets. No marvel then though some men, and some good men too perhaps, but young in goodness, as Joshua then was, envy them. They fret, and out of their own weakness are in agony, lest these divisions and subdivisions will undo us. The adversary again applauds, and waits the hour: when they have branched themselves out, saith he, small enough into parties and partitions, then will be our time. Fool! he sees not the firm root, out of which we all grow, though into branches: nor will beware until he see our small divided maniples cutting through at every angle of his ill-united and unwieldy brigade. And that we are to hope better of all these supposed sects and schisms, and that we shall not need that solicitude, honest perhaps, though over-timorous, of them that vex in this behalf, but shall laugh in the end at those malicious applauders of our differences, I have these reasons to persuade me.

First, when a city shall be as it were besieged and blocked about, her navigable river infested, inroads and incursions round, defiance and battle oft rumoured to be marching up even to her walls and suburb trenches, that then the people, or the greater part, more than at other times, wholly taken up with the study of highest and most important matters to be reformed, should be disputing, reasoning, reading, inventing, discoursing, even to a rarity and admiration, things not before discoursed or written of, argues first a singular goodwill, contentedness and confidence in your prudent foresight and safe government, Lords and Commons; and from thence derives itself to a gallant bravery and well-grounded contempt of their enemies, as if there were no small number of as great spirits among us, as his was, who when Rome was nigh besieged by Hannibal, being in the city, bought that piece of ground at no cheap rate, whereon Hannibal himself encamped his own regiment.

Next, it is a lively and cheerful presage of our happy success and victory. For as in a body, when the blood is fresh, the spirits pure and vigorous, not only to vital but to rational faculties, and those in the acutest and the pertest operations of wit and subtlety, it argues in what good plight and constitution the body is; so when the cheerfulness of the people is so sprightly up, as that it has not only wherewith to guard well its own freedom and safety, but to spare, and to bestow upon the solidest and sublimest points of controversy and new invention, it betokens us not degenerated, nor drooping to a fatal decay, but casting off the old and wrinkled skin of corruption to outlive these pangs and wax young again, entering the glorious ways of truth and prosperous virtue, destined to become great and honourable in these latter ages. Methinks I see in my mind a noble and puissant nation rousing herself like a strong man after sleep, and shaking her invincible locks: methinks I see her as an eagle mewing her mighty youth, and kindling her undazzled eyes at the full midday beam; purging and unscaling her long-abused sight at the fountain itself of heavenly radiance; while the whole noise of timorous and flocking birds, with those also that love the twilight, flutter about, amazed at what she means, and in their envious gabble would prognosticate a year of sects and schisms.

What should ye do then? should ye suppress all this flowery crop of knowledge and new light sprung up and yet springing daily in this city? Should ye set an oligarchy of twenty engrossers over it, to bring a famine upon our minds again, when we shall know nothing but what is measured to us by their bushel? Believe it, Lords and Commons, they who counsel ye to such a suppressing do as good as bid ye suppress yourselves; and I will soon show how. If it be desired to know the immediate cause of all this free writing and free speaking, there cannot be assigned a truer than your own mild and free and humane government. It is the liberty, Lords and Commons, which your own valorous and happy counsels have purchased us, liberty which is the nurse of all great wits; this is that which hath rarefied and enlightened our spirits like the influence of heaven; this is that which hath enfranchised, enlarged and lifted up our apprehensions, degrees above themselves.

Ye cannot make us now less capable, less knowing, less eagerly pursuing of the truth, unless ye first make yourselves, that made us so, less the lovers, less the founders of our true liberty. We can grow ignorant again, brutish, formal and slavish, as ye found us; but you then must first become that which ye cannot be, oppressive, arbitrary and tyrannous, as they were from whom ye have freed us. That our hearts are now more capacious, our thoughts more erected to the search and expectation of greatest and exactest things, is the issue of your own virtue propagated in us; ye cannot suppress that, unless ye reinforce an abrogated and merciless law, that fathers may dispatch at will their own children. And who shall then stick closest to ye, and excite others? not he who takes up arms for coat and conduct, and his four nobles of Danegelt. Although I dispraise not the defence of just immunities, yet love my peace better, if that were all. Give me the liberty to know, to utter, and to argue freely according to conscience, above all liberties.

What would be best advised, then, if it be found so hurtful and so unequal to suppress opinions for the newness or the unsuitableness to a customary acceptance, will not be my task to say. I only shall repeat what I have learned from one of your own honourable number, a right noble and pious lord, who, had he not sacrificed his life and fortunes to the Church and Commonwealth, we had not now missed and bewailed a worthy and undoubted patron of this argument. Ye know him, I am sure; yet I for honour's sake, and may it be eternal to him, shall name him, the Lord Brook. He writing of episcopacy, and by the way treating of sects and schisms, left ye his vote, or rather now the last words of his dying charge, which I know will ever be of dear and honoured regard with ye, so full of meekness and breathing charity, that next to his last testament, who bequeathed love and peace to his disciples, I cannot call to mind where I have read or heard words more mild and peaceful. He there exhorts us to hear with patience and humility those, however they be miscalled, that desire to live purely, in such a use of God's ordinances, as the best guidance of their conscience gives them, and to tolerate them, though in some disconformity to ourselves. The book itself will tell us more at large, being published to the world, and dedicated to the Parliament by him who, both for his life and for his death, deserves that what advice he left be not laid by without perusal.

And now the time in special is, by privilege to write and speak what may help to the further discussing of matters in agitation. The temple of Janus with his two controversial faces might now not unsignificantly be set open. And though all the winds of doctrine were let loose to play upon the earth, so Truth be in the field, we do injuriously, by licensing and prohibiting, to misdoubt her strength. Let her and Falsehood grapple; who ever knew Truth put to the worse, in a free and open encounter? Her confuting is the best and surest suppressing. He who hears what praying there is for light and clearer knowledge to be sent down among us, would think of other matters to be constituted beyond the discipline of Geneva, framed and fabricked already to our hands. Yet when the new light which we beg for shines in upon us, there be who envy and oppose, if it come not first in at their casements. What a collusion is this, whenas we are exhorted by the wise man to use diligence, *to seek for wisdom as for hidden treasures* early and late, that another order shall enjoin us to know nothing but by statute? When a man hath been labouring the hardest labour in the deep mines of knowledge, hath furnished out his findings in all their equipage: drawn forth his reasons as it were a battle ranged: scattered and defeated all objections in his way; calls out his adversary into the plain, offers him the advantage of wind and sun, if he please, only that he may try the matter by dint of argument: for his opponents then to skulk, to lay ambushments, to keep a narrow bridge of licensing where the challenger should pass, though it be valour enough in soldiership, is but weakness and cowardice in the wars of Truth.

For who knows not that Truth is strong, next to the Almighty? She needs no policies, nor stratagems, nor licensings to make her victorious, those are the shifts and the defences that error uses against her power. Give her but room, and do not bind her when she sleeps, for then she speaks not true, as the old Proteus did, who spake oracles only when he was caught and bound, but then rather she turns herself into all shapes, except her own, and perhaps tunes her voice according to the time, as Micaiah did before Ahab, until she be adjured into her own likeness. Yet is it not impossible that she may have more shapes than one. What else is all that rank of things indifferent, wherein Truth may be on this side or on the other, without being unlike herself? What but a vain shadow else is the abolition of *those ordinances, that hand-writing nailed to the cross*? What great purchase is this Christian liberty which Paul so often boasts of? His doctrine is, that he who eats or eats not, regards a day or regards it not, may do either to the Lord. How many other things might be tolerated in peace, and left to conscience, had we but charity, and were it not the chief stronghold of our hypocrisy to be ever judging one another?

I fear yet this iron yoke of outward conformity hath left a slavish print upon our necks; the ghost of a linen decency yet haunts us. We stumble and are impatient at the least dividing of one visible congregation from another, though it be not in fundamentals; and through our forwardness to suppress, and our backwardness to recover any enthralled piece of truth out of the gripe of custom, we care not to keep truth separated from truth, which is the fiercest rent and disunion of all. We do not see that, while we still affect by all means a rigid external formality, we may as soon fall again into a gross conforming stupidity, a stark and dead congealment of *wood and hay and stubble*, forced and frozen together, which is more to the sudden degenerating of a Church than many subdichotomies of petty schisms.

Not that I can think well of every light separation, or that all in a Church is to be expected *gold and silver and precious stones*: it is not possible for man to sever the wheat from the tares, the good fish from the other fry; that must be the Angels' ministry at the end of mortal things. Yet if all cannot be of one mind—as who looks they should be?—this doubtless is more wholesome, more prudent, and more Christian, that many be tolerated, rather than all compelled. I mean not tolerated popery, and open superstition, which, as it extirpates all religions and civil supremacies, so itself should be extirpate, provided first that all charitable and compassionate means be used to win and regain the weak and the misled; that also which is impious or evil absolutely either against faith or manners no law can possibly permit, that intends not to unlaw itself; but those neighbouring differences, or rather indifferences, are what I speak of, whether in some point of doctrine or of discipline, which, though they may be many, yet need not interrupt *the unity of Spirit*, if we could but find among us *the bond of peace*.

In the meanwhile if any one would write, and bring his helpful hand to the slow-moving Reformation which we labour under, if Truth have spoken to him before others, or but seemed at least to speak, who hath so bejesuited us that we should trouble that man with asking licence to do so worthy a deed? and not consider this, that if it come to prohibiting, there is not aught more likely to be prohibited than truth itself; whose first appearance to our eyes, bleared and dimmed with prejudice and custom, is more unsightly and unplausible than many errors, even as the person is of many a great man slight and contemptible to see to. And what do they tell us vainly of new opinions, when this very opinion of theirs, that none must be heard but whom they like, is the worst and newest opinion of all others; and is the chief cause why sects and schisms do so much abound, and true knowledge is kept at distance from us; besides yet a greater danger which is in it.

For when God shakes a kingdom with strong and healthful commotions to a general reforming, 'tis not untrue that many sectaries and false teachers are then busiest in seducing; but yet more true it is, that God then raises to his own work men of rare abilities, and more than common industry, not only to look back and revise what hath been taught heretofore, but to gain further and go on some new enlightened steps in the discovery of truth. For such is the order of God's enlightening his Church, to dispense and deal out by degrees his beam, so as our earthly eyes may best sustain it.

Neither is God appointed and confined, where and out of what place these his chosen shall be first heard to speak; for he sees not as man sees, chooses not as man chooses, lest we should devote ourselves again to set places, and assemblies, and outward callings of men; planting our faith one while in the old Convocation house, and another while in the Chapel at Westminster; when all the faith and religion that shall be there canonized is not sufficient without plain convincement, and the charity of patient instruction to supple the least bruise of conscience, to edify the meanest Christian, who desires to walk in the Spirit, and not in the letter of human trust, for all the number of voices that can be there made; no, though Harry VII himself there, with all his liege tombs about him, should lend them voices from the dead, to swell their number.

And if the men be erroneous who appear to be the leading schismatics, what withholds us but our sloth, our self-will, and distrust in the right cause, that we do not give them gentle meetings and gentle dismissions, that we debate not and examine the matter thoroughly with liberal and frequent audience; if not for their sakes, yet for our own? seeing no man who hath tasted learning, but will confess the many ways of profiting by those who, not contented with stale receipts, are able to manage and set forth new positions to the world. And were they but as the dust and cinders of our feet, so long as in that notion they may yet serve to polish and brighten the armoury of Truth, even for that respect they were not utterly to be cast away. But if they be of those whom God hath fitted for the special use of these times with eminent and ample gifts, and those perhaps neither among the priests nor among the Pharisees, and we in the haste of a precipitant zeal shall make no distinction, but resolve to stop their mouths, because we fear they come with new and dangerous opinions, as we commonly forejudge them ere we understand them; no less than woe to us, while, thinking thus to defend the Gospel, we are found the persecutors.

There have been not a few since the beginning of this Parliament, both of the presbytery and others, who by their unlicensed books, to the contempt of an Imprimatur, first broke that triple ice clung about our hearts, and taught the people to see day: I hope that none of those were the persuaders to renew upon us this bondage which they themselves have wrought so much good by contemning. But if neither the check that Moses gave to young Joshua, nor the countermand which our Saviour gave to young John, who was so ready to prohibit those whom he thought unlicensed, be not enough to admonish our elders how unacceptable to God their testy mood of prohibiting is; if neither their own remembrance what evil hath abounded in the Church by this let of licensing, and what good they themselves have begun by transgressing it, be not enough, but that they will persuade and execute the most Dominican part of the Inquisition over us, and are already with one foot in the stirrup so active at suppressing, it would be no unequal distribution in the first place to suppress the suppressors themselves: whom the change of their condition hath puffed up, more than their late experience of harder times hath made wise.

And as for regulating the press, let no man think to have the honour of advising ye better than yourselves have done in that Order published next before this, "that no book be printed, unless the printer's and the author's name, or at least the printer's, be registered." Those which otherwise come forth, if they be found mischievous and libellous, the fire and the executioner will be the timeliest and the most effectual remedy that man's prevention can use. For this authentic Spanish policy of licensing books, if I have said aught, will prove the most unlicensed book itself within a short while; and was the immediate image of a Star Chamber decree to that purpose made in those very times when that Court did the rest of those her pious works, for which she is now fallen from the stars with Lucifer. Whereby ye may guess what kind of state prudence, what love of the people, what care of religion or good manners there was at the contriving, although with singular hypocrisy it pretended to bind books to their good behaviour. And how it got the upper hand of your precedent Order so well constituted before, if we may believe those men whose profession gives them cause to inquire most, it may be doubted there was in it the fraud of some old patentees and monopolizers in the trade of bookselling; who under pretence of the poor in their Company not to be defrauded, and the just retaining of each man his several copy, which God forbid should be gainsaid, brought divers glossing colours to the House, which were indeed but colours, and serving to no end except it be to exercise a superiority over their neighbours; men who do not therefore labour in an honest profession to which learning is indebted, that they should be made other men's vassals. Another end is thought was aimed at by some of them in procuring by petition this Order, that, having power in their hands, malignant books might the easier scape abroad, as the event shows.

But of these sophisms and elenchs of merchandise I skill not. This I know, that errors in a good government and in a bad are equally almost incident; for what magistrate may not be misinformed, and much the sooner, if liberty of printing be reduced into the power of a few? But to redress willingly and speedily what hath been erred, and in highest authority to esteem a plain advertisement more than others have done a sumptuous bride, is a virtue (honoured Lords and Commons) answerable to your highest actions, and whereof none can participate but greatest and wisest men.

CRITICISM

Classic Criticism of *Paradise Lost*

ANDREW MARVELL

On Mr. Milton's *Paradise Lost* (1674)†

When I beheld the poet blind, yet bold,
In slender book his vast design unfold,
Messiah crowned, God's reconciled decree,
Rebelling Angels, the Forbidden Tree,
Heaven, Hell, Earth, Chaos, all; the argument
Held me a while, misdoubting his intent
That he would ruin (for I saw him strong)
The sacred truths to fable and old song,
(So Sampson groped the temple's posts in spite)
The world o'erwhelming to revenge his sight.
  Yet as I read, soon growing less severe,
I liked his project, the success did fear;
Through that wide field how he his way should find
O'er which lame faith leads understanding blind;
Lest he perplexed the things he would explain,
And what was easy he should render vain.
  Or if a work so infinite he spanned,
Jealous I was that some less skilful hand
(Such as disquiet always what is well,
And by ill imitating would excel)
Might hence presume the whole Creation's day
To change in scenes, and show it in a play.
  Pardon me, Mighty Poet, nor despise
My causeless, yet not impious, surmise.
But I am now convinced that none will dare
Within thy labours to pretend a share.
Thou hast not missed one thought that could be fit,
And all that was improper dost omit:

† From *The Complete Poems*, ed. Elizabeth Donno (Penguin Books, 1996).

So that no room is here for writers left,
But to detect their ignorance or theft.
That majesty which through thy work doth reign
Draws the devout, deterring the profane.
And things divine thou treat'st of in such state
As them preserves, and thee, inviolate.
At once delight and horror on us seize,
Thou sing'st with so much gravity and ease;
And above human flight dost soar aloft,
With plume so strong, so equal, and so soft.
The bird named from that paradise you sing
So never flags, but always keeps on wing.
  Where couldst thou words of such a compass find?
Whence furnish such a vast expense of mind?
Just heaven thee, like Tiresias, to requite,
Rewards with prophecy thy loss of sight.
  Well mightst thou scorn thy readers to allure
With tinkling rhyme, of thine own sense secure;
While the *Town-Bayes* writes all the while and spells,
And like a pack-horse tires without his bells.
Their fancies like our bushy points appear,
The poets tag them; we for fashion wear.
I too, transported by the mode, offend,
And while I meant to *praise* thee must *commend*.
Thy verse created like thy theme sublime,
In number, weight, and measure, needs not rhyme.

JOHN DRYDEN

Epigram†

Three poets in three distant ages born,
Greece, Italy, and England did adorn.
The first in loftiness of soul surpassed,
The next in majesty, in both the last.
The force of nature could no further go;
To make a third she joined the other two.

† "Under Mr. Milton's Picture before His *Paradise Lost*." From *Poems and Fables*, ed. James Kinsley (London: Oxford UP, 1962).

From Preface to Second Miscellany (1685)†

Imitation is a nice point, and there are few poets who deserve to be models in all they write. Milton's "Paradise Lost" is admirable; but am I therefore bound to maintain, that there are no flats amongst his elevations, when it is evident he creeps along sometimes for above an hundred lines together? Cannot I admire the height of his invention, and the strength of his expression, without defending his antiquated words, and the perpetual harshness of their sound? It is as much commendation as a man can hear, to own him excellent; all beyond it is idolatry.

JOSEPH ADDISON

From Spectator 297 (February 9, 1712)‡

* * *

There is another Objection against *Milton*'s Fable, which is indeed almost the same with the former, tho' placed in a different Light, namely, That the Hero in the *Paradise Lost* is unsuccessful, and by no means a Match for his Enemies. This gave occasion to Mr. *Dryden*'s Reflection, that the Devil was in reality *Milton*'s Hero. I think I have obviated this Objection in my first Paper. The *Paradise Lost* is an Epic, or a Narrative Poem, and he that looks for an Hero in it, searches for that which *Milton* never intended; but if he will needs fix the Name of an Hero upon any Person in it, 'tis certainly the *Messiah* who is the Hero, both in the Principal Action, and in the chief Episodes. Paganism could not furnish out a real Action for a Fable greater than that of the *Iliad* or *Æneid*, and therefore an Heathen could not form a higher Notion of a Poem than one of that kind, which they call an Heroic. Whether *Milton*'s is not of a sublimer Nature I will not presume to determine: It is sufficient that I shew there is in the *Paradise Lost* all the Greatness of Plan, Regularity of Design, and masterly Beauties which we discover in *Homer* and *Virgil*.

* * *

Milton's Sentiments and Ideas were so wonderfully Sublime, that it would have been impossible for him to have represented them in their full Strength and Beauty, without having recourse to these For-

† From *Works*, ed. Scott and Saintsbury, vol. 12.
‡ From *Spectator*, ed. Donald Bond, vol. 3 (Oxford: Clarendon, 1965).

eign Assistances. Our Language sunk under him, and was unequal to that greatness of Soul, which furnished him with such glorious Conceptions.

A second Fault in his Language is, that he often affects a kind of Jingle in his Words, as in the following Passages, and many others:

And brought into the World *a* World of *woe*.
. . . *Begirt th' Almighty throne*
Beseeching *or* besieging . . .
This tempted *our* attempt . . .
At one Slight bound *high overleapt all* bound.

I know there are Figures for this kind of Speech, that some of the greatest Ancients have been guilty of it, and that *Aristotle* himself has given it a place in his Rhetorick among the Beauties of that Art. But as it is in its self poor and trifling, it is I think at present universally exploded by all the Masters of Polite Writing.

The last Fault which I shall take notice of in *Milton's* Stile, is the frequent use of what the Learned call *Technical Words*, or Terms of Art. It is one of the great Beauties of Poetry, to make hard things intelligible, and to deliver what is abstruse of it self in such easy Language as may be understood by ordinary Readers: Besides that the Knowledge of a Poet should rather seem born with him, or inspired than drawn from Books and Systems. I have often wondered how Mr. *Dryden* could translate a Passage out of[a] *Virgil* after the following manner.

Tack to the Larboard, and stand off to Sea.
Veer Star-board Sea and Land . . .

Milton makes use of *Larboard* in the same manner. When he is upon Building he mentions *Doric Pillars, Pilasters, Cornice, Freeze, Architrave*. When he talks of Heavenly Bodies, you meet with *Eccliptick*, and *Eccentric*, the *trepidation*, *Stars dropping from the Zenith, Rays culminating from the Equator*. To which might be added many Instances of the like kind in several other Arts and Sciences.

I shall in my next Papers give an Account of the many particular Beauties in *Milton*, which would have been too long to insert under those general Heads I have already treated of, and with which I intend to conclude this Piece of Criticism.

From Spectator 303 (February 16, 1712)†

* * *

But there is no single Passage in the whole Poem worked up to a greater Sublimity, than that wherein his Person [the Devil] is described in those celebrated Lines:

. . . He, above the rest
In shape and gesture proudly eminent
Stood like a Tower, &c.

His Sentiments are every way answerable to his Character, and suitable to a created Being of the most exalted and most depraved Nature. Such is that in which he takes Possession of his Place of Torments.

. . . Hail Horrors, hail
Infernal World, and thou profoundest Hell
Receive thy new Possessor, one who brings
A mind not to be changed by place or time.

And afterwards,

. . . Here at least
We shall be free; th' Almighty hath not built
Here for his envy, will not drive us hence:
Here we may reign secure, and in my choice
To reign is worth ambition, tho' in Hell:
Better to reign in Hell, than serve in Heaven.

Amidst those Impieties which this Enraged Spirit utters in other places of the Poem, the Author has taken care to introduce none that is not big with absurdity, and incapable of shocking a Religious Reader; his Words, as the Poet describes them, bearing only a *Semblance of Worth, not Substance*. He is likewise with great Art described as owning his Adversary to be Almighty. Whatever perverse Interpretation he puts on the Justice, Mercy, and other Attributes of the Supreme Being, he frequently confesses his Omnipotence, that being the Perfection he was forced to allow him, and the only Consideration which could support his Pride under the Shame of his Defeat.

Nor must I here omit that beautiful Circumstance of his bursting out in Tears, upon his Survey of those innumerable Spirits whom he had involved in the same Guilt and Ruin with himself.

. . . He now prepared
To speak; whereat their doubled ranks they bend

† From *Spectator*, ed. Donald Bond, vol.3 (Oxford: Clarendon, 1965).

From wing to wing, and half enclose him round
With all his Peers: Attention held them mute.
Thrice he assay'd, and thrice in spite of Scorn
Tears, such as Angels weep, burst forth . . .

* * *

VOLTAIRE

From Candide (1759)†

[Candide and his companion Martin visit the palace of Pococurante ("Cares for Little"), a Venetian nobleman. In the library, Pococurante delivers himself of negative opinions on many great authors. The last author to be entertainingly abused is Milton. But in the numerous inaccuracies of this attack Pococurante lives up to his name. Voltaire is satirizing literary criticism of the day. His own *Essay on Epic Poetry* (1728) praises Milton in the highest terms.]

Seeing a volume of Milton's *Paradise Lost*, Candide asked Pococurante if he did not regard at least this author as a great man. "Who?" said Pococurante, "that barbarian who made a long commentary in ten books of turgid verse on the first chapter of Genesis? That clumsy imitator of the Greeks who disfigured Creation, and who, while Moses showed the Eternal Being producing the world by his word, has the Messiah take a huge pair of compasses out of his heavenly cupboard and trace out his work in advance? Can I possibly esteem an author who spoils both the Hell and the devil of Tasso, who disguises Lucifer sometimes as a toad and sometimes as a pygmy? Who makes him go over a hundred times the same stale arguments and theological disputes? Who takes up in all seriousness a comic episode in Ariosto and makes devils fire off canons in Heaven? Neither I nor anyone else in Italy could take pleasure in such pathetic extravagances! The union of Sin and Death, and the snakes Sin gives birth to, would cause any man of sensibility to vomit. And the long description of a hospital is good for no one except a gravedigger, or a grave-robber! This poem, which is obscure, bizarre, and disgusting, was despised from its birth in its own country, and I concur."

† Translated by the editor.

From Essay upon the Civil Wars of France . . . And also upon the Epick Poetry of the European Nations from Homer to Milton (1727)†

* * *

What Milton so boldly undertook, he performed with superior strength of judgment, and with an imagination productive of beauties not dreamed of before him. The meanness (if there is any) of some parts of the subject is lost in the immensity of the poetical invention.

* * *

I have often admired how barren the subject appears and how fruitful it grows in his hands.

The *Paradise Lost* is the only poem wherein are to be found in a perfect degree that uniformity which satisfies the mind and that variety which pleases the imagination.

* * *

The heathens always, the Jews often, and our Christian Priests sometimes, represent God as a tyrant infinitely powerful. But the God of Milton is always a creator, a father, and a judge; nor is his vengeance jarring with his mercy, nor his predeterminations repugnant to the liberty of man. There are the pictures which lift up indeed the soul of the reader. Milton in that point as well as in many others is as far above the ancient poets as the Christian religion is above the heathen fables.

* * *

It is observable that in all other poems love is represented as a vice; in Milton only 'tis a virtue. The pictures he draws of it are naked as the persons he speaks of, and as venerable. He removes with a chaste hand the veil which covers everywhere else the enjoyments of that passion. There is softness, tenderness and warmth without lasciviousness; the poet transports himself and us into that state of innocent happiness in which Adam and Eve continued for a short time.

* * *

† From *Le Bossu & Voltaire on the Epic*, ed. Stuart Curran (1970).

SAMUEL JOHNSON

From Lives of the English Poets (1779)†

* * *

I am now to examine *Paradise Lost*, a poem which, considered with respect to design, may claim the first place, and with respect to performance the second, among the productions of the human mind.

By the general consent of criticks the first praise of genius is due to the writer of an epick poem, as it requires an assemblage of all the powers which are singly sufficient for other compositions. Poetry is the art of uniting pleasure with truth, by calling imagination to the help of reason. Epick poetry undertakes to teach the most important truths by the most pleasing precepts, and therefore relates some great event in the most affecting manner. History must supply the writer with the rudiments of narration, which he must improve and exalt by a nobler art, must animate by dramatick energy, and diversify by retrospection and anticipation; morality must teach him the exact bounds and different shades of vice and virtue; from policy and the practice of life he has to learn the discriminations of character and the tendency of the passions, either single or combined; and physiology must supply him with illustrations and images. To put these materials to poetical use is required an imagination capable of painting nature and realizing fiction. Nor is he yet a poet till he has attained the whole extension of his language, distinguished all the delicacies of phrase, and all the colours of words, and learned to adjust their different sounds to all the varieties of metrical modulation.

Bossu is of opinion that the poet's first work is to find a *moral*, which his fable is afterwards to illustrate and establish. This seems to have been the process only of Milton: the moral of other poems is incidental and consequent; in Milton's only it is essential and intrinsick. His purpose was the most useful and the most arduous: 'to vindicate the ways of God to man'; to shew the reasonableness of religion, and the necessity of obedience to the Divine Law.

* * *

The subject of an epick poem is naturally an event of great importance. That of Milton is not the destruction of a city, the conduct of a colony, or the foundation of an empire. His subject is the fate of worlds, the revolutions of heaven and of earth; rebellion against the Supreme King raised by the highest order of created beings; the over-

† From vol. 1, ed. George Birkbeck Hill (Oxford: Clarendon Press, 1995).

throw of their host and the punishment of their crime; the creation of a new race of reasonable creatures; their original happiness and innocence, their forfeiture of immortality, and their restoration to hope and peace.

* * *

It is justly remarked by Addison that this poem has, by the nature of its subject, the advantage above all others, that it is universally and perpetually interesting. All mankind will, through all ages, bear the same relation to Adam and to Eve, and must partake of that good and evil which extend to themselves.

* * *

The thoughts which are occasionally called forth in the progress are such as could only be produced by an imagination in the highest degree fervid and active, to which materials were supplied by incessant study and unlimited curiosity. The heat of Milton's mind might be said to sublimate his learning, to throw off into his work the spirit of science, unmingled with its grosser parts.

* * *

The characteristick quality of his poem is sublimity. He sometimes descends to the elegant, but his element is the great. He can occasionally invest himself with grace; but his natural port is gigantick loftiness[1]. He can please when pleasure is required; but it is his peculiar power to astonish.

He seems to have been well acquainted with his own genius, and to know what it was that Nature had bestowed upon him more bountifully than upon others; the power of displaying the vast, illuminating the splendid, enforcing the awful, darkening the gloomy, and aggravating the dreadful: he therefore chose a subject on which too much could not be said, on which he might tire his fancy without the censure of extravagance.

The appearances of nature and the occurrences of life did not satiate his appetite of greatness. To paint things as they are requires a minute attention, and employs the memory rather than the fancy. Milton's delight was to sport in the wide regions of possibility; reality was a scene too narrow for his mind. He sent his faculties out upon discovery, into worlds where only imagination can travel, and delighted to form new modes of existence, and furnish sentiment and action to superior beings, to trace the counsels of hell, or accompany the choirs of heaven.

But he could not be always in other worlds: he must sometimes

1. Algarotti terms it *gigantesca sublimità Miltoniana*. JOHNSON.

revisit earth, and tell of things visible and known. When he cannot raise wonder by the sublimity of his mind he gives delight by its fertility.

* * *

But original deficience cannot be supplied. The want of human interest is always felt. *Paradise Lost* is one of the books which the reader admires and lays down, and forgets to take up again. None ever wished it longer than it is. Its perusal is a duty rather than a pleasure. We read Milton for instruction, retire harassed and overburdened, and look elsewhere for recreation; we desert our master, and seek for companions.

* * *

Milton's allegory of Sin and Death is undoubtedly faulty. Sin is indeed the mother of Death, and may be allowed to be the portress of hell; but when they stop the journey of Satan, a journey described as real, and when Death offers him battle, the allegory is broken. That Sin and Death should have shewn the way to hell might have been allowed; but they cannot facilitate the passage by building a bridge, because the difficulty of Satan's passage is described as real and sensible, and the bridge ought to be only figurative. The hell assigned to the rebellious spirits is described as not less local than the residence of man. It is placed in some distant part of space, separated from the regions of harmony and order by a chaotick waste and an unoccupied vacuity; but Sin and Death worked up a 'mole of aggregated soil,' cemented with asphaltus; a work too bulky for ideal architects.

This unskilful allegory appears to me one of the greatest faults of the poem; and to this there was no temptation, but the author's opinion of its beauty.

* * *

Through all his greater works there prevails an uniform peculiarity of *Diction*, a mode and cast of expression which bears little resemblance to that of any former writer, and which is so far removed from common use that an unlearned reader when he first opens his book finds himself surprised by a new language.

This novelty has been, by those who can find nothing wrong in Milton, imputed to his laborious endeavours after words suitable to the grandeur of his ideas. 'Our language,' says Addison, 'sunk under him.' But the truth is, that both in prose and verse, he had formed his style by a perverse and pedantick principle. He was desirous to use English words with a foreign idiom. This in all his prose is discovered and condemned, for there judgement operates freely, neither softened by the beauty nor awed by the dignity of his thoughts; but such is the power of his poetry that his call is obeyed without resistance, the reader feels himself in captivity to a higher and a nobler mind, and criticism sinks in admiration.

* * *

The highest praise of genius is original invention. Milton cannot be said to have contrived the structure of an epick poem, and therefore owes reverence to that vigour and amplitude of mind to which all generations must be indebted for the art of poetical narration, for the texture of the fable, the variation of incidents, the interposition of dialogue, and all the stratagems that surprise and enchain attention. But of all the borrowers from Homer Milton is perhaps the least indebted. He was naturally a thinker for himself, confident of his own abilities and disdainful of help or hindrance; he did not refuse admission to the thoughts or images of his predecessors, but he did not seek them. From his contemporaries he neither courted nor received support; there is in his writings nothing by which the pride of other authors might be gratified or favour gained, no exchange of praise nor solicitation of support. His great works were performed under discountenance and in blindness, but difficulties vanished at his touch; he was born for whatever is arduous; and his work is not the greatest of heroick poems, only because it is not the first.

* * *

FRANÇOIS-RENÉ, VICOMTE DE CHATEAUBRIAND

From Sketches of English Literature (1836)

* * *

Who ever wrote like this? What poet ever spoke such language? How miserable seem all modern compositions beside these strong and magnificent conceptions!

* * *

There is, in the poem, something which at first sight appears unaccountable: the infernal republic attempts to overthrow the celestial monarchy; Milton, though his sentiments are wholly republican, invariably ascribes justice and victory to the Almighty! The reason of this is that the poet was swayed by his religious opinions. In accordance with the Independents, he desired a theocratic republic, a hierarchical liberty, subject only to the dominion of Heaven; he had represented Cromwell as the lieutenant-general of God and the protector of the republic:—

> Cromwell, our chief of men, who, through a cloud
> Not of war only, but detractions rude,
> Guided by faith and matchless fortitude,
> To peace and truth thy glorious way hast plough'd,
> And on the neck of crowned fortune proud
> Hast rear'd God's trophies, and his works pursued,
> While Darwen stream, with blood of Scots imbrued,
> And Dunbar field resounds thy praises loud,
> And Worcester's laureat wreath. Yet much remains
> To conquer still; peace hath her victories
> No less renown'd than war: new foes arise
> Threat'ning to bind our souls, with secular chains:
> Help us to save free conscience from the paw
> Of hireling wolves, whose gospel is their maw.

Satan and his angels were pictured to Milton's imagination by the proud Presbyterians, who refused to submit to the *Saints*, Milton's own faction, of which he hailed the inspired Cromwell as the godly leader.

We discern in Milton a man of troubled spirit; still under the influence of revolutionary scenes and passions, he stood erect after the downfall of the revolution which had fled to him for shelter, and palpitated in his bosom. But the earnestness of that revolution overpowers him; religious gravity forms the counterpoise to his political agitations. Stunned, however, at the overthrow of his fondest illusions, at the dissipation of his dreams of liberty, he knows not which way to turn, but remains in a state of perplexity, even respecting religious truth.

* * *

WILLIAM BLAKE

From The Marriage of Heaven and Hell (1793)†

From The Voice of the Devil (Plates 5–6)

* * *

Those who restrain desire, do so because theirs is weak enough to be restrained; and the restrainer or Reason usurps its place & governs the unwilling.

And being restrain'd, it by degrees becomes passive, till it is only the shadow of desire.

The history of this is written in Paradise Lost, & the Governor or Reason is call'd Messiah.

And the original Archangel, or possessor of the command of the heavenly host, is call'd the Devil or Satan, and his children are call'd Sin & Death.

But in the Book of Job, Milton's Messiah is call'd Satan.

For this history has been adopted by both parties.

It indeed appear'd to reason as if Desire was cast out, but the Devil's account is, that the Messiah fell, & formed a heaven of what he stole from the Abyss.

This is shewn in the Gospel, where he prays to the Father to send the comforter, or Desire, that Reason may have Ideas to build on, the Jehovah of the Bible being no other than [the Devil *del.*] he who dwells in flaming fire.

Know that after Christ's death, he became Jehovah.

But in Milton, the Father is Destiny, the Son, a Ratio of the five senses, & the Holy-ghost, Vacuum!

Note: The reason Milton wrote in fetters when he wrote of Angels & God, and at liberty when of Devils & Hell, is because he was a true Poet and of the Devil's party without knowing it.

* * *

† From *William Blake's Writings*, vol. 1, ed. G. E. Bentley, Jr. (Oxford: Clarendon, 1978).

WILLIAM WORDSWORTH

London, 1802†

Milton! thou should'st be living at this hour:
England hath need of thee: she is a fen
Of stagnant waters: altar, sword, and pen,
Fireside, the heroic wealth of hall and bower,
Have forfeited their ancient English dower
Of inward happiness. We are selfish men;
Oh! raise us up, return to us again;
And give us manners, virtue, freedom, power.
Thy soul was like a Star, and dwelt apart:
Thou hadst a voice whose sound was like the sea:
Pure as the naked heavens, majestic, free,
So didst thou travel on life's common way,
In cheerful godliness; and yet thy heart
The lowliest duties on herself did lay.

SAMUEL TAYLOR COLERIDGE

From Lecture 4 (March 4, 1819)‡

* * *

In the mind itself purity, piety, an imagination to which neither the Past nor the Present were interesting except as far as they called forth and embraced the great Ideal, in which and for which he lived, a keen love of Truth which after many weary pursuits found an harbour in a sublime listening to the low still voice in his own spirit, and as keen a love of his Country which after disappointment, still more depressive at once expanded and sobered into a love of Man as the Probationer of Immortality, these were, these alone could be, the conditions under which such a work could be conceived, and accomplished.

* * *

Compared with the Iliad, many of the books of which might change places without any injury to the thread of the story—and 2ndly—with both the Iliad and more or less in all epic Poems whose

† From *William Wordsworth*, ed. Stephen Gill (Oxford: Oxford UP, 1984).
‡ From *Lectures 1808–1819 on Literature*, ed. R. A. Foakes (Princeton, NJ: Princeton UP, 1987).

subjects are from History, they have no *rounded* conclusion—they remain after all but a single chapter from the volume of History tho' an ornamented Chapter—. In Homer too the importance of his subject, namely, as the first effort of confederated Greece, an after thought of the critics—& the interest, such as it is, derived from the event as distinguished from the manner of representing these, languid to all but Greeks—The superiority of the Paradise Lost is obvious, but not dwelt on because it may be attributed to Christianity itself, tho' in this instance it comprehends the whole Mahometan World as well as Xtndom—and as the origin of evil, and the combat of Evil and Good, a matter of such interest to all mankind as to form the basis of all religions, and the true occasion of all Philosophy.

—Next the exquisite simplicity. It and it alone really possesses the Beginning, Middle, and End—the totality of a Poem or circle as distinguished from the ab ovo birth, parentage, &c or strait line of History.

* * *

Unassigned Lecture Notes [Milton and *Paradise Lost*]

* * *

The character of Satan is pride and sensual indulgence, finding in self the sole motive of action. It is the character so often seen *in little* on the political stage. It exhibits all the restlessness, temerity, and cunning which have marked the mighty hunters of mankind from Nimrod to Napoleon. The common fascination of men is, that these great men, as they are called, must act from some great motive. Milton has carefully marked in his Satan the intense selfishness, the alcohol of egotism, which would rather reign in hell than serve in heaven. To place this lust of self in opposition to denial of self or duty, and to show what exertions it would make, and what pains endure to accomplish its end, is Milton's particular object in the character of Satan. But around this character he has thrown a singularity of daring, a grandeur of sufferance, and a ruined splendour, which constitute the very height of poetic sublimity.

* * *

No one can rise from the perusal of this immortal poem without a deep sense of the grandeur and the purity of Milton's soul, or without feeling how susceptible of domestic enjoyments he really was, notwithstanding the discomforts which actually resulted from an apparently unhappy choice in marriage. He was, as every truly great poet has ever been, a good man; but finding it impossible to realize his own aspirations, either in religion, or politics, or society, he gave up his heart to the living spirit and light within him, and avenged himself on the world by enriching it with this record of his own transcendent ideal.

From Table Talk

[*Milton's Egotism, August 1833*]†

In the Paradise Lost—indeed in every one of his poems—it is Milton himself whom you see; his Satan, his Adam, his Raphael, almost his Eve—are all John Milton; and it is a sense of this intense egotism that gives me the greatest pleasure in reading Milton's works. The egotism of such a man is a revelation of spirit.

GEORGE GORDON, LORD BYRON

From Don Juan (1819–24)‡

From Dedication

x

If, fallen in evil days on evil tongues,
Milton appeal'd to the Avenger, Time,
If Time, the Avenger, execrates his wrongs,
And makes the word 'Miltonic' mean 'sublime,'
He deign'd not to belie his soul in songs,
Nor turn his very talent to a crime;
He did not loathe the Sire to laud the Son,
But closed the tyrant-hater he begun.

xi

Think'st thou, could he—the blind Old Man—arise
Like Samuel from the grave, to freeze once more

† From *Table Talk*, ed. Carl Woodring (Princeton, NJ: Princeton UP, 1990).
‡ From *Poetical Works*, ed. John Jump, 2nd ed. (Oxford: Oxford UP, 1970).

The blood of monarchs with his prophecies,
Or be alive again—again all hoar
With time and trials, and those helpless eyes,
And heartless daughters—worn—and pale—and poor;
Would he adore a sultan? he obey
The intellectual eunuch Castlereagh?

From Canto III

XCI

Milton's the prince of poets—so we say;
A little heavy, but no less divine:
An independent being in his day—
Learn'd, pious, temperate in love and wine;
But, his life falling into Johnson's way,
We're told this great high priest of all the Nine
Was whipt at college—a harsh sire—odd spouse,
For the first Mrs. Milton left his house.

PERCY BYSSHE SHELLEY

From the preface to Prometheus Unbound (1820)†

* * *

The only imaginary being resembling in any degree Prometheus, is Satan; and Prometheus is, in my judgement, a more poetical character than Satan because, in addition to courage and majesty and firm and patient opposition to omnipotent force, he is susceptible of being described as exempt from the taints of ambition, envy, revenge, and a desire for personal aggrandisement, which in the Hero of *Paradise Lost*, interfere with the interest. The character of Satan engenders in the mind a pernicious casuistry which leads us to weigh his faults with his wrongs and to excuse the former because the latter exceed all measure. In the minds of those who consider that magnificent fiction with a religious feeling, it engenders something worse. But Prometheus is, as it were, the type of the highest perfection of moral and intellectual nature, impelled by the purest and the truest motives to the best and noblest ends.

† From *Shelley's Poetry and Prose*, ed. Donald H. Reiman and Neil Fraistat, 2nd ed. (New York: Norton, 2002), pp. 206–7. Reprinted by permission of W. W. Norton & Company, Inc.

From A Defence of Poetry (1821)

* * *

The poetry of Dante may be considered as the bridge thrown over the stream of time, which unites the modern and antient world. The distorted notions of invisible things which Dante and his rival Milton have idealized, are merely the mask and the mantle in which these great poets walk through eternity enveloped and disguised. It is a difficult question to determine how far they were conscious of the distinction which must have subsisted in their minds between their own creeds and that of the people. Dante at least appears to wish to mark the full extent of it by placing Riphæaus, whom Virgil calls *justissimus unus*, in Paradise, and observing a most heretical caprice in his distribution of rewards and punishments. And Milton's poem contains within itself a philosophical refutation of that system of which, by a strange and natural antithesis, it has been a chief popular support. Nothing can exceed the energy and magnificence of the character of Satan as expressed in Paradise Lost. It is a mistake to suppose that he could ever have been intended for the popular personification of evil. Implacable hate, patient cunning, and a sleepless refinement of device to inflict the extremest anguish on an enemy, these things are evil; and although venial in a slave are not to be forgiven in a tyrant; although redeemed by much that ennobles his defeat in one subdued, are marked by all that dishonours his conquest in the victor. Milton's Devil as a moral being is as far superior to his God as one who perseveres in some purpose which he has conceived to be excellent in spite of adversity and torture, is to one who in the cold security of undoubted triumph inflicts the most horrible revenge upon his enemy, not from any mistaken notion of inducing him to repent of a perseverance in enmity, but with the alleged design of exasperating him to deserve new torments. Milton has so far violated the popular creed (if this shall be judged to be a violation) as to have alleged no superiority of moral virtue to his God over his Devil. And this bold neglect of a direct moral purpose is the most decisive proof of the supremacy of Milton's genius. He mingled as it were the elements of human nature, as colours upon a single pallet, and arranged them into the composition of his great picture according to the laws of epic truth; that is, according to the laws of that principle by which a series of actions of the external universe and of intelligent and ethical beings is calculated to excite the sympathy of succeeding generations of mankind. The Divina Commedia and Paradise Lost have conferred upon modern mythology a systematic form; and when change and time shall have added one more superstition to the mass of those which have arisen and decayed upon the earth, commentators will be learnedly employed in elucidating the religion of ancestral Europe, only not utterly forgotten because it will have been stamped with the eternity of genius.

* * *

WALTER SAVAGE LANDOR

From Imaginary Conversations (1846)†

* * *

Southey. In the *Paradise Lost* no principal character seems to have been intended. There is neither truth nor wit however in saying that Satan is hero of the piece, unless, as is usually the case in human life, he is the greatest hero who gives the widest sway to the worst passions. It is Adam who acts and suffers most, and on whom the consequences have most influence. This constitutes him the main character; although Eve is the more interesting, Satan the more energetic, and on whom the greater force of poetry is displayed. The Creator and his angels are quite secondary.

Landor. Must we not confess that every epic hitherto has been defective in plan; and even that each, until the time of Tasso, was more so than its predecessors? Such stupendous genius, so much fancy, so much eloquence, so much vigor of intellect, never were united as in *Paradise Lost*. Yet it is neither so correct nor so varied as the *Iliad*, nor, however important the action, so interesting. The moral itself is the reason why it wearies even those who insist on the necessity of it. Founded on an event believed by nearly all nations, certainly by all who read the poem, it lays down a principle which concerns every man's welfare, and a fact which every man's experience confirms: that great and irremediable misery may arise from apparently small offences. But will any one say that, in a poetical view, our certainty of moral truth in this position is an equivalent for the uncertainty *which* of the agents is what critics call the hero of the piece?

* * *

Yielded with coy submission, modest pride,
And sweet, reluctant, amorous delay.

I would rather have written these two lines than all the poetry that has been written since Milton's time in all the regions of the earth.

† Ed. Charles G. Crump (London: Dent, 1941).

We shall see again things equal in their way to the best of them; but here the sweetest of images and sentiments is seized and carried far away from all pursuers. Never tell me, what I think is already on your lips, that the golden tresses in their wanton ringlets implied nothing like subjection.

* * *

Southey. It appears, then, on record that the first overt crime of the refractory angels was *punning*: they fell rapidly after that.

* * *

Landor. My ear, I confess it, is dissatisfied with every thing, for days and weeks, after the harmony of *Paradise Lost*. Leaving this magnificent temple, I am hardly to be pacified by the fairy-built chambers, the rich cupboards of embossed plate, and the omnigenous images of Shakspeare.

* * *

After I have been reading the *Paradise Lost*, I can take up no other poet with satisfaction. I seem to have left the music of Handel for the music of the streets, or at best for drums and fifes. Although in Shakspeare there are occasional bursts of harmony no less sublime; yet, if there were many such in continuation, it would be hurtful, not only in comedy, but also in tragedy. The greater part should be equable and conversational. For, if the excitement were the same at the beginning, the middle, and the end; if, consequently (as must be the case), the language and versification were equally elevated throughout,—any long poem would be a bad one, and, worst of all, a drama. In our English heroic verse, such as Milton has composed it, there is a much greater variety of feet, of movement, of musical notes and bars, than in the Greek heroic; and the final sounds are incomparably more diversified. My predilection in youth was on the side of Homer; for I had read the *Iliad* twice, and the *Odyssea* once, before the *Paradise Lost*. Averse as I am to every thing relating to theology, and especially to the view of it thrown open by this poem,

I recur to it incessantly as the noblest specimen in the world of eloquence, harmony, and genius.

* * *

A rib of Shakspeare would have made a Milton; the same portion of Milton, all poets born ever since.

* * *

VICTOR HUGO

From Cromwell (1827)†

From Act 3

MILTON, *speaking to himself.*

The future is my judge and will understand my Eve, falling, as in a sweet dream, into the night of Hell. The future will understand my Adam, who is guilty, yet good. And the future will understand my indomitable archangel, who is proud of reigning over his own eternity: magnificent in his despair and in his very madness profound. See! He rises from the lake of fire and with his immense wing beats down the waves! Milton shall live in his own thoughts and console himself there. As I silently brood over my audacious, unheard-of design, an ardent genius flames in my breast. Yes! I dare to emulate the Creator Supreme. Through the power of my own words I shall create a whole world: my own Heaven, my own Hell, my own Earth.

ALFRED, LORD TENNYSON

Milton (1863)‡

O mighty-mouth'd inventor of harmonies,
O skill'd to sing of Time or Eternity,
God-gifted organ-voice of England,
Milton, a name to resound for ages;
Whose Titan angels, Gabriel, Abdiel,
Starr'd from Jehovah's gorgeous armouries,
Tower, as the deep-domed empyrean
Rings to the roar of an angel onset—
Me rather all that bowery loneliness,
The brooks of Eden mazily murmuring,
And bloom profuse and cedar arches
Charm, as a wanderer out in ocean,
Where some refulgent sunset of India
Streams o'er a rich ambrosial ocean isle,
And crimson-hued the stately palm-woods
Whisper in odorous heights of even.

† Translated by the editor.
‡ From *The Poems of Tennyson*, ed. Christopher Ricks (Harlow, Essex: Longman, 1987).

MATTHEW ARNOLD

From Milton (1888)†

* * *

Milton, from one end of *Paradise Lost* to the other, is in his diction and rhythm constantly a great artist in the great style.

* * *

That Milton, of all our English race, is by his diction and rhythm the one artist of the highest rank in the great style whom we have; this I take as requiring no discussion, this I take as certain.

The mighty power of poetry and art is generally admitted. But where the soul of this power, off this power at its best, chiefly resides, very many of us fail to see. It resides chiefly in the refining and elevation wrought in us by the high and rare excellence of the great style. We may feel the effect without being able to give ourselves clear account of its cause, but the thing is so. Now, no race needs the influences mentioned, the influences of refining and elevation, more than ours; and in poetry and art our grand source for them is Milton.

To what does he owe this supreme distinction? To nature first and foremost, to that bent of nature for inequality which to the worshippers of the average man is so unacceptable; to a gift, a divine favour. 'The older one grows,' says Goethe 'the more one prizes natural gifts, because by no possibility can they be procured and stuck on. Nature formed Milton to be a great poet. But what other poet has shown so sincere a sense of the grandeur of his vocation, and a moral effort so constant and sublime to make and keep himself worthy of it?

* * *

Continually he lived in companionship with high and rare excellence, with the great Hebrew poets and prophets, with the great poets of Greece and Rome. The Hebrew compositions were not in verse, and can be not inadequately represented by the grand, measured prose of our English Bible. The verse of the poets of Greece and Rome no translation can adequately reproduce. Prose cannot have the power of verse; verse-translation may give whatever of charm is in the soul and talent of the translator himself, but never the specific charm of the verse and poet translated. In our race are thousands of readers, presently there will be millions, who know not a word of Greek and Latin, and will never learn those languages. If this host of readers are ever to gain any sense of the power and charm

† From *Essays in Criticism*, Second Series, 1888.

of the, great poets of antiquity, their way to gain it is not through translations of the ancients, but through the original poetry of Milton, who has the like power and charm, because he has the like great style.

* * *

A. E. HOUSMAN

From Terence, this is stupid stuff (1896)†

* * *

O many a peer of England brews
Livelier liquor than the Muse,
And malt does more than Milton can
To justify God's ways to a man.

* * *

T. S. ELIOT

From Milton I (1936)‡

While it must be admitted that Milton is a very great poet indeed, it is something of a puzzle to decide in what his greatness consists. On analysis, the marks against him appear both more numerous and more significant than the marks to his credit. As a man, he is antipathetic. Either from the moralist's point of view, or from the theologian's point of view, or from the psychologist's point of view, or from that of the political philosopher, or judging by the ordinary standards of likebleness in human beings, Milton is unsatisfactory. The doubts which I have to express about him are more serious than these. His greatness as a poet has been sufficiently celebrated, though I think largely for the wrong reasons, and without the proper reservations. His misdeeds as a poet have been called attention to, as by Mr. Ezra Pound, but usually in passing. What seems to me necessary is to assert at the same time his greatness—in that what he could do well he did better than anyone else has ever done—and the serious charges to be made against him, in respect of the dete-

† From *A Shropshire Lad* (Oxford: Woodstock Books, 1994).
‡ From *On Poetry and Poets* (London: Faber & Faber, 1957). Reprinted by permission of the publisher.

rioration—the peculiar kind of deterioration—to which he subjected the language.

Many people will agree that a man may be a great artist and yet have a bad influence. There is more of Milton's influence in the badness of the bad verse of the eighteenth century than of anybody's else: he certainly did more harm than Dryden and Pope, and perhaps a good deal of the obloquy which has fallen on these two poets, especially the latter, because of their influence, ought to be transferred to Milton. But to put the matter simply in terms of 'bad influence' is not necessarily to bring a serious charge: because a good deal of the responsibility, when we state the problem in these terms, may devolve on the eighteenth-century poets themselves for being such bad poets that they were incapable of being influenced except for ill. There is a good deal more to the charge against Milton than this; and it appears a good deal more serious if we affirm that Milton's poetry could *only* be an influence for the worse, upon any poet whatever. It is more serious, also, if we affirm that Milton's bad influence may be traced much farther than the eighteenth century, and much farther than upon bad poets if we say that it was an influence against which we still have to struggle.

* * *

From Milton II (1947)†

* * *

It seems to me also that Milton's verse is especially refractory to yielding up its secrets to examination of the single line. For his verse is not formed in this way. It is the period, the sentence and still more the paragraph, that is the unit of Milton's verse; and emphasis on the line structure is the minimum necessary to provide a counter-pattern to the period structure. It is only in the period that the wave-length of Milton's verse is to be found: it is his ability to give a perfect and unique pattern to every paragraph, such that the full beauty of the line is found in its context, and his ability to work in larger musical units than any other poet—that is to me the most conclusive evidence of Milton's supreme mastery. The peculiar feeling, almost a physical sensation of a breathless leap, communicated by Milton's long periods, and by his alone, is impossible to procure from rhymed verse.

* * *

† From *On Poetry and Poets* (London: Faber & Faber, 1957). Reprinted by permission of the publisher.

Modern Criticism of *Paradise Lost*

On Satan

C. S. LEWIS

From Satan†

* * *

What the Satanic predicament consists in is made clear, as Mr Williams points out, by Satan himself. On his own showing he is suffering from a "sense of injur'd merit" (I, 98). This is a well known state of mind which we can all study in domestic animals, children, film-stars, politicians, or minor poets; and perhaps nearer home. Many critics have a curious partiality for it in literature, but I do not know that any one admires it in life. When it appears, unable to hurt, in a jealous dog or a spoiled child, it is usually laughed at. When it appears armed with the force of millions on the political stage, it escapes ridicule only by being more mischievous. And the cause from which the Sense of Injured Merit arose in Satan's mind—once more I follow Mr Williams—is also clear. "He thought himself impaired" (V, 662). He thought himself impaired because Messiah had been pronounced Head of the Angels. These are the "wrongs" which Shelley described as "beyond measure." A being superior to himself in kind, by whom he himself had been created—a being far above him in the natural hierarchy—had been preferred to him in honour by an authority whose right to do so was not disputable, and in a fashion which, as Abdiel points out, constituted a compliment to the angels rather than a slight (V, 823–843). No one had in fact done anything to Satan; he was not hungry, nor over-tasked, nor removed from his place, nor shunned, nor hated—he only thought himself impaired. In the midst of a world of light and love, of song and feast and dance,

† From *A Preface to* Paradise Lost (London and New York: Oxford UP, 1942). Reprinted by permission of the publisher.

he could find nothing to think of more interesting than his own prestige. And his own prestige, it must be noted, had and could have no other grounds than those which he refused to admit for the superior prestige of Messiah. Superiority in kind, or Divine appointment, or both, on what else could his own exalted position depend? Hence his revolt is entangled in contradictions from the very outset, and he cannot even raise the banner of liberty and equality without admitting in a tell-tale parenthesis that "Orders and Degrees Jarr not with liberty" (v, 789). He wants hierarchy and does not want hierarchy. Throughout the poem he is engaged in sawing off the branch he is sitting on, not only in the quasi-political sense already indicated, but in a deeper sense still, since a creature revolting against a creator is revolting against the source of his own powers—including even his power to revol. Hence the strife is most accurately described as "Heav'n ruining from Heav'n" (vi, 868), for only in so far as he also is "Heaven"—diseased, perverted, twisted, but still a native of Heaven—does Satan exist at all. It is like the scent of a flower trying to destroy the flower. As a consequence the same rebellion which means misery for the feelings and corruption for the will, means Nonsense for the intellect.

Mr Williams has reminded us in unforgettable words that "Hell is inaccurate," and has drawn attention to the fact that Satan lies about every subject he mentions in *Paradise Lost*. But I do not know whether we can distinguish his conscious lies from the blindness which he has almost willingly imposed on himself. When, at the very beginning of his insurrection, he tells Beelzebub that Messiah is going to make a tour "through all the Hierarchies . . . and give Laws" (v, 688–690) I suppose he may still know that he is lying; and similarly when he tells his followers that "all this haste of midnight march" (v, 774) had been ordered in honour of their new "Head." But when in Book i he claims that the "terror of his arm" had put God in doubt of "his empire," I am not quite certain. It is, of course, mere folly. There never had been any war between Satan and God, only between Satan and Michael; but it is possible that he now believes his own propaganda. When in Book x he makes to his peers the useless boast that Chaos had attempted to oppose his journey "protesting Fate supreame" (480) he may really, by then, have persuaded himself that this was true; for far earlier in his career he has become more a Lie than a Liar, a personified self-contradiction.

This doom of Nonsense—almost, in Pope's sense, of Dulness—is brought out in two scenes. The first is his debate with Abdiel in Book v. Here Satan attempts to maintain the heresy which is at the root of his whole predicament—the doctrine that he is a self-existent being, not a derived being, a creature. Now, of course, the property of a self-existent being is that it can understand its own existence; it is *causa sui*. The quality of a created being is that it just finds itself existing, it knows not how nor why. Yet at the same time, if a creature is silly enough to try to prove that it was not created, what is more natural than for it to say, "Well, I wasn't there to see it being done?" Yet what more futile, since in thus admitting ignorance of its own beginnings it proves that those beginnings lay outside itself? Satan falls instantly into this trap (850 *et seq.*)—as indeed he cannot help doing—and produces as proof of his self-existence what is really its disproof. But even this is not Nonsense enough. Uneasily shifting on the bed of Nonsense which he has made for himself, he then throws out the happy idea that "fatal course" really produced him, and finally, with a triumphant air, the theory that he sprouted from the soil like a vegetable. Thus, in twenty lines, the being too proud to admit derivation from God, has come to rejoice in believing that he "just grew" like Topsy or a turnip. The second passage is his speech from the throne in Book II. The blindness here displayed reminds one of Napoleon's utterance after his fall, "I wonder what Wellington will do now?—he will never be content to become a private citizen again." Just as Napoleon was incapable of conceiving, I do not say the virtues, but even the temptations, of an ordinarily honest man in a tolerably stable commonwealth, so Satan in this speech shows complete inability to conceive any state of mind but the infernal. His argument assumes as axiomatic that in any world where there is any good to be envied, subjects will envy their sovereign. The only exception is Hell, for there, since there is no good to be had, the sovereign cannot have more of it, and therefore cannot be envied. Hence he concludes that the infernal monarchy has a stability which the celestial lacks. That the obedient angels might love to obey is an idea which cannot cross his mind even as a hypothesis. But even within this invincible ignorance contradiction breaks out; for Satan makes this ludicrous proposition a reason for hoping ultimate victory. He does not, apparently, notice that every approach to victory must take away the grounds on which victory is hoped. A stability based on perfect misery, and therefore diminishing with each alleviation of that misery, is held out as something likely to assist in removing the misery altogether (II, 11–43).

What we see in Satan is the horrible co-existence of a subtle and incessant intellectual activity with an incapacity to understand anything. This doom he has brought upon himself; in order to avoid seeing one thing he has, almost voluntarily, incapacitated himself from seeing at all. And thus, throughout the poem, all his torments come, in a sense, at his own bidding, and the Divine judgement might have been expressed in the words "*thy* will be done." He says "Evil be thou my good" (which includes "Nonsense be thou my sense") and his prayer is granted. It is by his own will that he revolts;

but not by his own will that Revolt itself tears its way in agony out of his head and becomes a being separable from himself, capable of enchanting him (II, 749–766) and bearing him unexpected and unwelcome progeny. By his own will he becomes a serpent in Book IX; in Book X he is a serpent whether he will or no. This progressive degradation, of which he himself is vividly aware, is carefully marked in the poem. He begins by fighting for "liberty," however misconceived; but almost at once sinks to fighting for "Honour, Dominion, glorie, and renoune" (VI, 422). Defeated in this, he sinks to that great design which makes the main subject of the poem—the design of ruining two creatures who had never done him any harm, no longer in the serious hope of victory, but only to annoy the Enemy whom he cannot directly attack. (The coward in Beaumont and Fletcher's play, not daring to fight a duel, decided to go home and beat his servants.) This brings him as a spy into the universe, and soon not even a political spy, but a mere peeping Tom leering and writhing in prurience as he overlooks the privacy of two lovers, and there described, almost for the first time in the poem, not as the fallen Archangel or Hell's dread Emperor, but simply as "the Devil" (VI, 502)—the salacious grotesque, half bogey and half buffoon, of popular tradition. From hero to general, from general to politician, from politician to secret service agent, and thence to a thing that peers in at bedroom or bathroom windows, and thence to a toad, and finally to a snake—such is the progress of Satan. This progress, misunderstood, has given rise to the belief that Milton began by making Satan more glorious than he intended and then, too late, attempted to rectify the error. But such an unerring picture of the "sense of injured merit" in its actual operations upon character cannot have come about by blundering and accident. We need not doubt that it was the poet's intention to be fair to evil, to give it a run for its money—to show it *first* at the height, with all its rants and melodrama and "Godlike imitated state" about it, and *then* to trace what actually becomes of such self-intoxication when it encounters reality. Fortunately we happen to know that the terrible soliloquy in Book IV (32–113) was conceived and in part composed before the first two books. It was from this conception that Milton started and when he put the most specious aspects of Satan at the very beginning of his poem he was relying on two predispositions in the minds of his readers, which in that age, would have guarded them from our later misunderstanding. Men still believed that there really was such a person as Satan, and that he was a liar. The poet did not foresee that his work would one day meet the disarming simplicity of critics who take for gospel things said by the father of falsehood in public speeches to his troops.

It remains, of course, true that Satan is the best drawn of Milton's characters. The reason is not hard to find. Of the major characters whom Milton attempted he is incomparably the easiest to draw. Set a hundred poets to tell the same story and in ninety of the resulting poems Satan will be the best character. In all but a few writers the "good" characters are the least successful, and every one who has ever tried to make even the humblest story ought to know why. To make a character worse than oneself it is only necessary to release imaginatively from control some of the bad passions which, in real life, are always straining at the leash; the Satan, the Iago, the Becky Sharp, within each of us, is always there and only too ready, the moment the leash is slipped, to come out and have in our books that holiday we try to deny them in our lives. But if you try to draw a character better than yourself, all you can do is to take the best moments you have had and to imagine them prolonged and more consistently embodied in action. But the real high virtues which we do not possess at all, we cannot depict except in a purely external fashion. We do not really know what it feels like to be a man much better than ourselves. His whole inner landscape is one we have never seen, and when we guess it we blunder. It is in their "good" characters that novelists make, unawares, the most shocking self-revelations. Heaven understands Hell and Hell does not understand Heaven, and all of us, in our measure, share the Satanic, or at least the Napoleonic, blindness. To project ourselves into a wicked character, we have only to stop doing something, and something that we are already tired of doing; to project ourselves into a good one we have to do what we cannot and become what we are not. Hence all that is said about Milton's 'sympathy' with Satan, his expression in Satan of his own pride, malice, folly, misery, and lust, is true in a sense, but not in a sense peculiar to Milton. The Satan in Milton enables him to draw the character well just as the Satan in us enables us to receive it. Not as Milton, but as man, he has trodden the burning marl, pursued vain war with heaven, and turned aside with leer malign: A fallen man *is* very like a fallen angel. That, indeed, is one of the things which prevents the Satanic predicament from becoming comic. It is too near us; and doubtless Milton expected all readers to perceive that in the long run either the Satanic predicament or else the delighted obedience of Messiah, of Abdiel, of Adam, and of Eve, must be their own. It is therefore right to say that Milton has put much of himself into Satan; but it is unwarrantable to conclude that he was pleased with that part of himself or expected us to be pleased. Because he was, like the rest of us, damnable, it does not follow that he was, like Satan, damned.

Yet even the "good" characters in *Paradise Lost* are not so unsuccessful that a man who takes the poem seriously will doubt whether, in real life, Adam or Satan would be the better company. Observe their conversation. Adam talks about God, the Forbidden Tree, sleep, the difference between beast and man, his plans for the morrow, the stars, and the angels. He discusses dreams and clouds, the sun, the moon, and the planets, the winds, and the birds. He relates his own creation and celebrates the beauty and majesty of Eve. Now listen to Satan: in Book I at line 83 he starts to address Beelzebub; by line 94 he is stating his own position and telling Beelzebub about his "fixt mind" and "injured merit." At line 241 he starts off again, this time to give his impressions of Hell: by line 252 he is stating his own position and assuring us (untruly) that he is "still the same." At line 622 he begins to harangue his followers; by line 635 he is drawing attention to the excellence of his public conduct. Book II opens with his speech from the throne; before we have had eight lines he is lecturing the assembly on his right to leadership. He meets Sin—and states his position. He sees the Sun; it makes him think of his own position. He spies on the human lovers; and states his position. In Book IX he journeys round the whole earth; it reminds him of his own position. The point need not be laboured. Adam, though locally confined to a small park on a small planet, has interests that embrace "all the choir of heaven and all the furniture of earth." Satan has been in the Heaven of Heavens and in the abyss of Hell, and surveyed all that lies between them, and in that whole immensity has found only one thing that interests Satan. It may be said that Adam's situation made it easier for him, than for Satan, to let his mind roam. But that is just the point. Satan's monomaniac concern with himself and his supposed rights and wrongs is a necessity of the Satanic predicament. Certainly, he has no choice. He has chosen to have no choice. He has wished to 'be himself', and to be in himself and for himself, and his wish has been granted. The Hell he carries with him is, in one sense, a Hell of infinite boredom. Satan, like Miss Bates, is interesting to read about; but Milton makes plain the blank uninterestingness of *being* Satan.

To admire Satan, then, is to give one's vote not only for a world of misery, but also for a world of lies and propaganda, of wishful thinking, of incessant autobiography. Yet the choice is possible. Hardly a day passes without some slight movement towards it in each one of us. That is what makes *Paradise Lost* so serious a poem. The thing is possible, and the exposure of it is resented. Where *Paradise Lost* is not loved, it is deeply hated. As Keats said more rightly than he knew, "there is death" in Milton. We have all skirted the Satanic island closely enough to have motives for wishing to evade the full impact of the poem. For, I repeat, the thing is possible; and after a certain point it is prized. Sir Willoughby may be unhappy, but he *wants* to go on being Sir Willoughby. Satan *wants* to go on being Satan. That is the real meaning of his choice "Better to reign in Hell, than serve in Heav'n." Some, to the very end, will think this a fine thing to say; others will think that it fails to be roaring farce only because it spells agony. On the level of literary criticism the matter cannot be argued further. Each to his taste.

* * *

BALACHANDRA RAJAN

From The Problem of Satan†

"Satan", wrote Sir Walter Raleigh, "unavoidably reminds us of Prometheus, and although there are essential differences, we are not made to feel them essential. His very situation as the fearless antagonist of Omnipotence makes him either a fool or a hero, and Milton is far indeed from permitting us to think him a fool." Raleigh's conclusion reflects very fairly the trend of opinion in the preceding century, which, while not always insisting that Satan was a hero invariably endowed him with his share of heroic qualities. It is only recently that critics have become audible who prefer the less noble of the opposed alternatives. Charles Williams, the first of them, in a brief but thought-provoking introduction to Milton's poetry, spoke ominously of Satan's "solemn antics". C. S. Lewis then took the hint up and developed it more aggressively. Satan became for him "a personified self-contradiction", a being ultimately farcical, a creature who could not be brought into contact with the real without laughter arising "just as steam *must* when water meets fire". So challenging a formulation could naturally not pass unchallenged and Professor Stoll, backed by the resources of nineteenth century criticism, demanded at some length that the devil be given his due. Mr. Rostrevor Hamilton, using Raleigh's antithesis for a title, insisted that the poet had his reasons of which the Puritan knew nothing, and that the Satan created by Milton's imagination was nobler and more admirable than the devil conceived by his intellect. The controversy died away except for occasional salvoes in learned periodicals but the issues it raised are sufficiently important to be discussed again in somewhat different surroundings.

Now when a problem of this kind is presented to us the first thing we need to ask about is the adequacy of the vocabulary in which it is formulated. That "hero or fool?" is a leading question is not in itself regrettable. What is regrettable is that it is the sort of leading

† From Paradise Lost *and the Seventeenth-Century Reader* (London: Chatto & Windus, 1947; rpt. Ann Arbor: U of Michigan P, 1964). Reprinted by permission of the author.

question which is bound to result in a misleading answer. Given certain ethical systems Satan is ultimately heroic and given others he is ultimately farcical. But what we are concerned with is poetry rather than ethics and Satan considered as a poetic force is different from Satan as a cosmic principle. For when that principle becomes dramatically real, when it comes alive in the radius of human experience, you cannot bring to its poetic deployment the simple emotions of mirth or admiration. Your response to it must not be unconditional. You have to see it as an element in a concerted whole, a single fact in a poetic process. Therefore to understand its nature and function you need to relate it to the pattern it fulfils and the background of belief against which it is presented.

It is when we undertake this reconsideration that critical differences of shading begin to emerge. Our response to Satan is, I imagine, one of cautious interest. We think of him either as an abstract conception or else, more immediately, as someone in whom evil is mixed with good but who is doomed to destruction by the flaw of self-love. But with Milton's contemporaries the response was predominantly one of fear. If like Calvin they thought of Satan as "an enemie that is in courage most hardie, in strength most mightie, in policies most subtle, in diligence and celeritie unweariable, with all sorts of engins plenteously furnishd, in skill of warre most readie", that was only so that they could stand guard more vigilantly against their relentless opponent. If like Defoe they saw him as "a mighty, a terrible, an immortal Being; infinitely superior to man, as well in the dignity of his nature, as in the dreadful powers he retains still about him", the vision served to remind them inescapably that it was only by God's grace that they could hope to overcome the enormous forces against which they were contending. When Milton's great figure is silhouetted against this background the effect must be as Addison points out "to raise and terrify our imaginations". So the heroic qualities which Satan brings to his mission, the fortitude, the steadfast hate, the implacable resolution which is founded on despair are qualities not to be imitated or admired. They are defiled by the evil to which they are consecrated. If Milton dwells upon them it is because he knows that you will put them in their context, that you will see Satan's virtues as perverted by their end and darkening therefore to their inevitable eclipse, corroded and eaten out by the nemesis beyond them. The moral condemnation is never explicitly, or even poetically, denied. Touched on repeatedly in parenthesis, it is also always there as an undertone to the imagery. Words like Memphis and Alcairo may be nothing more than brilliant names to us. To Milton's contemporaries they were darkened with contempt. When Satan was described to them as a "great Sultan" the phrase would have reminded them of tyranny rather than splendour. When the fallen angels were likened to the cavalry of Egypt, a plague of locusts and a barbarian invasion, they would have given full weight to the mounting disapproval which lies behind the simile. As for the great Satanic defiances, they would have admired them for their strength and deplored them for their perversity. To quote Addison once more, Satan's sentiments "are every way answerable to his character, and suitable to a created Being of the most exalted and most depraved nature. . . . Amidst the impieties which this enraged Spirit utters . . . the author has taken care to introduce none that is not big with absurdity and incapable of shocking a religious reader". The sympathy for Satan which the poetry imposes, the admiration it compels for his Promethean qualities, are meant to be controlled by this sort of moral reaction. And the same sense of proportion should cover his intellectual argument. When Satan appeals to "just right and the fixt laws of Heav'n", when he grounds his mandate on the ultimate nature of things, and when, in betraying overtones, he couples God's "tyranny" with "the excess of joy", you are not supposed to take these statements at their face value. Other politicians have made claims somewhat similar, and Satan's assertions as the champion of liberty would amuse, rather than perplex, those who were brought up to think of him as the first liar.

But to set aside the problem at this point is to leave its most interesting elements unstated. It is right to insist that Milton's Satan is not presented in a moral vacuum, that there is a background of unremitting hostility against which his poetic presence must be built up. But though the system within which he exists is never questioned, though it is seldom ignored and frequently remembered, its immediate implications are progressively subdued. We know, and even Satan knows, that the God against whom he is contending is omnipotent. But against the settled strength of his heroism, against the desperate and deliberate valour of Hell, that fact dies down to an abstract and distant necessity. When the weight of the poetry is thus thrown in on Satan's side, the effect must be to equalize in our imaginations the relative magnitude of the contending forces. We see Satan so clearly that we can hardly see anything else, and though conscious, we are not always or inescapably conscious, of the strength and authority of the forces which control him. The conflict, then, is neither Promethean or farcical. It is dramatically real in proportion as you assent to the illusion of equality which the poem communicates.

That illusion, however, is not intended to last. In our first glimpse of the solemnities of heaven, in the deliberations of the celestial council, in the love and mercy which are poured into the Son's sacrifice, the stature of the whole infernal enterprise is meant to be implicitly reduced. But Milton's verse is not equal to the occasion.

His reliance on biblical phrasing undoubtedly meant far more to his contemporaries than it can ever mean to us, but even when every allowance has been made for this difference in impact, the drab legalities of Milton's celestial style are too curt and chill to be poetically successful. It is only in the speech on Mount Niphates, when the external magnificence surrounding Satan is stripped away, that we find his stature visibly reduced and his heroic grandeur battered and corroded by the endless siege of contraries within him.

* * *

In the fifth book we revert to a Satan who, chronologically, ought to be at his noblest. Instead, we find only a professional politician, a propagandist who, like all propagandists, is an ardent champion of the Rights of Man and is therefore able to be generously indignant about the despotic tendencies of government in Heaven. It is a Satan notably different from the Archangel of the first books, and those who feel this discrepancy are compelled either to assume that Milton changed his mind about Satan as he drew him, or else find ways of making the difference acceptable. One way of dealing with the evidence is to assume that Satan is chiefly what the occasion makes him. What he is, depends on what he does. The intruder in Eden is not quite the explorer of Chaos and both of them differ from the "false Archangel" whom Abdiel conquers in "debate of truth". The battle in Heaven is, we should remember, part of a Sermon preached to Adam; it is intended to warn him against an opponent who may conquer him by force of persuasion but cannot conquer him by force of arms. So the qualities stressed are Satan's specious plausibility in argument and, side by side with this, his very real ineptness when he is faced with the weapons of reason and the right. I have dealt in an earlier chapter with Satan's complaints and suggested that Milton's contemporaries could hardly have taken them seriously. But even if they were inclined to do so they would have been set right by the evidence of the Niphates soliloquy, with its betraying confession that God's service was never onerous, and that ambition, not altruism, drove Satan to revolt. The other half of Milton's poetic intention is to suggest Satan's tawdriness and triviality when he is measured against the values of Heaven. It is a tawdriness first felt in the Devil's encounter with Gabriel but confirmed now by a style which can be fantastically complicated, by speeches which bristle with the equipment of the orator, with jaunty sarcasm and irrelevant puns.

* * *

I have tried to suggest that what Satan is depends on his circumstances, and how his behaviour and implied stature are determined by his functions. I hope I have not suggested that he is nothing more than a collection of abstract properties, properties which can be irresponsibly shuffled to meet the demands of varying situations. But, if he is more than this, he is also more than a theological exercise, or a means of illustrating a preconceived theory of evil. He is, in short, a poetic representation, and Milton's special problem is to take those qualities which the general imagination associates with Satan and work them into a stable poetic whole. Those qualities are by no means interdependent and in juxtaposition may often seem contradictory. They can be brought together in poetry, or poetic prose, in the emotions kindled by antithesis and paradox. But, in the more spacious economy of a narrative poem, such lyrical insights are neither proper nor possible. The truth must be revealed in action, not reflection, and so the qualities which the poem portrays are most convincing when they are made to emerge from the situations in which they are presented. If Satan is heroic, he should be heroic in Hell. If he is melodramatic, he is best so in the serene peace of Eden. If he combines weakness in understanding with subtlety in debate, that combination is best revealed in circumstances which Milton's contemporaries would associate with Christian warfare. The qualities, then, are harmonized by their relationship to a fable which is constructed to imply them. They can be brought together still more closely by the disposition of that fable, that is by the divergence between the chronological and the reading order. Chronologically Satan's deterioration is neither continual nor consistent: before his fall from Heaven he is far less impressive than he is immediately after it. But the difference (made unavoidable by Satan's function in Heaven) is one submerged in the unity which the reading order stipulates, the inexorable law of Satan's degeneration which is exercised so evenly from the first books to the last.

Satan's history therefore is meant to be read poetically. You may bring to it (and indeed it is essential that you should bring to it) the preconceptions of an established moral outlook. But such preconceptions are no more than an equipment, an accepted means of reacting to the poem. They are what Milton assumes rather than what he demonstrates. Given the organization of sensibility they imply, the function of the poem is to play upon it, to use it as far as possible as a medium through which its own character is created and known. To vary the metaphor a little, the poem imposes its perspective on your feelings. The great figure of Satan and its inexorable decline confirms and yet insensibly rearranges the mass of beliefs and sentiments which you bring to it. You see it as a sermon on the weakness of evil and you learn more clearly than you can from any philosophy that evil must die by the logic of its being. But it is also a sermon on the strength of evil; because you see Satan created as he is, huge in the magnificence with which the first books surround him, you are compelled to know him as the Prince of Darkness and to admit his dominion over the forces of history. When two facts so apparently opposed are reconciled in one figure a poetic synthesis has been effected. Add to that synthesis the emotions which it orders, fear of the marauder and contempt for the liar, with wary admiration of the orator's resources, add to these the dramatic insights of soliloquy, and the result must make Satan symbolically alive within the universe which Milton's epic operates. In defining or interpreting this life, "hero" and "fool" are inadequate alternatives. They are descriptions, not so much of the poetry, as of the moral system which the poetry is said to recommend, or else of the intellectual convictions which Milton's imagination is taken to deny.

In opposition I have tried to maintain that Milton's heart was not at war with his head and that his Satan is on the whole what he intended to make him. Here and there Milton's execution may falter. But if we look at his picture through seventeenth century eyes, if we try not to impose upon it the deceptions of our own historic and personal perspectives, its implications should be plain and unmistakable. The failure lies not in the depiction of Satan but in that of the heavenly values which should subdue him. Those values are only imperfectly realized. So, though one half of the picture may be painted convincingly, the other half is sketched rather than painted. Milton's God is what his Satan never is, a collection of abstract properties, or, in his greatest moments, a treatise on free-will. The Son moves us more deeply, particularly in the quiet, firm monosyllables in which he announces his sacrifice. But the spare precision of the language Milton gives him is lit only seldom by the ardour which should inform it. Clothed in the language of Ezekiel's vision his triumph over Satan must have its moments of majesty, but it remains a moral rather than a poetic victory.

It is I think the barrenness of this victory which makes some misunderstanding of Satan's function inevitable. His regression faces us with a sort of vacuum and though the values which triumph over him are everywhere announced they are never brought to the foreground of our assent. Milton can describe pride, and in doing so condemn it; but love is to him never much more than loyalty, and humility teaches him only to "stand and wait". He may justify God's ways but he does not celebrate them. His sense of responsibility is too contractual, too persistently concerned with the mechanics of crime and punishment, for goodness or mercy to come into being within it. Because such goodness is so seldom real within the limits of Milton's poetry it becomes possible to claim that the poet was interested predominantly in evil, or even that evil was unconsciously his good. Such conclusions are to my mind untenable. Milton knows his Satan well enough to reject him and to make that rejection a poetic fact. If that dismissal is never stabilized in its transformation by a higher poetic acceptance, the failure should not blind us to the poverty of the values Milton condemns or to the reality and force of his depiction of evil.

A. J. A. WALDOCK

From Satan and the Technique of Degradation†

* * *

But quite apart from the inherent conditions of the theme—conditions that almost force him into pre-eminence—Satan, we understand well, was a predestined character for Milton. There need, surely, be no confusion here, no perplexity about the 'sympathy', conscious or unconscious, that Milton felt for his creation. Of course it does not mean that Milton, as we ordinarily use the phrase, was on Satan's side. It means merely that he was able, in a marked degree, to conceive Satan in terms of himself: in terms of the temptations to which he felt his own nature especially liable, and of the values, too, to which his own nature especially responded. I say 'to a marked degree', because there is nothing exclusive in Milton's sympathy with Satan. Milton seems to us often, as he writes of him, to be giving of his own substance, but he can give of his own substance anywhere. In those altercations, for example, between Satan and Abdiel in Books v and vi we *feel* Milton now in the lines of the one, now in the lines of the other, but chiefly, without any doubt, in the lines of Abdiel. In the concluding paragraph of Book v the sympathy is so close that there is virtually an identification: in speaking of Abdiel Milton might (as so many have noted) be speaking of himself: the lines come to us with the weight of some of the intensest memories of his life behind them.

There is, I think, a further distinction to be made. Mr Bernard Shaw once remarked that it is the habit of a sentimentalist to assume that human qualities come in neatly assorted sets, that they are 'matched' in people's natures like colours. In life, as he pointed out, such harmonious assortments of matched qualities are not so frequently found: a war hero may be spiteful and may turn out to be an unexpectedly bad loser at games; a lovable woman may be greedy, untrustworthy in financial affairs, and not a strict speaker of the

† From Paradise Lost *and Its Critics* (Cambridge: Cambridge UP, 1947). Reprinted with permission of Cambridge University Press.

truth; and so on. And just as we have to admit that lying and spitefulness are reprehensible (even though consisting in the same nature with charm and heroism) so we have to admit that courage in a gangster is still courage and therefore good. Now when Mr Lewis writes of Satan he writes for the moment, I think, as a sentimentalist. He wishes to see Satan's character as made up of aesthetically harmonious qualities—of qualities that match. He is reluctant to admit that we can condemn Satan for some things and at the same time find him extremely admirable for others. So he compiles for him a little list of traits that agree—a list, I think, that quite falsifies the impressions yielded by the first two books. We have in Satan, he says, an expression of Milton's 'own pride, malice, folly, misery, and lust'. But Milton expresses in Satan much more of himself than this, and such a picture of the Satan of the first two books is surely a very partial portrait. We hear about Satan's pride, see something of it, and have no difficulty in believing in it; the lust is tossed in gratuitously—I doubt if we ever really believe in it: there is no particular reason why we should;[1] we see something of his malice, we can perhaps deduce his folly, and we know that theoretically he and his mates are in misery. But what we are chiefly made to see and feel in the first two books are quite different things: fortitude in adversity, enormous endurance, a certain splendid recklessness, remarkable powers of rising to an occasion, extraordinary qualities of leadership (shown not least in his salutary taunts), and striking intelligence in meeting difficulties that are novel and could seem overwhelming. What we feel most of all, I suppose, is his refusal to give in—just that. How can Milton help sympathizing with qualities such as these? Obviously he sympathizes with them. In this sense and to this extent he *is* on Satan's side, as it was quite proper for him to be.

So far the situation seems very clear. But it is evident that portraiture so sympathetic, drawing such strength from Milton's own life and nature, could be very dangerous for Milton's scheme. Of course it was dangerous; and nothing is more interesting, technically, in the opening books than to note the nervousness that creeps on Milton as he becomes aware of what is threatening. It is an instructive and in some ways an amusing study. If one observes what is happening one sees that there is hardly a great speech of Satan's that Milton is not at pains to correct, to damp down and neutralize. He

1. Why we should believe in it, that is to say, in the sense in which we believe in his pride or his courage or his arrogance. In this respect the lust of Satan is not unlike the 'luxury' of Macbeth, which is also something *declared*, something extraneous, properly, to the portrait: take it away and the portrait is just the same. Take away Satan's lust and the portrait is just the same, for no matter what Milton may have had at the back of his mind in introducing it, artistically it is an extra. To say with M. Saurat that Satan represents 'in particular' sensuality seems to me absurd: absurd, indeed, in precisely the same way as it would be to say that Macbeth stands especially for viciousness and loose living.

will put some glorious thing in Satan's mouth, then, anxious about the effect of it, will pull us gently by the sleeve, saying (for this is what it amounts to): 'Do not be carried away by this fellow: he *sounds* splendid, but take my word for it. . . . ' We have in fact, once again, the two levels: the level of demonstration or exhibition, and the level of allegation or commentary; and again there is disagreement. What is conveyed on the one level is for a large part of the time not in accord with what is conveyed on the other. Milton's allegations *clash* with his demonstrations.

The process begins, indeed, quite early in the poem. After Satan's very first speech comes the comment:

> So spake th' Apostate Angel, though in pain,
> Vaunting aloud, but rackt with deep despare. (1, 125)

Has there been much despair in what we have just been listening to? The speech would almost seem to be incompatible with that. To accept Milton's comment here (as most readers appear to do) as if it had a validity equal to that of the speech itself is surely very naïve critical procedure. I emphasize the point again, because here too it becomes of the first importance for our estimate of what is happening in the poem—for our view, in fact, of what the poem actually *is*: in any work of imaginative literature at all it is the demonstration, by the very nature of the case, that has the higher validity: an allegation can possess no comparable authority. Of course they should agree; but if they do not then the demonstration must carry the day. In the present passage, had Milton very much in mind, one wonders, when he penned his comment? Did he really feel, when he wrote the words, that Satan *was* in 'deep despare'? It seems to me that if he had felt the despair he simply could not have written the speech as it is. Surely the truth is obvious that the phrase is half mechanical: it is the first of a long line of automatic snubs, of perfunctory jabs and growls. Each great speech lifts Satan a little beyond what Milton really intended, so he suppresses him again (or tries to) in a comment.

* * *

The technique, indeed, is almost comically transparent and in its nature (we may fairly say) is rather primitive. Using the method of allegation Milton can produce a trump card whenever he wishes. We have no defence against such tactics except, of course, to take due note of what is going on and to decline to play when the trump has appeared too obviously from Milton's sleeve. The most flagrant example of this kind of literary cheating occurs, I think, in Book IV. Gabriel, who has not been markedly successful in debate, retorts on the Adversary:

> And thou sly hypocrite, who now wouldst seem
> Patron of liberty, who more then thou
> Once fawn'd, and cring'd, and servilly ador'd
> Heav'ns awful Monarch?
>
> (IV, 957)

Are we, then, on Gabriel's undocumented assertion, to make an effort to accommodate the Satan we know to a Satan who 'once fawn'd, and cring'd, and servilly ador'd'? Why should we accept this high-handed piece of unsupported calumny? This seems beyond reasonable bounds, this is not keeping to the rules of the game at all.

But in the first two books of the poem such measures are really signs of nervousness and do not affect appreciably the single tremendous impression that Satan (rather in excess of Milton's will) has made. Everybody feels that the Satan of the first two books stands alone; after them comes a break, and he is never as impressive again. If we leave aside the unimportant 'accosting' of Uriel towards the end of Book III we hear him next in the famous 'address to the Sun' (IV, 32) in which he 'falls into many doubts with himself, and many passions, fear, envy, and despare'.

I do not think that it is possible to overestimate the effect of this break. Its significance, I think, is much greater than is usually admitted. It is in every respect, I would suggest, an interruption. It is not merely that the Satan of the first two books re-enters altered: the Satan of the first two books to all intents and purposes *disappears*: I do not think that in any true sense we ever see him again.

Milton's task in this, the second part of the delineation, is of course to trace the development of Satan. Now a character in process of change may affect us in either of two ways. If we have been given the requisite clues the development will seem, as it were, to carry its own guarantees with it. It is so with Macbeth. The preliminary glimpses we have of his nature, few and partial though they may seem to be, are enough; because of them we do not question the curiously unexpected turns his development takes. We could hardly have predicted those turns, but when they come we know that they are the right ones. It is as if the progress is self-proving; the keys with which we have been furnished fit; our feelings give us assurance that the man we saw could and would, in the given conditions, change into the man we see. And the progress of Lady Macbeth (so different in its course) is exactly the same in kind.

The progress of Satan is utterly distinct in its nature, and it seems to me that unless we recognize this we are not seeing the poem aright. The extreme simplification of the method in Books I and II leaves us with a memorable, indeed an overpowering, image: but the image is self-complete, finished. To expect it to develop is like expecting a statue of Michelangelo's to develop. We make, surely, a new start. The Satan of the address to the Sun is not a development from the old, he is not a changed Satan, he is a *new* Satan. We can make the transition from the one to the other, I think, in only one way: by spinning a bridge of theory across and above the visible presentment. A doctrine—that Pride, say, has certain consequences—will carry us across: I would suggest that we cannot make the crossing imaginatively. What it comes to is that we are obliged to take this new Satan, and, indeed, all the steps of this new Satan's subsequent history, on trust.

I do not think, in other words, that the term 'degeneration', applied to the downward course of Satan, has any real validity. Macbeth degenerates—in some respects, at least. A character in a piece of imaginative literature degenerates when we are in a position to check his progress by what we know of him: when we are made to feel that this or that change, once we are shown it, does follow, although we ourselves could not, perhaps, have foretold it. But what we have in the alleged 'degeneration' of Satan is really, on a large scale and in a disguised form, what we have had in the running fire of belittling commentary already noted. It is a pretended exhibition of changes occurring; actually it is of the nature of an assertion that certain changes occur. The changes do not generate themselves from within: they are imposed from without. Satan, in short, does not degenerate: *he is degraded*.

* * *

WILLIAM EMPSON

From Satan†

* * *

God says in III.90 that Satan will try to destroy or pervert Adam and Eve, "And shall pervert; For man will hearken to his glozing lies"; but Satan may believe in his offers up to the very moment when he makes them. The speech on Niphates' top has no reference to mankind, except to say in the last line that they will soon know his power. His next speech is the one now in question, so we do not reach it with much evidence that his intentions towards us are bad. He knows indeed that we will suffer bodily pain in Hell, as he and the other rebel angels do; but they can carry on life in a high manner, whereas

† From *Milton's God* (London: Chatto & Windus, 1961). Reprinted by permission of Curtis Brown Ltd., London, on behalf of The William Empson Estate. Copyright © William Empson.

Milton seems to accept the usual view that we can only remain in passive agony (II. 600). Satan evidently does not know this, and so far the irony of his offer belongs only to the God who made Hell. Satan may well think that it is worth enduring a period of suffering to be on the honest side, as Milton himself would. In his next soliloquy, around IV. 530, he expresses a rather self-indulgent pity for them and says he must bring upon them 'death' and 'long woes'; but in Milton's world death is a very subtle or almost meaningless term, and they might gain honour in the end as a reward for their long woes. By the way, C. S. Lewis need not have called Satan "a thing which peers in through bathroom windows" because he feels jealous here of the sexual pleasures of Adam and Eve; God has recently cut him off from his own corresponding pleasures, and he is straightforward enough about it. But I agree that his temper has begun to spoil, so that he eyes them "with leer malign"; indeed, his character rots away so fast now that his speech on first view of them is his only really puzzling one. Going by the sound-effects, as one should, the offer of high honour in Hell feels very sincere; we are to observe that Satan genuinely did find our parents less beneath his own angelic class then he had expected, so that he was gratified at least for a moment by sentiments of romantic generosity. But other lines of the speech are insinuatingly horrible.

I argued in my book *Pastoral* that Satan is not a consistent character, being something more basically dramatic instead; and I now think this wrong. There was a fashion for attacking 'character-analysis', especially in Shakespeare, which I have taken some time to get out of; maybe it has a kind of truth, but it is dangerously liable to make us miss points of character. I would still say, indeed, that there is an unnerving strain here between the two ways of reading the passage; you can either shudder at Satan's villainy or take the offer as sincere, and feel the agony of his ruined greatness. But both are within him; what I had not realized is that he has only just begun to doubt whether he has anything to offer them. He is still partly thinking of himself as a patron of Adam and Eve, who can save them from their wicked master; thus he seems genuinely indignant (520) at hearing the conditions of ignorance which God has imposed upon them. We could not expect him to stay in the mood of self-abasement reached on Niphates' top, accepting all God's claims, especially as even then he still found God intolerable. Thus his reasoning mind may probably be sincere when he offers high honour in Hell; but even as he speaks his lips are twisted by the new suspicion that God is only waiting to turn all he does to torture. I readily agree that from then on he is rotting away; but also, he rightly suspects that God is plotting to make him rot away; his story is more like the Orwell *1984* than anything else. The poetry of the offer is so haunting that I have long felt it must have meant something important to Milton, though I could not understand what; so I feel confident of this explanation now.

It seems best to consider the later details about Satan at once, which may be done briefly. The final soliloquy is in Book IX, before the Temptation, after going seven times round the world to hide in darkness for a week. His praise of the beauty of the world, though evidence of Milton's intention I think, is used by Satan merely to argue that the world ought not to have been made for such inferior persons; it is great indignity even for conformist angels to have to wait on them, and still more for himself to have to turn into a snake. His self-pity has reached the point of saying "Only in destroying find I ease", and he thinks it will be 'glorious' to mar the creation. We find him again uncertain whether God created the angels (God is evidently not still creating 'young' ones), but the doubt no longer gives him any moral support:

he to be aveng'd
And to repair his numbers thus impair'd,
Whether such virtue spent of old now fail'd
More Angels to create, if they at least
Are his Created or to spite us more
Determin'd to advance into our room
A Creature form'd of Earth, and him endow . . . (145)

I fully agree with the disgust felt by C. S. Lewis for Satan's character as it has now become, and could even agree that his doubts about God are now merely a means of deceiving himself. But surely one must also feel horror at the God who has deliberately reduced him to such a condition. Even now, he is still capable of being struck 'stupidly good' when first confronted with Eve alone (IX. 465). He is a less painful sight after the Fall, because totally corrupt and merely the Devil; as when he meets Sin and Death, on his way back to Hell, and urges them forward to enslave and destroy mankind (X. 400). His boastful speech on his return admits that God created the world, though still not that he created the angels. God then turns all the rebels into snakes, thus proving to them that he was only playing cat and mouse all the time; and then of course turns them back, so that they may continue to work upon mankind.

Most critics are now agreed that there is a gradual calculated degradation of Satan, but this bit of understanding gets obscured by a hunger to argue that he is very bad from the start. The chief merit of the shape of the poem, I think, which has often been called magnificent architecture, is that it presents the change in Satan with such force. We first meet him certain of the righteousness of his cause though defeated, follow him into doubt and despair, switch back in the narrative of Raphael to find him confident that his cause will be victorious as well as just, then return to the story and find his character rapidly rotting away. As there is no slip-up anywhere in this involved programme, we can at least be sure that it was intended.

* * *

KENNETH GROSS

From Satan and the Romantic Satan: A Notebook†

What kind of claims might I make on behalf of Milton's devil? It has become far too easy, or too easy to attack, to call him a hero, even if we see in him aspects of Milton in his roles of poet, visionary quester, rebel against tyranny, conspirator for liberty, propagandist, worshiper in a church of one. And yet he remains an inescapable object of attention, and of troubled admiration—whether we admire the character or the force that calls him into being. I might call him a modernist hero, a hero of the fallen imagination, though I am then not sure where or when I would place, or how describe, the Fall. Perhaps I could demonstrate his claims to a kind of heroism that one cannot identify as fully or as adequately in any other character of *Paradise Lost*. Of course, most of us presume that the battle has been fought already, that the heroic Satan (the Romantic Satan) is primarily an error of neophytes, a figure whose claims on the mind are admitted only to be cast out by a sophisticated appeal to Milton's way of testing and tempting the reader (and perhaps himself). But still I would want to account for so persistent a fascination, one that repeated readings in Milton criticism have, in my own case, clarified rather than dispelled. I would want to speak about Satan not as *advocatus diaboli*—almost always a tool of orthodoxy, a ventriloquist's dummy—nor as heretic—though real heresy, were it possible here, might sharpen debate more than any pluralism. I would rather speak as someone willing to take seriously his own naïveté, to examine its stakes.

"Don't for *heaven's sake*, be afraid of talking nonsense!" warns Wittgenstein. "But you must pay attention to your nonsense."

* * *

† From Mary Nyquist and Margaret Ferguson, eds., *Re-Membering Milton: Essays on the Texts and Traditions* (New York and London: Methuen, 1988). Reprinted by permission of the publisher.

One must say that Milton could scarcely have believed in anything like a heroic devil, indeed that the whole structure of his religious thinking committed him to an ultimate deprecation of the devil as absurd or ungrounded. (And why else are there devils and demons, if not to focus our will to deprecate?) Yet any appeal to Milton's beliefs (his categorical distinctions, his constitutive habits of representation, his usable or intractable authorities, his investments in possibility) is hardly unproblematic. And it is not only that the poet may seem to have had hidden or conflicting beliefs, divided loyalties, secret identifications, or that the burdens of poetry and belief are not always compatible—all recurrent and much studied issues. It is also that, even if I am convinced that Milton shared basic stances or habits of mind with, say, Luther or Calvin, and that these are powerfully incarnated in the poetry, I am not perfectly sure of what it means for us to try and ground our reading of the poetry on a hypothetical commitment to the polarized terms of the poet's belief. Such a commitment is often seen as a necessary, even a sufficient condition for reading Milton's epic. Yet this asks a kind of critical fideism, a *sacrificio intellectus*, that in this particular context can breed its own sort of pride and bad faith. Must one simply give up the game, then? A philosopher might say that our skepticism lies not simply in our not knowing what to believe, but in not knowing quite what belief itself looks like, how it speaks, though we may think we have a sense of how it *has* spoken. Even many of our sympathetic ways of talking about religious beliefs—assuming that we do not blandly deplore religion as divisive ideology, mystified politics, or spilt poetry—tend to mark an abysmal separation from the things they seek to name, the forms of life they seek to describe. And if I am uncertain of what belief looks like, what its grammar is, what its scope and stakes are, how can I calmly suspend disbelief, or speak coherently of the beliefs of another?

* * *

The lure of Satan, or the idea of Satan, lies partly in the dialectical leverage which he offers us in our attempts to construe the larger stakes of Milton's poem. But Satan possesses a less impersonal appeal as well, one that depends not so much on our sense of his relative heroism as on Satan's place as a dramatic myth of the self, or as a peculiar and persuasive illusion of what a self or a character might be. The sophisticated ironies of Romantic readers help one describe this appeal, but for the moment some flatter, more awkward impressions may do just as well.

The claims of Satan might be articulated as follows: it is not that I like Satan's voice, mind, or attitude better than those of other characters in the poem, but rather that Satan, at times, seems to be the only character *with* a voice, mind, or attitude of his own, or the one who places the stresses of voice, mind, and attitude most clearly. I am fascinated with Satan's character because he seems to be the only character. The lure of Satan is the lure of the dramatized mind; he is the vessel for what Milton learned from reading *Hamlet, King Lear*, or *Macbeth* (as well as a radical interpretation for translation of the spirit which haunts Shakespeare's voices of solitude, reason, suspicion, protest, and madness). To put it more strongly: I like to think about Satan because Satan is the only character in the poem who thinks, or in whom I best recognize what it feels like to think (though this may only mean, of course, to think like Satan). Satan is Milton's picture of what thinking looks like, an image of the mind, of subjectivity, of self-consciousness, a representation of the awkward pressures we put on ourselves to interpret our own situation within the mind's shifting circle of freedom and compulsion. Satan is the poet's most palpable image of what human thought is like as it is moved, wounded, or disowned by its memories, desires, intentions, sensations, as it confronts body and environment, inertia and pain, as it engages the words and stories which shape and misshape it. Satan is an image of the mind in its dividedness from both itself and others, in its illusions of inwardness and power. (It is fitting that Adam's discourse to Eve about her dream (V.95–121), about the conflicts of reason and fantasy and the dangerous vagaries of imagination, is occasioned by the intrusion of a Satanic presence, and hence a witness to Satan's problematic place in the realms of mind. (The beautifully ambiguous association of Satan and Eve in such a scene is another matter. Adam's accusatory identification, "thou serpent" (X.867) is merely the most obvious example of the links between the two, these being more subtly apparent in the fact that Eve is the only mortal in the poem with whom the devil has any sort of "conversation.")) What is crucial to the focus on mind, however, is not any specific evidence in Satan of unconscious mental processes (e.g. Oedipal conflicts or sado-masochistic instincts), though we may discover these as well. For the moment, what counts more is the diverse attention to the mind working itself in any way, to the phenomenology or figurations of subjectivity in general. This Satan is not necessarily Romantic, though he may foreshadow the burdens of Romantic subjectivity and self-centering, the self's anxious quests for what Byron called "concentered recompense."

Satan, despite his unresting intellect, gets a lot wrong, perhaps gets everything wrong. But it is less than obvious what we are to make of this. Milton lets us know that, as opposed to Satan, the innocent and reasonable Adam gets things right, as when he knows on awakening that he has come to be not of himself, but of some "great Maker . . . in goodness and in power præeminent" (VIII.278–

9); and yet the picture of thought here is unsatisfying. Adam's first speech sounds oddly like something learned by rote, or like a bit of preacherly ventriloquism (despite even the subtle pathos of his later words, which surmise that it is because of his creator that he can "feel that I am happier then I know" (282)). It may in fact be the compulsiveness, the unbending error of Satan's words which makes them feel like so proper an emblem of the mind's life, of the work of mind. The steady awareness of Satan's conscious and unconscious falsehoods—his lies against himself, his cohorts, his God—the feeling of things lost or evaded, the evidence in his speeches of a mind crossed by longing and pain, the awareness of contexts and unacknowledged truths which press in, threaten, and block: there is good reason why these also have carried more dramatic weight with readers than the accurate theology of a reasonable God who must have no inside, no underside, no shifts in motivation (indeed, no motivation at all), must in a sense have no mind. This is a God whose difficult, spare, authoritative, and often beautiful utterances may yet appear to us as more unabashedly "political," just because they come to us, as Satan's never do, with so little dramatic framing to remind us of the historical and rhetorical conditions of utterance (a framing which Empson, with novelistic fervor, tried nevertheless to sketch out for us).

It might be argued that we can study the unfolding of a more strictly poetic and prophetic subjectivity in the intricate movements of Milton's invocations, or that we witness the work of mind externalized, allegorized, and idealized in the dynamic account of the Son / Logos creating the world (one image of the poet's work as an "expence of mind"). Still, neither of these offers us the kind of dramatic center for our interest in the career of mind that Satan does. To understand Satan's affective power in this context, however, depends on our being careful not to condescend, on our resisting the temptation to literalize or divinize any apparent superiority to Satan which we may feel in reading his speeches; it depends on our allowing that there are occasions when we ourselves (for better or worse) may echo or be implicated in Satan's mode of self-description:

Hail, horrours, hail
Infernal World, an I thou profoundcest Hell
Receive thy new Possessor: One who brings
A mind not to be chang'd by Place or Time.
The mind is its own place, and in it self
Can make a Heav'n of Hell, a Hell of Heav'n.
What matter where, if I be still the same,
And what I should be . . .

(I.250–7)

Satan's conditional gets him into trouble: he is, of course, neither the same as he was nor what he thinks he should be ("all but less then hee / Whom Thunder hath made greater"). The text does not quite allow us to know whether *he* sees this clearly. In any case, even if Satan were the same, we might rightly doubt his claims to a property or power of mind, to an enabled privacy, which could continually stand free of the pressures of place and history. We may sense that, by means of an elegant but desperately protesting chiasmus, he has only succeeded in converting the words "Heaven" and "Hell" into empty, interchangeable ciphers, and that he does so without the sort of dialectical energy we may feel in similar reversals of Blake's. (Hence he fails to know what it means to inhabit either place.) The deep solipsism that the mind discovers in its fall decays quickly into self-aggrandisement, tyranny, gaudy display; it acquires a dependence on others which only thrusts the mind into situations of greater moral and experiential solitude. That solipsism becomes a deadening and divisive egotism, it flourishes and sickens in Satan's desire for revenge, for reducing God's best creatures to his own level of suffering. Finally, Satan's will that the mind be its own place returns upon him with a vengeance: viewing the created world from the top of Mount Niphates, he finds that the "Hell within him" is indeed independent of place, not to be avoided or abandoned by mere change of site, that he cannot escape from the Hell which now *is* his self, nor from the deeper, even shadowier Hell of his speculative fears (cf. IV.18–23, 75–8).

And yet we need not assume that this later, ironic evolution of Satan's "error" wholly proves his desire an inevitable disaster, or inescapably confirms the emptiness of the claims articulated in the lines I have quoted from Book I. The questioning of teleology is crucial here. Satan's initial vision of mental place, of the metamorphosis of place within mind, does suggest something willful or delusive, and yet it seems to me that his vision feeds on the same fantasy which legitimates, or is legitimated by, Michael's last promise to Adam and Eve: that they can through piety and struggle come eventually to possess "a paradise within" themselves, "happier farr" than the one they had lost (XII.587). This is not just a divine, retrospective correction of Satan's mistaken claims, the true measure of an idea of which his is but a demonic parody. If Michael's words point to a state of mind not owned by one person alone, but rather to a state which is the gift of God to man and of men and women to each other—a product of the career of love as well as the career of mind—that state may nevertheless be part of Satan's gift to the human future, no blessing or temptation but a "desperate hallow."

WILLIAM FLESCH

From The Majesty of Darkness: Idol and Image in Milton†

* * *

Determining which party Milton was of, then, depends on deciding which is the party of the iconoclasts. Percy Shelley—who can represent the radical tradition from Blake to Empson—sees Satan as a forerunner of his own explicitly revolutionary hero Prometheus, and it is hard to quarrel with him that even for Milton Satan was on the side which saw itself as resisting oppression. I agree that there are problems with Satan—I insist on it—but certainly he spends a lot of time defending his attempted regicide in terms like those of Milton's defenses of the English people. If we are to admire Milton's refusal to idolize the name of king—"a name then which there needs no more among the blockish vulgar, to make it wise, and excellent, and admir'd, nay to set it next the Bible, though otherwise containing little els but the common grounds of tyranny and popery, drest up, the better to deceiv" (*Complete* Prose, 3:339)—it is difficult not to admire much of what Satan says to the same purpose. Throughout the first two books of *Paradise Lost* Satan denounces what he sees as "the Tyranny of Heav'n" (1.124) or what Mammon calls a "state / Of splendid vassalage" (2.251–52). His incitement of the rebel angels can couch itself as a plea for liberty from servile pomp, whose ceremonies seem to be important in heaven. Satan's objection to God's command about the Son that "to him shall bow / All knees in Heav'n, and shall confess him Lord" (5.607–8) seems justified since the Son has not yet demonstrated his worth. While Milton wants us to admire the Son because he volunteers to redeem humanity through his sacrifice, this reason for exaltation comes after Satan's rebellion (although earlier in the poem). Satan's objection to the Son stems, at least in part, from the same impulse that caused Milton to inveigh against arbitrariness in law giving. It would not be out of character for Satan to urge, with Milton, that "in the publishing of humane lawes, which for the most part aime not beyond the good society, to set them barely forth to the people without reason or Preface, like a physicall prescript, or only with threatnings, as it were a lordly command, in the judgment of *Plato* was thought to be done neither generously not wisely." The judgment Milton is approving is about human and civil laws, it is true, but Milton's heaven (and

† From *Generosity and the Limits of Authority: Shakespeare, Herbert, Milton* (Ithaca: Cornell UP, 1992). Reprinted by permission of the publisher.

at this point, Milton's God) does not seem fundamentally different in quality from civil society. If God's purpose is to evoke love in the angels, one would think he'd do better to use persuasion which is "a more winning and more manlike way to keepe men in obedience than feare," since it "would so incite, and in a manner, charme the multitude into the love of that which is really good, as to imbrace it ever after, not of custome and awe, which most men do, but of choice and purpose, with true and constant delight" (*Complete Prose*, 1:746). But God does not give Satan any persuasive reason for the law proclaiming the Son's glorification; to Satan it does indeed seem an arbitrary and lordly command:

> by Decree
> Another now hath to himself ingross't
> All Power, and us eclipst under the name
> Of King anointed.
> (5.774–77)

There is no reason to doubt that Satan's expectations were encouraged by a genuine belief that God ruled only through what Milton scornfully calls "custome and awe" and Satan calls "Consent or custom" (1.640). Satan's grandeur, even if it is the grandeur of archangel ruined, comes from his iconoclasm, from his desire for liberty.

Obviously there is an important difference between Milton and Satan. Satan is both admirable and deluded in this speech: admirable in his rejection of royality ratified only by tradition; deluded in thinking that the only other ratification of God's regal power is force. Unlike Satan, Milton can ground his iconoclasm on the worship of the true God. Killing kings is permissible because, as he says in the *First Defense* (relying on the doctrine of the king's two bodies), God has not approved of the person who acts as magistrate but of his office (*Complete Prose*, 4:386). It would be idolatry to confuse the two, to equate the office with the person when speaking of the temporal order and so to mistake the particular for the general; but it is different on high. God, Milton very much wants to argue, combines both functions. If there is no power but of God, then a rebellion against God is not a rebellion against a temporary vessel of power but against the source of power itself. Satan's error is, first, in not understanding the difference between a normative iconoclasm, which has the worship of God as its end, and one without teleology, but it must be urged in his defense that he never had an opportunity to learn this difference because heaven is run so much like an earthly state.

Nevertheless, there are other problems with Satan. His superiority to his conception of God may consist in his perseverance "in some purpose which he has conceived to be excellent, in spite of adversity and torture," as Shelley put it in his "Defence of Poetry," but it is not at all clear how excellent his purpose is. Empson and Bloom see *Paradise Lost* as chronicling Milton's struggle with the nobility of his own conception of Satan, a struggle that forced him into debasing or "rotting" his own noble conception as Satan's grandeur threatened to get out of hand. But Shelley's analysis of Satan in the preface to *Prometheus Unbound*, that he is not "exempt from the taints of ambition, envy, revenge, and a desire for personal aggrandisement," seems as true of Satan early (both in the poem and in the time frame) as later. Satan desires to conquer God so that he can reign in God's place: the liberty he would achieve would be for himself alone. His rejection of Christ's authority comes ultimately from his sense that his own power is being diminished. He refuses to worship the name of king in God: yet for himself and his crew he claims that their "Imperial Titles . . . assert / Our being ordain'd to govern, not to serve" (5.801–2). He will not acknowledge as true of himself what he argues against God, that titles of nobility are "merely titular" (5.774). Satan's revolt is not against tyranny. It is against a tyrant whose place he wishes to usurp.

We should admire, then, the iconoclastic traits that urge Satan to revolt against a figure who looks and acts very much like a tyrant, but we should not overlook his own similar tendencies. Satan never sustains the iconoclasm that makes him admirable because it exists side by side with a desire to be the worshiped icon. I think this accounts for our ambivalent feeling about Satan: heroic in his rebellion against idolatry, he never gets beyond it himself.

* * *

REGINA M. SCHWARTZ

From "Yet Once More": Re-Creation, Repetition, and Return†

* * *

The Satanic Will

The relation of ritual repetition to time is inherently contradictory: on the one hand, ritual acknowledges the passing of time; to "remember" an event is to assume that it has occurred in the past and can only be recovered imaginatively. On the other hand, the function of

† From *Remembering and Repeating: Biblical Creation in* Paradise Lost (New York: Cambridge UP, 1988), pp. 94–103. Reprinted by permission of the publisher.

ritual is to escape time, to offer its participants entry into a separated time where event and commemoration are one. Compulsive repetition is predicated on a different relation to time. Such repetition reflects an attempt to "get even" for an insult or affront to the psychic apparatus, but because the continual passing of time renders the effort to "get even" or re-do an injury impossible, the compulsive repeater would stop time, as Miss Havisham stopped her clocks in *Great Expectations*. Satan would not only avenge himself against his accusor, but against time itself, and he depicts his fall not as any wound, but specifically, as a *change*.

> how chang'd
> From him, who in the happy Realms of Light
> Cloth'd with transcendent brightness didst outshine
> Myriads though bright:
>
> (I.84–87)

And that change immediately inspires him to refuse any further change.

> yet not for those,
> nor what the Potent Victor in his rage
> Can else inflict, do I repent or change,
> Though chang'd in outward luster;
>
> (I.94–97)

The distinction he grasps for here, between outward and inward change, is obviously specious; he knows, as we know, that the inner reflects the outer, and amidst his verbal flailing between "change" and "no change," the simple truth emerges that he *has* changed and that he now stubbornly wills that change to be irrevocable. Indeed, his conjunction might well be more forcefully causal: Satan does not seize upon his resolve "though" changed in outward luster, but "because" of that diminishment. He will fix the will or "harden the heart" toward a single purpose. It is fixity, a "fixt mind / And high disdain," that emerges from the "sense of injur'd merit" he cannot recover (I.98–99).

Having suffered loss, Satan grasps for that which can brook no loss. If heaven cannot be his eternally, then at least hate can be immortal. In his frustration that he cannot recapture the past, to undo and re-do it, he tries to seize control of change itself.

> What though the field be lost:
> All is not lost; the unconquerable Will,
> And study of revenge, immortal hate,
> And courage never to submit or yield:
> And what is else not to be overcome?
>
> (I.105–09)

These words are fraught with telling contradictions. "*Having lost*, I refuse to lose; *having been forced to yield*, I refuse to yield." And that last odd question, "what is else not to be overcome?" seductively suggests conflicting meanings. On the one hand, it suggests the tautology, "my will never to be overcome will never be overcome"; on the other, self-justification: "I must embrace revenge and hate for only they are of lasting consequence." But there is a more desperate underside to the sentiment: "We have been so thoroughly defeated that nothing is left us—'what is else?'—but defiance itself." The ostensibly heroic lines want to collapse into a plaintive "What have we left?" And the confusion we note here spills over into their sequel: "That Glory never shall his wrath or might / Extort from me" (I. 110–11). What glory? The glory of revenge and hate, the glory of resolve itself? Is there a "glory" left for Satan that has not been "extorted" already? Satan answers that question himself, deflating his own posturing less than thirty lines later: all glory is "extinct" (I.141). The contradictions in these lines stem from a fundamental one: Satan's will to be unconquerable is born of the essential impotence of his will.

Nietzsche speaks of this impotence of the will in the face of time as its prison.

> Willing liberates; but what is it that puts even the liberator himself in fetters? "It was"—that is the name of the will's gnashing of teeth and most secret melancholy. Powerless against what has been done, he is an angry spectator of all that is past. The will cannot will backwards; and that he cannot break time and time's covetousness, that is the will's loneliest melancholy.

It is a desperate assertion of mastery where there can be none that drives Satan to *choose* that hell of a bound will rather than suffer it. Satan's resolve of an unchanging mind and his appropriation of hell can now be seen as analogous efforts: to convert defeat into a choice. The victim of time and place would rule both time and place.

> Hail horrors, hail
> Infernal world, and thou profoundest Hell
> Receive thy new Possessor: One who brings
> A mind not to be chang'd by Place or Time.
> (I.250–53)

Nietzsche's words could be Satan's manifesto: "To recreate all 'it was' into a 'thus I willed it'—that alone I should call redemption." Like Hamlet, Satan could be bounded in a nutshell and count himself the king of infinite space—"the mind is its own place, and in itself / Can make a Heav'n of Hell" (I.254–55)—were it not that he has bad dreams—"which way I fly is Hell, myself am Hell" (IV.75).

Because of the irreversibility of the flow of time, the effort to re-do the past erupts in repetitions and substitutions. To avenge themselves on God, the fallen angels would repeat their fall in man. They would "drive as we were driven" (II.366). Nietzsche speaks of revenge as the logical consequence of time's restraint.

> what means does the will devise for himself to get rid of his melancholy and to mock his dungeon? Alas, every prisoner becomes a fool; and the imprisoned will redeems himself foolishly. That time does not run backwards, that is his wrath; "that which was" is the name of the stone he cannot move. And so he moves stones out of wrath and displeasure, and he wreaks revenge on whatever does not feel wrath and displeasure as he does. Thus the will, the liberator, took to hurting; and on all who can suffer he wreaks revenge for his inability to go backwards. This, indeed this alone, is what *revenge* is: the will's ill will against time and its "it was."

Re-inflicting his injury on others, Satan finds that it only redounds upon himself, and he falls forever. "Revenge, at first though sweet, / Bitter ere long back on itself recoils" (IX.171–72). Such repetitions only lock him in his injury, precluding any genuine change, precluding, that is, innovation. Ironically, Satan's drive for fixity is fulfilled in this iterative sense. Vengeful repetition is linked to fixity in another sense: born of a sense of impotence, it confirms the feeling of paralysis of the will—for repetitions which are derived from injury are not so much willed, as they are compelled.

When Freud linked the need to master an injury to the compulsive nature of repetition, he observed that a child at play could derive no obvious pleasure from reenacting the disappearance of his mother—hiding and recovering a spool in the *fort-da* game—except that now the child could control the absence and presence of the object. The formal expression of this attempted mastery, the game, has important implications. The *fort-da* game is not only motivated by the child's inability to control his mother's leave-takings; the very fact of the game itself confirms his ineffectuality. The real object of his frustration is never mastered. The mother's will is never subject to the child's. The child's domain, like Satan's hell, is no domain at all, and his substitutive and repetitive efforts to master, like Satan's, are only the semblance of control. Pandemonium is just such a play-domain. While it is erected in an effort to replace what is lost—with the roof of that "fabric huge" mirroring the floor of heaven, its "Starry Lamps and blazing Cressets . . . yielded light / As from a sky" (I.728–30)—the size similes that conclude Book I mock that effort, reducing the capital to a beehive. The game-world circumscribing the infernal will is underscored again in the account of the pursuits of the devils. Their philosophy, poetry, and war exercises are described, as we might expect, as means to "entertain / The irksome hours" (IV.526–27), that is, as play, not as solutions. Even that most serious business of the temptation and fall of man, where the real-life consequence is death, is enveloped by an aura of childsplay. Satan cannot heave his head from off the fiery flood without the "will / And high permission" (I.211–12) of his Father; and with his reiterated crime only redounding upon his own head, the redemption of man is implicit from the very beginning. The essential futility of re-doing by repeating is expressed most forcefully in that terrible game.

The quality that emerges most consistently in the portrayal of Satanic mastery, then, is that it is false.

> Nor hope to be myself less miserable
> By what I seek, but others to make such
> As I, though thereby worse to me redound:
> (IX.126–28)

The attempt to master past injuries by seeking revenge is grounded both in the sense that there is nothing to lose and that nothing could really be gained. Even amidst Satan's rallying efforts and contrivance of revenge plots during the debate in hell, the idea of achieving reparation, if entertained, is never seriously anticipated. We can detect little confidence in Satan's first proposal that the injured parties seek revenge.

> Thither let us tend
> From off the tossing of these fiery waves,
> There rest, if any rest can harbor there,
> And reassembling our afflicted Powers,
> Consult how we may henceforth most offend
> Our Enemy, our own loss how repair,
> How overcome this dire Calamity,
> What reinforcement we may gain from Hope,
> If not what resolution from despair.
> (I.183–91)

That repair/despair rhyme is suggestive. The effort to repair through repeating is born of despair, and such an attempt at reparation can only conclude in despair. The little optimism that begins this passage soon dissipates, until by the last line no "overcoming" is imaginable; we are left only with resolve. Even when Satan triumphantly proclaims that he leaves hell to seek deliverance, at the same time, he adjures the devils to search for a way to render hell more tolerable (II.456–66). Beelzebub seems to contradict Satan's realism, venturing the most hopeful lines uttered during the debate in hell. He envisions no less than the restoration of heaven's light to those who tempt man, and he speaks explicitly of the possibility of healing their injury. Still, this optimism is hedged with tentativeness, and like Satan's speeches, the "perhapses" and "we may chances" utterly collapse into the alternative vision—"or else"—and a fantasy of "some mild zone" ensues.

> Great things resolv'd, which from the lowest deep
> Will once more lift us up, in spite of Fate,
> Nearer our ancient Seat; perhaps in view
> Of those bright confines, whence with neighboring Arms
> And opportune excursion we may chance
> Re-enter Heav'n; or else in some mild Zone
> Dwell not unvisited of Heav'n's fair Light
> Secure, . . .
> . . . the soft delicious Air,
> To heal the scar of these corrosive Fires
> Shall breathe her balm.
>
> (II.392–402)

Beelzebub's shaky hope stands on even shakier ground, for his plan for this reparation—indeed, the entire argument to seduce man—is based wholly on the opposite conviction, that heaven is impenetrable: its "high walls fear no assault or Siege, / Or ambush from the Deep" (II.343–44). Moloch's imagined victories (turning "our Tortures into horrid Arms / Against the Torturer") also fade, like Satan's strained optimism, into his admission of complete ineffectuality. The devils' power may be sufficient to "disturb his Heaven", but then again, it may only "Alarm, / Though inaccessible, his fatal Throne" (II.103–4). His apologetic conclusion—"Which if not Victory is yet Revenge"—admits that the two are not at all synonymous.

The only significant difference between the plans of the roughhewn Moloch and Satan's more wily plot is substitution. Moloch would storm heaven again; Satan would also try again, on earth. Their common advocacy of desperate repetition far outweighs that difference. With his look of "desperate revenge," Moloch not only voices, he embodies the logic of Satanic repetition. The consequence Moloch imagines, falling again, is precisely the one Satan knows he will suffer for his "reiterated crimes" (I.214). In this sense, the infernal debate has already closed with its first, not its last, speaker. The fact that there is no substantive change from Moloch's to Satan's positions about how to rectify their plight—to "match torment with torment" is "to drive as we were driven"—reflects the characteristic stasis of revenge: for all their talk, they cannot move forward. Because revenge, by its very character, never achieves satisfaction, the effort to turn "it was" into "thus I willed it" through substitutions and repeatings can find "no end, in wand'ring mazes lost" (II.561).

Such repetitions of injury issue in death, or, more accurately, in the death-in-life that denies even an end to life's torments: it is not only as liminal figures, but as perpetual victims who perpetually victimize, that the devils become "neither living nor dead from one aspect and both living and dead from another." Satan is "to Death devote" (IX.901). He repeats his injury with the hope, not just of expelling mankind, but with the more comprehensive aim of wasting the whole creation. As we have seen, the fallen angels talk nervously of the possibility of being completely annihilated and Satan forms a natural alliance with the uncreated chaos. But to understand fully the relation between death and Satanic repetition, we must turn to the allegory of Sin and Death. Milton was willing to take this generic adventure, risk incurring the future wrath of a Samuel Johnson—"This unskillful allegory appears to me one of the greatest faults of the poem"—because only in allegory could the fundamental logic of compulsive repetition be fully addressed. Allegorical characters are projections of the self, and Satan's incestuous self-reproduction graphically illustrates that the issue of such repetition is not a new creation, but Death.

Doubling is the spatial form of temporal repetition, and its source, according to both Freud and Otto Rank, is narcissism. In Satan's refusal to confront a genuine Other—for such an Other would be an insult to the grandeur of the all-encompassing Self—he reproduced only projections of the Self. Like all regressive tendencies, narcissism has as its goal "the attempt to return to a state in which subject and object did not yet exist, to a time before that division occurred out of which the ego sprang," to a time when Self and Other were combined in an internal love union. Thus, we might expect narcissism ultimately to lead back to the womb. But Freud would see this return as a regression to a state even earlier—the state of non-being prior to birth. This becomes the ultimate return; for Freud, all compulsive repetitions, doubling included, are really disguised attempts to restore the original state of non-being. As the classical myth tells it, narcissism leads to death. While Freud tries to ground this theory of the death instinct organically in *Beyond the Pleasure Principle*, he might well have written the allegory of Sin and Death instead.

Satan's narcissism is most powerfully in evidence in his refusal to acknowledge the Other, his Creator. His claim to be self-begotten, his resistance to the Son, all bespeak a towering self-love. He responds to the elevation of the Son with more than denial: he responds by eproducig himself in his own image, conceiving Sin.

With Sin his "perfect image," "likest to [him] in shape and count'nance bright" (II.756), Satan's love for Sin is self-love. The doubling continues, until the repetitions issue in Death, but again, not a final death, for the deadly offspring of Sin and Death are "hourly conceiv'd / And hourly born" (II.796–97). What is most painful in that "Sight hateful, sight tormenting" of Adam and Eve "imparadis't in one another's arms" (IV.505, 506) is the fact that *two* are participating in that embrace. As Rank explains, noting the phenomenon in Oscar Wilde's *Dorian Gray*, narcissism precludes love for another: " 'I wish I could love,' cried Dorian Gray, with a deep note of pathos in his voice. 'But I seem to have lost the passion, and forgotten the desire. *I am too much concentrated on myself* [Rank's emphasis]. My own personality has become a burden to me. I want to escape, to go away, to forget.' " Satan acknowledges that not the least of his pains is his perpetual longing, and the narcissistic origins of that frustration are confirmed when Eve gazes at her fair image in the pool: she too would have "pin'd with vain desire" (IV.466).

While Milton reserves the classical type scene of narcissism for Eve, she echoes the doubling of Satan and Sin. Had the warning voice not led her away from her watery image to the Other, Eve would have succumbed to doubling.

> A Shape within the wat'ry gleam appear'd
> Bending to look on me, I started back,
> It started back, but pleas'd I soon return'd,
> Pleas'd it return'd as soon with answering looks
> Of sympathy and love;
>
> (IV.461–65)

Both Sin and Eve are engendered without mothers. Both are born—andthe detal must have been deliberate—from the left side of their parent/mate; Milton truncates his line that describes Sin's birth, allowing the ambiguity about the precise nature of that generation to echo for several verses before he clarifies that Sin is born from Satan's head and not from his rib.

> till on the left side op'ning wide,
> Likest to thee in shape and count'nance bright,
> Then shining heav'nly fair, a Goddess arm'd
> Out of thy head I sprung:
>
> (II.755–58)

When Eve does fall, she prophesies that the issue of her loins, like Sin's, will be "Food for so foul a Monster" (X.986). Conversely, Eve's initial renunciation of narcissism is proleptic of her later turn away from mothering generations and generations "devote" to death.

Eve, who is brought away from her image, taken "where no shadow stays / Thy coming" (IV.470–71), (where, that is, no double forestalls her) will not spawn endless doubles: she will be the mother of Life, not Death.

Self-love, the love of the double, does not suffice to explain the whole response to this shadow self; the reaction is far more ambivalent. Any notion of an ideal self involves the guilty rejection of those desires and instincts which do not fit that ideal image. When these internal anomalies are cast out, they also return externalized as the double. And so the individual is both attracted and repelled by this self-image. Satan is so abhorred by his Sin that he cannot, or will not, recognize it as his own.

> I know thee not, nor ever saw till now
> Sight more detestable than him and thee.
>
> (II.744–45)

While Satan's inability to recognize Sin and Death may become comic, that failure also suggests a profound insight into just this self-loathing. What Satan rejects as most offensive is, of course, his own mortality, and the double becomes a haunting reminder of that limitation. Satan sees, not just Death, but *his* death and that is why he recoils from it in horror.

> Whence and what are thou, execrable shape,
> That dar'st, though grim and terrible, advance
> Thy miscreated Front athwart my way
> To yonder Gates?
>
> (II.681–84)

Satan's will to master that which makes him most impotent asserts itself again. That will-to-master coupled with the loathing of the rejected self makes murder of the double his likely goal. But to master death, to kill the double, is to commit suicide. Satan's confrontation with death—"No second stroke intend" (II.713)—is ultimately a suicide scene. That implication becomes explicit when Death pursues but does not devour his other double, Sin; that too would be suicide, in this case, the end of Death itself.

> Before mine eyes in opposition sits
> Grim *Death* my Son and foe, who sets them on,
> And me his Parent would full soon devour
> For want of other prey, but that he knows
> His end with mine involv'd; and knows that I
> Should prove a bitter Morsel, and his bane,
> Whenever that shall be;
>
> (II.803–09)

Linking narcissism to thanatophobia, Rank points out that for the sufferer, it is not the fear of death, but "the *expectation* of the unavoidable destiny of death [that] is unbearable." Again, he aptly quotes Dorian Gray, " 'I have no terror of Death. It is only *the coming* of death that terrifies me.' "

> The normally unconscious thought of the approaching destruction of the self—the most general example of the repression of an unendurable certainty—torments these unfortunates with the conscious idea of their eternal, eternal [*sic*] inability to return, an idea from which release is only possible in death. Thus we have the strange paradox of the suicide who voluntarily seeks death in order to free himself of the intolerable thanatophobia.

If Satan's effort to master death, rather, to master his dread of death, is deferred here in Book II, it is only to be enacted later in the more involuted manner of the temptation and fall. Sin predicts that this aborted battle with Death will be resumed, conducted by "His wrath which one day will destroy ye both" (II.734). The narrator seconds Sin's comparison of the mock fight between Death and Satan to a final showdown between Satan and Christ.

> so matcht they stood;
> For never but once more was either like
> To meet so great a foe:
> (II.720–22)

Doubling proliferates temporally as well as spatially—the doubles will meet their doubles once more. This "once more," like the "once more" of "Lycidas," refers to the final battle at Judgment Day. That allusion suggests that doubling extends beyond Satan and Death: Satan is also Christ's double. Satan is the rejected self, the rejected son, who pursues and is pursued until he is killed, while Christ becomes a glorified suicide. Hebrews tells us that he is incarnated so that "through death he might destroy him who has the power of death, that is, the devil, and deliver all those who through fear of death were subject to lifelong bondage" (2:14b, 15).

* * *

On God

C. S. LEWIS

From the conclusion to A Preface to *Paradise Lost*†

* * *

In the second place, Milton's presentation of God the Father has always been felt to be unsatisfactory. Here again it is easy to look too deep for the causes. I very much doubt whether the failure is due to Milton's religious defects or whether it chiefly consists in giving us a cold, merciless, or tyrannical Deity. Many of those who say they dislike Milton's God only mean that they dislike God: infinite sovereignty *de jure*, combined with infinite power *de facto*, and love which, by its very nature, includes wrath also—it is not only in poetry that these things offend. To be sure, better men than Milton have written better than Milton of God; but the offence of his conception is not wholly due to its defects. And furthermore, I think the offence of his presentation is not wholly, or even mainly, due to his conception. The theological flaws (however we assess them) would not be *poetically* disastrous if only Milton had shown more poetical prudence. A God, theologically speaking, much worse than Milton's, would escape criticism if only He had been made sufficiently awful, mysterious, and vague. When the poet is content to suggest, our theological scruples are cast to the winds. When we read

> About him all the Sanctities of Heaven
> Stood thick as Starrs, and from his sight receiv'd
> Beatitude past utterance.
> (III, 60),

or

> Dark with excessive bright thy skirts appear
> (III, 380),

we are silenced. It is when the Son bows over His sceptre or the Father entertains the angels with "rubied Nectar" served "in Pearl, in Diamond, and massie Gold" that we are displeased. Milton has failed to disentangle himself from the bad tradition (seen at its worst in Vida's *Christiad* and at its best in the *Gierusalemme Liberata*) of trying to make Heaven too like Olympus. It is these anthropomorphic

† From *A Preface to* Paradise Lost (London and New York: Oxford UP, 1942), pp. 93–100. Reprinted by permission of the publisher.

details that make the Divine laughter sound merely spiteful and the Divine rebukes querulous; that they need not have sounded like this, Dante and the Hebrew prophets show.

* * *

To many it seems that the failure—even if it is only a partial failure—of Milton's God destroys *Paradise Lost* as a religious poem. And I think it is quite true that in some very important senses it is not a religious poem. If a Christian reader has found his devotion quickened by reading the medieval hymns or Dante or Herbert or Traherne, or even by Patmore or Cowper, and then turns to *Paradise Lost*, he will be disappointed. How cold, how heavy and external it will all seem! How many blankets seem to be interposed between us and our object! But I am not sure that *Paradise Lost* was intended to be a religious poem in the sense suggested, and I am sure it need not be. It is a poem depicting the objective pattern of things, the attempted destruction of that pattern by rebellious self love, and the triumphant absorption of that rebellion into a yet more complex pattern. The cosmic story—the ultimate *plot* in which all other stories are episodes—is set before us. We are invited, for the time being, to look at it from outside. And that is not, in itself, a religious exercise. When we remember that we also have our places in this plot, that we also, at any given moment, are moving either towards the Messianic or towards the Satanic position, then we are entering the world of religion. But when we do that, our epic holiday is over: we rightly shut up our Milton. In the religious life man faces God and God faces man. But in the epic it is feigned, for the moment, that we, as readers, can step aside and see the faces both of God and man in profile. We are not invited (as Alexander would have said) to *enjoy* the spiritual life, but to *contemplate* the whole pattern within which the spiritual life arises. Making use of a distinction of Johnson's we might say that the subject of the poem "is not piety, but the motives to piety." The comparison with Dante may be misleading. No doubt Dante is in most respects simply a better poet than Milton. But he is also doing a different kind of thing. He is telling the story of a spiritual pilgrimage—how one soul fared in its passage through the universe and how all may fear and hope to fare. Milton is giving us the story of the universe itself. Hence, quite apart from any superiority in Dante's art or Dante's spirituality (and I freely admit that he is often superior in both) the *Comedy* is a religious poem, a poetical expression of religious experience, as *Paradise Lost* is not. A failure in the last canto of the *Paradiso* would be disastrous because Dante is himself looking at God and inviting us to look with him. But Milton has only to describe how the angels and Adam looked at God: and a theologically inadequate symbol for God will not ruin the whole scheme—as in some large religious pictures it may be the position of the Christ that counts rather than the actual drawing of His face. No doubt the drawing of the face might be so bad that we could not get over it, and similarly Milton's God might be so bad as to spoil the whole pattern of which He is the centre. But I do not think He is as bad, or even nearly as bad, as that.

* * *

WILLIAM EMPSON

From Critics†

The extremely thorough reconsideration of *Paradise Lost* during this century, beginning with Sir Walter Raleigh's splendid handbook (1900), has made the poem more interesting and beautiful by greatly advancing our understanding of it; but the general reader has not been much encouraged to regard the contestants in this cooperative light, and may well suppose that the fighting has merely died down out of exhaustion. In trying to bring the results together I am inherently offering to act as mediator, though the position may only invite brickbats from all sides. The opinions of both attackers and defenders of the poem have evidently corresponded to their various theologies or world-views; most of them have not cared to drive their argument to the point of saying so, but the subject cannot be viewed in a purely aesthetic manner, as Milton himself would be the first to claim. His God is somehow 'embarrassing'; indeed, almost all the contestants have used that coy word, with its comforting suggestion of a merely social blunder. Professor C. S. Lewis let in some needed fresh air (*A Preface to Paradise Lost*, 1942) by saying, "Many of those who say they dislike Milton's God only mean that they dislike God" (p. 126); speaking as an Anglican, he decided that the poem merely uses beliefs which are central to any Christian theology, except for some minor and doubtful points; but even he was ready to grant that Milton might sometimes describe God 'imprudently' (p. 93). I am anxious to make my beliefs clear at the outset, because the revival of Christianity among literary critics has rather taken me by surprise. A number of young people nowadays, as one can readily understand, feel that 'modern' ideals and programmes, a very mixed bag of them, have worked out so badly that the traditional ones may be better; but

† From *Milton's God* (London: Chatto & Windus, 1961). Reprinted by permission of Curtis Brown Ltd., London, on behalf of The William Empson Estate.

how badly those used to work out too seems to have been successfully kept hidden. Thus young people often join a Church because they think it is the only way to avoid becoming a Communist, without realizing that a Renaissance Christian State was itself usually a thorough-going police terror. 'Dislike' is a question-begging term here. I think the traditional God of Christianity very wicked, and have done since I was at school, where nearly all my little playmates thought the same. I did not say this in my earlier literary criticism because I thought it could be taken for granted, and that to fuss about it would do no good (like anyone else, I have sometimes expressed a solemn interest in the ancient craving for human sacrifice and its protean reappearances, but this does not imply Christian belief); and it seems that nowadays the gap often makes a reader find my position evasive or illogical. Having had ten years teaching in Japan and China, and having only been interested in propaganda during the war, halfway through them, I am still rather ill-adjusted to the change of atmosphere. Lecturing at Government universities in the Far East, which means firmly nonmissionary ones, was not likely to prepare me for it; I gathered that those of my students who became interested in *Paradise Lost*, though too polite to express their opinion to me quite directly, thought "Well, if they worship such a monstrously wicked God as all that, no wonder that they themselves are so monstrously wicked as we have traditionally found them." Most Christians are so imprisoned by their own propaganda that they can scarcely imagine this reaction; though a missionary would have to agree that to worship a wicked God is morally bad for a man, so that he ought to be free to question whether his God is wicked. Such an approach does at least make Milton himself appear in a better light. He is struggling to make his God appear less wicked, as he tells us he will at the start (I.25), and does succeed in making him noticeably less wicked than the traditional Christian one; though, after all his efforts, owing to his loyalty to the sacred text and the penetration with which he makes its story real to us, his modern critics still feel, in a puzzled way, that there is something badly wrong about it all. That this searching goes on in *Paradise Lost*, I submit, is the chief source of its fascination and poignancy; and to realize that it is going on makes the poem feel much better at many points, indeed clears up most of the objections to it.

I thus tend to accept the details of interpretation which various recent critics have used to prove the poem bad, and then try to show that they make it good. The essay is by no means a complete survey; the field of Milton criticism has become very large, and maybe a man who had covered it all would not have much energy of judgement left; but I have tried to follow up the lines which seem to me important. Nor can I claim to digest all of the objections, and this first chapter is mainly concerned with points of radical disagreement. Thus I cannot agree with the following statement of Dr Leavis: that a man who writes in the style of Milton

> whatever he may suppose, is not really interested in the achievement of precise thought of any kind; he certainly hasn't the kind of energy of mind needed for sustained analytic and discursive thinking.

It is understandable to dislike the mind of the later Milton, but he was an experienced propagandist, very capable of deploying his whole case so as to convince his readers of what he had already decided they should believe. Certainly, his poetic style does not let us watch him in the process of deciding, but we happen to be able to do that in the *De Doctrina*, and his prose style there does not have the qualities which Dr Leavis finds to entail a contemptible mind in *Paradise Lost*. Dr Leavis seems to assume that Christianity must be at worst a neutral literary topic, so that anything ugly or confused in the poem must be the fault of the author; it strikes me that Dr Leavis is the one who failed to do the analytic and discursive thinking here. However, I recognize that many present-day Christians cheerfully agree with him, and would insist that Milton makes God bad by getting into muddles. My chief difference from them is that I do not believe the religion can so easily be reformed; I warmly agree so far as they regard the poem as an awful warning. Milton is a kind of historian here, recording a large public fact; this is so well recognized that many people agree on it while disagreeing about what the fact was. An enlightened view often held is that he expressed a large part of the public mind of Europe during his period, both Reformation and Counter-Reformation; in some damaging way they were both making God 'legalistic', and the poem illustrates the bad effects. This is probably the main thing a teacher should say on the question, as it is almost uncontroversial and yet enough to make a student feel free to read the poem intelligently (to point out the marks of Milton's Arianism helps the same purpose). My objection is that it uses the Renaissance thinkers as scapegoats, whereas really they were going back to the intellectual roots of the religion. Whether this is so or not, the poem enlarges the experience of most readers in an important way; it is an impressive example of one of the more appalling things the human mind is liable to do.

The recent controversy about the poem, on the other hand, has largely been conducted between attackers who find it bad because it makes God bad and defenders who find it all right because it leaves God tolerable, even though Milton is tactless about him. Surely this is an absurd spectacle; the poem is not good in spite of but especially because of its moral confusions, which ought to be clear in your mind when you are feeling its power. I think it horrible and wonderful; I regard it as like Aztec or Benin sculpture, or to come nearer home the novels of Kafka, and am rather suspicious of any critic who claims not to feel anything so obvious. Hence I also expect that most of the attackers would find their minds at rest if they took one step further and adopted the manly and appreciative attitude of Blake and Shelley, who said that the reason why the poem is so good is that it makes God so bad.

* * *

STANLEY FISH

From The Milk of the Pure Word†

* * *

Ingrate

The defence, however, cannot rest without admitting that the difficulties Milton's God poses for most readers remain. Northrop Frye's lifelong experience with the poem is a case in point:

> When as a student I first read the speech in Book Three of *Paradise Lost* in which 'God the Father turns a school divine', I thought it was grotesquely bad. I have been teaching and studying *Paradise Lost* for many years, and my visceral reaction to that speech is still exactly the same. But I see much more clearly than I did at first why Milton wanted such a speech at such a point.
>
> (*The Aims and Methods of Scholarship in Modern Languages and Literatures*, ed. James Thorpe, p. 64)

Frye's 'visceral reaction' is what all readers (who are not saints) feel to some extent—dismay, disappointment, and a reluctant hostility. The argument of the preceding pages holds, I think, through the phrase 'that shall redound'; but the confidence we have in the voice that intones this prediction soon becomes the source of new anxieties and discomforts. Milton has provided God with a dramatic moment so rhetorically effective that it secures for him a believing audience. This is fine when God is telling us what we want to hear—Satan will be defeated and the threat he represents in the poem

† From *Surprised by Sin: The Reader in* Paradise Lost, 2nd ed. (Cambridge: The Belknap Press of Harvard UP, 1998).

dispelled—but our complacence does not survive the inexorability of 'and shall pervert, / For Man will heark'n to his glozing lies, / And easily transgress the sole Command, / Sole pledge of his obedience' (92–95) * * * Where God had a willing audience at line 85, he holds us captive from line 92 on. (To dethrone him now would be only to add one more false deity to the roll call of Book I and one more error of judgment to a list already too long.)

The problem for the reader is compounded by the pace of the presentation. The closeness of God's methodical logic works against any effort to follow it. God dwells on a point only for the length of time it takes to state it concisely (truly), and that time is insufficient for a merely human mind to assimilate the various parts of a complex argument (Boethius spends five books saying something God says in six lines). Given no opportunity to make the psychological and mental adjustments the speech finally requires, the reader is always off balance as he struggles to place statements that refuse to stand still for him; his reactions lag behind his eye.

Contributing to his discomfort is the experience of overhearing a legal brief in which he is the defendant and pronounced guilty. We have seen how God's speech exists simultaneously on two levels within a single space: it is an exhaustive and objective description of what is; it is an oration delivered before auditors 'in a certain frame of mind'. For a few moments these two levels are perceived as one by the observer and draw from him an integrated response; but this harmony is disturbed when the diagramming of reality is discovered to involve the stating of facts that cannot be heard with equanimity. In other words, at some point, the formal and rhetorical proofs of deity cease to be complementary; the rhetorical proof fails as God does nothing to assure the good will of the jury; instead the traditional oratorical situation is reversed since the speaker judges the audience. To be sure, the oratorical situation does not actually exist for the expositor, who is unaware of his fallen auditors. Milton employs a familiar stage technique: a soliloquy is spoken within earshot of a character for whom it was not meant, and the result is a series of complications that are more or less created by this accident of coincidence. In this case the complication is the creation in the reader's mind of attitudes and modes of thought that have nothing to do with the intentions (if the word can be used) of the speaker, but which affect him as an object of worship and make the experience of the poem even more disquieting and arduous than it has been heretofore.

* * * The quality of the auditor's response measures his humility; if he can hear the judgment of the word—'They are corrupt, they have done abominable works, there is none that doeth good' (Psalm 14)—and answer with the psalmist 'cleanse me from my sin, For I

acknowledge my transgressions' (Psalm 51), his motions are godly; but if he protests at the accusation ('ingrate!') and turns aside to the flattery of worldly counsel or to the evasions of his own reason, he betrays his iniquity and is deficient in contrition.

* * *

Critics of Milton's God complain of his harshness and wish that the poet had been able 'to suggest a loving God' or at least a God less 'obstinately there', rather than this 'invitation . . . to stare God full in the face'; but Milton would be derelict in his duty if he were inconsiderately kind and protected his reader from the full force of the Truth.

* * *

The division some see in the logical and rhetorical aspects of God's public personality is a reflection of the division in the fallen reader, between that part of him which recognizes the truth and that part of him which rises, unbidden, against it, and resists its efforts to make him free. To God belongs the essence of the speech, the completeness, the logical perfection, the perfect accuracy of its perceptions; all else is the reader's, the harshness, the sense of irritation, the querulousness. The monologue of the divine expositor 'pointing out the connections among parts' is dispassionate, and if we find it unsatisfactory the fault (quite literally) is ours. 'If our understanding have a film of ignorance over it, or be blear with gazing on other false glisterings ['entising words'] what is that to Truth.' The emotional content of a word like 'ingrate' (if it is felt) is provided by the reader who receives it defensively, his pride resisting the just accusation, and confers on the speaker a tone compatible with his own reaction; the recalcitrance of the sinner, not the vindictiveness of his God, is the source of the difficulty. The word leads a double life; it leaps from the page to evoke a 'visceral' response and it falls into place as a perfect (accurate) definition of an object (you) in space; only one life, however, is real, the other is an illusion projected by the reaction of a guilty reader. Equally illusory is God's vaunted defensiveness. He does not argue, he asserts, disposing a series of self-evident axioms in an objective order, 'not talking to anyone in particular but meditating on objects'. (Of course, God technically addresses the Son, but he is not in any sense, we feel, initiating a discussion, although he is, as we discover, creating a situation within which the poem's first truly heroic act will be performed.) The most provocative of God's propositions, 'they themselves decreed / Thir own revolt, not I', is merely a stage in the impersonal unfolding of the discourse, and it reflects no attitude on the speaker's part towards man or towards himself. A logical proof in the Ramist (non-syllogistic) manner proceeds by contraries. The positive ('Whose but his own?') is proved by eliminating alternative possibilities; 'indeed in the establishment of any true axiom', Bacon insists, 'the negative instance is the more forcible.' The tendency to argue with God, like the sense of injury we feel at hearing his words, is *self*-revealing, a manifestation of the rebellion of the carnal reason in defiance of heavenly disposition; the flesh has not yet been mortified. This distinction—between the objective reality of the speech and the 'human impression', for which the fallen perspective, to the degree we are bound to it, is responsible—is not external to the reading experience. I make it as a reader in the confidence that Milton would have expected his contemporary reader, trained in analysis, committed to introspection, acutely aware of logical and rhetorical categories, to make it, consciously, while seeing in it evidence of his own intransigence.

The possibility of recovering an integrated response to God, of healing the split between the erected wit and the infected will, is represented by the poet, who joins in the heavenly songs of praise, and by the angelic audience:

> Thus while God spake, ambrosial fragrance fill'd
> All Heav'n, and in the blessed Spirits elect
> Sense of new joy ineffable diffus'd.
>
> (135–7)

Waldock wonders ironically, 'And it is in response to such words as these [i.e., as God's] that the blessed spirits . . . feel new joy suffusing them' (*Paradise Lost and Its Critics*, p. 103). The angels' joy, signifying as it does a recognition of God's goodness and glory, is a rebuke to those of us who cannot share it whole-heartedly. If the poem is successful, the reader will finally be able to hear the Word joyfully, and join, with Milton, in the angelic hallelujahs.

* * *

NORTHROP FRYE

From The Garden Within†

* * *

We have spoken of the similarity of the structure of the first three books of *Paradise Lost* to that of the Jonsonian masque, a murky disorganized antimasque being followed by a vision of splendour and

† From *The Return of Eden: Five Essays on Milton's Epics* (Toronto: U of Toronto P, 1965), pp. 60–72, 98–103. Reprinted by permission of the publisher.

glory. But the Jonsonian masque normally leads to compliments and praises of the person in whose honour the masque is being held, and that person never speaks himself: if he did the spell would be broken and the masque would vanish into its elements, an illusion of tinsel and candlelight. In Milton, God the Father, in flagrant defiance of Milton's own theology, which tells us that we can know nothing about the Father except through the human incarnation of the Son, does speak, and with disastrous consequences. The rest of the poem hardly recovers from his speech, and there are few difficulties in the appreciation of *Paradise Lost* that are not directly connected with it. Further, he keeps on speaking at intervals, and whenever he opens his ambrosial mouth the sensitive reader shudders. Nowhere else in Milton is the contrast between the conceptual and the dramatic aspects of a situation, already glanced at, so grotesque: between recognizing that God is the source of all goodness and introducing God as a character saying: "I am the source of all goodness." The Father observes the improved behaviour of Adam after the fall and parenthetically remarks: "my motions in him." Theologically, nothing could be more correct: dramatically, nothing is better calculated to give the impression of a smirking hypocrite.

The speech the Father makes in Book Three has perhaps been modelled on the speech of Zeus at the opening of the *Odyssey*. But that speech is in perfect dramatic propriety. Zeus is merely saying that men often blame the gods for disasters they bring upon themselves, and gives an example, the death of Aegisthus, which has already occurred. What God does in Milton is to embark on a profoundly unconvincing argument purporting to show that Adam is responsible for his own fall, although God, being omniscient, foreknew it. But if God had foreknowledge he must have known in the instant of creating Adam that he was creating a being who would fall. And even if the argument held together, the *qui s'excuse s'accuse* tone in which it is delivered would still make it emotionally unconvincing.

Nor are the Father's other words and actions any more reassuring. They often do not seem very sharply distinguished from those of Satan. He professes a great concern for his creation ("thou knowest how dear to me are all my works," he says to the Son), yet when the news is brought him that one-third of his angelic creation has revolted against him he merely smiles. And although the Son is a considerably more attractive figure than the Father, he too has caught the contagion of unconcern: he is a "gracious Judge without revile," but there is nothing in him of Blake's Holy Word—

> Calling the lapsed Soul,
> And weeping in the evening dew

—weeping such tears as even Satan has the grace to shed for his woebegone followers. Satan interprets his one-third as nearly half, and God the Father speaks of his two-thirds as "far the greater part," but there is little moral difference between the two communiqués. Satan is never shown sending his followers on pointless errands, though the Father, according to Raphael, frequently does so.

We understand Milton very well when he shows us Satan accommodating himself to his actions with "Necessity, the tyrant's plea," but the Father seems equally caught in the trap of his own pseudo-logic:

> I else must change
> Their nature, and revoke the high decree
> Unchangeable, eternal.

We understand very well also the fact that Satan, in the council in hell, volunteers to journey to the earth a split second too quickly, because he will have to go anyway and there is no point in letting a minor devil get the credit for volunteering. The insidious corruption of power could hardly have found a better image. But it is difficult to see why the Father should be teasing the angels for a volunteer, considering that they have just proved their courage by an entirely unnecessary display of it. It seems, to sum this up, very strange that the main "argument," in the more limited sense of the doctrinal coherence of the poem, should be so largely entrusted to the one character who is conspicuously no good at argument; and I find that the objections of students and many critics to the poem usually reduce themselves to a single one: Why is everything rational in *Paradise Lost* so profoundly unreasonable?

I am concerned with the twentieth-century reader, and for him there is no answer in what may be called the Great Historical Bromide: the assertion that such problems would not exist for the seventeenth-century reader, who could not possibly have felt such resentment against a character clearly labelled "God," and talking like a seventeenth-century clergyman. Even so, some of these questions can be answered at once if we adopt the view, mentioned earlier, that the angels are undergoing a spiritual education as well as Adam. The sentry-duty that Raphael and others are assigned, "to inure our prompt obedience," may be only a military metaphor for such education. Similarly with the calling for volunteers: it is not lack of courage but lack of understanding that holds the angels back—for one thing, they do not know how to die. The dramatizing of the Atonement is a greater mystery than anything they have encountered before, and is necessary if they are to watch the working out of that drama with any comprehension. But still two questions keep revolving around Milton's portrayal of the Father. First, why is he there, in defiance of all poetic tact? Second, what has happened to the great Promethean rebel who steered his way through four revolutions and then, in his crowning masterpiece, associates rebellion with Satan and goodness and virtue with this grinning reactionary mask? I shall try to answer these questions separately, and then see if I can combine the answers in a way that may give us some useful insight into the poem.

First, then, the fact that the Father in Book Three claims foreknowledge but disclaims foreordination is to be related to our earlier principle that liberty, for Milton, arrests the current of habit and of the cause-effect mechanism. We are not to read the great cycle of events in *Paradise Lost* cyclically: if we do we shall be reading it fatalistically. For inscrutable reasons the Father begets the Son; that inevitably causes the jealousy and revolt of Satan; that inevitably causes Satan's defeat and expulsion; that inevitably causes his attempt to assault the virtue of Adam and Eve, and so on through the whole dreary sequence. If we think of human life in time as a horizontal line, the Father is telling us that he is not to be found at the beginning of that line, as a First Cause from which everything inevitably proceeds. He is above the line, travelling along with human life like the moon on a journey. The great events in *Paradise Lost* should be read rather as a discontinuous series of crises, in each of which there is an opportunity to break the whole chain. We see these crises forming when Satan argues himself out of the possibility of submission to God, and when Adam (with the aid of some arm-twisting on the part of the poet) absolves God from any responsibility for his own sin. The failures, like the two great falls, look inevitable because they are failures, but the crucial victory, Christ's victory recorded in *Paradise Regained*, is not inevitable at all, at least from any point of view that we can take. At each crisis of life the important factor is not the consequences of previous actions, but the confrontation, across a vast apocalyptic gulf, with the source of deliverance. So whatever one thinks of the Father's argument, some argument separating present knowledge and past causation is essential to Milton's conception of the poem.

It seems to me—I have no evidence that this is Milton's view—that what God is saying in *Paradise Lost* is similar in many respects to what God is saying in the Book of Job. After the dialogue with the three friends and Elihu has reached a deadlock, God enters the argument himself with a series of rhetorical questions asking Job if he knows as much as God does about the creation. He seems to be trying to bully Job into submission by convicting him of ignorance of the divine ways. But perhaps his meaning can be taken differently. Perhaps he is merely discouraging Job from looking horizontally along a cause-effect sequence until he reaches a First Cause at the creation. Job is not even given the explanation that has been given the reader in the story of Satan's wager. It is not how he got into his calamity but how he can get out of it that is important, and this latter involves a direct and vertical relation between God and Job in the present tense.

* * *

On Adam and Eve

E. M. W. TILLYARD

From Paradise Lost: The Conscious Meaning *and* The Unconscious Meaning†

* * *

When the Son comes to the Garden to deliver judgment, his chief ground for blaming Adam seems to be his uxorious yielding. But we must remember that Adam's defence was that Eve gave him of the tree and he did eat. The Son replies to this defence:

Was shee thy God, that her thou didst obey
Before his voice, or was shee made thy guide,
Superior, or but equal, that to her
Thou did'st resigne thy Manhood, and the Place
Wherein God set thee above her made of thee,
And for thee, whose perfection farr excell'd
Hers in all real dignitie: Adornd
Shee was indeed, and lovely to attract
Thy Love, not thy Subjection, and her Gifts
Were such as under Government well seem'd,
Unseemly to beare rule, which was thy part
And person, had'st thou known thy self aright.[1]

The last line seems to show that Milton recognizes a prior cause of Adam's fall, lack of self-knowledge, itself implying a kind of triviality of mind. But still Milton cannot leave alone the theme of woman's delusiveness and indulges in a heartfelt outburst before Adam and Eve become reconciled.

† From *Milton*, rev. ed. (New York: Collier, 1967), pp. 224–25, 238–40.
1. x.145–56.

O why did God'd
Creator wise, that peopl'd highest Heav'n
With Spirits Masculine, create at last
This noveltie on Earth, this fair defect
Of Nature, and not fill the World at once
With Men as Angels without Feminine,
Or find some other way to generate
Mankind? this mischief had not then befall'n,
And more that shall befall, innumerable
Disturbances on Earth through Femal snares,
And straight conjunction with this Sex: for either
He never shall find out fit Mate, but such
As some misfortune brings him, or mistake,
Or whom he wishes most shall seldom gain
Through her perversness, but shall see her gaind
By a farr worse, or if she love, withheld
By Parents, or his happiest choice too late
Shall meet, alreadie linkt and Wedlock-bound
To a fell Adversarie, his hate or shame:
Which infinite calamitie shall cause
To Humane life, and household peace confound.[2]

This prophetic outburst of Adam, so entirely uncalled for, is very illuminating. It is of course Milton's own voice, unable through the urgency of personal experience to keep silent. And it may help to explain the curious shift, mentioned above, of the motive that prompted Adam's fall: the shift from gregariousness to sensuality. The qualities that ruin most men were not shared by Milton: he has no part in their levity and their terror of standing alone. But he cannot for long keep himself out of the poem. The one occasion when he allowed passion to gain the mastery over reason was when he made his first marriage: for him personally sex was the great pitfall. And so he cannot refrain from grafting sex onto the scheme of the Fall. The story in *Genesis* is too good an excuse to be missed for uttering his ancient grievance. Even in writing of the Fall, therefore, Milton is not exempt from the sin of sacrificing reason to passion.

The question remains: how many of the motives attributed to Adam and Eve are common to humanity, how many peculiar to one sex? Mental levity is common to both Adam and Eve, but stronger in Eve. It is the besetting sin of all humanity; fear of standing alone or gregariousness is of course common to it too, but it is a sin only in the man, for it is not woman's function to stand alone. Uxoriousness is a purely masculine failing.

* * *

2. x.888–908.

I did not mention Paradise among the themes that make up the main plan of Milton's conscious meaning, not because it is without all conscious meaning, but because much of that meaning breaks down. It is not very difficult to distinguish the two elements. The actual Paradise in Book Four consciously expresses Milton's yearning for a better state of things than this world provides: all the idealism of his youth is concentrated in that amazing description. Conscious and unconscious are at one in it. But when Milton attempts to introduce people into the picture, to present his age of innocence, he can be no more successful than any other human being in an attempt to imagine a state of existence at variance with the primal requirements of the human mind. He fails to convince us that Adam and Eve are happy, because he can find no adequate scope for their active natures.

> They sat them down, and after no more toil
> Of thir sweet Gardning labour then suffic'd
> To recommend coole *Zephyr*, and made ease
> More easie, wholsom thirst and appetite
> More grateful, to thir Supper Fruits they fell.[3]

Milton cannot really believe in such a way of life. Reduced to the ridiculous task of working in a garden which produces of its own accord more than they will ever need, Adam and Eve are in the hopeless position of Old Age Pensioners enjoying perpetual youth. Of course Milton makes it clear that he believed a state of regeneration arrived at after the knowledge of good and evil to be superior to a state of innocence, but he does not convince us, as he means to do, that a state of innocence is better than an unregenerate state of sin. On the contrary, we feel that Milton, stranded in his own Paradise, would very soon have eaten the apple on his own responsibility and immediately justified the act in a polemical pamphlet. Any genuine activity would be better than utter stagnation. I do not think these flippant thoughts about Paradise intrude in the Ninth Book, when Adam and Eve have turned into recognizable human beings, even before the Fall: we instinctively associate their characters with life as we know it, not with the conditions of life that prevailed in the Garden of Eden.

Here may be mentioned an interesting essay by Paul Elmer More in which he seeks for the central significance of *Paradise Lost*. Assuming that the poem has a permanent interest, that a successful epic must contain 'some great human truth, some appeal to universal human aspirations, decked in the garb of symbolism', although 'the poet himself may not be fully conscious of this deeper meaning', he concludes that the essence of *Paradise Lost* is Paradise itself:

3. iv.327–31.

> Sin is not the innermost subject of Milton's epic, nor man's disobedience and fall; these are but the tragic shadows cast about the central light. Justification of the ways of God to man is not the true moral of the plot: this and the whole divine drama are merely the poet's means of raising his conception to the highest generalisation. The true theme is Paradise itself; not Paradise lost, but the reality of that 'happy rural seat' where the errant tempter beheld
>
> To all delight of human sense exposed
> In narrow room nature's whole wealth, yea more,
> A heaven on earth.
>
> Milton's paradise is his presentation of that aspiration after a Golden Age that has existed at all times among all peoples. Set between the description of Hell and the description of the world after the fall it occupies the central position of the epic and commands our highest attention.

That Milton's Paradise (I mean Paradise itself, not the life of Adam and Eve in it) is described with passion no one can possibly deny. As I said, his lifelong search for perfection, for something better than the world can give, finds its fullest expression here. But More has not really finished his essay: he omits to say by what this passionate desire for a golden age is conditioned, of what profounder feeling it is really the expression. One of his sentences might easily have supplied him with the necessary sequel. Let us not forget, he writes,

> that the greatest period of our own literature, the many-tongued Elizabethan age, where the very wildernesses of verse are filled with Pentecostal eloquence and
>
> airy tongues that syllable men's names,
>
> let us not forget that the dramas and tales, the epics and lyrics, of that period, from Spenser to Milton, are more concerned with this one ideal of a Golden Age wrought out in some 'imitation of the fields of bliss', than with any other single matter.

And the reason, he might have added, lay in the very activity of the Elizabethan age. Only an active man can create a living picture of sedentary bliss. Similarly the poignant sweetness of Milton's descriptions of Paradise and his ardent desire for perfection have less an existence of their own than express the enormous energy of Milton's mind. The description of Paradise then, without being the centre, is in harmony with the main trend of the poem. It is only in the daily life of Adam and Eve that Milton's conscious intention breaks down.

* * *

C. S. LEWIS

The Fall†

Eve fell through Pride. The serpent tells her first that she is very beautiful, and then that all living things are gazing at her and adoring her (IX, 532–541). Next he begins to make her "feel herself impair'd." Her beauty lacks spectators. What is one man? She ought to be ador'd and served by angels: she would be queen of heaven if all had their rights (IX, 542–548). God is trying to keep the human race down: Godhead is their true destiny (703, 711), and Godhead is what she thinks of when she eats (790). The results of her fall begin at once. She thinks that earth is a long way from Heaven and God may not have seen her (811–816); the doom of Nonsense is already at work. Next she decides that she will not tell Adam about the fruit. She will exploit her secret to become his equal—or no, better still, his superior (817–825). The rebel is already aiming at tyranny. But presently she remembers that the fruit may, after all, be deadly. She decides that if she is to die, Adam must die with her; it is intolerable that he should be happy, and happy (who knows?) with another woman when she is gone. I am not sure that critics always notice the precise sin which Eve is now committing, yet there is no mystery about it. Its name in English is Murder. If the fruit is to produce deity Adam shall have none of it: she means to do a corner in divinity. But if it means death, then he must be made to eat it, in order that he may die—for that reason and no other, as her words make perfectly plain (826–830). And hardly has she made this resolve before she is congratulating herself upon it as a singular proof of the tenderness and magnanimity of her love (830–833).

If the precise movement of Eve's mind at this point is not always noticed, that is because Milton's truth to nature is here almost too great, and the reader is involved in the same illusion as Eve herself. The whole thing is so quick, each new element of folly, malice, and corruption enters so unobtrusively, so naturally, that it is hard to realize we have been watching the genesis of murder. We expect something more like Lady Macbeth's "unsex me here." But Lady Macbeth speaks thus after the intention of murder has already been fully formed in her mind. Milton is going closer to the actual moment of decision. Thus, and not otherwise, does the mind turn to embrace evil. No man, perhaps, ever at first described to himself the act he was about to do as Murder, or Adultery, or Fraud, or Treachery, or Perversion; and when he hears it so described by other men he is (in

† From *A Preface to* Paradise Lost (London and New York: Oxford UP, 1942). Reprinted by permission of the publisher.

a way) sincerely shocked and surprised. Those others "don't understand." If they knew what it had really been like for him, they would not use those crude 'stock' names. With a wink or a titter, or in a cloud of muddy emotion, the thing has slipped into his will as something not very extraordinary, something of which, rightly understood and in all his highly peculiar circumstances, he may even feel proud. If you or I, reader, ever commit a great crime, be sure we shall feel very much more like Eve than like Iago.

She has still a further descent to make. Before leaving the Tree she does "low Reverence" before it "as to the power that dwelt within," and thus completes the parallel between her fall and Satan's. She who thought it beneath her dignity to bow to Adam or to God, now worships a vegetable. She has at last become 'primitive' in the popular sense.

Adam fell by uxoriousness. We are not shown the formation of his decision as we are shown the formation of Eve's. Before he speaks to her, half-way through his inward monologue (896–916) we find the decision already made—"with thee Certain my resolution is to Die." His sin is, of course, intended to be a less ignoble sin than hers. Its half-nobility is, perhaps, emphasized by the fact that he does not argue about it. He is at that moment when a man's only answer to all that would restrain him is: "I don't care"; that moment when we resolve to treat some lower or partial value as an absolute—loyalty to a party or a family, faith to a lover, the customs of good fellowship, the honour of our profession, or the claims of science. If the reader finds it hard to look upon Adam's action as a sin at all, that is because he is not really granting Milton's premises. If conjugal love were the highest value in Adam's world, then of course his resolve would have been the correct one. But if there are things that have an even higher claim on a man, if the universe is imagined to be such that, when the pinch comes, a man ought to reject wife and mother and his own life also, then the case is altered, and then Adam can do no good to Eve (as, in fact, he does no good) by becoming her accomplice. What would have happened if instead of his "compliance bad" Adam had scolded or even chastised Eve and then interceded with God on her behalf, we are not told. The reason we are not told is that Milton does not know. And I think he knows he does not know: he says cautiously that the situation "*seemed* remediless" (919). This ignorance is not without significance. We see the results of our actions, but we do not know what would have happened if we had abstained. For all Adam knew, God might have had other cards in His hand; but Adam never raised the question, and now nobody will ever know. Rejected goods are invisible. Perhaps God would have killed Eve and left Adam "in those wilde Woods forlorn": perhaps, if the man had preferred honesty to party loyalty or established morals to adultery, a friend would have been ruined or two hearts broken. But then again, perhaps not. You can find out only by trying it. The only thing Adam knows is that he must hold the fort, and he does not hold it. The effects of the Fall on him are quite unlike its effects on the woman. She had rushed at once into false sentiment which made murder itself appear a proof of fine sensibility. Adam, after eating the fruit, goes in the opposite direction. He becomes a man of the world, a punster, an aspirant to fine raillery. He compliments Eve on her palate and says the real weakness of Paradise is that there were too few forbidden trees. The father of all the bright epigrammatic wasters and the mother of all the corrupting female novelists are now both before us. As critics have pointed out, Adam and Eve "become human" at this point. Unfortunately what follows is one of Milton's failures. Of course, they must now lust after each other. And of course this lusting must be something quite different from the innocent desires which Milton attributes to their unfallen intercourse. Wholly new, and perversely delicious, a tang of evil in sex is now to enter their experience. What will reveal itself on waking as the misery of shame now comes to them (they are growing "sapient," "exact of taste") as the delighted discovery that obscenity is possible. But could poetry suffice to draw such a distinction? Certainly not Milton's. His Homeric catalogue of flowers is wide of the mark. Yet something he does. Adam's hedonistic calculus—his cool statement that he has never (except perhaps once) been so ripe for "play" as now—strikes the right note. He would not have said that before he fell. Perhaps he would not have said "to enjoy thee." Eve is becoming to him a *thing*. And she does not mind: all her dreams of godhead have come to that.

A. J. A. WALDOCK

From The Fall (II)†

* * *

I add a few words on the aftermath. It would be profitless to raise again, I think, the logical difficulties. There was no way for Milton of making the transition from sinlessness to sin perfectly intelligible. It is obvious that Adam and Eve must already have contracted human weaknesses before they can start on the course of conduct that leads to their fall: to put it another way, they must already be fallen (tech-

† From *Paradise Lost and Its Critics* (Cambridge: Cambridge UP, 1947; rpt. Gloucester, MA: Peter Smith, 1959), pp. 17–19, 20–21, 22–24, 61–64, 75–79, 81–83. Reprinted by permission of the publisher.

nically) before they can begin to fall. Nor, again, is it possible to see just how the change from love to lust came about, or what it was in the act of disobedience that necessitated it. There is no help for these matters. Mr Lewis, it is true, makes a heroic effort to draw a distinction between fallen and unfallen sexuality, and suggests that Dante might have been able to portray the latter kind successfully. Even Milton, Mr Lewis thinks, if he had been less explicit—if he had been content to treat the loves of Adam and Eve 'remotely and mysteriously'—might have come near to succeeding. It may be so. It is perfectly obvious, of course, that nothing would have induced Milton to rest content with anything of the sort: he was not that kind of man—or poet. The poet who allowed Adam to turn the talk so neatly against Raphael with embarrassing questions about the love-life of angels was not likely to shy from the task of suggesting the innocent delights of Adam and Eve. It is perfectly evident, of course, that he very much enjoyed suggesting them. I cannot help thinking that Mr Lewis makes an unnecessary to-do about the provocativeness of Eve's sexual modesty. After the Fall a new self-consciousness enters, and we have sensuality itself. But how sensuality could have been absent from prelapsarian 'sex', if prelapsarian 'sex' be granted at all, is rather difficult to imagine. Milton, at any rate, could not imagine it and dismissed Augustine's efforts to square this particular circle (quite rightly) as nonsense.

Milton's triumph in what follows is, of course, the delineation of Eve. It is like watching some magic transformation; the Fall transmutes her into a woman, a person; one by one the human lineaments are etched in before our eyes. She has not spoken a dozen lines before she is there, alive:

> other care perhaps
> May have diverted from continual watch
> Our great Forbidder, safe with all his Spies
> About him.
>
> (ix, 813)

Already, as Professor Stoll puts it, she is showing a 'defensive reaction', dramatizing herself as in some obscure way injured: it makes her feel less guilty to reproach God, to suggest that it is all, in some indefinable sense, His fault. Do not let us be too hard on her for the jealous spasm that follows:

> but what if God have seen
> And Death ensue? then I shall be no more,
> And *Adam* wedded to another *Eve*,
> Shall live with her enjoying, I extinct;
> A death to think. Confirm'd then I resolve,
> *Adam* shall share with me in bliss or woe:

> So dear I love him, that with him all deaths
> I could endure, without him live no life.
>
> (IX, 826)

This, says Mr Lewis, is Murder. In a sense perhaps it is; and in a not dissimilar sense each of us commits murder five times a week; but we should not like to be called murderers. It is not as if she knew what death exactly was; nor is it quite fair, if we are to come down with a heavy hand on her jealous and possessive impulse here, to ignore (as Mr Lewis does) those other impulses—of love, heroism, self-sacrifice—that she shows in so many a later passage. Indeed we have only to move on forty lines to find one:

> Thou therefore also taste, that equal Lot
> May joyne us, equal Joy, as equal Love;
> Least thou not tasting, different degree
> Disjoyne us, and I then too late renounce
> Deitie for thee, when Fate will not permit.
>
> (IX, 881)

She means this, and who does not feel that she would be capable of it, that if Adam were to be left she would tear herself away from deity, if she could, to go back to him! She fibs sometimes. Carried away by Adam's loyalty, which so enhances her own value, she says:

> Were it I thought Death menac't would ensue
> This my attempt, I would sustain alone
> The worst, and not perswade thee, rather die
> Deserted.
>
> (IX, 977)

She is a liar, but who cares? She has found the right 'objective correlative' for her feelings.

The picture of the 'distemper' of Adam and Eve is itself a minor masterpiece, all the better for the glint of sardonic humour that Milton allows to intrude. Adam eats and is enraptured:

> if such pleasure be
> In things to us forbidden, it might be wish'd
> For this one Tree had bin forbidden ten.
>
> (IX, 1024)

'We can hear Eve's hectic, infatuate giggles at Adam's words', says Dr Tillyard; and so we can.

From now on, indeed, as far as Eve is concerned, Milton's bonds are fairly untied. The problem was somewhat different with Adam. He must remain stilted. He has so much still to exemplify, so much of the burden of the doctrine still to carry, that he can never win through to complete freedom as a man. But Eve's humanity only deepens as the poem moves towards its end. In the debates in Book x hers are the words that reach our hearts:

> While yet we live, scarse one short hour perhaps,
> Between us two let there be peace, both joyning.
> (x, 924)

And again:

> both have sin'd, but thou
> Against God onely, I against God and thee,
> And to the place of judgement will return,
> There with my cries importune Heaven, that all
> The sentence from thy head remov'd may light
> On me, sole cause to thee of all this woe,
> Mee mee onely just object of his ire.
> (x, 930)

Impetuous though the offer is, she is not pretending, and Adam, though he makes what she has said the text for another little lecture, scolds gently. On their joint problems she brings her realistic, ruthless woman's sense to bear. If the future of their 'descent' is what chiefly perplexes, then she advises: let there be no 'descent', prevent the race unblest. If that involves too hard an abstention, then she suggests the suicide pact. Both are eminently practical, drastic, knot-cutting proposals. Again she receives a slight scolding. But to our minds she has the better of it, and it is pleasant that the last words spoken in the poem should be hers. She regrets Eden, but Adam, after all, is her world. She links arms with him and faces the future.

* * *

NORTHROP FRYE

From Children of God and Nature†

In the soul of man, as God originally created it, there is a hierarchy. This hierarchy has three main levels: the reason, which is in control of the soul; the will, the agent carrying out the decrees of the reason, and the appetite. Reason and will, the decree and the act, are related in man much as the Father and the Son are related in the Godhead. The will is never free in the sense of being autonomous or detached

† From *The Return of Eden: Five Essays on Milton's Epics* (Toronto: U of Toronto P, 1965). Reprinted by permission of the publisher.

from some other aspect of the soul, but when reason is in charge of the soul the will is free because it participates in the freedom of the reason. In one of his academic Prolusions Milton says, as an axiom generally accepted: "the human intellect, as head and ruler, surpasses in splendor the other faculties of the mind; it governs and illuminates with its splendor the will itself, otherwise blind and dark, that like the moon shines with another's light."

The appetite is subordinate to both, and is controlled by the will from the reason. Of the appetites two are of central importance: the appetite for food and the sexual appetite. Both of these are part of the divine creation, and are therefore good. Even so, it is curious how emphatic Milton is about food as an element of both paradisal and heavenly life. In the unfallen world eating has something sacramental about it: Raphael explains how it is part of the upward movement in nature back toward its Creator, and even the form in which food is provided indicates the "providence" behind it:

> The savoury pulp they chew, and in the rind,
> Still as they thirsted, scoop the brimming stream.

The angels also eat and drink "in communion sweet," and Milton insists that, whatever the theologians may say, Raphael really ate the fruit salad provided for him by Eve. Not only does he eat it but he explains how he ate it. He appears to have no excretory organs except the pores of his skin—if angels have skin—but at any rate the upper end of his food pipe has been implanted in him by the Deity.

Milton also insists, again referring to objecting theologians, that sexual intercourse existed between Adam and Eve before the fall. There remains of course only the fourth question, the sexual life of angels, the subject of some curious speculations later on by Swedenborg. We are told that spirits can assume either sex, which seems to imply that sex has some point even in a spiritual nature. Adam's natural curiosity, combined with other elements we shall look at in a moment, prompts him to ask Raphael a direct question on this point. The question, not unnaturally, is not directly answered, but when it is asked Raphael blushes, mutters something about having just remembered another appointment, and bustles off. He does not leave however until he has given Adam a very strong hint what the answer is:

> Let it suffice thee that thou know'st
> Us happy, and without Love no happiness.
> Whatever pure thou in the body enjoy'st
> (And pure thou wert created) we enjoy
> In eminence, and obstacle find none
> Of membrane, joint, or limb, exclusive bars.

Or, as Blake was to say in a tone more ribald than either Milton's or Swedenborg's:

in Eternity
Embracings are comminglings from the head even to the feet,
And not a pompous high priest entering by a secret place.

There is a rough but useful correspondence between the hierarchy of reason, will and appetite in the individual and the social hierarchy of men, women and children that would have developed in Eden if Adam had not fallen. In this analogy the man would correspond to the level of the reason, the woman to that of the will united to the reason, and the child to that of the appetite, subordinate to both but still protected and cherished. We cannot prove this directly, as no unfallen society ever developed, but it seems implicit in Milton's argument. We are told that even in heaven there is such a thing as seniority, and when Satan disguises himself as a stripling cherub he makes all the deference to seniority toward Uriel that a young cherub ought to make, though how there could be young and old cherubim in eternity is not explained. The supremacy of husband over wife is taken for granted by Milton because he found it in the New Testament. When Milton says of Adam and Eve: "He for God only, she for God in him" he is merely putting a Pauline doctrine into pentameter verse. The correspondence of reason and will with man and woman is marked in the beginning of Book Nine, when Eve wants to go and work by herself and Adam allows her to go. Adam is right in doing so because he is leaving her will free, while retaining the natural supremacy of his own reason. He goes wrong only in accepting her (by then perverted) advice in connection with his own decision.

As far as the present world is concerned, we should remember something that many readers of Milton are apt to forget, that the authority of husband over wife is spiritual authority only. No man, except a man living entirely by the light of the gospel, would have the kind of integrity of which such an authority would be a by-product, nor could a woman who did not have a corresponding integrity be capable of responding to it. A bullying or dictatorial attitude toward one's wife would be merely one more example of what Milton calls man's effeminate slackness. Many theologians have asserted that the wife ought to be in subjection to her husband because woman brought sin into the world, but this is arguing directly from the unfallen to the fallen state, something Milton never does. Milton does say in *The Christian Doctrine* that the authority of the husband was increased after the fall, but this is an empirical observation on the patriarchal narratives in the Old Testament, not a deduction from the Eden story.

It is understandable however that Milton should see in the cult of courtly love, of *Frauendienst* or worship of women in the literary conventions of his time, one of the most direct and eloquent symbolic results of the fall of man. For this reason, Milton places the supremacy of Eve over Adam at the central point of the fall itself. "Was she thy God?" the real God asks what Adam must have found, in the context, an insensitively coarse remark:

> Not sunk in carnal pleasure; for which cause
> Among the beasts no mate for thee was found.

Adam is said to be "half" abashed by this; he is, as nearly as anyone can be in an unfallen state, shocked and angered. Yet what Raphael has been too anxious to correct does in fact turn out to be the cause of Adam's fall. The supremacy of Adam over Eve is the free and human relation; the supremacy of Eve could soon become a road leading to intellectual enslavement.

Milton's argument for divorce is really an argument for annulment, that is, an argument that if the relations between man and woman are intolerable, no marriage, in the gospel sense, has really taken place. The marriage Jesus describes as indissoluble is a lifetime companionship that can be consummated, or finished, only by the death of one of the partners. The union of Adam and Eve in Eden is the pattern of such a marriage, but not every legalized sex act in the fallen world achieves that pattern. But the argument for annulment really resolves itself into an argument against idolatry. The man has the right to divorce his wife (or the wife the husband) if she is a threat to his spiritual integrity, and she cannot be that without representing something of what idolatry means to Milton. When Eve, after her fall, comes to Adam and urges him to fall with her, that is the point at which Adam should have "divorced" Eve, hence the argument for divorce comes into the very act of the fall itself.

Few can have read *Paradise Lost* without being struck by the curiously domesticated nature of the life of Adam and Eve in Eden before the fall. Adam and Eve are suburbanites in the nude, and like other suburbanites they are preoccupied with gardening, with their own sexual relations, and with the details of their rudimentary housekeeping. Even what many would now regard as the horrors of suburban life are only delights to Adam and Eve. They do not mind that they are constantly under inspection by angelic neighbours, or by God himself, for, says Milton, "they thought no ill." Such extraordinary trustfulness is a natural part of the state of innocence. There's an angel up in the sky. So there is: how nice; perhaps he'll stay to lunch. And when Eve serves the meal, goes away and leaves the men to their masculine conversation, we feel that we are as close as Paradise can get to port and cigars. Commentators on Milton, at least since Taine a century ago, have said everything on this point that needs to be said. But the prevailing assumption has been that all this represents unconscious humour on the part of a humourless poet, and this assumption is quite wrong.

It is essential to Milton's argument to present Adam and Eve in this way. For it is Milton's belief that the original state of man was civilized, and that it was far closer to the average life of a seventeenth-century Englishman than it was to that of a noble savage. Savagery and primitivism came later, and were never intended by God to be part of man's life. Further, it would be a mistake to imagine, as the hasty reader often does, that because Adam and Eve are unfallen and sinless they must necessarily be insipid. They are not insipid at all, but lively, even explosive personalities. Adam has not been in the world five minutes before he is arguing with his Maker and pointing out to him the deficiencies of a life in which there is no other human being. This amuses his Creator, but it pleases him too to feel that there is so instant a response from the reason which he has planted in Adam's mind. When Raphael rebukes Adam, as Adam feels, unjustly, Adam makes a shrewd flanking attack by way of his question about Raphael's sex life, and on the way mentions in a parenthesis that he is sticking to his own views and is not allowing any angel to bully him out of them:

> Though higher of the genial bed by far,
> And with mysterious reverence, I deem.

Let us return to the episode in Book Nine in which we are told that Eve has suddenly taken it into her head to go and do her pruning by herself. Adam makes a long speech, in impeccable blank, verse, pointing out that, as they are about to be assailed by a clever and ruthless enemy, it might be better for them to stay together and not separate. Eve says that that is very true, and that she would like to go off and prune by herself. Adam makes another long speech, in equally impeccable blank verse, making the same point with elaborations. Eve says that all that is very true, and that she will now go off and prune by herself. At this point Adam attempts the manoeuvre which so many husbands have attempted, of trying to get the last word by telling her to go and do as she likes:

> Go in thy native innocence; rely.
> On what thou hast of virtue; summon all;
> For God towards thee hath done his part: do thine.
> So spake the Patriarch of Mankind; but Eve
> Persisted; yet submiss, though last, replied.

This unfallen spat indicates that there is room for explosive personalities in Paradise, because there is no malice in their explosion. Similarly with the liveliness of intellect that they display. When Eve has a troubling dream, and does not understand its meaning, Adam, who is several hours older, explains to her the origin of dreams, how they operate, and what their machinery is. The speech is intended to convey the sense of the freshness of discovery, not of the staleness of opinion.

The same applies to the kind of language they use, the language which has often puzzled readers and been ridiculed by them. Adam and Eve use the kind of stylized hierarchic language which indicates their exuberance in the possession of language as a new and fresh form of intellectual energy. The formality of their speeches is verbal play, and reflects the exuberance with which Milton himself, in addressing his own language in his early *Vacation Exercise* poem, described the appropriate epic diction:

> Such as may make thee search thy coffers round,
> Before thou clothe my fancy in fit sound.

Such formal rhetoric is at the opposite pole of human life from the dialogue in a Hemingway novel, which is equally appropriate to its purpose because it represents a weariness with human speech. Such communication, where nothing really needs to be said, is a parody of the kind of communication which according to Raphael the angels have, and which is intuitive rather than discursive. Adam and Eve are simply enjoying the possession of the power of discursive communication.

After the fall, the hierarchy implanted by God in the human soul is not merely upset, but reversed. Appetite now moves into the top place in the human soul, and by doing so it ceases to be appetite and is transformed into passion, the drive toward death. The appetites are a part of the creation, and like every other part of the creation they are an energy which seeks its fulfilment in form. Hunger is specifically satisfied with food, and the sexual desire by sexual intercourse. When appetite is perverted into passion, the drives of sex and hunger are perverted into lust and greed. Passion operates in the mind as though it were an external force, compelling the soul to obey against its own best interests, and the passions of greed and lust have two qualities that the appetites do not have: excess and mechanical energy. Hunger can be satisfied by food, but greed cannot be satisfied by anything: it seeks an excess of food, and when it runs out of food, it will seek to acquire other things out of mechanical habit. Eve is hungry before she eats the forbidden fruit, greedy immediately afterward, and her greed runs on into a desire to possess Adam.

After Adam has fallen with her, sexual intercourse between them is resumed, but this time its basis is entirely different. It is not the expression of the love of Adam for Eve, but rather the generalized and mechanical expression of the lust of a man for a woman, the woman being Eve because she is the only woman within reach. The will is now the agent of passion instead of reason, for the will must be the agent of one or the other. The behaviour of mankind takes on that mechanical and amorphous quality which Milton describes in chaos: he speaks elsewhere of the futility of efforts to define sin, "to put a girdle about that chaos." This inversion of the human mind, with passion on top and will its agent, reduces reason to the lowest point in the soul, where it is normally a helpless critic of what the passion is doing, able to point out the correct course, but, in the passion-driven mind, powerless to affect its decisions for long.

What happens in the human individual happens by analogy in fallen human society. Passion acts as though it were an external force, a tyrant of the mind, and a society made up of passionate individuals becomes a tyranny, in which the tyrant is the embodiment of the self-enslavement of his victims, as Michael explains to Adam:

> Reason in Man obscured, or not obeyed,
> Immediately inordinate desires
> And upstart passions catch the government
> From reason, and to servitude reduce
> Man, till then free. Therefore, since he permits
> Within himself unworthy powers to reign
> Over free reason, God, in judgement just,
> Subjects him from without to violent lords,
> Who oft as undeservedly enthrall
> His outward freedom.

Usually we have a secular tyrant and a spiritual tyrant or priest. The latter, in Christianity, is what Milton means by a prelate, a person who exerts temporal power in what ought to be the area of spiritual authority. Under the tyrant and the priest and their followers come the victims, the general public, and under them again come the few people equipped with enough reason to protest against what is happening and to try to rouse the conscience of the very small number who can be persuaded to agree and act with them. This is the situation of which the archetype is Abdiel among the rebel angels, which is also, as explained, the archetype of human heroism.

The distinction between lust and greed is that lust is a vice turned outward and affecting other people; greed is a vice that turns inward and affects oneself. These two forms of tyranny produce what for Milton are the two infallible signs of a perverted church: inquisition and indulgence, the desire to suppress freedom of thought and the tendency to provide easy formulas for the less dangerous vices. The former develops the censor who is attacked in *Areopagitica*; the latter develops what Milton calls the "hireling." Among the pamphlets written on the eve of the Restoration, the first two deal with these two forms of religious perversion. *A Treatise of Civil Power in Ecclesiastical Causes* is concerned mainly with the separation of spiritual and temporal authority necessary to avoid what Milton calls in *Areopagitica* "the laziness of a licensing church"; *The Likeliest Means to Remove Hirelings* is concerned with the complementary problem.

If we look at the visions which Michael shows Adam in Book Eleven, between the murder of Abel and the flood, we may be puzzled to find that some of them are not biblical. The story of Cain and Abel is naturally the first vision, and this story centres on one of Milton's central emblems, the altar of acceptable sacrifice, along with its demonic parody. This is followed by a vision of a lazar-house, the victims of which are said to have brought many of their evils on themselves by intemperance in eating and drinking, in other words by greed. We get a somewhat prosaic homily on the virtue of temperance at this point, yet the reason for it is clear: Milton is trying to define the origin of greed in the human body and its excessive appetite. The vision of the lazar-house is followed by another based on those mysterious verses in Genesis about the sons of God who discovered that the daughters of women were fair. The sons of God, according to Milton, were virtuous men and the daughters of women were daughters of women. The gigantic results of their union illustrate the physical origin of lust in the human body. These two visions are followed by two others, one of a cattle raid and one of a scene of riotous and drunken festivity. These two scenes are war and peace as they are usually understood in human life, war as a direct product of human greed, and "peace," that is, luxury, as a direct product of human lust. These four antediluvian scenes thus make up a vision of greed and lust spilling excessively and mechanically, over all human life in a moral flood of which the physical one seems the only possible outcome.

* * *

BARBARA K. LEWALSKI

From "Higher Argument": Completing and Publishing *Paradise Lost*†

* * *

At the center of his epic, Milton set a richly imagined representation of prelapsarian love, marriage, and domestic society. It is a brilliant though sometimes conflicted representation, in which Milton's internalization of contemporary assumptions about gender hierarchy, his idealistic view of companionate marriage, his own life experiences, and his deeply felt emotional needs sometimes strain against each other. Most profoundly, he explores through Adam and Eve the fundamental challenge of any love relationship: the uneasy, inevitable, and ultimately creative tension between autonomy and interdependence.

In a sublime epithalamion, Milton celebrates marriage as the foundation of human society, and also gives his representation of Edenic marriage political resonance as he contrasts Adam and Eve's joyous and fulfilled marital love with the sterility and licentious indulgence of "Court Amours"—Charles I's cavaliers and the Bacchic "revelers" of Charles II's Restoration court:

> Haile wedded Love, mysterious Law, true source
> Of human ofspring, sole proprietie
> In Paradise of all things common else.
> By thee adulterous lust was driv'n from men
> Among the bestial herds to raunge, by thee
> Founded in Reason, Loyal, Just, and Pure,
> Relations dear, and all the Charities
> Of Father, Son, and Brother first were known . . .
>
> Here Love his golden shafts imploies, here lights
> His constant Lamp, and waves his purple wings,
> Reigns here and revels; not in the bought smile
> Of Harlots, loveless, joyless, unindeard,
> Casual fruition, nor in Court Amours
> Mixt Dance, or wanton Mask, or Midnight Bal. (4.750–68)

This paean elides female relationships: no mention is made of mothers and sisters, though the Bard implies, with modern anthropologists, that these social bonds are forged through women. He also imagines Adam and Eve's archetypal marriage according to the forms

† From *The Life of John Milton: A Critical Biography* (Oxford: Blackwell, 2000), pp. 479–88. Reprinted by permission of the publisher.

of the Early Modern institution, as an arrangement between the father and the husband which the woman is to accept or (in rare cases) decline. After brief resistance Eve accepts the husband offered by God the Father and the role prescribed for her: to produce "multitudes like thy self," and to be for Adam "an individual solace dear" (4.449–91).

Milton's epic inscribes gender hierarchy, though in a complex and nuanced version. Adam and Eve are described first in terms of their shared nobility, majesty, and authority over all other creatures; their moral and spiritual equality is based on their creation as God's images, exhibiting "Truth, wisdome, Sanctitude severe and pure" (4.287–95). Then their different physical qualities are interpreted as emblems of their unequal natures and roles: "For contemplation hee and valour formd, / For softness shee and sweet attractive Grace, / Hee for God only, shee for God in him" (4.297–9). Later Adam, after admitting to Raphael his unsettling passion for Eve, says that he knows she is inferior to himself in qualities both of mind and body:

> For well I understand in the prime end
> Of Nature her th'inferiour, in the mind
> And inward Faculties, which most excell,
> In outward also her resembling less
> His image who made both, and less expressing
> The character of that Dominion giv'n
> O'er other Creatures. (8.540–6)

Raphael confirms this judgment, urging Adam not to attribute "overmuch to things / Less excellent," to cultivate proper self-esteem so that Eve will "acknowledge thee her Head," to eschew passion, and to love Eve's higher qualities as a means to make a Neoplatonic ascent to heavenly love (8.565–75). More authoritative still, the Son, judging Adam after the Fall, confirms that Adam's proper role is to act as Eve's head and governor, not make an idol of her to set in place of God:

> Was shee thy God, that her thou didst obey
> Before his voice, or was shee made thy guide,
> Superior, or but equal, that to her
> Thou did'st resigne thy Manhood, and the Place
> Wherein God set thee above her made of thee,
> And for thee, whose perfection far excell'd
> Hers in all real dignitie: Adornd
> Shee was indeed, and lovely to attract
> Thy Love, not thy Subjection, and her Gifts
> Were such as under Government well seem'd,
> Unseemly to beare rule, which was thy part
> And person, had'st thou known thy self aright.
> (10.145–56)

Yet this conventional view of gender is destabilized by elements of Milton's imaginative vision that invite a more egalitarian conception: if Milton could not fully work through such conflicts, he did provide liberalizing perspectives upon which some later feminists could and did build. One such is the poem's unusually fluid concept of hierarchy, the concomitant of Milton's monist ontology: if humans and angels differ only in degree and humans can expect the gradual refinement of their natures to angelic status, the distance between male and female on the hierarchical scale must be minimal. Moreover, Raphael's comment that creatures hold their place on that scale "as neerer to him [God] plac't or neerer tending" (5.476) allows that if Adam is at first "plac't" marginally higher than Eve, their final places will depend on how they develop, whither they "tend." In line with this, in Milton's unique representation of the state of innocence, Adam and Eve are both expected to grow, change, and develop in virtue by properly pruning and directing their erroneous apprehensions and perilous impulses, as well as their burgeoning garden.

Another complicating element is Milton's concept of companionate marriage, an advanced notion as he developed it in the divorce tracts, and he imagined it in much more gracious and idealized terms in the poem. Pleading with God for a mate, Adam points to the great disparity between humans and beasts and to the infinite distance between humans and God, then asks for an equal life partner:

Among unequals what societie
Can sort, what harmonie or true delight?
Which must be mutual, in proportion due
Giv'n and receiv'd; . . .
Of fellowship I speak
Such as I seek, fit to participate
All rational delight. (8.383–91)

God states that he always intended exactly such a mate for Adam: "Thy likeness, thy fit help, thy other self, / Thy wish exactly to thy hearts desire" (8.450–1). Consonant with this vision of marriage, Adam and Eve's roles and talents are not sharply segregated by gender, as convention would dictate. Eve performs certain domestic tasks—ornamenting the couple's bedroom bower and preparing and serving the noonday meal when Raphael visits—but otherwise the couple share the physical and intellectual activities of Edenic life. They take equal responsibility for their world, laboring together to maintain its eco-system: in Milton's unique version of Eden their pruning, cutting, and cultivating activities are absolutely necessary to keep the garden from returning to wild. Unique to Milton's Eden also is the fact that Eve names the plants and thereby shares in the authority over nature, the intuitive knowledge, and the power of symbolization that Adam's naming of the animals signifies, albeit in lesser degree. She also receives the same education as Adam, though not in the same manner. As decorum dictated, Adam asked Raphael questions (often framing them faultily) while Eve listened in silence as the angel explained the nature of being, rendered an account of the War in Heaven as a brief epic, and recounted his story of Creation as a hexaemeron. For both, the Edenic curriculum included ontology, metaphysics, moral philosophy, history, epic poetry, and divine revelation. Eve missed the astronomy lesson when she left to tend her flowers, but the Miltonic Bard insists that she both delighted in and was fully capable of that knowledge and would obtain it later in discussion with Adam—thereby gaining the educational benefit of dialogic interaction that Adam enjoyed with Raphael (8.48–50). Milton portrays Eve as an accomplished reasoner and debater in the marital dispute in Book IX and underscores her intellectual "sufficiency" in the temptation scene by her wry response to Satan's fulsome flattery and her precise statement of the terms of the prohibition as a divine command outside the law of nature.

Milton also accords Eve important areas of initiative and autonomy that further qualify patriarchal assumptions. Both before and after the Fall Eve often proposes issues for discussion, initiates action, and leads in some new direction. She first raises questions about the order of the cosmos; she proposes the proto-capitalist idea of the division of labor to help meet the problem of the garden's burgeoning growth; she first responds to "prevenient grace" and makes the first motion to repentance; she proposes suicide or sexual abstinence to prevent visitation of the Fall's effects on all humankind. When their dialogic interchanges are working properly, Adam responds to, develops, and where necessary corrects Eve's initiatives, as Raphael does Adam's, to advance their common understanding. In the realm of literary creativity, Eve constructs the first autobiographical narrative as she recounts her earliest recollections—with the implications autobiography carries of coming to self-awareness, probing one's own subjectivity, interpreting one's own experience, and so becoming an author (4.449–91). She is as much a lyric poet as Adam, perhaps more so. Their hymns and prayers are joint expressions, but Eve creates the first love lyric in Eden—the delicate, rhetorically artful, sonnet-like pastoral that begins "Sweet is the breath of Morn" (4.641–56). And if Adam brought this lyric form to higher perfection in his *aubade* echoing the Song of Songs (5.17–25), Eve after the Fall perfects the tragic lyric. Adam's agonized complaint, "O miserable of happy" (10.720–862), ends in despair, while Eve's moving lament, "Forsake me not thus, *Adam*" (10.914–36), opens the way to repentance, forgiveness, and reconciliation.

Also, Milton brings the ideology of gender hierarchy up against the characters' different experiences and psychology. Eve and Adam offer very different autobiographical accounts of their creation, first encounter, and marriage, accounts that evidently reflect Milton's reading of female and male psychology. Eve tells of constructing herself first through pleasurable self-contemplation, which she mistakes as a response to another female "shape," and then by freely accepting a marriage relationship; but she does not express any need for completion by another. She recounts as an episode "oft remembered" (4.449–91) how she woke on a flowery bank in some wonderment about herself, and how she then followed a murmur of waters to a pool that reflected a female image bending toward her as she to it "with answering looks / Of sympathie and love" (4.464–5). As a version of the Narcissus myth, Eve's story suggests her potential for self-love, but in most respects she is defined against the Narcissus story. She did not remain fixed forever, enamoured of her watery image, but after listening to the arguments of God and Adam, freely agreed ("I yielded") to reject narcissism, to share love and companionship with Adam in marriage, and to create human society—living images, not watery reflections. Eve's story also presents a classic Lacanian mirror scene: initial symbiosis with maternal earth and water in a place of pleasure before language, then a rupture when God's voice (the Law of the Father) intervenes, leading her to a husband and thereby into language and culture. She at first turns away, finding masculine Adam "Less winning soft, less amiablie milde, / Then that smooth watry image" (4.479–80), but he wins her as his mate by urging his "paternal" claim to her as well as his ardent love. Eve, however, complicates the reading of her story as a simple submission to patriarchy. As she recounts the words spoken to her by God, she almost concludes that God made Adam for her, not vice versa, and that he instituted matriarchy, not patriarchy:

> hee,
> Whose image thou art, him thou shalt enjoy
> Inseparablie thine, to him shalt beare
> Multitudes like thy self [not, like himself], and thence be call'd
> Mother of human Race. (4.471–6)

Moralizing her story, Eve claims to have learned from the first events of her life "How beauty is excelled by manly grace / And wisdom, which alone is truly fair" (490–1). On one reading this seems to be a forthright testimony to male superiority in mind and body. But on another, Eve hereby proclaims (after a brief homoerotic hesitation) her heterosexual attraction to Adam's "manly grace" over female beauty, and then distinguishes wisdom from both physical qualities, implying that it may pertain both to Adam's and her own self-knowledge and wise choices.

Adam's narrative (8.355–99), by contrast, testifies to a psychological and emotional neediness that in some ways undercuts gender hierarchy and recalls Milton's similar testimony in the divorce tracts. Adam reports his initial attempts to discover who he is by contemplating nature and his immediate inference that "some great Maker" created both it and him. Then he recounts his eloquent pleas with God for a mate, emphasizing his keen sense of incompleteness and loneliness without an "equal" companion. Recounting the courtship event he explains Eve's hesitation not as she herself did but by projecting onto her a serene consciousness of self-worth, "That would be woo'd, and not unsought be won," and a demeanor of "obsequious Majestie" in accepting his suit (8.500–10). He underscores the conflict between ideology and experience by emphasizing the disconnect between what he "knows" of Eve's inferiority to him and what he experiences when he is with her:

> when I approach
> Her loveliness, so absolute she seems
> And in herself compleat, so well to know
> Her own, that what she wills to do or say,
> Seems wisest, vertuousest, discreetest, best, . . .
>
> Authority and Reason on her waite,
> As one intended first, not after made
> Occasionally, and to consummate all,
> Greatness of mind, and nobleness thir seat
> Build in her loveliest, and create an awe
> About her, as a guard Angelic plac't. (8.546–59)

Though Raphael rightly rebukes Adam for such potentially dangerous sentiments Milton allows Adam to qualify the angel's apparently rigid Neoplatonism from the perspective of his (and our) experience of something beyond Raphael's ken, the "mysterious reverence" due the marriage bed and marriage itself, an institution angels do not have (8.598–9). Adam also scores a point, and shows that he understands the implications of monism, as he leads Raphael to acknowledge that happiness for angels as for humans involves some version of sexual love. After Eve's Fall, Adam's instant decision to fall with her arises from his desperate fear of returning to his lonely life before her creation:

> How can I live without thee, how forgoe
> Thy sweet Converse and Love so dearly joyn'd,
> To live again in these wilde Woods forlorn?

> Should God create another *Eve*, and I
> Another Rib afford, yet loss of thee
> Would never from my heart. (9.908–13)

Milton's most brilliant analysis of human psychology occurs in a scene without precedent in other literary versions of the Genesis story: the dispute which occasioned Adam and Eve's separation (9.205–386). In that dialogue, as Adam and Eve enmesh themselves in ever greater misunderstandings, the reader feels on his or her pulses the truth of this archetypal version of all those familiar scenes in which love or friends, by no one's design, exacerbate slight disagreements into great divide leading to unwise decisions and dire results. Eve advances her well-meaning but misguided proposal for temporary separation to meet a genuine problem: the tendency of the garden to "wanton growth." Adam reminds her of the enemy who, they met him together, "each / To other speedie aid might lend at need" (9.259–60). He might have won his point had he stopped there, but he talks on, unintentionally affronting Eve with a pompous platitude emphasizing the wife's need of her husband's guardianship. Eve, hurt by the implication that she would easily be seduced, responds "as one who loves, and some unkindness meets" (9.271), throwing Adam off balance. Logic deserts him, leading him to assert that the temptation itself would bring dishonor, and Eve picks up on his error. She enjoys having the better of the argument for the moment as she insists, quite rightly, that both must have been created "sufficient" to stand alone against temptation and that temptation itself can be no dishonor. But she goes on to cast herself as a Romance heroine eager to exhibit heroic self-sufficiency and to gain honor in victorious single combat with the enemy: "And what is Faith, Love, Vertue unassaid / Alone, without exterior help sustaind?" (9.335–6). She here goes beyond *Areopagitica's* warfaring Christian who "sallies out and sees her adversary," and echoes, faintly, the Satanic claim to absolute autonomy. She is right to insist that both are sufficient to stand, but quite wrong to infer that "exterior help," divine or human, should therefore be shunned, or that reasonable precautions in the presence of danger violate Edenic happiness. She thinks the goods of autonomy and interdependence are in conflict, but it is precisely the challenge of this first couple to hold them in balance.

Adam's fervent reply speaks both to the logical and the psychological issues involved: explaining how reason may be deceived and lead the will to sin, he ends with an eloquent testimony to the mutual aid the couple continually give each other, and a reminder that temptation will inevitably come unsought, affording Eve an opportunity to win the praise she seeks. Had he stopped here, with this strong argument offering Eve a clear choice, she would almost certainly have given way (if a bit reluctantly), announcing herself convinced by his arguments and comforted by his loving sentiments. But Adam, still off balance and still attributing overmuch wisdom to Eve, talks on and gives away his case:

> But if thou think, trial unsought may finde
> Us both securer then thus warnd thou seemst,
> Go; for thy stay, not free, absents thee more;
> Go in thy native innocence, relie
> On what thou hast of vertue, summon all,
> For God towards thee hath done his part, do thine. (9.370–5)

Besides offering Eve a better rationale for going than any she has thought of, Adam unwittingly intensifies the psychological pressure on her by his repeated imperatives—"Go . . . go . . . rely . . . do"—making it much more difficult for her to stay without seeming to back down ignominiously. It was not Adam's place in prelapsarian Eden to command Eve to stay and thereby control her free choice in the moral sphere; but neither was it his place to help her choose such a dangerous course of action by giving over his proper leadership role. Neither has sinned in this debate because there has been no deliberate choice of evil. Eve has not disobeyed and Adam has tried to act for the best, so the theological imperatives of the biblical story and of Milton's Arminianism are preserved: Adam and Eve remain innocent until they consciously decide to eat the fruit. But as their imperfectly controlled emotions sabotage their dialogic exchange and their misunderstandings result in physical separation, we experience the mounting sense of inevitability proper to tragedy.

In the Fall sequence and its aftermath, it is hardly an exaggeration to say that Milton's epic turns into an Eviad, casting Eve rather than Adam in the role of central protagonist. The biblical story of course requires that she be the object of the serpent's temptation, but Milton's poem goes much further. Eve initiates the marital dispute, she engages in a lengthy and highly dramatic dialogue with Satan embodied in the serpent, and she analyzes her motives and emotions in probing soliloquies before eating the fruit and before offering it to Adam. After the Fall she accepts God's judgment humbly, while Adam, dismayed to find his grand gesture of falling with Eve unappreciated by her, blames both Eve and the God who gave her to him. Eve responds first to "prevenient grace," and so first breaks out of the seemingly endless cycle of accusations and recriminations, becoming the human means to lead Adam back from the paralysis of despair to love, repentance, and reconciliation, first with his wife and then with God. In her lament/petition to Adam, Eve echoes the Son's offer in the Council in Heaven to take on himself God's wrath for Adam's sin—"Behold mee then, mee for him . . . / On mee let thine anger fall" (3.236–7)—as she proposes to invite God to wreak all his anger on her: "On me, sole cause to thee of all this woe, / Mee mee onely just object of his ire" (10.932–6). While she cannot play the Son's redemptive role, she does become the first human to reach toward the new standard of epic heroism (9.31–2).

Milton designed the last segment of his poem around the issue of postlapsarian education, for Adam, Eve, and the reader. At this juncture Adam and Eve have to learn how to read biblical history (which to them is prophecy), and specifically, how to interpret the *proto-evangelium* or messianic promise of redemption signified by the metaphorical curse on the serpent: that the seed of the woman will bruise his head. For Adam, its meaning is progressively clarified by a revelation of future times from his own age to the Apocalypse, presented by the archangel Michael in a series of visionary pageants (Book XI) and narratives (Book XII). Adam has to learn to interpret what he sees and hears by a process, much more strenuous than with Raphael, of faulty formulation, improper response, and correction. He also learns by vicarious experience, identifying so closely with his progeny that he seems almost to live their history with them: he is enraged by the wickedness of Cain, laments the terrors of pestilence and death in a lazar house, weeps for the destruction of the world by the flood, rejoices in the steadfast faith of Abraham, Moses, and the other righteous, and waxes ecstatic over the eventual triumph of Christ with his saints. Under Michael's correction he learns to read history emblematically, as a series of episodes displaying again and again the proliferation of evils his sin has unleashed upon the world. He also learns to read it typologically, as a movement "From shadowie Types to Truth" (12.303) in which the meaning of the messianic promises becomes ever clearer, so that at last, despite sin and death and all our woe, he can proclaim the goodness of God's ways to man: "O goodness infinite, goodness immense! / That all this good of evil shall produce, / And evil turn to good" (12.469–71). Michael then offers him further consolation in the far-off prospect of the Last Judgment and the Millennium, placing less emphasis on heavenly bliss than on the restoration of the fallen earth to its paradisal beauty, so that "the Earth / Shall all be Paradise, far happier place / Than this of *Eden*, and far happier daies" (12.463–5). Michael also points to the apocalyptic climax of this period, the Son's final epic victory against Satan, Sin, and Death, followed by the dissolution in flames of "*Satan* with his perverted World," and the emergence of a new, purged, and refined creation: "New Heav'ns, new Earth, Ages of endless date / Founded in righteousness and peace and love / To bring forth fruits Joy and eternal Bliss" (12.547–51). Then Adam can apply the messianic promise to himself, acknowledging Christ as "my Redeemer ever blest" and as a model for the new heroism (12.560–73).

Adam and the reader are also to take a political lesson from history, as they see how, over and over again, one or a few righteous humans stand out against, but are at length overwhelmed by, the many wicked, resulting in the collapse of all attempts to found a permanent version of the Kingdom of God on earth. Michael sums up that pattern as he comments on the way of the world after Christ's ascension: "so shall the World goe on, / To good malignant, to bad men benigne, / Under her own waight groaning" until Christ's second coming (12.537–51). That tragic vision of an external paradise irretrievably lost, along with the promise of "A paradise within thee, happier far" might seem a recipe for quietism, indicating Milton's retreat from the political arena. But the entire thrust of Michael's prophecy is against any kind of passivity, spiritual, moral, or even political. He shows that in every age the few just have the responsibility to oppose, if God calls them to do so, the Nimrods, or the Pharaohs, or the royalist persecutors of Puritans, even though—like the loyal angels in the War in Heaven—they can win no decisive victories and can effect no lasting reforms until the Son appears. Michael offers Adam and his progeny examples of both kinds of heroism: heroic martyrdom and heroic action. And Adam understands. He has learned that "suffering for Truths sake / Is fortitude to highest victorie," and also that God often uses weak humans to accomplish great things: "by things deemed weak / Subverting worldly strong" (12.563–70).

Eve also learns something of this history by a mode of prophecy that validates her distinct order of experience. She claims to have received in dreams directly from God some understanding of the "great good" to come. Dreams were a recognized vehicle of prophecy, though inferior to vision. How much history Eve's dreams conveyed is left unclear, but they lead her to recognize her own divinely appointed agency in bringing the messianic promise into history. As she speaks the last words we hear in Eden, she voices her own version of the new heroism and claims her central role in God's plan and Milton's poem, as primary protagonist of the Fall but also primary human agent in redemption:

> This further consolation yet secure
> I carry hence, though all by mee is lost,
> Such favour I unworthie am voutsaft,
> By mee the Promis'd Seed shall all restore. (12.620–3)

Milton's poignant, quiet, marvelously evocative final lines are elegiac in substance and tone, conjoining loss and consolation. Prophecy and Providence provide part of that consolation, but so does Adam and Eve's loving union: its continuing comforts and challenges are underscored by the paradoxical description of the pair going forth "hand-in-hand" and "solitarie." The final lines also effect a sharp adjustment of the perspective glass, as we are suddenly translated from the end of time back to the beginning, and watch Adam and Eve go forth to live out all our woe and to enact all that has been foreseen.

> Som natural tears they drop'd, but wip'd them soon;
> The World was all before them, where to choose
> Thir place of rest, and Providence thir guide:
> They hand in hand, with wandring steps and slow,
> Through *Eden* took thir solitarie way.

On Style and Versification

DOUGLAS BUSH

From The Restoration: 1660–74†

* * *

Any long poem, at least until recent times, demanded stylization, and Renaissance theory and practice, looking back to the highly stylized Virgil and Homer, to some degree codified devices for achieving epic magnificence. For Milton the poetry of Della Casa and Tasso and Tasso's critical discourses were probably of special value. But, even if the Italians had never existed, Milton's classical instincts and his conception of the religious and prophetic function of poetry would have led him toward Roman, Greek, and Hebraic grandeur. In composing *Paradise Lost* he was not merely "a poet soaring in the high region of his fancies with his garland and singing robes about him." His epic style must be "answerable" to his divine subject; it must raise the mind above mundane concerns to contemplation of first and last things. Although "sublimity" has dropped out of the modern critical lexicon, no other word is adequate. In Dr. Johnson's phrase, Milton's "natural port is gigantick loftiness." Most everything said so far has had to do with Miltonic sublimity, but a little must be, and

† From *John Milton: A Sketch of His Life and Writings* (New York: Collier, 1967), pp. 174–80. Reprinted by permission of the publisher.

only a little can be, said about matters of style; proper discussion would need another book.

Elements of the grand style had appeared in Milton's earlier poems, especially the sonnets, and in the roughness and toughness of language, syntax, and image in the soaring or snorting prose, English and Latin. Under diction go unusual, exalted, and arresting words, coinages, words used in new meanings, punning plays on words, the shifting of parts of speech (adjectives as adverbs and nouns—"the vast abrupt"), the use of Latin derivatives in their literal sense ("error" for "wandering"). Then there are condensed and elliptical syntax, at once fluid and muscular; the placing of words and phrases for emphasis rather than in the order of prose; periodic sentences (like those that open books one and two); periphrases (which, like similes, do not merely elevate the fact but assess its significance). These and other devices—some of which had been used by Spenser, Sylvester, and George Sandys in his translation of Ovid—compel attention, heighten dignity, energy, and intensity, and govern imaginative and emotional responses. Milton's unique power in the exploitation of them has led to the common charge that he made English a foreign language. Yet to discount the charge one has only to open the poem almost anywhere and read; and close reading will show that the epic devices are richly functional and hardly ever mechanical. For all the bold and cunning pressures Milton exerts upon language, in its total effect his style is one of grand simplicity; it is only after rapidly assimilating the large cinematic impressions that we study the subtle details.

The placing of words and phrases with the freedom of an inflected language—something already practiced in Milton's prose—yields continual advantages in expressive emphasis:

> Him the Almighty Power
> Hurled headlong flaming from th' ethereal sky
> With hideous ruin and combustion down.
> To bottomless perdition, there to dwell
> In adamantine chains and penal fire,
> Who durst defy th' Omnipotent to arms.

Recast in the order of prose (and bereft of rhythm, this would be flat and limp. The force of the initial and alliterative "Him" and "Hurled headlong" (Milton is fond of a monosyllabic verb as the first word in a line) carries on until, as a critic has said, Satan hits bottom where he is held by the regularity of "there . . . fire," and the last line is the stronger for being delayed five lines beyond its antecedent; the stock epithets, like Homer's, recall accepted facts and free the imagination to receive the central impact. The explosive but ordered finality of that passage may be contrasted with the disorderly violence of evil energy, expressed partly by word order, partly by the jostling of many verbs, in the lines where Sin and Death, in parody of God's creativity, begin to build their bridge to the world (X.282 f.):

> Then both from out hell gates into the waste
> Wide anarchy of Chaos damp and dark
> Flew diverse, and with power (their power was great)
> Hovering upon the waters; what they met
> Solid or slimy, as in raging sea
> Tossed up and down, together crowded drove
> From each side shoaling towards the mouth of hell.

Yet within the necessary stylization there is infinite variety of diction and tone (including the serious use of the comic or grotesque), and one pervasive thread is quiet and direct simplicity, from "Brought death into the world, and all our woe" or "There rest, if any rest can harbor there" (the rhetorical pattern, *a:b:b:a*, though potent, is hardly noticed) to the last lines of the poem which were quoted above. In sublime simplicity nothing could surpass the invocation to Light. After the opening phrase, "Hail, holy Light," which sets the tone as religious, not scientific, the first few lines of theological speculation are technical and latinate, but the rest are in another vein. The change of scene from hell to heaven recalls—as we observed on an early page—the journeys of Orpheus and Aeneas to and up from the underworld, the blind poet's continuing love of the classics and above them of the Bible, his place in the line of blind prophet-poets, his visual darkness and his inner light:

> Yet not the more
> Cease I to wander where the Muses haunt
> Clear spring, or shady grove, or sunny hill,
> Smit with the love of sacred song; but chief
> Thee, Sion, and the flow'ry brooks beneath
> That wash thy hallowed feet, and warbling flow,
> Nightly I visit; nor sometimes forget
> Those other two equaled with me in fate,
> So were I equaled with them in renown,
> Blind Thamyris and blind Maeonides,
> And Tiresias and Phineus prophets old:
> Then feed on thoughts that voluntary move
> Harmonious numbers, as the wakeful bird
> Sings darkling, and in shadiest covert hid
> Tunes her nocturnal note. Thus with the year
> Seasons return; but not to me returns
> Day, or the sweet approach of ev'n or morn,
> Or sight of vernal bloom, or summer's rose,

Or flocks, or herds, or human face divine;
But cloud instead, and ever-during dark
Surrounds me, from the cheerful ways of men
Cut off, and for the book of knowledge fair
Presented with a universal blank
Of Nature's works to me expunged and razed,
And wisdom at one entrance quite shut out.
So much the rather thou, celestial Light,
Shine inward, and the mind through all her powers
Irradiate, there plant eyes, all mist from thence
Purge and disperse, that I may see and tell
Of things invisible to mortal sight.

If we want to know what "classical" writing is, this is it. One general impression is of Milton's feeling of normality, of community with mankind; there is no trace of sentimental softness, nothing of the self-pity and sense of uniqueness found in some poems of the romantic age. In keeping with that is the depersonalizing and generalizing of both personal emotions and their objects. In the first lines Milton records his unabated love of classical poetry, though he sets it below the Bible; while the lines are, as always, self-sufficient, they work a beautiful variation on the passage (*Georgics* II.475 f.) in which Virgil declares his love of the Muses—*ingenti percussus amore*—and his delight in the country even if he cannot attain to higher cosmic themes. Milton gives a "prosaic" list (in ascending order) of the everyday things of nature and life from which a blind poet is cut off. Such an atmosphere has been created that the mere naming of the items is—along with the rhythm—enough; and the list ends with a quietly paradoxical phrase, the first adjective suggesting the association of "friend with friend," the second the creation of man in God's image and the miracle of the human face. No less "prosaic," apart from the strongly charged Miltonic "turn" (a phrase repeated in slightly altered form), are the personal lines quoted above in the second paragraph of this section. And neither passage exhibits the predominantly Latin diction and syntax that supposedly make the grand style a stiff brocade; indeed many impressionistic judgments on this point, in regard to the whole poem, are simply not in accord with the facts. In any case, however bold or complicated Milton's syntax at times may be, his meaning is scarcely ever in doubt—as it often is in Shakespeare, though Shakespeare is always taken to represent the true genius of English.

As Milton said in his short and vigorous preface (which may reflect the recent debate on rhyme between Dryden and Sir Robert Howard), the use of blank verse for a heroic poem was a great innovation, and in using it he created a new world of expressive sound. His rhythms are so much a part of his total effect, indeed of his very meaning, that he has to be read aloud; even a few remarks on his style could not avoid rhythm. But the subtleties of Milton's versification are as impossible to deal with briefly as the subtleties of his style, and only a little can be said about some main principles. The basic fact is that Milton's unit is the ten-syllable line; it is essential to think of it in that way and not as an iambic pentameter with many substitutions, an idea which suggests contrived mechanics rather than complete freedom and flexibility. In Milton's blank verse the ten syllables (often achieved through elision and slurring, as in excerpts quoted here) are commonly grouped in pairs, which are most often iambs; but that is as far as one can go toward a general rule. The lines contain any number of stresses from three to eight, and these may differ markedly in degree and in position. The caesura or natural pause in the line falls most often of course in the middle section but is continually varied, and it may come even after the first syllable (as, in the extract above from the invocation to Light, "Day" is poised so arrestingly); the weight of the caesura varies like its position. Although, for the reasons indicated, the infinite variety of stress and tempo cannot begin to be measured with the usual blunt instrument, marks for stressed and unstressed syllables, the familiar opening lines may be crudely charted:

> Ŏf mán's / fírst dís / ŏbéd / ĭĕnce, / / aňd / thĕ frúit
> Ŏf thát / fŏrbíd / dĕn trée, / / whŏse mór / tăl táste
> Broúght deáth / ĭntŏ / thĕ wórld, / / aňd áll / oŭr wóe,
> Wĭth lóss / ŏf Éd / ĕn, / / tĭll / óne gréat / ĕr Mán
> Rĕstóre / us, / / aňd / rĕgaín / thĕ blíss / fŭl séat,
> Síng, Héav'n / lў̆ Múse, / / thăt ŏn / thĕ séc / rĕt tóp. . . .

Here only one line is a regular iambic, and its movement carries an effect of irrevocable finality, an effect felt likewise in "and all our woe" (a phrase that becomes a leitmotiv throughout the poem). In the first line and the beginning of the third the grouping of strong stresses accentuates the thematic ideas. In line four the feminine caesura (one that comes after a weak syllable) heightens the idea of something gone wrong, while the phrases that follow are mostly in the rising rhythm of reassurance. Readers might differ in stressing or not stressing such words as "till," "us," and "that," in the last three lines. In general, we read the weighted words slowly and slide quickly over the rest.

This opening sentence has sixteen lines, a sufficient example of what Milton in his preface refers to as "the sense variously drawn out from one verse into another." We observed how the use of run-on lines and strong medial pauses (with some wrenching of normal word order) gave the sonnets the character of blank-verse paragraphs, and in the epic Milton had full scope for his planetary wheelings. While the ten-syllable line (with its endless internal variations) remains in our ear as a norm, there is another system comprising the irregular rhythmic units that flow from one caesura to another, so that we have the combined pleasures of recurrence and surprise manipulated by a supreme artist; and all these effects contribute immeasurably to the sense of what is being said. The continual changes of pace and stress operate within "the enormous onward pressure of the great stream on which you are embarked." In general Milton compels a reading much more rapid than most blank verse allows. As Mr. Eliot, a master of expressive rhythm, has said, Milton's verse is never monotonous; its strength and intricate refinements every reader must experience for himself.

In the world of Hobbes and Newton and the Royal Society, of travesties of the classical epics and *Hudibras* and *The Country Wife, Paradise Lost* was an anachronism when it was published (although, as we shall see, its fame soon mounted). But the science and skepticism of the Augustan Enlightenment have now only historical interest and *Paradise Lost* remains, an anachronism still. No long poem in the world is maintained throughout at concert pitch, not even the *Iliad* or *Odyssey* or *Aeneid* and certainly not the *Divine Comedy*, which is often used as a stick to beat Milton with. In its texture and structure, in all its imaginative variety and power, *Paradise Lost* is an inexhaustible source of aesthetic pleasure of a kind unique in English poetry. And, whatever theological elements some readers may choose to ignore, the essential myth, the picture of the grandeur and misery of man, remains "true," and infinitely more noble and beautiful than anything modern literature has been able to provide. The question is not how far the poem is worthy of our attention, but how far we can make ourselves worthy of it.

CHRISTOPHER B. RICKS

From Enhancing Suggestions†

* * *

With the Fall of Man, language falls too. The prophecy which Sin makes includes words, as was inevitable:

> Till I in Man residing through the Race,
> His thoughts, his looks, words, actions all infect. (x.607–8)

† From *Milton's Grand Style* (Oxford: Clarendon, 1963), pp. 109–12. Reprinted by permission of Oxford University Press.

So one of the reasons why Milton often uses 'words in a proper and primary signification' (Newton) is because he thereby re-create something of the pre-lapsarian state language. Mr. Stein has brilliantly drawn attention to play with the word 'error' in the account of the river Paradise, 'With mazie error under pendant shades' (iv.239).

> Here, before the Fall, the word *error* argues, from its original meaning, for the order in irregularity, for the rightness in wandering, before the concept of error is introduced into man's world and comes to signify wrong wandering. Back of the phrase are the echoes from hell, Belial's precious thoughts that wander, and the debates of the philosophical angels 'in wandering mazes lost'.

Error here is not exactly a pun, since it means only 'wandering'—but the 'only' is a different thing from an absolutely simple use of the word, since the evil meaning is consciously and ominously excluded. Rather than the meaning being simply 'wandering', it is 'wandering (not error)' Certainly the word is a reminder of the Fall, in that it takes us back to a time when there were no infected words because there were no infected actions.

Not that one can *prove* that the word is not simple Latinism. But 'error' is frequent enough in its fallen meaning in the poem for such Latinism to be of a powerfully and unusually obtuse kind: 'I also err'd in overmuch admiring'; 'I rue that errour now'; 'inmost powers made erre'. And the same pre-lapsarian play occurs during the Creation, when it is fortified with *serpent*: the waters are 'with Serpent errour wandring (vii 302). It is surely easier to believe in a slightly ingenious Milton than in one who could be so strangely absent-minded as to use both 'serpent' and 'error' without in some way in voking the Fall. And when Milton uses 'error' elsewhere than in *Paradise Lost*, it always has the fallen meaning.

Many of the Latinisms involve just this choice: is Milton reaching back to an earlier purity—which we are to contrast with what has happened to the word, and the world, since? Or is he simply being forgetful? The answer is likely to depend on one's general estimate of Milton. When in Paradise we hear the 'liquid Lapse of murmuring Streams' (viii. 263), the meaning may be 'falling (not the Fall)'. Certainly many of Milton's finest effects come from just this invoking of what is then deliberately excluded: 'Not that faire field of Euna . . . ', or the story of the fall of Mulciber, or the beauty of the bower:

In shadier Bower
More sacred and sequesterd, though but feignd,

Pan or Silvanus never slept, nor Nymph,
Nor Faunus haunted. (IV.705–8)

The Miltonic style is very much of a piece, and the habits so fruitfully at work in the allusions may well be the same as those that inspire the words themselves. To invoke, and then to exclude; so that a 'Lapse' become 'falling, not the Fall', Milton uses 'lapse' enough times for the Fall for it to be improbable that such a meaning is merely forgotten: 'I will renew his lapsed powers'; 'Man whom they triumph'd once lapst'; 'thy original lapse'; 'Which would but lead me to a worse relapse, And heavier fall'. How tragically far we are from the 'liquid Lapse of murmuring Streams'. The irrevocable Fall has degraded language too, and turned those innocent notes to tragic.

The Paradisal state of language is naturally most clear in descriptions of Paradise, where there is not yet any grave distinction between 'luxuriant' and 'luxurious':

the mantling Vine
Layes forth her purple Grape, and gently creeps
Luxuriant . . . (IV.258–60)

The work under our labour grows,
Luxurious by restraint . . . (IX.208–9)

Both words are innocent; but both remind us ominously that innocence will soon be gone, and that instead of luxurious plants we shall know of 'luxurious Cities', 'wealth and luxurie', 'luxurious wealth', 'luxurie and riot'.

Once again, outside *Paradise Lost* Milton does not use the word in its 'unfallen' sense. (And the *O.E.D.* shows how old and powerful is the meaning 'unchaste, excessive, voluptuous.') In the same way the 'wantonness' of Eden, or of its inhabitants, is neither mere description nor moral condemnation: it is 'mere description (not moral condemnation)'.

For Nature here
Wantond as in her prime, and plaid at will
Her Virgin Fancies. (V.294–6)

Such wantonness is still virginal (Herrick's 'cleanly-wantonness'), as it is in the 'wanton growth' of the branches, or—poignantly—in the 'wanton ringlets' of Eve. But in Hell we have already heard the fallen word, have heard of 'wanton rites' and 'wanton passions'; and Satan brings fallen wantonness to the seduction of Eve, so that the word is infected before our eyes:

and his tortuous Traine
Curld many a wanton wreath in sight of Eve,
To lure her eye. (IX.516–18)

So it is not long after the Fall that Adam and Eve become liable to the grimmer meaning:

> hee on Eve
> Regan to cast lascivious Eyes, she him
> As wantonly repaid. (IX.1013–15)

* * *

Through such delicate anticipations and echoes, Milton creates a style which is not only grand but also suggestive, as the eighteenth-century commentators saw. It does not seem true that 'the mind that invented Milton's Grand Style had renounced the English language'. On the contrary, he triumphantly combined what might well seem to be incompatible greatnesses. His style is not only grand in its explicitness, but also—as Arnold insisted—pregnant and allusive: 'Milton charges himself so full with thought, imagination, knowledge, that his style will hardly contain them. He is too full-stored to show us in much detail one conception, one piece of knowledge; he just shows it to us in a pregnant allusive way, and then he presses on to another'.

ARCHIE BURNETT

From "Sense Variously Drawn Out": The Line in *Paradise Lost*†

* * *

Of approximately seventy occurrences of the name [Satan] in *Paradise Lost*, one-third are found at the beginning of a line (and there are others very near it). Sometimes the immediate context adds to the drama:

> . . . . At interview both stood
> A while, but suddenly at head appeared
> Satan. . . . (6.555–57)

An apt pause follows "stood," making "A while" in the next line linger aptly. One recalls Satan playing for time at the start of book 3 of *Paradise Regained*:

> So spake the Son of God, and Satan stood
> A while as mute confounded what to say.

† From *Literary Imagination* 5.1 (2003): 74–83. Reprinted by permission of the Association of Literary Scholars and Critics.

"Both stood / A while, but suddenly"—the adverb puts us on the alert for Satan's dramatic entrance—"at head appeared / Satan." He cannot be hidden:

> In with the river sunk, and with it rose
> Satan involved in rising mist, then sought
> Where to lie hid . . . (9.74–76)

In spite of "sunk . . . involved . . . hid," the masking of "rose" in "rising," and the beguiling camouflage of alliteration and assonance, the emphatic placing of "Satan" blows his cover. Similarly, in 3.418–22—

> Mean while upon the firm opacous globe
> Of this round world, whose first convex divides
> The luminous inferior orbs, enclosed
> From Chaos and the inroad of darkness old,
> Satan alighted walks . . .

—Satan emerges, eventually, from the obscurity of "enclosed . . . Chaos . . . inroad . . . darkness." (Note, too, how responsively the rhythmic stress of "Satan alighted walks" represents the bumpy landing—"Satan alighted"—finally stabilized in "walks.") Even in the timing of "for now / Satan" (4.8–9) Satan's presence is announced with a brief shiver of apprehension. By this device alone, Milton regularly requires the reader to greet the appearance of "our grand foe / Satan" (10.1033–43) with wary attention.

In the passage describing the creation of the animals (7.463–72), the play of syntax against lineation creates a sense of muscular effort and release. Such effects are again not isolated in the poem, but, noticeably, they are a principal means of registering the pain of hell:

> So he with difficulty and labour hard
> Moved on, with difficulty and labour he; (2.1021–22)

The placing of the verb, already delayed by the adverbial phrase "with difficulty and labour hard," intensifies the impression given by the verbal repetition of striving to get nowhere. Instead of a comparatively straightforward statement—

> So he with difficulty and labour and moved on

—the versification takes on the suggestion of the words, and the movement feels like driving with the brake slightly engaged:

> So he with difficulty and labour hard
> Moved on. . . .

The answer to Donald Davie's perverse comment on these lines—that the repetition reveals "a refusal to profit by syntactical resources, so as to weave the anticipation into the narrative"—is that Milton's poem need not be only narrative; that narrative need not involve anticipation at all times; and that at this particular moment the profit to be had from syntax is legitimately as much dramatic as narrative.

The torment of hell is often registered powerfully by the friction of syntax against the line. When, for instance, Satan counsels the devils to consider

> . . . what best may ease
> The present misery, and render hell
> More tolerable; if there be cure or charm
> To respite or deceive, or slack the pain
> Of this ill mansion: . . . (2.458–62)

the lines unsettle the sentence structure so fundamentally that Satan's optimistic speculations, already shaky in "may . . . if . . . or" and in the slide through "cure or charm / To respite or deceive, or slack," are completely undermined. The unease of hell in "ease / The present misery" is felt at other times in hell when the line break again separates verb from object:

> Yet with a pleasing sorcery could charm
> Pain for a while or anguish, and excite
> Fallacious hope . . . (2.566–68)

"Charm" and "pain" are separated, yet still sufficiently juxtaposed, to highlight the difficulty, the futility even, of applying charm to pain; and "fallacious hope" extinguishes the brief optimism of "excite." The "hell within" (4.20) Satan (a contrast to the later "paradise within," 12.587) is dramatized by the same play of grammar against lineation:

> . . . Horror and doubt distract
> His troubled thoughts, and from the bottom stir
> The hell within him, for within him hell
> He brings, and round about him . . . (4.18–21)

In hell physical movement, and particularly vertical movement, is arduous, as when a verb turns out to be transitive:

> Forthwith upright he rears from off the pool
> His mighty stature . . . (1.221–22)

Comparable difficulty with raising and rising in hell is announced in

> Nor want we skill or art, from whence to raise
> Magnificence . . . (2.272–73)

And, with a different dislocation of syntax, in

> . . . with grave
> Aspect he rose . . . (2.300–301)

Such examples show that a principled versification need not mean a constrainedly unexpressive one. In fact, Milton characteristically eschewed such constraint. As Paul Fussell remarks, "[T]here is always something in fixed forms that stimulates Milton to mild rebellion or exhibitions of technical independence." This is nowhere more evident than in the preliminary note on "The Verse," inserted before October 26 in the issue of the first edition with the 1668 title page. In defense of "English heroic verse without rhyme," Milton cites Homer and Vergil as classical precedents, and argues that modern poets who have conformed to the custom of rhyming have as a result experienced "vexation, hindrance, and constraint" in expression. "True musical delight," he argues, "consists only in apt numbers, fit quantity of syllables, and the sense variously drawn out from one verse into another." On these grounds Milton claims that his chosen verse form is "an example set, the first in English, of ancient liberty recovered to heroic poem."

The political overtones are significant. Barbara K. Lewalski comments: "His note on 'The Verse' aggressively challenges not only the new poetic norms but also, by implication, the debased court culture and royalist politics that underpin them." Defiantly, Milton lays claim to liberty of style at a time when the Restoration must have seemed to have stifled the ideals of the "Good Old Cause" and the "liberty" he had so fervently championed. As late as 1653, he had greeted the restoration of the Rump parliament with elation, hailing its members as "authors, assertors, and now recoverers of our liberty." Perhaps in the note on the verse there is a grim if defiant, acknowledgement that stylistic freedom is all that remains? It is not that the poem entirely lacks rhyme: John Diekhoff noted in 1934 that some two hundred lines of the poem contain rhyme, and that the rhymes were no accident. Milton's insistence is on not being constrained by rhyme, on exercising liberty in a use of the line at once principled and flexible, "the sense variously drawn out from one verse into another."

It is the sheer range of effects that impresses, and not only in the "physical sensation of a breathless leap, communicated by Milton's long periods" which T. S. Eliot praise. The verse can creep along too:

> . . . yet, when they list, would creep,
> If aught disturbed their noise, into her womb,
> And kennel there . . . (2.656–58)

. . . the mantling vine
Lays forth her purple grape, and gently creeps
Luxuriant . . . (4.258–60)

Forth flourished thick the clustering vine, forth crept
The swelling gourd . . . (7.320–21)

. . . First crept
The parsimonious emmet, provident
Of future . . . (7.484–86)

In each case the verb is placed at the end of the line, just before a slight pause. Notice how the interposed conditional clause "if aught disturbed their noise" further slows up the completion of "would creep . . . into her womb"; how the adverb "gently" prepares the transition as the monosyllabic "creeps" flourishes into "luxuriant"; and how "crept" develops through assonance into "swelling." Milton does not write

Forth crept the swelling gourd

or

First crept the parsimonious emmet

but rather

. . . forth crept
The swelling gourd

and

. . . First crept
The parsimonious emmet.

The result, as in the many dramatic acts of naming, is an increase in what Donald Davie termed "eventfulness," and it is a quality much more in evidence in the effects of lineation in *Paradise Lost* than he seemed to estimate. Milton attentively distinguishes between the headlong profusion of "Forth flourished thick the clustering vine" and the slower maturation of ". . . forth crept / The swelling gourd," and makes lines progress as warily as the ant.

At the other extreme, the sensation of flight across great distances is suggested when the syntax, prompted by the word "over," significantly runs over:

Who shall tempt with wandering feet
The dark unbottomed infinite abyss
And through the palpable obscure find out
His uncouth way, or spread his airy flight

Upborne with indefatigable wings
Over the vast abrupt, ere he arrive
The happy isle. . . . (2.204–10)

. . . set forth
Their airy caravan high over seas
Flying, and over lands with mutual wing
Easing their flight . . . (7.427–30)

Enjambment is similarly evocative in the description of the bridge built from hell to earth by Sin and Death, where the syntax, again taking the prompt of the word "over," analogously makes links over the lines:

. . . Sin and Death amain
Following his track, such was the will of heaven,
Paved after him a broad and beaten way
Over the dark abyss, whose boiling gulf
Tamely endured a bridge of wondrous length
From hell continued reaching the utmost orb
Of this frail world . . . (2.1024–30)

. . . the mole immense wrought on
Over the foaming deep high arched, a bridge
Of length prodigious joining to the wall
Immovable of this now fenceless world
. . . .
. . . and over Hellespont
Bridging his way, Europe with Asia joined
. . . .
Now had they brought the work by wondrous art
Pontifical, a ridge of pendent rock
Over the vexed abyss . . . (10.300–303, 309–10, 312–14)

The syntax runs over but never runs away with itself. Momentousness and control of momentum go together. Momentousness need not involve heavy-handedness, however, and a simple pause can be delicately acknowledged:

. . . yet first
Pausing a while, thus to herself she mused. (9.743–44)
As one who in his journey baits at noon,
Though bent on speed, so here the archangel paused
Betwixt the world destroyed and world restored. (12.1–3)

So spake the archangel Michael, then paused,
As at the world's great period. . . . (12.466–67)

It is particularly apt, too, when the line division coincides with other divisions and partings:

> . . . the angelic choirs
> On each hand parting, to his speed gave way . . . (5.251–52)

> . . . to right and left the front
> Divided, and to either flank retired. (6.569–70)

> . . . thy saints unmixed, and from the impure
> Far separate, circling the holy mount . . . (6.742–43)

> And light from darkness by the hemisphere
> Divided . . . (7.250–51)

> The waters underneath from those above
> Dividing . . . (7.268–69)

> . . . on either side
> Disparted chaos over built exclaimed . . . (10.415–16)

In the account of the Israelites passing through the Red Sea, other effects of lineation complement the mimetic division. The sea

> . . . them lets pass
> As on dry land between two crystal walls,
> Awed by the rod of Moses so to stand
> Divided, till his rescued gain their shore: (12.196–99)

"Pass" occurs at the moment of passing from one line to the next, and the pause after "stand" effects a momentary stasis. But the syntax runs on to stand divided over the line break, and "shore" is gained at the limit of the sentence and line. The sustained strong stress on "stand" and "divided" supports the syntactic linkage, accentuating a miracle of stable division.

The line break can also represent instability. Milton turns it to particular expressive use in accounts of shaky foundations, associated in the poem with hell and Satanic forces. In the catalogue of devils—

> The chief were those who from the pit of hell
> Roaming to seek their prey on earth, durst fix
> Their seats long after next the seat of God (1.381–83)

—the detachment of "their seats" from "fix" threatens the security of the fixing. The site of Solomon's temple, chosen under Moloch's influence, is similarly undermined by the precarious position of the words "build," "stood," and "built":

> . . . the wisest heart
> Of Solomon he led by fraud to build
> His temple right against the temple of God
> On that opprobrious hill, . . .
> . . . .
> . . . where stood
> Her temple on the offensive mountain, built
> By that uxorious king . . . (1.400–403, 422–44)

Babel too seems to quake momentarily:

> Of brick, and of that stuff they cast to build
> A city and tower, whose top may reach to heaven; (12.43–44)

And an ambiguity at the line break sends a tremor through Pandemonium:

> Built like a temple, where pilasters round
> Were set . . . (1.713–14)

"Round" may be an adverb reinforcing "were set"; but the momentary hesitation at the line break suggests that it may also be an adjective postmodifying "pilasters," and the stability of sentence and building alike is disturbed. The poem intimates dramatically that it is impossible to achieve equilibrium in hell, as in a countermovement within Belial's speech advocating composure:

> . . . All things invite
> To peaceful counsels, and the settled state
> Of order, how in safety best we may
> Compose our present evils . . . (2.278–81)

"The settled state of order" is split unsettlingly into "the settled state / Of order"; whether "may" signifies permission (God's, ultimately) or possibility hangs tellingly unresolved; and the pause before "Compose" serves to discompose. It is just this instability that Satan introduces into the lives of Adam and Eve, feeling that he has

> . . . fair foundation laid whereon to build
> Their ruin! (4.521–22)

The full force, literal and metaphorical, of "ruin" is released as a seemingly steady and complete line ending in "build" totters bathetically into the paradox of "ruin": syntax and line break work (as Satan does) to deceive, and provide an ominous premonition of the Fall. At such moments the line break runs through the syntax like a crack.

* * *

On Christian Ideology

A. S. P. WOODHOUSE

From Paradise Lost, I: Theme and Pattern†

* * *

II

Paradise Lost is the outcome of Milton's deliberate effort to write a classical epic on a Christian theme, and specifically on the fall of man. Any attempt to isolate and explain the effect of the poem must seek to draw out the implications of this truism, and essay once more some comparison of *Paradise Lost* with its two great models, the *Iliad* and the *Aeneid*. It must watch the poet imposing an analogous pattern upon very different materials, and be alert to detect the modifications and extensions of the pattern which his Christian theme, outlook, and purpose demand or permit.

When full allowance is made for Milton's heresies, *Paradise Lost* remains unequivocally a Christian poem. It assumes the two orders of nature and grace and the priority of the order of grace. Its theme is man's fall from grace and it adumbrates the terms on which, by divine intervention, he will be restored. *Paradise Lost* cannot be adequately described as an epic which substitutes Christian machinery for Olympian, or even Christian legend for pagan, though it does both: it is an epic which finds its subject at the heart of Christian revelation. Implicit in the difference between *Paradise Lost* and its classical models is the whole difference between Christianity and the Graeco-Roman religions and philosophies which it replaced. The points, relevant to our discussion, at which the Christian view of things and the classical most sharply diverge must be set down, at whatever risk of oversimplification.

The classical recognizes only one order of existence, the natural, though it acknowledges gradations within this order, whereas Christianity adds to the order of nature the superior order of grace, which alone holds the key to the enigma of life. And this addition of a second order which, in man, intersects with the first may serve to remind us that the Christian view of existence, like every great system of thought, is itself a pattern, and consequently contains elements which can be readily incorporated in the aesthetic patterns of

† From *The Heavenly Muse: A Preface to Milton* (Toronto: U of Toronto P, 1972), pp. 177–80, 188–90. Reprinted by permission of the publisher.

the poet, as Dante would illustrate and as Milton will. But let us pursue for a moment the more obvious results of the single order in the classical systems and the twofold order in the Christian. The essential naturalism of the classical systems permeates any conceptions of the supernatural they may entertain, whether in the pantheon of Homer or in the religion of Virgil, who saw 'Universal Nature moved by Universal Mind.' In Christianity, on the contrary, the supernatural dominates the natural. Though it ratifies many of the natural virtues before transcending them, Christianity will not rest content therewith, but adds its own special virtues of piety, humility, and love; and the Christian virtues combine to produce an ideal of heroism, realized in Christ, and very different from classical conceptions of the heroic, a fact which impinges directly upon epic poetry. Nor may we ignore the way in which Christianity extends what I will call the vertical range of human experience: in the classical view man may rise to the specifically human or sink to the level of the barbarian or the beast; in the Christian vision he is confronted by the dizzy alternatives of rising to heaven or plunging to the bottomless pit. I am the more insistent on this fact since Christianity is often thought merely to restrict the poet's outlook. It does not, I think, at all restrict him in his treatment of evil, but it does afford him a new orientation in several ways and with important results. Thus providence replaces the classical fate. 'Necessitie and Chance Approach not mee,' says Milton's God, 'and what I will is Fate' (7:172–3). This is something very different from fate in Homer, or even from the fate which in Virgil plays providence to the Roman race. One result is that on a total view there can be no such thing as divine tragedy, but only a divine comedy. We do not, however, always take total views, and in the divine comedy there is ample provision for tragic episodes. To prove it, one need not invoke the most moving spectacle in all history, Christ on the Cross: it will suffice to remember that as he turns to the story of man's actual fall, Milton, as he says, 'now must change Those notes to Tragic' (9.5–6). And well he may; for this tragic episode, 'with loss of *Eden*' brings 'Death into the World, and all our woe' (1.3–4). But on a total view the episode takes its place in the divine comedy as the *felix culpa*, the fortunate fall, and the lost Eden is replaced by 'a paradise within thee, happier farr' (12.587). Christianity does not eliminate the tragic from human life: it may even accentuate the tragic; but it places the tragic episode in the divine comedy, and thus invites us to take of it a double view. This Milton perfectly understood when he summed up the tragedy of Samson the man, with its human mitigations as well as its human miseries, before he permitted the Chorus to raise its eyes to the place of Samson's sacrifice in the divine scheme.

And so in *Paradise Lost* the fall is none the less tragic in its immediate impact for turning out at last to be the fortunate fall. But does not the sense of an all-encompassing providence, we may ask, reduce the human character to the dimensions of a puppet—such an Adam as, in Milton's phrase, we see in the motions? And does not the Christian epic here fall far short of Homer and even of Virgil? Not necessarily. In Homer and Virgil the individual is encompassed by the decrees of fate. And for the Christian, even Calvinism never really succeeded in eliminating free will and contingency from his life and actions; and to the attempt of Calvinism to do so, Milton is strongly opposed. He insists upon free will: 'when God gave [Adam] reason he gave him freedom to choose, for reason is but choosing' (*Areopagitica*, Col. 4:319). The absolute decree which bestowed on man free will meant that every subsequent decree, as it bore upon the life of the individual, was not absolute but contingent on the choice he made. If there is a difference between Homer and Milton, and there is a great difference, it is not because providence leaves man's destiny less in his own hands than does fate (rather, indeed, the reverse), but because the end which providence proposes is recognized as good and because under its standard the good man does not fight alone or unsupported. In Homer the hero is by no means the master of his fate, but he is the captain of his soul. In Milton he is in some degree the master of his individual destiny, but Christ is the captain of his soul.

Nothing, indeed, in this brief preliminary attempt to isolate and appraise, in general terms, the effect upon Milton's epic of his Christian theme and outlook is intended to obscure the large degree of accommodation achievable between Christianity and classical humanism, and by the Christian humanists of the Renaissance actually achieved. It is simply intended to remind us of a certain evident difference between them, rediscovered from time to time, and clearly so in the seventeenth century under the impulse of Puritanism.

Of Milton's growing sense of this difference something may be inferred from his resolute turning to scriptural subjects in all his later poetry, from distinctively Christian judgments repeatedly expressed in *Paradise Lost*, from his changed attitude to classic myth, and from his specific rejection, in *Paradise Regained*, of the heritage of Greece and Rome when they came into competition with Christianity. At the same time, however, we find his classical humanism reasserting itself in his increasingly close adherence to ancient forms and models in epic and tragedy, with but one partial effort, in *Paradise Regained*, to implement his theoretic conviction that the Bible will yield forms and models at least comparable with the classics. In *Paradise Lost* (as also, in its different way, in *Samson Agonistes*) Milton undertakes to present a Christian theme in a classical form, and, sacrificing nothing of the purity of either, to adapt them the one to the other.

* * *

IV

Despite the strong inclination of Christian humanism to approximate the Virgilian and the Christian ideals, there was a point, as Dante saw, beyond which Virgil could not go. And in the particular matter of the heroic Milton is equally categorical. For him the ideal of heroism is realized once and for all in Christ. Long ago he had described Christ as 'most perfect *Heroe*' (*The Passion* 13), and significantly it was in connection with the heroic martyrdom of the crucifixion and the seeming defeat. The experience of the intervening years had brought home to Milton with a new urgency the idea of heroism in defeat, and this accounts for his exclusive emphasis upon it in the prologue to Book 9. But the idea does not subsist alone: the temporary defeat is part of the divine purpose which cannot fail of victory in the end, and Christian piety, yet more definitely than the Roman *pietas*, means complete submission to, and co-operation with, the divine purpose. Christ, then, is the real hero of *Paradise Lost* in the sense that, like Achilles and Aeneas, he sets the standard of heroism. It is not Christ the heroic martyr, however, that actually figures in the poem, though he is clearly adumbrated there. It is Christ the victor, clad with the Father's irresistible might, who drives Satan out of heaven, and thus performs, like Achilles, what a lesser hero could not achieve. In the successive stages of the heroic, and as it is brought under the control of morality and religion, the element of power, represented by the strength, prowess, and courage of Achilles, is not eliminated, but, by its alliance with the divine purpose, sustained and exalted. Something like this is the context in which Milton's statement on the true heroic requires to be read.

It is not only in its conception of the heroic, however, that *Paradise Lost* deviates from its classical models. At the moment of crisis, which is approaching when Milton pauses to comment on the heroic, his protagonist, as we have said, fails utterly in heroism, exhibits indeed, in Milton's earlier phrase, 'the cowardice of doing wrong' (*Of Education*, Col. 4: 288), and only after repentance, when he has learned the fortitude of patience, does he begin to approach the Miltonic standard of the heroic.

In the *Iliad* and the *Aeneid* the protagonist manifests in fullest measure the qualities, whatever they may be, which the poet recognizes as heroic; in *Paradise Lost* he does not. In Homer and Virgil hero and protagonist are, accordingly, one: in Milton they are two. This has confused the critics, who have quite rightly rejected Adam as hero and have sought another, but in their search have unfortunately stumbled on Satan. In reality Adam is the protagonist and Christ the hero, while Satan is reserved for another role, that of antagonist. To separate hero and protagonist was a bold step necessitated by Milton's theme. To have identified hero and antagonist would have been not boldness, but imbecility, since it would have wrecked that theme—as indeed in the theory of these critics it does. On Milton's plan, the qualities manifested by the hero are the criteria by which protagonist and antagonist alike are to be judged; they reveal the weakness of the one, and the wickedness, which is also the weakness, of the other.

But the strong impression that Satan, though not the hero of the poem, is still in some sense heroic will not be easily relinquished and need not be. In epic protagonist and antagonist must meet as mighty opposites, and this demands in the antagonist certain marks of heroism. Hector indeed contends for our admiration and pity with Achilles himself. And if Turnus appears less admirable it is because, as we have suggested above, he represents an outmoded form of the heroic and seems like a pale reflection of Achilles; and he is not unworthy of Aeneas' steel. But how does this affect Satan? If he had had to encounter only Adam one is tempted to say that no very high degree of heroism would have been necessary: a woman and a serpent might have made up the sum. One would of course be wrong: Adam in his innocence appears to Satan formidable enough. But, in any case, Satan has, as we shall see, much more to do than that. And to equip him for his role, Milton follows Virgil's lead and betters the instruction. He bestows upon Satan, in the beginning, all the qualities of the Homeric hero. Satan has the strength, prowess, and daring of Achilles, the same irresponsibility and recklessness, the same egoistic desire for glory and impatience of constraint, and like Achilles, though for a different reason, the pathos of the doomed. The intended dilemma of Raleigh's question about Satan, 'Hero or fool?' is no dilemma at all. He is both—like Achilles and Turnus.

It has been convenient to speak thus far as if the dichotomy of hero and protagonist in *Paradise Lost* were absolute: to speak of Adam as the protagonist and Christ as the hero; but this is to oversimplify and to give less weight than one should to the supernatural action, which is, as we shall observe, peculiarly important in *Paradise Lost*. The story of the revolt of the angels and their ejection from heaven, which stands in a causal relation to the fall of man, is told at length; and of that story Christ is not only hero but protagonist. So, in effect, Milton's epic has one hero, Christ, and two protagonists, Adam and Christ, the one defeated, the other victorious. The demanded unity is secured in several ways. In part it is secured by the causal relation between the two actions and the encompassing function of Christ, who in the preliminary action defeats Satan and hurls him down to hell, but in the predicted consequence of man's fall will descend to earth for the second defeat of Satan and the rescue and restoration of man. It is secured also by the enforced parallel (with, of course, vital difference) between the two protagonists: Adam is man whose disobedience spelled defeat; Christ is one greater Man, the second Adam, whose perfect obedience spelled victory and the fulfilment of the divine purpose. The role of protagonist in the poem is then filled by Christ-Adam, and the protagonist thus conceived includes the standard of heroism. This is the corrected and completed statement of the relation of hero and protagonist in *Paradise Lost*. And it permits two further observations.

We see now that it is because Satan is pitted against Christ, not because he is pitted against Adam, that Milton is obliged to bestow upon him marks of the heroic. But it must be a heroism compatible with folly and wickedness, that is, a pagan heroism; and for this Milton looks in the ancient epics. Such heroism Satan has in abundance at the beginning; but, as the story proceeds, and Satan sinks deeper into wickedness, he is gradually divested even of this, as if Milton were saying that without virtue, without Christian heroism, all heroism is an illusion.

We also see a little further into Milton's relation to his classical models. If the three poems be set side by side, it is evident that Achilles, Aeneas, and Christ-Adam are the protagonists in the actions and furnish, each for his own poem, the standard of heroism, and that Hector, Turnus, and Satan are the antagonists. But it is equally evident that in point of character and motive the grouping is different: Hector, Aeneas, Christ-Adam; Achilles, Turnus, Satan. Nor should one overlook a similarity, not at first glance obvious, but real and significant, between Adam and Hector. Though one is protagonist, the other antagonist, each has, and is conscious of having, a vast burden of responsibility committed to his charge, and each, though for very different reasons, fails in his charge; so that in Hector, antagonist in the *Iliad*, but protagonist of Ilium, one has some premonition of a figure without counterpart in the *Aeneid*, and peculiar to *Paradise Lost*, the figure of the defeated protagonist.

* * *

STANLEY FISH

From With Mortal Voice: Milton Defends against the Muse†

* * *

Gladly Mixing

It is a truth Milton was continually proclaiming, yet one he could never fully accept; and his conflicted relationship with the ideal of submission is acted out in the careers of even his most exemplary heroes. The Lady of *Comus* has her moment of doubt and disequilibrium before she recovers the equanimity of perfect faith; both the speaker of *Lycidas* and the Samson of *Samson Agonistes* are inveterate murmurers who respond with bitterness to a world they never made and find impossible to understand; and even the Christ of *Paradise Regained* recalls moments when the desire to perform "victorious deeds" and "heroic acts" flamed in his heart. It is only when Milton creates a character more or less out of whole cloth that he can even imagine what it would be like not to feel the stirrings he describes as "that last infirmity of Noble mind." That character is Abdiel, the zealous loyalist, whose finest moment is not seen by anyone, including himself. It is a moment that follows upon something more visibly heroic, his rising to affirm his fidelity to the Father even in the midst of the Satanic host. Now he is on the way back to his friends, but the surprise that awaits him when he arrives is anticipated in the syntax of book VI's opening lines:

> All night the dreadless Angel unpursu'd
> Through Heav'n's wide Champaign held his way, till Morn,
> Wak't by the circling Hours, with rosy hand
> Unbarr'd the gates of Light. (*PL*, VI, 1–4)

"Unpursu'd" is an early clue as to what will soon happen—or, rather, not happen: Abdiel's flight is without the temporal pressure, at least in one direction, that usually gives such actions point. The significant shift, however, occurs at the end of the second line. When we first read it, "till Morn" seems an adverbial phrase modifying "held his way" and therefore a gloss on *Abdiel's* action; but line 3 reveals that in the fuller syntax "till Morn" is the object of the participle "Wak't" (the morn is waked) and then the subject of "Unbarr'd." What this means is that in the course of these lines the agency is taken away

† From *ELH* 62.3 (1995): 522–25.

from Abdiel and given to the Morn, who now has the forward initiative. It is *her* way, not his, and moreover it is a way that will proceed independently of anything Abdiel does or doesn't do. The hours circle—that is, they don't go in a straight line but describe motions that return always to the same appointed place.

The effect of this image is to further undercut the urgency and point of Abdiel's linear flight; and that effect is itself redoubled when that flight is interrupted by a leisurely explanation of the subordinate and indeed decorative role of time in the realm of the heavens:

There is a Cave
Within the Mount of God, fast by his Throne,
Where light and darkness in perpetual round
Lodge and dislodge by turns, which makes through Heav'n
Grateful vicissitude, like Day and Night. (4–8)

That is, for the sake of variety (here a purely aesthetic category) there is a light show in heaven that *simulates* day and night, that simulates the "Diurnal Sphere" in which the passing of time is attended by crisis, choice, and unpredictable consequences. In Heaven, time's passing is devoid of such risks because everything is always and already centered on the central and informing value of the universe; so that when in line 12 Raphael tells us that "now went forth the Morn," we are meant to understand that "now" merely marks a turn-taking and not a moment of poised urgency; and if we miss the point, the verse quickly reminds us of it: "Such as in highest Heav'n" (13). "Shot through with orient Beams" (15) further dissipates the already attenuated energy of Abdiel's flight, and for all intents and purposes Abdiel disappears from the passage, reemerging only as the *object* of the effect he had hoped to cause:

When all the Plain
Cover'd with thick embattl'd Squadrons bright,
Chariots and flaming Arms, and fiery Steeds
Reflecting blaze on blaze, first met his view.
(15–18)

The "first" in line 18 is very precise: the view *precedes* his "taking it in." It is before him in two senses of the word: it is in front of him, and it was there before he saw it. In relation to it, he is superfluous; it doesn't need him, and the extent of his inefficacy is given a slow deliberate gloss: "War he perceiv'd, war in procinct, and found / Already known what he for news had thought / To have reported" (19–21). That is, Abdiel had thought that there was something he could *do*, something he could *say*, words that only he could produce, words that would make a difference because they would *be* different, not already spoken in the eternal present; but that thought, and the vision of self and identity of which it is an extension, are countermanded by a reality that has no place for them—the reality of the "Omnific Word."

At this moment Abdiel is exactly in the position the epic narrator occupies in the opening of book VII, confronted by the suffocating omnipresence of the deity he serves. What distinguishes the two is their reaction, or, rather, the fact that Abdiel doesn't have a reaction. The hinge between what he has just "met"—the castrating sight of his undeniable impotence—and what he now does is the word "gladly": "Already known what he for news had thought / To have reported: gladly then he mixt" (20–21). The extraordinary thing about "gladly" is that it participates in both actions (because it participates in two syntactic structures) and thereby acknowledges no difference between them: Abdiel would have been glad to report and he just as gladly mixes—that is, loses himself in a host already composed without his reportorial aid. I don't mean that he says to himself, "Well, that was a disappointment (not to have reported), but I can still enjoy the fellowship of my peers"; he doesn't say *anything* to himself. The two possible modes of action which for us would be seen as active and passive respectively are for him absolutely continuous, of a piece, alternative forms of service. He can take no credit for not feeling aggrieved at having his great moment snatched from him, because it never occurs to him to be aggrieved, and therefore he deserves credit precisely in the measure he would not think to claim it. As far as he is concerned, he just does what he does, or is what he is, and as he is named, the servant of God.

Thus, when God says to him, "Servant of God, well done" (29), he is really saying, "Good job at being Abdiel, Abdiel." Being Abdiel is being just one thing, all the time, being what Christ declares himself to be—"Mee hung'ring . . . to do my father's will"—and what Milton sometimes claims to be: "I conceav'd my selfe to be now not as mine own person." But even here, the language betrays him: he *conceives* himself to have a corporate identity, but the act of conceiving, of thinking about himself in that way, is performed at a distance from what it contemplates; and so he fails of his claim and of his goal. But is it his goal? Does not a part of him want to fail, want to fall and wander erroneous and desolate on the plain, so that he can make his way, make his mark, make his career, speak with a mortal voice, a voice that sounds only because it is far from home, from *patria*, in exile, but a voice that sounds a note the exile loves as he loves himself?

On Feminism

JOSEPH A. WITTREICH JR.

From Critiquing the Feminist Critique†

* * *

In the aftermath of his announced "dislodgment," Milton's name continues to turn up unexpectedly: in the poetry of Allen Ginsberg and the novels of Margaret Drabble; in the autobiographies of both Malcolm X and Frank Reynolds, former secretary to the Hell's Angels; in the *Washington Post's* editorializing on the crisis in Iran and in the *New York Times'* account of Anita Bryant's divorce trial; in the reflections of Shirley MacLaine in *Out on a Limb*; and most recently in Bill Moyers' remarks on the venality of White House rhetoric—but also in a well-publicized commendatory citation written by a superior officer for J. D. Hicks, gay cop of San Francisco. It is startling to find Milton as a presence here, only because the rift between the popular culture and the academic culture has become so huge and because—through a curious turn in sexual politics, an act of male appropriation—*Paradise Lost* is no longer thought to be a poem in which Milton curries favor with women. This is instead a text with which women enter into a fiercely adversarial relationship; it is a target on which they can heap their frustrations and often rage. If we can glimpse our own historical moment through a *Saturday Review* demonstration of sexual difference—"He begins with the new Miltonic poem, and finds she has never looked into it" or even into Milton, for that matter)—our moment is an aberration.

In the eighteenth century, when there was perhaps a deeper gulf between the sexes but not nearly so great a distance between the popular culture and the intellectual elite, Milton's name was a strong presence in both cultures, but it was also a name revered particularly by women. We hear of him in accounts of Ann Yearsley, a Bristol milkmaid who knew little poetry but knew *Paradise Lost* inordinately well, and in stories of the twelve-year-old Caroline Symmons, who seems to have been especially enamored of the same poem. One representative woman of the age writes: " 'The mind is its own place,' says the great Milton; the mind is its own place, says the little Elizabeth Montagu." Yet Montagu's intent is not so much to align herself with Satan as to suggest that Satan is a Prometheus, that the plight

† From *Feminist Milton* (Ithaca: Cornell UP, 1987). Reprinted by permission of the publisher.

of women requires of them a Promethean patience and endurance. Not all, but certainly some, of these women share in Montagu's sentiment that "old virginityship is . . . Milton's hell, 'where hope ne'er comes that comes to all' "—and share too in her resolve " 'to gather the rose of love while yet 'tis time.' "

Mary Wollstonecraft is said to have done just that, but with dire consequences. Only when she is in the throes of passion for Henry Fuseli is she able to redeem Milton, and then only by surrendering her feminist ideology and ceasing to attack Milton as a cultural authority. Otherwise and earlier, according to Mary Poovey, Milton's Eve is regarded by Wollstonecraft as "one of the masculine stereotypes of female nature" in which some women sought their identity and still others found their female nature grossly distorted, indeed subjugated. Wollstonecraft, this argument goes, discovers in Milton's Eve a "commentary not on women but on men from whose imagination she sprang—from Milton's Adam and, before him, from Milton himself." Her strategy is therefore to quote Milton against himself by turning Eve's words back upon the poet. What is concealed by such an argument is Wollstonecraft's own recognition, which is not very different from Christopher Hill's, that "Milton's attitude to Eve is as full of paradoxes as his attitude towards women in general." Another turn of the critical lens reveals a Wollstonecraft who is not faithless to a feminist ideology, but faithful to a text torn by ideological contradictions that do not do irreparable damage and are evidence of Milton's subversion of stereotypical representations of Eve and of women generally, a Wollstonecraft determined to represent Milton's text in all its paradoxes and ambiguities. No less than those of his early female readership, Milton's writings participate in ideology without being ruthlessly determined by it, and as keenly as this readership, Milton seems to have been sensitive to the ideological tensions inherent in his calculated contradictions and to have implanted them in his texts for instructive purposes. It is only right that in the eighteenth and early nineteenth centuries a poem about the education of humanity should be turned to that end.

However detached Milton may have become from our present educational system, he was securely attached to it in an earlier time, when *Paradise Lost* was recommended reading for young children, a particularly important part of the educational system for women, and, in America, a book through which simultaneously white women were being taught submission and black women were being shown the way to liberation. Judging from the observation of the German critic C. P. Moritz, this poem was common fare for landladies (and tailors' wives no less!), indeed for all women who saw themselves victimized by a male-dominated society and who, finding their own situation mirrored in Satan's, fastened their attention on his soliloquy in Book IV. Women seemed all too like Satan, who "bore about with him a hell in his own bosom." Yet it was not just Satan who analogized their condition—there was also Eve. Thus the elderly Hannah More, to some "appearing a patroness of vice" and therefore deciding to dismiss her servants and leave her home, relates her situation to Eve's. As she was helped into her carriage, she is reported to have "cast one pensive parting look upon her bower, saying, 'I am driven like Eve out of Paradise; but not, like Eve, by angels.' " Among these women a shared recognition of the advantages in knowing history was coupled with the realization that for women to know their history was for them to know their Milton. Women, no less than men, were engaged by Milton, especially in times of fierce strife when freedom was being crushed beneath the despot's sway and when a tempest of evil days was seen blackening the English nation. Indeed, women were especially engaged, for they found in *Paradise Lost*, with its urgent sexual and social awareness, an acculturating narrative—a forging ground for their own ideal of educated and responsible womanhood, an ideal then founded upon sexual equality rather than, as today, upon sexual difference.

The place of *Paradise Lost* in the popular culture, and especially its allure for women, affords a valuable perspective on the history of reading and of interpretation, on what was allowably said of this poem or, as was sometimes the case particularly in the eighteenth century, on what was being sidestepped or silenced. Particularly in women's paradigmatic responses to *Paradise Lost*, which are not always the same, and in the responses women then provoked, we find a ground on which to follow, as Hans Robert Jauss might say, the footprints of the poem's immediate reception. The horizon of expectations that greeted *Paradise Lost* was created largely by Milton's own political posture and manifestations of it in his prose writings; but such expectations were also altered, even corrected, thereby steering reception, determining interpretation, but paradoxically delaying understanding of the poem. Furthermore, there was at the very outset an effort to anathematize as misleading and incompetent any interpretations that were heretical or simply unorthodox. There was also an effort to create distance between expectations of *Paradise Lost* and Milton's supposed achievement. This was done through a maneuver that, first, disengages the poem from the context of Milton's prose writings with which it enjoys an elaborate and meaningful intertextuality and that, then, realigns this poem with the literary and generally conservative tradition of epic.

We see this situation best in the respective comments of Andrew Marvell and Theodore Haak, where Marvell, in his dedicatory verses on *Paradise Lost*, empties Milton's poem of the same subversive political content that Haak credits it with holding. The history of the reception of *Paradise Lost* is especially multifaceted and multilayered, the meanings embedded therein coming available in successive unfoldings through a slow and halting process in which newly articulated experiences of the poem, especially by women, are raised to consciousness, producing a "gradual and belated understanding." In the case of *Paradise Lost*, the first reception is not the only, and perhaps not the most important, reception. The poem's later reception, especially during the Romantic period, is more than a distorted echo of its initial reception, and something other than simply a reflex of newly emergent myths and experience.

* * *

MARY NYQUIST

From The Genesis of Gendered Subjectivity in the Divorce Tracts and in *Paradise Lost*†

It appears that one can now speak of "third-wave feminism" as well as "post-feminist feminism." Like other labels generated by the historical moment to which they refer, these await a lengthy period of interrogation. But if they should stick, their significance will be associated with the variety of attacks mounted against Western bourgeois or liberal feminism over the past decade and a half. Now, as never before, what has to be contended with—precisely because it has been exposed in the process of contestation and critique—is the historically determinate and class-inflected nature of the discourse of "equal rights." The questions, equal with whom, and to what end? have been raised in ways that have begun to expose how, ever since the early modern period, bourgeois man has proved the measure. They have also shown how the formal or legal status of this elusive "equality" tends by its very nature to protect the status quo.

Because much academic criticism on *Paradise Lost*, especially that produced in North America, has been written within a liberal-humanist tradition that wants Milton to be, among other things, the patron saint of the companionate marriage, it has frequently made use of a notion of equality that is both mystified and mystifying. The undeniable emphasis on mutuality to be found in *Paradise Lost*—the mutual dependency of Eve and Adam on one another, their shared responsibility for the Fall—is for this reason often treated as if it

† From Mary Nyquist and Margaret W. Ferguson, eds., *Re-Membering Milton: Essays on the Texts and Traditions* (New York and London: Methuen, 1988), pp. 99–102, 115–23. Reprinted by permission of the publisher.

somehow entailed a significant form of equality. Differences that in *Paradise Lost* are ordered hierarchically and ideologically tend to be neutralized by a critical discourse interested in formal balance and harmonious pairing. To take just one, not especially contentious, example, Milton is said to go out of his way to offset the superiority associated with Adam in his naming of the animals by inventing an equivalent task for Eve: her naming of the flowers. In this reading, Milton, a kind of proto-feminist, generously gives the power of naming to both woman and man. The rhetorical effectiveness of this point obviously depends in important ways upon the suppression of features suggestive of asymmetry. Left unquestioned must be the differences between Adam's authoritative naming of the creatures—an activity associated with the rational superiority and dominion of "Man" when it is presented by Adam, who in Book VIII relates to Raphael this episode of the creation story in the second chapter of Genesis—and Eve's naming of the flowers, which is revealed only incidentally in her response to the penalty of exile delivered in Book XI. In a speech that has the form of a lament for the garden she has just been told they are to leave, Eve's naming in Book XI appears in such a way that it seems never to have had the precise status of an event. It is, instead, inseparably a feature of her apostrophic address to the flowers themselves: "O flow'rs / . . . which I bred up with tender hand / From the first op'ning bud, and gave ye Names" (XI. 273–7) here Eve's "naming" becomes associated not with rational insight and dominion but rather with the act of lyrical utterance, and therefore with the affective responsibilities of the domestic sphere into which her subjectivity has always already fallen.

In recent years, a remarkably similar critical current, intent on neutralizing oppositions, has been at work in feminist biblical commentaries on Genesis. Within the Judeo-Christian tradition, claims for the spiritual equality of the sexes have very often had recourse to Genesis 1.27, "So God created man [*hā'ādām*, ostensibly a generic term] in his own image, in the image of God created he him; male and female created he them." This verse, which is part of what is now considered the Priestly or "P" creation account (Genesis 1–2.4a), has always co-existed somewhat uneasily with the more primitive and more obviously masculinist Yahwist or "J" creation account in chapter 2, where the creator makes man from the dust of the ground (thereby making *hā'ādām* punningly relate to *hā'ădāmâ*, the word for ground or earth) and woman from this man's rib. Within a specifically Christian context, the relationship between the two accounts has been—at least potentially—problematical, since 1 Timothy 2:11–14 uses the Yahwist account to bolster the prohibition against women taking positions of authority within the Church: "Let the woman learn in silence with all subjection. But I suffer not a woman to teach, nor to usurp authority over the man, but to be in silence for Adam was first formed, then Eve. And Adam was not deceived, but the woman being deceived was in the transgression." Recently, in an effort to reconcile feminism and Christianity, Phyllis Trible has tried to harmonize the differences between the Priestly and the Yahwist creation accounts. Trible holds that the exegetical tradition alone is responsible for the sexist meanings usually attributed to the Yahwist creation story, which she renarrates using methods that are basically formalist.

More specifically, Trible argues that the second chapter of Genesis tells the story not of the creation of a patriarchal Adam, from whom a secondary Eve is derived, but the story of the creation of a generic and androgynous earth creature or "man" to whom the sexually distinct woman and man are related as full equals. Throughout, Trible's retelling is strongly motivated by the desire to neutralize the discrepancy between the "P" and the "J" accounts by assimilating "J" to "P," which is assumed to recognize the equality of the sexes and therefore to provide the meaning of the two creation accounts taken together as one. Because "P" suggests the possibility of a symmetrical, non-hierarchical relationship between male and female, "J" is said by Trible to tell the story of the creation of a sexually undifferentiated creature who becomes "sexed" only with the creation of woman. The simultaneous emergence of woman and man as equals is signalled, she argues, when Yahweh brings the newly fashioned partner to the previously undifferentiated *hā'ādām* or "man," who responds with the lyrically erotic utterance: "This is now bone of my bones, and flesh of my flesh: she shall be called Woman, because she was taken out of Man" (Genesis 2:23) (in Trible's reading "taken out of" means "differentiated from").

Trible's revisionary and profoundly ahistorical reading is significant in large part because it has been so widely influential. Among feminist theologians it would seem to have established a new orthodoxy. And it has recently been ingeniously elaborated for a secular readership by Mieke Bal, who assumes with Trible that the commentator can, by an effort of will, position herself outside the traditions of masculinist interpretation; and that Genesis bears no lasting traces of the patriarchal society which produced it. Yet it is far too easy to adopt the opposing or rather complementary view that Genesis is a text inaugurating a transhistorically homogeneous patriarchal culture. This is, unfortunately, a view that is frequently expressed in connection with *Paradise Lost*. For in spite of the existence of scholarly studies of Genesis in its various exegetical traditions, the view that the relationship of *Paradise Lost* to Genesis is basically direct or at least unproblematically mediated continues to flourish. And so, as a result, does an entire network of misogynistic or idealizing commonplaces and freefloating sexual stereotypes, relating, indifferently, to Genesis and to this institutionally privileged text by Milton, English literature's paradigmatic patriarch.

The notion of a timeless and ideologically uninflected "patriarchy" is of course vulnerable on many counts, not least of which is its capacity to neutralize the experience of oppression. I would therefore like to attempt to situate historically Milton's own appropriation of the Genesis creation accounts. In the process, I hope also to draw a preliminary sketch, in outline, of the genealogy of that seductive but odd couple, mutuality and equality. It is certainly not difficult to recognize the reading given Genesis by Trible and Bal as a product of its time. Especially in North America, the notion of an originary androgyny has had tremendous appeal to mainstream or liberal feminism. Taken to represent an ideal yet attainable equality of the sexes, androgyny is often associated metaphorically with an ideal and egalitarian form of marriage. A passionate interest in this very institution makes itself felt throughout Milton's divorce tracts, in which his interpretation of the two creation accounts first appears. Milton's exegesis, too, is the product of an ideologically overdetermined desire to unify the two different creation accounts in Genesis. Not surprisingly, at the same time it is representative of the kind of masculinist "mis"-reading that Trible and Bal seek to overturn. By emphasizing its historical specificity, however, I hope to show that it is so for reasons that cannot be universalized.

* * *

IV

One of the questions concerning *Paradise Lost* that this discussion of the divorce tracts has, I hope, made it possible to address is: why does Milton's Eve tell the story of her earliest experiences first, in Book IV? Why, if Adam was formed first, then Eve, does Adam tell *his* story to Raphael *last*, in Book VIII? An adequate response to this question would require a full-scale analysis of the ways in which *Paradise Lost* articulates a putative sequential order of events or story with the narrative discourse that distributes this story. As a genre, epic is of course expected to develop complicated relations between a presumed chronological and a narrative ordering of events. But *Paradise Lost* would seem to use both retrospective and prospective narratives in a more systematic and motivated manner than does any of its predecessors, in part because it is so highly conscious of the problematical process of its consumption. I would like to argue here that *Paradise Lost*'s narrative distribution of Adam and Eve's first experiences is not just complexly but ideologically motivated, and that the import of this motivation can best be grasped by an analysis aware of the historically specific features of Milton's exegetical practice in the divorce tracts.

This practice is crucially important to *Paradise Lost*'s own use of the Genesis creation texts. In the case of the passage it most obviously informs, Raphael's account of the creation of "man" on the sixth day of creation in Book VII, certain features are intelligible only in the light of this historically specific context. If commenting on this passage at all, critics have tended to suggest that Raphael gives something like a heavenly, as compared with Adam's later more earthly, account of creation. This doesn't, however, even begin to do justice to the intricately plotted relations of the "P" and "J" accounts in the following:

> Let us make now Man in our image, Man
> In our similitude, and let them rule
> Over the Fish and Fowl of Sea and Air,
> Beast of the Field, and over all the Earth,
> And every creeping thing that creeps the ground.
> This said, he form'd thee, *Adam*, thee O Man
> Dust of the ground, and in thy nostrils breath'd
> The breath of Life; in his own Image hee
> Created thee, in the Image of God
> Express, and thou becam'st a living Soul.
> Male he created thee, but thy consort
> Female for Race; then bless'd Mankind, and said,
> Be fruitful, multiply, and fill the Earth,
> Subdue it, and throughout Dominion hold
> Over Fish of the Sea, and Fowl of the Air,
> And every living thing that moves on the Earth.
> Wherever thus created, for no place
> Is yet distinct by name, thence, as thou know'st
> He brought thee into this delicious Grove,
> This Garden, planted with the Trees of God,
> Delectable both to behold and taste;
> And freely all thir pleasant fruit for food
> Gave thee, all sorts are here that all th' Earth yields,
> Variety without end; but of the Tree
> Which tasted works knowledge of Good and Evil,
> Thou may'st not; in the day thou eat'st, thou di'st;
> Death is the penalty impos'd, beware,
> And govern well thy appetite, lest sin
> Surprise thee, and her black attendant Death.
> Here finish'd hee.
>
> (VII. 519–48)

Genesis 1:26–8 is here given in what is virtually its entirety. But the principal acts of Genesis 2:7–17 are also related: Yahweh's making of "Man" from the dust of the ground (2:7), his taking of this man into the garden of Eden (2:15), and his giving of the prohibition (2:16,17). One could argue that even Milton's "artistry" here hasn't received its proper due, since this splicing economically makes from two heterogeneous accounts a single one that is both intellectually and aesthetically coherent.

Yet it does more, far more, than this. For Raphael's account removes any trace of ambiguity—the residual generic dust, as it were—from the Priestly account of the creation of *hā'ādām* or "man" in the image of God. This it does by a set of speech-acts unambiguously identifying this "man" with Raphael's interlocutor, Adam. The direct address in "he form'd thee, *Adam*, thee O Man / Dust of the ground" has what amounts to a deictic function, joining the representative "Man" to Raphael's gendered and embodied listener, who is specifically and repeatedly addressed here, while Eve (though still an auditor) very pointedly is not. It is clearly significant that these very lines effect the joining of the Priestly and Yahwistic accounts. By placing "thee O Man / Dust of the ground" in apposition to the named "Adam," it is suggested that this individualized "Adam" actually *is hā'ādām* or representative man and the punning *hā'ādāmâ* "ground," an identity that only the joining of the two accounts reveals.

The impression this joining creates is that the two accounts have always already been one in narrating the creation of Adam. The same cannot be said of Raphael's account of the creation of Eve, however. For in contrast (I would like to say something like "in striking contrast," yet it has not really been noticed) to the ingenious joining that takes place for the sake of Adam, Raphael refers to Eve's creation only in the statement immediately following, which is again, significantly, addressed to Adam: "Male he created thee, but thy consort / Female for Race" (529–30). Outside of this meagre "but thy consort / Female for Race," Raphael's account does not otherwise even allude to the creation of Eve, although, as we have seen, other details of the narrative in the second chapter are included in it. Indeed, if we examine the matter more closely, it appears that the Yahwist account is made use of only up to and including Genesis 2:17 (the giving of the prohibition) precisely because Genesis 2:18 inaugurates the story of the creation of a help meet for Adam.

But of course the story of Eve's creation is not excised from *Paradise Lost* altogether, which is, presumably, why readers have not protested its absence here. It is told later, by another narrator, Adam. One of the effects of this narrative distribution is that in Milton's epic Adam's story comes to have exactly the same relation to

Raphael's as in the divorce tracts and in Protestant commentaries the second chapter of Genesis has to the first: it is an exposition or commentary upon it, revealing its true import. Yet the second telling can have this status only because it is Adam's. As my discussion indicates, Milton's argument in the divorce tracts rests on a radical privileging of "J" over "P" in the specific form of a privileging of the words of divine institution in Genesis 2:18. Had Milton interpolated the story of Eve's creation into Raphael's creation account, he would have had to record these words in the form of indirect speech (as he does the words of prohibition in lines 542–7) or else to have reproduced both the creator's speech and Adam's. In either case, the instituting words would have been displaced from their centres of authority. By transferring the entire narrative to Adam and by interpolating a dramatic colloquy into this narrative, *Paradise Lost* ensures the coincidence of narrator and auditor of the instituting words, of narrator and of the first man's instituting response. By dramatizing this commentary, this necessary supplement to Raphael's account, in the form of a colloquy narrated by *Adam*, *Paradise Lost* makes sure that the doctrine of marriage is both produced and understood by the person for whom it is ordained, just as in the divorce tracts it is the privileged male voice, Milton's, which expounds the true doctrine of divorce.

As the divorce tracts never tire of insisting, the true doctrine of marriage relates only to the satisfaction of that which the wanting soul needfully seeks. In *Paradise Lost* this doctrine is co-authored by Adam and the "Presence Divine," who work it out together. It is also communicated, formally, by the extraordinary emphasis placed on Adam's subjectivity, on his actual experience of desire. As Milton has masterminded the exchange, the divine instituting words come *after* Adam has been got to express his longing for a fitting companion (VIII.444–51), so that this longing has the kind of priority that befits the first man. Yet the longing is also clearly a rational burning. With its strong filiations to the disputation, the very form of the colloquy establishes that this desire is rational, and that merely reproductive ends are certainly not what Adam has in mind. Although procreation is referred to, it is presented as a kind of necessary consequence of the conjunction of male and female, but for that very reason as a subordinate end. Adam's language cleverly associates it with a prior lack, a prior and psychological defect inherent in his being the first and only man (VIII.415–25). The way Milton's Adam responds to the deity's formal presentation to him of his bride, Eve, is just as motivated. The Genesis 2:23–4 speech is cited, but only after it has been introduced in a way that joins it explicitly to the causes implicit in the deity's instituting words:

> This turn hath made amends; thou hast fulfill'd
> Thy words, Creator bounteous and benign,
> Giver of all things fair, but fairest this
> Of all thy gifts, nor enviest. I now see
> Bone of my Bone, Flesh of my Flesh, my Self
> Before me; Woman is her Name, of Man
> Extracted; for this cause he shall forgo
> Father and Mother, and to his Wife adhere;
> And they shall be one Flesh, one Heart, one Soul.
> (VII.491–9)

This speech is presented as a species of spontaneous lyrical utterance ("I overjoy'd could not forbear aloud" (490)) and according to Adam is "heard" by Eve. Yet it is obviously addressed *not* to her but to her maker, who is thanked for the gift itself, but not until he has been praised for having kept his word. Before letting Adam commit himself to the project of becoming one flesh with Eve, Milton has to make it clear that Adam does so believing that the "Heav'nly Maker" has done what he has promised, that is, created a truly fit help.

Not only the placement of Adam's narrative after Raphael's but also its most salient formal features can thus be seen to be motivated ideologically, and to illustrate the causes joining the divorce tracts and *Paradise Lost*. Before turning to Eve, I would like to summarize the discussion so far by emphasizing that these causes are joined, and to man's advantage, both when "P" and "J" are united and when they aren't. By joining "P" and "J" as it does, Raphael's account specifies the gendered Adam of *Paradise Lost* as the "man" who is made in the divine image. By disjoining them, Raphael's account lets Adam himself tell the story of the creature made to satisfy his desire for an other self.

We can now, more directly, take up the question, why does heaven's last best gift tell her story first? One way of approach might be to suggest that had Eve's narrative of her earliest experiences appeared where "naturally," in the order of creation, it should have, that is *after* Adam's, *Paradise Lost* might have risked allowing her to appear as the necessary and hence in a certain sense superior creature suggested by what Jacques Derrida has called the logic of the supplement, undeniably set in motion by Adam's self-confessed "single imperfection." *Paradise Lost*'s narrative discourse would seem to want to subvert this logic by presenting Eve's narrative first. And it seems to want to subvert it further by placing immediately *after* Adam's narrative a confession in which Eve's completeness and superiority is made to seem an illusion to which Adam is, unaccountably, susceptible. In this part of Adam's dialogue with Raphael, the language of supplementarity as artificial exteriority seems curiously insistent: Eve has been given "Too much of Ornament" (VIII.538); she is "Made so adorn for thy delight the more" (VIII.576) and so on.

Yet a displaced form of the logic of supplementarity may nevertheless be at work in the place of priority given Eve's narrative. For if Eve is created to satisfy the psychological needs of a lonely Adam, then it is necessary that *Paradise Lost*'s readers experience her from the first as expressing an intimately subjective sense of self. From the start she must be associated in a distinctive manner with the very interiority that Adam's need for an other self articulates. Or to put this another way, Eve's subjectivity must be made available to the reader so that it can ground, as it were, the lonely Adam's articulated desire for another self. Appearing as it does in Book IV, Eve's narrative lacks any immediately discernible connection with the Genesis creation accounts on which the narratives of both Raphael and Adam draw. Its distance from Scripture as publicly acknowledged authority is matched by Eve the narrator's use of markedly lyrical, as opposed to disputational, forms. Set in juxtaposition to the rather barrenly disputational speech of Adam's which immediately precedes in Book IV, Eve's narrative creates a space that is strongly if only implicitly gendered, a space that is dilatory, erotic, and significantly, almost quintessentially, "private."

In a recent essay, Christine Froula reads Eve's first speech thematically and semi-allegorically, as telling the story of Eve's (or woman's) submission of her own personal experience and autonomy to the voices (the deity's, then Adam's) of patriarchal authority. As the very title of her essay—"When Eve Reads Milton"—indicates, Froula wants to find in Milton's Eve if not a proto-feminist then a potential ally in contemporary academic feminism's struggle to interrogate the academic canon together with the cultural and political authority it represents. Milton's Eve can play the part of such an ally, however, only because for Froula the privacy of Eve's earliest experiences and the autonomy she thereby initially seems to possess are equivalent to a potentially empowering freedom from patriarchal rule. Given the liberal assumptions of the feminism it espouses, Froula's argument obviously does not want to submit the category of personal experience to ideological analysis.

In attempting to give it such an analysis, I would like to suggest that Eve's speech plays a pivotal role, historically and culturally, in the construction of the kind of female subjectivity required by a new economy's progressive sentimentalization of the private sphere. It is possible to suggest this in part because the subjective experiences Eve relates are represented as having taken place before any knowledge of or commitment to Adam. That is, they are represented as taking place in a sphere that has the defining features of the "private" in an emerging capitalist economy: a sphere that appears to be autonomous and self-sustaining even though not "productive" and in so appearing is the very home of the subject. In Book VIII Adam recalls having virtually thought his creator into existence and having come up with the idea of Eve in a dialogue with his fellow patriarch. By contrast, Eve recalls inhabiting a space she believed to be uninhabited, autonomous, hers—but for the "Shape within the wat'ry gleam." It is, however, precisely because this belief is evidently *false* that it is possible to see this space as analogous to the "private" sphere, which is of course constituted by and interconnected with the "public" world outside it. Illusory as this autonomy is, inhabiting a world appearing to be her own world nevertheless seem to be the condition of the subjectivity Eve here reveals.

It has long been a commonplace of commentaries on *Paradise Lost* that a network of contrasts is articulated between Eve's narration of her earliest experiences and Adam's, the contrasts all illustrating the hierarchically ordered nature of their differences. Yet it has not been recognized clearly enough that while shadowing forth these bi-polar oppositions, Eve's narrative is supposed to rationalize the mutuality or intersubjective basis of their love. For by means of the Narcissus myth, *Paradise Lost* is able to represent her experiencing a desire equivalent or complementary to the lonely Adam's desire for an "other self." It is not hard to see that Adam's own desire for an other self has a strong "narcissistic" component. Yet Adam's retrospective narrative shows this narcissism being sparked, sanctioned and then satisfied by his creator. By contrast, though in Book IV Eve recalls experiencing a desire for an other self, this desire is clearly and unambiguously constituted by illusion, both in the sense of specular illusion and in the sense of error. Neo-Platonic readings of the Narcissus myth find in it a reflection of the "fall" of spirit into matter. Milton transforms this tragic tale into one with a comic resolution by instructing Eve in the superiority of spirit or, more exactly, in the superiority of "manly grace and wisdom" over her "beauty." But because this happily ending little *Bildungsroman* also involves a movement from illusion to reality, Eve is made to come to prefer not only "manly grace and wisdom" as attributes of Adam but also, and much more importantly, Adam as embodiment of the reality principle itself: he whose image she really is, as opposed to the specular image in which her desire originated.

To become available for the mutuality the doctrine of wedded love requires, Eve's desire therefore must in effect lose its identity, while yet somehow offering itself up for correction and reorientation. As has often been noted, Eve's fate diverges from that of Narcissus at the moment when the divine voice intervenes to call her away from her delightful play with her reflection in the "waters." We have seen that in Book VIII Adam's desire for an other self is sanctioned by the divine presence's rendering of "It is not good that the man should be alone; I will make him an help meet for him." When the divine voice speaks to Eve, it is to ask that she redirect the desire she too experiences for an other self:

> What thou seest,
> What there thou seest fair Creature is thyself,
> With thee it came and goes: but follow me,
> And I will bring thee where no shadow stays
> Thy coming, and thy soft imbraces, hee
> Whose image thou art, him thou shalt enjoy
> Inseparably thine.
>
> (IV.467–73)

Unlike the instituting words spoken to Adam in Book VIII, these have no basis in the Yahwist creation account. Yet they are clearly invented to accompany the only part of that account which Milton has to work with here, the brief "and brought her unto the man" (Gen. 2:22), which in Genesis immediately precedes Adam's words of recognition. Marked inescapably by literary invention and uttered by a presence that is invisible to Eve, the voice's words have a curiously secondary or derivative status, at least compared with those spoken to Adam. They seem indeed, fittingly, to be a kind of echo of the divine voice.

In so far as it effects a separation of Eve from her physical image, this word in a way echoes what Milton calls the creator's originary "divorcing command" by which "the world first rose out of Chaos" (*DDD* 273). But the separation of Eve from her image is not the only divorce effected here. Before this intervention the "Smooth Lake" into which Eve peers seems to her "another Sky," as if the waters on the face of the earth and the heavens were for her indistinguishable or continuous. The divine voice could therefore much more precisely be said to recapitulate or echo the paternal Word's original division of the waters from the waters in Genesis 1:6–7. Before describing her watery mirror and her other self, Eve mentions "a murmuring sound / Of waters issu'd from a Cave"—murmurs, waters and cave all being associated symbolically with maternality, as critics have pointed out. When the paternal Word intervenes, Eve's specular auto-eroticism seems to become, paradoxically, even more her own, in part because it no longer simply reflects that of Ovid's Narcissus. And when Eve responds to the verbal intervention by rejecting not only his advice but also Adam, "hee / Whose image" she is, preferring the "smooth wat'ry image," an analogical relationship gets established between female auto-eroticism and the mother-daughter dyad. But—and the difference is of crucial importance—this implicit and mere analogy is based on specular reflection and error alone.

Grounded in illusion, Eve's desire for an other self is therefore throughout appropriated by a patriarchal order, with the result that in *Paradise Lost*'s recasting of Ovid's tale of Narcissus, Eve's illusion is not only permitted but destined to pass away. In its very choice of subject, Milton's epic seems to testify to the progressive privatization and sentimentalization of the domestic sphere. That this privatization and sentimentalization make possible the construction of a novel female subjectivity is nowhere clearer than in Eve's first speech, in which the divine voice echoes the words originally dividing the waters from the waters, words which in their derived context separate Eve from the self which is only falsely, illusorily either mother or other.

This takes us to the very last feature of Eve's story-telling to be considered here. As has been suggested, Protestant exegetes consider Adam's declaration in Genesis 2:24, "This is now bone of my bones, and flesh of my flesh," to be part of the first wedding ceremony. A version of this ceremonial utterance appears in Adam's narrative and (highly abridged) in Eve's. In Genesis, this declaration follows "and brought her unto the man," a verse which is translated into action in both of *Paradise Lost*'s accounts. Calvin, when commenting on this phrase, views the action from Adam's point of view, as involving the exchange of a gift: "For seeing Adam tooke not a wife to him selfe at his owne will: but tooke her whome the Lord offered and appointed unto him: hereof the holinesse of matrimonie doeth the better appeare, because we know that God is the author thereof." Yet Milton is not alone in seeing this moment from Eve's point of view as well as from Adam's, for Diodati, commenting on "And brought her unto him," says: "As a mediator, to cause her voluntarily to espouse her self to Adam and to confirm and sanctify that conjunction." In *Paradise Lost*, the story Eve tells stresses with remarkable persistence both the difficulty and the importance of Eve's "voluntarily" espousing herself to Adam. Many years ago Cleanth Brooks mentioned that Eve's speech in Book IV seemed to anticipate Freud's observations on the comparative difficulty the female has in the transition to adult heterosexuality. But if it does so, it is in a context that constitutes female desire so as to situate the process of transition within competing representational media, within what is almost a kind of hall of voices and mirrors.

This entire discussion of the relation between *Paradise Lost*'s retrospective creation narratives and the divorce tracts can therefore be put in the following, summary terms. If in Book VIII's recollected colloquy Adam is revealed articulating the doctrine of marriage, in Book IV's recollected self-mirroring Eve is portrayed enacting its discipline. Or to formulate this somewhat differently, by associating Eve with the vicissitudes of courtship and marriage, and by emphasizing her voluntary submission both to the paternal voice and to her "author" and bridegroom, Adam, *Paradise Lost* can *first* present the practice for which Adam *then*, at the epic's leisure, supplies the theory. In doing so, *Paradise Lost* manages to establish a paradigm for the heroines of the genre Milton's epic is said to usher in. In the Yahwist's creation account, Adam may have been formed first, then Eve. But Milton's Eve tells her story first because the domestic sphere with which her subjectivity associates itself will soon be in need of novels whose heroines are represented learning, in struggles whose conclusions are almost always implicit in the way they begin, the value of submitting desire to the paternal law.

* * *

JULIA M. WALKER

From Eve: The First Reflection†

* * *

Engender in and by the Pool

In books 4 and 5, Eden is gendered feminine and given an identity inextricably linked with Eve's. As Eve's face is bounded by the edge of the mirroring lake, so is the question of gender identity and self-knowledge framed by the gendered geography of Eden. Eve neither recognizes nor names herself. Eve's ultimate act in her book 4 creation narrative is to yield, not to learn. She submits to the arbitrary gender displacement, coming to see Adam as at once the generative image of and better than herself, but thus learning—or accepting—that she can know herself only in herself only in relation to Adam. There is no place for interiority in this construction of selfhood. Milton presents Eve to herself and to the reader only in relation to Adam and to the gendered universe of which she and Eden are each a part. As the relationships among the valley and the river and the lake are not perfectly separable, neither can the identities of Eden, Eve, and Adam be neatly categorized, although the latter will be given an interior self. Milton reiterates at many points his gendering of the Earth as feminine, but Adam seems to have no sense that it is from this feminine Earth from which he was formed. He draws

† From *Medusa's Mirrors: Spenser, Shakespeare, Milton, and the Metamorphosis of the Female Self* (Newark: U of Delaware P, 1998), pp. 166–70. Reprinted by permission of the publisher.

his self-identity solely from his maker and not from matter, but expects Eve to privilege his absent rib above any other aspect of her being.

At what point does Eve cease to be a part of Adam, becoming not his rib but her self?

Never.

At what point does Eve cease to seek for self-knowledge from her reflection?

Never.

Can a narrative act of gender displacement generate a representation of self-knowledge—even in its most simple form, physical self-recognition—sufficient to stand as self-identity, the sort of simple self-identity Adam exhibits when he peruses his own body, calling it *Myself* (8.267)?

No.

Does she ever see Adam, "hee whose image thou art," as her own image?

She does not.

Literally, then, Eve never recognizes anything; she does not "know again"; she simply accepts the cognition given to her by the voice and hand of God and by the voice and hand of Adam. In the gendered geography of Eden—the geography of the river, the valley, and the lake—Milton presents his readers with a pattern of displacement, a paradigm of arbitrarily gendered causality, which he immediately repeats in human terms in Eve's cognition scene. Milton does not here rely on mere conjunction. By using the first displacement as the generative locus for the second, by having Eve turn without recognition of her identity in the re-gendered mirror of the lake's water, Milton emphasizes the necessity of reading one reinscription through and by the other, thus calling attention to the arbitrary nature of both types of gendering and to their inextricable relation.

With the scene at the lake we are given a second geographical subtext for Eve's identity, the pool of Narcissus in Ovid's *Metamorphoses*. Not only does "Eve's interaction with her own image in the water . . . [raise] the specter of narcissism," as Marshall Grossman puts it, but this subtext invades and becomes part of the text with stunning effect. Critics from James Holly Hanford to Stanley Fish speak of Eve and of "the mirror of the pool," of Eve "at the pool." Yet nowhere in Eve's description or in the narrator's framing of it does the word "pool" occur; it is always "lake," always. The reader supplies "pool" just as the reader—cued by Milton's visual allusion—supplies the subtext of Ovid's Narcissus. But Eve's narrative is properly both an invocation and a rejection of Ovid's story. Eve is not only herself pleased with what she sees in the pool, as is Narcissus, but she identifies pleasure and admiration (this she does recognize) when she describes this Other as also pleased: "Pleas'd it return'd as soon with answering looks / Of sympathy and love" (464–65). Eve, like Narcissus, is unknowingly, "unwittingly" self-absorbed. Milton reminds us of this, as the Voice of God both informs and warns Eve:

> What there thou seest,
> What there thou seest fair Creature is thyself,
> With thee it came and goes: but follow me,
> And I will bring thee where no shadow stays
> Thy coming.
>
> (4.467–71)

those phrases echo almost exactly the words with which Ovid's narrator tries to warn Narcissus:

> quod petis, est nusquam; quod amas, avertere, perdes!
> ista repercussae, quam cernis, imaginis umbra est:
> nil habet ista sui; tecum venitque manetque;
> tecum discedet, si tu discedere possis!
>
> (2.433–36)

> (What you seek is nowhere; but turn yourself away, and the object of your love will be no more. That which you behold is but the shadow of a reflected form and has no substance of its own. With you it comes, with you it stays, and it will go with you—if you can go.)

Richard J. DuRocher, in his discussion of these two passages, acknowledges that the "correspondences between the passages reside in syntax . . . and in diction," but argues that "the distinct tonal qualities of these two voices—Ovid's taunting, condescending; Milton's gracious, magnanimous—register widely divergent evaluations of the situations of Narcissus and Eve." DuRocher goes on to take issue with Arnold Stein's distinction between the two passages, discussing thematic issues at some length. But, surprisingly, neither of these critics focuses on the most concrete difference between Narcissus and Eve: Narcissus eventually recognizes that he is gazing at himself; Eve never recognizes that image as herself. When she sees herself in the water, she does not know that "it"—literally and grammatically neuter—is herself that she sees. She is soon told by the voice of God, but is never allowed to see the image while knowing that she gazes at herself. Tradition, particularly the medieval tradition of moral allegory, links vanity and self-absorption to the Narcissus story, but Ovid's story offers a less judgmental account of the fair young man, Ovid's narrator expressing regret at the youth's initial inability to recognize himself and pity at his subsequent grief. In

Ovid's narrative we find no hint of self-gratification—quite the reverse. In the tradition of moral allegory Narcissus becomes an icon of destructive self-love, but this is not the tradition invoked by Milton's syntactical parallel; he quotes Ovid, but we hear the narrative of Vanity from the *Romance of the Rose*. And yet we should not be too quick to convict ourselves of careless reading, for Eve's phrase "with vain desire" (however strongly "vain" may be glossed as "fruitless") makes our misreading almost inevitable.

Not only is Eve's initial encounter with Eden rendered problematic by Milton's invocation of the Narcissus story, but as a narrative it lacks the specificity of Adam's in many ways. Not the least important is her omission of any gendered pronouns. Even though this narrative is presented as memory, memory that we might expect to be embellished by subsequent knowledge, Eve's speech does not gender. She quotes the "voice" who will take her to "hee / Whose image thou art, him thou shalt enjoy." That voice gives her two names, Eve and Mother, but these names are not gendered by the voice of God or by Eve, only by our fallen knowledge. Eve also quotes Adam's odd third-person identification of himself, "whom thou fli'st, of him thou art, / His flesh, his bone," but she uses no other gendered pronouns in this narrative. Neither Eve nor God's voice nor Adam genders her. She is drawn to the feminine lake; the mirror of that lake gives her the first vision she has of another human form; but she is not allowed to identify herself with that vision, nor indeed does she identify by gender anything that she sees. She speaks of "it"; she is first told of and then shown "he," and she quotes God and Adam's use of the masculine pronoun; but there are no feminine pronouns in this narrative. Only the reader's knowledge of the feminine lake and of fallen sexuality gender Eve's identity. Eve herself genders nothing and the voices she hears speak only of maleness, leaving her otherness unnamed. How, then, can she identify herself as physically different and individual from either Adam or her surroundings? She cannot know herself as separate and particular, as an individual entity unique in the cosmos, as Adam knows himself. As she is allowed to know her image only in relation to Adam, so can she know her function only in relation to the fruitful earth with which she is associated, not seeing herself as a unique Other—which explains why, in book 9, she worries that Adam might enjoy "another Eve" (9.827). As the poem progresses, Eve's sense of self becomes important in its absence. Milton gives us a more extreme version of Britomart's negative description of what she sees in the mirror, for Eve is never allowed to know what she is supposed to see.

As Eve "yields" to Adam's voice in book 4, satisfying his need for her, so does the Earth on which they live yield to them that which will satisfy their other needs. To honor Raphael's arrival in book 5,

Adam sends Eve out to find the fruits of the Earth, and the narrative of his order, Eve's activities, and Raphael's response further tie Eve to the fruitful, yielding, feminine earth. Adam orders:

> But go with speed,
> And what thy stores contain, bring forth and pour
> . . . .
> well we may afford
> Our givers thir own gifts, and large bestow
> From large bestow'd, where Nature multiplies
> Her fertile growth.
> (5.313–14, 316–19)

Eve goes forth to gather "Whatever Earth all-bearing Mother yields" (5.338). Earth, gendered female, "yields" as did Eve in her book-4 narrative, and the fruit of that yielding is both implicitly feminine and explicitly under the control of Eve as "She gathers . . . and. . . . Heaps with unsparing hand," "She crushes," and "She tempers" the moist and creamy fruits for the feast. Fifty lines later Raphael greets Eve: "Hail Mother of Mankind, whose fruitful Womb / Shall fill the World" (5.388–89). Because Eve "yields" to the voice of God and to the voice of Adam in book 4, she will ultimately yield, as does the earth, the fruit of her womb to "fill the World." In the context of epic gender roles, this passage of book 5 offers a most interesting set of allusions in relation to Eve's identity. Eve goes to gather the feminine fruits of the feminine Earth, fruits that the "all-bearing mother" also yields on "the Punic coast, or where / Alcinöus reigned" (340–41); the narrator's specific geographical and patriarchal allusions thus link Eve—at least superficially—to Dido and Naussica. Although Eve is called (oddly) "the fairest of her daughters" (4.324), those daughters of Eve that Milton actually associates with her are usually at least as ominous as fair: Pandora (4.714), Aphrodite at the choice of Paris (5.381–82), Dalilah (9.1061). While it's true that less than fifty lines after invoking Dido and Naussica Raphael gives Eve the greeting of Mary, I would suggest that this seemingly positive identification is made problematic by the prior references to two other women who nurtured epic heroes and who were subsequently left behind in the narrative wake of male destiny, their own female identities left undeveloped and ultimately submerged. The words of Adam and of the narrator and of Raphael all associate Eve with the feminine identity of Nature and with the womb of the world, an association that confirms—or foretells, if we speak of narrative rather than chronological order—not simply Mary but the feminine cosmos Raphael describes in book 7.

* * *

On the Poet Himself

HELEN VENDLER

From Milton's Epic Poem†

* * *

The enlargement of the mind by time and space, seen from afar or up close, conveyed sometimes in the decrees of God, sometimes in the account of an angel, sometimes through the eye of the human narrator, is only a material reflection of the true enlargement of the mind at which the epic aims: the expansion of our thinking about human experience. Since God looks on from His privileged vantage-point in eternity, to Him the whole story is ever-present. Stationed at any point in the story, He can see both backward and forward. At the moment of Christ's birth, for instance, Noah's Flood belongs to the past, and would be presented in a flash-back; but at the moment of the Creation the Flood is yet to come, and would have to be voiced as a flash-forward. This omniscient position proper to God is adopted by the narrator of the poem, who is both the blind and aging seventeenth-century John Milton ("On evil days . . . fall'n, and evil tongues") and the all-seeing tale-teller, who knows, by the divine inspiration of his Muse, what is happening on earth, in Heaven, and in Hell; now, in the past, and in the future. It is Milton's Godlike ambition to know all of space and span all of time: no other Western poet has taken on, and successfully carried out, such a task. Only from God's point of view, Milton realizes, can he "justify the ways of God to men".

To conceive of that justification, Milton had to begin to think of himself not as a just man, but as a sinner. Of course he had always believed that he, like every other person since Adam's fall, had suffered the consequences of that "original sin"—the darkening of the intellect and the weakening of the will that make human beings susceptible to actual present sin. Yet he had—or thought he had—sternly fortified himself against those consequences, training his intellect vigorously in all its faculties, disciplining his will to diligence in the service of God. In his earlier writings Milton never represented himself as someone who had fallen into actual sin in his active life. No concession, then, could have been more humbling to a man of Milton's temperament—proud, competitive, unyielding, and aggres-

† From John T. Shawcross, ed., Paradise Lost: *A Poem in Twelve Books* (San Francisco: Arion, 2002), pp. xv–xxi, xxvi–xxviii. Reprinted by permission of the publisher.

sive—than to admit that he had been deeply mistaken in his political conviction that the cause of good must succeed in this life. He had fallen unawares into the deadly sins of pride and ambition, Satan's own vices.

When Milton was in his thirties, hatred of his enemies, and the certainty of his own righteousness, had reached a point of unbridled violence visibly unleashed in his prose: in one tract he imagined his enemies finally consigned to Hell, where they would be tortured in the most savage manner, and made the slaves, the "negroes" of the other damned souls:

> But they . . . after a shameful end in this life (which God grant them), shall be thrown down eternally into the darkest and deepest gulf of hell, where, under the despiteful control, the trample and spurn of all the other damned, that in the anguish of their torture, shall have no other ease than to exercise a raving and bestial tyranny over them as their slaves and negroes, they shall remain in that plight forever, the basest, the lower-most, the most dejected, most underfoot, and down-trodden vassals of perdition.
>
> (*Of Reformation*, 1641)

Now in the catastrophe of his fifties, Milton could echo Job: "If I justify myself, mine own mouth shall condemn me: if I say, I am perfect, it shall also prove me perverse" (9.20). God's providence was a darker force than he had realized: "He destroyeth the perfect and the wicked," Job declared (9.22). The thoughts of the fallen angels mirror Milton's own tortured meditations on fate, God's foreknowledge, and free will:

> Others apart sat on a hill retir'd,
> In thoughts more elevate, and reason'd high
> Of providence, foreknowledge, will, and fate,
> Fix'd fate, free will, foreknowledge absolute,
> And found no end, in wand'ring mazes lost.
> Of good and evil much they argu'd then,
> Of happiness and final misery,
> Passion and apathy, and glory and shame.
>
> (II, 557–64)

As Milton revolved within himself his own bafflement, pain, misery, and shame, he saw his former erring judgments as ones that, stemming from pride, had drawn him into his present blighted state. To find archetypes of his own post-calamity suffering, Milton began to investigate Aftermath in all its forms: we can say that *Paradise Lost* is in its entirety a meditation on Aftermath.

The poem opens in the sulfurous aftermath of the angels' fall, as we see Satan tormented by "the thought / Both of lost happiness and lasting pain". He finds himself in a region "where peace / And rest can never dwell, hope never comes / That comes to all; but torture without end / Still urges". When Satan arrives in Eden to tempt Eve, the angels themselves are shadowed over by the pall of aftermath: "Dim sadness did not spare / That time celestial visages". The Fall of Man brings about a bitter aftermath in the relations of Adam and Eve: one of mutual shame, accusation, blame, and passionate repudiation. While these psychological aftermaths occur within the "realistically drawn" characters of the poem, Milton adds a hideous allegorical story of aftermath as well. From Satan's head, at his Fall, there sprang forth (in a parody of the birth of Athena) a daughter, Sin; Satan copulates incestuously with his daughter, who brings forth a son, Death; Death in turn copulates incestuously with his mother Sin, whereupon she gives birth to the barking hellhounds of mortal vice. This philosophically motivated chain of personified consequences sexualizes aftermath into generational perpetuity, as though evil becomes unstoppable once the Tempter knows Sin and Sin knows Death.

There are recurrent historical aftermaths, too, throughout *Paradise Lost*, many of them drawn from the first books of the Bible: the Flood comes to destroy the sinful population of the world; mutually incomprehensible speech follows on the building of Babel; fire incinerates Sodom and Gomorrah. All of these aftermaths are shown to be caused by human sin. If Milton then finds himself in aftermath, has he too not sinned by yielding to the same worldly ambition that built the vain tower of Babel? And is not his fate the fate of the whole human race? Milton's encyclopedic internalizing of history documents for him, as one aftermath of the Fall, the endless suffering of the human tribe. Within the poem, however, Milton turns his knowledge of the past into prophecies of the future, as the angel Michael shows Adam a pageant of human time in which every sort of historically recorded evil—war, genocide, murder, theft, and rape, as well as the bodily and mental suffering that would so appall Keats—pass before his eyes. "What else should I have expected?" Milton must have asked himself as he contemplated his ruined state in 1660: "Who was I that I thought myself exempt from the common human fate displayed in every history I have read?" "In what sort of pride did I imagine I could help establish the kingdom of God on earth in a material government?"

The gravest aftermath of the Fall is of course the death of the Son of God. It is also the hinge on which aftermath turns into something else. After the Atonement, aftermath is transformed into its second and unexpected phase, which can be called by many names. The theological name for it is Resurrection; Milton's psychological name for it is "a paradise within thee, happier far"; the literary name for it is symbol, in which intractable fact is projected on to an aesthetic plane where it finds resolution. Milton had reflected on the achievement of a paradise within (though not in those terms) in 1644 in *Areopagitica*, his prose-poem on liberty and faith:

> It was from out of the rind of one apple tasted, that the knowledge of good and evil, as two twins cleaving together, leaped forth into the world. And perhaps this is that doom which Adam fell into of knowing good and evil, that is to say, of knowing good by evil. . . .
>
> I cannot praise a fugitive and cloistered virtue, unexercised and unbreathed, that never sallies out and sees her adversary, but slinks out of the race where that immortal garland is to be run for, not without dust and heat. Assuredly we bring not innocence into the world, we bring impurity much rather: that which purifies us is trial, and trial is by what is contrary.

"That which purifies us is trial, and trial is by what is contrary." Milton lived to see this truth cruelly proved on his own person, and he was chastened by it, and purified. *Paradise Lost* is the poem of that chastening. But the chastened sometimes forget the emotions that attended them in their earlier passion of pride and vaunting desire. Milton's genius is that he forgets nothing—not his resentment, not his fear, not his envy, not his anger, nor his sense of being unjustly treated, nor his earlier conviction of superiority to others. He pours all these emotions, in unquestionably authentic form, into his Satan stretched on the burning marl, plotting with his fellow rebels, defying God, and deviously seeking revenge as he crosses the turbulent realm of Chaos on his way to seduce Eve into disobedience.

Because Satan is the first dramatic figure in the epic, his emotions have uncorrected power over us at the beginning (Blake's judgment testifies to that power). Because Adam and Eve stand at the human center of the poem, their recriminations and mourning after the Fall strike us as if they were our own. Because we, like Milton, have read history, we can ratify the grief attending on Michael's pageant of human evil and interminable suffering. But what are the emotions we are to feel about the other half of the poem's aftermath-testimony—the paradise within?

That positive, or "comic", aftermath has proved harder for many readers to credit, because Milton's language framing it comes from theological formulations of the mercy of God mediated by the atonement of Christ. The redeeming aftermath is announced in the most abstract passages of the poem, those spoken by God enthroned in heaven and replied to by the Son of God sitting at his right hand. Blake was right in saying that Milton's imagination was "in fetters" here, because almost every statement that God utters is drawn from his speeches in the Bible. To invent imaginative digressions for God was in Milton's eyes blasphemous; and so in these passages he subjected his powerful pen to the voice of biblical revelation, confining his imagination as he did not feel obliged to do when writing of the fallen angels or of Adam and Eve.

But Milton was not mechanically rephrasing Christian doctrine. The redeeming aftermath—following on the rage of failure—had certainly been experienced by him, or he could not have written his epic. He firmly believed that ultimately truth, mercy, and justice will be seen to be truth, mercy, and justice, and that lies and vices will be unveiled as lies and vices. Although such exposure can sometimes occur within historical time, Christian faith puts this revelation in its ultimate form at the Last Judgment; in this life, as recorded history witnesses, the wicked flourish as the bay tree. Although human confidence may be shaken by the victories of sinners, in God's view, since all is ever-present, there is no need to wait for apocalypse: truth and justice and mercy are always in sight, here and now. By seeing through God's eyes, one can possess that happier paradise, finding oneself always in the presence of the real, the just, and the true no matter how compassed round by evil one might be. It was by imagining what it would be to see through God's eyes that Milton found his own second paradise (and decided on the perspective of his narrator). How does the poet represent God, and God's speech, so as to convey to us what it would be like to speak always from that interior faith in which all is as it should be—redeemed, justified, at peace?

In the epic, God is not shaken, God is not afraid, God is not vengeful; he is serene, secure, and (usually) unswayed by temporary emotions. He repudiates special pleading; he cannot, seeing all, see without judging. Another name for his judgment is the anthropomorphized "wrath", but God's wrath is a self-evident decree, not anger in the human sense. Transgression, in the mathematics of justice, requires punishment; but in the compassion of mercy, transgression requires alleviation. In the long loop of God's foreknowledge, the seed of the woman will bruise the heel of the serpent, and mankind will be brought into a new and closer relation to the divine because the Son of God will become man. When God speaks of these things in *Paradise Lost*, his tone is one of veracity and serene acknowledgment.

Milton is convinced that the entity he names God embodies the most authentic justice, the truest estimation of events, the best providential intent, and the wisest and most merciful disposition. We perhaps find it hard to imagine the Good, the True, and the Radiant in one uncreated Being—"Bright effluence of bright essence increate"—but Milton did not. God, he intimates, speaks as we would speak if we ourselves were virtuous and saw clearly and without personal bias. Nonetheless, the anthropomorphizing of deity is the most difficult for us of the poem's strategies, biblical though it is. (And it is true that Milton's God sometimes—as in his anger in Book x at Satan, Sin, and Death—speaks with passion and derision, as Milton's sardonic irony grimly escapes its divine "fetters".)

* * *

Milton was lucky in inheriting, from the antecedent biblical script, such grand phenomena as stimuli to his imagination. But he inherited, too, one large stumbling-block which he needed to explore and understand: the command laid by God on the newly created pair that they shall not eat of the fruit of one tree in the garden. It is a purely arbitrary rule; there is nothing intrinsically sinful in eating fruit. It is not as though God had commanded Adam not to be cruel to Eve, or commanded Eve not to kill her children. Such commands would introduce ordinary moral evil, and obscure the intrinsic moral fable of Genesis, in which God makes a single rule: his creatures are to obey his command. As long as they grant him wisdom and goodness superior to their own, they are safe. As soon as they believe their own judgment to be the equal of his—or superior to his—they have disturbed the hierarchy of goodness and flouted the conclusions of reason. How can God *not* be superior to them in wisdom and goodness, since he created them and established them in supreme happiness? When Adam and Eve sin, their sin is one of disobedience (not one of carnal appetite) and of pride (estimating themselves as creatures above their creator). By God's explicit command, the angel Raphael has already alerted them to the tempter and his malice; and in disregarding God's forewarning, Adam and Eve rank their own judgment superior to his. When they lose their faith in God's wisdom, they will fall. Raphael bids farewell to Adam with a single injunction:

> Stand fast; to stand or fall
> Free in thine own arbitrament it lies.
> Perfect within, no outward aid require;
> And all temptation to transgress repel.
> (VIII, 640–43)

Because for Milton the indispensable condition for happiness is liberty, liberty was for him the essential quality of Paradise, and liberty requires the availability of choice. By this reasoning he could ratify God's establishing of a single test, giving his creatures the power to choose for or against the good. Milton too had had liberty to act as he thought best: to make common cause with the Puritans, to take part in their government and their pamphlet-wars, to serve

Cromwell as Cromwell took up arms against his enemies. He perceived that like Adam, he had forgotten the warnings of God distinguishing between material and spiritual success, and had fallen. His sin was putting his trust in earthly gains and believing himself to be God's appointed messenger. In his anger against his enemies, he had betrayed love and charity, on which all other virtues depend. Milton's poem traces his own choices, made through pride and moral blindness, back to their archetypes in the pride of Satan and the heedless disobedience of Adam and Eve.

By the end of the poem, Adam has learned "that suff'ring for truth's sake / Is fortitude to highest victory". The Archangel Michael reminds him, however, that knowledge by itself is not virtue: Adam must add "deeds to thy knowledge answerable". As Michael enumerates those "deeds", we see that they are not the warlike ones of the Puritan "saints" raising an army to establish God's kingdom on earth. Rather, they are deeds of Christian forbearance, patience, and faithful love:

> . . . only add
> Deeds to thy knowledge answerable, add faith,
> Add virtue, patience, temperance, add love,
> By name to come call'd charity, the soul
> Of all the rest: then wilt thou not be loath
> To leave this Paradise, but shall possess
> A paradise within thee, happier far.
> (xii, 581–87)

When we compare the tone of this passage with the virulent rage of the early Milton imagining with unleashed glee the fate of his enemies in Hell, we can understand how much his character was deepened by undergoing, and then meditating on, his own fate, experienced first as tragedy but subsequently as a redemptive chastening and a source of deeper self-understanding.

* * *

MARY ANN RADZINOWICZ

From How Milton Read the Book of Psalms: His Formal, Stylistic, and Thematic Analysis†

Milton read the Book of Psalms as the record of a journey through life traversing all the tempers, moods, passions, and uneven reactions

† From *Milton's Epics and the Book of Psalms* (Princeton: Princeton UP, 1989), pp. 3–6.

that mark the psalmist's search for an adequate faith. Such a mode of reading was common to Englishmen in his day, guided by the Geneva Bible's representation of Psalms as a course of life by which "at length [to] atteine to [an] incorruptible crowne of glorie." Since the journey is not a consistent progress toward enlightenment, individual psalms register backsliding, fear, self-deception, even inadequacy of response no less truly than nobility of spirit. Milton did not congratulate the psalmist or censure him for this or that response. Rather, the generation of each psalm from an occasion in the life of its speaker gave him examples of the impassioned voices in which human beings record significant moments in their life's journey. He thought its whole course showed the power of experience to ripen the human soul.

Milton read Psalms, however, not simply as an anthology of moral, intellectual, and psychological episodes in the journey. He also read it as encompassing a variety of genres, each marked by a distinctive decorum, rhetorical structure, and poetical figures. While many English psalm paraphrasts grouped some psalms by mood or theme, Milton showed awareness of a fuller range of psalm kinds. He did not distribute psalms among various psalmists and attributed none to any poet other than David. When he translated Psalms 80 through 88, for example, he ignored the superscriptions to Asaph and to Heman the Ezrahite. He particularly noticed, however, the variety of distinctive speaking parts that David plays in Scripture—musician, believer, prophet, teacher, witness, and penitent among them. By distinguishing in David that range of feelings and intentions. Milton registered the genres or formal kinds in the Book of Psalms. Hence he was able to write into *Paradise Lost* a range of lyrics based on a variety of psalm genres. He initiated hymns, laments, wisdom songs, thanksgivings, blessings, and prophecies, each genre by convention having an appropriate form and structure, a distinctive decorum and rhetoric, an individual voice and stance. Milton's recognition of psalm kinds put at his disposal a variety of religious lyrics to be incorporated into the epic, brief or diffuse, to function there in much the same way that individual genres in the religious anthology of the personal and national journey in the Book of Psalms contribute variety and emotional strength to the comprehensive spiritual achievement that the book as a whole traces. He read it as a book unified by its paideutic journey; he stressed the aptness of single psalms for special occasions in the religious life of each believer, he responded to the patterns of genres that move across the Psalter, interrelating individual songs.

A consequence of interweaving diverse psalm genres in both *Paradise Regained* and *Paradise Lost* is what we may call multivocality, and that multivocality plays an important role in the architecture of each epic. Each is received by the reader not just as one speaker's continuous delivery of a transcendent mimesis drawn either from Luke or from Genesis and its aftermath, but also as a blending of many voices, rhetorically as well as psychologically and intellectually distinctive. Thus each epic reveals both a powerful, unifying, personal impulse urging Milton to express in poetry a lyrical act of worship and an equally powerful, comprehensive, impersonal impulse urging him to express in poetry a fullness of knowledge. Milton nowhere claimed to have seen in the unified diversity of the Book of Psalms a comprehensive formal pattern for epic; other books of the Bible performed that function for him, when he looked to scriptural authority to strengthen classical models for epic—Genesis for *Paradise Lost*, Job for *Paradise Regained*. Rather his attentiveness to the psalms taught him something not learnt elsewhere about the generation of a long heroic poem out of the impassioned speech of brief poems. The distinctive psalmic genres act as choral voices creating multivocality for the epic, as arcs uniting the work while spacing the process of change and variety within it. To some of the genres or kinds, Milton adds his own voice. He too laments, warns, hymns, expostulates, and teaches upon occasions anticipated by the groups of psalms, in decorum anticipated by their intentions. But he is not limited to them, nor obliged to give his own voice to all. When, for example, in *Paradise Lost*, the proems draw on prophetic psalms or the angelic songs imitate hymns, Milton capably unites his voice to that of bard or angel. To some of Adam's laments he adds his personal voice, while from others he withholds it to encourage our ironic awareness of original, ordinary self-pity. As the Book of Psalms in Milton's reading is more than the sum of its lyrical parts in representing a journey of wisdom learned through suffering, so the multivocality of *Paradise Lost* draws all speakers and the audience as well into *paideia*. Similarly, in the briefer narrated dialogues of *Paradise Regained*, Milton constructs from psalms the two angelic hymns and the laments of Mary and of the disciples, now more rarely but pointedly merging his voice with those of his speakers. His epics are not univocal but multivocal; the vatic voice is not composed of short self-reflexive songs but takes its color from alterations in mood and occasion; the unity of the heroic intellectual enterprise not only controls, but is qualified by, a diversity of lyric energies.

Milton's recognition of psalm genres coexisted with his reading of the unity of the Book of Psalms as an encyclopedic representation of the heroic idea that human suffering is purposive and educative. The limitations of lyric from Milton's point of view drove him to write the heroic poem; the lyrical effects of intensity and unity checked for him the potential endlessness of epic. The heroic poem confronts for a whole society those threats to high achievement posed by its own experience of chaos. The narrative of that confrontation glorifies the active virtues its society must attain as alone sufficient to perfect its culture. The epic poet undertakes to narrate the deeds of heroic figures best suited to exemplify the actual or potential achievements of his civilization in that confrontation. His own responses—lyrical, reflexive, or didactic—are part of the story; he encompasses in his own person a quest for the heroic mode. But the virtues that preserve a state and make it happy are as many as are the dangers that threaten it; the poet seeking to render them in epic faces a centrifugal energy in the conception of his poem that puts him to the choice between what Milton called a "diffuse" and a "brief" model. No matter how well-made either model might be, a proliferation of journeys or tests, of achievements or educative failures, endangers the coherence of his epic, as the unity of *The Faerie Queene*, for example, may be threatened by the multiplicity of virtues Spenser represented as generative of the achievement of English Renaissance civilization. It is then that an equivalent lyric impulse—to interject one's own passion to control chaos in one's own voice in lyric compression—acts to check epic endlessness. Psalm reading was of enormous value to Milton in showing him models both of intense lyricism and of comprehensive heroism, just as it was of value in showing him models of generic multivocality and of an intellectually unified journey toward abstract comprehensive knowledge.

Milton, then, practiced a threefold reading of psalms. He made a thematic analysis of the whole Book of Psalms as figuring both a personal and public religious journey, both of the individual believer and of the Hebrew people. He made a generic analysis of the individual kinds to be found in the Book of Psalms, and he made a further stylistic or figural analysis of its tropes and prosody. He read the psalms as inspired truth, as individual instances of psalmic genres, and as compositions in a scriptural poetic medium. Only reading in the first or thematic way did Milton read Scripture differently from any other literary text. The third kind of analysis of Scripture, the stylistic, he actually blended with techniques grounded in his education in classical literature and in classical and Renaissance rhetoric.

* * *

WILLIAM FLESCH

From The Majesty of Darkness: Idol and Image in Milton†

* * *

There is, then, something seriously deficient about the angelic and unfallen conception of God. Empson remarks that book 6 reads like bad science fiction (*Milton's God*, p. 54), which seems a good way of summing up our discomfort with heaven according to Raphael. Therefore, I suggest that the Fall of humanity turns out to be fortunate (to argue that it's not, as Danielson does, is inevitably to prefer God's poetry in book 3 to Milton's) because it enables a much deeper understanding of God. Satan verges on such an understanding when he is closest to Milton, when he is thinking least materially, most poetically, most like an Arian. If the angels are Arians at all, it is in a trivial way; for them God is only unknowable and inaccessible because he is just the other side of knowledge and accessibility. For Adam and Eve, however, the Fall produces a sense of drastic discontinuity between finite intelligences and the unknowable God. This sense of discontinuity is at first primarily negative (as when Adam asks how he will be able henceforth to tolerate the insupportably dazzling sight of God or angel, or when Eve feels that heaven is high and remote), but even in its negative aspect Milton equates discontinuity with poetic power. His dismissal, in his invocation to book 9, of Raphael's account of the war in heaven seems every bit as imperious as Empson's. It is for the "Sad task" of describing the Fall that Milton requests "answerable style" (9.13 and 20); this seems odd at first, since he had shown little anxiety about whether he would be able to ventriloquize a seraphic description of the war in heaven. But he goes on in the invocation to reject poetry about "tilting Furniture" (9.34) and thereby himself voices our half-suppressed embarrassment about the silliness of what's gone on in heaven. Milton is not interested in the standard topics that give

> Heroic name
> To Person or to Poem. Mee of these
> Nor skill'd nor studious, higher Argument
> Remains, sufficient of itself to raise
> That name, unless an age too late, or cold

† From *Generosity and the Limits of Authority: Shakespeare, Herbert, Milton* (Ithaca: Cornell UP, 1992). Reprinted by permission of the publisher.

> Climate, or Years damp my intended wing
> Depress; and much they may, if all be mine,
> Not Hers who brings it nightly to my Ear.
> (9.40–47)

More interesting than the implication that Raphael's narrative is not up to the poetry Milton finally aspires to is the contrast with twilit Eden presented by the opening of book 9. There is more poetic affect in Milton's intense apprehension of his mortality in these lines than in any of the descriptions of the events in heaven. Even the cautious optimism of the last two lines is suffused with a sense of loss. Perhaps he will live to finish the poem, but he will still be susceptible to all the dampening influences of his mortal condition. These lines feel rather like *The Tempest*: the island is magical, but when you leave, every third thought will be of death. I think this passage is so moving because of the contrast between Urania's radiance and Milton's mortal blindness. We get a sense of her radiance but also a sense that the power of that radiance is not a saving but a consoling one. "Nightly" seems to be the key word. For Urania, night is like the nights in paradise before the fall, illumined by the stars, planets, and moon, or like night in heaven: "grateful Twilight (for Night comes not there / In darker veil)" (5.645–46). For Milton, however, it ultimately means the night of his Sonnet 23, forgotten for a moment but returning after his nightly muse has fled. The radiance that illuminates him also intensifies his sense of loss, as when Caliban wakes and cries to sleep.

In the invocation to book 9, Milton both asserts and demonstrates that loss of Eden, the fall into mortality, produces poetic affect. Of course, this is a position that he cannot be comfortable with. One feels that the choiring angels hymning praise to the works of God provide the model of poetry that Milton is least anxious about. But the affect actually derives from the impossibility of sustaining the apparent radiance of that poetry in a fallen condition. For a long time, I think, Milton felt ambivalent about his sense that poetic power is enabled by loss, and at least twice before he tried to dissipate that ambivalence by splitting its antinomies into paired poems: "L'Allegro" / "Il Penseroso" and "On the Morning of Christ's Nativity" / "The Passion." But in *Paradise Lost* he combines celebration and lamentation. This combination reflects Milton's ambivalence about the poetry he writes most powerfully, but this ambivalence also produces the most powerful moments in that poetry. As an evil rhetorician whose language is sublimely intensified in hell, Satan represents the negative side of that ambivalence. The Romantics, however, seem right in thinking that Milton could not avoid, through much of the poem, feeling a strong identity with Satan, an identity that he understood as a real problem: the identification seems to stem from their both having a deeper conception of godliness than does the rest of heaven. This conception seems indissolubly linked to ambivalence. Satan and Milton are both suspicious of the origins of their poetic power, but Satan's final response is to get rid of ambivalence by reifying that origin and by making it either an icon to be rejected (if the icon is God) or worshiped (if it is himself). Milton, on the other hand, had a lot invested in not identifying poetic and iconic thinking. If he calls books the image of God in "Areopagitica" (*Complete Prose*, 2:492), he is very careful to explode the notion that one could call "idols the layman's books" (6:693). Satan cannot sustain the drastically iconoclastic sense that his poetic power springs from something radically unknowable, from unknowability itself. He does not have the negative capability that would enable him to accept ambivalence itself as a condition of power. He does not have the patience that enables a mortal to choose long and begin late and to risk the dissipation of the power of his mortal voice in its own exercise. This is not just another way of saying what the angels say, that his overweening pride made him reject an invisible God who nevertheless should obviously be obeyed. Satan's deep sense that the origin of poetic power is inaccessible far outdoes, in its deep and powerful sublimity, the angels' conceptions of God. But it finally founders, while Milton's does not.

Empson and Bloom see Milton's response to his ambivalence as cutting the Gordian knot by scapegoating Satan and making him despicable (or, more subtly, by recounting how unjust rebellion necessarily makes the highest nobility vile). But *Paradise Lost* seems ultimately to resolve this problem positively too, which is, I think, its greatest strength. In giving up Satan it does not give up God or an ambivalent conception of God. Early on, Milton was ambivalent about a poetry based on loss; in *Paradise Lost* he bases his poetry on the very loss that that ambivalence entails, the loss of angelic certainty about the origin of power.

* * *

General Criticism

E. M. W. TILLYARD

Paradise Lost: Possible Inconsistency†

By examining the construction of the poem it became plain that a rigorous conscious unity had been imposed on it. The question remains how far the unconscious meaning affects this conscious unity. That Milton's belief in the redeeming Christ was held with small conviction makes little difference, because he did believe in some sort of regeneration, quite apart from Christian theology, and some sort of mythology is convenient for building up an epic. Anyhow there is no upsetting of balance. When we come to Satan the case is different. I have said that Satan best expresses the heroic energy which was a part of Milton's nature. If it appears that the treatment of the Fall, round which the rest of the incidents are grouped and which consequently should express all the more important feelings in the poem, has no connection with what Satan expresses, it will have to be admitted that the unity of the poem has been very badly impaired by this insubordinate creature of Milton's imagination.

I have tried to show that in his treatment of the Fall Milton meant to condemn the mental levity of Man, who is prone to forget the importance of his every action. His condemnation is the more weighty because of the solemnity with which by the art of his construction he invests the struggle. He clears the stage, gives us all heaven for audience, and the wretched human actors have hardly begun to grasp the fateful significance of their parts. Feebly they commit what they imagine is a trifling error, for which they are punished with a doom out of all apparent proportion to their crime. To their crime, yes; but not to the mental triviality that accompanied it: by their miserable inadequacy before the issues of life mankind have deserved their fate. Milton's treatment of the Fall yields the obvious meaning that it is the first business of man to understand the issues of life, and to be aware of the importance of every trivial act. This he believed, because not only his own nature but the trend of Puritan thought fostered this awareness. The present life, and the right use of every moment of it, were Milton's principal concern. Now, a belief that every moment is critical, that every action is irrevocable and determining, must heighten the pressure at which life is lived. Life

† From *Milton*, rev. ed. (New York: Collier, 1967).

will have nothing of routine in it, but will consist of one gala performance, never to be repeated. A man holding such beliefs will be in the temper to do heroic deeds. This is the strenuous Western temper at its height, the temper of the discoverers and of the other great men of the Renaissance. Thus it is that the immense weight of emphasis put on the eating of the apple does imply the heroic temper expressed most powerfully by Satan.

Satan then does not go counter to the meaning of *Paradise Lost* as implied by the construction, but he does somewhat upset the balance. He gives us the positive statement: the Fall the negative only, the implication. The negative is the weaker, and occurs just where from motives of balance we crave the greatest emphasis. Milton prepares with perfect craft for the climax, and when the climax comes, though sincere and in harmony with the rest of the poem, it does not come up to our expectations. Indeed it could not. Adam and Eve have no power of heroic action. They are hopelessly limited to inactive virtues. The myth Milton chose was of too intractable a stuff to allow of a perfect climax: he is forced to the method of negative implication; and the most powerful expression of heroic energy is found elsewhere.

We now see what it was that Milton sacrificed by abandoning his Arthuriad. He sacrificed a subject whose climax might easily have expressed his own energy, for one which had wider scope, but whose climax could not express that energy in a straightforward way. It is possible that the weakness inherent in the myth of the Fall as a subject impelled him to write his two last poems: the first a clear-cut struggle between opposing forces, with good victorious; the second a drama exhibiting the rebirth of heroic energy.

Milton's unadmitted pessimism also affects the unity. It is present in some degree throughout, but far more strongly in the last four or five books. And this difference is much more than a relative frequency of passages in which pessimism is latent: it amounts to a change of attitude. In the last books pessimism has got somehow into the texture of the verse, causing a less energetic movement. Not that energy is ever absent: in particular the Ninth Book shows a rise over the Eighth, perhaps because it may contain relics of the projected tragedy. It is also true that as the scene is more confined in the last books the verse movement will naturally be less expansive. But that is not enough to account for the change of tone. The only explanation is that Milton himself had altered during the writing of the poem. The change is very clear. In the first four books Milton gives energy out: in the last four or five he turns it inward into himself. In the first it is active: in the last books it has been converted into a stoical resistance. Satan aspiring after a new world is Milton, the Renaissance man seeking after experience and truth: Michael is equally Milton, but a different Milton, when he adapts the words of Seneca the Stoic into

> Nor love thy Life, nor hate; but what thou livest
> Live well, how long or short permit to Heav'n.

It is in the last books that Milton most speaks of reason contending with passion and of the necessity of imposing limits on the desire for knowledge. Control has become more important than energy. When we remember Milton's early lust for knowledge and that he thought such a lust no bad thing, if we can trust the tone of his *Tractate on Education*, we must admit that the later books of *Paradise Lost* show a change from his earlier beliefs. And if we admit, as I think we should, that the variety and range of the first four books, as well as Satan himself, express this love of knowledge which Milton did not think bad, another discrepancy of tone between the beginning and the end of the poem will have been detected. This is how Raphael ends his account of the creation and constitution of the universe:

> Sollicit not thy thoughts with matters hid,
> Leave them to God above, him serve and feare;
> Of other Creatures, as him pleases best,
> Wherever plac't, let him dispose: joy thou
> In what he gives to thee, this Paradise
> And thy fair *Eve*; Heav'n is for thee too high
> To know what passes there; be lowlie wise:
> Think onely what concernes thee and thy being.[1]

But most important of all for the doctrine of self-limitation and self-sufficiency are Adam's words to Michael near the end of the poem when the history of the world has been brought to a close, and Michael's reply. These two speeches sum up, with a simplicity whose impressiveness one cannot describe but can merely note with profound admiration, Milton's mature, one may say middle-aged, philosophy of life. They must be quoted in full.

> He ended; and thus Adam last reply'd.
> How soon hath thy prediction, Seer blest,
> Measur'd this transient World, the Race of time,
> Till time stand fixt: beyond is all abyss,
> Eternitie, whose end no eye can reach.
> Greatly instructed I shall hence depart,
> Greatly in peace of thought, and have my fill
> Of knowledge, what this Vessel can containe;
> Beyond which was my folly to aspire.
> Henceforth I learne, that to obey is best,
> And love with fear the onely God, to walk

1. viii. 167–74.

As in his presence, ever to observe
His providence, and on him sole depend,
Merciful over all his works, with good
Still overcoming evil, and by small
Accomplishing great things, by things deemd weak
Subverting worldly strong, and worldly wise
By simply meek; that suffering for Truths sake
Is fortitude to highest victorie,
And to the faithful Death the Gate of Life;
Taught this by his example whom I now
Acknowledge my Redeemer ever blest.
  To whom thus also th' Angel last repli'd:
This having learnt, thou hast attained the summe
Of wisdome; hope no higher, though all the Starrs
Thou knewst by name, and all th' ethereal Powers,
All secrets of the deep, all Natures works,
Or works of God in Heav'n, Air, Earth, or Sea,
And all the riches of this World enjoydst,
And all the rule, one Empire; onely add
Deeds to thy knowledge answerable, add Faith,
Add vertue, Patience, Temperance, add Love,
By name to come call'd Charitie, the soul
Of all the rest: then wilt thou not be loath
To leave this Paradise, but shalt possess
A Paradise within thee, happier farr.[2]

All is turned inwards: the inner paradise is the only paradise that matters. It is a different Milton from the one who wrote the *Defensio Secunda* and such lines as

But first whom shall we send
In search of this new world, whom shall we find
Sufficient? who shall tempt with wandering feet
The dark unbottom'd infinite Abyss
And through the palpable obscure find out
His uncouth way, or spread his aerie flight
Upborn with indefatigable wings
Over the vast abrupt.[3]

The conclusion I would draw is that Milton was in some respects a changed man after the Restoration. In dealing with the prose I said that we could not be certain how the Restoration affected him, how far he had reconciled himself to what should have appeared to be inevitable. *Paradise Lost* gives the answer. He had not reconciled himself: he could not believe that the dreaded event would really come. And when it did come, his activity turned itself into resistance.

2. xii. 552–87.
3. ii. 402–9.

What we know of the composition of *Paradise Lost* is in keeping with this supposition. If Milton had begun to plan the poem in 1655, to write it in 1658, and finished it in 1663, it is probable that by the Restoration he had written the first four books; in unrevised form at least. The middle books concern us less. Much of them Milton may have had in his head before the Restoration, or he may have written them while still in doubt what the Restoration would mean and how permanent it was. The last four or five would probably belong to the Restoration period alone.

That the Restoration should have been the greatest shock Milton received during his life was almost inevitable. Always sanguine by temper and joining tenacity to hope, he could not have persuaded himself that the Parliamentary cause could fail, until its ruin was quite complete. For all the forebodings and disillusion of the last pamphlets, a great store of hope must have remained. We need not be so surprised that he turned his energies inward as that he did not fall into despair and inertia. It must be remembered too that Milton was at one with Aristotle in exalting the political virtues, and to exercise them political liberty was necessary. Cut off from freedom of speech by the Restoration, no wonder if like the Romans under the Empire he sought a stoical comfort in the fortitude of his own mind.

The pessimism, then, causes a change of tone and thereby somewhat impairs the unity of the poem. But it calls forth Milton's courage, the courage of resistance, and courage is the link with the more active form of that virtue displayed in the early books. Nor do I think that the dominance either of Satan in the earlier, or of pessimism in the later, books altogether impairs the design. The gradual working out of the action on to earth and into the heart of man remains the expression of one of the most powerful of human wills.

A. J. A. WALDOCK

From The Poet and the Theme†

* * *

It is possible, I think, to overrate very much Milton's *awareness* of the peculiar difficulties of his theme. The difficulties are of the kind that fairly leap to our eyes. That is partly because, owing to certain types of literary development during the last two centuries or so, we

† From Paradise Lost *and Its Critics* (Cambridge: Cambridge UP, 1947; rpt. Gloucester, MA: Peter Smith, 1959). Reprinted by permission of the publisher.

have received an intensive training in the business of estimating the sort of literary problem that is radical in *Paradise Lost*. We have acquired, in plain fact—through the novel, and in other ways—certain types of literary experience that Milton was without. It is not absurd to mention the novel in connection with *Paradise Lost*, for the problems of such a poem and the characteristic problems of the novel have elements in common. The novel has given us an enormous store of precedents. Largely as a result of its history we have built up a technique for assessing at once the practicability of certain themes for literary treatment, a technique that it is not ridiculous to suggest that Milton did not possess in quite the same sense. We have only to look at the material that he was bent on disposing in his epic to see that some of the problems he faced were virtually insoluble. A glance at the story of the Fall as it is given in Genesis shows that it is lined with difficulties of the gravest order. God, to begin with, does not show to advantage in that particular story: the story is a bad one for God. Within that set of events to make God attractive to our common human sensibilities (and it is not to be forgotten that the *raison d'être* of the whole poem lies in its appeal to common human sensibilities) will be hard. Again, it will be necessary to mark the transition from innocence to guilt; somehow sinlessness has to give place to sin; and in a large narrative such a transition may not be easy to make plausible. There is, once more, the disproportion (cruel at least on the face of it) between the offence and the punishment—bringing us back again to God. That apparent disproportion may not trouble us in the biblical story, the miniature; but what of it when the story is magnified a hundred times? Looking back at *Paradise Lost* from what in some real senses is our vantage-point and bringing to bear on it, quite frankly, the whole weight of our own literary experience, we almost catch our breath at the manifold drawbacks of the fable. Could any writer with an instinct for narrative, we ask ourselves, have failed to see what problems those first three chapters of Genesis held, and to shrink back deterred? At half-a-dozen points difficulties lay in wait that at the slightest prompting might become acute; in any large treatment of the story some of them would necessarily become acute. The story in Genesis was like a stretch of film minutely flawed. Milton's plan was to take this and project it on an enormous canvas. Must he not (we wonder sometimes) have foreseen the effect of the tremendous enlargement: that every slight imperfection would show, that every rift would become a gulf?

He foresaw, it is obvious, nothing of the kind, and one reason, I would suggest, is that he had not the technique for assessing such complications that we (quite involuntarily) possess. The classical epic, it is true, was behind him, but that was not enough. There were no precedents for what he was about to try; so deceptive and difficult a theme on so grandiose a scale *was* something, unattempted yet in prose or rhyme.

* * *

Here is one of the great paradoxes of *Paradise Lost*. We know that Milton came to his theme gradually and steadily, drawn to it by the deep needs of his nature. Only the highest would suffice him, and of all 'arguments' this was the highest he knew. His choice, then, of form and theme conjoined was in one sense an act of majestic daring. 'He would not take any risk', writes the late Professor Elton, 'short of the heaviest.' And yet in another sense there was *no* risk, provided only he did his own part well, for what theme could be more fully guaranteed, what theme could possibly be safer, than this? It is hardly a wonder if he embarked on it, though with self-searching and awe, yet without excessive anxiety or trepidation. We ponder, as I say, its many disadvantages and are amazed that he himself could ever have overlooked them; must he not have guessed, even if dimly, how in the enormous magnification he intended every tiny rift in the original story would show? The answer of course is that for him there were no rifts; it was out of the question for Milton to admit to himself difficulties in the scriptural story of the Fall—impossible for him, really, to see them. As his work progressed it is clear that he came on problems that he had not expected to encounter. It is of great interest in reading *Paradise Lost* to note that here, or here, a sudden difficulty has checked Milton slightly—that here, or here, a faint uneasiness shows itself. And yet we may take it for granted, I suppose, that Milton never to the end became aware of the real nature of the gravest of the narrative problems he had been grappling with. Just as he began with what must have seemed to him the perfect story, with nothing really that *could* be wrong with it, so at the end, having done his work faithfully and well, it was natural that he should feel that his poem stood four-square, firm-based, an unassailable imaginative whole.

* * *

We cannot say that Milton did not believe what he was writing when he penned this account of the multitudinous guilt of our first parents; we can only say that he most definitely did not believe in it in the way in which he believed in the inferiority of the Son (for that doctrine made strong sense to him) or in which he believed in the freedom of man and his responsibility of choice (for those convictions were part of his life).

Nor did he believe, in that way, in the primal happiness. What, after all, has Milton—the Milton of the great famous sayings in the prose works, the Milton who could not praise a fugitive and cloistered virtue unexercised and unbreathed—to do with the effortless innocence, the 'blank' virtue, of prelapsarian man? It is another of the paradoxes of the poem. In many senses *Paradise Lost* was his predestined theme, and yet in a sense it put him in a false position, cut clean against the grain of his nature. Believing rather more intensely than the average man that our dignity consists in independent and strenuous thought, and feeling with the same rather exceptional intensity that the essence of life is struggle, he must deplore the coming of thought into the world (for that is what it really amounts to) and represent man's best state as that original featureless blessedness. He was trapped, in a sense, by his theme, and from the trap there was no escape. It is true, as Mr Basil Willey has pointed out, that he bends the myth slightly this way and that, rejecting for example, the 'magic sciential apple' which itself confers knowledge and substituting a taboo. 'It was necessary', he wrote in the *Christian Doctrine*, 'that something should be forbidden or commanded as a test of fidelity, and that an act in its own nature indifferent, in order that man's obedience might be thereby manifested.' Again, with all his regard for learning, certain types of inquiry, as we know, were suspect for Milton, or had become so: these he has no hesitation in associating with the Fall. Raphael says:

> Sollicit not thy thoughts with matters hid; (VIII, 167)

and Adam is adjured to keep to knowledge within bounds. Milton's feelings, no doubt, went with these cautions. In such ways he is able to adapt the story very slightly to his purposes, to win a little freedom and make a private point or two. But there is not, after all, very much that he can do. He can read the myth (or make a valiant attempt to do so) in terms of Passion and Reason, the twin principles of his own humanistic thinking; but with all that, the myth obstinately remains, drawing him away from what most deeply absorbs him (effort, combat, the life of the 'way-faring Christian') to the celebration of a state of affairs that could never have profoundly interested him, and that he never persuades us does.

An immediate consequence could have been predicted. In a sense Milton's central theme denied him the full expression of his deepest interests. It was likely, then, that as his really deep interests could not find outlet in his poem in the right way they might find outlet in the wrong way. And to a certain extent they do; they find vents and safety-valves often in inopportune places. Adam cannot give Milton much scope to express what he really feels about life: but Satan is there, Satan gives him scope. And the result is that the balance is somewhat disturbed; pressures are set up that are at times disquieting, that seem to threaten more than once, indeed, the equilibrium of the poem.

STANLEY FISH

From Not so much a Teaching as an Intangling†

* * *

I would like to suggest something about *Paradise Lost* that is not new except for the literalness with which the point will be made: (1) the poem's centre of reference is its reader who is also its subject; (2) Milton's purpose is to educate the reader to an awareness of his position and responsibilities as a fallen man, and to a sense of the distance which separates him from the innocence once his; (3) Milton's method is to re-create in the mind of the reader (which is, finally, the poem's scene) the drama of the Fall, to make him fall again exactly as Adam did and with Adam's troubled clarity, that is to say, 'not deceived'. In a limited sense few would deny the truth of my first two statements; Milton's concern with the ethical imperatives of political and social behaviour would hardly allow him to write an epic which did not attempt to give his audience a basis for moral action; but I do not think the third has been accepted in the way that I intend it.

A. J. A. Waldock, one of many sensitive readers who have confronted the poem since 1940, writes: '*Paradise Lost* is an epic poem of singularly hard and definite outline, expressing itself (or so at least would be our first impressions) with unmistakable clarity and point.'

* * *

By 'hard and definite outline' I take Waldock to mean the sense of continuity and direction evoked by the simultaneous introduction of the epic tradition and Christian myth. The 'definiteness' of a genre classification leads the reader to expect a series of formal stimuli—martial encounters, complex similes, an epic voice—to which his response is more or less automatic; the hardness of the Christian myth predetermines his sympathies; the union of the two allows the assumption of a comfortable reading experience in which conveniently labelled protagonists act out rather simple roles in a succession of familiar situations. The reader is prepared to hiss the devil off the

† From *Surprised by Sin: The Reader in* Paradise Lost, 2nd ed. (Cambridge: The Belknap Press of Harvard UP, 1998). Copyright © 1967, 1997 by Stanley Fish. Reprinted by permission of Harvard University Press and Palgrave Macmillan.

stage and applaud the pronouncements of a partisan and somewhat human deity who is not unlike Tasso's 'il Padre eterno'. But of course this is not the case; no sensitive reading of *Paradise Lost* tallies with these expectations, and it is my contention that Milton ostentatiously calls them up in order to provide his reader with the shock of their disappointment. This is not to say merely that Milton communicates a part of his meaning by a calculated departure from convention; every poet does that; but that Milton consciously wants to worry his reader, to force him to doubt the correctness of his responses, and to bring him to the realization that his inability to read the poem with any confidence in his own perception is its focus.

Milton's programme of reader harassment begins in the opening lines; the reader, however, may not be aware of it until line 84 when Satan speaks for the first time. The speech is a powerful one, moving smoothly from the *exclamatio* of 'But O how fall'n' (84) to the regret and apparent logic of 'till then who knew / The force of those dire Arms' (93–94), the determination of 'courage never to submit or yield' (108) and the grand defiance of 'Irreconcilable to our grand Foe, / Who now triumphs, and in th' excess of joy / Sole reigning holds the Tyranny of Heav'n' (122–124). This is our first view of Satan and the impression given, reinforced by a succession of speeches in Book 1, is described by Waldock: 'fortitude in adversity, enormous endurance, a certain splendid recklessness, remarkable powers of rising to an occasion, extraordinary qualities of leadership (shown not least in his salutary taunts)'. But in each case Milton follows the voice of Satan with a comment which complicates, and according to some, falsifies, our reaction to it:

> So spake th' Apostate Angel, though in pain,
> Vaunting aloud, but rackt with deep despair.
> (125–6)

Waldock's indignation at this authorial intrusion is instructive:

> If one observes what is happening one sees that there is hardly a great speech of Satan's that Milton is not at pains to correct, to damp down and neutralize. He will put some glorious thing in Satan's mouth, then, anxious about the effect of it, will pull us gently by the sleeve, saying (for this is what it amounts to): 'Do not be carried away by this fellow: he *sounds* splendid, but take my word for it. . . . ' Has there been much despair in what we have just been listening to? The speech would almost seem to be incompatible with that. To accept Milton's comment here . . . as if it had a validity equal to that of the speech itself is surely very naïve critical procedure . . . in any work of imaginative literature at all it is the demonstration, by the very nature

> of the case, that has the higher validity; an allegation can possess no comparable authority. Of course they should agree; but if they do not then the demonstration must carry the day.
> (pp. 77–78)

There are several assumptions here:

(1) There is a disparity between our response to the speech and the epic voice's evaluation of it.
(2) Ideally, there should be no disparity.
(3) Milton's intention is to correct *his* error.
(4) He wants us to discount the effect of the speech through a kind of mathematical cancellation.
(5) The question of relative authority is purely an aesthetic one. That is, the reader is obliged to hearken to the most dramatically persuasive of any conflicting voices.

Of these I can assent only to the first. The comment of the epic voice unsettles the reader, who sees in it at least a partial challenge to his own assessment of the speech. The implication is that there is more (or less) here than has met the ear; and since the only ear available is the reader's, the further implication is that he has failed in some way to evaluate properly what he has heard.

* * *

* * * The reader is made aware that Milton is correcting not a mistake of composition, but the weakness all men evince in the face of eloquence. The error is his, not Milton's; and when Waldock invokes some unidentified critical principle ('they should agree') he objects to an effect Milton anticipates and desires.

But this is more than a stylistic trick to ensure the perception of irony. For, as Waldock points out, this first epic interjection introduces a pattern that is operative throughout. In Books I and II these 'correctives' are particularly numerous and, if the word can be used here, tactless. Waldock falsifies his experience of the poem, I think, when he characterizes Milton's countermands as gentle; we are not warned ('Do not be carried away by this fellow'), but accused, taunted by an imperious voice which says with no consideration of our feelings, 'I know that you *have been* carried away by what you have just heard; you should not have been; you have made a mistake, just as I knew you would'; and we resent this rebuke, not, as Waldock suggests, because our aesthetic sense balks at a clumsy attempt to neutralize an unintentional effect, but because a failing has been exposed in a context that forces us to acknowledge it. We are angry at the epic voice, not for fudging, but for being right, for insisting that we become our own critics. There is little in the human situation more humiliating, in both senses of the word, than the public acceptance of a deserved rebuke.

* * *

GORDON TESKEY

From Milton's Choice of Subject in the Context of Renaissance Critical Theory†

I

To ask how Milton finally chose "Mans First Disobedience" as the subject of his epic is to address something too large, and too fundamental, to be contained by the form of our question. "Choice," after all, is a complicated and mysterious notion and if we are not to be led too far from Milton some reliable, though admittedly crude, assumptions about it are necessary. Let us assume that there are two kinds of choices: those that are relatively specialized and can be directed from above, as it were, by a metadiscourse of rational selection—what move to make in a chess game, for instance, or which muse to call on when telling of actions forepast—and then those rare, self-defining choices that engage all parts of the mind in a subtle and complicated exchange from which the faculty of reason cannot escape to become a detached referee—choices such as whether one should enter the priesthood, a problem Milton confronted at Cambridge, or what subject to choose for an epic.

I do not mean to suggest that the first kind of choice is less important than the second: a specialized rational decision on a matter that is perfectly clear to the chooser can have consequences far greater than a decision taken after much anxious self-searching. But because the second kind of choice places the identity of the chooser at stake, it can arouse anxiety as to what one will become after the choice has been made. Which of several possible selves should I choose to be in the next instant? Only in the state of innocence, as Milton conceives it, can one confront such a question continually without being mad. For the rest of us, radical change, and the liberty that goes with it, is economized by rites of passage, public or private.

There is a tendency, therefore, to think of one's life as a chain of relatively stable selves linked together by points of transition, or thresholds, where the individual is transformed into a new self that,

† From *English Literary History* 53.1 (Spring 1986): 53–72.

while continuous with the old, is radically changed. In this way the intolerable anxiety we would feel about gradual and disorderly change is managed by a double strategy of *restricting* change within the narrow bounds of a sudden transformation, and of *defining* change in ritual terms as a passage from one stable state to another.

* * *

II

We could therefore expect Milton to engage the question what subject he would choose for his first epic by referring that question, at least at the outset, to an external framework of theory that was shared by other Renaissance poets. Such a framework was available in the aggressively new discipline of poetics which promised, after the dissemination of Aristotle's rediscovered treatise in the early sixteenth century, to get the untidy business of literature firmly established on a rational basis. For critics of the period the most pressing task of this new discipline was to derive laws for constructing an epic poem—"that critical abstraction of the century" as F. T. Prince calls it—that would be as rigorous as those geometrical laws, discovered in the same period, for constructing a dodecahedron: "a sublime art," as Milton himself did not hesitate to call it, "which teaches what the laws are of a true epic poem" (YP 2:404–5).

Milton's enthusiasm for the new critical theory was at its height, not surprisingly, shortly after his return from Italy, where the debate, or "*famosa questione*," as his friend Manso had called it, still continued over the heroic decorum of Tasso's great epic. While the technical theory of the heroic poem could not indicate directly to Milton, or to any other poet, what he should choose as his subject, it nevertheless formed his conception of what it was he had to choose from: a class of distinct historical events each member of which would be suitable for enlarging, by poetic invention, into a unified action that would somehow be contained in itself. It is of course true that other things had some general bearing on Milton's choice—his disappointment in the revolution, his scepticism about British legend, and his demonstrated interest in accommodating Biblical materials to classical forms—but in the complex process of choosing, I would argue that the very concept of a subject in Renaissance poetics, carrying as it did an implied theory of history, played a critical, though a negative, role. For rather than eliminating each member within a general class of possible subjects—Arthur against the Saxons or Alfred the Danes, or, if a tragedy were wanted, "Hardiknut dying in his cups an example to riot" (*CE* 18:244)—Milton had to reject entirely the underlying principle of classification defining such things as fit subjects. At the heart of this principle is an abstract model, or *idea*, as some critics called it, of "the true epic poem" from which actual poems would derive the authority to call themselves "epics" by a relationship of *similarity*. It is, in the generalized, Jakobsonian sense of the word, a "metaphorical" principle of authority of which the most obvious consequence is the privileging of formal treatment over what Tasso had significantly called the "bare matter" of the subject.

Whatever its subject, an epic had in some way to refer to a generic ideal inferred from the examples of Homer and Virgil or understood by the abstract "laws" of poetics. Only when Milton had freed himself from this way of seeing the problem was his view of the obvious choice clear. The subject of *Paradise Lost* differs from the normal conception of a subject in Renaissance critical theory because it is based on a *contiguous* or "metonymical" principle of authority by descent from an origin, one in which the term "heroic" may now be applied not to formal treatment but to what actually occurs in the poem.

It is convenient, for our purposes at least, that Milton should have made his first effort to write a heroic poem shortly after his return from the continent. As he tells it in the *"Epitaphium Damonis,"* he had applied his lips to a new set of pipes that fell apart when their fastening broke under the "weighty sounds" of his theme.

Et tum forte novis admoram labra cicutis,
Dissiluere tamen rupta compage, nec ultra
Ferre graves potuere sonos . . .
("Epitaphium Damonis," 157–59)

The theme carried by these sounds includes, among other things, the coming of Brutus to Britain and Arthur's mysterious birth, that is, the legendary materials of the "Briton moniments," as Spenser had called them, that were thought indispensable to any national epic. It seems likely that Milton's *novae cicutae*, or "new pipes," refer specifically to his recently formed theoretical conception of "what the laws are of a true epic poem." It is noteworthy that at this stage the failure is not blamed on any fault in his choice of subject but on his technical competence to do justice to such a high theme: his pipes could not hold up under the strain. We might well imagine Milton terminating this effort to write about Britain's "indigenous kings," as he calls them in *"Mansus"* (l. 80), with the same words he was soon to attach, in the *Poems* of 1645, to a youthful failure entitled "The Passion": "This Subject the Author finding to be above the yeers he had, when he wrote it, and nothing satisfi'd with what was begun, left it unfinisht."

* * * The real problem with an *Arthuriad* was neither its doubtful

basis in fact nor the use of Arthur by royalists as an icon of kingship. It is that all those stories in Geoffrey of Monmouth's bouquet—stories of Saxon phalanxes (*"Manses,"* ll. 82–84) and of Uther's disguise (*"Epitaphium Damonis,"* ll. 162–68)—belong to a theoretically defined class of separate events taking place within history: within it, and therefore, despite any effort to impose unity of action upon them, subject to the underlying disorder that such a conception of history entails. Only when he had put behind him the theoretical abstraction of an ideal heroic poem could Milton relegate this class of events to the final two books of *Paradise Lost*.

* * *

In the invocation to *Paradise Lost* . . . the poet sees his poem, now identified with its subject, as an *extension*, rather than an *imitation*, of the original Word. When we consider what was described at the outset as Milton's ritualized conception of choice—a sudden transformation into something defined from outside the self—we realize how important for the release of his creative powers was that moment, whenever it was, that he chose "paradise lost." For the new, vatic "self" emerging from that moment is fully an extension of what it describes: in Milton's terms as a continuation of the Word, and perhaps also in ours since the myth of the fall is now, as Lévi-Strauss would say, thinking through him.

Glossary of Names in *Paradise Lost*

Aaron *3.598* Older brother of Moses. The first high priest of Israel. The jewels in his breastplate had beneficent magical powers. Exodus 29:9. See MOSES, URIM.

Abarim *1.408* A ridge of mountains east of the Jordan, in Moab, including Nebo and Pisgah. Contemporary sources suggested to Milton that they were in the "wilds" to the south. Numbers 21:11.

Abássin kings *4.280* Abyssinian, or Ethiopian. See AMARA.

Abbana *1.469* See DAMASCUS.

Abdiel *5.805* A seraph, whose name means "Servant of God." He confronts and rebukes Satan.

Abraham *12.152* Father, or patriarch, of the Hebrews and the Arabs. His name was changed from "Abram" so as to mean "Father of many nations." Genesis 17:5. See CANAAN and UR OF CHALDEA.

Accaron *1.466* Later "Ekron," the northernmost of the five Philistine cities associated with the worship of Beëlzebub. 2 Kings 1:2 and Zephaniah 2:4.

Acheron *2.578* One of the traditional four rivers of Hell; its name means "without joy." Mentioned by Virgil, Dante, and Spenser. The other rivers are Lethe ("oblivion"), Phlegethon ("fiery") and Styx ("horror").

Achilles *9.15* Hero of the *Iliad* who pursued Hector around the walls of the city and killed him. See TROY.

Adam *4.323* The first man, formed from dust and given life when God breathes into him: "And the Lord God formed man of the dust of the ground, and breathed into his nostrils the breath of life: and man became a living soul" (Genesis 2:7). In Hebrew, Adam's name means "dust" or "earth," and God plays on this meaning when he judges Adam: "For dust thou art, and unto dust shalt thou return" (Genesis 3:19). In the account of creation that was added to the Bible at a later date but placed at the beginning (Genesis 1–2:3), Adam and Eve are made in the *image* of God without reference to dust, bone, or breath: "So God created man in his own image, in the image of God created he him; male and female created he them" (Genesis 1:27). See EVE.

Ades *2.964* A personification of darkness and uncertainty associated with the classical underworld.

Adonis *1.450* River in Lebanon named after the boy who was beloved of Aphrodite and fatally wounded by a boar. Aphrodite turned him into a flower so that he would be annually reborn. The river runs red annually, supposedly discolored with Adonis's blood. See Shakespeare's "Venus and Adonis" and Spenser's *Faerie Queene* 3.6. 29–47. See THAMMUZ.

Adramelech *6.365* "Splendid king," an idol worshiped in Samaria, to whom children were sacrificed by being burned alive. 2 Kings 17:31. See MOLOCH.

Adria *1.520* Adriatic Sea, which washes Italy's east coast.

Aegean *1.746* The sea of Greece and its islands in the eastern Mediterranean.

Afer *10.702* A southwest wind.

Agra *11.391* Great Mogul capital in northwestern India.

Aialon *12.266* Broad valley west of Jerusalem over which the moon stood still at Joshua's prayer. Joshua 10:12. See GIBEON.

Aladule *10.435* Aladule, king of the mountainous country of Armenia. He trained assassins in a paradisal garden.

Alcairo *1.718* Ancient Memphis, capital of Egypt, where Osiris, Serapis, and other gods were worshiped. Famous for its magnificence, identified by Milton with nearby Cairo.

Alcides *2.542* Hercules.

Alcinous *5.341* King of the Phaeacians on the island of Scheria who welcomed Odysseus at his court, which had an orchard paradise Milton associated with Eden. *Odyssey* 7.112–21.

Aleian field *7.19* The wide plain onto which Bellerophon fell from Pegasus. See BELLEROPHON.

Algiers *11.404* A country in north Africa, its chief city of the same name.

Almansor *11.403* Muslim ruler in Spain and Northern Africa.

Amalthea *4.278* In older tradition, the nymph who raised the infant Zeus (Jove) on Mount Ida, in Crete, concealing the young god from his father, Cronos, who wished to devour him. She is sometimes identified with the goat who supplied the infant with milk and whose horn, when broken off by the infant, became the horn of plenty, which is magically replenished with fruit and flowers. Milton alludes to a later tradition in which Amalthea is the mother of Bacchus, the wine god (hence "florid son," 4.278) by Ammonian Jove. See AMMON.

Amara *4.281* A fabulous paradise on a high rock where the younger sons of the emperor of Ethiopia were kept so that they could not overthrow their father. Another false, pagan version of Eden.

Amazonian targe *9.1111* The shield of an Amazon. The Amazons, better known for their bows and arrows, are mythical female warriors.

Ammon *4.277* Son of Zeus (Jove) by a daughter of Atlas, and king of Libya, or North Africa generally. See BARCA and CYRENE. Identified with Jove—Milton's "Libyan Jove" and "Ammonian Jove" (9.508)—and said to be the father of the wine god Bacchus, the "florid son" of Amalthea. Milton identifies Ammon with "old Cham" (4.276), that is, Ham, the son of Noah and patriarch of the African peoples. Typically for Milton, the fabulous, pagan myth is a distortion of biblical truth, which is historical. In the Bible, it is Noah who first cultivates wine. Rather than being the father of the wine god, Ham merely sees his father drunk (Genesis 9:20–27). See AMALTHEA, CHAM, NYSEAN ISLE, OLYMPIAS.

Ammonite(s) *1.396* Semitic people, often at war with the Israelites. See MOLOCH.

Amphisbaena *10.524* Mythical serpent with a head at each end. Greek for "going both ways."

Amram *1.339* Father of Moses.

Andromeda *3.559* In Greek mythology, a princess chained to a rock to be devoured by a monster. A constellation next to Aries.

Angels *1.38* Immortal beings created by God before human beings. Most of the angels' names are derived from Hebrew words ending with *El* ("of God"). See, e.g., GABRIEL. The angels serve God in various ways, according to their orders, or degrees. See CHERUBIM. The Greek word *angelos* means "messenger." In *Paradise Lost*, Raphael and Michael perform the most important angelic missions. Other missions are Uriel's steering the sun (3.645–53) and warning Gabriel of Satan's approach (4.124–30, 549–75), Gabriel's guarding the Garden, (4.543–54) and Zephon and Ithuriel's mission (assigned them by Gabriel) to find and arrest the intruder in the Garden (4.788–96). See CHERUBIM, MICHAEL, RAPHAEL.

Angola *11.401* A rich African kingdom, comparable in power to the kingdom of the Congo.

Aonian Mount *1.15* Mount Parnassus in Greece, sacred to the Muses and Apollo.

Apostate *5.852* One who stands apart, a rebel.

Arabian shore *3.537* The shore of the Arabian peninsula, on the Red Sea.

Arcadian pipe *11.132* Arcadia is a remote, mountainous province of Greece in the central Peloponnesian peninsula, where pastoral poetry, sung to the accompaniment of the pipe, is said to have begun.

Archangel *5.660* An angel of the highest rank.

Argestas *10.699* A west-northwest wind.

Argo *2.1017* Ship of Jason and the Argonauts on their quest for the Golden Fleece.

Argob *1.398* Pagan kingdom of Og, Deuteronomy 3:4. See BASAN.

Argus *11.131* Many-eyed herdsman who was set to guard Io and was lulled to sleep and beheaded by Hermes. After his death, Juno put his eyes in the tail of the peacock. Ovid, *Metamorphoses* 1.624–29, 1.717–23; 2.531–33.

Ariel *6.371* "Lion of God" or "divine light," one of the rebel angels.

Aries *10.329* Constellation of the Ram. The constellation between the Centaur and the Scorpion is Anguis, the Serpent.

Arimaspian *2.945* Fabulous one-eyed people who steal gold from gryphons. Herodotus 3.116, 4.27; Pliny 7.2; Lucan 3.280.

Arioch ***6.371*** "Lion-like."

Armoric knights ***1.581*** Knights of Brittany.

Arnon ***1.399*** A river that flows into the Dead Sea from the east. Deuteronomy 3:8. The northern boundary of Moab. Numbers 21:13.

Aroer ***1.407*** Northern Moabite town.

Ascalon ***1.465*** One of the five cities of the Philistines, on the Mediterranean Sea. Judges 14:19; 2 Samuel 1:20; Zephaniah 2:4.

Ashtaroth ***1.422*** Plural of the goddess Astoreth and, in her Phoenician form, Astarte, a fertility goddess worshipped throughout Palestine and associated with the moon, whence the "crescent horns" (1.439) with which she was often depicted. She is also associated with the Greek goddess of love, Aphrodite. See ADONIS.

Asmadai ***6.365*** A rebel angel. See ASMODEUS.

Asmodeus ***4.168*** A jealous spirit who killed a young woman's seven husbands before being driven off by the eighth, Tobias, aided by the angel Raphael, who instructed Tobias to burn the entrails of a fish, the smell of which drove Asmodeus into upper Egypt, where Raphael bound him. Tobit 8:3. See RAPHAEL and TOBIAS.

Asphaltic pool ***1.411*** The Dead Sea, so called for its oily scum or bitumen.

Asphaltic slime ***10.298*** Binding agent used by Sin and Death to hold together the substance of chaos for the bridge across Hell. Greek *asphaltos* is mentioned in the Septuagint (the Greek translation of the Hebrew scriptures) as the substance used to build the tower of Babel. Genesis 11:3. Also the tarry remains of the cities of Sodom and Gomorrah. See NAPHTHA.

Aspramont ***1.583*** A mountain in Calabria, southern Italy, where Charlemagne won a victory over the Saracens.

Assyria ***1.721*** A great kingdom in upper Mesopotamia, its capital, Nineveh, on the Tigris river. At one time its power extended over the entire Near East and into Egypt.

Assyrian mount ***4.126*** See MOUNT NIPHATES.

Astarte ***1.439*** See ASHTAROTH.

Astoreth ***1.438*** See ASHTAROTH.

Astraea ***4.998*** The constellation Virgo. Goddess of justice who lived on earth in the Golden Age but fled to heaven when men became wicked.

Astracan ***10.432*** Astrakhan. A city near the mouth of the Volga river, which empties into the Caspian Sea.

Atabalipa ***11.409*** Inca ruler, whose kingdom, Cusco, in Peru, was plundered by Pizarro.

Athens ***9.671*** The most famous ancient Greek city, the birthplace of the arts, of democracy, and of political oratory, famous especially for its leadership in the war against the tyranny of the Persians.

Atlantic sisters ***10.674*** See PLEIADES.

Atlas ***4.987*** Mount Atlas in the extreme west of northern Africa. Atlas was a Titan who for rebelling against Zeus was compelled to hold up the sky. He was changed to a mountain by Perseus. See GORGON.

Auran *4.211* The western boundary of the large country of Eden (of which the garden, Paradise, is but a small part).
Ausonian land *1.739* *Ausonia* is an ancient name for Italy.
Azazel *1.534* A rebel angel, Satan's standard-bearer, and a chief devil in the Book of Enoch.
Azores *4.592* A group of islands in the Atlantic, eight hundred miles west of Portugal, representing the extreme west where the sun sets.
Azotus *1.464* Ashdod, one of the five Philistine cities and a center of Dagon worship. The ark of the covenant, after its capture by the Philistines, was taken to Ashdod and put in the temple of Dagon where the idol was mysteriously knocked down and mutilated. 1 Samuel 5:1–7. See DAGON.
Baälim *1.422* A plural form of Hebrew *Baal*, which means "lord." See BEËLZEBUB, BELIAL, and BELUS.
Babel *1.694* The tower intended to reach to Heaven. God frustrated the project by causing the builders to speak different languages. Genesis 11:1–9. Milton supposed Nimrod to be the builder and associated the tower with Babylon. Cf. 12.24–62.
Babylon *1.717* The great city on the lower Euphrates near the Persian Gulf, famous for its brick buildings, associated with the tower of Babel. The Israelites were taken into captivity there after the conquest of Jerusalem. Thus Babylon, like Egypt, is a place of captivity and a symbol of bondage.
Bacchus *4.279* The Roman name for Dionysus, the god of wine.
Bactrian Sophy *10.433* Persian ruler.
Barca *2.904* North African or Tunisian desert region called Cyrenaica. See CYRENE. *Aeneid* 4.42–3.
Basan *1.398* Bashan, a country east of the Jordan ruled by Og, an enemy of Israel; also associated with the Ammonites, enemies of Israel. Deutoronomy 3:1.
Beëlzebub *1.81* *Baal-Zebub*, "Lord of Flies." In Matthew 12:24 he is called "the prince of the devils." Perhaps originally a god with the power to deliver a city from an infestation of flies. See ACCARON. 2 Kings 1:1–3.
Beersaba *3.536* Beersheba, in southern Palestine.
Belial *1.490* Hebrew for "worthlessness." Belial is named as a devil in the New Testament (2 Corinthians 6:15). In the Old Testament, however, the phrase "sons of Belial" means men given over to shameless, dissolute, and murderous lives. See GIBEAH and SODOM.
Bellerophon *7.18* The hero who tried to reach the home of the gods by riding the winged horse Pegasus up Mount Olympus. Zeus sent a gadfly to sting Pegasus, who threw Bellerophon. See PEGASEAN WING. See ALEIAN
Bellona *2.922* Roman goddess of war.
Belus *1.720* A version of *Bel*, *Baal*, a Babylonian god whose name means "lord."
Bengala *2.638* A great Indian kingdom.
Bethel *1.485* "House of the Lord." In the idolatrous northern kingdom

of Israel, King Jeroboam set up two places in which golden calves were worshiped: Bethel and Dan, Bethel in the extreme south of the northern kingdom, Dan in the extreme north. 1 Kings 12:28–9. This act repeats and doubles the crime of the worship of the golden calf in Exodus 32:1–6. See JACOB.

Biserta *1.585* A Mediterranean seaport in Tunisia, North Africa, from which a Saracen army prepares to sail for France. *Orlando Innamorato* 2.29.1–22.

Bizance *11.395* Byzantium or Constantinople, modern Istanbul, conquered by the Turks in 1453 and so in Milton's day ruled by a sultan. It guards the Bosphorus, the narrow strait that is the boundary between Asia and Europe.

Book of Knowledge *3.47* The Book of Nature, God's revelation in his creatures.

Books of Life *1.363* Records of the angels' now blotted out, glorious titles. Cf. Revelation 3:5, "I will not blot out his name out of the book of life."

Boreas *10.699* A north wind.

Bosphorus *2.1018* Narrow strait between Asia and Europe where the clashing rocks, the Symplegades, threatened the ship of Jason and the Argonauts. Apollonius of Rhodes, *Argonautica* 2.317–23, 552–67.

Briareos *1.199* The hundred-handed monster who aided Zeus against the other gods when they sought to bind him. Briareos fought with the gods against the Titans. *Iliad* 1.396–406.

Busiris *1.307* Legendary Egyptian tyrant identified with Pharaoh of the Book of Exodus.

Cadmus *9.506* Legendary founder and king of Thebes. Zeus turned him and his wife, Hermione, into snakes. Ovid, *Metamorphoses* 4.571–601.

Caecias *10.699* An east-northeast wind.

Calabria *2.661* The southern part of mainland Italy across the strait of Messina from Sicily. See PELORUS, TRINACRIAN SHORE, and TYPHON.

Cambalu *11.388* Peking (Beijing), capital of China.

Canaan *12.135* The Promised Land of the Hebrews, corresponding (roughly) with modern Israel and the West Bank. Bounded on the north by the mountains of Lebanon, on the south by the desert and the borders of Egypt, on the east by the Jordan River and the Dead Sea, and on the west by the "Great Sea," or Mediterranean. Canaan is promised first to Abraham and his descendants and again to the Israelites when they leave Egypt. Canaan is named after Noah's grandson, whose father was Ham. Enraged by Ham's disrespect, Noah cursed Canaan's descendants, justifying the conquest of the Promised Land under Joshua and the subjection of the Canaanites. For Abraham, see Genesis 12:1–7. For Noah, see Genesis 9:18–27. For the division of the land under Joshua, see Joshua 15–21. See CHAM.

Cape of Hope *4.160* The southern tip of Africa, which had to be rounded on the sea route to the east.

Capitoline Jove *9.508* An epithet of Jove referring to his temple on the Capitoline hill in Rome. See SCIPIO.

Capricorn *10.677* Constellation of the Goat, and the southern tropic, or "turning place" from which the sun begins its journey north across the equator to the Tropic of Cancer. See CRAB.

Carmel, Mount *12.144* A high promontory on the Mediterranean coast marking the westernmost point of the Promised Land, scene of the contest between Elijah and the prophets of Baal (1 Kings 18).

Casbeen *10.436* Kazvin in northern Persia, a former capital.

Casius, Mount *2.593* A mountain between Egypt and Arabia.

Castalian spring *4.274* A spring at the Oracle of Delphi, on Mount Parnassus, sacred to Apollo. Its waters inspired those who drank them with the gift of poetry. See AONIAN MOUNT and DELPHI.

Cathayan coast *10.293* Cathay, an ancient kingdom occupying the northern half of China. Often identified with China.

Cathayan Khan *11.388* Ruler of Cathay, descendant of Genghis Khan.

Centaur *10.328* The constellation Sagittarius, the archer.

Ceres *4.271* Latin name for Greek Demeter, goddess of crops, especially grain, whence *cereal*. Ceres was mother of Proserpina (Persephone), who was seized by the god of the underworld, Hades (or Pluto), while she was gathering flowers in the field of Enna, in Sicily. Mourning her daughter, Ceres refused to let crops grow, whereupon Persephone was allowed to return to the earth for two-thirds of the year. For the remaining third of the year, winter, the earth is barren.

Chaldea *12.130* See UR.

Cham *4.276* Ammon, father of Bacchus, identified with Jove and with the constellation Aries, the Ram. Also identified with Noah's son Ham. See AMMON and CANAAN.

Chaos *1.10* Chaos is three things: a cosmological concept, a narrative scene (although not, strictly speaking, a place), and a personification. Only in this last sense should *Chaos* be capitalized. As a cosmological concept, chaos is the region surrounding the three created systems of Milton's cosmos: Heaven, Hell, and the universe. Chaos is infinitely extended and utterly disorganized. There is no limit to chaos and no measure within it: no time, no space. Chaos is not a vacuum, however. It is filled with "materials" in a wildly turbulent state that is often compared to the ocean, the most turbulent system visible on earth. These materials were originally in God the Father, who extended to infinity. When the Father withdraws from infinity and situates himself in Heaven (which he creates), the materials of chaos are left behind. Being now entirely distinct from the Father, the materials of chaos are neither evil nor good. But of these materials the Son, assisted by the Spirit, forms the created universe, which *is* good. See 2.890–91 and 7.210–34.

As a narrative scene, chaos does have distance, time, and direction, an "up" and a "down" (1.75–81). This chaos is the "wasteful deep" (6.862) through which the rebel angels can fall for nine days (6.871); it is the "unvoyageable gulf" (10.366) across which Satan does voyage from Hell to the universe (2.917–50); and it is the "gulf / Impassable" across which Sin and Death nevertheless form a "stupendious bridge" (10.351 and 10.283–320). Finally, as a personification, Chaos is the king of chaos, the "power of that place" (2. Argument), enthroned beside his queen, "sable-vested Night" (2.959–62). Milton confers on him the inspired title *Anarch* (2.98), from Greek *a* ("without") + *arche* ("origin, rule"). As a king, Chaos is indignant at divine incursions into his realm (2.999–1003). In Book Six, Chaos is still a fairly close personification when he "roar[s]" at the fall of the rebel angels "Through his wild anarchy" (6.871–73). By Book Ten, Chaos has become a vestigial personification, "vexed" (10.314) at the bridge built by Sin and Death and exclaiming against it: "On either side / Disparted Chaos overbuilt exclaimed / And with rebounding surge the bars assailed" (10.415–17).

Charlemagne *1.586* "Charles the Great." King of the Franks in the eighth to ninth century A.D. Holy Roman emperor and defender of Christendom against Saracen aggression, particularly from Spain. His rear guard, commanded by the great hero Roland (Orlando), was obliterated by a Saracen army at Roncesvalles, a pass in the Pyrenees near Fontarabbia (Fuenterrabia). In the Old French epic poem *The Song of Roland*, neither Charlemagne nor his peerage fell.

Charybdis *2.1020* A monster in Homer's *Odyssey* 12.55–126, 222–59, a giant whirlpool or sucking gulf on one side of the narrow strait between Sicily and Italy. Charybdis sucks ships down into her gulf and vomits them out. On the other side of the strait, on a cliff, is the monster Scylla, who has six fierce dog heads. One monster seizes from below, the other from above (Ovid, *Metamorphoses* 7.62–65 and 13.730–31).

Chemos *1.406* Chemosh "Subduer." National deity of the Moabites, long-standing enemies of Israel. Yet Chemosh was idolatrously worshiped in Israel from the reign of Solomon to Josiah, who purged the worship of foreign gods. Numbers 21:29; Jeremiah 48:4–7, 13, 46; 1 Kings 11:7; 2 Kings 23:13–14. See PEOR.

Chersonese *11.392* Remotely derived from a Greek word for "dry land." Milton probably means the peninsula of Malacca, east of India. The ancient Jewish historian Josephus (8.6) says that Solomon sent a fleet to the Chersonese to obtain gold.

Cherubim *1.665* Hebrew plural of cherub, the second of the nine orders of angels: seraphim, cherubim, thrones, dominations, virtues, powers, principalities, archangels, and angels. Only archangels and angels function as intermediaries between God and Man. Cherubim were responsible for guarding the presence of God from profanity. In Genesis 3:24, a cherub guards the tree of life after the expulsion of Adam and Eve. In Exodus 25:18, two golden figures of the cherubim guard the ark. Later, huge sculptures of the cherubim overshadow the ark of the covenant in Solomon's temple. 1 Kings 6:27. Milton audaciously represents cherubim among the fallen angels in Hell. See ZOPHIEL.

Chimera *2.628* Fire-breathing monster with a lion's head, a goat's body, and a serpent's tail.

Circean call *9.522* Circe, a witch-goddess in Homer's *Odyssey* 10.210–19, transforms men into obedient beasts.

Cleombrotus *3.473* A Greek youth who, wanting to enjoy sooner the afterlife promised in Plato's *Phaedo*, leaped from a high wall into the sea.

Cocytus *2.579* A river of Hell whose name comes from a Greek word meaning "to shriek and wail over the dead." See ACHERON.

Congo *11.401* In Milton's day, a region covering most of West Africa south of the Sahara.

Crab *10.675* The constellation Cancer, which marks the farthest point north that the sun travels away from the equator before turning south (hence *tropic*, "turning"). These movements of the sun belong to the astronomical system in which everything moves around a stationary Earth. See CAPRICORN; see also PLEIADES, SPARTAN TWINS, TAURUS, VIRGIN, and ZODIAC.

Cronian Sea *10.290* The Arctic Ocean, frequently a barrier of ice, named after Cronos, often identified with Saturn, who was driven by his son Zeus from Olympus and into the northern regions of the earth.

Cusco *11.408* See ATABALIPA.

Cyclades *5.264* A group of islands forming a circle in the southern Aegean Sea.

Cyrene *2.904* Ancient North African city in the region of Barca.

Cytherea's son *9.19* Cytherea, the goddess Venus, whose son is Aeneas, the hero of Virgil's *Aeneid*.

Dagon *1.462.* Philistine fish-god. When the Philistines captured the ark of the covenant and set it beside the idol of Dagon, the idol fell on its face. When they repeated the experiment on a second night, they found in the morning that the head and hands of Dagon were cut off: "only the stump of Dagon was left to him" (Samuel 5.1–4).

Dalila *9.1061* Lover of Samson who betrayed him to the Philistines by putting him to sleep and having a man cut off his hair, the source of his strength (Judges 16:19).

Damasco *1.584* See DAMASCUS.

Damascus *1.468* Capital of Syria, where Naaman, a leper, was captain of the army. When told by the prophet Elisha that he would be cured by bathing seven times in the Jordan River, he compared the Jordan unfavorably with Abbana and Pharphar, the rivers of Damascus. But when he bathed in the Jordan he was cured (2 Kings 5.1–14). In Ariosto's *Orlando Furioso* 16.1–16, Muslim and Christian knights joust at "Damasco." See 1.584.

Damiata *2.593* An ancient city on the delta of the Nile.

Dan *1.485* A city in the extreme north of Palestine at the headwaters of the Jordan (1 Kings 12:28–33). See BETHEL.

Danaw *1.353* The Danube River, forming, with the Rhine, the northern boundary of the Roman Empire. It flows east through central Europe into the Black Sea. In the fifth century A.D. it was crossed by the barbarian hordes, which destroyed the Empire. See RHENE.

Danite *9.1059* One who is of the tribe of Dan.

Daphne *4.273* A nymph, daughter of the river god Peneus, beloved of Apollo. When fleeing Apollo, she prayed to her father to save her, whereupon she was transformed into a laurel tree, thence sacred to Apollo. Ovid, *Metamorphoses* 1.452–567. See ORONTES for the grove named after her.

Darien *9.81* The isthmus of Panama, barring the ocean from flowing between the Atlantic and the Pacific. See Job 38:8–11.

David *12.326* The second king of Israel. He captured Jerusalem, made it his capital city and transferred the ark of the covenant there. David is the type of man who is a sinner but has a passionate faith. He was traditionally supposed to be the author of the Psalms and is often portrayed with a harp. The prophets said that the Messiah would be of the royal line of David (Psalm 89:34–37; Isaiah 11:10). Jesus' kingship rests on his being a descendant of David: "the Lord God shall give unto him the throne of his father David" (Luke 1: 32).

Death *2.787* The son of Sin and Satan, Death is described as dark and shapeless but with the appearance of a crown on his head. He is armed with a javelin and a whip of scorpions (1.672 and 701). His body is later described as a vast, loose-skinned corpse that cannot be filled even by all the prey that waits for him on earth (10.599–601). Death is described in Hell smelling the flesh of living creatures by raising "His nostril wide into the murky air" (10.280). Death is born to Sin soon after she is placed at the gates of Hell. Once out of her, he rapes her, whereupon she gives birth to the hell hounds that torment her at his urging (2.778–809). At the end of time, the Son will defeat Sin and Death and "fix their stings" in Satan's head (12.431–33). The Son will then hurl Sin and Death back through chaos to Hell, where their bodies will seal up the gates. Until then, Sin resides in all of mankind and prepares them as a meal for her son: "Till I in Man residing . . . season him thy last and sweetest prey" (10.607–9). See SIN.

Deccan *9.1103* In Milton's day, the region of India lying inland from the port of Goa on the northwest coast. See MALABAR.

Delia *9.387* A name for Diana, so called for her birthplace on the island of Delos.

Delos *5.265* The smallest of the Greek islands in the Cyclades. It is sacred to Apollo and Diana, who were born there.

Delphian cliff *1.517* High on Mount Parnassus, overlooking the gulf of Corinth, Delphi is one of the holiest sites of ancient Greece. It is home to the oracle of Apollo and the Pythian games in honor of Apollo, the most important games after those held at Olympia in honor of Zeus. Because of its height, Milton would associate the worship of the pagan gods that took place at Delphi with the devils who would occupy the "middle air." Delphi is analogous to the "high places" of pagan worship which are often mentioned in the Bible, 1 and 2 Kings. See PYTHIAN FIELDS, PYTHIAN VALE, and PYTHON.

Demogorgon *2.965* In medieval (but not classical) mythography, the most ancient and terrible of the gods, whose name is dreadful to utter or to hear. Demogorgon is given prominence by Boccaccio in his *Genealogy of the Pagan Gods* and is mentioned by Spenser in *The Faerie Queene* 1.1.37: "Great *Gorgon*, Prince of Darknesse and dead night, / At which *Cocytus* quakes, and *Styx* is put to flight."

Deucalion *11.12* With his wife, Pyrrha, was saved from the flood with which Zeus destroyed the men of the Bronze Age. For Milton, their story is a pagan version of the true story of Noah's Flood. After praying at the shrine of Themis, goddess of law, they restored the human race by throwing stones over their shoulders. The stones Deucalion threw became men, those Pyrrha threw became women.

Dipsas *10.526* Monster whose bite causes overpowering thirst.

Dis *4.270* Pluto, or Hades, king of the underworld. See CERES.

Dodona *1.518* The site of a very ancient oracle of Zeus, where Zeus's instructions were uttered by the rustling leaves of a sacred oak tree. Homer, *Odyssey* 19.296–7.

Dominations *2.11* Fourth of the nine orders of angels. See CHERUBIM (Colossians 1:16).

Dominic *3.479* Founder of an order of monks (Dominicans) known for their white robes.

Dorian *1.550* An ancient musical mode associated with military discipline. Plato, *Republic* 398e–99a.

Doric land *1.519* Greece.

Dothan *11.217* A town in northern Palestine that was besieged by a Syrian king attempting to capture Elisha (2 Kings 6:13–18). At Elisha's request, God struck the armies of the Syrian king blind.

Dryad *9.387* A tree nymph. Greek *drus*, "tree."

Ecbatan *11.393* Hamadan, ancient summer capital of Persian kings. *Paradise Regained* 3.286: "Ecbatana her structure vast there shows."

Eden *1.4* The large country between the upper Tigris and Euphrates Rivers in which the garden of Paradise, where Adam and Eve live, is situated. Since the Tigris forms the eastern boundary of Eden and, in *Paradise Lost*, flows under the mount of Paradise, the garden is in the easternmost place possible in the land of Eden. Genesis 2:8: "And the Lord God planted a Garden eastward in Eden; and there he put the man he had formed." See 4.208–14 and 9.71–73. In the final line of *Paradise Lost*, Adam and Eve have been expelled from the Garden but are still in the vast territory of Eden, through which they pass: "Through Eden took their solitary way." See PARADISE.

El Dorado *11.411* "The Golden." Fabled capital of Guiana sought by the Spanish and later by Sir Walter Raleigh in the expeditions of 1595 and 1616.

Elealè *1.411* One of the towns in Moab that the tribes of Reuben and

Gad wished to occupy with their cattle. These tribes asked Moses not to bring them across the Jordan River into the Promised Land but to let them settle in Elealè and the surrounding towns, a request that contributed to God's decision to allow none of the men who left Egypt to enter the Promised Land, except Caleb and Joshua (Numbers 32:1–12). See HESEBON.

Eli's sons ***1.495*** The wicked sons of the aged high priest: "They lay with the women that assembled at the door of the tabernacle of the congregation" (1 Samuel 2:22). Eli's sons are, for Milton, types of the wicked priests in the established church.

Ellops ***10.525*** A kind of serpent-fish, like the lamprey eel.

Elysian flowers ***3.359*** Elysium, the classical paradise, situated in Virgil's underworld.

Empedocles ***3.471*** Pre-Socratic philosopher-poet who was fabled to have leaped into the volcanic tube of Mount Etna to ensure his fame. See Horace, *Art of Poetry* 463–66.

Enna ***4.269*** The meadow in Sicily where Persephone was abducted by Hades, king of the underworld. See CERES.

Epidaurus ***9.507*** Greek town on the eastern coast of the Peloponnesus and home of Asclepius (Latin, Aesculapius), the god of healing. The god took the form of a holy serpent. The symbol of Asclepius is two snakes entwined around a staff.

Ercoco ***11.398*** Modern Archico, port on the west, or African, coast of the Red Sea. In Milton's day, the only port of the empire of Negus.

Erebus ***2.883*** A place of darkness between earth and Hades, the classical underworld.

Esau ***3.512*** The elder of Isaac's two sons, and the hairier, tricked out of his inheritance by his smooth brother Jacob, who wore "skins of the kids of the goats" on his hands and neck to deceive the blind Isaac on his deathbed (Genesis 27). See JACOB.

Estotiland ***10.686*** A fabled, utopian island off the northeast coast of North America. Milton means only an extremely cold northern region.

Ethiopian (sea) ***2.641*** The Indian Ocean off the east coast of Africa.

Etna ***1.233*** An active volcano in Sicily, visible from the strait of Messina, the prison of the giant Enceladus, and also of the monster, Typhon, both of whom Jove struck down with his thunderbolt and pinned beneath the mountain. Etna is also the subterranean forge where the Cyclopes made Jove's thunderbolts (Virgil, *Georgics*, 4.170–75; *Aeneid* 3.568–82; 8.424–53). See TYPHON.

Etrurian shades ***1.303*** Etruria, the ancient name of Tuscany, in north central Italy. Mountainous and heavily wooded. See VALLOMBROSA.

Euboic Sea ***2.546*** The strait between Thessaly, in northern Greece, and the large island of Euboea. The strait is overlooked by Mount Oeta, in Thessaly. See LICHAS.

Euphrates ***1.420*** One of the two rivers of Mesopotamia ("land between the rivers") and one of the four rivers of Paradise (Genesis 2:14). Spenser calls the Euphrates "immortal" (*The Faerie Queene* 4.11.21). The Euphrates rises in the mountains of Anatolia, in

Turkey, and flows south-southeast for seventeen hundred miles to join the Tigris near the Persian Gulf. The upper Euphrates forms the northeastern boundary of the land promised to the Jews: "Unto thy seed have I given this land, from the river of Egypt [not the Nile, but a stream south of Gaza] unto . . . the river Euphrates" (Genesis 15:18).

Eurus *10.705* East-southeast wind.

Eurynome *10.581* Milton interprets her name to mean "wide-encroaching." With her husband, Ophion, a serpent-god sometimes identified with the serpent who tempted Eve in Eden, she ruled Olympus until expelled by Cronos and Rhea.

Eve *1.364* The first woman, formed from a rib taken from the side of the first man, Adam. Eve's name is taken to mean "life" in Hebrew, which it does when breathed with an *H*: "And Adam called his wife's name Eve; because she was the mother of all living" (Genesis 3:20). In the Greek Septuagint Bible, Eve's name is *Zoê*, "life." See ADAM.

Ezekiel *1.455* The prophet who went into exile in Babylon with the Israelites in the sixth century B.C. Famous for his vision of God in the opening chapter of his book.

Father *3.56* See GOD.

Faunus *4.708* Benevolent Roman god of shepherds and woods identified with the Greek Pan. See PAN and SILVANUS.

Fesole *1.289* Fiesole, the town above Florence where Galileo lived under house arrest by order of the Inquisition. See TUSCAN ARTIST and GALILEO.

Fez *11.403* A walled desert city inland in northern Africa, famous for its marble palaces and temples and its pink stone. In his *Commonplace Book*, Milton notes the great honor in which poets were held there.

Flora *5.16* Roman goddess of flowers. In Ovid's *Fasti* 5.193–207, Flora is beloved of Zephyr, the god of the west wind. Milton draws on Zephyr's pursuit of Flora for his account of the first meeting of Adam and Eve.

Fontarabbia *1.587* See CHARLEMAGNE.

Fount of life *3.357* Milton takes the idea of a paradisal fountain of life from the last chapter of Revelation 22:1: "And he shewed me a pure river of water of life, clear as crystal, proceeding out of the throne of God and of the land." The phrase, "Fountain of Life," is from Psalm 36:9. See TREE OF LIFE.

Furies *2.596* The Greek female spirits of vengeance, the Erinyes, are in Latin called the *Dirae* or *Furiae*. Milton recalls the Erinyes' first intelligible utterance in Aeschylus's *Eumenides* (130), when they cry "seize!" repeatedly. For the Furies in Latin literature, see Cicero, *On the Nature of the Gods* 3.18.46; Virgil, *Aeneid* 6.570–72, 7.323–560, 12.845–69; Ovid, *Metamorphoses* 4.451–54. See also *Iliad* 9.454; *Odyssey* 2:135. See HARPIES.

Gabriel *4.549* "Strength of God," one of the four archangels, he commands the troop of angels set to guard the Garden of Eden and confronts Satan there (4.866–1015).

Galileo *5.262* Great Italian scientist and astronomer, the first to look into the heavens with a telescope, disproving the time-honored, geocentric, Ptolemaic system and proving the Copernican hypothesis: that the earth revolves around the sun. He also noted erosion on the moon. See TUSCAN ARTIST.

Ganges *3.436* One of the two great rivers of northern India, sacred to the Hindus, which flows into the Bay of Bengal, on the east side of the Indian subcontinent. Identified with the first of the four rivers of Eden, the Pison (Genesis 2:11). See HYDASPES.

Gath *1.465* One of the five Philistine cities. See AZOTUS.

Gaza *1.466* The southernmost of the five Philistine cities. See AZOTUS.

Gehenna *1.405* The word for Hell in the Greek text of the New Testament. Matthew 5:22 and 10:28: "fear him which is able to destroy both soul and body in hell [gehenne]." It is derived from Hebrew *gê-hinnôm*, literally the valley Hinnom, also called "Tophet" ("drum"), to the southwest of Jerusalem. A grove in this valley was sacred to Moloch, to whom children were sacrificed by being burned alive.

Gentiles *4.277* People who are not Jews. Milton uses the term twice in *Paradise Lost* to refer specifically to Greek-speaking peoples. See 12.310: "Joshua whom the gentiles Jesus call."

Geryon *11.410* A red, winged, three-headed, cattle-hording monster killed by Hercules. He is associated by Spenser with Spanish tyranny and aggression: "He that whylome in Spaine so sore was dred, / For his huge powre and great oppression" (*The Faerie Queene* 5.10.9). Milton therefore refers to the Spanish conquistadors in the New World as "Geryon's sons."

Giants *1.576* In classical mythology, the giants are incited to war against the Olympian gods to avenge the Titans. See TITAN.

Gibeah *1.504* A city near Jerusalem in the territory of Benjamin where a Levite and his concubine (improved by Milton to "matron") were, during a journey, hospitably received for the night by an old man. "Certain sons of Belial" (Judges 19:22) beat at the door demanding that the Levite be sent out to them to be raped. The concubine was sent out instead and was raped to death. This crime was the occasion of the civil war in Israel against the tribe of Benjamin.

Gibeon *12.265* The place over which Joshua prays to the sun to stand still so that he can complete his slaughter of the Amorites (Joshua 10:9). See AIALON.

Gibraltar *1.355* The promontory on the south coast of Spain at its closest point to Africa, separating the Atlantic from the Mediterranean. The barbarian hordes passed through Spain, crossed the strait of Gibraltar, and spread across North Africa, or Libya.

Goblin *2.688* Ugly demon.

God *1.42* The infinite, all-knowing, all-powerful being, who withdraws from infinity to occupy Heaven, which he creates. God is called the Father of all things because he is their creator and ruler. But in some special sense God is father of the Son, who participates in

God's being and is God's creative Word. Milton wishes us to understand that God is not only all-powerful but also good, just, merciful, and loving. He leaves these last two attributes to be shown by the Son. God sees all times at once and therefore knows, well in advance of the event, that Adam and Eve will fall (3.92). But God adds that, because Adam and Eve are free, his foreknowledge is not a cause of their fall, even though his foreknowledge makes it certain (3.117–19). Despite this certainty, God says he made mankind "Sufficient to have stood though free to fall" (3.98–99). Because God is just, mankind must be punished (3.210). Because God is merciful, mankind must be redeemed from punishment, which would otherwise be eternal. The Son achieves this redemption by becoming incarnate, as Jesus, and dying for mankind: "on me let thine anger fall" (3.237). See CHAOS, MESSIAH, SON, SPIRIT, and WORD.

Golgotha *3.477* "Place of the skull," also called Calvary. Latin *calva* "skull." The hill of execution outside Jerusalem on which Jesus was crucified.

Gonfalons *5.589* Heraldic banners suspended from crossbars, as opposed to being fastened to flag poles, as "standards" are.

Gordian *4.348* Referring to the Gordian knot in Asia. Legend said that whoever untied it would rule Asia. Alexander the Great cut it with his sword.

Gorgon(s) *2.628* Three female monsters with snakes for hair, the sight of whom turned viewers to stone. One of them was Medusa, who was killed by the hero Perseus and her head put on Athena's shield. Numerous references in Ovid's *Metamorphoses*. For example, at 4.655–62, Perseus uses the head of Medusa to turn the Titan Atlas into the mountain of that name in northern Africa, across from Gibraltar. See OPHIUSA.

Gorgonian terror *2.611* Having the power to turn to stone. Cf. the "Gorgonian rigor" of Death's "look" (10.296–97).

Goshen *1.309* Where the captive Israelites lived in Egypt (Genesis 47:6).

Graces *4.267* The Charites, attendants of Aphrodite, commonly represented in art as three naked young women, their arms interlocked, two facing toward us and one away. Aglaia ("splendor"), Euphrosyne ("mirth"), and Thalia ("blossoming").

Great Mogul *11.391* The Mogul emperor in India.

Gryphon *2.943* Fabled bird with eagle's wings and beak, and lion's body. Gryphons guard gold in the deserts of north India. See ARIMASPIAN.

Guiana *11.410* Region of northern South America, much larger than the present country of that name. It is "yet unspoiled" because the Spaniards had not yet found and sacked it. Sir Walter Raleigh failed in his two attempts to do so.

Hamath *12.139* In Syria on the river Orontes.

Haran *12.131* A city, far up the Euphrates valley, on the Belikh, a south-flowing tributary of the Euphrates, to which Abraham's father, Terah, traveled with his family when he left Ur on the lower Euphrates. From Haran, at God's command, Abraham would journey south into Canaan (Palestine).

Harpies *2.596* Female winged demons with eagle-clawed feet who carry off children and souls. Their name is derived from a Greek verb meaning "to seize." Hesiod says that they are as swift as winds, birds, and time (*Theogony* 267–69). In Virgil, they carry food off or defile it and are also among the monsters at the doors of Hell. (*Aeneid* 3.211–18, 6.289). See FURIES.

Heaven *1.30* The place of God's presence, populated by the angels whom he created and who serve and praise him. First described in Book Three of *Paradise Lost*, especially 3.344–71, modeled on the heavenly Jerusalem of Revelation 21–22. Milton situates Heaven outside the created universe, which is suspended from it by a golden chain. Seen by Satan from far off, it has jeweled towers and battlements, which are alive. In Book Six, when the war in Heaven is recounted, Heaven appears as a vast country, much more extensive than the lands on earth.

Hell *1.28* Not situated in the earth but far off in chaos, at a great distance from Heaven and the created universe. As a place of eternal punishment, Hell was created to receive the rebel angels as they fell. Also the place of punishment at the end of time for reprobate men. Milton's Hell seems to be circular, like a furnace. See 1.542, 2.635. Yet it is also like a vast continent, with four infernal rivers—Styx, Acheron, Cocytus, and Phlegethon—and a landscape that the angels explore. See 2.570–628. There is a burning lake on which the angels lie unconscious for nine days before being wakened by Satan and going to the shore, which also burns under their feet. See 1.50–74, 1.227–37. The rebel angels build a palace in Hell, Pandaemonium. See 1.700–30. The gates of Hell, guarded by Sin and Death, are made of brass, iron, and adamantine rock and are encircled with fire. When opened, fire and smoke belches through them into chaos. See 2.645–48, 2.876–89. See GEHENNA.

Hellespont *10.309* Now called the Dardenelles, the strait between Asia and Europe. When invading Greece, the Persian emperor Xerxes commanded a bridge to be made across the Hellespont. When the bridge was destroyed by a storm, Xerxes ordered that the bridge makers be beheaded, that the waves of the Hellespont be scourged with three hundred strokes of the lash, and that the men with the whips utter barbarous insults while doing so. This act of hubris brought disaster on Xerxes' campaign (Herodotus, *The Histories* 7.33–36).

Herculean (Hercules) *9.1060* A hero and demigod who performed twelve great labors and, like Samson, was undone in the end by a woman. His wife, Deianeira, hoping to regain his love, sent him a robe dyed in what she supposed to be a love potion but was actually poison. In his agony, Hercules climbed Mount Oeta, raised his own funeral pyre, and burned away his mortal part, ascending to heaven as a god. In the madness caused by his agony, Hercules threw his companion Lichas into the Euboic sea. See LICHAS.

Hermes *3.603* Winged-footed messenger of the gods, himself a god. Mercury to the Romans. Milton uses the name as the technical term in alchemy, where mercury was supposed to be "bound" in the process of obtaining gold from baser metals.

Hermione *9.506* See CADMUS.

Hermon *12.141* Mount Hermon, snowcapped peak in Palestine, northeast of the Sea of Galilee. The headwaters of the Jordan are at its feet. Mount Hermon was regarded by the Israelites as their northern border, but Milton follows contemporary cartographers in supposing it to be the eastern boundary.

Hesebon *1.408* A Moabite, later an Amorite, town to the east of the Jordan River, northeast of Mount Nebo. It is included in the towns mentioned in Isaiah's prophecy of the destruction of Moab. Isaiah 15:4: "And Heshbon shall cry, and Elealeh . . . therefore the armed soldiers of Moab shall cry out." See ELEALÈ.

Hesperian gardens *3.568* A fabled paradisal garden located in the far west of the world on the border of the ocean, where the sun sets. See 8.632. A tree planted there by Jove grew golden apples that were guarded by the Hesperides, daughters of Night and Darkness. In this office they were assisted by a multiheaded dragon. Because the apples recall the fruit in the Garden of Eden and the dragon recalls the serpent, Milton regards the Hesperides as being, like other Greek fables, a deformation of biblical truth. See 4.250–151: "Hesperian fables true, / If true, here only."

Hesperus *4.605* The first star to appear in the evening, and the brightest. Actually the planet Venus.

Hinnom *1.404* See GEHENNA.

Hispahan *11.394* Ispahan, a Persian capital city.

Horonaim *1.409* A city of Moab mentioned in Isaiah's prophecy against Moab: "My heart shall cry out for Moab . . . for in the way of Horonaim they shall raise up a cry of destruction" (Isaiah 15:5). See also HESEBON.

Hours *4.267* Female deities, *Horae*, responsible for changes of season.

Hydaspes *3.436* A river in India, rising in the Himalayas, and a tributary of the Indus. The limit of Alexander's conquest. Milton's reference to it probably is intended to take in the Indus. See INDUS.

Hydra *2.628* A venemous serpent with nine heads, one of the offspring of Echidna, Typhon's mate. Killed by Hercules.

Hymen *11.591* The Roman god of marriage.

Ida *1.515* Mountain on the island of Crete that is the birthplace of Zeus. See AMALTHEA.

Ilium *1.578* The city of Troy, where the action of Homer's *Iliad* unfolds. For Milton, the men of the "heroic race" that fought at Ilium are midway in stature between men and giants.

Illyria *9.505* Illiricum, ancient Roman province extending around the Adriatic Sea from Italy to Macedonia, and north to the Danube.

Imaus *3.431* Mountains extending north from the Himalayas through central Asia, around which lived the Tartars and the Scythians. The name was supposed by Pliny to mean "full of snow."

Ind *2.2* India.

India *5.339* In Milton's day, India was known for spices and as a source of wealth. In his readings on India, especially Samuel Purchase's *Pilgrimage* (1625), Milton seems to have been excited by Indian fruits and shocked by Hindu religious rites.

Indus *9.82* One of the two great rivers of northern India (see GANGES) which rises in the Himalayas, in Tibet, and flows into the Arabian sea on India's west coast. See HYDASPES.

Ionian gods *1.508* Ionia is that part of the shore and islands of Asia Minor that was inhabited by Greeks. Homer and the early Greek philosophers came from Ionia. The "Ionian gods" are therefore the Greek gods, whom Milton supposes to have been men of "Javan's issue." Javan is the son of Japhet, one of the three sons of Noah, who are the patriarchs of the Semitic, African, and Indo-European (Greek and Hittite) peoples. Milton suggests that the Greek gods, like the gods of Syria, Palestine, and Egypt, are fallen angels disguised as gods. But he also speculates (following ancient euhemeristic tradition) that the Greek gods are remote ancestors of the Greeks elevated to the status of gods.

Iris *11.244* A messenger of the gods, herself a goddess, whose multicolored scarf is the rainbow.

Isaac *12.268* Hebrew patriarch, father of Esau and Jacob. See ESAU and JACOB.

Isis *1.478* Egyptian goddess with the head of a cow, wife to Osiris.

Israel *1.413* Not the geographical country (see CANAAN) but the nation of the Hebrews.

Ithuriel *4.788* Angel whose name means "discovery of God."

Jacob *3.510* After cheating his brother, Esau, out of their father's blessing, Jacob fled to Bethel (near Padan-Aran) in Syria, where he dreamed of angels ascending and descending on a ladder between Earth and Heaven (Genesis 28). See ESAU.

Janus *11.129* Double-faced Roman god of gateways.

Japhet *4.717* Noah's son, patriarch of the Greeks (see IONIAN GODS), identified with Epimetheus ("afterthought"), son of the titan Iapetus and brother of Prometheus ("forethought"). Pandora ("all gifts") was given to Epimetheus as punishment for Prometheus's having stolen fire from heaven. The large wine jar Pandora brought with her, when opened, released into the world all the ills that afflict mankind (Hesiod, *Works and Days* 54–105).

Javan *1.508* See IONIAN GODS.

Jehovah *1.386* God the Father, Yahweh.

Jesus *10.183* The Latin form of Greek *Iesous* and Hebrew *Yeshua*, which Englished is *Joshua*. See 12.310. See JOSHUA.

John *3.623* The author of the Book of Revelation. In Milton's day identified with the author of the fourth gospel.

Jordan *3.535* The holy river of Israel and the eastern boundary of

Israel above the Dead Sea, into which the Jordan flows from the north (see HERMON). The name *Jordan* is from the Hebrew *Yarad* "to go down." When the Israelites crossed the Jordan to enter the Promised Land, the river stood back to let them pass, just as the Red Sea parted when they fled from Pharaoh (Joshua 3).

Joshua *12.310* Joshua is the severe leader of the Hebrews who after Moses's death conquers the Promised Land. Greek *Iesous* (Latin *Jesus*) is the translation of the Hebrew *Joshua*, or *Yeshua*. In medieval biblical exegesis, Joshua is a *type*, or symbolic anticipation, of Jesus: as Joshua led the Israelites across the Jordan into the Promised Land, so Jesus will lead all mankind through death to eternal life. Milton follows Christian tradition in seeing Moses as a symbol of the Law, and so incapable of leading the people into the Promised Land. Joshua therefore bears the "name and office" of Jesus, who will lead humanity "Through the world's wilderness . . . Safe to eternal Paradise of rest." See 12.313–14.

Josiah *1.418* King of Judah 637–608 B.C., a religious reformer who violently purged the nation of the worship of false gods. 2 Kings 22–23, 25: "And like unto him was there no king before him, that turned to the Lord, with all his heart, and with all his soul, and with all his might, according to all the law of Moses; neither after him arose there any like him." A figure much admired by Milton, who saw Cromwell as a figure like Josiah. Josiah died at Megiddo in battle against Necho, king of Egypt (2 Chronicles 35:20–24).

Jove *1.198* See JUPITER.

Judah *1.457* The southern kingdom remaining after the division of Israel into two kingdoms following Solomon's death. The northern kingdom was thence called "Israel." Although the kingdom of Judah had Jerusalem as its capital, and the temple with the Ark of the Covenant, it was much smaller than the northern kingdom, made up of only two small tribes, as opposed to the ten in the north. Judah is "alienated" because its leaders are in captivity in Babylon. Milton is referring to Ezekiel's vision (Ezekiel 8) of the idolatrous worship practiced in and near the temple in Jerusalem.

Juno *4.500* The Roman equivalent of Hera, the wife of Zeus.

Jupiter *4.499* The Roman equivalent of the Greek king of the gods, Zeus.

Laertes' Son *9.441* Odysseus. See ULYSSES.

Lahore *11.391* Mogul capital in northern India.

Lapland *2.665* The extreme north of Scandinavia, associated with storm-causing wizards and witches.

Lavinia *9.17* Turnus's promised bride, given to Aeneas instead. See TURNUS.

Lazar-house *11.479* A place of confinement for sufferers of leprosy.

Lebanon *1.447* The mountainous country to the north of Israel where the Adonis river runs, discolored each summer with reddish mud, or the petals of the anemone, supposedly the blood of Thammuz. See ADONIS.

Lemnos *1.746* Large island in the northern Aegean Sea to which Hephaistos fell when Zeus threw him from Olympus (*Iliad* 1.590–3).
Leo *10.676* Constellation of the Lion.
Lethe *2.583* See ACHERON.
Leucothea *11.135* "White goddess," associated with dawn and with sea spray.
Leviathan *1.201* The whale or sea monster, associated with Satan.
Libecchio *10.706* Italy's southwest wind.
Libra *3.558* Constellation of the Scales.
Libya *1.355* In Milton's day, most of North Africa, including the Sahara Desert. See GIBRALTAR.
Libyan Jove *1.277* See Ammon.
Lichas *2.545* Hercules' companion and the innocent bearer of the poisoned cloak. See HERCULES.
Living Strength *1.433* Jehovah, God the Father.
Lucifer *5.760* "Light bearer," the morning star, perhaps the name of Satan before his fall: "Satan, so call him now, his former name / Is heard no more in Heav'n" (5.658–9). Milton uses the name *Lucifer* to recall the prophecy of Isaiah (14:12–14) against Babylon, a figure of Satanic pride: "How art thou fallen from Heaven, O Lucifer, son of the morning! . . . For thou hast said in thine heart I will ascend into Heaven, I will exalt my throne above the stars of God: I will sit also upon the mount of the congregation, in the sides of the north: I will ascend above the heights of the clouds; I will be like the most High."
Luz *3.513* The earlier name of *Bethel*. See also JACOB.
Maeonides *3.35* Homer's patronymic, "son of Maon."
Maeotis *9.78* The Sea of Azov, north of the Black Sea and connected to it by a narrow channel. Shallow, reedy, semifresh water. Milton calls it "the *pool* Maeotis" from the Latin "palus Maeotis," where *palus* can mean "a marsh."
Magellan *10.687* Strait of Magellan, which cuts through near the southern tip of South America. Named after the Portugese navigator Magellan.
Mahanaim *11.214* The place east of the Jordan River where Jacob met the angels of God encamped like an army in tents.
Maia's son *5.285* Hermes, messenger of the gods.
Malabar *9.1103* Region on the western coast of Hindustan in India, famous in Milton's day for fig trees, the extended branches of which take root in the ground, forming an extensive system of arches.
Mammon *1.678* One of the devils, his name proverbial for greed. In Matthew 6:24 Jesus says, "Ye cannot serve God and Mammon." See MULCIBER.
Mary *5.387* Virgin mother of Jesus, called the "second Eve" because, being innocent of all sin, she is able to bear Christ, who will restore humanity to the state from which Eve fell. Milton emphasizes that it is through Eve too that what was lost shall be restored: "though

all by me is lost. . . . By me the promised Seed shall all restore" (12.621–23).

Media *4.171* Persia.

Medusa *2.611* See GORGON.

Megaera *10.560* One of the three Furies, the others being Alecto and Tisiphone, depicted in ancient literature and art with serpents for hair and with serpents in their hands. See FURIES.

Meliboean purple *11.242* A famous, rare, purple dye produced in Meliboea, on the coast of Thessaly. This is the best and brightest purple there is, yet Michael's cloak is "Livelier." See SARRA.

Melind *11.399* Malindi, on the coast of Africa, in modern Kenya, the port from which Vasco da Gama crossed the Indian Ocean to Goa, in India.

Memnonian palace *10.308* Persian winter palace (also called Susa) named after its founder Memnon, the son of Tithonus and Eos, or Dawn.

Memphian chivalry *1.307* Cavalry of Memphis, ancient capital of Egypt.

Messiah *5.664* "The anointed one" in Hebrew, the general term for a king. Jesus. The first king, Saul, was anointed by the prophet Samuel (1 Samuel 10.1), as was the great king David (1 Samuel 16.1–13). In Psalm 89:20, God says, "I have found David my servant; with my holy oil have I anointed him." In the prophetic books of the Bible, a messiah is prophesied who will sit on David's throne and govern all the nations of the earth in a time of universal peace: Isaiah 11:1–12, 32:1–2; Jeremiah 33:14–16; Ezekiel 37:24–28; Zechariah 10:9, 12:10; Zephaniah 1:1; Zechariah 14:1; Malachi 4. The Christian gospels would apply these prophecies to Jesus, whose name "Christ" (Greek *ho christos*, "the anointed one") means "messiah": "We have found the Messias, which is, being interpreted, the Christ" (John 1:41; cf. 4:25). In Milton's Heaven, before the Creation of the World, the Son is proclaimed Messiah.

Michael *2.294* The name means "who is like El (the Lord)." The chief of the archangels, Michael contends with Satan at the apocalypse (Jude 9; Revelation 12:7). Although he appears seldom in the Bible, Michael is an important figure in later Christian literature and art, notably in Milton. In the war in Heaven, Michael is commander of the celestial armies (6.44, 202–03, 411–13, 686–87, 777–78) and the greatest of the angelic warriors (6.320–23, 250–61). Abdiel knocks Satan backwards (6.193–95), but Michael alone wounds him (6.320–27; see 2.293–5). As executor of divine justice, Michael is sent with a troop of cherubim at his command to expel Adam and Eve from Paradise.

Moab *1.406* The kingdom to the east of Israel on the other side of the Dead Sea, its people closely related to the Israelites. (In some periods, Moab extended far enough north to border on the Jordan River as well.) Israel and Moab often fought (Numbers 22–24; Judges 3:

12–30, 11:17; 1 Samuel 14:47–48; 2 Samuel 8:2). Moses, the most sacred of Israel's leaders, was buried by God in an unknown location in Moab: "And the children of Israel wept for Moses in the plains of Moab thirty days" (Deuteronomy 34:1–8). Despised for their idolatry, which was associated with sexual license, the Moabites (and the Ammonites) were said to be descended from Lot's incestuous union with his daughters, after the destruction of Sodom and Gomorrah (Genesis 19:30–38). Ruth, the great-grandmother of David, came from Moab. (Ruth 1:22, 4:13–22). See HORONAIM.

Moloch *1.392* "King," cf. Hebrew *Melech*, "king." God of the Ammonites, who were said to be descendants of the incestuous union of Lot with his daughters. See MOAB. Moloch was worshiped in Rabba, the capital city of the Ammonites, and his worship spread to Israel. See GEHENNA. Moloch's idol was a large brass figure, enthroned and crowned, with arms extended, and with the head of a bull, through the mouth of which infants were thrown to be incinerated within. As Milton's friend John Selden reports in his treatise on the gods of Syria, drums and other instruments were sounded to drown out the screams. Leviticus 18:21: "And thou shalt not let any of thy seed pass through the fire to Molech."

Mombaza *11.399* Mombasa in modern Kenya, in East Africa.

Montalban *1.583* Rinaldo's castle (Ariosto, *Orlando Furioso* canto 30, stanza 93). In Boiardo's *Orlando Innamorato*, book 2, canto 23, book 3, canto 4, there is a large battle around Montalban between Charlemagne and the Saracens. See CHARLEMAGNE.

Moreh *12.137* The site of Sichem (Shechem; modern Nablus), the first place in the land of Canaan where Abraham made camp (Genesis 12:6).

Moses *12.170* The most sacred of Israel's leaders, Moses led the Hebrews out of Egypt and through the wilderness to the borders of the Promised Land, Canaan. While in the wilderness, at Mount Sinai, Moses received from God the covenant of the Law, the basis of Jewish ritual. Moses was led by God to the top of Mount Pisgah and shown the Promised Land, which he was not allowed to enter. First named in *Paradise Lost* as "that shepherd who first taught the chosen seed . . . how the heav'ns and earth / Rose out of chaos" (1.8–10), Moses is the supposed author of the Pentateuch, the first five books of the Bible, including the first, Genesis (Deuteronomy 31:24). It was supposed that the Pentateuch was dictated to Moses by God on Mount Sinai (Exodus 24:3–12). Milton gives more space to the Hebrews' Exodus from Egypt and journey to the Promised Land under Moses' leadership than to any other event recounted in the historical books (11 and 12) of *Paradise Lost* (12.169–260). This emphasis is due in part to Milton's seeing the Israelites' journey in the wilderness, from bondage in Egypt to freedom in Canaan, as a type of the English Revolution. See JOSHUA and AARON.

Mount of God **5.643** In *Paradise Lost*, the place of the presence of God in Heaven and the site of God's throne. Based on the two most sacred mountains in the Bible, Mount Sinai, where Moses received the Law, and Mount Sion (Zion) in Jerusalem. See 6.5 and 7.584–86.

Mozambique *4.161* In Milton's day, district of East Africa that had been settled by Arab traders and colonized by the Portuguese.

Mulciber *1.740* The devil Mammon. Along with Vulcan, a Latin name of the Greek god Hephaistos, famous for elaborate metal work. In the *Iliad* he fashions the shield of Achilles and in the *Aeneid* he fashions the shield of Aeneas. At the end of the first book of the *Iliad* (590–94), he describes being thrown from heaven by Zeus and falling onto the Greek isle of Lemnos. Typically, Milton regards the Greek story as a deformation of the truth, which is his own account of the fall of the rebel angels into Hell. See MAMMON.

Muse *1.6* The Muses are the daughters of Zeus and Mnemosyne ("Memory"). Milton follows the great epic poets, chiefly Homer, in invoking the muse at the outset of his epic. Classical tradition names nine muses, who were patrons of the various arts and sciences, including Clio, the muse of history, and Calliope, the muse of epic poetry. Since his poem is both an epic and an account of the origin of history, Milton would intend both these muses to be suggested in his invocation. However, the only classical muse Milton names is Urania (7.1), whose name is from the Greek, *ouraniê*, "of the sky." Urania is the muse of astronomy and, for Christian poets, of religious poetry. Milton suggests that the classical muses are but a distorted memory of God's wisdom (7.3–8). In the invocation with which *Paradise Lost* opens, Milton's muse is the Word of God as he spoke to Moses on Mount Sinai and to David (in the Psalms) on Mount Sion. The heavenly muse is further specified in line 1.17 as the Spirit, or inner light, associated with reason and conscience. This inner light is identified, in line 1.20, with the Spirit in Genesis 1:2, which moves on the waters of chaos at the creation of the world. At 1.375, Milton re-invokes the muse before his catalog of the leaders of the rebel angels who in the future will be the pagan gods of Egypt, Palestine, Greece, and Rome. In this Milton imitates Homer's catalog of the ships and their commanders who went to Troy (*Iliad* 2.483–877). Recalling that the muses are the daughters of Memory, epic catalogs function as guarantees of the factual truth of what the poet sings.

Naphtha *1.729* The fuel for the lamps in Pandemonium. It is a liquid form of asphalt tar, or bitumen. See ASPHALTIC SLIME.

Nebo *1.407* A headland of the northern plateau of Moab, east of the Jordan River. From one part of it, Mount Pisgah, Moses was shown the Promised Land (Deuteronomy 32:49, 34:1). Milton's phrase is from 1 Chronicles 5:8: "Who dwelt in Aroer, even unto Nebo."

Negus *11.397* Title of the emperor of Abyssinia, in East Africa. See ERCOCO.

Neptune *9.18* Roman god of the sea and of earthquakes. His Greek name was Poseidon. Milton is referring to the Greek god, who was angry with Odysseus.

Niger *11.402* Great river in West Africa flowing eastward and then south into the Atlantic, in the Gulf of Guinea. Adam's gaze sweeps northward from the Niger across the Sahara to Mount Atlas on the Mediterranean.

Night 2.962 The consort of Chaos, whom Milton calls "eldest of things." See Spenser, *The Faerie Queene* 1.5.20–28, where the chariot of Night is drawn by coal-black steeds from Hell whose mouths foam with tar.

Nile *1.344* The great river of Egypt, longest river in the world, flowing 4,160 miles from the Abyssinian highlands through the desert to the Mediterranean Sea.

Nilus 4.283 The Nile River.

Niphates, Mount 3.742 Armenian mountain near the Assyrian-Mesopotamian border; source of the Tigris River.

Nisroch 6.447 One of the rebel angels who will become the Assyrian idol worshiped by Sennacherib (2 Kings 19:36–37).

Norumbega *10.696* A town vaguely situated in Maine or farther north, perhaps on the Penobscot River.

Notus *10.702* The south wind.

Nyseian isle 4.275 The isle of Nysa in the Triton River in north Africa, an earthly paradise, birthplace of Bacchus (Diodorus Siculus 3.67). See AMMON.

Ob 9.78 A river in Siberia, Milton's Muscovy, flowing north to the Arctic Ocean.

Ocean 4.*165* Oceanus, the eldest of the Titans, the father of rivers and a personification of the ocean that surrounds the terrestrial world.

Oechalia 2.542 A town in Euboea, in northern Greece, conquered by Hercules, from which he was returning when he put on a poisoned robe sent him by his wife, Deianeira, causing the mortal part of him to die. See HERCULES.

Oeta 2.545 Mountain in southern Thessaly by the Euboic Sea. See HERCULES.

Olympias 9.509 Wife of Philip II of Macedon, impregnated by Ammonian Jove in the form of a serpent. The child born of this union was Alexander the Great. A similar story accompanies the birth of Scipio. See SCIPIO.

Olympus *1.516* A snowcapped mountain in the far north of mainland Greece, on the border of Macedonia, home of the Greek gods, especially of Zeus after his departure from Mount Ida on the island of Crete.

Ophion *10.581* A serpent-god who ruled with his consort Eurynome before Cronos and Rhea, the parents of Zeus. The name means "serpent." See EURYNOME.

Ophir *11.400* Fabulous land where Solomon was thought to have obtained gold of exceptional purity for his temple. It was sometimes identified with Sofala, a wealthy port on the east coast of Africa.

Ophiuchus 2.709 Northern constellation, the "serpent bearer."

Ophiusa 10.528 Perhaps one of the Balearic Islands, which are off the coast of Spain in the western Mediterranean. The name means "full of serpents." These sprang from drops of Medusa's blood when Perseus flew over the islands. See GORGON.

Ops *10.584* Rhea, or Cybele, wife to Cronos, or Saturn. She became the Roman goddess of plenty.

Optic glass *1.288* Telescope, invented in the sixteenth century in northern Europe for observing ships at sea, much improved and adopted for astronomical observation by Lippershey and Galileo in Padua, Italy.

Orcus *2.964* Roman god of death, closely identified with Pluto, or Hades.

Oread *9.387* A mountain nymph. Greek *oros* "mountain." See DRYAD.

Oreb *1.7* Horeb, Sinai in Exodus 3:1, where Moses met God, who appeared to him as a burning bush. See SINAI.

Orion *1.305* A constellation, represented as a hunter or an armed giant, the rising of which is associated with the season of storms. See *Aeneid* 1.535.

Ormus *2.2* City of great wealth on an island in the Persian Gulf. The name survives in the strait of Hormuz.

Orontes *4.273* A Syrian river that flows into the Mediterranean. A grove of Daphne stood beside it. See 9.80.

Orpheus *3.17* See also 7.32–38. Legendary shamanistic poet who descended to the underworld to retrieve his wife, Eurydice, and, because of the beauty of the music he made, was allowed to return to the upper world with her, on condition that he not look back. He did look back, and Eurydice was lost. Milton says he sings with "other notes" than those that Orpheus used because he is inspired by the true God. Orpheus' music, which caused rocks, animals, and trees to listen spellbound, became a symbol of the power of poetry over the natural world. A troop of maenads, female worshipers of Bacchus, tore Orpheus to pieces and threw his head into the Hebrus River. The head floated to the island of Lesbos, where it was buried with full honors by the inhabitants of that island. (Ovid *Metamorphoses* 10.1–60). For this act of piety, the people of Lesbos would always have fine poets among them. The greatest of these poets was Sappho, a woman who wrote love poems to women. Hence the term *lesbian* originates in the love of song.

Orus *1.478* Horus, Egyptian sky god, son of Osiris and Isis. He has a hawk's head. The Pharaoh is a human incarnation of Horus.

Osiris *1.478* Egyptian god of fertility and of the dead, dismembered by his brother, Seth. The scattered parts were collected by his wife, Isis, who gave them life, making him god of the underworld.

Oxus *11.389* A large river in Asia that flows into the Aral Sea in Kazakhstan. Maps in Milton's day show it flowing into the Caspian Sea.

Padan-Aram *3.513* Territory in Syria, north of Palestine, adjacent to the upper Euphrates, in which Jacob had his vision of the stairs ascending from earth to heaven.

Pales *9.393* Roman goddess of flocks and pastures.

Pan *4.707* Roman god of nature, shepherds, and flocks. He is depicted as a goat-god who is mostly human from the waist up (though with horns and goatlike features including large ears) and a goat from the waist down. See FAUNUS and SILVANUS.

Pandemonium *1.756* Literally, "assembly-place of all demons."

Pandora *4.714* See JAPHET.

Paneas *3.535* A city near Mount Hermon in northern Palestine at a spring of the Jordan, now Banias. Identified with Dan.

Paquin *11.390* Peking (Beijing), capital of China, which was thought to be a kingdom distinct from Cathay.

Paradise *3.354* The Greek word *paradeisos*, "garden." The word used for the garden of Eden in the ancient Greek translation of the Hebrew Scriptures. Paradise is situated in the northeasternmost part of the large country, Eden, on the top of a high mountain. Milton's paradise is unusual in including work and sexual intercourse. For Milton, the ideal natural state must include having children. The unfallen state, therefore, is an open system in which humans are spread throughout the earth: "Hail mother of mankind whose fruitful womb / Shall fill the world more numerous with thy sons / Than with these various fruits the trees of God / Have heaped this table" (5.388–91). Unlike Dante, Milton does not enclose human innocence within the confines of the garden. Innocence and happiness are destined to spread over the earth (11.339–46). Politically, the Garden is the "capital seat" (11.343; cf. "high seat," 4.371) of Adam, who is intended to be a benevolent, yet august, ruler over all his descendants. In paradise, Adam and Eve represent not only the perfect human marriage but also the ideal polity, with Adam as the ruler and Eve as its only citizen. (But Eve contains all future citizens of that polity.) When Adam and Eve fall, they lose not only their ideal relation to the natural world but also the ideal political state, leaving humanity to suffer all the political evils to be manifested in history, especially tyranny. See EDEN.

Pegasean wing *7.4* The winged horse Pegasus created the source of the Hippocrene spring on Mount Helicon by striking the rock with his hoof. The Hippocrene spring is identified with poetry, especially epic poetry, in dactylic meter, which can sound like hoofbeats. See BELLEROPHON.

Pelorus *1.232* The promontory on the northeast corner of Sicily, near the volcanic Mount Etna. Ovid, Metamorphoses 13.727. The name is chosen partly for the strong assonance with "torn" but chiefly because it is from the ancient Greek adjective for something huge, of monstrous proportions: *pelōros*. In the 48 lines from Hesiod's *Theogony* (820–68) on Zeus's war against Typhon, this adjective is used five times. Later tradition identified the place where Typhon is buried with Mount Etna and with the promontory thence named *Pelorus*. See CALABARIA, TRINACRIAN SHORE, and TYPHON.

Peor *1.412* Alternate name for CHEMOS. Canaanite god associated with sexual orgies on Mount Peor in Moab. In Numbers 25, many of the Israelites, during their journey in the wilderness, "commit whoredom with the daughters of Moab" and make sacrifices to Baal-Peor (Numbers 25:1–3), whereupon God commands Moses to have the offenders killed and brings on a plague that kills twenty-four thousand people.

Peter, Saint *3.484* The disciple Jesus names as the rock upon whom he will found his church (Matthew 16:18–19). Peter was the first bishop of Rome, and in Roman Catholic eyes the popes are his successors as heads of the Church. In postbiblical tradition, Peter is stationed at the gates of Heaven where, before the Last Judgment, he admits or refuses to admit each human soul. Those not admitted go to Hell or to Purgatory. Milton thinks that the text of the Bible warrants belief only in the Last Judgment.

Petsora *10.292* The river Pechora in Siberia, which flows from the Urals to the Arctic Ocean.

Pharphar *1.469* See DAMASCUS.

Phineus *3.36* Thracian king and blind prophet.

Phlegethon *2.580* See ACHERON.

Phlegra *1.577* A headland in the Aegean where the gods and the giants fought. Pindar speaks of it as a "plain" (*Nemean Odes* 1.67).

Phoenix *5.272* Mythical bird that immolates itself on a pyre and rises again from its own ashes. It then flies with those ashes to Heliopolis ("city of the sun") in Egypt. See also Ovid, *Metamorphoses* 15.391–407.

Plato *3.472* Greek philosopher. See CLEOMBROTUS.

Plebeian *10.442* A Roman term for a person of the lowest class.

Pleiades *7.374* A dense cluster of stars, known as the Seven Sisters and the Atlantic Sisters, that rises in the spring when it is time to plow the earth. They are thought to pour, by benign *influence* ("flowing-in"), fertility into the earth (Hesiod, *Works and Days* 383–84). See CRAB and TAURUS.

Plutonian hall *10.444* Hall of Pluto, Roman god of the underworld. See DIS.

Pomona *5.378* Roman goddess of fruit.

Pontus *5.340* The Black Sea.

Potentates *5.749* See CHERUBIM.

Powers *6.22* See CHERUBIM.

Proserpine *4.269* Roman name of Persephone. See CERES.

Proteus *3.604* A sea god under Neptune, or Poseidon. He is the "shepherd" of all the creatures in the ocean, especially seals. Proteus can change his form into any shape. He also has the power of prophecy. See *Odyssey* 4.365–570. Alchemists took the god Proteus to be a symbol of the many forms of matter, yet they also thought that matter has one true, essential form, as the god Proteus does. Alchemists attempted to isolate this true essential form of matter in their alembics, or retorts, in the vain attempt to turn base matter into gold. See HERMES.

Punic coast *5.340* The south coast of the Mediterranean sea at Carthage, in North Africa. The Romans called the Carthaginians the *Poeni* (Gr. *Phoinix*) from their Phoenician origin, and referred to their own wars with the Carthaginians as the "Punic wars," *Punica bella*.

Pyrrha *11.12* See DEUCALION.

Pythian vale *10.530* The mountain valley at Delphi, where Apollo slew Python. See DELPHIAN CLIFF and PYTHON.

Pythian Fields *2.530* At Delphi, the site of the Pythian games, sacred to Apollo.

Python *10.531* A monstrous serpent born from the slime deposited by Deucalion's flood. Python was slain by Apollo.

Quiloa *11.399* Kilwa-Kisiwani, an island port off the east coast of Africa.

Rabba *1.397* Principal city of the Ammonites, worshipers of Moloch. It is situated east of the Jordan, to the north. In 2 Samuel 12:27, Rabbah is called "the city of waters." See Jeremiah 49.

Ramiel *6.372* His name means "one who exalts himself against God." In the pseudepigraphical book, 1 Enoch (6:7), Ramiel is among the angels who take a vow to fornicate with women. They do so and bring forth a race of cannibalistic giants. The episode is based on the tamer account given in Genesis 6:1–4. Ramiel's violence recalls Virgil's phrase, "the violence of Turnus," *violentia Turni* (*Aeneid* 11.376).

Raphael *5.221* "Health of God." In Tobit 3:17, the angel Raphael is a healer and an exorcist, driving out and binding the evil spirit Asmodeus. See ASMODEUS and TOBIAS.

Red Sea *1.306* The sea whose waters, at Moses' command, divide so that the Israelites may pass. When the army of Pharaoh pursues, the sea closes over it. Exodus 14.

Rhea *1.513* Wife of Cronos. Because her husband ate their children as soon as they were born, Rhea hid the infant Zeus in a cave on Mount Ida in Crete, deceiving Cronos by throwing into his gullet a stone wrapped in swaddling bands. See AMALTHEIA.

Rhene *1.353* The Rhine River, major waterway of western Europe, which, with the Danube, formed the northern boundary of the Roman Empire. It flows northwest into the North Sea. In the fifth century C.E., barbarian tribes crossed the Rhine, sweeping everything in their path, sacking Rome, deposing the last emperor, and establishing their own kingdoms in the territories of the former Empire. See DANAW.

Rhodope *7.35* A mountain range in northern Thrace, sacred to Dionysus, where Orpheus made music and was torn apart by the maenads (Ovid, *Metamorphoses* 10.77). See ORPHEUS.

Rimmon *1.467* Syrian god, worshiped in Damascus. See DAMASCUS.

River Dragon *12.191* The Pharaoh. Ezekiel (29:1–5) speaks a tremendous prophecy against the Pharaoh: "Behold I am against thee, Pharaoh king of Egypt, the great dragon that lieth in the midst of his rivers, which hath said, My river is mine own, and I have made it for myself. But I will put hooks in thy jaws, and I will cause the fish of thy rivers to stick unto thy scales, and I will bring thee up out of the midst of thy rivers."

River horse *7.474* Hippopotamus, from Greek *hippos* "horse," + *potamos* "river."

Rome, free *9.671* The state of Rome under the Republic, before the emperors. Political oratory flourished under the Republic.

Samarchand *11.389* The capital city of Tamburlaine's vast Asian empire. A city of the same name is in Uzbekistan. In Marlowe's *The Second Part of Tamburlaine the Great*, Tamburlaine describes his city: "Then shall my native city Samarcanda, / And crystal waves of fresh Jaertis' stream, / The pride and beauty of her princely seat, / Be famous through the furthest continents; / For there my royal palace shall be plac'd, / Whose shining turrets shall dismay the heavens" (4.3.107–12). See TEMIR.

Samoed shore *10.696* Samoedia, northeastern Siberia.

Samos *5.265* An island in the Aegean, not one of the Cyclades but one of the Sporades; it is the birthplace of Hera. The two islands, Delos and Samos, are associated by Ovid in *Metamophoses* 8.220 and by Milton because they are both places of sacred birth. See DELOS.

Samson *9.1060* Hebrew hero from the book of Judges whose divine strength depended on his hair not being cut. See DALILA.

Sarra *11.243* Tyre, a Phoenician seaport on an island just off the Mediterranean's eastern shore. It was famous for, and wealthy because of, its rich, purple dye, obtained from the murex sea snail. See MELIBOEAN.

Satan *1.82* The Hebrew *ha–satan* (used also in the Greek New Testament) means " the adversary."

Saturn *1.512* Roman counterpart of the Greek Cronos, ruler of the gods until deposed by his son Jupiter (the Greek Zeus). See RHEA.

Scales *10.676* The constellation Libra.

Scipio *9.510* Scipio the Great, or Scipio Africanus, so named because of his victory over Hannibal in North Africa, which ended the Second Punic War. Considered the greatest Roman, he was said to have had a conception like that of Alexander the Great, whose mother was impregnated by Ammonian Jove in the form of a serpent. The serpent with which Scipio's mother dallied was Capitoline Jove. See OLYMPIAS.

Scorpion *10.328* The constellation Scorpio.

Scylla *2.660* In Homer's *Odyssey*, 12.55–126, 229–59, a monster on a cliff on the strait between Italy and Sicily. Opposite her is the monster Charybdis. See CHARYBDIS. In Ovid's *Metamorphoses*, 13.730–33 and 14.40–67, Scylla is a maiden who is beloved of Glaucus and resented for that reason by the enchantress Circe, who transforms Scylla's lower body into heads of barking dogs.

Sechem *12.136* See MOREH.

Seleucia *4.212* The city that marks the eastern limit of the large country of Eden. For Milton, the more recent name of Telassar, built by the Macedonians ("Grecian kings") in the wake of Alexander the Great's conquest of Palestine. Seleucia is situated on the Tigris River (the great river to the east of the Euphrates) below Baghdad.

Under the name *Telassar,* Seleucia is twice mentioned in the Bible as the place where the "children of Eden" lived. See 2 Kings 19:12 and Isaiah 37:12. See AURAN and EDEN.

Senir *12.146* The ridge of mountains of which Mount Hermon is a part. The northern limit of the Promised Land (Deuteronomy 3:8–9).

Sennaär 3.467 Shinar, in Babylonia, the plain on which the tower of Babel was built.

Seon *1.409* Sihon, king of the Amorites who refused the Israelites passage through his land when they were traveling to the Promised Land. He was therefore destroyed and his land taken. Among the cities occupied was his capital, Heshbon, which was named after him (Numbers 21:23–28).

Seraphim *6.249* The highest order of angels. Unlike the cherubim, who guard God, and therefore turn their attention away from Him, the seraphim are forever gazing upon and praising God. They are seen only once in the Bible, in Isaiah 6:1–3, where they have six wings, two covering the face, two covering the feet, and two used for flight. They chant, "Holy holy holy, is the Lord of hosts: the whole earth is full of his glory." In Milton's more active vision they are, at least once, in the war in Heaven, "fighting Seraphim." One of the most impressive characters in *Paradise Lost*, and one of the most militantly active of the angels, is Abdiel, "than whom none with more zeal adored / The Deity" (5.805–06). See ABDIEL and CHERUBIM.

Serapis *1.720* A combination of Osiris and Apis, the bull-god. The worship of Serapis was introduced into Greece by the first Ptolemy to establish a common worship for the Egyptians and the Greeks.

Serbonian bog 2.592 A vast region of quicksands in Egypt that devoured whole armies (Diadorus Siculus [1.30.5–7]). See also Lucan, *Pharsalia* 8.539. Herodotus (*Histories* 3.8) says that Lake Serbonis is where Typhon is supposed to be buried. See TYPHON and SYRTIS.

Sericana 3.438 Serica. The longer form is used by Boiardo and Ariosto. Broad, arid plains to the south of the mountains of Imaus, in Scythia. Milton imagines the plains of Sericana north of the Himalayas. Maps in Milton's day depicted sailing wagons on Sericana.

Serraliona *10.703* Sierra Leone, a cape on the west coast of Africa.

Sibma *1.410* A Moabite town, noted for vines and fruits. The "vine of Sibma" is mentioned in Isaiah's (16:8–9) prophecy of the destruction of Moab.

Sidon *1.441* A wealthy Phoenician seaport where the moon goddess Astarte (identified with Aphrodite) was worshiped. She may have been worshiped by "virgins," but not all her priestesses were such. Temple prostitution, where priestesses engaged with worshipers in sexual practices regarded as religious rites, was common in Palestine and is one reason why idolatry is so often described in the Bible as a kind of prostitution. Solomon himself is "Beguiled by fair idolatresses" (1.445).

Siloa *1.11* Siloam, a spring (Gihon) in the Kidron Valley immediately to the east of Jerusalem. The waters of Gihon pass through a passage cut in the rock to the Pool of Siloam, the overflow from which waters the king's garden (Nehemiah 3:15). Jesus cures a blind man with the waters of Siloam (John 9:1–11). Because Siloam is associated with David, the supposed author of the psalms, Milton sees it as the true form of the Heliconian springs that inspire Greek poetry. See PEGASUS.

Silvanus *4.707* A Roman divinity of woods, not clearly distinct from Faunus and often identified with Pan. He is represented as an old man with the strength of youth, living in sacred groves removed, but not remote, from human habitation. See FAUNUS and PAN.

Sin *2.760* Satan's consort in Heaven, born from the left side of Satan's head and impregnated by him with their son Death. Sin falls with the rebel angels but is given a key and charged to keep the gates of Hell. There, her son Death is born and immediately rapes her. From this union the hellhounds are born and are ranged about her middle, barking ceaselessly. Periodically they re-enter her womb and gnaw her insides. Below Sin's loins her body becomes that of a serpent with a "mortal sting" (1.653). The image of Sin as a beautiful woman above and a serpent below is traditional; but Milton may be drawing more particularly on Spenser's monster, Error, who is a woman above and a serpent below, armed with a sting. Error's brood of eyeless frogs, toads, and small serpents creep in and out of her mouth (not her womb) until the Redcross knight cuts her head off. They then drink her blood, swell up, and burst. See *The Faerie Queene* 1.1.14–26. The hellhounds barking about Sin's middle are derived, as Milton indicates (1.659–61), from Ovid's Scylla, whose lower body is composed of the heads of barking hounds. See SCYLLA. When Satan and Death confront each other at Hell's gates, Sin reconciles them, reveals that Death is Satan's son by her, and opens the gates of Hell, allowing Satan to pass through them into chaos. After Adam and Eve fall, Sin and Death build a bridge across chaos from Hell to the created universe, thus making it easy for devils to come into the world. When Satan meets Sin and Death at the head of their completed bridge, he tells them what to do with mankind: "Him first make our thrall and lastly kill" (10.402). The killing is Death's business; the enthralling is Sin's. See DEATH.

Sinaean kings *11.390* Chinese kings. See PAQUIN.

Sinai *1.7* The holy mountain in the desert of the Sinai. The Israelites encamp there at the beginning of their journey to the Promised Land. Sinai is the same mountain as *Oreb* ("Horeb," Exodus 3:1), but they are different peaks, Sinai being the higher of the two. It was on the top of Sinai that Moses received from God the Hebrew Law inscribed on tablets of stone (Exodus 19–20). In addition to being a symbol of the Hebrew Law, Mount Sinai is for Milton a site of divine inspiration. Its "top" is "secret" in the Latin sense of being removed from common sight, for Moses ascended the mountain alone (12.227–30). Its summit is hidden in dark clouds and smoke.

Sion *1.10* Zion. The low mountain on which Jerusalem is situated. The site of the Temple and, more important for Milton, the place where King David was inspired to compose sacred songs, the psalms.

Sirocco *10.706* The Italian name (Scirocco) for the southeast wind. It is warm, moist, dusty, and is thought to bring disease.

Sittim *1.413* Shittim, the place where the Israelites were encamped on the east side of the Jordan River, across from Jericho. There, the Israelites committed "whoredom with the daughters of Moab." The sexual crime was compounded by idolatry (Numbers 25:1–3, 33: 49–56; Joshua 2:1, 3:1; Michah 6:6). See PEOR.

Sodom *1.503* One of the two wicked cities on the plain at the southeast end of the Dead Sea, the other being Gomorrah. While living in Sodom, Abraham's nephew Lot hospitably receives in his house two visiting angels. The men of Sodom surround the house and call to Lot to deliver the visitors over to them to be sexually abused (Genesis 19:5). Lot offers to send out his two daughters instead and is refused. The angels then strike the men in the street blind "So that they wearied themselves to find the door" (19:11). After Lot escapes the city with his daughters, God rains fire and brimstone on Sodom and Gomorrah so that nothing is left living there (Genesis 19:12–28). Against instructions, Lot's wife looks back at the burning city and is changed to a pillar of salt (19:26).

Sofala *11.400* See OPHIR.

Soldan *1.764* Sultan.

Solomon *1.401* Son of King David by Bathsheba and king of Israel after David's death. Unlike his father, Solomon was permitted to build the temple at Jerusalem, where the ark of the covenant would be housed. Solomon was legendary for his wealth and wisdom.

Son *3.79* Milton's Son is not inseparable from God the Father (and the Holy Ghost), as in the orthodox Christian view of the Trinity: "on [God's] right / The radiant image of his glory sat, / His only son" (3.62–64). The Son is begotten by God, as a true son, but he is also the first being created by God: "of all creation first, / Begotten Son, divine similitude" (3.383–4). He is the agent of all the Father's actions, but he is also the wisdom, or forethought, behind those actions. The Father calls him "My word, my wisdom, and effectual might" (3.170). In these capacities the Son defeats the rebel angels, creates the world (and Adam and Eve), goes to earth as the man Jesus, teaches humans, and dies to redeem them. At the end of time it is the Son who executes judgment.

Some of Milton's terms suggest that the Son is subordinate to the Father, as when the Father calls the Son "Effulgence of my glory" (6.680), an echo of the first chapter of Hebrews: "the brightness of [God's] glory, and the express image of his person." But the Son is also the "Filial Godhead" (7.175), participating in the being of Father as God. The supposed heresy of Milton's subordinationist view of the Son is not so important for the poem as it has been made to seem. The Son is certainly God's equal and is himself God, notably in the Creation narrative of Book 7. While Milton cannot see how the Son can be anything other than a creation of the Father, the Father confers on the Son the dignity of a son, as in Roman adoption. This dignity, because it has been earned by the Son's merit ("By merit more than birthright Son of God" 3.309), is a higher dignity than being simply "begotten." As the Father explains at 3.305–12, the Son rises to the dignity of oneness with the Father's glory because of his willingness to sacrifice himself "to save a world from utter loss" (3.7–8). Finally, as the Father himself declares, the Son's love of humanity outshines the Father's glory: "love hath abounded more than glory abounds" (3.312). See GOD, MESSIAH, SPIRIT, and WORD.

Spartan twins *10.674* The constellation of the twins, Gemini, through which the sun is here imagined to pass as it moves north toward the tropic of Cancer. See CRAB.

Spirit *1.17* In traditional Christianity, the Spirit, or Holy Ghost, is the third person of the Trinity and one of the three equal parts of God. In Milton, the Spirit represents God's creative power and is subordinate to the Father and to the Son. When the Father sends the Son into chaos to create the world, he says, "My overshadowing Spirit and might with thee / I send along" (7.165–66). Milton identifies this Spirit with his own creative power, too. The power that assists in creating the world is also the power that assists Milton in writing his poem. See 1.17–22. See GOD, SON, WORD.

Stygian flood *1.239* Waters of the infernal river *styx*: "horror." See ACHERON.

Styx *2.577* See ACHERON.

Sus *11.403* Like FEZ, another North African Muslim kingdom, in southwest Morocco, stretching from the coast inland through the desert.

Susa *10.308* See MEMNONIAN.

Synod *2.391* A council of potentates, officials, or clergymen, and the like, gathered to consider some important question. *Synod* can also refer to a conjunction of stars. The word *consider* (*con* "with" + *sider* "star": to study the position of the stars before taking some action) also carries an astrological metaphor.

Syrian king *11.218* See DOTHAN.

Syrtis *2.939* A region of huge sandbanks and quicksands off the North African shore in which ships are lost. The region appeared to be neither water nor land, being impossible either to sail in or to walk on. The Roman poet Lucan mentions the quicksands as an image of matter in its chaotic state before nature gave it form (*Pharsalia* 9.303–4). See SERBONIAN BOG.

Tantalus *2.614* The son of Zeus and the titaness, Pluto. Among other crimes, Tantalus offered the gods a stew containing the dismembered body of his son, Pelops, after whom the Peloponnesian peninsula, in Greece, is named. The gods discerned the ruse and restored Pelops to life. Tantalus was condemned in the underworld to a punishment from which we take the word *tantalize*. He suffered intense thirst and hunger, even as he stood in water up to his chin and beneath overhanging boughs of fruit. When he attempted to drink, the water receded before him. When he attempted to eat, the wind blew the boughs out of his reach (Homer, *Odyssey* 11.582–92).

Tarsus ***1.200*** An important biblical city on the south coast of modern Turkey, ancient Cilicia, the birthplace of Saint Paul. Milton mentions Tarsus in connection with the monster Typhon, who, according to Pindar (*Pythian Odes* 1.16–17), formerly resided in his "honored-under-many-names cave" in Cilicia. See TYPHON.

Tartar(s) ***3.432*** Nomadic Mongols of Central Asia.

Tartarian Sulphur ***2.69*** Sulphur of Tartarus, the deepest region of the world, beneath Hades itself. Although Tartarus is commonly identified as Hell, or Hades, it is as far beneath Hades as earth is beneath heaven. The gods stowed their divine enemies in Tartarus, not in Hades, which is for human souls.

Tauris ***10.436*** Tebriz, in northwestern Persia (modern Iran).

Taurus ***1.769*** The constellation of the bull, containing the Pleiades, through which the sun passes as it returns north from the tropic of Capricorn in the spring. See CRAB and PLEIADES.

Telassar ***4.214*** See SELEUCIA.

Temir ***11.389*** Tamburlaine. See SAMARCHAND.

Teneriffe ***4.987*** A high peak in the Canary Islands, visible from a great distance at sea.

Ternate ***2.639*** With Tidore, one of the "spice islands" in the Moluccas.

Thammuz ***1.446*** Syrian dying god associated with Adonis and idolatrously worshiped by women before the temple (Ezekiel 8:14).

Thamyris ***3.35*** A Thracian poet blinded by the Muses. (Homer, *Iliad* 2.594–600).

Thebes ***1.578*** After Ilium (Troy), the most famous besieged city of antiquity, where great heroes fought. It was the subject of a tragedy by Aeschylus and an epic by the late Roman poet Statius.

Themis ***11.14*** The goddess of law, in the lineage of the Titans, daughter of Ouranos (sky) and Ge (earth). See DEUCALION.

Thracian ***7.34*** Of Thrace, mountainous semi-wild region of northern Greece, associated with the worship of Dionysus and with the poet Orpheus. See ORPHEUS.

Thrascias ***10.700*** A north-northwest wind from Thrace.

Thyestean banquet ***10.688*** Atreus killed the sons of his brother Thyestes and served them in a stew to him, a crime that began the curse on the house of Atreus (Aeschylus, *Agamemnon* 1591–1602). Seneca (*Thyestes* 776–77 and 784–884) says the sun went dark at the crime.

Tidore ***2.639*** See TERNATE.

Tiresias ***3.36*** Prophet of Thebes whose prophetic powers were divine compensation for the loss of his sight.

Titan ***1.510*** The oldest son of the sky, Ouranos, and brother of Zeus, who fought with the other titans against the Olympians.

Tobias *5.222* In the apocryphal book of Tobit, Tobias, the son of Tobit, is sent on a long journey by his father. Tobias is accompanied on this journey by a benevolent friend, later revealed to be the angel Raphael. With Raphael's help, Tobias rescues his kinswoman Sarah from the power of the demon Asmodeus and marries her (Tobit 5–9). See ASMODEUS and RAPHAEL.

Tobit's son *4.170* Tobias.

Tophet *1.404* In the valley of Hinnom, southwest of Jerusalem, where children were sacrificed to Moloch. The practice was stopped by the religious reformer, King Josiah: "And he defiled Topheth, which is in the valley of the children of Hinnom, that no man might make his son or his daughter to pass through the fire to Molech" (2 Kings 23:10). See GEHENNA, JOSIAH, and MOLOCH.

Trebizond *1.584* A rich Byzantine city on the Black Sea.

Tree of Knowledge of Good and Evil *4.221* The tree on which the forbidden fruit grows. After he creates Adam, God says, "But of the Tree of the Knowledge of Good and Evil, thou shalt not eat of it: for in the day that thou eatest thereof thou shalt surely die" (Genesis 2:17). Eve repeats this to the serpent when he tempts her (Genesis 3:2–3), to which the serpent replies that God has forbidden the fruit to prevent Adam and Eve from becoming gods themselves: "For God doth know that in the day ye eat thereof, then your eyes shall be opened, and ye shall be as gods, knowing good and evil" (Genesis 3:4–5). Eve then sees that the fruit of the tree is attractive to eat, that it is beautiful to look at and that it is desirable for the wisdom it affords. Milton carefully follows these three phases of attraction. His Eve calls the fruit "this fruit divine, / Fair to the eye, inviting to the taste, / Of virtue to make wise." (9.776–78). In the Bible, the knowledge the fruit gives is closely tied to sexual shame: "And the eyes of them both were opened, and they knew that they were naked; and they sewed fig leaves together, and made themselves aprons" (Genesis 3:7). Although Milton's account of the knowledge of good and evil includes sexual shame and its related but opposite feeling, lust, he understands knowledge of good and evil in the larger, ethical sense of those words. His interpretation, which he had developed in *Areopagitica*, is that to know a thing is to take it into oneself, to taste it (Latin *sapio* means "to taste, to know," whence our *sapience*). For Adam and Eve to know good and evil (good being already in them) is to lose the absolute goodness that they had before: "We know / Both good and evil: good lost and evil got" (9.1071–72).

Tree of Life *3.354* One of the more mysterious elements of the Genesis story, the Tree of Life seems to come from older folkloric legends of a magical tree, the fruit of which has the power to confer eternal life. The Tree of Life is mentioned alongside the Tree of the Knowledge of Good and Evil: "And out of the ground made the Lord God to grow every tree that is pleasant to the sight, and good for food; the tree of life also in the midst of the garden, and the tree of knowledge of good and evil" (Genesis 2:9.) The two trees are mentioned again when Adam and Eve are expelled from the garden: "And the Lord God said, Behold, the man is become as one of us, to know good and evil: and now, lest he put forth his hand, and take also of the tree of life, and eat, and live forever: therefore the Lord God sent him forth from the garden of Eden, to till the ground from whence he was taken (Genesis 3:22–3). To protect the Tree of Life, God places at the east gate of the garden a guard of cherubim and also a magic flaming sword (Genesis 3:24). The Tree of Life reappears in the final chapter of the Bible, Revelation 22:2, where it grows on both sides of the river of water of life, bearing twelve kinds of fruit through the entire year, and healing the nations—the gentiles—with its leaves. This image blends the tree in the garden of Eden with those trees seen by Ezekiel in his vision of the holy waters flowing from the sanctuary: "And by the river upon the bank thereof, on this side and on that side, shall grow all trees for meat, whose leaves shall not fade, neither shall the fruit thereof be consumed . . . and the fruit thereof shall be for meat, and the leaf thereof for medicine" (Ezekiel 47:12). See FOUNT OF LIFE.

Tremisen *11.404* A North African city in Nubia, noted, like FEZ, for the honor it confers on poets. For sites in North Africa, Milton draws on Ariosto, *Orlando Furioso* 33.98–107; "Tremisenne" appears in stanza 101.

Trinacrian shore *2.661* Sicilian shore, opposite Calabria on the straits separating Sicily from the Italian mainland. Ovid, *Metamorphoses* 5.346–53, refers to Sicily (when it is thrown on top of Typhon) as the "vast Trinacrian isle." See CALABRIA and PELORUS.

Triton *4.276* See NYSEIAN ISLE.

Troy *9.16* The great city in Asia Minor besieged by a confederacy of Greek (Achaean) kingdoms in Homer's *Iliad*. Also called "Ilium." The fate of the city is sealed when the Greek hero Achilles pursues and kills Troy's chief defender, Hector.

Turnus *9.17* In the second half of Virgil's *Aeneid*, Turnus, incensed by the loss of his promised bride, Lavinia, leads a confederacy of native Italian (Ausonian) kingdoms against the Trojans, led by Aeneas.

Tuscan artist *1.288* Galileo, who was from Tuscany and was confined by the Inquisition in a villa in Fiesole, above Florence. See GALILEO and OPTIC GLASS.

Typhoean rage *2.539* See TYPHON.

Typhon *1.199* Born of the union of Earth with Tartarus after the defeat of the titans, Typhon is the most dangerous opponent of the Olympian gods and the only one who is a continuing threat. He has one hundred bellowing, fire-breathing dragon heads, and his vast body terminates in vipers, which is how Milton describes him in "Ode on the Morning of Christ's Nativity": "Typhon huge ending in snaky twine" (line 227). A symbol of arrogant pride and open violence, Typhon alone puts the Olympians to flight, all except Zeus and Athene, who for Milton are the types of the Father and the Son.

The other gods flee to Egypt, where they disguise themselves as animals and are worshiped in that form, an event alluded to by Milton when he calls the Egyptian gods "wandering gods disguised in brutish forms" (1.481). Zeus at last pins Typhon under the volcano Etna, in Sicily, or under the entire island of Sicily and the volcanic region of southern Italy. In the passage on Typhon in Aeschylus's *Prometheus Bound* (lines 351–72), many elements of Milton's Hell and Milton's Satan appear, e.g., the "gorgonian gleam" of Typhon's eyes (see GORGONIAN TERROR); the continuing effect of Zeus's lightning not only on Typhon's body but also on his mind (see *Paradise Lost* 1.94 and 1.126); the prostration of Typhon's huge body, not on a lake of fire but beneath the "roots" of Mount Etna; Typhon's boast, spoken in high language, that he will overthrow "the tyranny of Zeus" (*Prometheus Bound*, line 357; cf. *Paradise Lost* 1.124); and Prometheus's prophecy that Typhon's continuing inner torment will one day cause him to vomit fire that will destroy the fruitful fields of Sicily. Numerous references in ancient poetry to the fruitfulness of Sicily made it for Milton a type of Eden. See CERES. Hesoid, *Theogony* 820–68; Pindar, *Pythian Odes* 1.15–28 and 8.15–18; *Olympian Odes* 4.6–7; Fragments 18; and Ovid, *Metamorphoses* 5.346–53. See PELORUS.

Ulysses *2.1019* Latin name for the hero of the *Odyssey*, Odysseus, who suffers much and passes many dangers returning from Troy to his kingdom on the island of Ithaca. See CHARYBDIS and SCYLLA.

Ur of Chaldea *12.130* An ancient city on the west bank of the lower Euphrates River, near the Persian Gulf. The original home of Terah, father of Abraham, and a place where idolatry and polytheism were practiced. The Chaldeans were also famous for astronomy. Terah and his family left Ur and traveled up the Euphrates valley to Haran, to the northeast of Palestine. From Haran, Abraham was called by God to enter the Promised Land. See ABRAHAM and CANAAN.

Urania *7.1* See MUSE.

Uriel *3.648* Angel, whose name means "light (or fire) of God" (2 Esdras 4:1).

Urim *6.761* Together with the Thummim, mysterious, symbolic, and magical objects (Milton imagines them as jewels) on the breastplate of the high priest: "and thou shalt put in the breastplate of judgement the Urim and the Thummim; and they shall be upon Aaron's heart, when he goeth before the Lord" (Exodus 28:30). They were used for divination and casting lots, and had some role to play when people wished to seek counsel of God (Numbers 27:21). See AARON.

Uther's son *1.580* Arthur, later King Arthur, who defended Britain against Saxon invasions and is a patriotic symbol for the English. At an early stage, Milton considered writing an epic poem on Arthur.

Uzziel *4.782* Angel whose name means "strength of God." He is Gabriel's lieutenant in the troop guarding the garden.

Valdarno *1.290* Valley of the Arno River, which flows through Florence.

Vallombrosa *1.303* "Shadowy valley." A remote monastery on a mountain in Tuscany overlooking the valley of the Arno. Milton means the whole valley.

Vertumnus *9.395* Roman god of gardens who pursues Ceres, goddess of fruit.

Virgin *10.676* The constellation Virgo, through which (in the earth-centered, Ptolemaic system) the sun passes on its way south from the tropic of Cancer, which is north of the equator, to the tropic of Capricorn, which is south of the equator. See CRAB.

Virtue, angelic *5.371* An expression in Greek and Latin epic poetry, where a character is referred to as a "strength" or "force," as when Homer speaks of "the strength of Priam," the "force of Hector," and "the force of Alcinous" (*Iliad* 3.105, 14.418; *Odyssey* 7.167), or when Virgil speaks of the "smelling-strength of dogs," *odora canum vis* (*Aeneid* 4.132).

Well of life *11.416* See FOUNT OF LIFE and TREE OF LIFE.

Word *3.170* When *Word* is capitalized it refers to the Son of God (Greek *logos*, "word" and "reason principle"). When he is incarnate in the world, the Son of God is Jesus. When the Father addresses the Son as "My Word," he goes on to define what this title means: "my wisdom and effectual might" (3.170). The Christian belief that the Son is both the Word of God and the power that created the world by spoken command (Genesis 1:3) is based on the opening verses of the Gospel According to John (1:1–5): "In the beginning was the Word (*logos*), and the Word was with God, and the Word was God. The same was in the beginning with God. All things were made by him; and without him was not anything made that was made. In him was life; and the life was the light of men. And the light shineth in the darkness; and the darkness comprehended it not." In Book 7 Milton shows the actual creation of the world as acts of the Son. At two moments, however—when mankind is created and when the Son returns to heaven—Milton asserts that the Father is really present with the Son when the Son creates. 7.516–19 and 7.588–90. By doing so, Milton makes his own account of creation consistent with that of Genesis. See MESSIAH, SPIRIT, and SON.

World *2.347* The entire created universe, formed by the Son from chaos, provided with an outer, protective shell, on the outside of which Satan lands (3.418–22), and containing the sun, the stars, the planets, and the earth. This World is attached to Heaven by a golden chain (2.1005 and 2.1051). Although the World contains the entire universe observable from earth, when it is first spotted by Satan, when he is in chaos, it appears extremely small: "in bigness as a star / Of smallest magnitude" (2.1052–53). The World appears in its true, vast proportions, however, when the Son uses his huge golden compasses to draw its circumference: "One foot he centered and the other turned / Round through the vast profundity obscure" (7.228–29).

Xerxes *10.307* The Persian king who invaded Greece in 480 B.C.E. See HELLESPONT.

Zephon *4.788* Angel whose name means "searcher of secrets."

Zephyr *4.329* See FLORA.

Zodiac *11.247* A band of stars marking the apparent paths of the sun, moon, and planets about the earth, assuming the earth to be the center of the astronomical system. This band is divided into twelve constellations resembling (when lines are drawn between the stars) certain mythological animals and persons. For the movement of the sun through the zodiacal signs to either side of the equator, see CRAB.

Zophiel *6.535* Angel whose name means "spy of God." During the war in Heaven, Zophiel, "of cherubim the swiftest wing," discerns the approach of the rebel angels and in brilliant language urges the loyal angels to prepare to fight.

Suggestions for Further Reading

• indicates a work included or excerpted in this Norton Critical Edition.

Achinstein, Sharon. *Milton and the Revolutionary Reader*. Princeton, N.J., 1994.

Adams, Robert Martin. *Ikon: John Milton and the Modern Critics*. Ithaca, N.Y., 1955.

Allen, Don Cameron. *The Harmonious Vision: Studies in Milton's Poetry*. Baltimore, Md., 1954.

Barker, Arthur E. *Milton and the Puritan Dilemma, 1641–1660*. Toronto, 1942.

Belsey, Catherine. *John Milton: Language, Gender, Power*. Oxford, 1988.

Bennett, Joan S. *Reviving Liberty: Radical Christian Humanism in Milton's Great Poems*. Cambridge, Mass., 1989.

Broadbent, John B. *Some Graver Subject: An Essay on* Paradise Lost. London, 1960.

•Burnett, Archie. " 'Sense Variously Drawn Out': The Line in *Paradise Lost*." *Literary Imagination* 5.1 (2003): 69–92.

Burrow, Colin. *Epic Romance: Homer to Milton*. Oxford, 1993.

•Bush, Douglas. *John Milton: A Sketch of His Life and Writings*. London, 1964.

Campbell, Gordon. *A Milton Chronology*. London, 1977.

Corns, Thomas N. *Milton's Language*. Oxford, 1990.

Daiches, David. *Milton*. London, 1957.

Demaray, John G. *Cosmos and Epic Representation: Dante, Spenser, Milton, and the Transformation of Renaissance Heroic Poetry*. Pittsburgh, Pa., 1991.

Diekhoff, John S. *Milton on Himself*. London, 1965.

DuRocher, Richard J. *Milton and Ovid*. Ithaca, N.Y., 1985.

•Empson, William. *Milton's God*. London, 1961.

Evans, J. Martin. *Milton's Imperial Epic:* Paradise Lost *and the Discourse of Colonialism*. Ithaca, N.Y., 1996.

Fallon, Robert Thomas. *Divided Empire: Milton's Political Imagery*. University Park, Pa., 1996.

Fallon, Stephen M. *Milton among the Philosophers: Poetry and Materialism in Seventeenth-Century England*. Ithaca, N.Y., 1991.

Ferry, Anne D. *Milton's Epic Voice: The Narrator in* Paradise Lost. Cambridge, Mass., 1963.

Fish, Stanley E. *How Milton Works*. Cambridge, Mass., 2001.

•———. *Surprised by Sin: The Reader in* Paradise Lost, 2nd ed. Cambridge, Mass., 1997.

•———. "With Mortal Voice: Milton Defends against the Muse." *English Literary History* 62.3 (1995): 522–25.

•Flesch, William. *Generosity and the Limits of Authority: Shakespeare, Herbert, Milton*. Ithaca, N.Y., 1992.

•Frye, Northrop. *The Return of Eden: Five Essays on Milton's Epics*. Toronto, 1965.

Gardner, Helen. *A Reading of* Paradise Lost. Oxford, 1965.

Gilbert, Allan H. *A Geographical Dictionary of Milton*. New Haven, Conn., 1914.

Gregerson, Linda. *The Reformation of the Subject: Spenser, Milton, and the English Protestant Epic*. Cambridge, UK, 1995.

Grose, Christopher. *Milton and the Sense of Tradition*. New Haven, Conn., 1988.

•Gross, Kenneth. "Satan and the Romantic Satan: A Notebook." In *Re-Membering Milton: Essays on the Texts and Traditions*, eds. Mary Nyquist and Margaret W. Ferguson. New York, 1987.

Grossman, Marshall. *The Story of All Things: Writing the Self in English Renaissance Narrative Poetry*. Durham, N.C., 1998.

Guillory, John. *Poetic Authority: Spenser, Milton, and Literary History*. New York, 1983.

Hanford, James Holly. *John Milton: Englishman*. New York, 1949.

Haskin, Dayton. *Milton's Burden of Interpretation*. Philadelphia, Pa., 1994.

Hill, Christopher. *The Experience of Defeat: Milton and Some Contemporaries*. London, 1977.
———. *Milton and the English Revolution*. London, 1984.
Hollander, John. *The Figure of Echo: A Mode of Allusion in Milton and After*. Berkeley, Calif., 1981.
Kendrick, Christopher. *Milton: A Study in Ideology and Form*. London, 1986.
Kerrigan, William. *The Sacred Complex: On the Psychogenesis of* Paradise Lost. Cambridge, Mass., 1983.
Knoppers, Laura Lunger. *Historicizing Milton: Spectacle, Power, and Poetry in Restoration England*. Athens, Ga., 1994.
Kolbrener, William. *Milton's Warring Angels: A Study of Critical Engagements*. Cambridge, UK, 1997.
Leonard, John. *Naming in Paradise: Milton and the Language of Adam and Eve*. Oxford, 1990.
•Lewalski, Barbara Kiefer. *The Life of John Milton: A Critical Biography*. Cambridge, Mass., 2000.
———. Paradise Lost *and the Rhetoric of Literary Forms*. Princeton, N.J., 1985.
•Lewis, C. S. *A Preface to* Paradise Lost. London, 1942.
Lieb, Michael. *Milton and the Culture of Violence*. Ithaca, N.Y., 1994.
Loewenstein, David. *Milton and the Drama of History*. Cambridge, UK, 1990.
MacCaffrey, Isabel. Paradise Lost *as Myth*. Cambridge, Mass., 1959.
MacCallum, Hugh. *Milton and the Sons of God: The Divine Image in Milton's Epic Poetry*. Toronto, 1986.
Martin, Catherine Gimelli. *The Ruins of Allegory:* Paradise Lost *and the Metamorphosis of Epic Convention*. Durham, N.C., 1998.
Martz, Louis L. *Poet of Exile: A Study of Milton's Poetry*. New Haven, Conn., 1980.
McColley, Diane Kelsey. *Milton's Eve*. Urbana, Ill., 1983.
Moyles, R. G. *The Text of* Paradise Lost: *A Study in Editorial Procedure*. Toronto, 1985.
Mulryan, John. *"Through a Glass Darkly": Milton's Reinvention of the Mythological Tradition*. Pittsburgh, Pa., 1996.
Murrin, Michael. *History and Warfare in Renaissance Epic*. Chicago, 1994.
Newlyn, Lucy. Paradise Lost *and the Romantic Reader*. Oxford, 1992.
Norbrook, David. *Writing the English Republic: Poetry, Rhetoric, and Politics, 1627–1660*. Cambridge, UK, 1999.
Nyquist, Mary. "The Genesis of Gendered Subjectivity in the Divorce Tracts and in *Paradise Lost*." In *Re-Membering Milton: Essays on the Texts and Traditions*, eds. Mary Nyquist and Margaret W. Ferguson. New York, 1987.
•Nyquist, Mary, and Margaret W. Ferguson, *Re-Membering Milton: Essays on the Texts and Traditions*. New York, 1987.
Patrides, C. A. *Milton and the Christian Tradition*. Oxford, 1986.
Quilligan, Maureen. *Milton's Spenser: The Politics of Reading*. Ithaca, N.Y., 1983.
•Radzinowicz, Mary Ann. *Milton's Epics and the Book of Psalms*. Princeton, N.J., 1989.
———. *Towards* Samson Agonistes: *The Growth of Milton's Mind*. Princeton, N.J., 1972.
•Rajan, Balachandra. Paradise Lost *and the Seventeenth-Century Reader*, 2nd ed. London, 1962.
———. *The Lofty Rhyme: A Study of Milton's Major Poetry*. Miami, 1970.
Rappaport, Herman. *Milton and the Postmodern*. Lincoln, Neb., 1983.
Redman, Harry Jr. *Major French Milton Critics of the Nineteenth Century*. Pittsburgh, Pa., 1994.
•Ricks, Christopher. *Milton's Grand Style*. Oxford, 1963.
Rogers, John. *The Matter of Revolution: Science, Poetry, and Politics in the Age of Milton*. Ithaca, N.Y., 1996.
Rosenblatt, Jason P. *Torah and Law in* Paradise Lost. Princeton, N.J., 1994.
Rumrich, John. *Milton Unbound: Controversy and Reinterpretation*. Cambridge, UK, 1996.
Sauer, Elizabeth. *Barbarous Dissonance and Images of Voice in Milton's Epics*. Montreal and Kingston, 1996.
•Schwartz, Regina M. *Remembering and Repeating: On Milton's Theology and Poetics*, 2nd ed. Chicago, 1993.
Shawcross, John T. *John Milton and Influence: Presence in Literature, History and Culture*. Pittsburgh, Pa., 1991.
———. "A Note on the Text." *In* Paradise Lost: *A Poem in Twelve Books, The Author John Milton*. Ed. John T. Shawcross. San Francisco, 2002.
Smith, Nigel. *Literature and Revolution in England, 1640–1660*. New Haven, Conn., 1994.
Sprott, Ernest S. *Milton's Art of Prosody*. Oxford, 1953.
Summers, Joseph. *The Muse's Method: An Introduction to* Paradise Lost. London, 1962.
Taylor, Edward W. *Milton's Poetry: Its Development in Time*. Pittsburgh, Pa., 1979.

•Tillyard, E. M. W. *Milton*, 2nd ed. New York, 1966.
Turner, James G. *One Flesh: Paradisal Marriage and Sexual Relations in the Age of Milton*. Oxford, 1987.
•Vendler, Helen. "Introduction." In Paradise Lost: *A Poem in Twelve Books, the Author John Milton*. Ed. John T. Shawcross. San Francisco, 2002.
•Waldock, A. J. A. Paradise Lost *and Its Critics*. Cambridge, Mass., 1947.
Walker, Julia M. *Medusa's Mirrors: Spenser, Shakespeare, Milton, and the Metamorphosis of the Female Self*. Newark, Del., 1998.
•———. *Milton and the Idea of Woman*. Urbana Ill., 1988.
Webber, Joan. *Milton and His Epic Tradition*. Seattle, Wash., 1979.
•Wittreich, Joseph A. Jr. *Feminist Milton*. Ithaca, N.Y., 1987.
———. *Milton and the Line of Vision*. Madison, Wis., 1975.
•Woodhouse, A. S. P. *The Heavenly Muse: A Preface to Milton*. Toronto, 1972.